Early Library in: Franciscus Philippus Florinus [pseud.] Oeconomus prudens et legalis Nurnberg, 1722.
p. 125 18th c. (modified, 1994)

NATIONAL LIBRARY of MEDICINE CLASSIFICATION

**A Scheme for the Shelf Arrangement
of Library Materials in the Field of
Medicine and Its Related Sciences**

Fifth Edition 1994

U.S. DEPARTMENT OF HEALTH
AND HUMAN SERVICES
Public Health Service
National Institutes of Health

NATIONAL LIBRARY OF MEDICINE
8600 Rockville Pike
Bethesda, Maryland 20894

NIH Publication No. 95-1535

First edition 1951
Second edition 1958
Third edition 1964
Third edition (with supplement 1969)
Fourth edition 1978
Fourth edition, revised 1981
Fourth edition, second printing 1992
Fifth edition 1994

National Library of Medicine Cataloging in Publication

National Library of Medicine (U.S.)
   National Library of Medicine classification : a scheme for the shelf arrangement of library materials in the field of medicine and its related sciences. -- 5th ed. -- Bethesda, Md. : U.S. Dept. of Health and Human Services, Public Health Service, National Institutes of Health, National Library of Medicine ; Washington, D.C. : For sale by the Supt. of Docs., U.S. G.P.O., 1994.

   -- (NIH publication ; no. 95-1535)

   Includes bibliographical references and index.

   1. Classification 2. Medicine I. Title II. Series

Z 697.M4 U63c 1994

Cit. No. 9440818

This book is printed on acid-free paper for permanence.

The Secretary of Health and Human Services has determined that the publication of this monograph is necessary in the transaction of the public business required by law of this Department. Use of funds for printing this monograph has been approved by the Director of the Office of Management and Budget through September 30, 1995.

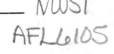

For sale by the U.S. Government Printing Office
Superintendent of Documents, Mail Stop: SSOP, Washington, DC 20402-9328
ISBN 0-16-045397-6

TABLE OF CONTENTS

PREFACE

The 1994 fifth edition of the *NLM Classification* updates the fourth revised edition published in 1981 and reprinted in 1992. The fifth edition contains a number of new classification numbers for new concepts and knowledge; however few changes were made to existing numbers. The Index to the Classification schedules was significantly expanded with descriptors from the Medical Subject Headings (MeSH ®) vocabulary.

Many people, but above all NLM Cataloging Section's staff, contributed to the revision of the *Classification*. Wen-min Kao, Principal Cataloger, was its editor. Christa Hoffmann, Head Cataloging Section, managed the project and worked with John Cox, Office of Computer and Communications Systems, to make essential programming and database changes which assisted in a more systematic updating and verification of data against MeSH. Senior Cataloging staff - Evelyn Bain, Chong Chung, Grace Rawsthorne and Sharon Willis - reviewed MeSH vocabulary for inclusion in the Index and assigned appropriate class numbers to the terms. Other staff members of the Cataloging Section provided valuable intellectual and editorial assistance. Peri Schuyler, Head Medical Subject Headings Section, and her staff of subject specialists; Dr. Elizabeth Van Lenten, Index Section; and Dr. Sue Goo Rhee from the NIH/National Heart Lung and Blood Institute, contributed their subject expertise. Ronald Gordner, NLM Reference Section, provided the public services point of view. Pauline Cochrane, University of Illinois at Urbana-Champaign GSLIS, performed important preliminary work that assisted in developing the update and revision process.

The following reviewed and commented on the *Classification* schedules, and many of their constructive suggestions were incorporated into the final publication:

Wilma Bass
    Georgetown University, Dahlgren Memorial Library
Elizabeth Crabtree
    American Hospital Association, AHA Resource Center
Susan L. Gullion
    University of California Los Angeles, L. Darling Biomedical Library
Lynn El-Hoshy
    Library of Congress, Cataloging Policy & Support Office
Mary Kreinbring
    Northwestern University, The Dental School Library
Robert Pisciotta
    University of Kansas Medical Center, Dykes Library
Wendy Skinner
    Crouse Irving Memorial Hospital, School of Nursing Library
Margaret Stangohr
    East Carolina University, Health Sciences Library
Steven Squires
    University of North Carolina at Chapel Hill, Health Sciences Library
Margaret Wineburgh-Freed
    University of Southern California, Norris Medical Library

The revision of the *National Library of Medicine Classification* benefits both NLM and the many health science libraries in the United States and abroad which use it to arrange their materials or to browse their online catalogs. All who contributed to its successful completion deserve our gratitude and commendation.

Donald A.B. Lindberg, M.D.
Director
National Library of Medicine

INTRODUCTION

The *National Library of Medicine Classification* covers the field of medicine and related sciences, utilizing schedules QS-QZ and W-WZ permanently excluded from the *Library of Congress Classification Schedules*. The various schedules of the *Library of Congress (LC) Classification* supplement the *NLM Classification* for subjects bordering on medicine and for general reference materials. The LC schedules for Human Anatomy (QM), Microbiology (QR) and Medicine (R) are not used at all by the National Library of Medicine since they overlap the *NLM Classification*.

The genesis of the *NLM Classification* is a *Survey Report* on the Army Medical Library, published in 1944, which recommended that the "Library be reclassified according to a modern scheme," and that the new scheme be a mixed notation (letters and numbers) resembling that of the Library of Congress. Subsequently a classification committee was formed, chaired by Keyes D. Metcalf and including Mary Louise Marshall who compiled the schedules. Medical specialists acted as consultants to the committee. Based on the consultants' advice, that of the committee and of the NLM cataloging staff, Ms. Marshall produced a preliminary edition of the Library's *Classification* which was issued in 1948.

The preliminary edition was revised by Frank B. Rogers and the first edition of the new classification was published in 1951 as the U.S. Army Medical Library *Classification*. It firmly established the current structure of the classification and NLM's classification practices. The headings for the individual schedules were given in brief form (e.g., WE - Musculoskeletal System; WG - Cardiovascular System) and together they provided an outline of the subjects that constitute the *National Library of Medicine Classification*. These headings were interpreted broadly as including the physiological system, the specialty or specialties connected with them, the regions of the body chiefly concerned and subordinate related fields. Within each schedule, division by organ usually has priority. All schedules, including some of their sections, are preceded by a group of form numbers ranging generally from 1-39 which are employed as mnemonic devices throughout the *Classification*.

Scope of Revision

The objectives of the current revision were to incorporate all additions and changes made since publishing the fourth revised edition, to revise selected schedules which needed updating, to integrate new MeSH descriptors used in cataloging but not represented in the fourth edition, and to update the terminology used in the index, captions and scope notes to conform to current usage. New classification numbers for new concepts were introduced following guidelines designed to maintain the structure of the *Classification*. In general, new numbers were added when:

a) there was no suitable number available for a subject; for example, WL 103.7 was added to cover the new discipline of Psychoneuroimmunology. In addition, new numbers were added by expanding the use of subdivision by special topics where needed and by adding new "A-Z" entries under established lists of Special Topics. For example, QT 37.5 for specific Biomedical and biocompatible materials was added with the special topics Ceramics (.C4) and Polymers (.P7)

b) there was scattered placement of a subject in many different numbers; for example, WB 101 was added for Ambulatory care (General) to provide a classification for ambulatory care beyond the hospital setting.

c) a classification number was heavily used and needed to be further broken down; for example, the new form number "18.2 Educational materials" was established to separate materials about education from materials used in education. This separation of Education and Educational materials is employed in all schedules throughout the *Classification*.

d) there was sufficient material on diseases already classified with materials on the specialty and/or organ system under "General works" to warrant a new classification number for the diseases; for example WG 210 was added for Heart diseases, WH 120 for Hematologic diseases, WL 140 for Nervous system diseases, etc.

e) form numbers not previously assigned to a schedule or section were incorporated; for example, "17" for Atlases.

In keeping with the structure of the *Classification*, preference was given to the use of whole numbers over decimals when establishing a new classification number. However, logical placement of a subject or publication form was the predominant factor when introducing a new classification number into an established range of numbers. Whenever possible the mnemonic characteristic for a form number was maintained. For example, the number "17" is used to identify classification numbers for atlases. Atlases on Operative dentistry are classed in WU 317 and atlases on Orthodontics in WU 417. Some exceptions to this principle are WU 507 for atlases on Prosthodontics and WU 600.7 for atlases on Oral surgery. In the former case, the number "507" is used to insert the form number for atlases on prosthodontics between WU 500 General Works and WU 515 Partial dentures... , and in the latter case, the number "600.7" is used to insert the form number for atlases on oral surgery between WU 600 General Works and WU 605 Tooth extraction.

Relationship to MeSH

The schedules with their special requirements for use with all types and forms of materials preclude strict adherence to the hierarchical arrangement of the Medical Subject Headings (MeSH), the Library's thesaurus for indexing and cataloging. The schedules maintain their own character in order to provide for material, old as well as new, acquired for the collection, including dictionaries, atlases, directories and other items which are not suitable for the arrangements found in MeSH. However, an effort was made to make schedule headings, subheadings and class number captions compatible with MeSH terminology. The *MeSH Tree Structures* were used extensively to determine the proper placement of a concept in a schedule and to relate index headings to one another. Since the representation of subjects in the schedules of the *Classification* is intentionally broad, the captions do not enumerate all of the subordinate concepts that are to be classified in a given number. MeSH descriptors for these subordinate concepts do appear in the index with the appropriate references to the classification numbers.

Index

The **Index** to the *Classification* provides access to classification numbers through the terminology of Medical Subject Headings (MeSH). Index entries were updated to reflect additions and changes to the MeSH vocabulary through 1995. Because resource limitations did not permit the verification of all classification numbers that previously appeared in *see* references in the **Index**, the classification numbers were removed from these entries. For additional information on the Index see the Introduction to the Index to the Classification, p. I-i.

NLM CLASSIFICATION PRACTICES

GENERAL

The Library applies subject classification primarily to materials treated as monographs. Serial publications are separated by form and are assigned classification numbers within several broad categories.

The classification practices outlined below are current conventions. They are provided as explanation, stating NLM's general classification approach using the National Library of Medicine's and the Library of Congress's schedules, rather than 'how to classify' instructions.

Basic Rules

The classification number assigned to a work is determined by the main focus or subject content of the work.

A work dealing with several subjects that fall into different areas of the classification is classed by emphasis, or if emphasis is lacking, by the first subject treated in the work.

A work on a particular disease is classified with the disease which in turn is classified with the organ or region chiefly affected, regardless of special emphasis on diet, drug, or other specific form of therapy.

Form Numbers

Each schedule, as well as some sections within a schedule (e.g., WO 201-233.1), contains a group of form numbers, generally 1-39, that are used to classify material by form within the general subject area of the schedule. In general, classification by form (such as *13* for dictionaries and encyclopedias, *15* for classification and nomenclature, etc.) takes precedence over classification by subject.

Special cases for classification by form number:

1. Collections by several authors or by individual authors, and works comprised of addresses, essays, and lectures are classed in their respective form numbers when the works cover the overall subject of the schedule. Collections of works or essays that cover a particular subject within the schedule are classed by subject. For example, Psychiatry - collected works is classified in WM 5 or 7 while Psychotherapy - collected works is classified in WM 420.

2. Some numbers in the range of 1-39 are not true form numbers, that is, they are used to classify material with a special emphasis, such as 26.5 for Medical informatics, computers, and automatic data processing (General) when the emphasis applies to the overall subject of the schedule. If the material covers a particular aspect of the overall subject, it is classified by subject. For example, Computers in cardiology is classified in WG 26.5 while Computers in heart surgery is classified in WG 169).

3. In general, the form number 11 is used for works dealing with the history of any aspect of a subject within a classification schedule. For example, WM 11 is used for both Psychiatry - history and Psychotherapy - history. There are exceptions to the use of the form number for history which are generally noted under the particular form number or in the Index. Furthermore, the form number 11 is not assigned to the schedules W and WB. The history of health professions and the practice of medicine are instead classified in the WZ schedule.

Because many form numbers correlate with a form subdivision in the subject headings assigned in cataloging, the definitions for form subdivisions given in the Appendix to the 'Cataloging Practices' section of any current *Medical Subject Headings -- Annotated Alphabetic List*, may also assist in determining when to classify by form number.

Table G

Geographic subdivision is provided for certain subjects in the NLM schedules by the application of **Table G** (see p. xvii). The use of geographical breakdown is restricted to those classes which are annotated with "Table G" in the schedules and includes both monographs and serials.

If a work on a subject that is geographically subdivided covers an area larger than what is represented in a **Table G** notation it is classified in the **General coverage (Not Table G)** number, directly following the class number that provides for geographic subdivision. For example WG 11 History (Table G) is the number for the history of cardiology in particular geographic areas and WG 11.1 General coverage (Not Table G) is the number for books with general coverage of the history of cardiology.

SPECIAL PLANS

Several types of monographic publications are classified according to special plans: Nineteenth century titles, Early printed books, and Bibliographies.

Nineteenth Century Titles

A simplified subject classification derived from the letters that represent the preclinical and clinical subjects covered by the *NLM Classification* is used for nineteenth century (1801-1913) monographs. This abbreviated classification is limited to combinations of letters and the classification notations W1-6, W 600, WX 2 and the form number 22 which appears throughout the schedule. In addition, the entire WZ schedule, History of Medicine, is used for nineteenth century titles. When the subject falls outside of the schedules of the *NLM Classification*, only the letters of the LC schedule representing the subject are used, e.g., BF Psychology, SF Veterinary Medicine, etc. Facsimiles and reprints of entire nineteenth century works are classified in the 19th Century Schedule. Bibliographies imprinted in the nineteenth century use the special plan for Bibliographies rather than the 19th Century Schedule.

Early Printed Books

Works published before 1801 and Americana, i.e., early imprints from North, South and Central America and the Caribbean islands, are considered early printed books and are classified in a special part of the WZ schedule, WZ 220-270. These books are arranged alphabetically by author within each century or in the Americana number. (See WZ 270 for specific guidance by state for the coverage of Americana.) Reprints and translations of pre-1801 works are classified in WZ 290.

Bibliographies

A bibliography within the scope of the *NLM Classification* is classified in the number for the subject, prefixed by a capital Z. Bibliographies outside the scope of the NLM Classification are classed in LC's Z schedule for Bibliography. Numbers for bibliographies are seldom given in the Index but are derived by using the instructions below for formulating the call number of a bibliography. Unless otherwise noted, the classification numbers for bibliographies may be used for both monographs and serials.

BIBLIOGRAPHIES -- Classification	CLASS NUMBERS
General medical serials	ZW 1
General medical serials in one library	ZW 1
General medical monographs and/or serials issued periodically	ZW 1
Monographic works on general medicine	ZWB 100 (mono-graphs only)
General holdings of libraries in special fields (including private libraries)	[Not LC practice]
Chiropractic	Z 675.C48
Dentistry	Z 675.D3
Hospital	Z 675.H7
Medicine	Z 675.M4
Mental health	Z 675.M43
Nursing	Z 675.N8
Occupational health	Z 675.O22
Pharmacy	Z 675.P48
Veterinary medicine	Z 675.V47
Others, A-Z as listed in LC's Z schedule under Z 675	
General monographic holdings of non-specialized libraries, university, public, etc., by country	Z 881-977
General serials holdings of non-specialized libraries and union lists of serials	Z 6945
Specific topics in medicine and allied fields	Z + NLM schedule letters
Specific topics in fields outside scope of NLM classification	Z 5051-7999
Exception: ZQ 1 is used for bibliography of general scientific periodicals and ZSF [and number] for subjects in the SF schedules. Other exceptions made in the past will no longer be used.	
General materials published in a particular country (national bibliographies)	Z 1201-4980
General serials published in a particular country	Z 6947-6964
Private library catalogs, other than those in Z 675	Z 997
Booksellers catalogs	
Monographs	Z 998-1000.5
Serials	Z 6946-6964
Dissertations	
General	Z 5053-5055
Of schools of dentistry, medicine, nursing, pharmacy, public health, veterinary medicine, etc.	
Foreign	
Individual (with the university)	W4
Collective	ZW 4
United States (by subject)	ZSF, ZQS-ZWZ
General bibliographies of periodicals	Z 6941

SERIAL PUBLICATIONS

NLM follows the *Anglo-American Cataloguing Rules*, second edition, revised 1988, in defining serials. A serial is a "... publication in any medium issued in successive parts bearing numeric or chronological designations and intended to be published indefinitely. Serials include periodicals; newspapers; annuals (reports, yearbooks, etc.); the journals, memoirs, proceedings, transactions, etc. of societies; and numbered monographic series."

Serials are classified in the form number W1 with the exceptions noted below.

Exceptions

Government Administrative Reports or Statistics (W2)
Serial government publications that are administrative or statistical in nature are classed in W2. Integrated reports of administrative and/or statistical information on several hospitals under government administration are classed in W2. Serials classified in W2 are sub-arranged by jurisdiction according to "Table G."

Hospital Administrative Reports or Statistics (WX 2)
Serial hospital publications that are administrative or statistical in nature, including reports of single government hospitals, are classed in WX 2. Serials classified in WX 2 are sub-arranged geographically according to "Table G."

Directories, Handbooks, etc.
Certain publication types, such as directories, handbooks, etc., issued serially are classed in form numbers used also for monographs. For example, directories, whether monographic or serial in nature, are classed in form number 22. Numbers used for both types of publications are identified in the schedules with an asterisk (*). The appropriate LC schedule is used for the above defined publication types when their subject falls outside the scope of the *NLM Classification*.

Bibliographies and Indexes
Serial publications of bibliographies or indexes are classed according to the instructions in the section on Bibliographies above.

LIBRARY OF CONGRESS CLASSIFICATION SCHEDULES

The LC schedules for Human anatomy (QM), Microbiology (QR) and Medicine (R) are not used at all by the National Library of Medicine since they overlap the *NLM Classification*. Otherwise, the Library of Congress schedules augment the *NLM Classification* for subjects related to medicine. NLM rarely uses LC's schedule for Law (K) except for general works. Legal works related to medicine are classified with the subject rather than the law.

LC class numbers are provided in the Index to the *NLM Classification*. Although these numbers were verified against the LC schedules for this revision, the pertinent LC schedules should also be consulted since the numbers may change over time.

Special Instructions

Below are listed those LC schedules with special instructions for subjects that fall within both the NLM and LC schedules.

QD - *Chemistry* -- Use QU or QV if any portion of a work is devoted to biochemistry or pharmacology.

QH - *Natural Sciences (General)* -- Classify here general works on genetics and evolution.

QL - *Zoology* -- Classify here non-pathogenic invertebrates. Pathogenic invertebrates are classed in NLM's QX schedule.

Vertebrates -- Anatomy and physiology of domestic animals are classed in SF (see below). Care and clinical use of laboratory animals in QY 50-60. Works on experimental studies in the interest of learning more about human disease are classed in the appropriate NLM schedule numbers.

QP - *Physiology* -- Classify here physiology of wild animals in general. Physiology of domestic animals is classed in SF. Special topics in this area, when applicable to humans, are for the most part classed in the appropriate NLM numbers; for example, Altitude, **WD 710-715**, Body temperature regulation, **QT 165**.

SF - *Animal cultures* -- Classify here anatomy and physiology of domestic animals.

T - *Technology* -- Classify here Human engineering **TA**, Biotechnology **TP**; however, works on Biomedical engineering are classed in NLM's **QT** schedule.

U - *Military Science* -- Classify here Military medicine.

CHANGES IN CLASSIFICATION PRACTICES

Numbered Congresses -- W3, W 3.5 and ZW 3

NLM no longer classifies serial publications of congresses or sequentially issued, numbered and dated monographic congresses in W3. All newly acquired monographic congresses, including those of named meetings previously classified in W3, are classed in the appropriate subject classification number. Serial publications that are proceedings or reports of meetings are classified in W1.

Nurses' instruction

Since 1984 background materials on specific subjects, in any format, prepared for a nursing audience have been classified with the subject with the form subdivision "nurses' instruction" added to the subject headings. Prior to 1984 these materials were classified in the WY schedule together with materials dealing with nursing techniques in special fields of medicine.

TABLE G

General

Table G is a system of notations that provides geographical or jurisdictional arrangement of materials under specific class numbers in the *NLM Classification*. The use of Table G permits a shelving order which is controlled geographically and alphabetically. Table G is applied only when a class number heading is annotated by "(Table G)." When *LC Classification* numbers are used, the geographical breakdown or tables provided in the LC schedules are applied.

The geographic tables of the *NLM Classification* consist of nine geographic regions. Additionally, special provision is made for international agencies that frequently publish materials related to medicine. Each region or group is identified by a letter.

A--United States	J--Middle East and Asia
D--Americas	K--Australasia
F--Great Britain	L--Islands of the Pacific and Indian Oceans
G--Europe	M--International Agencies
H--Africa	P--Polar Regions

The notation is composed of two letters and one or two numbers from the Cutter-Sanborn tables. The first letter of a notation represents the geographical region or jurisdiction, and the second one is the first letter of the name of a country or, in the case for the states of the United States, a state.

New geographic notations are interpolated into Table G when needed following the established pattern. When a country changes its name a Table G notation is assigned to the new name. The notation for the latest form of a name is used regardless of which form of name is found in the item or when the item was produced.

The Table provides a state or political unit break down only for the United States and Great Britain. A work that is limited to a city, or a state, province or its equivalent, takes the geographic notation for the state or country, or for the smallest area below the national level that has its own notation. Other heavily used state or country notations may be modified to form county (province, state, etc.) or city notations by the addition of .1 (county) or .2 (city) to the appropriate notation.

Examples:

AM3--Maryland	DC2--Canada	FE5--England
AM3.1 M7--Montgomery County	DC2.1 B8--British Columbia	FE5.1 M6--Middlesex
AM3.2 B2--Baltimore	DC2.2 V2--Vancouver	FE5.2 L6--London

Table G notations no longer in use are found below under the heading "Obsolete Table G Notations," preceding the Australian example for an "Expanded Country Notation."

United States -- Special Instructions

Special provisions are made for United States government documents published at the federal, state or local level. Works pertaining to the internal affairs of the various departments or agencies of the U.S. Federal Government, with the exception of the Armed Forces, take the designation "A."

Publications pertaining to the internal affairs of the Armed Forces take the following designations:

A1 Department of Defense
A2 Department of the Army
A3 Army Air Forces (to 1947)
A4 Department of the Air Force
A5 Department of the Navy

AA1 is used for materials pertaining to the United States as a whole but not to the internal affairs of the government. AA1 is used also for materials that span four or more states or territories, unless there is a number for the region.

As noted above, each state is provided with a separate number. The only city appearing in Table G is New York City. For other subordinate political units in the United States it is the individual state number which is so modified, as indicated above.

Examples for Applying Table G

1. Application of Table G to monographic materials.

United States

WZ 70	Hume, Ruth Fox, 1922-
AM3	Medicine in Maryland

WA 546	Ziegler, Mark V., 1891-
AM3.1	A survey of the Health Department of Montgomery
M7	County, Maryland / ...

WA 546	United States. Bureau of the Census
AC2.2	Social and health indicators system, Los Angeles
L86	

Foreign

WZ 70	Anning, Stephen T.
FE5	The history of medicine of Leeds

WM 11	Psychoanalyse in Berlin
GG4	

WA 900	Health on the march, 1948-1960, West Bengal
JI4.1	("W5" represents West Bengal, the state)
W5	

2. The application of Table G to serial documents (W2)

United States

W2	United States. Army. Air Corps. Materiel Division
A3	Air Corps technical report

W2	Connecticut Commission on Alcoholism
AC	Annual report

Foreign

W2	Great Britain. General Register Office
FA1	Quarterly return of marriages, births, and death ...

W2	Saskatchewan. Bureau of Public Health
DC2.1	Annual report
S2	

3. The application of Table G to hospital reports

As instructed in the WX schedule under "WX 2   Serial hospital reports" these serials are arranged geographically and cuttered for the hospital. Decimal subdivisions .1 and .2 for subordinate political divisions are not used, but a notation is added to represent the city.

Civilian hospitals

WX	Cedars of Lebanon Hospital (Los Angeles, Calif.)
2	Staff journal
AC2	
L8	

WX	Hahnemann Hospital tidings
2	
AP4	
P5	

WX	Lasarettet i Landskrona
2	Aarsberättelse
GS8	
L2	

WX	St. Luke's Hospital (Jacksonville, Fla.)
2	Annual report
AF4	
J2	

U.S. Military Hospitals.

Named hospitals have fixed locations and are cuttered the same way as civilian hospitals except that the military symbol precedes the geographical notation. Numbered hospitals did not have fixed locations and geographical notation is not applied to them.

WX	United States. Army. Walter Reed Army Hospital, Washington, D.C.
2	Annual report
A2	
D6	

WX	United States. Army. General Hospital No. 141
2	Year book
A2	
141	

I. SUMMARY

A--United States (Federal Government)
AA1--United States (as geographical area)
D--Americas
F--Great Britain
G--Europe
H--Africa

J--Middle East and Asia
K--Australasia
L--Islands of the Pacific and Indian Oceans
M--International Agencies
P--Polar Regions

II. UNITED STATES (Federal Government)

A--United States (as author)
A1--Department of Defense
A2--Department of the Army
A3--Army Air Forces (to 1947)
A4--Department of the Air Force
A5--Department of the Navy

III. UNITED STATES

AA1--United States
AA4--Alabama
AA5--Alaska
AA6--Appalachian Region
AA7--Arizona
AA8--Arkansas
AC2--California
AC6--Colorado
AC8--Connecticut
AD4--Delaware
AD6--District of Columbia
AF4--Florida
AG4--Georgia
AG7--Great Lakes Region
AH3--Hawaii
AI2--Idaho
AI3--Illinois
AI6--Indiana
AI8--Iowa
AK3--Kansas
AK4--Kentucky
AL6--Louisiana
AM2--Maine
AM3--Maryland
AM4--Massachusetts
AM5--Michigan
AM53--Mid-Atlantic Region

AM56--Midwestern United States
AM6--Minnesota
AM7--Mississippi
AM8--Missouri
AM9--Montana
AN1--Nebraska
AN2--Nevada
AN25--New England
AN3--New Hampshire
AN4--New Jersey
AN5--New Mexico
AN6--New York (State)
AN7--New York City
AN8--North Carolina
AN9--North Dakota
AO3--Ohio
AO5--Oklahoma
AO7--Oregon
AP4--Pennsylvania
AR4--Rhode Island
AS6--South Carolina
AS8--South Dakota
AT2--Tennessee
AT4--Texas
AU8--Utah
AV5--Vermont
AV8--Virginia

UNITES STATES Continued

AW2--Washington

AW4--West Virginia

AW6--Wisconsin

AW8--Wyoming

IV. AMERICAS

DA1--Americas

DA15--Latin America

DA2--North America

DA3--Central America

DA4--South America

DA7--Argentina

DB3--Bahamas

DB34--Barbados

DB38--Belize

DB4--Bermuda

DB6--Bolivia

DB8--Brazil

   British Guiana see Guyana

   British Honduras see Belize

DC2--Canada

DC5--Chile

DC7--Colombia

DC8--Costa Rica

DC9--Cuba

DD6--Dominican Republic

   Dutch Guiana see Suriname

DE2--Ecuador

DF3--Falkland Islands

DG5--Guatemala

DG6--Guyana

DG8--French Guiana

DH2--Haiti

DH7--Honduras

DJ2--Jamaica

DM3--Martinique

DM4--Mexico

DN4--Netherlands Antilles

DN5--Nicaragua

DP2--Panama

DP3--Panama Canal Zone

DP4--Paraguay

DP6--Peru

DP8--Puerto Rico

DS2--Salvador

DS9--Suriname

DT7--Trinidad and Tobago

DU7--Uruguay

DV4--Venezuela

DV5--Virgin Islands

DW5--West Indies

V. GREAT BRITAIN

FA1--Great Britain

FE5--England

FI7--Northern Ireland

FM2--Isle of Man

FS2--Scotland

FW3--Wales

VII. EUROPE

GA1--Europe

GA4--Albania

GA5--Andorra

GA7--Armenia

GA8--Austria

GA85--Azerbaijan

GA9--Azores

GB4--Belgium

GB5--Bosnia-Herzegovina

GB8--Bulgaria

GB9--Byelarus

GC5--Croatia

GC7--Cyprus

GC75--Czech Republic

EUROPE Continued

GC8--Czechoslovakia
GD4--Denmark
GE7--Estonia
GF5--Finland
GF7--France
GG3--Georgia (Republic)
GG4--Germany
GG5--Gibraltar
GG6--Greece
GG7--Greenland
GH8--Hungary
GI3--Iceland
GI6--Ireland
GI8--Italy
GL3--Latvia
GL4--Liechtenstein
GL5--Lithuania
GL8--Luxembourg
GM2--Macedonia (Republic)

GM3--Malta
GM4--Moldova
GM5--Monaco
GM6--Montenegro
GN4--Netherlands
GN6--Norway
GP6--Poland
GP7--Portugal
GR8--Romania
GR9--Russia
GS3--Scandinavia
GS4--Serbia
GS45--Slovakia
GS5--Slovenia
GS6--Spain
GS8--Sweden
GS9--Switzerland
GU5--Ukraine
GY8--Yugoslavia

VII. AFRICA

HA1--Africa
HA12--Africa South of the Sahara
HA14--Central Africa
HA15--Eastern Africa
HA2--North Africa
HA21--Western Africa
HA4--Algeria
HA6--Angola
HA7--African Atlantic Islands
HA71--Ascension
HA72--St. Helena
HA73--Tristan de Cunha
   Basutoland see Lesotho
   Bechuanaland see Botswana
HB35--Benin
HB4--Botswana
HB8--Burundi
HC3--Cameroon
HC4--Cape Verde Islands
HC43--Central African Republic
HC45--Chad
HC5--Congo (Brazzaville)
   Congo (Kinshasa) see Zaire
HC7--Côte d'Ivoire
   Dahomey see Benin

HD6--Djibouti
HE3--Egypt
HE7--Eritrea
HE8--Ethiopia
   French Somaliland see Djibouti
HG2--Gabon
HG3--Gambia
HG6--Ghana
HG66--Guinea
HG7--Guinea-Bissau
HG9--Equatorial Guinea
   Ivory Coast see Côte d'Ivoire
HK4--Kenya
HL3--Lesotho
HL5--Liberia
HL6--Libya
HM3--Madagascar
   Malagasy Republic see Madagascar
HM4--Malawi
HM45--Mali
HM48--Mauritania
HM5--Morocco
HM7--Mozambique
HN2--Namibia
HN4--Niger

AFRICA Continued

HN5--Nigeria
    Nyasaland see Malawi
    Portuguese Guinea see Guinea-Bissau
    Rhodesia, Northern see Zambia
    Rhodesia, Southern see Zimbabwe
HR8--Rwanda
HS1--Senegal
HS3--Sierra Leone
HS5--Somalia
HS8--South West Africa
    Spanish Guinea see Equatorial Guinea
HS86--Sudan

HS9--Swaziland
    Tanganyika see Tanzania
HT3--Tanzania
HT6--Togo
HT8--Tunisia
HU4--Uganda
HU5--South Africa
HZ15--Zaire
HZ2--Zambia
    Zanzibar see Tanzania
HZ7--Zimbabwe

VII. MIDDLE EAST AND ASIA

JA1--Asia
JA2--Middle East
JA4--Afghanistan
JA7--Arabia
JB15--Bahrain
JB2--Bangladesh
    Burma see Myanmar
JC2--Cambodia
    Ceylon see Sri Lanka
JC6--China
    Formosa see Taiwan
JH6--Hong Kong
JI4--India
JI5--Indochina
JI7--Iran
JI8--Iraq
JI9--Israel
JJ3--Japan
JJ6--Jordan
JK2--Kazakhstan
JK6--Korea
JK8--Kuwait
JK9--Kyrgyzstan
JL2--Laos

JL4--Lebanon
JM1--Macao
JM2--Malaysia
    Malaya see Malaysia
    Manchuria see China
JM6--Mongolia
JM9--Myanmar
JN4--Nepal
JP2--Palestine
JP3--Pakistan
JS2--Saudi Arabia
JS6--Singapore
JS8--Sri Lanka
JS9--Syria
JT2--Taiwan
JT23--Tajikistan
JT3--Thailand
JT5--Tibet
JT8--Turkey
JT9--Turkmenistan
JU9--Uzbekistan
JV6--Vietnam
JY4--Yemen

IX. AUSTRALASIA

KA8--Australia

KN4--New Zealand

X. ISLANDS OF THE PACIFIC AND INDIAN OCEANS

LA1--Pacific Islands
LA2--Indian Ocean Islands
LB6--Borneo
LB7--Brunei
LC7--Comoros
LF4--Fiji
LI4--Indonesia
LM4--Mauritius
LM6--Micronesia

Netherlands East Indies see Indonesia
LN6--New Caledonia
LP2--Papua New Guinea
LP5--Philippines
LP7--Polynesia
LR4--Reunion
LS5--Seychelles
LV2--Vanuatu

XI. INTERNATIONAL AGENCIES

M--International agencies
    (General or not listed below)
MA4--Allied Forces
MF6--Food and Agricultural Organization of the
        United Nations
MI3--International Labour Office
ML4--League of Nations
MP2--Pan American Sanitary Bureau
MP3--Pan American Union

MP4--Pan American Zoonoses Center
MS7--SEATO (South East Asia Treaty
        Organization)
MS9--Supreme Commander of the Allied Powers
MU5--United Nations
MU7--Unesco
MU8--Unicef
MW6--World Health Organization

XII. POLAR REGIONS

PA6--Antarctic

PA7--Arctic

OBSOLETE *TABLE G* NOTATIONS

OBSOLETE NOTATION	GEOGRAPHIC NAMES	NEW NOTATION
AMERICAS		
DA5	Lesser Antilles	None
DG7	Dutch Guiana	DS9
DH8	British Honduras	DB38
EUROPE		
GT8	Turkey	JT8
AFRICA		
HB3	Basutoland	HL3
HC6	Congo (Kinshasa)	HZ15
HF4	French Equatorial Africa	None

TABLE G — continued

OBSOLETE NOTATION	GEOGRAPHIC NAMES	NEW NOTATION
	AFRICA Continued	
HF8	French West Africa	None
HM6	Spanish Morocco	None
HN8	Nyasaland	HM4
HR4	Rhodesia	None
HR5	Rio de Oro	HM48
HS6	French Somaliland	HD6
HT4	Tangier	None
HZ3	Zanzibar	HT3
	MIDDLE EAST AND ASIA	
JB8	Burma	JM9
JC4	Ceylon	JS8
JF6	Formosa	JT2
JM3	Manchuria	JC6
JT7	Trans-Jordan	None
	ISLANDS OF THE PACIFIC AND INDIAN OCEANS	
LN4	Netherlands Indies	LI4
	INTERNATIONAL AGENCIES	
MI8	Islamic Countries	None

EXPANDED COUNTRY NOTATION

The expanded country notation below for Australia is an example of how a cataloging agency may expand the notation of a state, country, etc. when the need arises. NLM has used this method; however, since these expansions are infrequent and on an ad hoc basis they are not printed in the *Classification*.

KA8   Australia
.C6 Commission of Inquiry into Poverty
.D3 Department of Health
.D32   Department of Labor and Immigration
.D34   Department of Science
.D4 Department of Social Security
.H6 Hospitals and Health Services
etc.

TABLE G — continued

KA8.1
    .A8 Australian Capital Territory
    .N3 New South Wales
    .N6 Northern Territory
    .Q3 Queensland
    etc.

KA8.2
    .A3 Adelaide
    .B8   Brisbane
    .C2 Canberra
    etc.

This kind of pattern can be used for any single country number.

OUTLINE OF SCHEDULES

PRECLINICAL SCIENCES

MEDICINE AND RELATED SUBJECTS

QS

HUMAN ANATOMY

Classify here general material on normal human anatomy including that of men, women, or children treated separately. Classify material on anatomy of a part of the body with the part, on surgical anatomy in WO 101, on artistic anatomy of human or animal in NC 760–783.8, on anatomy of animals in QL or SF.

QS 1–132	**Anatomy**
QS 504-532.5	**Histology**
QS 604–681	**Embryology**

ANATOMY

Note that other form numbers are used under Histology (QS 504–539) and under Embryology (QS 604–681).

* 1 **Societies (Cutter from the name of society)**
Includes ephemeral membership lists issued serially or separately. Classify substantial lists with directories. Classify annual reports, journals, etc., in W1.

4 **General works**
Classify here works on regional anatomy. If written for the surgeon, classify in WO 101 Surgical anatomy. Classify material on comparative anatomy in QS 124.

Collections (General)
5 **By several authors**
7 **By individual authors**

9 **Addresses. Essays. Lectures (General)**

11 **History (Table G)**
11.1 **General coverage (Not Table G)**

* 13 **Dictionaries. Encyclopedias**

* 15 **Classification. Nomenclature. Terminology**

* 16 **Tables. Statistics**

17 **Atlases. Pictorial works**

*NUMBER CAN BE USED FOR BOTH MONOGRAPHS AND SERIALS.

18   **Education**
Classify here works about education.

* 18.2   **Educational materials**
Classify here educational materials, e.g., outlines, questions and answers, programmed instruction, catalogs, computer-assisted instruction, etc., regardless of format. Classify textbooks, regardless of format, by subject.

20.5   **Research (General)**
Classify here works about research in general. Classsify works about research on a particular subject by subject.

21   **Anatomy as a profession**

* 22   **Directories (Table G)**
* 22.1   **General coverage (Not Table G)**

Laboratories, institutes, etc.
23   **Collective**
24   **Individual (Cutter from name of agency)**

25   **Laboratory manuals. Technique**

* 26   **Equipment and supplies**
Classify catalogs here.

26.5   **Medical informatics. Automatic data processing. Computers (General)**
Classify works on use for special subjects by subject.

Museums, exhibits, etc.
27   **Collective (Table G)**
27.1   **General coverage (Not Table G)**
28   **Individual (Table G)**

[32]   **[This number not used]**
Classify laws on dissection in QS 132.

* 39   **Handbooks**

124   **Comparative anatomy of humans and animals**
Classify works on artistic anatomy of humans and animals in NC 760–783.8; on comparative anatomy limited to animals in QL 801–950.9.

130   **Dissection manuals**

* 132   Laws concerning dissection. Discussion of law

HISTOLOGY

504   General works

          Collections (General)
505   By several authors
507   By individual authors

509   Addresses. Essays. Lectures (General)

511   History (Table G)
511.1   General coverage (Not Table G)

* 513   Dictionaries. Encyclopedias

* 515   Classification. Nomenclature. Terminology

* 516   Tables. Statistics

517   Atlases. Pictorial works

518   Education
         Classify here works about education.

* 518.2   Educational materials
         Classify here educational materials, e.g., outlines, questions and answers, programmed instruction, catalogs, computer–assisted instruction, etc., regardless of format. Classify textbooks, regardless of format, by subject.

520   Research (General)
         Classify here works about research in general. Classify works about research on a particular subject by subject. Cf. 530 Experimental histology.

521   Histology as a profession

* 522   Directories (Table G)
* 522.1   General coverage (Not Table G)

Tissue banks

523   Collective

524   Individual (Cutter from name of bank)

525   Laboratory manuals. Technique

* 526   Equipment and supplies
       Classify catalogs here.

526.5   Medical informatics. Automatic data processing. Computers (General)
       Classify works on use for special subjects by subject.

* 529   Handbooks

530   Experimental histology
       Classify works on cytology of normal tissue in QH. Classify works about research in QS 520.

531   Histocytochemistry

532   Types of normal tissue (General)
       Classify works on aging tissue of the elderly in WT 104; on lymphoid tissue in WH 700; on fetal membranes in WQ 210 or in QS 645 if written for the embryologist.

532.5   Specific types of tissue, A–Z

     .A3   Adipose tissue
     .C7   Connective tissue
     .E5   Elastic tissue
     .E7   Epithelium
     .M3   Membranes (General)
     .M8   Mucous membrane
     .N3   Nerve tissue

EMBRYOLOGY

604   General works

Collections (General)

605   By several authors

607   By individual authors

609   Addresses. Essays. Lectures (General)

611	**History (Table G)**
611.1	**General coverage (Not Table G)**

* 613   **Dictionaries. Encyclopedias**

* 615   **Classification. Nomenclature. Terminology**

* 616   **Tables. Statistics**

617   **Atlases. Pictorial works**

618   **Education**
Classify here works about education.

* 618.2   **Educational materials**
Classify here educational materials, for example, outlines, questions and answers, programmed instruction, catalogs, computer–assisted instruction, etc., regardless of format. Classify textbooks, regardless of format, by subject.

620   **Research (General)**
Classify here works about research in general. Classify works about research on a particular subject by subject.

621   **Embryology as a profession**

* 622   **Directories (Table G)**
* 622.1   **General coverage (Not Table G)**

625   **Laboratory manuals. Technique**

* 626   **Equipment and supplies**
Classify catalogs here.

626.5   **Medical informatics. Automatic data processing. Computers (General)**
Classify works on use for special subjects by subject.

* 629   **Handbooks**

638   **Sex determination (Embryogenic)**

640   **Sex differentiation**

642   **Twinning**

*NUMBER CAN BE USED FOR BOTH MONOGRAPHS AND SERIALS.

645   **Placentation.   Fetal membranes**

675   **Congenital abnormalities (General or not elsewhere classified)**
        Classify works on specific abnormalities with anatomical part involved, e.g., Cleft lip WV 440. Classify works on inborn errors of metabolism, general and systemic, in WD 205, etc.

677   **Chromosome abnormalities, including experimental works**
        Classify works on chromosome aberrations in QH 462.

679   **Drug–induced abnormalities, including experimental works**

681   **Radiation–induced abnormalities, including experimental works**
        Classify works on specific abnormalities with anatomical part involved, e.g., of the central nervous system in WL 101.

QT

PHYSIOLOGY

*Classify here material on general physiology; classify physiology of a part of the body
with the part; classify animal physiology in QP, QL, or SF. The last part of QT
covers the broad areas of hygiene.*

QT 1–33.1	General
QT 34–37.5	Physics, Mathematics, and Engineering
QT 104–172	Human Physiology
QT 180–275	Physiology and Hygiene

GENERAL

* 1   **Societies (Cutter from name of society)**
       *Includes ephemeral membership lists issued serially or separately. Classify substantial
       lists with directories. Classify annual reports, journals, etc., in W1.*

4   **General works, including comparative physiology**
       Classify material on comparative physiology limited to animals in QP.

       Collections (General)
5   **By several authors**
7   **By individual authors**

9   **Addresses. Essays. Lectures (General)**

11   **History (Table G)**
11.1   **General coverage (Not Table G)**

* 13   **Dictionaries. Encyclopedias**

* 15   **Classification. Nomenclature. Terminology**

* 16   **Tables. Statistics**

17   **Atlases. Pictorial works**

18   **Education**
Classify here works about education.

* 18.2   **Educational materials**
Classify here educational materials, e.g., outlines, questions and answers, programmed instruction, catalogs, computer–assisted instruction, etc., regardless of format. Classify textbooks, regardless of format, by subject.

* 19   **Schools, departments, and faculties of physiology or physical education**

20.5   **Research (General)**
Classify here works about research in general. Classify works about research on a particular subject by subject. Cf. QT 25 Experimental physiology.

21   **Physiology as a profession. Ethics. Peer review**

* 22   **Directories (Table G)**
* 22.1   **General coverage (Not Table G)**

Laboratories, institutes, etc.
23   **Collective**
24   **Individual (Cutter from name of agency)**

25   **Laboratory manuals. Experimental physiology. Technique**

* 26   **Equipment and supplies**
Classify catalogs here.

26.5   **Medical informatics. Automatic data processing. Computers (General)**
Classify works on use for special subjects by subject.

Museums, exhibits, etc.
27   **Collective**
28   **Individual (Cutter from name of museum, etc.)**

* 29   **Handbooks**

* 32   **Laws (Table G)**
* 32.1   **General coverage (Not Table G)**

* 33   **Discussion of law (Table G)**
* 33.1   **General coverage (Not Table G)**

PHYSICS, MATHEMATICS, AND ENGINEERING

Include here only general works on physics, mathematics, and engineering as applied to physiological and medical phenomena. Classify works on their applications to specific problems by subject.

34 **Biophysics**
Cf. WN Radiology. Diagnostic imaging

35 **Biomedical mathematics**
Cf. WA 950 Theory or methods of medical statistics. Classify works for the biologist in QH 323.5.

36 **Biomedical engineering**

37 **Biomedical and biocompatible materials**
Classify works on dental materials in WU 180–190.

37.5 **Specific materials, A–Z**

    .C4   Ceramics
    .P7   Polymers

HUMAN PHYSIOLOGY

104 **General works**

120 **Homeostasis (General)**

140 **Environmental exposure. Physiological adaptation**

145 **Acclimatization**

150 **Hot climates**

160 **Cold climates**

Environmental exposure. Physiological adaptation - Continued

162 **Other environmental factors acting on human physiology, A–Z**
Classify works on animals in general and on wild animals in QP 82–82.2; on domestic animals in SF 768–768.2. Classify works on environmental factors relating to personal health and hygiene in QT 230; to disease, in QZ 57; to public health, in WA. For other environmental factors not listed here, consult the Index to the classification.

.A5 **Air ionization**
.E4 **Electrolytes**
.G7 **Gravitation**
.H8 **Humidity**
.L5 **Light**
.M3 **Magnetics**
.S8 **Stress**
.U4 **Ultraviolet rays and other non–ionizing radiation not classified elsewhere.**
Cf. WB 117 for general medical use; WB 288 for diagnostic use; WB 480 for therapeutic use; WD 605 for adverse effects.

165 **Body temperature regulation**

167 **Physiological periodicity**

172 **Exocrine glands (General)**
Classify works on specific glands with the system where located, e.g., Sebaceous glands WR 410.

PHYSIOLOGY AND HYGIENE

180 **Physiology. General hygiene**
Include college level texts.

200 **Teachers' manuals, books for nurses, etc., on physiology and hygiene**
Classify works about study and teaching of public health in WA 18. Classify works on informal health education (community, radio, etc.) in WA 590.

School texts of physiology and hygiene
Classify material on hygiene of adolescence in WS 460.

210 **Secondary**

215 **Juvenile**

225 **Sex education**
Classify in HQ material on sex education other than school texts.

230 **Lighting. Air. Sunlight. Living space**

235   **Diet**
Classify works on particular foods and beverages in the numbers for diet in health and disease, WB 400–449; on diets for particular diseases with the disease.

240   **Cleanliness**

245   **Clothing**

250   **Recreation. Outdoor activities**

255   **Physical fitness. Gymnastics. Physical education**
Cf. WB 541 Medical gymnastics.

260   **Athletics. Sports**
Classify works on first aid in WA 292.

260.5   **Special activities, A–Z**

     .B2   **Baseball**
     .B3   **Basketball**
     .B5   **Bicycling**
     .B7   **Boxing**
     .D6   **Diving**
     .F6   **Football**
     .G6   **Golf**
     .H6   **Hockey**
     .J6   **Jogging**
     .M3   **Martial arts**
     .M9   **Mountaineering**
     .R9   **Running**
     .S6   **Skiing**
     .S7   **Soccer**
     .S9   **Swimming**
     .T3   **Tennis**
     .T7   **Track and field**
     .W2   **Walking**
     .W4   **Weight lifting**
     .W9   **Wrestling**

261   **Sports medicine**
Classify works on first aid in WA 292; on specific pathological conditions with the condition.

265   **Relaxation. Rest. Sleep (Hygiene)**
Classify works on therapeutic use of rest, etc., in WB 545; on disorders of sleep in WM 188; on physiology of sleep in WL 108.

275   **Hygienic aspects of beauty culture**
Classify works on hair care in WR 465; on public health aspects of barber shops, beauty salons, and cosmetics in WA 744.

QU

BIOCHEMISTRY

* 1   **Societies (Cutter from name of society)**
        Includes ephemeral membership lists issued serially or separately.   Classify substantial lists with directories; annual reports, journals, etc. in W1.

4   **General works**

        Collections (General)
5   **By several authors**
7   **By individual authors**

9   **Addresses. Essays. Lectures (General)**

11   **History (Table G)**
11.1   **General coverage (Not Table G)**

* 13   **Dictionaries.   Encyclopedias**

* 15   **Classification. Nomenclature. Terminology**

* 16   **Tables.   Statistics**
        Classify nutrition tables or food value tables in QU 145–145.5.

17   **Atlases.   Pictorial works**

18   **Education**
        Classify here works about education.

* 18.2 **Educational materials**
        Classify here educational materials, e.g., outlines, questions and answers, programmed instruction, catalogs, computer–assisted instruction, etc., regardless of format. Classify textbooks, regardless of format, by subject.

20   **Research (General)**
        Classify here works about research in general. Classify works about research on a particular subject by subject.

21   **Biochemistry as a profession**

*NUMBER CAN BE USED FOR BOTH MONOGRAPHS AND SERIALS.

* 22   **Directories (Table G)**
* 22.1   General coverage (Not Table G)

       Laboratories, institutes, etc.
23   Collective
24   Individual (Cutter from name of agency)

25   **Laboratory manuals. Technique**

* 26   **Equipment and supplies**
       Classify catalogs here.

26.5   **Medical informatics. Automatic data processing. Computers (General)**
       Classify works on use for special subjects by subject.

* 32   **Laws (Table G)**
* 32.1   General coverage (Not Table G)

* 33   **Discussion of law (Table G)**
* 33.1   General coverage (Not Table G)

34   **Biochemical phenomena (General or not elsewhere classified)**
       Classify here works on binding sites, diffusion, energy transfer, osmosis, etc., when related to biochemistry in general.

* 39   **Handbooks**

50   **Chemistry of food substances (General)**

54   **Nitrogen and related compounds (General or not elsewhere classified)**
       Classify works on nitrogen compounds that work primarily on a particular body system in QV.

55   **Proteins (General or not elsewhere classified)**
       Classify here works on proteins in general or those in foods. Classify works on proteins that work primarily on a particular body system in QV; on those that are localized, by site, e.g., eye proteins in WW 101; on those that are enzymes or coenzymes in QU 135–141 or with the system acted upon; on blood proteins in WH or in clinical pathology QY 455; on immunoglobulins in QW 601; on other immunoproteins in appropriate QW number.

56   **Nucleoproteins**

57   **Nucleosides. Nucleotides**

*NUMBER CAN BE USED FOR BOTH MONOGRAPHS AND SERIALS.

58   **Nucleic acids and derivatives (General or not elsewhere classified)**
           Classify works on derivatives acting on blood and blood formation in QV 185.

58.5   **DNA**

58.7   **RNA**

60   **Amino acids (General or not elsewhere classified)**

61   **Amines. Amidines (General or not elsewhere classified)**
           Classify works on catecholamines in WK 725; on amino alcohols in QV 82–84.

62   **Amides (General or not elsewhere classified)**

65   **Heterocyclic compounds associated with amino acid synthesis and metabolism**
           e.g., Allantoin. Indoleacetic acids

68   **Peptides (General or not elsewhere classified)**

70   **Nitrogen fixation**

75   **Carbohydrates**
           Cf. QY 470 under Blood chemistry.

83   **Polysaccharides and derivatives**
           e.g., Dextrins. Glycogen

84   **Sugar acids and their salts and esters (General or not elsewhere classified)**

85   **Lipids (General or not elsewhere classified)**
           Cf. QY 465 under Blood chemistry.

86   **Fats. Oils**

87   **Lipotropic factors**
           Classify works on methionine in QU 60.

90   **Fatty acids**

93   **Phospholipids**
           e.g., Phosphatidylethanolamines

Lipids - Continued

95   **Sterols**
      e.g., Cholesterol

98   **Carboxylic acids and their salts and esters (General or not elsewhere classified)**

99   **Aldehydes (General or not elsewhere classified)**

100   **Body composition**

105   **Body fluids**
      Classify here works on acid–base equilibrium, hydrogen–ion concentration, and water–electrolyte balance in body fluids. Cf. WD 220 Water–electrolyte imbalance, etc.

107   **Growth substances. Growth inhibitors (General or not elsewhere classified)**

110   **Pigments (General or not elsewhere classified)**

120   **Metabolism**
      Classify works on metabolism of a particular substance with the substance, e.g., Metabolism of proteins in QU 55.

125   **Energy metabolism. Calorimetry**

130   **Inorganic substances (General or not elsewhere classified)**
      Cf. QY 480 under Blood chemistry.

130.5   **Trace elements**

131   **Organometallic compounds. Organophosphorus compounds. Organothiophosphorus compounds (General or not elsewhere classified)**

133   **Colloids (General or not elsewhere classified)**

135   **Enzymes. Coenzymes (General or not elsewhere classified). Enzymology**
      Classify works on enzyme deficiency in WD 105 or with the diseases resulting.

136   **Hydrolases (General or not elsewhere classified)**

137   **Isomerases (General or not elsewhere classified)**

Enzymes. Coenzymes. Enzymology - Continued

138   **Ligases (General or not elsewhere classified)**

139   **Lyases (General or not elsewhere classified)**

140   **Oxidoreductases (General or not elsewhere classified)**

141   **Transferases (General or not elsewhere classified)**

142   **Enzyme precursors (General or not elsewhere classified)**

143   **Enzyme inhibitors (General or not elsewhere classified)**

144   **Enzyme reactivators (General or not elsewhere classified)**

145   **Nutrition. Nutritional requirements**
Classify works on infant nutrition in WS 115–125; on child nutrition in WS 115–130; on geriatric nutrition in WT 115.

145.5   **Nutritive values of food**

146   **Nutritional surveys (Table G)**
146.1   **General coverage (Not Table G)**

160   **Vitamins. Vitamin requirements**
Cf. QY 350 Assay of vitamins; QZ 109 Vitamin deficiencies; SF 98.V5 Vitamins in animal nutrition; WD 105 Deficiency diseases.

165   **Fat soluble vitamins**

167   **Vitamin A, A1, etc.**

173   **Vitamin D, D2, etc.**

179   **Vitamin E**

181   **Vitamin K**

185   **Water soluble vitamins**

187   **Vitamin B complex (General)**

Vitamins. Vitamin requirements
  Water soluble vitamins
    Vitamin B complex - Continued

QV

PHARMACOLOGY

Classify here works on pharmacology in general or on the pharmacology of individual drugs or types of drugs grouped according to their specific action. Classify works on an individual drug according to its principal action. Classify works on the use of an individual drug in the treatment of a particular disease with the disease. Classify works on the purely chemical or technological use of chemicals in the QD or the T schedules. Classify a drug derived from a plant with the drug.

Classify works on vitamins in QU; on endocrine preparations (including synthetic substitutes) in WJ, WK, or WP; and non-endocrine biologicals in QW. Note that occasionally agents are classed together because they are frequently treated together regardless of their different actions, e.g., sulfur and sulfur compounds in QV 265. Classify works dealing with the general aspects of pharmacy and pharmaceutics in the section beginning with QV 701. Note that Pharmacy and Pharmaceutics section also has many of the early range or form numbers found under Pharmacology.

QV 1–370	General
QV 600–667	Toxicology
QV 701–835	Pharmacy and Pharmaceutics

GENERAL

* 1   **Societies (Cutter from name of society)**
Includes ephemeral membership lists issued serially or separately. Classify substantial lists with directories; annual reports, journals, etc., in W1.

4   **General works**

Collections (General)
5   By several authors
7   By individual authors

9   **Addresses. Essays. Lectures (General)**

11   **History (Table G)**
11.1   **General coverage (Not Table G)**
Classify works on the history of a specific drug with the drug.

* 13   **Dictionaries. Encyclopedias**

* 15   **Classification. Nomenclature. Terminology**

*NUMBER CAN BE USED FOR BOTH MONOGRAPHS AND SERIALS.

* 16   **Tables. Weights and measures. Statistics**

17   **Atlases. Pictorial works**
         Classify pictorial works on medicinal plants or materia medica in QV 717.

18   **Education**
         Classify here works about education.

* 18.2   **Educational materials**
         Classify here educational materials, e.g., outlines, questions and answers, programmed instruction, catalogs, computer-assisted instruction, etc., regardless of format. Classify textbooks, regardless of format, by subject.

* 19   **Schools and colleges**
         Classify courses of study, catalogs, etc., in W 19.5.

20   **Graduate and continuing education in pharmacy (including fellowships, internships, residencies, etc.)**

20.5   **Research (General)**
         Classify here works about research in general. Classify works about research on a particular subject by subject. Cf. QV 34 Experimental pharmacology.

21   **Pharmacology as a profession. Pharmacy as a profession. Ethics. Peer review**

21.5   **Pharmacists' aides**

* 22   **Directories (Table G)**
* 22.1   **General coverage (Not Table G)**

         Laboratories, institutes, etc.
23   **Collective**
24   **Individual (Cutter from name of agency)**

25   **Laboratory manuals, including those on microscopic and chemical analysis. Technique**
         Cf. QV 744 Pharmaceutical chemistry.

* 26   **Equipment and supplies**
         Classify drug catalogs in QV 772. Cf. QV 785–835 for pharmaceutical supplies.

26.5   **Medical informatics. Automatic data processing. Computers (General)**
         Classify works on use for special subjects by subject.

	Museums, exhibits, etc.
27	Collective
28	Individual (Cutter from name of museum, etc.)

| 29 | Registration of pharmacists (Table G) |
| 29.1 | General coverage (Not Table G) |

| * 32 | Laws (Table G) |
| * 32.1 | General coverage (Not Table G) |

| * 33 | Discussion of law. Jurisprudence (Table G) |
| * 33.1 | General coverage (Not Table G) |

34   Experimental pharmacology (General)
Classify here works that discuss the experimental work itself. Classify works about research in QV 20.5. Classify works on specific subjects by subject.

38   Drug action (including absorption, distribution, excretion of drugs; mechanism of drug action; synergism, antagonism, tolerance; factors modifying drug action, including genetic factors)

* 39   Handbooks

50   Dental pharmacology
Cf. WU 180–190 Dental materials.

55   Drugs (General)
Cf. QV 38 Drug action; QV 704 Pharmacy; QY 450–490 Blood chemistry.

60   Dermatologic agents
Classify works on topical anti–inflammatory agents here. Cf. QV 247 for other anti–inflammatory agents. Classify works on local anti–infective agents in QV 220.

63   Protectives
e.g., Adsorbents. Demulcents. Emollients

65   Irritants. Astringents

66   Gastrointestinal agents (General or not elsewhere classified)
Cf. WI 703 Bile acids, salts, etc.

69   Antacids. Anti–ulcer agents

71   Antidiarrheals

*NUMBER CAN BE USED FOR BOTH MONOGRAPHS AND SERIALS.

Gastrointestinal agents - Continued

73   **Emetics. Antiemetics**

75   **Cathartics**

76   **Antitussive agents**

76.5   **Neuropharmacology. Drugs acting on the nervous system (General or not elsewhere classified)**

77   **Psychopharmacology**

77.2   **Psychotropic drugs (General or not elsewhere classified)**

77.5   **Antidepressive agents**

77.7   **Hallucinogens**

77.9   **Tranquilizers**

80   **Depressants of the central nervous system**
            Note that some of the agents classed in this group of numbers, QV 80–98, are here because of their relation to the depressant listed.

81   **Agents of general anesthesia**
            Classify here works on anesthetics in general also. Cf. QV 110–115 Local anesthetics. Classify works on the barbiturates (except hexobarbital) in QV 88.

82   **Alcohols**

83   **Methyl**

84   **Ethyl**

85   **Hypnotics. Sedatives. Anticonvulsants**

87   **Bromides**

88   **Barbiturates**
            Classify works on hexobarbital in QV 81.

89   **Opioid analgesics.   Narcotics and narcotic antagonists**
            Cf. QV 95   Anti–inflammatory analgesics.

90   **Opium alkaloids**

92   **Morphine and derivatives**

95   **Anti–inflammatory analgesics.   Non–narcotic analgesics**
            Classify general works on analgesics here.   Cf. QV 89   Opioid analgesics; WO 234 Preanesthetic medication.

98   **Gout suppressants**

100   **Stimulants of the central nervous system**

101   **Analeptics**

102   **Amphetamines**

103   **Convulsants**

107   **Xanthines**
            e.g., Caffeine.   Theobromine.   Theophylline

110   **Local anesthetics (General or not elsewhere classified)**

113   **Cocaine and derivatives**

115   **Synthetic local anesthetics**

120   **Autonomic agents (General or not elsewhere classified)**
            Classify general works on bronchodilator agents here.   Classify works on theophylline in QV 107.   Classify works on autonomic agents that are also anti–inflammatory agents in QV 247; that are also histamine antagonists in QV 157; that are also sympathomimetics in QV 129; that are also vasodilator agents in QV 150.

122   **Parasympathomimetics**
            e.g., Pilocarpine

124   **Cholinesterase inhibitors and reactivators**

Parasympathomimetics - Continued

126   **Neurotransmitters (General or not elsewhere classified)**
         Classify works on epinephrine, norepinephrine, and other catecholamines in WK 725.

129   **Sympathomimetics**
         e.g., Ephedrine
         See note under QV 126 above. Classify works on amphetamines in QV 102.

132   **Sympatholytics. Parasympatholytics**
         Classify works on cholinesterase reactivators in QV 124.

134   **Atropine and allied compounds**

137   **Nicotine**

138   **Non–metallic elements and their compounds, A–Z**
         The substances classed here are used largely in experimental pharmacology, toxicology, and/or biochemistry for various purposes. Classify by specific use where possible.

     .C1   **Carbon**
     .P4   **Phosphorus**
     .S5   **Selenium**

140   **Neuromuscular agents**
         e.g., Curare
         Classify works on tranquilizers in QV 77.9.

150   **Drugs acting on the cardiovascular system**

153   **Digitalis. Cardiac glycosides**

155   **Quinidine and related compounds**

156   **Nitrates, nitrites, etc.**

157   **Histamine. Histamine antagonists. Histamine receptor blockaders**

160   **Diuretics. Antidiuretics**

170   **Drugs acting on the reproductive organs**

173   **Oxytocics**

Drugs acting on the reproductive organs
    Oxytocics - Continued

174   **Ergot and its derivatives**

175   **Abortifacient agents**

177   **Contraceptives (including those with indirect action)**
             Classify works on contraceptive devices in WP 640.

180   **Drugs acting on blood cells and blood formation (General or not elsewhere classified)**
             Classify works on folic acid and vitamin B12 in QU 188 and QU 194, respectively.

181   **Hematinics**

183   **Iron.   Iron salts**

184   **Liver extracts**

185   **Nucleic acid derivatives**
             Cf. QU 58 for works on biochemistry of nucleic acid derivatives.

190   **Drugs affecting blood coagulation**

193   **Anticoagulants**
             e.g., Coumarins.   Heparin

195   **Hemostatics.   Coagulants**

220   **Local anti-infective agents.   Disinfectants (General or not elsewhere classified)**

223   **Phenols.   Cresols (General or not elsewhere classified)**

225   **Formaldehyde.   Nitrofurazone**

229   **Oxidizing antiseptics**
             e.g., Hydrogen peroxide.   Potassium permanganate

231   **Halogen antiseptics**
             e.g., Iodine

233   **Detergents and other surface-active agents**

Local anti-infective agents. Disinfectants - Continued

235   **Dyes**
        Cf. QV 240 for general works on the pharmacology of dyes, etc.

239   **Boron compounds**

240   **Dyes and related compounds used in diagnosis or as reagents, indicators, etc.**

241   **Tars. Balsams**

243   **Urinary anti-infective agents**
        e.g., Methenamine. Mandelic acids

247   **Anti-inflammatory agents (General or not elsewhere classified)**
        Classify works on anti-inflammatory analgesics in QV 95; on topical anti-inflammatory agents in QV 60.

250   **Anti-infective agents (General or not elsewhere classified)**
        Classify works on local anti-infective agents in QV 220-239.

252   **Antifungal agents. Antifungal antibiotics**

253   **Anthelmintics**

254   **Antiprotozoal agents (General or not elsewhere classified)**

255   **Amebicides**

256   **Antimalarials**

257   **Cinchona and its derivatives**

258   **Synthetic drugs**

259   **Leprostatic agents**
        e.g., Chaulmoogra oil

261   **Antisyphilitics**
        e.g., Mercury compounds. Bismuth compounds. Iodides

262   **Arsenicals (General or not elsewhere classified)**

Anti-infective agents - Continued

265   **Sulfonamides. Sulfur and other sulfur compounds (General or not elsewhere classified)**

268   **Antitubercular agents. Antitubercular antibiotics**
Cf. WF 360 Drug therapy of pulmonary tuberculosis. Classify works on streptomycin in QV 356.

268.5   **Antiviral agents (General or not elsewhere classified)**

269   **Antineoplastic agents. Antineoplastic antibiotics**
Cf. QZ 267 Drug therapy of neoplasms. Classify works on azaserine in QV 252 Antifungal antibiotics or in QW 920 Immunosuppressive agents.

270   **Water. Inorganic ions. Electrolytes (General or not elsewhere classified)**
Cf. QU 105 Water-electrolyte balance; WD 220 Water-electrolyte imbalance.

273   **Water. Sodium salts**

275   **Cations and related compounds. Alkali and alkaline earth metals (General or not elsewhere classified)**
Cf. QV 290–298 Heavy metals and their compounds.

276   **Calcium**

277   **Potassium**

278   **Magnesium**

280   **Anions. Halogens**
Classify works on antiseptic halogens in QV 231.

282   **Fluorine. Fluorides**
Cf. QV 50 Dental pharmacology.

283   **Iodine. Iodides and related compounds**
Cf. QV 231 for iodines, etc. as antiseptics.

285   **Phosphates**
Classify works on sugar phosphates in QU 75.

290   **Heavy metals and their compounds (General or not elsewhere classified)**
Include works on rare earth metals not indexed elsewhere. Classify works on toxicological effects here also. Classify here works on chelating agents in general, but classify works on particular chelating agents with specific metal.

Heavy metals and their compounds - Continued

292	Lead
293	Mercury (General or compounds not elsewhere classified)
294	Arsenic (General or compounds not elsewhere classified)
295	Antimony
296	Gold
297	Silver
298	Zinc
310	Gases and their compounds (General or not elsewhere classified)
312	Oxygen and its compounds (General or not elsewhere classified)
314	Carbon dioxide
318	Helium

350   Antibiotics (General or not elsewhere classified)
Classify works on antifungal, antineoplastic, and antitubercular antibiotics in QV 252, QV 269, and QV 268, respectively.

350.5   Specific drugs, A–Z

       .C3   Cephalosporins
       .C5   Chloramphenicol
       .E7   Erythromycin
       .G3   Gentamicins

354	Penicillins
356	Streptomycin
360	Tetracyclines

370   **Tissue extracts**
Classify works on tissue therapy in WB 391; on therapy of specific diseases with the disease. Classify works on liver extracts in QV 184.

TOXICOLOGY

Classify general works on industrial poisons and poisoning in WA 465; general works on food poisoning in WC 268; on public health aspects of food poisoning in WA 695–722; on animal poisons in WD 400–430; on plant poisons in WD 500–530; on poisons acting on plants or animals in the appropriate LC schedules (See Index to this Classification). Classify works on agents that are primarily air, water, or soil pollutants in WA or WN. Classify works on chemicals used extensively in drug therapy or in experimental pharmacology in the pharmacology numbers.

600   **General works**

601   **Antidotes and other therapeutic measures**

602   **Detection of poisons. Tests. Laboratory manuals. Technique**
Classify works on medicolegal aspects in W 750.

* 605   **Directories of poison control centers. Lists of poisons, antidotes, etc. (Table G)**
* 605.1   **General coverage (Not Table G)**

* 607   **Handbooks**

610   **Inorganic poisons**

612   **Acids. Alkalies**

618   **Irritant poisons**
Cf. QV 664 Lung irritants; QV 666 Irritant gases.

627   **Organic poisons**

628   **Alkaloids**

632   **Non–alkaloids**

633   **Hydrocarbons. Volatile poisons. Solvents**

*NUMBER CAN BE USED FOR BOTH MONOGRAPHS AND SERIALS.

662   **Gas poisons and poisoning**
        Cf. QV 81   Anesthetic gases; QV 310   Gases used in therapy.

663   **Chemical warfare agents**
        Classify here works on the agent even if its war use is not part of the discussion.

664   **Lung irritants**
        e.g., Chloropicrin.   Phosgene
        Cf. QV 666 for works on irritant gases.

665   **Tear gases.   Toxic smokes**

666   **Irritant gases**
        Cf. QV 644 for general works on lung irritants.

667   **Systemic poisons.   Paralysants**

PHARMACY AND PHARMACEUTICS

Classify works on pharmacy as a profession in QV 21; on pharmacy education in QV 18–20.

* 701   **Societies (Cutter from name of society)**
        Includes ephemeral membership lists issued serially or separately.   Classify substantial lists with directories.   Classify annual reports, journals, etc., in W1.

704   **General works**

        Collections (General)
705   **By several authors**
707   **By individual authors**

709   **Addresses.   Essays.   Lectures (General)**

711   **History (Table G)**
711.1   **General coverage (Not Table G)**

* 715   **Classification.   Nomenclature.   Terminology**

717   **Atlases.   Pictorial works**

* 722   Directories (Table G)
* 722.1   General Coverage (Not Table G)

* 732   Laws (Table G)
* 732.1   General coverage (Not Table G)

* 733   Discussion of law. Jurisprudence (Table G)
* 733.1   General coverage (Not Table G)

* 735   Handbooks

736   Drug industry. Economics of pharmacy. Advertising

737   Pharmaceutical services. Community pharmacy services. Pharmacies
     Classify works on hospital pharmacy service in WX 179; on public health aspects in WA 730.

* 738   Pharmacopoeias (Official, i.e., one adopted by a government or other authoritative pharmaceutical body) (Table G)
* 738.1   General coverage (Not Table G)

* 740   Dispensatories, formularies, etc. (Unofficial) (Table G)
* 740.1   General coverage (Not Table G)

744   Pharmaceutical chemistry
     Classify works on techniques of drug analysis and laboratory manuals in QV 25.

746   Drug incompatibility (Pharmaceutical aspects)

748   Prescription writing. Dosage

752   Pharmacognosy. Natural history of drugs

754   Collection and preservation of drugs
     Cf. QV 820 Preservatives.

760   Materia medica

* 766   Medicinal plants (General and without geographic application)

767   Herbs

Medicinal plants - Continued

770   **Geographic distribution (Table G)**
770.1   **General coverage (Not Table G)**
General geographic coverage with more than three areas.

771   **Standardization and evaluation of drugs**
Classify works on monitoring drugs in WB 330; on monitoring those used for a particular disease, with the disease.

* 772   **Commercial preparations.   Patent medicines**
Include here drug catalogs issued singly or serially.

773   **Fraud in manufacturing of drugs**

778   **Pharmaceutical processes.   Drug compounding**

785   **Types of pharmaceutical preparations.   Dosage forms (General or not elsewhere classified)**

786   **Solutions**

787   **Tablets**

800   **Vehicles.   Pharmaceutic aids**

810   **Flavoring agents**

820   **Preservatives**
Cf. QV 754   Collection and preservation of drugs.

825   **Packaging**

835   **Labels and labeling**

QW

MICROBIOLOGY AND IMMUNOLOGY

Classify works on a particular species of bacteria with the order to which that species belongs, according to the classification in Bergey's Manual of Determinative Bacteriology.

QW 1–300   **Microbiology**
QW 501–949   **Immunology**

MICROBIOLOGY

* 1   **Societies (Cutter from name of society)**
    Includes ephemeral membership lists issued serially or separately. Classify substantial lists with directories. Classify annual reports, journals, etc., in W1.

4   **General works**
    Classify here works on microbiology as a whole. Classify works on bacteriology alone in QW 50; on virology alone in QW 160–170; on mycology alone in QW 180–180.5, or appropriate LC numbers.

    Collections (General)
5   **By several authors**
7   **By individual authors**

9   **Addresses. Essays. Lectures (General)**

11   **History (Table G)**
11.1   **General coverage (Not Table G)**

* 13   **Dictionaries. Encyclopedias**

* 15   **Classification. Nomenclature. Terminology**

* 16   **Tables. Statistics**

17   **Atlases. Pictorial works**

18   **Education**
    Classify here works about education.

*NUMBER CAN BE USED FOR BOTH MONOGRAPHS AND SERIALS.

* 18.2   **Educational materials**
       Classify here educational materials, e.g., outlines, questions and answers, programmed instruction, catalogs, computer–assisted instruction, etc., regardless of format. Classify textbooks, regardless of format, by subject.

20.5   **Research (General)**
       Classify here works about research in general. Classify works about research on a particular subject by subject.

21   **Microbiology and immunology as professions**

* 22   **Directories (Table G)**
* 22.1   **General coverage (Not Table G)**

     Laboratories, institutes, etc.
23   **Collective**
24   **Individual (Cutter from name of agency)**

25   **Laboratory manuals. Technique**

25.5   **Specific techniques, A–Z**

       .M6   **Microbial sensitivity tests**
       .V7   **Virus cultivation**

* 26   **Apparatus, equipment, etc.**
       Classify catalogs here.

26.5   **Medical informatics. Automatic data processing. Computers (General)**
       Classify works on use for special subjects by subject.

     Museums, exhibits, etc.
27   **Collective**
28   **Individual (Cutter from name of museum, etc.)**

* 32   **Laws (Table G)**
* 32.1   **General coverage (Not Table G)**

* 33   **Discussion of law (Table G)**
* 33.1   **General coverage (Not Table G)**

* 39   **Handbooks**

50   **Bacteria (General). Bacteriology**

*NUMBER CAN BE USED FOR BOTH MONOGRAPHS AND SERIALS.

51   **Morphology and variability of bacteria. Bacterial genetics**
         Classify works on fungi in QW 180; on viruses in QW 160 or with the specific fungi or virus group.

52   **Physiology and chemistry of bacteria. Metabolism**
         Classify works on fungi in QW 180; on viruses in QW 160 or with the specific fungi or virus group.

55   **Environmental microbiology**

60   **Plant and soil microbiology**
         Classify works on specific microorganisms by subject, e.g., Plant viruses QW 163.

65   **Dental microbiology**

70   **Veterinary microbiology**

75   **Industrial microbiology**

80   **Water and sewage microbiology**

82   **Air microbiology**

85   **Microbiology of food, milk, and other beverages**

115   **Actinomycetes and related organisms**

118   **Coryneform group**

120   **Propionibacteriaceae**

125   **Actinomycetales**

125.5   **Specific organisms, A–Z**

         .A2   **Actinomycetaceae**
         .M9   **Mycobacteriaceae**
         .S8   **Streptomycetaceae**

127   **Bacillaceae**

Bacillaceae - Continued

127.5   Specific groups, A–Z

     .B2   Bacillus
     .C5   Clostridium

128   Gliding bacteria

131   Gram–negative bacteria (General). Gram–negative aerobic bacteria (include cocci and rods)

133   Gram–negative anaerobic bacteria (include cocci and rods)

135   Gram–negative chemolithotrophic bacteria

137   Gram–negative facultatively anaerobic rods (General or not elsewhere classified)

138   Enterobacteriaceae

138.5   Specific organisms, A–Z

     .E5   Enterobacter
     .E8   Escherichia
     .K5   Klebsiella
     .P7   Proteus
     .S2   Salmonella
     .S3   Serratia
     .S4   Shigella
     .Y3   Yersinia

139   Haemophilus

140   Pasteurella

141   Vibrionaceae

142   Gram–positive bacteria (General or not elsewhere classified)

142.5   Specific organisms, A–Z

     .A8   Asporogenous rods
     .C6   Cocci

143   **Mollicutes**

145   **Phototrophic bacteria**

149   **Rickettsias and chlamydias**

150   **Rickettsiales**

152   **Chlamydiales**

153   **Sheathed bacteria.   Budding or appendaged bacteria**

154   **Spiral and curved bacteria**

155   **Spirochaetales**

160   **Viruses (General).   Virology**
        Classify works about a virus disease with the disease.

161   **Bacteriophages**

161.5   **Specific phages, A–Z**

        .C6   **Coliphages**
        .M9   **Mycobacteriophages**
        .S8   **Staphylococcus phages**

162   **Insect viruses**
        Classify works on diseases of insects in SB 942.

163   **Plant viruses**
        Classify works on virus diseases of plants in SB 736.

164   **Vertebrate viruses**

165   **DNA viruses**

165.5   **Specific DNA groups, A–Z**

        .A3   **Adenoviridae**
        .H3   **Herpesviridae**

Vertebrate viruses
DNA viruses
Specific DNA groups, A-Z - Continued

.I6   Iridoviridae
.P2   Papovaviridae
.P3   Parvoviridae
.P6   Poxviridae

166   Oncogenic viruses

168   RNA viruses

168.5   Specific RNA groups, A-Z

.A7   Arboviruses
.A8   Arenaviridae
.B9   Bunyaviridae
.C8   Coronaviridae
.H6   HIV
.O7   Orthomyxoviridae
.P2   Paramyxoviridae
.P4   Picornaviridae
.R15   Reoviridae
.R18   Retroviridae
.R2   Rhabdoviridae
.R8   Rubivirus. Rubella virus

169   Vertebrate viruses, unclassified

170   Hepatitis viruses

180   Pathogenic fungi. Mycology
Classify general non-medical works on mycology and non-pathogenic fungi in QK 600–635.

180.5   Specific fungi, A-Z

.A8   Ascomycetes
.B2   Basidiomycetes
.D3   Dermatophytes
.D38   Deuteromycetes
.M9   Myxomycota
.P4   Phycomycetes
.Y3   Yeasts
         Classify specific yeasts under the appropriate number for the class.

190   Bacterial and fungal spores
Classify works on bacterial spores alone in QW 51; on fungal spores alone in QW 180.

300   Biological warfare

IMMUNOLOGY

Classify works on immunologic diseases in WD 300–330.

* 501   **Societies (Cutter from name of society)**
Includes ephemeral membership lists issued serially or separately. Classify substantial lists with directories. Classify annual reports, journals, etc., in W1.

504   **General works**

504.5   **Immunochemistry. Immunohistochemistry**

      Collections (General)
505   **By several authors**
507   **By individual authors**

509   **Addresses. Essays. Lectures (General)**

511   **History (Table G)**
511.1   **General coverage (Not Table G)**

* 513   **Dictionaries. Encyclopedias**

* 515   **Nomenclature. Classification. Terminology**

* 516   **Tables. Statistics**

517   **Atlases. Pictorial works**

518   **Education**
Classify here works about education.

* 518.2   **Educational materials**
Classify here educational materials, e.g., outlines, questions and answers, programmed instruction, catalogs, computer-assisted instruction, etc., regardless of format. Classify textbooks, regardless of format, by subject.

520   **Research (General)**
Classify here works about research in general. Classify works about research on a particular subject by subject.

*NUMBER CAN BE USED FOR BOTH MONOGRAPHS AND SERIALS.

[521]   [This number not used]
           Classify works on immunology as a profession in QW 21.

* 522   Directories (Table G)
* 522.1   General coverage (Not Table G)

           Laboratories, institutes, etc.
523   Collective
524   Individual (Cutter from name of agency)

525   Laboratory manuals. Technique
           Classify works on immunodiagnostic tests in QY 250–275.

525.5   Specific techniques, A–Z

           .E6   Enzyme–linked immunosorbent assay
           .F6   Fluorescent antibody technique
           .I3   Immunoassay
           .I32   Immunoblotting
           .I34   Immunoenzyme techniques
           .L6   Leukocyte adherence inhibition test
           .R15   Radioallergosorbent test
           .R2   Radioimmunoassay

* 526   Equipment and supplies
           Classify catalogs here.

* 539   Handbooks

540   Immunity (General or not elsewhere classified)

541   Natural immunity. Immunogenetics

545   Autoimmunity

551   Acquired immunity. Artificial immunity
           Classify preparations producing artificial immunity in QW 800–815.

552   Active immunity

553   Passive immunity

563   Local immunity

568	Cellular immunity. Immunologic cytotoxicity. Immunocompetence. Immunologic factors (General or not elsewhere classified)
570	Antigens. Antibodies. Serology
573	Antigens
573.5	Specific antigens, A–Z

.H6   Histocompatibility antigens
.H7   HLA antigens

575	Antibodies
575.5	Specific antibodies, A–Z

.A6   Antibodies, Monoclonal

601	Immunoglobulins
630	Toxins. Antitoxins

Classify works on toxoids, antitoxins, etc., as preparations producing immunity in QW 800–815.

630.5   Specific toxins and antitoxins, A–Z

.B2   Bacterial toxins
.C9   Cytotoxins
.E5   Endotoxins
.E6   Enterotoxins
.I3   Immunotoxins
.M3   Marine toxins
.M9   Mycotoxins
.N4   Neurotoxins
.R5   Ricin

640   Agglutination. Precipitation
Classify works on immunodiagnostic tests in QY 265.

660   Lysis and bacterial action

680   Complement. Complement fixation
Classify works on immunodiagnostic tests in QY 265.

690   **Phagocytosis**

700   **Infection. Mechanisms of infection and resistance**

730   **Virulence. Invasiveness**

800   **Biological products producing immunity**
          Classify works on vaccines and vaccination for a specific disease, with the disease, e.g., Smallpox vaccination, WC 588.

805   **Vaccines. Antitoxins. Toxoids**
          Classify works on toxins or antitoxins formed in the body in QW 630–630.5.

806   **Vaccination**

815   **Immune serums**

900   **Anaphylaxis and hypersensitivity. Allergens**
          Classify works on diseases of hypersensitivity in general in WD 300–375. Classify specific allergic reactions with the system affected.

920   **Immunosuppression. Immunosuppressive agents**
          Classify transplantation immunology in WO 680.

940   **Immunotherapy**
          Classify works on therapy of a particular disease with the disease.

945   **Serotherapy**

949   **Active immunotherapy**

QX

PARASITOLOGY

* 1   **Societies (Cutter from name of society)**
        Includes ephemeral membership lists issued serially or separately. Classify substantial lists with directories. Classify annual reports, journals, etc., in W1.

4   **General works**

        Collections (General)
5   **By several authors**
7   **By individual authors**

9   **Addresses. Essays. Lectures (General)**

11   **History (Table G)**
11.1   **General coverage (Not Table G)**

* 13   **Dictionaries. Encyclopedias**

* 15   **Classification. Nomenclature. Terminology**

* 16   **Tables. Statistics**

17   **Atlases. Pictorial works**

18   **Education**
        Classify here works about education.

* 18.2 **Educational materials**
        Classify here educational materials, e.g., outlines, questions and answers, programmed instruction, catalogs, computer-assisted instruction, etc., regardless of format. Classify textbooks, regardless of format, by subject.

* 19   **Schools, departments, and faculties of parasitology**

20   **Research (General)**
        Classify here works about research in general. Classify works about research on a particular subject by subject.

*NUMBER CAN BE USED FOR BOTH MONOGRAPHS AND SERIALS.

21	Parasitology as a profession
* 22	Directories (Table G)
* 22.1	General coverage (Not Table G)
	Laboratories, institutes, etc.
23	Collective
24	Individual (Cutter from name of agency)
25	Laboratory manuals. Technique
* 26	Equipment and supplies
	Classify catalogs here.
26.5	Medical informatics. Automatic data processing. Computers (General)
	Classify works on use for special subjects by subject.
	Museums, exhibits, etc.
27	Collective
28	Individual (Cutter from name of museum, etc.)
* 32	Laws (Table G)
* 32.1	General coverage (Not Table G)
* 33	Discussion of law (Table G)
* 33.1	General coverage (Not Table G)
* 39	Handbooks
45	Host–parasite relations
50	Protozoa
55	Sarcodina (Amoebae)
70	Mastigophora
	e.g., Giardia. Trichomonas. Trypanosoma. Leishmania
123	Sporozoa
135	Plasmodia

*NUMBER CAN BE USED FOR BOTH MONOGRAPHS AND SERIALS.

Protozoa
  Sporozoa - Continued

Arthropods - Continued

463   **Crustacea**

467   **Arachnida**

469   **Scorpions**

471   **Spiders**

473   **Acari**

475   **Sarcoptidae (Mites)**
      e.g., Sarcoptes scabiei

479   **Ticks**

483   **Trombiculid mites**

500   **Insects**
      Classify works on diseases of insects in SB 942.

501   **Phthiroptera**

502   **Lice**

503   **Hemiptera**
      e.g., Bedbugs

505   **Diptera**

510   **Mosquitoes**

515   **Anopheles**

525   **Aedes**

530   **Culex**

550   **Siphonaptera (Fleas)**

555   **Coleoptera (Beetles)**

Diptera - Continued

560   **Lepidoptera (Moths.   Butterflies)**

565   **Hymenoptera (Bees.   Wasps.   Ants)**

570   **Orthoptera**
            e.g., Grasshoppers

600   **Insect control.   Tick control**
            Classify works on pest control in general and other public health aspects in WA 240.

650   **Insect vectors**

675   **Mollusca**

QY

CLINICAL PATHOLOGY

Classify here works on general clinical pathology and diagnostics. Classify works on tests for a particular disease or for diseases of a particular system with the disease or system, except for works on syphilis tests, which are classed here.

QY 1–350	General
QY 400–490	Blood

GENERAL

* 1   **Societies (Cutter from name of society)**
     Includes ephemeral membership lists issued serially or separately. Classify annual reports, journals, etc., in W1.

4   **General works**

   Collections (General)
5   **By several authors**
7   **By individual authors**

9   **Addresses. Essays. Lectures (General)**

11   **History (Table G)**
11.1   **General coverage (Not Table G)**

* 13   **Dictionaries. Encyclopedias**

* 15   **Classification. Nomenclature. Terminology**

* 16   **Tables. Statistics**

17   **Atlases. Pictorial works**

18   **Education**
     Classify here works about education.

* 18.2   **Educational materials**
Classify here educational materials, e.g., outlines, questions and answers, programmed instruction, catalogs, computer–assisted instruction, etc., regardless of format. Classify textbooks, regardless of format, by subject.

* 19   **Schools and colleges**
Classify courses of study, catalogs, etc., in W 19.5.

20   **Research (General)**
Classify here works about research in general. Classify works about research on a particular subject by subject.

21   **Medical technology as a profession. Ethics. Peer review**

* 22   **Directories of medical technology (Table G)**
Classify directories of all pathologists in QZ 22.
* 22.1   **Directories of medical technology (Not Table G)**

Laboratories, institutes, etc.
Classify hospital laboratories in WX 207.
23   **Collective**
24   **Individual (Cutter from name of agency)**

25   **Laboratory manuals. Technique**
Classify works on specific tests by type.

* 26   **Equipment and supplies**
Classify catalogs here.

26.5   **Medical informatics. Automatic data processing. Computers (General)**
Classify works on use for special subjects by subject.

Museums, exhibits, etc.
27   **Collective**
28   **Individual (Cutter from name of museum, etc.)**

* 32   **Laws (Table G)**
* 32.1   **General coverage (Not Table G)**

* 33   **Discussion of law (Table G)**
* 33.1   **General coverage (Not Table G)**

35   **Molding and casting of anatomic models. Moulages**

* 39   **Handbooks**

50   **Laboratory animals (General or not elsewhere classified)**
       Classify works on diseases of laboratory animals in SF 996.5; on vivisection as experimental surgery in WO 50; and on antivivisection in HV 4905-4959.

52   **Acquisition and transportation**
       Classify catalogs in QY 26; directories of users and sources for obtaining, in QY 22.

54   **Care and breeding**

56   **Environment**
       e.g., Germ-free life

58   **Experimental techniques**
       Cf. QY 25   Laboratory manuals.

60   **Special classes of animals, A-Z**

       .A6   **Amphibia**
       .B4   **Birds**
       .C2   **Cats**
       .D6   **Dogs**
       .F4   **Fishes**
       .L3   **Lagomorpha (Rabbits, etc.)**
       .M2   **Mammals (General or not elsewhere classified)**
       .P7   **Primates**
       .R6   **Rodents**
       .S8   **Swine**

90   **Chemical techniques**

95   **Cytological techniques**
       Cf. QH 585   Methods in cytology.

100   **Bacteriological techniques**

110   **Methods in medical mycology**

120   **Sputum**

125   **Saliva**

130   **Gastric and duodenal contents**

140	Liver tests
143	Bile pigments
147	Function tests
160	Feces
175	Kidney function tests
185	Urinalysis
190	Semen
210	Puncture fluids (Peritoneal. Pleural. Pericardial)
220	Cerebrospinal fluid
250	Immunodiagnostic tests *Cf. QW 525 for techniques of administering other immunologic tests.*
260	Diagnostic skin tests
265	Agglutination, precipitation, flocculation, and complement fixation tests
275	Serodiagnostic tests for syphilis
330	Assay of hormones
335	Pregnancy tests
350	Assay of vitamins

BLOOD

400	General works *Classify works on morphology, physiology, and clinical aspects of diseases of blood in WH. Cf. WG for works on the cardiovascular system.*

402	**Cellular elements**
408	**Physical examination** e.g., Sedimentation. Volume index, etc.
410	**Coagulation** e.g., Bleeding time, clotting time, etc.
415	**Typing**
450	**Blood chemistry**
455	**Nitrogenous constituents**
465	**Lipids**
470	**Carbohydrates**
480	**Inorganic substances**
490	**Enzymes**

QZ

PATHOLOGY

* 1   **Societies (Cutter from name of society)**
        Includes ephemeral membership lists issued serially or separately. Classify substantial lists with directories. Classify annual reports, journals, etc., in W1.

4   **General works**
        Classify material on comparative pathology in QZ 33.

        Collections (General)
5   **By several authors**
7   **By individual authors**

9   **Addresses. Essays. Lectures (General)**

11   **History (Table G)**
11.1   **General coverage (Not Table G)**

11.5   **Paleopathology**

* 13   **Dictionaries. Encyclopedias**

* 15   **Classification. Nomenclature. Terminology**

* 16   **Tables. Statistics**

17   **Atlases. Pictorial works**
        Classify here atlases on tissue pathology in disease.

18   **Education**
        Classify here works about education.

* 18.2 **Educational materials**
        Classify here educational materials, e.g., outlines, questions and answers, programmed instruction, catalogs, computer–assisted instruction, etc., regardless of format. Classify textbooks, regardless of format, by subject.

* 19   **Schools, departments, and faculties of pathology**

20.5   **Research (General)**
Classify material on cancer research in QZ 206.

21   **Pathology as a profession. Ethics. Peer review**

* 22   **Directories (Table G)**
* 22.1   **General coverage (Not Table G)**

      Laboratories, institutes, etc. Cancer hospitals
23   **Collective**
24   **Individual (Cutter from name of agency)**

25   **Laboratory manuals. Technique**

* 26   **Equipment and supplies**
Classify catalogs here.

26.5   **Medical informatics. Automatic data processing. Computers (General)**
Classify works on use for special subjects by subject.

      Museums, exhibits, etc.
27   **Collective**
28   **Individual (Cutter from name of agency)**

* 32   **Laws (Table G)**
* 32.1   **General coverage (Not Table G)**

* 32.3   **Discussion of law (Table G)**
* 32.4   **General coverage (Not Table G)**

33   **Comparative pathology**

35   **Postmortem examination**
Classify works on examination of dead bodies for medicolegal purposes in W 800–867.

* 39   **Handbooks**

40   **Pathogenesis of disease**
Classify here works on causative factors and development. Classify works on diagnosis, therapy, etc., of the resultant disease with the disease or system.

42   **Iatrogenic disease (General). Adverse effects of drugs. Medication errors**
Classify works with emphasis on drug action in QV 38.

Pathogenesis of disease - Continued

45   **Developmental defects**

50   **Heredity. Body constitution. Medical genetics**
                Classify works on pharmacogenetics in QV 38.

53   **Age factors. Sex factors**
                Classify works on age factors or sex factors relating to a particular disease, with the disease.

55   **Trauma (Physical)**

57   **Physical agents**
                e.g., Light. Vibration
                Cf. QT 162 for physiological effects.

59   **Chemical agents**

65   **Bacteria. Fungi. Viruses. Rickettsia (General)**
                Classify works on specific organisms in QW regardless of the subject.

85   **Animal parasites**

105   **Nutrition disorders**
                Cf. WD 100–175 for clinical aspects.

109   **Vitamin deficiencies**

140   **General manifestations of disease**

150   **Local reactions to injury and disease**

160   **General reactions to injury and disease. Stress**

170   **Circulatory disorders**

180   **Degenerative processes. Disorders of metabolism**
                Cf. WD 200–226 for clinical aspects.

190   **Local disorders of growth**
                e.g., Hyperplasia

200   **Neoplasms. Cysts (General)**
                Classify works on neoplasms by site or tissue if applicable.

Neoplasms. Cysts (General) - Continued

201   **Popular works**
          Classify here popular works on all aspects of neoplasms.

202   **Etiology. Metastasis. Regression. Invasiveness**

204   **Precancerous conditions**

206   **Research (General)**
          Classify works on specific topics by subject, e.g., on experimental work on the etiology
             of neoplasms in QZ 202.

241   **Diagnosis**

266   **Therapy**

267   **Drug therapy**

268   **Surgical techniques**

269   **Radiotherapy**

275   **Pediatric oncology. Adolescent oncology (General)**
          Classify here all aspects of pediatric and adolescent neoplasms in general;
             classify works on particular neoplasms with the neoplasms. Classify
             works on neoplasms by site or tissue if applicable.

Specific types of neoplasms
          Classify books on neoplasms by site when possible, especially when the emphasis
             is on dysfunction, symptomatology, and treatment. Emphasis in this section
             is on the pathology of tissues rather than on organ. Classify works on dental
             or oral tissue in WU 280.

310   **Embryonal and mixed tumors**

340   **Connective, muscle, and vascular tissues**

345   **Sarcoma**

350   **Leukemia. Lymphoma**
          Cf. WH 250 and WH 525 for clinical aspects.

365   **Glandular epithelial tissues. Carcinoma (General or not elsewhere**
           classified)

Specific types of neoplasms - Continued

380   **Nerve tissue**

W

HEALTH PROFESSIONS

Classify here general and miscellaneous material relating to the health professions.

W 1–96	General
W 100–275	Medical, Dental, and Pharmaceutical Service Plans
W 322–323	Other Medical Services
W 601–925	Forensic Medicine and Dentistry

GENERAL

* 1   **Serials. Periodicals**

* 2   **Serial documents (Table G)**
Classify here government administrative reports and statistics, including administrative reports and statistics on several hospitals under governmental administration. Cf. WX 2 Hospital administrative reports and statistics.

* 3   **Congresses**
Classify here monographic and serial publication of recurring congresses on medicine and related subjects. Note that as of July 1, 1988, NLM no longer assigns W3 to newly acquired publications, with the exception of analytics to ongoing serial publication already classified in W3.

* 3.5   **Directories of congresses**
Classify bibliographies of congress publications in ZW 3.   Note that as of July 1, 1988, NLM no longer assigns W 3.5 or ZW 3 to newly acquired publications.

* 4   **Dissertations, by university**

* 4A   **American dissertations, by author**
Classify dissertations which qualify as Americana in WZ 270.

     Collections (General)
5   **By several authors**
6   **Pamphlet volumes. Miscellaneous reprint volumes**
7   **By individual authors**

9   **Addresses. Essays. Lectures (General)**
Classify works on specific topics by subject.

*NUMBER CAN BE USED FOR BOTH MONOGRAPHS AND SERIALS.

10   Voyages. Expeditions. Travels

* 13   Dictionaries. Encyclopedias
            Classify material on medical shorthand here if it is the primary subject of book.

* 15   Nomenclature. Terminology
            Classify works on classification of disease and on disease eponyms in WB 15.

* 16   Tables. Statistics

18   Education
            Classify here works about education.

* 18.2   Educational materials
            Classify here educational materials, e.g., outlines, questions and answers, programmed instruction, catalogs, computer–assisted instruction, etc., regardless of format. Classify textbooks, regardless of format, by subject.

* 19   Schools and colleges

* 19.5   Courses of study, catalogs, announcements, etc., of all schools (including schools of dentistry, nursing, etc.) (Table G)

20   Graduate and continuing medical education (including fellowships, internships, residencies, etc.)

20.5   Medical research (General)
            Classify here material on the various aspects and accomplishments of medical research. Classify works on research limited to a particular subject with the subject.

20.55   Special topics, A–Z

            .A5   Animal testing alternatives
            .H9   Human experimentation

20.9   Fraternities in medicine and allied fields (Cutter from name of fraternity)

21   Medicine as a profession. Peer review
            Classify here works about medical careers. Classify those about other specific careers with the specialty, e.g., those about nursing in WY 16. Classify works on the specialities in general in W 87.

21.5   **Allied health personnel. Allied health professions**
Classify here works about supply and distribution as well as those about careers. Classify works on specific personnel in more specific number when available, e.g., those on nurses aides in WY 193. Classify works on health manpower including physicians in W 76.

* 22   **Directories (Table G)**
* 22.1   **General coverage (Not Table G)**

           Laboratories, institutes, etc.
23   **Collective**
24   **Individual (Cutter from name of agency)**

* 26   **Equipment and supplies**
Classify here medical and surgical supply and instrument catalogs as well as catalogs of special equipment, e.g., tables and chairs in doctors' waiting rooms. Include works on history of instruments in general.

26.5   **Medical informatics. Health informatics**
Classify works on use for special subjects by subject.

26.55   **Special topics, A–Z**

        .A7   **Artificial intelligence. Expert systems**
        .A9   **Automatic data processing**
        .C7   **Computers**
        .D2   **Decision making, Computer-assisted**
                Classify works on computer–assisted diagnosis (general) in WB 141; on computer–assisted therapy (general) in WB 300.
        .I4   **Information systems. Information storage and retrieval**
        .S6   **Software**

           Museums, exhibits, etc.
27   **Collective**
28   **Individual (Cutter from name of agency or exhibit)**

* 32   **Laws (General) (Table G)**
* 32.1   **General coverage (Not Table G)**

* 32.5   **Discussion of law. Medical jurisprudence (General) (Table G)**
Include here works on legal advice, court decisions and opinions, legal rights and obligations. Cf. W 700, etc., Forensic medicine.
* 32.6   **General coverage (Not Table G)**

* 33   **Laws governing medical practice (Table G)**
* 33.1   **General coverage (Not Table G)**

*NUMBER CAN BE USED FOR BOTH MONOGRAPHS AND SERIALS.

Laws - Continued

40	Licensure (Table G)	
40.1	General coverage (Not Table G)	

44	Malpractice (Table G)
44.1	General coverage (Not Table G)

* 49   **Handbooks**

50   **Medical ethics**

58   **Advertising. Fee–splitting**

61   **Medical philosophy and logic**

62   **Social relations of the physician (including relations with patients; relations with public, clubs, societies, etc.) Attitude**

64   **Referral and consultation (General)**
       Classify here works on referral, etc., initiated by the physician. Classify works on particular medical problems by subject; works on problems referred by specialists with the specialty.

74   **Medical economics. Health care costs (General)**
       Cf. W 58 for economic aspects of medical ethics.

76   **Health manpower and services, distribution and characteristics**
       Classify works limited to allied health manpower in W 21.5.

79   **Income of physicians**

80   **Practice management (including business administration)**
       Classify here medical secretaries' handbooks.

84   **Health services. Quality of health care (General) (Table G)**
       Classify works on public health administration in appropriate WA number. Classify works on quality of health care relating only to private practice in WB 50.

84.1	**General coverage (Not Table G)**
84.3	**Research (General)**

84.5   **Comprehensive health care. Community medicine**
       Cf. WA 546 Community health service.

84.6   **Primary health care**

Health services. Quality of health care - Continued

84.7   **Patient care planning. Progressive health care (General)**
Classify works on care of hospital patients in WX 162.

84.8   **Patient care team**
Classify works on hospital teams in WX 162.5.

85   **Patients. Attitude and compliance. Satisfaction**
Classify works on attitude toward particular subject with the subject.

85.5   **Right to die. Advance directives. Living wills**
Cf. WB 310 Hospice care. Terminal care.

87   **Professional practice**
Cf. W 21 Medicine as a profession. Include here general works about types of practice in medicine and allied fields. Classify works on specific medical specialties or allied fields by subject, e.g., on surgery in WO 21; on nursing in WY 101–145, etc.

88   **Administrative work. Teaching. Research**
Classify here works about planning for administrative, teaching, or research careers. Classify works on practice management in W 80, etc.; on education and how to teach in W 18, etc.; on research itself in W 20.5, etc.

89   **Family practice (As a specialty) Private practice**
Classify texts and treatises for general practitioner or family doctor in WB 110.

90   **Specialism (General)**
Classify works on a particular specialty with the specialty.

92   **Group practice. Partnership practice**

94   **Government services**

96   **Institutional practice**

MEDICAL, DENTAL, AND PHARMACEUTICAL SERVICE PLANS

Classify works on Medicare and medical care plans for the aged in WT 31.

100   **General works**
Cf. W 275 General service plans by country.

125 Voluntary pre–payment plans (General or not elsewhere classified) (Table G)
125.1 General coverage (Not Table G)

130 Managed care plans (General or not elsewhere classified) (Table G)
130.1 General coverage (Not Table G)

132 Health maintenance organizations (Table G)
132.1 General coverage (Not Table G)

160 Hospitalization insurance. Major medical insurance. Long–term care insurance. Medigap insurance (Table G)
160.1 General coverage (Not Table G)

185 Compulsory pre–payment plans (not a function of the state) (General or not elsewhere classified) (Table G)
185.1 General coverage (Not Table G)

225 Medicine as function of the state (Table G)
    Classify here material on health protection for everyone as a function of the state, supported by taxation, with medical services subject to regulation by the state.
225.1 General coverage (Not Table G)

250 Medical care for low–income and indigent groups. Medicaid (Table G)
250.1 General coverage (Not Table G)

255 Nursing insurance

260 Dental insurance. State dentistry (Table G)
260.1 General coverage (Not Table G)

265 Pharmaceutical insurance (Table G)
265.1 General coverage (Not Table G)

270 Psychiatric insurance (Table G)
270.1 General coverage (Not Table G)

275 Medical, dental, pharmaceutical and/or psychiatric service plans, by country (Table G)
    Classify here works covering both compulsory and voluntary plans. Cf. W 100 General works.

OTHER MEDICAL SERVICES

322   **Medical social work**
Include works on social service in hospitals here.   *Cf. WM 30.5*
Psychiatric social work.

323   **Medical missions**
Classify biographical or autobiographical works of medical missionary doctors and nurses in WZ 100.

FORENSIC MEDICINE AND DENTISTRY

* 601   **Societies (Cutter from name of society)**
Includes ephemeral membership lists issued serially or separately. Classify substantial lists with directories. Classify annual reports, journals, etc., in W1.

     Collections (General)
605   **By several authors**
607   **By individual authors**

609   **Addresses. Essays. Lectures (General)**

611   **History (Table G)**
611.1   **General coverage (Not Table G)**

* 613   **Dictionaries. Encyclopedias**

* 615   **Classification. Nomenclature. Terminology**

* 616   **Tables. Statistics**

617   **Atlases. Pictorial works**
Classify here atlases and pictorial works on any phase of forensic medicine, etc.

618   **Education**
Classify here works about education.

* 618.2   **Educational materials**
Classify here educational materials, e.g., outlines, questions and answers, programmed instruction, catalogs, computer-assisted instruction, etc., regardless of format. Classify textbooks, regardless of format, by subject.

* 622   Directories (Table G)
* 622.1   General coverage (Not Table G)

             Laboratories, institutes, etc.
  623   Collective
  624   Individual (Cutter from name of agency)

  625   Laboratory manuals. Technique

  626   Equipment and supplies
             Classify catalogs in W 26.

  626.5   Medical informatics. Automatic data processing. Computers (General)
             Classify works on use for special subjects by subject.

             Museums, exhibits, etc., on medicolegal subjects
  627   Collective
  628   Individual (Cutter from name of agency, exhibit, etc.)

  [632]   [This number not used]
             Classify works on medical jurisprudence only, in W 32.5–32.6. Cf. W 700.

* 639   Handbooks

  700   General works
             *Classify here works on medical and pathological examination of criminal evidence,
             as well as works including material on medical jurisprudence. Classify works on
             medical jurisprudence only, in W 32.5–32.6.*

  705   Medicolegal dentistry

  725   Medical evidence in the establishment of responsibility

  740   Forensic psychiatry
             Classify works on commitment in WM 32–33.

  750   Examination of evidential material. Forensic chemistry

  775   Medicolegal examination

  780   Examination of the living

  783   Malingering

Medicolegal examination - Continued

786   Identification

789   Legal establishment of the beginning of life

791   Consanguinity. Paternity. Pregnancy

795   Rape. Sexual offenses

800   Examination of dead bodies. Duties of coroners

820   Signs of death. Time of death. Sudden death

822   Destruction and attempted destruction of the human body

825   Determination of cause of death. Medicolegal autopsy

843   Trauma

860   Criminal violence. Homicide

864   Suicide

867   Criminal abortion. Infanticide
           Cf. WQ 225 for spontaneous abortion; WQ 440 for medical aspects of therapeutic or induced abortion; HQ 767 for social aspects of induced abortion.

900   Medicolegal aspects of insurance
       Classify works on liability insurance in form number 44 with malpractice when available in NLM schedules or in HG 9990 if general material.

910   Medicolegal aspects of compensation to victims of criminal violence

925   Medicolegal aspects of occupational disease and injury
       Cf. WV 32 for estimation of disability in otolaryngology; WW 32 for estimation of disability in ophthalmology.

WA

PUBLIC HEALTH

GENERAL

* 1   **Societies (Cutter from name of society)**
        Include ephemeral membership lists issued serially or separately. Classify substantial lists with directories. Classify annual reports, journals, etc., in W1.

4   **Works on general hygiene (including in one volume personal hygiene, public health, etc.)**
        Classify general works on public health in WA 100.

        Collections (General)
5   **By several authors**
7   **By individual authors**

9   **Addresses. Essays. Lectures (General)**

11   **History (Table G)**
11.1   **General coverage (Not Table G)**

* 13   **Dictionaries. Encyclopedias**

* 15   **Classification. Nomenclature. Terminology**

* 16   **Tables. Statistics**

17   **Atlases. Pictorial works**

18   **Education**
Classify here works about education.

* 18.2   **Educational materials**
Classify here educational materials, e.g., outlines, questions and answers, programmed instruction, catalogs, computer–assisted instruction, etc., regardless of format. Classify textbooks, regardless of format, by subject.

* 19   **Schools, colleges, and specialized departments and facilities**
Classify courses of study, college catalogs, etc., in W 19.5.

20.5   **Research (General)**
Classify here works about research in general. Classify research limited to a particular subject with the subject.

21   **Public health as a profession. Ethics. Peer review**

* 22   **Directories (Table G)**
* 22.1   **General coverage (Not Table G)**

     Laboratories, institutes, etc.
23   **Collective**
24   **Individual (Cutter from name of agency)**

25   **Laboratory manuals. Technique**

26   **Equipment and supplies**
Classify catalogs in W 26. Classify works on safety equipment in general in WA 260; on industrial safety equipment in WA 485.

26.5   **Medical informatics. Automatic data processing. Computers (General)**
Classify works on use for special subjects by subject.

     Museums, exhibits, etc.
27   **Collective**
28   **Individual (Cutter from name of museum or exhibit)**

30   **Social, economic, and environmental factors in public health (General)**
Classify works on rural health and hygiene in WA 390; on urban health and hygiene in WA 380.

31   **Social medicine. Medical sociology**

* 32   **Laws (Table G)**
Classify pure food laws in WA 697.
* 32.1   **General coverage (Not Table G)**

*NUMBER CAN BE USED FOR BOTH MONOGRAPHS AND SERIALS.

Laws - Continued

* 33	Discussion of law (Table G)	
* 33.1	General coverage (Not Table G)	

* 39   **Handbooks**

54   **Registration and certification of the dead**

55   **Registration of notifiable diseases**

100   **General works**

105   **Epidemiology**
            Classify statistics in WA 900.

106   **Disease reservoirs**

PREVENTIVE MEDICINE

108   **Preventive health services. Preventive medicine (General)**

110   **Prevention and control of communicable diseases. Transmission of infectious diseases**
            Classify works on immunological aspects in QW 700; on parasitological aspects of insect control in QX 600; on control of sexually transmitted diseases in WC 142.

230   **Quarantine**
            Classify material on laws in WA 32–33.

234   **Port and maritime quarantine**

240   **Disinfection. Disinfestation. Pesticides (Including diseases caused by)**
            Classify works on immunological aspects in QX 650. Classify works on ectoparasitic infestations and disinfestations in WC 900.

243   **Diagnostic services**
            Classify works on mass chest X–ray in WF 225; on mobile health units in WX 190.

245   **Mass screening. Multiphasic screening**

PREVENTION OF ACCIDENT AND OF INJURY

250   **General works**
Classify works on occupational accidents and their prevention in WA 485.

260   **Protective devices (General)**

275   **Traffic accidents. Public health aspects of automobile driving**

288   **Accidents in the home, office, etc. Consumer protection and product safety (General)**
Include works on household articles and products as causes of accidents

292   **First aid in illness and injury, e.g., Bandaging. Minor injuries**
Classify works on resuscitation in anesthesiology in WO 250; on resuscitation of the newborn in WQ 450. Classify military first aid manuals in UH 396.

HEALTH PROBLEMS OF SPECIAL POPULATION GROUPS

300   **General works**
Classify general works on diseases generally associated with particular ethnic groups in WB 720. Include works on particular groups not elsewhere classified.

305   **Mental health of special population groups**
Classify works on particular diseases in WM. Cf. WM 105 for general works on mental health.

308   **Family health**
Cf. W 89 Family practice as a specialty; WB 110 for works for the family doctor

309   **Women's health**
Cf. WA 491 Protection of women in the workplace.

310   **Maternal welfare. Maternal and child welfare. Maternal health services**

320   **Child welfare. Child abuse. Child health services**

350   **School health and hygiene services. School dental health services**
Classify works on diseases of school children in WS. Cf. WU 113 for dental hygiene.

351   **Universities and colleges**

352   **School mental health services**
Classify works on diseases in WM.

353   **Universities and colleges**

380   **Urban health and hygiene**
Cf. WA 546 Local health administration.

390   **Rural health and hygiene**
Classify agricultural workers' diseases in WA 400.

395   **Health in developing countries**

OCCUPATIONAL MEDICINE, HEALTH AND HYGIENE

400   **General works (including occupational diseases)**
Classify works on particular diseases by system, etc.   Cf. WF 405 Tuberculosis in the workplace; WR 600 Occupational dermatitis; WW 505 Occupational ophthalmology.

412   **Medical and dental services**

440   **Prevention and control of occupational diseases**

450   **Control of atmospheric conditions**

465   **Industrial poisons and poisoning (General)**
Classify works on toxicology of chemicals with no industrial health emphasis and on specific chemicals in QV 600–662; or if insecticides in WA 240.

470   **Illumination. Noise. Radiation. Vibration**

475   **Occupational fatigue and its prevention**

485   **Occupational accidents. Safety equipment**

487   **Accidents in professional work**
Use only for works on professions not ordinarily considered industrial

Accidents in professional work - Continued

487.5   By profession, A–Z

         .A78   Art
         .D4   Dancing
         .F4   Firefighting

491   Protection of women in the workplace
           Cf. WA 309 Women's health.

495   Occupational mental health services

HEALTH ADMINISTRATION AND ORGANIZATION

525   General works

530   International health administration (Table G)
530.1   General coverage (Not Table G)

540   National and state health administration (Table G)
540.1   General coverage (Not Table G)

541   Regional health planning (Table G)
541.1   General coverage (Not Table G)

546   Local health administration. Community health services (Table G)
546.1   General coverage (Not Table G)

590   Health education
           Classify here works on informal health education (community, radio, etc.). Classify works on study and teaching of public health in WA 18; classify teachers' manuals on physiology and hygiene in QT 200.

SANITATION AND ENVIRONMENTAL CONTROL

670   General works

671   Sanitary engineering. Environmental control (General)
           Classify works on entraterrestrial environment in WD 758; on sealed cabin ecology in WD 756.

672   Inspection. Surveys (Table G)
           Classify works on inspection in particular areas by subject.
672.1   General coverage (Not Table G)

675   **Water. Water supply. Sources**
           Include works on sanitary aspects of ice and ice making here.

686   **Analysis**
           Cf. QW 80   Water microbiology.

687   **Saline water conversion**

689   **Pollution**
           Classify works on radioactive pollution in WN 615; general works on industrial seawater pollution in WA 788; on pollution of bathing beaches in WA 820.

690   **Purification**

695   **Food. Food supply. Food inspection**

697   **Pure food laws**
           Classify here food and drug laws discussed together. Classify works on drug laws alone in QV 32–33.

701   **Adulteration and contamination**
           Classify works on radioactive contamination in WN 612.

703   **Fresh foods (Vegetables. Fruits. Eggs. Fish)**

707   **Meat and poultry inspection**

710   **Preserved foods (canned, dried, frozen, salted, smoked, etc.)**

712   **Food additives**

715   **Milk. Milk supply. Dairy products**

716   **Analysis**

719   **Pasteurization**

722   **Fats. Oils. Margarine**

730   **Drugs. Drug adulteration and contamination. Pharmacies**
           Classify here works on refrigeration of biological products. Classify works on fraud in QV 773; on drug legislation in QV 32–33.

744   Cosmetics. Barber shops. Beauty salons

750   Air sanitation and hygiene

754   Pollution and pollutants
       Cf. QW 82 Air microbiology; WA 450 Industrial pollution. Classify works on radioactive pollutions and pollutants in WN 615. Classify works on agents used extensively in biochemistry or pharmacology in QU or QV.

770   Ventilating. Heating

774   Air conditioning

776   Noise and noise abatement

778   Waste products. Waste disposal

780   Refuse and garbage disposal

785   Sewage disposal. Soil pollution
       Classify works on radioactive pollution and pollutants in WN 615.

788   Hazardous waste. Industrial waste (including radioactive waste)
       Cf. WN 650 for general works on radiation safety.

790   Medical waste. Dental waste

795   Housing

799   Public buildings. Restaurants

810   Public transportation

820   Bathing beaches. Public baths. Swimming pools

830   Toilet facilities

840   Mortuary practice

844   Embalming

Mortuary practice - Continued

846   **Burial. Cemeteries**

847   **Cremation**

STATISTICS AND SURVEYS

900   **Public health statistics (including narrative reports on health conditions and health surveys) (Table G)**
            Classify mortality statistics with causes of death here. Classify works on mortality statistics alone in HB. Classify works on nutrition surveys in QU 146–146.1.

900.1   **General coverage (Not Table G)**

950   **Theory or methods of medical statistics**
            Classify works on biometry in its broader sense in QH 323.5.

WB

PRACTICE OF MEDICINE

WB 1–130   **General**
WB 141–293   **General Diagnosis**
WB 300–962   **Therapeutics**

GENERAL

* 1   Societies (Table G)
Includes ephemeral membership lists issued serially or separately. Classify substantial lists with directories. Classify annual reports, journals, etc., in W1.

Collections (on clinical medicine, diagnosis, special therapeutic systems)
Classify collections on a specific subject with the subject. Cf. W5–7 on the medical profession.

5   By several authors
7   By individual authors

9   Addresses. Essays. Lectures (General)

[11]   [This number not used]
Use WZ for history of medical practice. Classify works on the history of special systems of therapeutics in the numbers for those specialities (WB 900–962). The latter are the only numbers used for history in the WB schedule.

13   Encyclopedias
Classify dictionaries in W 13.

* 15   Classification. Nomenclature. Terminology
Classify works that consist of general medical nomenclature or terminology in W 15.

* 16   Tables. Statistics

17   Atlases
e.g., those on special devices or forms of therapy, such as Acupuncture.
Cf. QZ 17 for tissue pathology of disease.

18   **Education**
Classify here materials on education in the special systems of therapeutics or other topics specific to this schedule. Classify materials on general medical education in W 18.

* 18.2   **Educational materials**
Classify here educational materials, e.g., outlines, questions and answers, programmed instruction, catalogs, computer–assisted instruction, etc., regardless of format. Classify textbooks, regardless of format, by subject.

* 22   **Directories (of health resorts and/or special systems of therapeutics) (Table G)**
* 22.1   **General coverage (Not Table G)**

Institutes. Laboratories of experimental research
23   **Collective**
24   **Individual (Cutter from name of agency)**

25   **Technique of research in internal medicine**
Classify works on technique of research limited to a particular subject with the subject.

26   **Equipment and supplies**
Classify medical and surgical supply and instrument catalogs in W 26. Classify works on self help devices in WB 320.

[26.5]   **[This number not used]**
Classify works on medical informatics, data processing or computers used in medicine in W 26.5 or by subject.

Hospitals, dispensaries and clinics for specialized types of therapy e.g., Homeopathy. Diathermy. Hydrotherapy
Classify works on general hospitals in WX; others in specialty numbers.
27   **Collective (Table G)**
27.1   **General coverage (Not Table G)**
28   **Individual (Table G)**

29   **Rehabilitation centers. Residential facilities. Sheltered workshops**
Cf. WM 29–29.1 Mental health facilities.

* 32   **Laws relating to special systems of therapeutics (Table G)**
* 32.1   **General coverage (Not Table G)**

* 33   **Discussion of law (Table G)**
* 33.1   **General coverage (Not Table G)**

* 39   **Handbooks**

50 **Medical practice (Table G)**
Classify here works dealing only with private practice.   Classify works on health services in general in W 84–84.3.

50.1 **General coverage (Not Table G)**

100 **General works**

101 **Ambulatory care (General)**
Cf. WX 205   Hospital outpatient clinics, ambulatory care facilities.

102 **Clinical medicine**

103 **Behavioral medicine**

104 **Medical psychology**

105 **Emergency medicine.   Medical emergencies**
Classify works on emergency hospital service in WX 215; on first aid in WA 292.

110 **Family practice (including general practice)**
Classify works on general or family practice as a specialty in W 89.

115 **Internal medicine**

117 **Medical uses of non–ionizing radiation (General)**
Cf. WB 288 for diagnostic use; WB 480 for therapeutic use.

120 **Popular medicine (General)**
e.g., Household medical books.   Self medication
Example: Mayo Clinic family health book computer file.

130 **General works for laymen**
Classify here books on general medicine written in style suitable for laymen.   Example: The frontiers of medicine.

GENERAL DIAGNOSIS

141 **General works**
Cf. QY 4   General works on clinical pathology.

141.4 **Health status**

141.5 **Differential diagnosis**

THERAPEUTICS

300   **General works**

305   **Instructions or non–drug prescriptions for devices or therapy (General)**
Classify specific devices or therapies by subject.

310   **Hospice care. Palliative treatment. Terminal care**
Cf. W85.5 Right to die; WY 152 Nursing care of terminal patients.

320   **Rehabilitation of the disabled (General)**
Classify here works on physical and medical rehabilitation in general as well as those that include in addition educational, social, and vocational rehabilitation. Classify works on specific types, by type, e.g., Physical therapy WB 460. Classify works with no medical slant in HD 7255–7256.

325   **Aftercare**
Cf. WM 29–29.1 for mental patients; WO 183 Postoperative care; WY 100 Nursing care.

327   **Self care**

330   **Drug therapy**
Cf. QV Pharmacology.

340   **Administration of medicine**

342   **Inhalation. Intranasal**

344   **Rectal**

350   **Oral**

354   **Injections. Infusions**

356   **Blood transfusion**

365   **Various other therapeutic and diagnostic procedures (General or not elsewhere classified)**

369   **Acupuncture. Moxibustion**

Various other therapeutic and diagnostic procedures - Continued

371   **Cupping.   Counterirritation**
         e.g., Mustard plasters

373   **Punctures (General or not elsewhere classified)**

377   **Spinal, cisternal and ventricular puncture**

379   **Biopsy**

381   **Bloodletting**

391   **Tissue therapy.   Organotherapy**

400   **Dietetics.   Diet therapy**
         Classify works on diets to be used with particular diseases with the disease, e.g.,
         atherogenic diet in WG 550.   Classify works on nutrition and food values in
         QU 145–145.5.

405   **Dietary cookbooks (General)**

410   **Special methods of feeding, e.g., parenteral; tube**

420   **Fasting**

422   **Macrobiotic diet**

424   **Low sodium diets.   Salt–free diets**

425   **Fat control**
         Classify works on reducing diets in WD 210–212.

426   **Meat diets.   Protein control**

427   **Carbohydrate control**

428   **Milk diets.   Calcium control**

430   **Vegetable diets.   Fruit diets**

431   **Cereals.   Grains.   Seeds.   Breads**

Dietetics. Diet therapy - Continued

432   Raw food diets

433   Beverages

438   Coffee. Tea. Chocolate

442   Water. Mineral waters
                 Classify general works on hydrotherapy in WB 520.

444   Wines. Liquors. Cordials. Beer

447   Miscellaneous food preparations
                 e.g., Yeast

449   Diet fads (Critical and historical material)

460   Physical medicine. Physical therapy

469   Heat therapy. Induced hyperthermia

473   Cryotherapy. Therapeutic use of cold

480   Ultraviolet therapy. Sunlight. Light therapy

495   Electric stimulation therapy

510   Diathermy

515   Ultrasonic therapy

520   Hydrotherapy (General)

525   Balneology

535   Mechanotherapy. Massage, exercise, rest, etc., treated together

537   Massage

541   Exercise therapy. Medical gymnastics
                 Cf. QT 255 Physical education

Physical medicine. Physical therapy
Mechanotherapy. Massage, exercise, rest, etc. treated together - Continued

545   Rest. Relaxation
             Classify works on hygienic aspects of rest and relaxation in QT 265.

550   Therapeutic use of music
             Classify works on therapeutic use of music in psychiatry in WM 450.5.M8.

555   Occupational therapy
             Classify works on occupational therapy in psychiatry in WM 450.5.O2.

700   Medical climatology. Geography of disease

710   Diseases of geographic areas

720   Diseases of ethnic groups (General or not elsewhere classified)
             Classify here works on diseases that are associated primarily with a particular ethnic group, when treated as such. Classify works on general health problems of ethnic groups in WA 300–305. Classify works on specific diseases with the disease.

750   Climatotherapy
             Cf. WF 330 Climatotherapy of pulmonary tuberculosis.

760   Health resorts (Table G)
             Includes history.
760.1   General coverage (Not Table G)

880   Mental healing

885   Faith healing. Christian Science healing

890   Special systems of therapeutics. Alternative medicine (General or not elsewhere classified)
             Classify works on cupping in WB 371; on diet fads in WB 449; on vegetarianism in WB 430; on mental healing in WB 880–885. Classify works on a specific disease with the disease.

900   History of special systems or alternative medicine (General or not elsewhere classified)

903   Anthroposophy (used in medicine)
             Cf. BP 595–597 General works.

905   Chiropractic

905.6   History and philosophy

Special systems of therapeutics. Alternative medicine
Chiropractic - Continued

905.7   **Chiropractic as a profession. Ethics. Peer review**
Classify works on education in WB 18.

905.8   **Diagnosis**

905.9   **Therapeutics**

920   **Eclecticism**

925   **Herbalism**

930   **Homeopathy**

935   **Naturopathy**

940   **Osteopathy**

960   **Radiesthesia**

962   **Reflexotherapy**

WC

COMMUNICABLE DISEASES

Classify here all major systemic infectious diseases with the exception of tuberculosis, which classes in WF 200–415. A few infectious diseases, usually local in character, are classed with the part affected (e.g., those classed in Dermatology, WR 220–245). Classify diseases for which no specific class number exists here on the basis of likeness, e.g. pseudoglanders with glanders in WC 330. Note that some related diseases are classed together regardless of the affecting organism, e.g., the pneumonias (WC 202–209) and the dysenteries (WC 280–285). Classify works on an infection which affects a single organ with the organ.

* 1 **Societies (Cutter from name of society)**
    Includes ephemeral membership lists issued serially or separately. Classify substantial lists with directories. Classify annual reports, journals, etc., in W1.

    Collections (General)
5   **By several authors**
7   **By individual authors**

9   **Addresses. Essays. Lectures (General)**

11 **History (General) (Table G)**
    Classify history of a single infectious disease with the disease.
11.1 **General coverage (Not Table G)**

* 13 **Dictionaries. Encyclopedias**

* 15 **Classification. Nomenclature. Terminology**

* 16 **Tables. Statistics**

17 **Atlases. Pictorial works**
    Classify here also atlases on single infectious diseases.

18 **Education**
    Classify here works about education.

* 18.2 **Educational materials**
    Classify here educational materials, e.g., outlines, questions and answers, programmed instruction, catalogs, computer-assisted instruction, etc., regardless of format. Classify textbooks, regardless of format, by subject.

* 19   Schools, colleges, and specialized departments and facilities

20   Research (General)
            Classify here works about research in general.   Classify works about research on a particular subject by subject.

* 22   Directories (Table G)
* 22.1   General coverage (Not Table G)

            Laboratories, institutes, etc.
23   Collective
24   Individual (Cutter from name of agency)

25   Laboratory manuals.   Technique

26   Equipment and supplies
            Classify catalogs in W 26.

26.5   Medical informatics.   Automatic data processing.   Computers (General)
            Classify works on use for special subjects by subject.

            Isolation and quarantine hospitals, leprosaria, prophylaxis stations, clinics, dispensaries, etc.
27   Collective (Table G)
27.1   General coverage (Not Table G)
28   Individual (Table G)

[32]   [This number not used]
            Classify laws relating to infectious diseases under appropriate topics in WA Public Health.

[33]   [This number not used]
            Classify discussion of laws realting to infectious diseases under appropriate topics in WA Public Health.

* 39   Handbooks

100   General works

140   Sexually transmitted diseases
            Classify works on AIDS and HIV infections in WC 503–503.7.

142   Control measures

144   Prevention

*NUMBER CAN BE USED FOR BOTH MONOGRAPHS AND SERIALS.

Sexually transmitted diseases - Continued

150   **Gonorrhea**
            Classify works on gonorrhea in the female in WP 157.

155   **Chancroid**

160   **Syphilis**

161   **Congenital**

162   **Primary. Secondary**

164   **Tertiary**

165   **Neurosyphilis. Paresis**
            Cf. WM 220 for general works on organic psychoses.

168   **Cardiovascular**

170   **Treatment**

180   **Granuloma inguinale**

185   **Lymphogranuloma venereum**

195   **Infection. Cross infection. Laboratory infection**
            Cf. WX 167 for prevention and control of cross infection in hospitals.

200   **Bacterial infections (General or not elsewhere classified)**
            Classify works on localized bacterial infections by site.

202   **Pneumonia (General)**

204   **Lobar pneumonia. Staphylococcal pneumonia**

207   **Viral pneumonia**

209   **Other**

210   **Streptococcal infections (General or not elsewhere classified)**
            Classify works on endocarditis in WG 285; on impetigo in WR 225.

Bacterial infections
Streptococcal infections - Continued

214 Scarlet fever

217 Pneumococcal infections
Classify works on lobar pneumonia in WC 204.

220 Rheumatic fever. Chorea in rheumatic fever
Classify works on rheumatic heart disease in WG 240.

230 Focal infection
Cf. WU 290 in dentistry.

234 Erysipelas

240 Bacteremia. Septicemia. Toxemias
Classify works on pregnancy toxemias in WQ 215.

242 Listeria infections

245 Meningococcal infections

246 Mycoplasmatales infections

250 Staphylococcal infections
Classify works on infectious skin diseases in WR; on hordeolum in WW 205; on staphylococcal pneumonia in WC 204; on food poisoning in WC 268.

255 Wound infection
Cf. WO 185 Surgical wound infection.

260 Enterobacteriaceae and other enteric infections
Classify works on Yersinia infections in WC 350.

262 Cholera

264 Epidemics

266 Paratyphoid fevers

268 Bacterial food poisoning
Classify works on contamination of food by specific chemicals with the chemical involved. Classify works on food poisoning caused by pesticides in WA 240. Classify works on plant poisoning in WD 500–530.

Bacterial infections
    Enterobacteriaceae and other enteric infections - Continued

269   **Salmonella infections**
          Classify works on salmonella food poisoning in WC 268; on paratyphoid fevers in WC 266.

270   **Typhoid**

280   **Dysentery**

282   **Bacillary dysentery**

285   **Amebic dysentery. Amebiasis**
          Classify works on amebic liver abscess in WI 730.

290   **Escherichia coli infections**

302   **Actinomycetales infections. Mycobacterium infections**
          Classify works on leprosy in WC 335; on maduromycosis in WR 340; on tuberculosis in WF, etc.

305   **Anthrax**

310   **Brucellosis**

318   **Corynebacterium infections**

320   **Diphtheria**

330   **Pseudomonas infections. Glanders**

335   **Leprosy**

340   **Bordetella infections. Whooping cough**

350   **Yersinia infections. Plague**

355   **Epidemics**

368   **Clostridium infections**
          Classify works on botulism in WC 268; on bacillary hemoglobinuria in WJ 344.

370   **Tetanus. Trismus**

Bacterial infections
Clostridium infections - Continued

375   Gas gangrene

380   Tularemia

390   Rat-bite fever

400   Spirochete infections

406   Borrelia infections. Lyme disease

410   Relapsing fever

420   Leptospirosis. Weil's disease

422   Treponemal infections
          Classify works on syphilis in WC 160–170.

425   Yaws

450   Mycoses (General or not elsewhere classified)
          Classify works on dermatomycoses in WR 300–340; on fungal lung diseases in WF 652.

460   Coccidioidomycosis. Paracoccidioidomycosis

465   Histoplasmosis

470   Candidiasis
          Classify works on cutaneous candidiasis in WR 300.

475   Cryptococcosis. Sporotrichosis

500   Virus diseases (General or not elsewhere classified)

501   RNA virus infections (General or not elsewhere classified)

502   Retroviridae infections (General or not elsewhere classified)

503   Acquired immunodeficiency syndrome. HIV infections

Virus diseases
    RNA virus infections
        Retroviridae infections
            Acquired Immunodeficiency syndrome. HIV infections - Continued

503.1   **Diagnosis**

503.2   **Therapy**

503.3   **Etiology. Transmission**

503.4   **Epidemiology (Table G)**
503.41   **General coverage (Not Table G)**

503.5   **Complications**

503.6   **Prevention and control**

503.7   **Psychosocial aspects**

505   **Viral respiratory tract infections (General or not elsewhere classified)**

510   **Common cold**

512   **Orthomyxoviridae infections (General or not elsewhere classified)**

515   **Influenza**

518   **Paramyxovirus infections (General or not elsewhere classified)**
            Classify works on measles in WC 580.

520   **Mumps**

522   **Infectious mononucleosis**

524   **Arbovirus infections (General or not elsewhere classified)**
            Classify works on epidemic encephalitis in WC 542; on lymphocytic choriomeningitis
               in WC 540.

526   **Phlebotomus fever**

528   **Dengue**

530   **Yellow fever**

Virus diseases
  Arbovirus infections
    Yellow fever - Continued

532   **Epidemics**

534   **Viral hemorrhagic fevers**

536   **Human viral hepatitis**

540   **Neurotropic virus diseases (General or not elsewhere classified)**

542   **Epidemic encephalitis. Equine encephalomyelitis (in humans)**
         Classify works on encephalomyelitis of the horse in SF 959.E5.

550   **Rabies**

555   **Poliomyelitis**

556   **Prevention and control**

570   **Infectious viral skin diseases (General or not elsewhere classified)**

571   **Herpesvirus infections (General or not elsewhere classified)**
         Classify works on infectious mononucleosis in WC 522; on Burkitt's lymphoma
         in WH 525; on other infections with no skin manifestations in WC 500.

572   **Chickenpox**

575   **Herpes zoster**

578   **Herpes simplex**

580   **Measles**

582   **Rubella**

584   **Poxviridae infections (General or not elsewhere classified)**

585   **Smallpox**

588   **Prevention and control**

590   **Epidemics**

Virus diseases - Continued

593   **Cat–scratch disease**

600   **Rickettsial and chlamydial infections. Tick–borne diseases (General or not elsewhere classified)**

602   **Trench fever**

605   **Epidemic louse–borne typhus**

610   **Epidemics**

615   **Endemic flea–borne typhus**

620   **Rocky Mountain spotted fever**

625   **Other tick–borne rickettsial infections**
           e.g., Q fever

630   **Scrub typhus**

635   **Other mite–borne rickettsial infections**
           e.g., Rickettsialpox

640   **Bartonellaceae infections**

660   **Ornithosis**

680   **Tropical diseases (General)**
           Cf. WR 350 Tropical diseases of the skin.

695   **Parasitic diseases (General or not elsewhere classified)**
           Classify general works on localized infections by site, e.g., Parasitic skin diseases in WR 345.

698   **Parasitic intestinal diseases (General or not elsewhere classified)**
           Classify works on amebic dysentery in WC 285.

700   **Protozoan infections (General or not elsewhere classified)**
           Classify works on amebiasis in WC 285; on trichomonas vaginitis in WP 258. See also other localized infections indexed.

705   **Trypanosomiasis**

Parasitic diseases
   Protozoan infections - Continued

715   Visceral leishmaniasis
         Classify general works on leishmaniasis and on mucocutaneous leishmaniasis in WR 350.

725   Toxoplasmosis (General or not elsewhere classified)

730   Coccidiosis

735   Balantidiasis

750   Malaria

755   Epidemiology

765   Prevention and control

770   Therapy

800   Helminthiasis (General or not elsewhere classified)

805   Trematode infections (General or not elsewhere classified)

810   Schistosomiasis

830   Cestode infections (General or not elsewhere classified)

838   Cysticercosis.   Taeniasis

840   Echinococcosis
         Classify works on hepatic echinococcosis in WI 700; on pulmonary echinococcosis in WF 600.

850   Nematode infections (General or not elsewhere classified)

855   Trichinosis

860   Trichuriasis.   Oxyuriasis

865   Strongyloidiasis

Parasitic diseases
  Helminthiasis
    Nematode infections - Continued

870   Ascariasis

880   Filariasis and related conditions (General or not elsewhere classified)

885   Onchocerciasis

890   Hookworm infections (General or not elsewhere classified)

900   Ectoparasitic infestations (General or not elsewhere classified)
      Disinfestation
Classify works on pediculosis in WR 375; on scabies in WR 365 or if veterinary in SF 810. Cf. WC 625 and WC 635 for tick and mite–borne rickettsial infections.

950   Zoonoses (General)
Classify work on specific diseases of animals in SF.

The WD schedule consists of a series of small tables which deal with subjects that cannot be readily integrated into other schedules because of the underlying framework of the Classification. Classify works on history or societies in the general number for each table.

WD 100–175	**Nutrition Disorders**
WD 200–226	**Metabolic Diseases**
WD 300–375	**Immunologic and Collagen Diseases. Hypersensitivity**
WD 400–430	**Animal Poisons**
WD 500–530	**Plant Poisons**
WD 600–670	**Diseases and Injuries Caused by Physical Agents**
WD 700–758	**Aviation and Space Medicine**

NUTRITION DISORDERS

Classify works on nutrition disorders in infancy and childhood in WS 115–130; in the aged in WT 115.

100   **General works**
   Classify here works on particular nutrition disorders not included below or elsewhere classified.

* 101   **Handbooks**

105   **Deficiency diseases (General or not elsewhere classified)**
   Classify works on deficiency of hormones in WK; on deficiencies as etiological factors in particular diseases with the disease.

110   **Vitamin A deficiency**
   e.g., Night blindness

120   **Vitamin B deficiency**

122   **Thiamine deficiency**
   e.g., Beriberi

124   **Riboflavin deficiency**

126   **Pellagra**

140   **Ascorbic acid deficiency**
             e.g., Scurvy

145   **Vitamin D deficiency**
             e.g., Rickets

150   **Vitamin E deficiency**

155   **Vitamin K deficiency**

175   **Celiac disease. Sprue**

METABOLIC DISEASES

200   **General works**
             Classify works on diabetes and related conditions in WK; on achlorhydria in WI 308.

* 200.1   **Handbooks**

200.5   **Specific diseases or groups of diseases not classified elsewhere, A–Z**

             .C2   **Calcium metabolism disorders**
                     Classify works on deficiency diseases in WD 100–175.
             .H8   **Hyperlipemia**
             .H9   **Hyperprolactinemia**
             .M2   **Malabsorption syndromes**
                     Classify works on celiac disease and sprue in WD 175. Classify works for the gastroenterologist in WI 500.
             .P4   **Phosphorus metabolism disorders**
             .P7   **Protein–losing enteropathies**

205   **Inborn errors of metabolism (General)**
             Classify works on the hemolytic anemias in WH 170; on chronic idiopathic jaundice in WI 703; on errors of renal tubular transport in WJ 301.

205.5   **Specific errors or groups of errors not elsewhere classified, A–Z**

             .A5   **Amino acid metabolism**
                     Classify works on albinism in WR 265.
             .A6   **Amyloidosis**
             .C2   **Carbohydrate metabolism**

*NUMBER CAN BE USED FOR BOTH MONOGRAPHS AND SERIALS.

.H9	Hyperbilirubinemia, Hereditary	
.L5	Lipid metabolism	
.M3	Metal metabolism (General)	
	Classify works on specific disorders separately.	
.M4	Minerals	
.P2	Paralysis, Familial periodic	
.P6	Porphyria	
.P8	Purine–pyrimidine metabolism	
	Classify works on gout in WE 350.	
.X2	Xanthomatosis	

210   **Obesity**
Classify works on reducing diets here or in WD 212 below.

212   **Popular works**

214   **Adiposis dolorosa. Lipomatosis. Lipodystrophy**
Classify works on panniculitis in WR 220; on lipochondrodystrophy in WD 205.5.C2.

220   **Water–electrolyte imbalance. Acid–base imbalance**
Classify works on water–electrolyte balance and acid base equilibrium in QU 105.

222   **Acidosis**
Classify works on diabetic acidosis in WK 830; on renal tubular acidosis in WJ 301; on respiratory acidosis in WF 140.

226   **Alkalosis**

IMMUNOLOGIC AND COLLAGEN DISEASES. HYPERSENSITIVITY

This schedule is for works on diseases that are largely systemic. Classify works on the hematologic diseases in WH; on disorders associated with transplantation in WO 680; on phagocytic bactericidal dysfunction and associated conditions in QW 690.

300   **General works**
Classify works on asthma in WF 553; on hay fever in WV 335; on dermatitis in WR 160; on respiratory hypersensitivity in WF 150.

* 301   **Handbooks**

305   **Autoimmune diseases (General)**

HYPERSENSITIVITY

308   **Immune complex disease. Immunologic deficiency syndromes (General or not elsewhere classified)**
Classify works on acquired immunodeficiency syndrome (AIDS) and other HIV infections in WC 503–503.7.

310   **Food hypersensitivity**

320   **Drug hypersensitivity**

330   **Serum sickness**

375   **Collagen diseases and other connective tissue diseases (General)**
Cf. WE 346 Rheumatoid arthritis; WG 240 Rheumatic heart disease; WC 220 Rheumatic fever; WG 518 Periarteritis nodosa; WG 520 Thromboangiitis obliterans; WR 152 Lupus erythematosus, Systemic; WR 260 Scleroderma, Systemic.

ANIMAL POISONS

400   **General works**

* 401   **Handbooks**

405   **Marine forms**

410   **Reptiles**

420   **Spiders. Scorpions. Centipedes. Leeches**

430   **Insects**

PLANT POISONS

500   **General works**
Cf. QV 627 Organic poisons.

* 501   **Handbooks**

505   **Ergotism**

515   **Favism**

520   **Mushroom poisoning**

530   **Milk sickness**

DISEASES AND INJURIES CAUSED BY PHYSICAL AGENTS

600   **General works**
       Classify material on burns in WO 704; on blast injuries in WO 820; on radiation injuries in WN 610.

* 601   **Handbooks**

602   **Electric injuries**

605   **Non–ionizing radiation injuries (General)**

610   **Heat exhaustion. Sunstroke**

630   **Motion sickness**
       e.g., Seasickness. Airsickness

640   **Vibration disorders (General)**
       Classify works on vibration as a cause of disease in QZ 57; on aviation effects in WD 735; on control in industry in WA 470; on therapeutic use in WB 535.

650   **High air pressure. Submarine medicine**

655   **Anoxia. Anoxemia**
       Cf. WF 143 Respiratory symptoms; WD 715 Aviation medicine.

670   **Hypothermia**
       Classify here works written for the practicing physician, such as those on diagnosis, treatment, etc. Classify works on pathogenesis of hypothermia in QZ 57; studies of normal physiological effects of cold in QT 160; on induced hypothermia in WO 350.

*NUMBER CAN BE USED FOR BOTH MONOGRAPHS AND SERIALS.

AVIATION AND SPACE MEDICINE

Classify works combining both atmospheric and space flight in WD 700–745; on Space flight alone in WD 750–758. Classify here works on diseases associated with high altitude on earth as well as in the air.

700   **General works**
      Classify material on aerotitis media in WV 232; on vision in WW.

* 701   **Handbooks**

* 703   **Dictionaries. Encyclopedias**

704   **Research (General)**
      Classify here works about research in general, in aviation medicine alone or in aviation medicine and space medicine combined. Classify works about research in space medicine alone in WD 751. Classify works about research on a particular subject, by subject.

705   **Personnel selection and fitness. Physical standards**

710   **Altitude effects**

712   **Decompression sickness**

715   **Anoxia. Inert gas narcosis**

720   **Speed. Acceleration. Deceleration. Gravitation. Rotation**
      e.g., G force
      Classify works on airsickness in WD 630.

730   **Psychological aspects**
      e.g., Fear. Stress

735   **Fatigue. Effect of noise. Effect of vibration**

740   **Aviation accidents. Protective devices**

745   **Aviation dentistry**

SPACE MEDICINE

750   **General works (including works on broad aspects of space flight)**

*NUMBER CAN BE USED FOR BOTH MONOGRAPHS AND SERIALS.

SPACE MEDICINE

751   **Research (General)**
Classify works about research on a particular subject by subject.

751.6   **Medical informatics. Automatic data processing. Computers (General)**
Classify works on use for special subjects by sbuject.

752   **Physiological aspects**

754   **Psychological aspects**

756   **Closed ecological systems**

758   **Extraterrestrial environment**

WE

MUSCULOSKELETAL SYSTEM

Classify general works on the musculoskeletal system and its diseases in WS 270 when related to children; in WY 157.6 when related to nursing. Classify works on nursing of patients with specific diseases in WY also. Classify works on skin diseases in WR.

WE 1–190	**General**
WE 200–600	**By Tissue**
WE 700–890	**By Region**

GENERAL

* 1   **Societies (Cutter from name of society)**
Includes ephemeral membership lists issued serially or separately. Classify substantial lists with directories. Classify annual reports, journals, etc., in W1.

        Collections (General)
5   **By several authors**
7   **By individual authors**

9   **Addresses. Essays. Lectures (General)**

11   **History (Table G)**
11.1   **General coverage (Not Table G)**

* 13   **Dictionaries. Encyclopedias**

* 15   **Classification. Nomenclature. Terminology**

* 16   **Tables. Statistics**

17   **Atlases. Pictorial works**
Classify atlases limited to a particular part of the system here also.

18   **Education**
Classify here works about education.

* 18.2 **Educational materials**
Classify here educational materials, e.g., outlines, questions and answers, programmed instruction, catalogs, computer–assisted instruction, etc., regardless of format. Classify textbooks, regardless of format, by subject.

* 19 **Schools, departments and faculties of orthopedics**

20 **Research (General)**
Classify here works about research in general. Classify works about research on a particular subject by subject.

21 **Orthopedics as a profession. Ethics. Peer review**

* 22 **Directories (Table G)**
* 22.1 **General coverage (Not Table G)**

Laboratories, institutes, etc.
23 **Collective**
24 **Individual (Cutter from name of agency)**

25 **Laboratory manuals. Technique**

26 **Equipment and supplies**
Classify catalogs in W 26. Classify works on bone plates and screws in WE 185.

26.5 **Medical informatics. Automatic data processing. Computers (General)**
Classify works on use for special subjects by subject.

Hospitals, clinics, dispensaries, etc.
27 **Collective (Table G)**
27.1 **General coverage (Not Table G)**
28 **Individual (Table G)**

* 32 **Laws (Table G)**
* 32.1 **General coverage (Not Table G)**

* 33 **Discussion of law (Table G)**
* 33.1 **General coverage (Not Table G)**

* 39 **Handbooks**

100 **General works**
Classify works on specialty and on the specialty and diseases here. Classify works on diseases alone in WE 140.

*NUMBER CAN BE USED FOR BOTH MONOGRAPHS AND SERIALS.

101   **Anatomy. Histology. Embryology (General)**

102   **Physiology. Biochemistry**

103   **Movement. Locomotion. Posture. Exertion**

104   **Kinesthesis. Weight perception**

140   **Diseases (General)**

141   **Examination. Diagnosis. Diagnostic methods. Radiography**
               Classify material on a single organ with the organ.

168   **Orthopedics (General)**

170   **Amputation**

172   **Prosthesis**
               Classify catalogs in W 26.

175   **Fractures. Dislocations. Sprains**

180   **Fractures**

182   **Open fractures**

185   **Fracture fixation**

190   **Reconstructive orthopedics. Transplantation of bone and bones**

BY TISSUE

200   **Bone and bones (General)**
               Include works on structure and function of bones in general. Classify works on specific bones with part or system involved.

225   **Bone diseases**
               Classify works on eosinophilic granuloma in WH 650.

Bone diseases - Continued

250   **Congenital abnormalities. Disorders of metabolism, growth, or development**
Classify works on abnormalities of specific bones or regions with the bone or region. Classify works on systemic metabolic disorders involving the bones in WD 200–205.5.

251   **Osteomyelitis and other infectious diseases**

253   **Tuberculosis of bones and joints**

258   **Neoplasms. Cysts**
Classify works on neoplasms of specific bones by site.

259   **Osteochondritis**

300   **Joints. Ligaments. Synovial membranes and fluid. Cartilage**

304   **Joint diseases**

312   **Surgery (including arthrodesis and arthroplasty) (General)**

344   **Arthritis**

346   **Rheumatoid arthritis. Ankylosis**
Cf. WU 140 Temporomandibular joint ankylosis; WE 725 Ankylosing spondylitis.

348   **Degenerative joint disease. Osteoarthritis**

350   **Gout**

400   **Bursae**

500   **Muscles. Fascia**
Include works on structure and function. Classify works on diseases in general in WE 550. Classify works on specific muscles with part or system involved.

544   **Myositis. Fibrositis. Rheumatism**

545   **Contracture**
Classify works on muscle contraction in WE 500; on muscle cramp and myoclonus in WE 550.

Muscles. Fascia - Continued

550   **Muscular diseases. Neuromuscular diseases**
Classify works on neuromuscular diseases of the eye in WW 400–475.

555   **Myasthenia gravis**

559   **Muscular dystrophy**

600   **Tendons. Tendon sheaths**

BY REGION

700   **Head and trunk**

705   **Head. Face**
Cf. WU 101 works for the dentist. Classify works on the jaw in WU; on the temporal bone written for the otolaryngologist in WV 201.

706   **Injuries**

707   **Neoplasms (Head and neck)**

708   **Neck**

715   **Thorax. Ribs**
Classify material on anatomy and physiology here as well as that on bone disorders and malformations. Classify material on diseases of organs or systems within the thoracic cavity, as well as thoracic surgery, in WF.

720   **Back**

725   **Spine. Vertebrae**
Classify works on lumbar and sacral vertebrae in WE 750; on spinal tuberculosis in WE 253.

730   **Congenital anomalies**
e.g., Spinal dysraphism

735   **Curvatures**
e.g., Scoliosis. Kyphosis. Lordosis

740   **Intervertebral disks**

750   Lumbosacral region.   Sacrococcygeal region.   Pelvis

755   Low back pain.   Sciatica

800   Extremities

805   Upper extremity

810   Shoulder.   Upper arm

812   Axilla

820   Elbow.   Forearm

830   Wrist.   Hand

832   Infections of the hand

835   Fingers.   Toes

850   Lower extremity
       Classify works on varicose veins in WG 620.

855   Hip.   Upper leg

860   Hip joint

865   Femur.   Thigh

870   Knee.   Lower leg

880   Ankle.   Foot
       Classify works on toes in WE 835.

883   Deformities
        e.g., Clubfoot

886   Flat feet

890   Podiatry

WF

RESPIRATORY SYSTEM

Classify general works on the respiratory system and its diseases in WS 280 when related to children; in WY 163 when related to nursing. Classify works on nursing of patients with specific diseases in WY also.

WF 1–900	General
WF 970–985	Thorax and Thoracic Surgery

GENERAL

* 1   **Societies (Cutter from name of society)**
        Includes ephemeral membership lists issued serially or separately. Classify substantial lists with directories. Classify annual reports, journals, etc., in Wl.

        Collections (General)
5   **By several authors**
7   **By individual authors**

9   **Addresses. Essays. Lectures (General)**

11   **History (Table G)**
11.1   **General coverage (Not Table G)**

* 13   **Dictionaries. Encyclopedias**

* 15   **Classification. Nomenclature. Terminology**

* 16   **Tables. Statistics**

17   **Atlases. Pictorial works**
        Classify atlases limited to a particular part of the system here also.

18   **Education**
        Classify here works about education.

* 18.2   **Educational materials**
        Classify here educational materials, e.g., outlines, questions and answers, programmed instruction, catalogs, computer–assisted instruction, etc., regardless of format. Classify textbooks, regardless of format, by subject.

* 19   **Schools, colleges, and specialized departments and facilities**

20   **Research (General)**
        Classify here works about research in general. Classify works about research on a particular subject by subject.

21   **Pneumology as a profession. Ethics. Peer review**

* 22   **Directories (Table G)**
* 22.1   **General coverage (Not Table G)**

        Institutes. Laboratories of experimental research
23   **Collective**
24   **Individual (Cutter from name of agency)**

25   **Laboratory manuals. Technique**

26   **Equipment and supplies**
        Classify catalogs in W 26.

26.5   **Medical informatics. Automatic data processing. Computers (General)**
        Classify works for use on special subjects by subject.

        Hospitals, sanatoriums, clinics, etc.
27   **Collective (Table G)**
27.1   **General coverage (Not Table G)**
28   **Individual (Table G)**

* 32   **Laws (Table G)**
        Classify legislation on tuberculosis in WF 200.
* 32.1   **General coverage (Not Table G)**

* 33   **Discussion of law (Table G)**
* 33.1   **General coverage (Not Table G)**

* 39   **Handbooks**

100   **General works**
        Classify works on specialty and on the specialty and diseases here. Classify works on diseases alone in WF 140.

*NUMBER CAN BE USED FOR BOTH MONOGRAPHS AND SERIALS.

101   **Anatomy. Histology. Embryology. Abnormalities**

102   **Physiology of respiration**

110   **Biochemistry of respiration and the respiratory system**

140   **Diseases of the respiratory system (General)**

141   **Examination. Diagnosis. Radiography. Monitoring**

141.5   **Specific techniques, A–Z**

         .B8   **Bronchial provocation tests**
         .P7   **Plethysmography, Whole body**

143   **Symptomatology**

145   **Therapeutics**

150   **Respiratory hypersensitivity (General)**
         Classify localized reactions with organs affected, e.g., Hay fever in WV 335.

200   **Tuberculosis (General)**
         Classify works on tuberculosis of organs of other systems, with the organ or system.
         Classify here also legislation on tuberculosis.

205   **Epidemiology**

215   **Pathology**

220   **Diagnosis. Prognosis**

225   **Mass chest X-ray**

250   **Immunological aspects**
         e.g., BCG vaccine

290   **Lymph node tuberculosis. Scrofula**

300   **Pulmonary tuberculosis**
         Classify works on silicotuberculosis in WF 654.

Pulmonary tuberculosis - Continued

310   Therapy

315   Diet. Rest. Exercise. Home care

330   Hospitalization. Climatotherapy. Heliotherapy

350   Surgery

360   Drug therapy

380   Miliary tuberculosis

390   Pleural tuberculosis

405   Tuberculosis in the workplace

415   Tuberculosis in childhood

450   Neoplasms (General)

490   Pharynx. Trachea
           Classify works for the otolaryngologist in WV 410. Classify works on tracheoesophageal fistula in WI 250.

500   Bronchi

544   Bronchiectasis

546   Bronchitis. Tracheitis

553   Asthma

600   Lungs
           Classify works on the pneumonias in WC 202-209; on pulmonary tuberculosis in WF 300-360.

645   Atelectasis

648   Emphysema

Lungs - Continued

651   **Lung abscess**

652   **Fungal lung diseases**

654   **Pneumoconiosis**

658   **Neoplasms**
           Include works on lung neoplasms of bronchial origin.

668   **Surgery**
           e.g., Pneumonectomy

700   **Pleura. Pleural cavity**

744   **Pleurisy. Pleuritis**

745   **Empyema**

746   **Pneumothorax. Hemothorax**

768   **Artificial pneumothorax**

800   **Diaphragm**

805   **Functional disorders**
           e.g., Hiccup

810   **Diaphragmatic hernia**

900   **Mediastinum**

THORAX AND THORACIC SURGERY

970   **General works**
       *Classify here works on two or more systems within the thoracic cavity, e.g., on
       respiratory and cardiovascular systems. Classify works on anatomy, physiology,
       bone structure and abnormalities of the skeletal portion of the thorax in WE 715.*

975   **Diagnosis. Radiography**

980   **Surgery**

985   **Injuries**

WG

CARDIOVASCULAR SYSTEM

Classify general works on the cardiovascular system and its diseases in WS 290 when related to children; in WY 152.5 when related to nursing. Classify works on nursing of patients with specific diseases in WY also. Classify works on blood supply of specific parts of other body systems with system or part.

WG 1–170	**General**
WG 200–460	**Heart**
WG 500–700	**Blood Vessels**

GENERAL

* 1 **Societies (Cutter from name of society)**
Includes ephemeral membership lists issued serially or separately. Classify substantial lists with directories. Classify annual reports, journals, etc. in W1.

Collections (General)
5 **By several authors**
7 **By individual authors**

9 **Addresses. Essays. Lectures (General)**

11 **History (Table G)**
11.1 **General coverage (Not Table G)**

* 13 **Dictionaries. Encyclopedias**

* 15 **Classification. Nomenclature. Terminology**

* 16 **Tables. Statistics**

17 **Atlases. Pictorial works**
Classify atlases limited to a particular part of the system here also.

18 **Education**
Classify here works about education.

* 18.2   **Educational materials**
> *Classify here educational materials, e.g., outlines, questions and answers, programmed instruction, catalogs, computer–assisted instruction, etc., regardless of format. Classify textbooks, regardless of format, by subject.*

* 19   **Schools, colleges, and specialized departments and facilities**

20   **Research (General)**
> *Classify here works about research in general. Classify works about research on a particular subject by subject. Cf. WG 110 Experimental studies.*

21   **Cardiology as a profession. Ethics. Peer review**

* 22   **Directories (Table G)**
* 22.1   **General coverage (Not Table G)**

Institutes. Laboratories of experimental research
23   **Collective**
24   **Individual (Cutter from name of agency)**

25   **Laboratory manuals. Technique**
> *Cf. WG 140 for clinical examination and diagnosis.*

26   **Equipment and supplies**
> *Classify catalogs in W 26. Classify works on artificial and mechanical hearts in WG 169.5. Classify works on artificial pacemakers here. Cf. WG 168 for artificial cardiac pacing.*

26.5   **Medical informatics. Automatic data processing. Computers (General)**
> *Classify works on use for special subjects by subject.*

Hospitals, clinics, dispensaries, etc.
27   **Collective (Table G)**
27.1   **General coverage (Not Table G)**
28   **Individual (Table G)**

* 32   **Laws (Table G)**
* 32.1   **General coverage (Not Table G)**

* 33   **Discussion of law (Table G)**
* 33.1   **General coverage (Not Table G)**

* 39   **Handbooks**

100   **General works**
Classify works on specialty and on the specialty and diseases here. Classify works on diseases alone in WG 120.

101   **Anatomy. Histology. Embryology**

102   **Physiology. Biochemistry**

103   **Circulation (General)**
Classify works on blood circulation of a system or part with system or part.

104   **Microcirculation (General)**

106   **Hemodynamics. Blood velocity, volume, pressure, etc.**
Classify works on hypertension and hypotension in WG 340; on measurement of blood pressure in clinical diagnosis in WB 280.

110   **Experimental studies**
Classify here works that discuss the experimental work itself. Classify works about research in WG 20. Classify works on specific subjects by subject.

113   **Popular works**
Classify here works on heart and vascular diseases in general or on coronary disease and congestive heart failure in particular. Classify works on other specific disorders with the disorder.

120   **Cardiovascular diseases (General or not elsewhere classified)**

140   **Electrocardiography. Vectorcardiography. Monitoring (General)**

141   **Examination. Diagnosis. Diagnostic methods (General and heart specifically)**

141.5   **Specific diagnostic methods, A–Z**

       .A3   **Angiocardiography**
       .A9   **Auscultation, Heart**
       .B2   **Ballistocardiography**
       .C15   **Cardiography, Impedance**
       .C2   **Catheterization, Heart**
       .E2   **Echocardiography**
       .F9   **Function tests, Heart (General)**
       .K5   **Kinetocardiography**
       .K9   **Kymography**
       .P4   **Phonocardiography**
       .P7   **Plethysmography**

Examination. Diagnosis. Diagnostic methods
Specific diagnostic methods, A-Z - Continued

.R2   Radiography (General)
.R3   Radionuclide imaging
.T6   Tomography

142   **Pathology**

166   **Therapeutics**
             Classify works on drugs acting on the cardiovascular system in QV 150.

166.5   **Specific therapeutic methods, A–Z**

.A5   Angioplasty, Laser
.B2   Balloon dilatation. Balloon angioplasty

168   **Cardiovascular surgery. Artificial cardiac pacing**
             Classify works on surgery for a particular disorder with the disorder.

169   **Heart surgery. Heart transplantation**
             Classify works on surgery of coronary vessels in general, heart valves, myocardium, etc., here. Classify works on surgery of the aorta in WG 410. Classify works on surgery of a particular disorder with the disorder.

169.5   **Artificial heart. Mechanical heart**

170   **Vascular surgery**
             Classify works on surgery of arteries and veins in general here. Cf. WG 410 Aorta and numbers for other specific vessels.

HEART

200   **General works**
             Note that popular works are classed in WG 113; works on examination, in WG 140–141.5; on surgery, in WG 169–169.5.

201   **Anatomy. Histology. Embryology**

202   **Physiology. Mechanism of the heart beat**

205   **Cardiac emergencies**

210   **Heart diseases (General or not elsewhere classified)**

220	**Congenital heart disease. Abnormalities of the heart and the cardiovascular system (General)**
240	**Rheumatic heart disease**
260	**Valves**
262	**Mitral**
265	**Aortic**
268	**Tricuspid**
269	**Pulmonary**
275	**Pericardium**
280	**Myocardium** *Classify material on myocardial infarct in WG 300.*
285	**Endocardium**
298	**Angina pectoris**
300	**Coronary vessels. Coronary disease**
320	**Functional heart disease** e.g., Neurocirculatory asthenia
330	**Disorders of the heart beat**
340	**Hypertension. Hypertensive heart disease. Hypotension**
370	**Congestive heart failure**
410	**Aorta** *Cf. WC 168 for aortic involvement in syphilis.*
420	**Pulmonary embolism and related disorders. Pulmonary heart disease**

460   **Special cardiac problems in anesthesia, dentistry, surgery**
         e.g., Choice of anesthetic
         Cf. WO 235 for general works on choice of anesthetic. Classify works on problems in pregnancy in WQ 244; in labor specifically in WQ 330.

BLOOD VESSELS

Classify works on blood supply of the extremities here, but classify works on blood supply of specific parts of other body systems with that system or part. Classify works on coronary vessels in WG 300; on the aorta specifically in WG 410; on circulation in WG 103–104; on vascular resistance in WG 106; on vascular surgery in WG 170.

500   **General works. Radiography**

510   **Arteries (General or not elsewhere classified)**

515   **Inflammation**

518   **Polyarteritis nodosa**

520   **Thromboangiitis obliterans**

530   **Immersion foot. Frostbite**

540   **Arterial embolism. Arterial thrombosis**

550   **Arteriosclerosis and related disorders**

560   **Vasomotor regulation and disorders**
         Classify material on carotid sinus syndrome here.

570   **Raynaud's disease**

578   **Vasodilator disorders**

580   **Aneurysms**
         Classify works on aortic aneurysm in WG 410; on heart aneurysm in WG 300; on cerebral aneurysm in WL 354–355.

590   **Arteriovenous anastomosis. Arteriovenous fistula**

Arteries - Continued

595   **Specific arteries, A–Z**
Classify works on the aorta in WG 410; on coronary arteries in WG 300.

.A9	Axillary artery
.B2	Basilar artery
.B7	Brachial artery
.B72	Brachiocephalic trunk
.B76	Bronchial arteries
.C2	Carotid arteries
.C3	Celiac artery
.C37	Cerebral arteries
.F3	Femoral artery
.H3	Hepatic artery
.I5	Iliac artery
.M2	Maxillary artery
.M3	Meningeal arteries
.M38	Mesenteric arteries
.O7	Ophthalmic artery
.P6	Popliteal artery
.P8	Pulmonary artery
.R3	Renal artery
.R38	Retinal artery
.S7	Splenic artery
.S8	Subclavian artery
.T3	Temporal arteries
.T4	Thoracic arteries
.U6	Umbilical arteries
.V3	Vertebral artery

600   **Veins**

610   **Thrombosis. Phlebothrombosis. Thrombophlebitis and related disorders**

620   **Varicose veins**

625   **Specific veins, A–Z**
Classify works on coronary veins in WG 300; on the portal system in WI 720.

.A9	Axillary vein
.A99	Azygos vein
.B7	Brachiocephalic veins
.C3	Cerebral veins
.C7	Cranial sinuses
.F3	Femoral vein
.H3	Hepatic veins
.I5	Iliac vein
.J8	Jugular vein
.P6	Popliteal vein
.P8	Pulmonary veins
.R3	Renal veins

Veins
  Specific veins, A-Z - Continued

.R38	Retinal vein
.S2	Saphenous vein
.S8	Subclavian vein
.V3	Venae cavae

700   **Capillaries**
    Classify works on capillary resistance in WG 106; on microcirculation in WG 104.

WH

HEMIC AND LYMPHATIC SYSTEMS

Classify general works on the hemic and lymphatic systems and their diseases in WS 300 when related to children; in WY 152.5 when related to nursing. Classify works on nursing of patients with specific diseases in WY also.

* 1   **Societies (Cutter from name of society)**
         Includes ephemeral membership lists issued serially or separately. Classify substantial lists with directories. Classify annual reports, journals, etc., in W1.

         Collections (General)
5   **By several authors**
7   **By individual authors**

9   **Addresses. Essays. Lectures (General)**

11   **History (Table G)**
11.1   **General coverage (Not Table G)**

* 13   **Dictionaries. Encyclopedias**

* 15   **Classification. Nomenclature. Terminology**

* 16   **Tables. Statistics**

17   **Atlases. Pictorial works**
         Classify atlases limited to a particular part of the system here also.

18   **Education**
         Classify here works about education.

* 18.2   **Educational materials**
         Classify here educational materials, e.g., outlines, questions and answers, programmed instruction, catalogs, computer-assisted instruction, etc., regardless of format. Classify textbooks, regardless of format, by subject.

* 19   **Schools, departments and faculties of hematology**

20   **Research (General)**
         Classify here works about research in general. Classify works about research on a particular subject by subject.

*NUMBER CAN BE USED FOR BOTH MONOGRAPHS AND SERIALS.

21   **Hematology as a profession. Ethics. Peer review**

* 22   **Directories (Table G)**
* 22.1   **General coverage (Not Table G)**

Institutes. Laboratories of experimental research. Blood banks
23   **Collective**
24   **Individual (Cutter from name of agency)**

25   **Laboratory manuals. Technique**
Classify works on laboratory examination of blood in QY 400–490.

26   **Equipment and supplies**
Classify catalogs in W 26.

26.5   **Medical informatics. Automatic data processing. Computers (General)**
Classify works on use for special subjects by subject.

Hospitals, clinics, etc.
28   **Individual (Table G)**

* 32   **Laws (Table G)**
* 32.1   **General coverage (Not Table G)**

* 33   **Discussion of law (Table G)**
* 33.1   **General coverage (Not Table G)**

* 39   **Handbooks**

100   **General works**
Classify works on specialty and on the specialty and diseases here. Classify works on diseases alone in WH 120.

120   **Hematologic diseases (General or not elsewhere classified)**

140   **Hematopoietic system and hematopoiesis. Developmental theories. Blood cells (General)**
Classify material on blood chemistry in QY 450.

150   **Erythrocytes**

155   **Anemia**
Classify works on neonatal anemia in WS 420; on splenic anemia in WH 600; on blood group incompatibility in WH 420.

*NUMBER CAN BE USED FOR BOTH MONOGRAPHS AND SERIALS.

Erythrocytes
    Anemia - Continued

160   **Hypochromic anemia**

165   **Macrocytic anemia. Pernicious anemia**

170   **Hemolytic anemia**
             e.g., Sickle cell anemia
             Classify works on favism in WD 515; on hemoglobinuria in WJ 344; on kernicterus in WL 362.

175   **Anemias of bone marrow dysfunction**
             e.g., Aplastic anemia

180   **Polycythemia. Polycythemia vera**

190   **Hemoglobin and other hemeproteins. Porphyrins (Associated with hemoglobin)**
             Classify general works on porphyrins in QU 110; on porphyria in WD 205.5.P6.

200   **Leukocytes. Leukocyte disorders (General)**

250   **Leukemia**
             Classify works on histology and pathology of leukemia in QZ 350.

300   **Blood platelets**

310   **Mechanism of blood coagulation. Hemostasis**
             Classify works on blood coagulation disorders in WH 322-325.

312   **Hemorrhagic diathesis (General)**
             Classify works on blood platelet disorders in WH 300.

314   **Purpura (General)**

315   **Thrombopenic purpura**

320   **Non-thrombopenic purpuras**

322   **Blood coagulation disorders (General)**

325   **Hemophilia. Hemarthrosis**

380   **Bone marrow. Bone marrow diseases (General or not elsewhere classified) Sternal puncture**
Cf. WH 175 Anemias; WH 180 Polycythemia vera.

400   **Fluid elements. Plasma. Serum. Blood proteins. Blood protein disorders**
Classify works on blood chemistry in QY 450–490; on inborn errors of protein metabolism in WD 205–205.5. Cf. WH 540 Multiple myeloma.

420   **Blood groups. Blood group incompatibility (General)**
Classify works on blood typing in QY 415; on medicolegal examination in W 791.

425   **Rh–Hr blood group system. Fetal erythroblastosis**
Classify works on kernicterus in WL 362.

450   **Whole blood. Blood derivatives. Plasma substitutes. Blood expanders**

460   **Blood bank procedures**
e.g., Procurement, processing, preservation, storage, shipment, etc. Blood donors. Plasmapheresis
Classify material on blood banks in WH 23 or WH 24; on blood transfusion in WB 356.

500   **Hodgkin's disease**

525   **Lymphoma**
e.g., Lymphosarcoma. Leucosarcoma
Classify here works which deal collectively with subjects classed in WH 250 Leukemia, WH 500 Hodgkin's disease, and WH 525 Lymphoma; include works on chemotherapy of hematological neoplastic disease. Classify works on histology and pathology of lymphomas in QZ 350.

540   **Multiple myeloma**

600   **Spleen**

650   **Reticuloendothelial system**
Classify works on the lipoidoses alone in WD 205.5.L5.

700   **Lymphatic system. Lymphatic diseases (General)**
Classify works on cells in general in WH 140; on blood cells by type in the numbers provided above.

WI

DIGESTIVE SYSTEM

Classify general works on the digestive system and its diseases in WS 310–312 when related to children; in WY 156.5 when related to nursing. Classify works on nursing of patients with specific diseases in WY number also. Classify works on liver and biliary tract treated together in WI 700–740 and in WI 770 if applicable. Classify works on gallbladder and other specific parts in WI 750–765 as indicated.

WI 1–250	General
WI 300–387	Stomach
WI 400–575	Intestines
WI 600–650	Anus and Rectum
WI 700–770	Liver and Biliary Tract
WI 800–820	Pancreas
WI 900–970	Abdomen and Abdominal Surgery

GENERAL

* 1 **Societies (Cutter from name of society)**
Includes ephemeral membership lists issued serially or separately. Classify substantial lists with directories. Classify annual reports, journals, etc., in W1.

Collections (General)
5 **By several authors**
7 **By individual authors**

9 **Addresses. Essays. Lectures (General)**

11 **History (Table G)**
11.1 **General coverage (Not Table G)**

* 13 **Dictionaries. Encyclopedias**

* 15 **Classification. Nomenclature. Terminology**

* 16 **Tables. Statistics**

17 **Atlases. Pictorial works**
Classify atlases limited to a particular part of the system here also.

*NUMBER CAN BE USED FOR BOTH MONOGRAPHS AND SERIALS.

18   **Education**
Classify here works about education.

* 18.2   **Educational materials**
Classify here educational materials, e.g., outlines, questions and answers, programmed instruction, catalogs, computer–assisted instruction, etc., regardless of format. Classify textbooks, regardless of format, by subject.

* 19   **Schools, departments, and faculties of gastroenterology**

20   **Research (General)**
Classify here works about research in general. Classify works about research on a particular subject by subject.

21   **Gastroenterology as a profession. Ethics. Peer review**

* 22   **Directories (Table G)**
* 22.1   **General coverage (Not Table G)**

Laboratories, institutes, etc.
23   **Collective**
24   **Individual (Cutter from name of agency)**

25   **Laboratory manuals. Technique**

26   **Equipment and supplies**
Classify catalogs in W 26.

26.5   **Medical informatics. Automatic data processing. Computers (General)**
Classify works on use for special subjects by subject.

Hospitals, clinics, etc.
27   **Collective (Table G)**
27.1   **General coverage (Not Table G)**
28   **Individual (Table G)**

* 32   **Laws (Table G)**
* 32.1   **General coverage (Not Table G)**

* 33   **Discussion of law (Table G)**
* 33.1   **General coverage (Not Table G)**

* 39   **Handbooks**

100   **General works**
          Classify works on surgery of the digestive or gastrointestinal system in general in WI 900.

101   **Anatomy. Histology. Embryology**

102   **Physiology. Biochemistry. Digestion**

113   **Popular works (General). Hygiene**

140   **Diseases (General)**

141   **Examination. Diagnosis. Diagnostic methods. Monitoring (General)**
          Classify works on examination of organ with the organ.

143   **Symptomatology. Manifestations of disease**

145   **Dyspepsia and related conditions**

146   **Nausea. Vomiting**

147   **Abdominal pain**

149   **Neoplasms**
          Classify works on neoplasms of specific organ with the organ.

150   **Functional disorders**

200   **Lips. Mouth**
          Classify works for the dentist in WU 140; on neoplasms written for the dentist in WU 280.

210   **Tongue. Taste buds**

230   **Salivary glands**

250   **Esophagus**

STOMACH

300 **General works**
Classify works on analysis of stomach contents in QY 130.

301 **Anatomy. Histology. Embryology. Congenital abnormalities**

302 **Physiology**

308 **Achlorhydria**

310 **Gastritis**

320 **Neoplasms**

350 **Peptic ulcer**

360   **Stomach ulcer**

370   **Duodenal ulcer**

380 **Surgery. Postgastrectomy syndromes**

387 **Pylorus. Pyloric antrum. Pyloric stenosis**

INTESTINES

400 **General works**

402 **Physiology**

405 **Symptomatology**

407   **Diarrhea**

409   **Constipation**

412 **Congenital malformations**

420   **Inflammation**
         e.g., Enteritis; inflammatory bowel diseases
         Classify works on regional enteritis in WI 512.

425   **Diverticulitis.   Diverticulosis**

430   **Polyps.   Polyposis**

435   **Neoplasms**

450   **Intussusception**

460   **Intestinal obstruction.   Ileus**

480   **Surgery (General)**

500   **Small intestine.   Mesentery**

505   **Duodenum**
         Classify works on duodenal ulcer in WI 370; on analysis of duodenal contents
         in QY 130.

510   **Jejunum**

512   **Ileum**

520   **Colon**
         Classify works on diverticulitis and diverticulosis in WI 425.   Cf. WC 280   Dysentery.

522   **Inflammation**
         e.g., Colitis

528   **Megacolon**
         e.g., Hirschsprung's disease

529   **Neoplasms.   Polyps**
         Classify works on colorectal neoplasms here.

530   **Cecum**

535   **Appendix**

560   **Sigmoid**

575   **Peritoneum. Omentum. Peritoneal cavity. Retroperitoneal space**

ANUS AND RECTUM

600   **General works**

605   **Hemorrhoids. Fissure in ano. Rectal fistula**

610   **Neoplasms**
          Classify works on colorectal neoplasms in WI 529.

620   **Proctoscopy. Sigmoidoscopy**

650   **Proctological surgery**

LIVER AND BILIARY TRACT

700   **General works**

702   **Physiology. Liver circulation**

703   **Bile. Bile acids, alcohols, and salts. Jaundice (General or not elsewhere classified)**

704   **Liver function in food metabolism**

720   **Circulatory disorders. Portal system. Portal hypertension**

725   **Cirrhosis**

730   **Abscess**

735   **Neoplasms**

740   **Degenerative diseases. Hepatolenticular degeneration**

750	Gallbladder. Bile ducts. Vater's ampulla. Cholecystography
755	Cholecystitis. Cholelithiasis
765	Neoplasms
770	Surgery (General)

PANCREAS

800	General works
	Classify works on the islands of Langerhans in WK 800–885.
802	Physiology. Secretions
805	Pancreatitis
810	Neoplasms. Cysts
820	Cystic fibrosis
830	Surgery (General)

ABDOMEN AND ABDOMINAL SURGERY

Classify works on surgery of the digestive or gastrointestinal system in general here.

900	General works
940	Umbilical region
950	Hernia
955	Ventral
960	Inguinal

WJ

UROGENITAL SYSTEM

Classify general works on the urogenital system and its diseases in WS 320–322 when related to children; in WY 164 when related to nursing. Classify works on nursing of patients with specific diseases in WY numbers also.

WJ 1–190	General
WJ 300–378	Kidney
WJ 400	Ureter
WJ 500–504	Bladder
WJ 600	Urethra
WJ 700–875	Male Genitalia

GENERAL

* 1   **Societies (Cutter from name of society)**
Includes ephemeral membership lists issued serially or separately. Classify substantial lists with directories. Classify annual reports, journals, etc., in W1.

Collections (General)
5   **By several authors**
7   **By individual authors**

9   **Addresses. Essays. Lectures (General)**

11   **History (Table G)**
11.1   **General coverage (Not Table G)**

* 13   **Dictionaries. Encyclopedias**

* 15   **Classification. Nomenclature. Terminology**

* 16   **Tables. Statistics**

17   **Atlases. Pictorial works**
Classify atlases limited to a particular part of the system here also.

18   **Education**
Classify here works about education.

*NUMBER CAN BE USED FOR BOTH MONOGRAPHS AND SERIALS.

* 18.2   Educational materials
Classify here educational materials, e.g., outlines, questions and answers, programmed instruction, catalogs, computer–assisted instruction, etc., regardless of format. Classify textbooks, regardless of format, by subject.

* 19   Schools, departments, and faculties of urology

20   Research (General)
Classify here works about research in general. Classify works about research on a particular subject by subject.

21   Urology as a profession. Ethics. Peer review

* 22   Directories (Table G)
* 22.1   General coverage (Not Table G)

Laboratories, institutes, etc.
23   Collective
24   Individual (Cutter from name of agency)

25   Laboratory manuals. Technique

26   Equipment and supplies
Classify catalogs in W 26.

26.5   Medical informatics. Automatic data processing. Computers (General)
Classify works on use for special subjects by subject.

Hospitals, clinics, dispensaries, etc.
27   Collective (Table G)
27.1   General coverage (Not Table G)
28   Individual (Table G)

* 32   Laws (Table G)
* 32.1   General coverage (Not Table G)

* 33   Discussion of law (Table G)
* 33.1   General coverage (Not Table G)

* 39   Handbooks

100   General works
Classify works on specialty and on the specialty and diseases here. Classify works on diseases alone in WJ 140.

101   **Anatomy. Histology. Embryology. Abnormalities**

102   **Physiology. Biochemistry**

140   **Urologic diseases (General)**

141   **Urologic examination (General). Monitoring**
         Classify material on examination of single organ with the organ. Classify works on urinalysis in QY 185.

146   **Urination and urination disorders**

151   **Urinary tract infections**

160   **Neoplasms (General)**

166   **Urologic therapeutics**
         Classify works on the pharmacodynamics of diuretics in QV 160; on the pharmacodynamics of anti–infective agents in QV 243.

168   **Urologic surgery**

190   **Gynecologic urology**
         Classify works that include obstetrical urology here. Classify those on urologic diseases in pregnancy (when treated separately) in WQ 260. Cf. WP 180 Vesicovaginal fistula.

KIDNEY

300   **General works**
         Classify works on kidney functions tests in QY 175; on urinalysis in QY 185.

301   **Anatomy. Histology. Embryology. Physiology. Abnormalities**

302   **Diagnosis. Radiography. Pyelography. Monitoring**

303   **Urinary secretion. Anuria (General)**

340   **Nephrosis**

342   **Kidney failure. Crush syndrome**

343   **Proteinuria. Albuminuria. Renal aminoaciduria**

344   **Hemoglobinuria. Hematuria. Myoglobinuria**

348   **Uremia**

351   **Infections**
          e.g., Pyelitis, Pyelonephritis

353   **Nephritis**

356   **Kidney calculi. Nephrocalcinosis**

358   **Neoplasms. Cystic kidney**

368   **Surgery. Kidney transplantation**

378   **Artificial kidney. Hemodialysis. Peritoneal dialysis**
          Classify works on hemodialysis and peritoneal dialysis used in treatment of diseases
          of other parts of the body with the diseases or part.

URETER

400   **Ureter**

BLADDER

500   **Bladder. Cystoscopy. Cystoscopic surgery**
          Classify works on vesicovaginal fistula in WP 180.

504   **Neoplasms**

URETHRA

600   **Urethra**

MALE GENITALIA

700   **General works**
Classify here also works which include both male and female genitalia.

701   **Anatomy. Histology. Embryology**

702   **Physiology**

706   **Neoplasms (General)**

709   **Impotence. Infertility**
Cf. WP 570 for general works on infertility.

710   **Male contraception**
Classify general works on medical aspects of contraceptives in WP 630. Classify works on sociological and religious aspects in HQ 763–766.5. Classify works on contraceptive drugs in QV 177.

712   **Sex differentiation disorders**

750   **Prostate. Seminal vesicles. Ejaculatory ducts**

752   **Diseases of the prostate. Prostatic neoplasms**

768   **Surgery**

780   **Vas deferens. Spermatic cord**

790   **Penis. Foreskin. Circumcision**

800   **Scrotum. Scrotal contents. Epididymis. Tunica vaginalis**

830   **Testis**

834   **Spermatogenesis. Spermatozoa**
Cf. QY 190 Semen (clinical analysis).

840   **Cryptorchidism. Eunuchism and related disorders**

858   **Neoplasms**

Testis - Continued

868   **Surgery. Castration**

875   **Testicular hormones and antagonists**
         Include works on related synthetic hormones here. Classify works on anabolic steroids in WK 150.

WK

ENDOCRINE SYSTEM

Classify general works on the endocrine system and its diseases in WS 330 when related to children; in WY 155 when related to nursing. Classify works on nursing of patients with specific diseases in the WY number also.

WK 1–190	General
WK 200–280	Thyroid Gland
WK 300	Parathyroid Glands
WK 350	Pineal Body
WK 400	Thymus Gland
WK 500–590	Pituitary Gland
WK 700–790	Adrenal Glands
WK 800–885	Islets of Langerhans
WK 900–920	Gonads

GENERAL

* 1   **Societies (Cutter from name of society)**
               Includes ephemeral membership lists issued serially or separately. Classify substantial lists with directories. Classify annual reports, journals, etc., in W1.

              Collections (General)
5   **By several authors**
7   **By individual authors**

9   **Addresses. Essays. Lectures (General)**

11   **History (Table G)**
11.1   **General coverage (Not Table G)**

* 13   **Dictionaries. Encyclopedias**

* 15   **Classification. Nomenclature. Terminology**

* 16   **Tables. Statistics**

17   **Atlases. Pictorial works**
               Classify atlases limited to a particular part of the system here also.

18   **Education**
Classify here works about education.

* 18.2   **Educational materials**
Classify here educational materials, e.g., outlines, questions and answers, programmed instruction, catalogs, computer-assisted instruction, etc., regardless of format. Classify textbooks, regardless of format, by subject.

* 19   **Schools, departments and faculties of endocrinology**

20   **Research (General)**
Classify here works about research in general. Classify works about research on a particular subject by subject.

21   **Endocrinology as a profession. Ethics. Peer review**

* 22   **Directories (Table G)**
* 22.1   **General coverage (Not Table G)**

Laboratories, institutes, etc.
23   **Collective**
24   **Individual (Cutter from name of agency)**

25   **Laboratory manuals. Technique. Experimental studies (General)**

26   **Equipment and supplies**
Classify catalogs in W 26.

26.5   **Medical informatics. Automatic data processing. Computers (General)**
Classify works on use for special subjects by subject.

Hospitals, clinics, dispensaries, etc.
27   **Collective (Table G)**
27.1   **General coverage (Not Table G)**
28   **Individual (Table G)**

* 32   **Laws (Table G)**
* 32.1   **General coverage (Not Table G)**

* 33   **Discussion of law (Table G)**
* 33.1   **General coverage (Not Table G)**

* 39   **Handbooks**

NUMBER CAN BE USED FOR BOTH MONOGRAPHS AND SERIALS.

100   **Endocrine glands (General)**
Classify works on specialty and on the specialty and diseases here. Classify works on diseases alone in WK 140.

102   **Physiology. Biochemistry. Hormones and antagonists (General)**

140   **Endocrine diseases (General)**

150   **Steroid hormones (General or not elsewhere classified)**
Classify works on hormones of a particular gland with the gland.

170   **Gastrointestinal hormones**
e.g., Secretin. Enterogastrone

180   **Renal hormones**

185   **Other hormones**
e.g., Peptide hormones

187   **Synthetic hormones (General or not elsewhere classified)**
Classify works on specific synthetic hormones with the hormones synthesized.

190   **Hormone therapy**

THYROID GLAND

200   **General works**

201   **Anatomy. Histology. Embryology. Abnormalities**

202   **Physiology. Biochemistry (including iodine metabolism). Thyroid hormones and antagonists**

250   **Hypothyroidism and related disorders (General or not elsewhere classified)**

252   **Cretinism. Myxedema**

259   **Goiter**
Classify here works on goiter in general and on specific goiters, except exophthalmic goiter which is classed in WK 265.

265   Hyperthyroidism. Thyrotoxicosis. Exophthalmic goiter

267   Medical therapy

270   Neoplasms. Cysts

280   Surgery

PARATHYROID GLANDS

300   Parathyroid glands

PINEAL BODY

350   Pineal body

THYMUS GLAND

400   Thymus gland

PITUITARY GLAND

500   General works

501   Anatomy. Histology. Embryology

502   Physiology. Biochemistry

510   Anterior pituitary gland (Adenohypophysis)
         Include here works on the pituitary–adrenal system.

515   Hormones and antagonists
         e.g., Corticotropin. Growth hormones
         Include works on release and release inhibiting hormones.

520   **Posterior pituitary gland (Neurohypophysis).   Hormones and antagonists**
Classify works on antidiuretic vasopressin in QV 160; on oxytocin in QV 173.

550   **Diseases**
e.g., Diabetes insipidus.   Pituitary dwarfism.   Gigantism.   Acromegaly.   Hypopituitarism.   Froehlich's syndrome, etc.

585   **Neoplasms**
Include works on the anterior and posterior pituitary glands here also.

590   **Surgery**

ADRENAL GLANDS

700   **General works**

701   **Anatomy.   Histology.   Embryology.   Abnormalities**

702   **Physiology.   Biochemistry**

725   **Adrenal medulla.   Epinephrine.   Norepinephrine and other catecholamines**
Classify works on methyldopa in QV 150 or with the disorder being treated.

750   **Adrenal cortex**
Classify works on neoplasms in WK 780; on surgery, in WK 790; on the pituitary–adrenal system, in WK 510.

755   **Adrenal cortex hormones**
e.g., Cortisone

757   **Synthetic substitutes for cortical hormones**
Classify works on topical glucocorticoids in QV 60.

760   **Diseases of the adrenal cortex**

765   **Adrenal cortex hypofunction**
e.g., Addison's disease

770   **Adrenal cortex hyperfunction**
e.g., Adrenogenital syndrome.   Virilism

780   **Neoplasms**

790   Surgery

ISLETS OF LANGERHANS

800   General works

801   Anatomy. Histology. Embryology

810   Diabetes mellitus

815   Therapy

818   Diet

819   Diet lists. Diabetic cookery

820   Insulin and its modifications

825   Other hypoglycemic agents

830   Diabetic ketoacidosis. Diabetic coma

835   Complications of diabetes

840   Diabetes as a complication in other conditions
              Classify works on diabetes in pregnancy in WQ 248.

850   Diabetic patients' manuals. Self care

870   Glycosurias

880   Hyperinsulinism. Hyperglycemia. Hypoglycemia

885   Neoplasms

GONADS

900   **Gonads. Sex hormones (General)**
Cf. WJ 830 Testis; WP 320 Ovary; WJ 875 Androgens; WP 522 Estrogens; WK 515 Pituitary gonadotropins; WP 530 Corpus luteum hormones.

920   **Placental hormones**

WL

NERVOUS SYSTEM

Classify general works on the nervous system and its diseases in WS 340 when related to children; in WY 160.5 when related to nursing. Classify works on nursing of patients with specific diseases in WY also.

WL 1–203	General
WL 300–405	Central Nervous System
WL 500–544	Peripheral Nerves
WL 600–610	Autonomic Nervous System
WL 700–710	Sense Organs

GENERAL

* 1 **Societies (Cutter from name of society)**
Includes ephemeral membership lists issued serially or separately. Classify substantial lists with directories. Classify annual reports, journals, etc. in W1.

Collections (General)
5   **By several authors**
7   **By individual authors**

9   **Addresses. Essays. Lectures (General)**

11   **History (Table G)**
11.1   **General coverage (Not Table G)**

* 13   **Dictionaries. Encyclopedias**

* 15   **Classification. Nomenclature. Terminology**

* 16   **Tables. Statistics**

17   **Atlases. Pictorial works**
Classify atlases limited to a particular part of the system here also.

18   **Education**
Classify here works about education.

* 18.2   **Educational materials**
         Classify here educational materials, e.g., outlines, questions and answers, programmed instruction, catalogs, computer–assisted instruction, etc., regardless of format.
         Classify textbooks, regardless of format, by subject.

* 19   **Schools, departments, and faculties of neurology**

20   **Research (General)**
         Classify here works about research in general. Classify works about research on a particular subject by subject.

21   **Neurology as a profession. Ethics. Peer review**

* 22   **Directories (Table G)**
* 22.1   **General coverage (Not Table G)**

         Laboratories, institutes, etc.
23   **Collective**
24   **Individual (Cutter from name of agency)**

25   **Laboratory manuals. Technique**

26   **Equipment and supplies**
         e.g., For electroencephalography
         Classify catalogs in W 26.

26.5   **Medical informatics. Automatic data processing. Computers (General)**
         Classify works on use for special subjects by subject.

         Hospitals, clinics, dispensaries, etc.
27   **Collective (Table G)**
27.1   **General coverage (Not Table G)**
28   **Individual (Table G)**

30   **Administration of services**
         e.g., Services for the epileptic

* 32   **Laws (Table G)**
* 32.1   **General coverage (Not Table G)**

* 33   **Discussion of law (Table G)**
* 33.1   **General coverage (Not Table G)**

* 39   **Handbooks**

100   **General works**
> *Classify works on specialty and on the specialty and diseases here. Classify works on diseases alone in WL 140.*

101   **Anatomy. Histology. Embryology. Abnormalities (General)**

102   **Physiology (General)**

102.5   **Neurons**

102.7   **Motor neurons**

102.8   **Synapses**

102.9   **Nerve endings**

103   **Psychophysiology (General)**
> *Classify works on specific topics by subject. See MeSH tree structure F2 and Index to this Classification.*

103.5   **Neuropsychology**

103.7   **Psychoneuroimmunology**

104   **Neurochemistry**

105   **Neuroendocrinology**

106   **Reflexes**
> *Classify works on conditioned reflexes, etc., in BF 319–319.5.*

108   **Physiology of sleep**
> *Classify works on disorders of sleep WM 188.*

140   **Nervous system diseases (General)**

141   **Neurologic examination. Diagnostic principles. Radiography of the brain**
> e.g., Ventriculography
> *Classify works on pediatric neuroradiography in WS 340.*

150   **Electroencephalography. Monitoring (General)**

154   **Echoencephalography**

160   **Nervous system neoplasms (General)**

200   **Meninges.   Blood–brain barrier**
          Classify works on listeria meningitis in WC 242; on meningococcal meningitis in WC 245; on viral meningitis in WC 540.

203   **Cerebrospinal fluid**
          Cf. QY 220 Clinical analysis; WB 377 Spinal, cisternal and ventricular puncture.

CENTRAL NERVOUS SYSTEM

300   **General works (Include works on brain alone)**
          Cf. WL 348 Brain diseases. Classify works on diagnosis in WL 141 General; WL 150 Electroencephalography; WL 154 Echoencephalography; WL 405 Myelography or in a specific number for the disorder.

302   **Cerebrovascular circulation**
          Cf. WG 595.C37 Cerebral arteries.

307   **Cerebrum.   Cerebral cortex.   Telencephalon**
          Classify here works on basal ganglia, corpus callosum and cerebral ventricles.

310   **Brain stem**

312   **Diencephalon.   Thalamus**

314   **Limbic system**

320   **Cerebellum**

330   **Cranial nerves (General or not elsewhere classified)**

335   **Localization of function.   Cerebral dominance.   Brain mapping**

340   **Neurologic manifestations (General or not elsewhere classified)**
          Cf. WL 390 Movement disorders; WW 460 Neurologic manifestations of eye disease.

340.2   **Communicative disorders.   Speech–language pathology**
          Classify here all works on communicative disorders except those of psychogenic origins. Classify communicative disorders of psychogenic origins in WM 475-475.6.

Neurologic manifestations
Communicative disorders. Speech-language pathology - Continued

340.5   Aphasia
         Classify works on aphasia of psychogenic origin in WM 475.5.

340.6   Dyslexia
         Classify works on dyslexia of psychogenic origin in WM 475.6.

341   Consciousness. Unconsciousness

342   Headache

344   Migraine and other vascular headaches

346   Paralysis (General or not elsewhere classified)

348   Diseases of the brain

350   Congenital (General or not elsewhere classified)

351   Inflammatory
         e.g., Abscess. Encephalitis. Encephalomyelitis
         Cf. WC 542 Epidemic encephalitis.

354   Traumatic
         e.g., Concussion. Skull fracture. Brain damage

355   Cerebrovascular disorders
         e.g., Cerebral hemorrhage

358   Neoplasms of the brain and of the central nervous system in general

359   Degenerative
         e.g., Parkinsonism

360   Multiple sclerosis

362   Kernicterus

368   Brain surgery. Neurosurgery (General)
         Classify works on sympathectomy in WL 610.

370   Psychosurgery

385   **Epilepsy**

390   **Movement disorders (General or not elsewhere classified)**
           Classify works on muscular diseases in WE 550–559; on psychomotor disorders in WM 197.

400   **Spinal cord.   Spinal nerves (General or not elsewhere classified).   Nerve roots.   Pyramidal tracts**

405   **Myelography**

PERIPHERAL NERVES

500   **General works**
           Cf. WL 330   Cranial nerves; WL 400   Spinal nerves.

544   **Neuritis.   Neuralgia**

AUTONOMIC NERVOUS SYSTEM

600   **General works**
           Classify here works on specific autonomic nerve groups, not included below.

610   **Sympathetic nervous system.   Parasympathetic nervous system**
           Classify works on cranial nerves in WL 330.

SENSE ORGANS

700   **General works**
           Classify works on specific sense organs with the system involved.

702   **Psychophysics.   Sensation (General)**
           Do not confuse with psychophysiology WL 103.

704   **Pain**
           Classify works on individual sense organ and/or pain relating to it with the organ.

705   **Perception.   Perceptual distortion**

Classify works on psychological aspects of perception in BF 311. Classify works on perceptual distortion and disorders associated with psychoses in WM 204. Classify works on visual perception in WW 105; on auditory perception in WV 272, etc.

710   **Sensation disorders (General or not elsewhere classified)**

Cf. WR 280 for sensory disorders of the skin.

WM

PSYCHIATRY

Classify material on medicolegal psychiatry in W 740; on child psychiatry in WS 350; on adolescent psychiatry in WS 463; on geriatric psychiatry in WT 150; on psychiatric nursing in general and on specific diseases in WY 160. Classify in WM, however, works on specific mental disorders of childhood, adolescence, or old age unless specifically instructed to do otherwise.

* 1   **Societies (Cutter from name of society)**
           Includes ephermeral membership lists issued serially or separately. Classify substantial lists with directories. Classify annual reports, journals, etc., in W1.

           Collections (General)
  5   **By several authors**
  7   **By individual authors**

  9   **Addresses. Essays. Lectures (General)**

  11   **History (Table G)**
  11.1   **General coverage (Not Table G)**

* 13   **Dictionaries. Encyclopedias**

* 15   **Classification. Nomenclature. Terminology**

* 16   **Tables. Statistics**

  17   **Pictorial works**

  18   **Education**
           Classify here works about education.

* 18.2   **Educational materials**
           Classify here educational materials, e.g., outlines, questions and answers, programmed instruction, catalogs, computer–assisted instruction, etc., regardless of format. Classify textbooks, regardless of format, by subject.

* 19   **Schools and colleges**
           Classify courses of study, catalogs, etc., in W 19.5.

19.5   Graduate and continuing education in psychiatry (including fellowships, internships, residencies, etc.)

20   Research (General)
> *Classify here works about research in general. Classify works about research on a particular subject by subject.*

21   Psychiatry, psychoanalysis, etc. as professions. Careers in mental health. Types of practice. Peer review
> *Classify works for and about psychiatric aides in WY 160.*

* 22   Directories (Table G)
* 22.1   General coverage (Not Table G)

Laboratories, institutes, etc.
23   Collective
24   Individual (Cutter form name of agency)

25   Techniques in experimental psychiatry

26   Equipment and supplies
> *Classify catalogs in W 26.*

26.5   Medical informatics. Automatic data processing. Computers (General)
> *Classify works on use for special subject by subject.*

Hospitals, clinics, dispensaries, etc.
> *Classify works limited to psychiatric hospitals for children in WS 27–28.*
27   Collective (Table G)
27.1   General coverage (Not Table G)
28   Individual (Table G)

29   Community mental health centers. Rehabilitation centers. Halfway houses. Sheltered workshops. Aftercare. Day care (Table G)
29.1   General coverage (Not Table G)

29.5   Patients. Attitude and compliance. Satisfaction

30   Administrative psychiatry
> e.g., Management of hospitals, etc. Supervision of students. Mental health services
> *Cf. WM 401 for general works on crisis intervention; WA 305 for special population groups.*

30.5   Psychiatric social work

30.6   Community psychiatry (General)

31   Socioeconomic and environmental factors in mental illness

31.5   Preventive measures in psychiatry

* 32   Laws (Table G)
            e.g., Commitment
            Cf. W 740 Forensic psychiatry.
* 32.1   General coverage (Not Table G)
            Include international law.

* 33   Discussion of law (Table G)
* 33.1   General coverage (Not Table G)

* 34   Handbooks

35   Practices in the care of the mentally ill
            e.g., Ward attendance. Use of restraints. Technique of home care
            Cf. WY 160 Psychiatric nursing.

40   Case histories (General)
            *Classify here case books, biographies and autobiographies of the mentally ill. Classify
            case histories limited to one disease with the disease. Classify works on famous
            persons in WZ 313.*

49   Art and literature as related to psychiatry. Symbolic case histories
            e.g., Electra, Hamlet, Oedipus, Don Juan, etc.

55   Counseling on psychological problems

61   Pastoral care

62   Social relations of the psychiatrist (including relations with patients; relations
            with public, clubs, societies, etc.) Attitude. Ethics

64   Referral and consultation (General)

75   Popular works (General)

90   Psychophysiologic disorders (General) Psychosomatic medicine (General
            works about the profession)
            Classify general works on psychophysiologic sex disorders in WM 611.

*NUMBER CAN BE USED FOR BOTH MONOGRAPHS AND SERIALS.

100   General works

Classify works on specialty and on the specialty and diseases here. Classify works on diseases alone in WM 140.

102   Biological psychiatry

105   Clinical psychology. Mental health

Classify popular works in WM 75. Classify works on counseling in WM 55.

140   Mental disorders (General)

141   Psychiatric examination and diagnosis

145   Psychological tests (General or not elsewhere classified)

Classify works on intelligence tests in BF 431–432.5.

145.5   Specific tests, A–Z

     .B4   Bender–Gestalt test
     .C3   Cattell personality factor questionnaire
     .I5   Ink blot tests
     .M6   MMPI
     .N4   Neuropsychological tests
     .P8   Projective techniques
     .R7   Rorschach tests
     .R8   Rosenzweig picture–frustration study
     .S9   Szondi test
     .T3   Thematic apperception test
     .W9   Word association tests

165   Behavioral symptoms (General or not elsewhere classified)

Classify here works on behavioral symptoms for which there are no classification numbers for related disorders. Classify specific symptoms with related disorders, e.g., Anxiety with Anxiety disorders in WM 172; Depression with Depressive disorder in WM 171.

170   Neuroses

171   Affective symptoms

Include works on depression and depressive disorder here. Cf. WM 207 Manic depressive psychoses.

172   Anxiety. Anxiety disorders

173   Hysteria and associated disorders

Neuroses
     Hysteria and associated disorders - Continued

173.5   Conversion disorder

173.6   Dissociative disorders

173.7   Amnesia and other memory disorders

174   Neurasthenia. Mental fatigue

175   Eating disorders associated with neuroses. Anorexia nervosa
         Cf. WI 143 for eating disorders in general; WS 115–130 for disorders of children and infants.

176   Obsessive–compulsive neuroses. Compulsive behavior. Obsessive behavior

178   Phobic disorders. Hypochondriasis. Sick role
         Classify works on sick role associated with a particular disease with the disease.

184   Combat disorders

188   Sleep disorders and associated conditions
         Classify here material on all disorders of sleep regardless of severity. Include popular works. Cf. WL 108 Physiology of sleep.

190   Personality disorders (General or not elsewhere classified)
         e.g., Inadequate personality. Passive–dependent personality

193   Defense mechanisms
         Cf. WM 173.5 Conversion reaction; WS 350.8.D3 Defense mechanism in children. Classify works on purely psychological aspects of various defense mechanisms in appropriate BF numbers.

193.5   Special topics, A–Z

         .A2   Acting out
         .D3   Denial (Psychology)
         .D5   Displacement (Psychology)
         .P3   Perceptual defense
         .P7   Projection
         .R1   Rationalization
         .R2   Regression
         .R4   Repression
         .S8   Sublimation. Fantasy

197   **Psychomotor disorders (General or not elsewhere classified)**
Classify specific disorders by subject, e.g., Apraxia WL 340.

200   **Psychoses**

202   **Functional**

203   **Schizophrenia and schizophrenic syndromes**

203.5   **Autism**

204   **Cognition and perceptual disorders associated with psychoses**

205   **Paranoid disorders**

207   **Manic–depressive psychoses and affective syndromes**
Classify works on reactive depression and on non-psychotic affective symptoms in WM 171.

[210]   **[This number not used]**
Classify works on antisocial personality in WM 190.

220   **Organic (General or not elsewhere classified)**
e.g., Psychoses associated with infections, convulsive disorders, neurologic disorders

270   **Substance dependence.   Substance abuse**

274   **Alcohol**

276   **Cannabis**

280   **Cocaine**

284   **Narcotics**

286   **Opium alkaloids**

288   **Diacetylmorphine**

290   **Nicotine**

300   **Mental retardation. Down syndrome**
Classify works on mental retardation of children WS 107; on education of the mentally retarded in LC 4601–4640.5.

302   **Case studies. Biographical accounts**

304   **Evaluation. Prognosis**

307   **Special problems, A–Z**

        .C6   **Communication**
        .M5   **Mental disorders**
        .S3   **Sex problems (General)**
        .S6   **Social problems (General)**

308   **Rehabilitation and training (General)**

400   **Therapy**
Cf. WL 370 Psychosurgery.

401   **Emergency psychiatric services. Crisis intervention (including work with victims of rape and other crimes)**
Classify works on community mental health programs in WM 30.

402   **Drug therapy**

405   **Physical therapy (General or not elsewhere classified)**
e.g., Induced hyperthermia

410   **Shock. Insulin shock therapy**

412   **Electric. Electronarcosis**

415   **Hypnosis**

420   **Psychotherapy (General or not elsewhere classified)**
Classify works on psychotherapy in childhood in WS 350.2, in adolescence in WS 463, and in old age in WT 150.

420.5   **Special types, A–Z**

        .A2   **Abreaction. Catharsis**
        .G3   **Gestalt therapy**

Therapy
  Psychotherapy
    Special types, A-Z - Continued

.N8	Nondirective therapy	
.P5	Psychotherapy, Brief	
.P7	Psychotherapy, Multiple	
.P8	Psychotherapy, Rational–Emotive	

425	Behavior therapy

425.5	Special types, A–Z

.A9	Aversive therapy	
.B6	Biofeedback (Psychology)	
.C6	Cognitive therapy	
.D4	Desensitization, Psychologic. Implosive therapy	
.R3	Relaxation techniques	

426	Self–help groups

428	Socioenvironmental therapy

430	Group psychotherapy

430.5	Special types, A–Z

.F2	Family therapy	
.H2	Disabled	
.M3	Marital therapy	
.P8	Psychodrama	
.S3	Sensitivity training groups. Encounter groups	

Cf. HM 134 for general sociological works.

440	Milieu therapy. Therapeutic community

445	Residential treatment (General)

450	Activity therapy

450.5	Special types, A–Z	
	.A8	Art therapy
	.B5	Bibliotherapy
	.D2	Dance therapy
	.M8	Music therapy
	.O2	Occupational therapy
	.P5	Photography
	.V5	Videotherapy
	.W9	Writing

Therapy - Continued

460   Psychoanalysis.   Psychoanalytic theory

460.5   Special topics associated with psychoanalysis, psychoanalytic therapy or interpretation, A–Z

.B7	Bonding, Human–Pet
.C5	Communication
.C7	Creativeness
.D8	Dreams. Symbolism
.E3	Ego. Self
.E8	Existentialism. Logotherapy
.E9	Extraversion. Introversion
.F8	Free association
.I4	Identification
.I5	Individuation
.L2	Language
.M5	Memory
.M6	Motivation
.O2	Object attachment
.P3	Personality
.P5	Pleasure–pain principle
.P7	Political systems
.R2	Reinforcement
.R3	Religion. Church. Morals. Superego
.S3	Sex
.U6	Unconscious. Id
.W6	Women

460.6   Psychoanalytic therapy

460.7   Psychoanalytic interpretation

475   Communicative disorders.   Speech–language pathology
Classify works communicative disorders of neurologic origins in WL 340.2.

475.5   Aphasia
Classify works on aphasia of neurologic origin in WL 340.5.

475.6   Dyslexia
Classify works on dyslexia of neurologic origin in WL 340.6.

600   Social behavior disorders (General)
Cf. WS 350.8.S6 for works about children.

610   Paraphilias
e.g., Sadism.   Fetishism.   Transvestitism.   Exhibitionism.   Pedophilia

611   Psychosexual disorders (General or not elsewhere classified)
Cf. WJ 712 Sex differentiation disorders; WP 610 Female sexual adjustment.

WN

RADIOLOGY. DIAGNOSTIC IMAGING

Classify material on ionizing radiation used in the diagnosis and treatment of a specific disease, organ or system with the disease, organ or system. General diagnostic uses of ultrasound and magnetic resonance imaging are included here. Classify material on non–ionizing radiation in WB or other applicable numbers (See Index to this Classification).

WN 1–160	General
WN 180–240	Diagnostic imaging. Radiography
WN 250–250.5	Radiotherapy
WN 300–340	Radium
WN 415–665	Radioactivity (Excluding Roentgen Rays and Radium)

GENERAL

* 1   Societies (Cutter from name of society)
        Includes ephemeral membership lists issued serially or separately.   Classify annual reports, journals, etc., in W1.

        Collections (General)
5   By several authors
7   By individual authors

9   Addresses. Essays. Lectures (General)

11   History (Table G)
11.1   General coverage (Not Table G)

* 13   Dictionaries. Encyclopedias

* 15   Classification. Nomenclature. Terminology

* 16   Tables. Statistics

17   Atlases. Pictorial works
        Classify atlases limited to a particular radiological subject here also.

*NUMBER CAN BE USED FOR BOTH MONOGRAPHS AND SERIALS.

18   **Education**
           Classify here works about education.

* 18.2   **Educational materials**
           Classify here educational materials, e.g., outlines, questions and answers, programmed instruction, catalogs, computer–assisted instruction, etc., regardless of format. Classify textbooks, regardless of format, by subject.

* 19   **Schools and colleges**
           Classify courses of study, catalogs, etc., in W 19.5.

20   **Research (General)**
           Classify here works about research in general. Classify works about research on a particular subject by subject.

21   **Radiology, diagnostic imaging and nuclear medicine as professions. Ethics. Peer review**

* 22   **Directories (Table G)**
* 22.1   **General coverage (Not Table G)**

           Radiological laboratories, institutes, etc.
23   **Collective**
24   **Individual (Cutter from name of agency)**

25   **Laboratory manuals. Technique**

[26]   **[This number not used]**
           Classify works on equipment in WN 150; catalogs of equipment in W 26.

26.5   **Medical informatics. Automatic data processing. Computers (General)**
           Classify works on use for special subjects by subject.

           Hospitals, clinics, etc.
27   **Collective (Table G)**
27.1   **General coverage (Not Table G)**
28   **Individual (Table G)**

* 32   **Laws (Table G)**
* 32.1   **General coverage (Not Table G)**

* 33   **Discussion of law (Table G)**
* 33.1   **General coverage (Not Table G)**

* 39   **Handbooks**

*NUMBER CAN BE USED FOR BOTH MONOGRAPHS AND SERIALS.

100	**General works. Stereoscopy. Electrokymography**
105	**Ionizing radiation**
110	**Health physics** *Include here works on the physics of radiation and nuclear medicine.*
150	**Equipment and supplies** e.g., Film. Screens. Generators. Radiation counters *Classify works on use of counters, etc., in radiation protection in WN 650. Classify catalogs in W 26.*
160	**Technology. Contrast media** e.g., Positioning *Classify works on contrast media for particular types of radiography with the specific type. Classify works on laboratory techniques in WN 25.*

DIAGNOSTIC IMAGING. RADIOGRAPHY

Classify works on diagnosis of a system, region or organ with the specific area.

180	**Diagnostic imaging (General or not elsewhere classified)**
185	**Magnetic resonance imaging**
200	**Radiography (General or not elsewhere classified)**
203	**Radionuclide imaging**
205	**Thermography**
206	**Tomography**
208	**Ultrasonography**
210	**Foreign body localization**
220	**Fluoroscopy**
230	**Dental diagnostic imaging**

240   **Pediatric diagnostic imaging**

RADIOTHERAPY

250   **General works**

250.5   **Special types, A–Z**
        .B7   **Brachytherapy**
        .R2   **Radiotherapy, Computer–assisted**
        .R3   **Radiotherapy, High–energy**
        .X7   **X–ray therapy**

RADIUM

300   **General works**

340   **Therapeutic use**
        e.g., Use of radon seeds, radium needles, etc.

RADIOACTIVITY (EXCLUDING ROENTGEN RAYS AND RADIUM)

Classify here works on specific elements as well as general works. Classify works on medical applications for a specific disease or organ with the disease or organ.

415   **General works (On nuclear physics, atomic energy, radioisotopes slanted toward the biological sciences)**
        Classify works slanted toward the physical sciences in QC.

420   **Radioisotopes. Radioactive elements**
        Classify works on medical applications in WN 440–450.

440   **Nuclear medicine**

445   **Diagnosis**
        Classify works on radionuclide imaging in WN 203.

450   **Therapeutics**

600   **Radiobiology**

Classify here works on general effects of radiation to man, animals, and plant life.

610   **Radiation injuries**

Classify general works on radiation–induced abnormalities in QS 681.

612   **Food contamination**

615   **Air, soil, and water pollution and pollutants (General)**

Classify general works on air pollution in WA 754; on industrial air pollution in WA 450; on soil pollution in WA 785; on water pollution in WA 689.

620   **Injurious effects on man and animals**

630   **Injurious effects on plant life (related to human ecology)**

650   **Radiation protection**

Cf. WA 788 Industrial wastes.

660   **Radiometry**

665   **Radiation dosage**

WO

SURGERY

Note form numbers used also under Anesthesia WO 201–233.1.

WO 1–75	General
WO 100–149	General Surgery
WO 162–198	Surgical Procedure and Armamentarium
WO 200–460	Anesthesia
WO 500–517	Operative Surgery and Surgical Techniques
WO 600–640	Plastic Surgery
WO 660–690	Transplantation
WO 700–820	Traumatic, Industrial, and Emergency Surgery
WO 925–950	Surgery in Special Age Groups

GENERAL

* 1　Societies (Cutter from name of society)
Includes ephemeral membership lists issued serially or separately. Classify substantial lists with directories. Classify annual reports, journals, etc., in W1.

Collections (General)
5　By authors
7　By individual authors

9　Addresses. Essays. Lectures (General)

11　History (Table G)
11.1　General coverage (Not Table G)

* 13　Dictionaries. Encyclopedias

* 15　Classification. Nomenclature. Terminology

* 16　Tables. Statistics. Collected surgical case reports (General)

[17]　[This number not used]
Classify atlases in WO 517.

18   **Education**
Classify here works about education.

* 18.2   **Educational materials**
Classify here educational materials, e.g., outlines, questions and answers, programmed instruction, catalogs, computer–assisted instruction, etc., regardless of format. Classify textbooks, regardless of format, by subject.

* 19   **Schools, departments, and faculties of surgery**

20   **Research (General)**
Classify here works about research in general. Classify works about research on a particular subject by subject. Cf. WO 50 Experimental surgery.

21   **Surgery as a profession. Ethics. Peer review**

* 22   **Directories (Table G)**
* 22.1   **General coverage (Not Table G)**

Laboratories, research institutes, organ banks, etc.
23   **Collective**
24   **Individual (Cutter from name of agency)**

[25]   **[This number not used]**
Classify laboratory manuals in WO 500–512, etc.

[26]   **[This number not used]**
Classify material on surgical instruments and equipment in WO 162; on instruments and equipment used in anesthesia in WO 240; catalogs in W 26.

Hospitals, clinics, dispensaries, etc.
27   **Collective (Table G)**
27.1   **General coverage (Not Table G)**
28   **Individual (Table G)**

* 32   **Laws (Table G)**
* 32.1   **General coverage (Not Table G)**

* 33   **Discussion of law (Table G)**
* 33.1   **General coverage (Not Table G)**

* 39   **Handbooks**

50   **Experimental surgery (General)**
Classify works on experimental work in a particular area by subject. Classify works about research in WO 20.

*NUMBER CAN BE USED FOR BOTH MONOGRAPHS AND SERIALS.

62   Social relations of the surgeon (including relations with patients, relations with public, clubs, societies, etc.). Attitude

64   Referral and consultation (General)

75   Popular works (General)

GENERAL SURGERY

100   General works
     Cf. WF 980 Thoracic surgery; WI 900 Abdominal surgery; WO 500 Operative surgery.

101   Surgical anatomy

102   Physiology

113   Antisepsis. Sterilization. Asepsis

140   Surgical diseases (General)
     Classify here works that discuss diagnosis, prognosis, treatment. Classify works limited to pathology in WO 142 below.

141   Surgical examination. Surgical diagnosis. Exploratory surgery

142   Surgical pathology (Examination of tissues or organs removed in course of surgery. Examination of biopsy or frozen section material, etc.)
     Cf. WO 140 Surgical diseases.

149   Surgical shock

SURGICAL PROCEDURE AND ARMAMENTARIUM

162   Surgical equipment, instruments and other supplies
     Classify catalogs in W 26. Cf. WO 240 for equipment used in anesthesia.

166   Sutures. Ligatures. Tissue adhesives

167   Surgical dressing. Bandaging technique. Adhesive plaster

Surgical equipment, instruments and other supplies
Surgical dressing. Bandaging technique. Adhesive plaster - Continued

170   Surgical casts

176   Artificial organs
        Classify works on specific organs in the surgery number or lacking that, in the general number for the organ being replaced. Cf. WG 169.5 Artificial heart; WJ 378 Artificial kidney.

178   Principles of surgical care

179   Preoperative care

181   Intraoperative Care

183   Postoperative care

184   Postoperative complications and treatment

185   Surgical wounds. Surgical wound infection. Wound healing (including healing of non–surgical wounds)

188   Closure of wounds. Drainage

192   Minor surgery. Ambulatory surgery (General)

198   Electrosurgery. Cautery. Laser and electrocoagulation (General)
        Classify works on use in particular fields with the field or the condition, e.g., in ophthalmology WW 168.

ANESTHESIA

200   Surgical anesthesia. Analgesia (General)
        Do not confuse with general anesthesia WO 275.

* 201   Societies (Cutter from name of society)
        Includes ephemeral membership lists issued serially or separately. Classify substantial lists with directories. Classify annual reports, journals, etc., in W1.

       Collections (Gemeral)
205   By several authors
207   By individual authors

209   Addresses. Essays. Lectures (General)

*NUMBER CAN BE USED FOR BOTH MONOGRAPHS AND SERIALS.

211 History (Table G)
211.1 General coverage (Not Table G)

* 213 Dictionaries. Encyclopedias

* 215 Classification. Nomenclature. Terminology

218 Education
    Classify here works about education.

* 218.2 Educational materials
    Classify here educational materials, e.g., outlines, questions and answers, programmed instruction, catalogs, computer–assisted instruction, etc., regardless of format. Classify textbooks, regardless of format, by subject.

* 219 Schools, departments, and faculties of anesthesiology

220 Research (General)
    Classify here works about research in general. Classify works about research on a particular subject by subject.

221 Anesthesiology as a profession. Ethics. Peer review

* 222 Directories (Table G)
* 222.1 General coverage (Not Table G)

[226] [This number not used]
    Classify equipment and supplies for anesthesia in WO 240; catalogs in W 26. Cf. WO 162 Surgical equipment.

* 231 Handbooks

* 232 Laws (Table G)
232.1 General coverage (Not Table G)

* 233 Discussion of law (Table G)
233.1 General coverage (Not Table G)

234 Preanesthetic medication. Preparation of patient

235 Choice of anesthesia
    Classify works on choice of anesthesia for patients with cardiac problems in WG 460.

240   **Equipment and supplies**
          Classify catalogs in W 26. Cf. WO 162 Surgical equipment.

245   **Accidents. Complications**
          e.g., Laryngospasm. Cardiac failure. Vomiting
          Classify works written for the cardiologist in WG 460.

250   **Asphyxia. Methods of resuscitation**
          Classify here general works on asphyxia and resuscitation. Classify works on first aid in WA 292; on resuscitation of the newborn in WQ 450.

275   **General anesthesia**

277   **Inhalation anesthesia**

280   **Intratracheal anesthesia. Technique of intubation**

285   **Intravenous**

290   **Rectal**

297   **Muscle relaxants and tranquilizing agents in conjunction with anesthesia and analgesia**

300   **Conduction anesthesia**
          e.g., Regional anesthesia or local anesthesia

305   **Spinal. Epidural**

340   **Infiltration and topical**

350   **Induced hypothermia, and related topics**

375   **Diagnostic and therapeutic anesthetic procedures**
          e.g., Nerve block

440   **Pediatric anesthesia**

445   **Geriatric anesthesia**

450   **Obstetrical anesthesia**

460   **Anesthesia in dentistry.   Dental hypnosis**

OPERATIVE SURGERY AND SURGICAL TECHNIQUES

500   **General works**
         Classify works on abdominal surgery in WI 900; on thoracic surgery in WF 980; on general surgery in WO 100.

511   **Laser surgery**

510   **Cryogenic surgery**

512   **Microsurgery**

517   **Atlases.   Pictorial works**
         Classify all types of surgical atlases in this number, except those relating to a particular body system or part.   Classify the latter by system.

PLASTIC SURGERY

600   **General works**
         Classify material on plastic surgery of a condition, e.g., burns, with the condition. Classify material on plastic surgery of a region, system or organ with the area covered, e.g., plastic surgery of the nose, in WV 312.

610   **Skin transplantation, tube grafts, etc.**

640   **Prosthesis in plastic surgery**
         Cf. WO 176   Artificial organs (General).

TRANSPLANTATION

660   **General works**
         Classify works on specific organs in the surgery number or lacking that, in the general number for the organ being replaced.   Classify general works on artificial organs in WO 176.

665   **Tissue preservation**

680   **Immunology**
         Classify works on immunosuppressive agents in QW 920.

690   **Legal, ethical, and religious aspects**
         Classify the text of laws in WO 32.

TRAUMATIC, INDUSTRIAL, AND EMERGENCY SURGERY

700   **General works**

704   **Burns**

800   **Military surgery**

807   **Gunshot wounds**

820   **Blast injuries**

SURGERY IN SPECIAL AGE GROUPS

925   **Pediatric surgery**
         Classify works on pediatric anesthesia in WO 440; on surgery of individual organs in WS 260–360.

950   **Geriatric surgery**
         Classify works on geriatric anesthesia in WO 445.

WP

GYNECOLOGY

Classify general works on pediatric gynecology in WS 360; on gynecological nursing and nursing of gynecological diseases in WY 156.7. Classify works on male and female reproductive organs treated together in WJ 700–702; on human reproduction in WQ 205, etc.

WP 1–390	**General**
WP 400–480	**Uterus and Cervix Uteri**
WP 505–660	**Physiology and Functional Disorders**
WP 800–910	**Breast**

GENERAL

* 1   **Societies (Cutter from name of society)**
Includes ephemeral membership lists issued serially or separately. Classify substantial lists with directories. Classify annual reports, journals, etc., in W1.

Collections (General)
5   **By several authors**
7   **By individual authors**

9   **Addresses. Essays. Lectures (General)**

11   **History (Table G)**
11.1   **General coverage (Not Table G)**

* 13   **Dictionaries. Encyclopedias**

* 15   **Classification. Nomenclature. Terminology**

* 16   **Statistics. Tables**

17   **Atlases. Pictorial works**
Classify here also atlases on specific organs.

18   **Education**
Classify here works about education.

*NUMBER CAN BE USED FOR BOTH MONOGRAPHS AND SERIALS.

* 18.2   **Educational materials**
Classify here educational materials, e.g., outlines, questions and answers, programmed instruction, catalogs, computer–assisted instruction, etc., regardless of format. Classify textbooks, regardless of format, by subject.

* 19   **Schools, departments, and faculties of gynecology**

20   **Research (General)**
Classify here works about research in general. Classify works about research on a particular subject by subject.

21   **Gynecology as a profession. Ethics. Peer review**

* 22   **Directories (Table G)**
* 22.1   **General coverage (Not Table G)**

Laboratories, institutes, etc.
23   **Collective**
24   **Individual (Cutter from name of agency)**

25   **Laboratory manuals. Technique**

26   **Equipment and supplies**
Classify catalogs in W 26.

26.5   **Medical informatics. Automatic data processing. Computers (General)**
Classify works on use for special subjects by subject.

Hospitals, dispensaries, clinics, etc.
27   **Collective (Table G)**
27.1   **General coverage (Not Table G)**
28   **Individual (Table G)**

* 32   **Laws (Table G)**
* 32.1   **General coverage (Not Table G)**

* 33   **Discussion of law (Table G)**
* 33.1   **General coverage (Not Table G)**

34   **Malpractice (Table G)**
34.1   **General coverage (Not Table G)**

* 39   **Handbooks**

100   **General works**
         Classify works on specialty and on the specialty and diseases here. Classify works on diseases alone in WP 140.

101   **Anatomy**

120   **Popular works (General)**

140   **Diseases (General)**

141   **Examination. Diagnosis. Radiography. Monitoring**

145   **Neoplasms. Cysts (General)**
         Classify works on neoplasms of specific organs with the organ.

150   **Embryology. Congenital abnormalities**

155   **Pelvis. Pelvic inflammations**

157   **Gonorrhea in the female**

160   **Genital tuberculosis**

170   **Perineal injuries**

180   **Rectovaginal fistula. Vesicovaginal fistula**

200   **Vulva**

250   **Vagina**

255   **Vaginitis. Leukorrhea**

258   **Trichomonas vaginitis**

275   **Adnexa uteri**

300   **Fallopian tubes**
         Classify works on tubal pregnancy in WQ 220.

520   **Endocrine functions of the ovaries**

522   **Estrogenic hormones, synthetic substitutes, and antagonists**

530   **Corpus luteum hormones and related compounds**
           Classify works on progestational hormones here unless those produced by other organs are discussed exclusively.

540   **Ovulation. Ovarian function. Menstrual cycle**

550   **Menstruation and its disorders**

552   **Amenorrhea. Hypomenorrhea. Oligomenorrhea**

555   **Menorrhagia. Metrorrhagia**

560   **Dysmenorrhea. Premenstrual tension**

565   **Fertility**

570   **Infertility (General). Infertility in the female**
           Cf. WJ 709 Infertility in the male only.

580   **Menopause**

610   **Problems of the female in sexual adjustment**
           e.g., Dyspareunia. Frigidity

630   **Contraception**
           Classify works on religious and sociological aspects in HQ 763–766.5.

640   **Contraceptive devices (General and female)**
           Classify works only on male contraceptive devices in WJ 710. Classify works on contraceptive agents (chemical) in QV 177.

650   **Gynecological therapy**

660   **Gynecological surgery**
           Classify works on female sexual sterilization here. Classify works on surgery of particular organs with the organ.

BREAST

800   **General works**

815   **Examination.   Diagnosis.   Radiography**

825   **Functional changes**
             e.g., In pregnancy and lactation

840   **Diseases of the breast**

870   **Neoplasms**

900   **Therapy**
             Classify works on therapy of neoplasms in WP 870.

910   **Surgery**

WQ

OBSTETRICS

Classify works on obstetrical nursing in WY 157.

WQ 1–175	General
WQ 200–260	Pregnancy
WQ 300–330	Labor
WQ 400–450	Obstetrical Surgery
WQ 500–505	Puerperium

GENERAL

* 1 **Societies (Cutter from name of society)**
Includes ephemeral membership lists issued serially or separately. Classify substantial lists with directories. Classify annual reports, journals, etc., in W1.

Collections (General)
5 **By several authors**
7 **By individual authors**

9 **Addresses. Essays. Lectures (General)**

11 **History (Table G)**
11.1 **General coverage (Not Table G)**

* 13 **Dictionaries. Encyclopedias**

* 15 **Classification. Nomenclature. Terminology**

* 16 **Tables. Statistics**

17 **Atlases. Pictorial works**
Classify atlases limited to a particular part of the system here also.

18 **Education**
Classify here works about education.

* 18.2   **Educational materials**
Classify here educational materials, e.g., outlines, questions and answers, programmed instruction, catalogs, computer–assisted instruction, etc., regardless of format. Classify textbooks, regardless of format, by subject.

* 19   **Schools, departments, and faculties of obstetrics**

20   **Research (General)**
Classify here works about research in general. Classify works about research on a particular subject by subject.

21   **Obstetrics as a profession. Ethics. Peer review**

* 22   **Directories (Table G)**
* 22.1   **General coverage (Not Table G)**

Clinics, dispensaries, etc.
23   **Collective (Table G)**
23.1   **General coverage (Not Table G)**
24   **Individual (Table G)**

25   **Laboratory manuals. Technique**

26   **Equipment and supplies**
Classify catalogs in W 26.

26.5   **Medical informatics. Automatic data processing. Computers (General)**
Classify works on use for special subjects by subject.

Maternity hospitals
27   **Collective (Table G)**
27.1   **General coverage (Not Table G)**
28   **Individual (Table G)**

* 32   **Laws (Table G)**
* 32.1   **General coverage (Not Table G)**

* 33   **Discussion of law (Table G)**
* 33.1   **General coverage (Not Table G)**

34   **Malpractice (Table G)**
34.1   **General coverage (Not Table G)**

* 39   **Handbooks**

100	General works
150	Popular works on pregnancy and childbirth
152	Natural childbirth
155	Home childbirth
160	Midwifery
165	Manuals for midwives
175	Prenatal care

PREGNANCY

200	General works
202	Diagnosis *Cf. QY 335 Pregnancy tests.*
205	Fertilization. Development of ovum. General physiology of reproduction
206	Sex determination (Diagnostic)
208	Artificial insemination
209	Prenatal diagnosis. Fetal monitoring
210	Fetus. Fetal membranes. Umbilical cord. Perinatology (General) *Classify works on fetal experimentation in general in W 20.5.*
210.5	Fetal anatomy, physiology, and biochemistry
211	Fetal diseases (General or not elsewhere classified)
212	Placenta *Cf. WK 920 Placental hormones.*

215   **Toxemias**
         e.g., Eclampsia

220   **Ectopic pregnancy**

225   **Abortion. Fetal death**
         Cf. WQ 440   Induced abortion; W 867   Criminal abortion.

235   **Multiple pregnancy**

240   **Pregnancy complications (General or not elsewhere classified)**
         Classify works on pregnancy toxemias in WQ 215.

244   **Cardiovascular complications**

248   **Diabetes**

252   **Hematologic complications**

256   **Infectious diseases**

260   **Urologic complications**

LABOR

300   **General works**

305   **Physiology. Clinical course**

307   **Presentation**

310   **Dystocia**

320   **Disproportions of the pelvis**

330   **Complications of labor**
         e.g., Postpartum hemorrhage

OBSTETRICAL SURGERY

400   **General works**
           Classify works on obstetrical anesthesia in WO 450.

415   **Delivery (including preparatory manipulation)**

425   **Use of forceps**

430   **Cesarean section. Symphysiotomy and similar techniques**

435   **Embryotomy**

440   **Induction of labor. Therapeutic abortion. Techniques of induced abortion**
           Classify works on sociological and religious aspects of induced abortion in HQ 767–767.52.

450   **Resuscitation of the newborn**

PUERPERIUM

500   **General works. Postnatal care**

505   **Puerperal infection**

WR

DERMATOLOGY

Classify general works on dermatology in WS 260 when related to children; in WY 154.5 when related to nursing. Classify works on nursing of patients with specific skin diseases in the WY number also.

* 1 **Societies (Cutter from name of society)**
Includes ephemeral membership lists issued serially or separately. Classify substantial lists with directories. Classify annual reports, journals, etc., in W1.

    Collections (General)
5   **By several authors**
7   **By individual authors**

9 **Addresses. Essays. Lectures (General)**

11 **History (Table G)**
11.1   **General coverage (Not Table G)**

* 13 **Dictionaries. Encyclopedias**

* 15 **Classification. Nomenclature. Terminology**

* 16 **Tables. Statistics**

17 **Atlases. Pictorial works**
Classify here also atlases on single skin diseases.

18 **Education**
Classify here works about education.

* 18.2 **Educational materials**
Classify here educational materials, e.g., outlines, questions and answers, programmed instruction, catalogs, computer–assisted instruction, etc., regardless of format. Classify textbooks, regardless of format, by subject.

* 19 **Schools, departments, and faculties of dermatology**

20 **Research (General)**
Classify here works about research in general. Classify works about research on a particular subject by subject.

*NUMBER CAN BE USED FOR BOTH MONOGRAPHS AND SERIALS.

21   Dermatology as a profession. Ethics. Peer review

* 22   Directories (Table G)
* 22.1   General coverage (Not Table G)

     Laboratories, institutes, etc.
23   Collective
24   Individual (Cutter from name of agency)

25   Laboratory manuals. Technique

26   Equipment and supplies
     Classify catalogs in W 26.

26.5   Medical informatics. Automatic data processing. Computers (General)
     Classify works on use for special subjects by subject.

     Hospitals, dispensaries, clinics, etc.
27   Collective (Table G)
27.1   General coverage (Not Table G)
28   Individual (Table G)

* 32   Laws (Table G)
32.1   General coverage (Not Table G)

* 33   Discussion of law (Table G)
* 33.1   General coverage (Not Table G)

* 39   Handbooks

100   General works
     Classify works on specialty and on the specialty and diseases here. Classify works on diseases alone in WR 140.

101   Anatomy. Histology. Embryology

102   Physiology. Chemistry and metabolism of the skin. Sensory functions. Skin temperature

105   Pathology

140   Skin diseases (General)

Skin diseases - Continued

141   **Diagnosis. Monitoring**

143   **Skin manifestations**

150   **Erythemas**
            e.g., E. multiforme. E. nodosum

152   **Lupus erythematosus**

160   **Diseases associated with hypersensitivity. Dermatitis**
            Cf. WD 300 for general works on hypersensitivity. Classify works on dermatitis herpetiformis in WR 200; on occupational dermatitis in WR 600; on neurodermatitis in WR 280.

165   **Drug eruptions**

170   **Urticaria. Angioneurotic edema**
            Classify works on urticaria pigmentosa in WR 267.

175   **Contact dermatitis**
            Cf. WR 600 Occupational dermatitis.

180   **Dermatitis exfoliativa**

190   **Eczema**

200   **Bullous skin diseases of obscure etiology**
            Classify works on erythema multiforme in WR 150.

204   **Papulosquamous dermatoses**
            Classify works on exfoliative dermatitis in WR 180; on seborrhea in WR 415.

205   **Psoriasis**

215   **Lichen planus**

218   **Genetic skin diseases (General or not elsewhere classified)**

220   **Infectious skin diseases (General, bacterial, or not elsewhere classified)**
            Classify works on viral skin infections in WC 570–590; parasitic skin diseases in WR 345.

225   **Impetigo. Ecthyma**

Infectious skin diseases - Continued

235   **Furunculosis.   Carbuncle**

245   **Cutaneous tuberculosis**
        e.g., Lupus

260   **Scleroderma**

265   **Pigmentation disorders**
        e.g., Lentigo.   Vitiligo

267   **Of metabolic origin**
        e.g., Hemochromatosis.   Albinism

280   **Neurodermatitis and related sensory disorders**
        Classify works on causalgia in WL 544.

282   **Pruritus.   Prurigo**

300   **Dermatomycoses**

310   **Tinea.   Tinea pedis**

330   **Tinea capitis**

340   **Maduromycosis**

345   **Parasitic skin diseases (General or not elsewhere classified)**
        Classify works on mucocutaneous leishmaniasis in WR 350.

350   **Tropical diseases of the skin (General or not elsewhere classified)**
        e.g., Leishmaniasis
        Cf. WC 715   Visceral leishmaniasis.

360   **Skin diseases caused by arthropods (General or not elsewhere classified)**

365   **Scabies**

375   **Pediculosis**

390   **Skin appendages**

Skin appendages - Continued

400   Sweat glands. Disorders of the sweat glands

410   Sebaceous glands. Disorders of the sebaceous glands

415   Seborrhea

420   Epidermal cyst

430   Acne. Acneform lesions

450   Hair. Scalp. Diseases of the hair and scalp

455   Hypertrichosis

460   Alopecia

465   Care of the hair

475   Nails. Diseases of the nails

500   Neoplasms. Keratosis (General or not elsewhere classified)

598   Decubitus ulcer and other skin ulcers
                Classify works on leg ulcer in WE 850.

600   Occupational dermatitis
                Cf. WR 175 Contact dermatitis.

650   Therapy of skin diseases

660   Radiotherapy

WS

PEDIATRICS

Classify works on diseases of specific body systems in children in WS 260–368. Classify works on anatomy and physiology of the child in QS or QT. Classify pediatric works on topics other than body systems per se with the topic, e.g., surgery of the child in WO 925. Classify works on specific diseases with the disease, e.g., pneumonia in infants in WC 202; schizphrenia in childhood in WM 203, etc. Classify works on diseases limited to the newborn in WS 421; diseases limited to the premature infant in WS 410.

WS 1–141	**General**
WS 200–463	**Diseases of Children**
WS 260–368	**By System**
WS 405–463	**By Age Group**

GENERAL

* 1   **Societies (Cutter from name of society)**
             Includes ephemeral membership lists issued serially or separately. Classify substantial lists with directories. Classify annual reports, journal, etc., in W1.

           Collections (General)
    5   **By several authors**
    7   **By individual authors**

    9   **Addresses. Essays. Lectures (General)**

    11   **History (Table G)**
    11.1   **General coverage (Not Table G)**

* 13   **Dictionaries. Encyclopedias**

* 15   **Classification. Nomenclature. Terminology**

* 16   **Tables (development, height, nutrition, weight, etc.) Statistics**

    17   **Atlases. Pictorial works**
             Cf. QZ 17 for tissue pathology of disease.

*NUMBER CAN BE USED FOR BOTH MONOGRAPHS AND SERIALS.

18   **Education**

Classify here works about education.

* 18.2   **Educational materials**

Classify here educational materials, e.g., outlines, questions and answers, programmed instruction, catalogs, computer–assisted instruction, etc., regardless of format. Classify textbooks, regardless of format, by subject.

* 19   **Schools, departments, and faculties of pediatrics**

20   **Research (General)**

Classify here works about research in general. Classify works about research on a particular subject by subject.

21   **Pediatrics as a profession. Ethics. Peer review**

* 22   **Directories (Table G)**
* 22.1   **General coverage (Not Table G)**

Institutes

Classify here works on organizations which provide public or private services for disabled children which include medical, nursing and hygienic aspects, rehabilitation, etc. Cf. WA 320 for public health aspects.

23   **Collective (Table G)**
23.1   **General coverage (Not Table G)**
24   **Individual (Table G)**

25   **Laboratory manuals. Technique**

26   **Equipment and supplies**

e.g., Eating utensils for spastic children
Classify catalogs in W 26.

26.5   **Medical informatics. Automatic data processing. Computers (General)**

Classify works on use for special subjects by subject.

Hospitals, dispensaries, etc. (including psychiatric hospitals for children)

Classify here works on psychiatric hospitals for children only. Classify works on community mental health services for children in WM 30.

27   **Collective (Table G)**
27.1   **General coverage (Not Table G)**
28   **Individual (Table G)**

29   **Hospital staff manuals**

* 32   **Laws (Table G)**
* 32.1   **General coverage (Not Table G)**

*NUMBER CAN BE USED FOR BOTH MONOGRAPHS AND SERIALS.

Laws - Continued

* 33	**Discussion of law (Table G)**
* 33.1	**General coverage (Not Table G)**

* 39   **Handbooks**

100   **General works**
           Classify works on specialty and on the specialty and diseases here. Classify works on diseases alone in WS 200.

103   **Normal physical growth and development**

104   **Growth disorders. Failure to thrive**

105   **Normal mental growth and development. Child psychology**
           Classify works on psychophysiological aspects in WL, e.g., on physiology of sleep in WL 108; on laterality in WL 335; or with the system involved; on vision and visual perception in WW 103–105; on motor skills in WE 103–104.

105.5   **Special topics, A–Z**

.A8	**Attitudes and adjustments (to death, illness, divorce, etc.)**
.C3	**Child rearing (Psychological aspects)**
	Classify general works including physiological problems with child care in WS 113.
.C7	**Cognition. Fantasy. Imagination**
.C8	**Communication. Verbal behavior**
.D2	**Decision making. Logic. Thinking. Concept formation. Perception (Psychological)**
	Classify works on neurophysiological perception and specific types of perception in WL 705 or with the organ involved.
.D3	**Deprivation (economic, parental, etc.) and security**
.D8	**Dreams**
.E5	**Emotions. Frustrations, etc.**
.E8	**Evaluation of psychological development (General)**
.E9	**External influences (literature, motion pictures, television, war, etc.)**
.F2	**Family relations. Birth order. Only child. Twins. Parent–child relations. Father–child relations. Mother–child relations. Sibling relations, etc.**
.H2	**Disabled child (Psychological problems)**
.H7	**Hospitalized child**
	Cf. WA 310–320 Maternal and child welfare.
.I5	**Interpersonal relations (doctor, peer, stranger, etc.)**
	Cf. WS 105.5.S6 Race relations. Classify works on dentist's relation to the child in WU 480; on nurse's relation to the child in WY 159.
.M2	**Memory**
.M3	**Mental health**
	Classify works on school mental health in WA 352.
.M4	**Morals**
.M5	**Motivation**
.P3	**Personality development**

Normal mental growth and development. Child psychology
Special topics, A-Z - Continued

.P5	Play
.S3	Self
.S4	Sex behavior
.S6	Social behavior. Social problems. Race relations

Cf. WS 105.5.I5 Interpersonal relations.

107   The retarded child. Down syndrome
Classify other material on child psychiatry in WS 350; on education of the mentally retarded in LC 4601–4640.4; on adult mental retardation in WM 300.

107.5   Special topics when related to the retarded child, A–Z

.B4	Biochemistry. Genetics
.C2	Case studies. Biographical accounts
.C6	Communication
.D3	Development. Prognosis
.F6	Foster homes
.I4	Institutionalization

Cf. WS 27–28 Hospitals; WS 105.5.H7 Hospitalized child (General).

.P7	Psychomotor problems
.P8	Psychosocial problems
.R3	Rehabilitation and training (General)
.R4	Relations with doctor, nurse, etc.
.R5	Relations with family. Family adjustment

110   Learning disorders (physical, mental, and neurologic)
Classify works on specific disorders in appropriate numbers, e.g., Aphasia WL 340.5. Classify works for the educator in LC 4704.

113   Care and training
Cf. WS 105.5.C3 for psychological aspects.

115   Nutritional requirements. Nutrition disorders

120   In infancy

125   Breast feeding

130   In childhood

135   Prophylactic immunizations

141   Physical examination and diagnosis. Mass screening
Classify works on examination and diagnosis of specific age groups in WS 405–460.

DISEASES OF CHILDREN

Classify works on communicable diseases of children, not associated with a system, in the WC schedule.

200	**General works**
205	**Pediatric emergencies**

BY SYSTEM

In the numbers for each system, include general works on the diseases of the organs of the system or on special groups of diseases of the system. Classify works on surgery of a single organ here in WS, e.g., Gastrectomy of the child in WS 310. Classify works on surgery of a system with the system, e.g., Neurosurgery of the child in WL 368. Classify works on particular diseases with the disease except for the three disease numbers in WS 312, 322 and 342.

260	**Skin**
270	**Musculoskeletal system**
280	**Respiratory system**
290	**Cardiovascular system**
300	**Hemic and lymphatic system**
310	**Digestive or gastrointestinal system**
312	**Diarrheal disorders**
320	**Urogenital system**
322	**Enuresis**
330	**Endocrine system**
340	**Nervous system**

Nervous system - Continued

342   Cerebral palsy

350   **Child psychiatry. Child guidance. Psychoses (General)**
         Cf. WS 107 The retarded child. Classify works on specific disorders in WM.

350.2   **Therapy**
         Classify here works on all types of therapy for mental disorders of children. Classify therapy of a particular disorder with the disorder.

350.5   **Psychoanalysis**

350.6   **Behavior disorders. Development disorders. Neuroses (General)**
         Classify works on particular neurotic disorders in WM 171–197.

350.8   **Special topics in child psychiatry, A–Z**

       .A4   Aggression. Violence. Dangerous behavior
       .A8   Attention deficit disorder with hyperactivity
       .D3   Defense mechanisms
       .H9   Hyperkinesis
       .I3   Identity crisis
       .I4   Inhibition
       .L9   Lying
       .P3   Personality disorders
       .R9   Runaway reaction
       .S6   Social behavior disorders
         Classify works on aggression in WS 350.8.A4.

360   **Pediatric gynecology (General)**

366   **Pediatric therapeutics (General)**

368   **Medical rehabilitation of physically disabled children**

BY AGE GROUP

405   **Birth injuries**

410   **Premature infants. Diseases of premature infants**
         Classify specific diseases with the disease except those of the premature infants only.

420   **Newborn infants. Neonatology**

421 **Diseases of newborn infants**
Classify specific diseases with the disease except those of the newborn only.

430 **Infancy**

440 **Preschool child**

450 **Puberty**

460 **Adolescence (General)**

462 **Adolescent psychology. Adolescent behavior**

463 **Psychiatric problems of adolescents. Behavior disorders. Psychotherapy. Psychoanalysis. Psychoses.**
Classify specific mental disorders with the disorder in WM.

WT

GERIATRICS. CHRONIC DISEASE

Classify works on geriatric nursing in WY 152.

WT 1–39	General
WT 100–166	Geriatrics
WT 500	Chronic Disease

GENERAL

* 1 **Societies (Cutter from name of society)**
Includes ephemeral membership lists issued serially or separately. Classify substantial lists with directories. Classify annual reports, journals, etc., in W1.

Collections (General)
5 **By several authors**
7 **By individual authors**

9 **Addresses. Essays. Lectures (General)**

11 **History (Table G)**
11.1 **General coverage (Not Table G)**

* 13 **Dictionaries. Encyclopedias**

* 15 **Classification. Nomenclature. Terminology**

* 16 **Tables. Statistics**

17 **Atlases. Pictorial works**
Cf. QZ 17 for tissue pathology of disease.

18 **Education**
Classify here works about education.

* 18.2   **Educational materials**
          Classify here educational materials, e.g., outlines, questions and answers, programmed instruction, catalogs, computer–assisted instruction, etc., regardless of format. Classify textbooks, regardless of format, by subject.

* 19   **Schools, departments, and faculties of geriatrics**

20   **Research (General)**
          Classify here works about research in general. Classify works about research on a particular subject by subject.

21   **Geriatrics as a profession. Ethics. Peer review**

* 22   **Directories (Table G)**
* 22.1   **General coverage (Not Table G)**

       Laboratories, institutes, etc.
23   **Collective**
24   **Individual (Cutter from name of agency)**

25   **Laboratory manuals. Technique**

26   **Equipment and supplies**
          Classify catalogs in W 26.

26.5   **Medical informatics. Automatic data processing. Computers (General)**
          Classify works on use for special subjects by subject.

       Hospitals, dispensaries, clinics, old age homes, etc.
27   **Collective (Table G)**
27.1   **General coverage (Not Table G)**
28   **Individual (Table G)**

29   **Day care centers and programs (Table G)**
29.1   **General coverage (Not Table G)**

30   **Surveys. Medicosocial problems of gerontology and chronic disease.**

31   **Medical care plans. Long term care**
          Include here works on Medicare. Classify works on nursing care only in WY 152.

* 32   **Laws (Table G)**
* 32.1   **General coverage (Not Table G)**

Laws - Continued

* 33   Discussion of law (Table G)
* 33.1   General coverage (Not Table G)

* 39   Handbooks

GERIATRICS

100   **General works**
Classify works on specific diseases with the disease in other schedules; on nursing of specific diseases in WY 152; on anesthesia in WO 445; on surgery in WO 950.

104   **Anatomical, biochemical and physiological changes in senescence. The aging process.**
Classify works on aging tissue here. Classify works on the aging organ or system with the organ or system.

115   **Nutritional requirements. Nutrition disorders**

116   **Longevity. Life expectancy. Death**
Cf. WS 200 for death of children, and other specific topics related to death, e.g., Attitude to death BF 789.D4, etc.

120   **Popular works (General). Geriatric hygiene**
Include here autobiographical case histories. Example: Mills. Notings of a nonogenarian. Classify popular works on a particular subject by subject.

141   **Physical examination and diagnosis**

145   **Geriatric psychology. Mental health**
Classify works on geriatric psychiatry in WT 150.

150   **Geriatric psychiatry. Mental disorders of senescence**
Classify works on specific disorders with the disorder; on geriatric psychology in WT 145.

155   **Senile dementia. Alzheimer's disease**
Cf. WM 220 for dementia and presenile dementia.

166   **Therapeutics (General or not elsewhere classified)**

*NUMBER CAN BE USED FOR BOTH MONOGRAPHS AND SERIALS.

CHRONIC DISEASE

500   **General works**

WU

DENTISTRY. ORAL SURGERY

GENERAL

* 1   **Societies (Cutter from name of society)**
    Includes ephemeral membership lists issued serially or separately. Classify substantial lists with directories. Classify annual reports, journals, etc., in W1.

    Collections (General)
5   **By several authors**
7   **By individual authors**

9   **Addresses. Essays. Lectures (General)**

11   **History (Table G)**
11.1   **General coverage (Not Table G)**

* 13   **Dictionaries. Encyclopedias**

* 15   **Classification. Nomenclature. Terminology**

* 16   **Tables. Statistics**

17   **Atlases**
    Classify atlases limited to a particular part of the system with the part in the form number for atlases where available, e.g., WU 317, WU 417, WU 507, or WU 600.7.

18   **Education**
    Classify here works about education.

* **18.2**   **Educational materials**
Classify here educational materials, e.g., outlines, questions and answers, programmed instruction, catalogs, computer–assisted instruction, etc., regardless of format. Classify textbooks, regardless of format, by subject.

18.5   **Education of dental assistants, hygienists, and technicians**

* **19**   **Schools and colleges**
Classify courses of study, catalogs, etc., in W 19.5.

20   **Graduate and continuing dental education (including fellowships, internships, residencies, etc.)**

20.5   **Dental research (General)**
Classify here works about research in general. Classify works about research on a particular subject by subject.

21   **Dentistry as a profession. Peer review**

* **22**   **Directories (Table G)**
* **22.1**   **General coverage**

Laboratories, institutes, etc., including research institutes
23   **Collective**
24   **Individual (Cutter from name of institution)**

24.5   **Banks (Table G)**
24.51   **General coverage (Not Table G)**

25   **Laboratory manuals (General). Technique**
Classify manuals of prosthetic dentistry in WU 500–530.

26   **Equipment and supplies (General)**
Classify catalogs in W 26; works on dental materials in WU 180–190; on orthodontic appliances in WU 426.

26.5   **Medical informatics. Automatic data processing. Computers (General)**
Classify works on use for special subjects by subject.

Hospitals, clinics, dispensaries, etc.
27   **Collective (Table G)**
27.1   **General coverage (Not Table G)**
28   **Individual (Table G)**

29   **Dental care (including comprehensive dental care)**
Cf. W 260 Dental insurance.

30   **Surveys**

* 32   **Laws (Table G)**
* 32.1   **General coverage (Not Table G)**

* 33   **Discussion of law (Table G)**
* 33.1   **General coverage (Not Table G)**

40   **Licensure of dentists and dental hygienists (Table G)**
40.1   **General coverage (Not Table G)**

44   **Malpractice (Table G)**
44.1   **General coverage (Not Table G)**

* 49   **Handbooks**

50   **Dental ethics**

58   **Advertising. Fee–splitting**

61   **Dentist's relation to public, patients and physicians. Attitude**

77   **Dental economics. Practice management**

79   **Group practice. Partnership practice**

80   **Popular works (General)**
      Classify works for children in WU 113.6

90   **Auxiliary personnel**
      e.g., Duties, professional opportunities, work manuals
      Classify works on dental technicians in WU 150.

95   **Dental records**

100   **General works**
      Classify works on specialty and on the specialty and diseases here. Classify works on diseases alone in WU 140. Include here works about dentistry written for practitioners of other specialties.

101   **Anatomy. Histology. Morphology. Embryology**
      Include works on the jaw.

101.5   **Malformations and abnormalities of jaws, mouth, and/or teeth (General)**

102   **Physiology**
        e.g., Mastication
        Include works on the jaw.

105   **Dental emergencies (General)**

113   **Oral health and hygiene. Preventive and prophylactic dentistry**
        Classify here works on school education and prophylactic programs. Cf. WA 350
        School dental services. Classify popular works for the adult in WU 80.

113.6   **Works for and about children**
        Classify general works on pediatric dentistry in WU 480.

113.7   **Nutrition and oral health (General)**
        Cf. WU 270 Caries. Etiology of caries.

140   **Stomatognathic diseases (General). Oral pathology**
        Classify works on mouth diseases written for the dentist here; classify works for the
        gastroenterologist in WI 200; classify works on jaw diseases alone in WU 140.5.

140.5   **Jaw diseases**
        Classify here works on temporomandibular joint syndrome also. Cf. WU 600–610
        Injuries and surgery of the jaw.

141   **Examination. Diagnosis. Diagnostic methods (General)**
        Classify works on X-ray diagnosis in WN 230.

141.5   **Specific diagnostic methods, A–Z**

        .C3   **Cephalometry**
        .O2   **Odontometry**

150   **Dental technology (General) Dental technicians**
        Classify works on technology for particular procedures with that procedure.

158   **Oral and dental injuries (General)**
        Classify works on maxillofacial injuries and jaw fractures and dislocations in WU
        610.

166   **Oral and dental therapeutics**

170   **Dental chemistry (General)**

180   **Dental alloys and metals**

190   **Dental materials (General and those not classed in WU 180)**

210   **Dentition**

220   **Enamel. Dentin**

230   **Dental pulp. Tooth root. Root canals. Dental cementum (Endodontics)**
        Classify works on reimplantation in WU 640.

240   **Periodontium. Alveolar process. Gingiva (Periodontics)**

242   **Periodontitis and related diseases**

250   **Dental deposits**

270   **Caries. Etiology of caries. Effect of fluoridation**

280   **Oral and dental neoplasms**

290   **Oral manifestations**
        Classify works on oral manifestations of specific diseases with the disease.

OPERATIVE DENTISTRY

300   **General works**

317   **Atlases**

350   **Cavities. Cavity treatment**

360   **Inlays**

ORTHODONTICS

400   **General works**

417   Atlases

426   Orthodontic appliances

440   Occlusion. Malocclusion

SPECIAL GROUPS

470   Dental care for the disabled

480   Pediatric dentistry

490   Geriatric dentistry. Dental care for the aged

PROSTHODONTICS

Classify works on cleft palate prosthesis in WV 440; on maxillofacial and mandibular prosthesis in WU 600.

500   General works. Dental prosthesis (General)

507   Atlases

515   Partial dentures. Bridges. Crowns

530   Complete dentures

ORAL SURGERY

600   General works
              Cf. WO 460 Anesthesia in dentistry. Include here general works on mandibular and maxillofacial prosthesis.

600.7   Atlases

605   Tooth extraction

610   Maxillofacial injuries.   Mandibular injuries.   Fractures and dislocations of
         the jaw

640   Dental implantation.   Tooth reimplantation.   Transplantation

WV

OTOLARYNGOLOGY

Classify works on nursing of patients with ear, nose, or throat diseases in WY 158.5. Note that the numbers WV 1–39 are assigned to works on the specialties otology, rhinology, and laryngology when treated individually as well as in combination.   WV 100–190 are for general works only.

WV 1–190	General
WV 200–290	Ear
WV 300–358	Nose and Paranasal Sinuses
WV 400–440	Pharyngeal Region
WV 500–540	Larynx

GENERAL

* 1 **Societies (Cutter from name of society)**
     Includes ephemeral membership lists issued serially or separtely.   Classify substantial lists with directories.   Classify annual reports, journals, etc., in W1.

Collections (General)
5   **By several authors**
7   **By individual authors**

9   **Addresses.   Essays.   Lectures (General)**

11   **History (Table G)**
11.1   **General coverage (Not Table G)**

* 13   **Dictionaries.   Encyclopedias**

* 15   **Classification.   Nomenclature.   Terminology**

* 16   **Tables.   Statistics**

17   **Atlases.   Pictorial works**
     Classify here also atlases on a specific organ.

18   **Education**
     Classify here works about education.

* 18.2   **Educational materials**
Classify here educational materials, e.g., outlines, questions and answers, programmed instruction, catalogs, computer-assisted instruction, etc., regardless of format. Classify textbooks, regardless of format, by subject.

* 19   **Schools, departments, and faculties of otolaryngology**

20   **Research (General)**
Classify here works about research in general. Classify works about research on a particular subject by subject.

21   **Otolaryngology as a profession. Ethics. Peer review**

* 22   **Directories (Table G)**
* 22.1   **General coverage (Not Table G)**

Laboratories, institutes, etc.
23   **Collective**
24   **Individual (Cutter from name of agency)**

25   **Laboratory manuals. Technique**

26   **Equipment and supplies**
Classify catalogs in W 26.

26.5   **Medical informatics. Automatic data processing. Computers (General)**
Classify works on use for special subjects by subject.

Hospitals, clinics, dispensaries, etc.
27   **Collective (Table G)**
27.1   **General coverage (Not Table G)**
28   **Individual (Table G)**

* 32   **Laws. Estimation of disability for compensation (Table G)**
* 32.1   **General coverage (Not Table G)**

* 33   **Discussion of law (Table G)**
* 33.1   **General coverage (Not Table G)**

* 39   **Handbooks**

100   **General works**
Classify works on specialty and on the specialty and diseases here. Classify works on diseases alone in WV 140.

101   **Anatomy. Physiology. Biochemistry. Embryology. Abnormalities**

140   **Otorhinolaryngologic diseases (General)**

150   **ENT symptomatology and diagnosis. Monitoring**

168   **ENT surgery**
         Classify works on surgery of a particular organ with the organ.

180   **Intracranial complications of ENT diseases**

190   **Otorhinolaryngologic neoplasms (General)**

EAR

200   **General works**

201   **Anatomy. Physiology**
         Cf. WV 272 for physiology and testing of hearing.

210   **Examination. Diagnosis**

220   **External ear**

222   **Ear canal. Foreign bodies. Cerumen**

225   **Tympanic membrane**

230   **Middle ear. Eustachian tube. Petrous bone**

232   **Otitis media (including aerotitis)**

233   **Mastoid region**

250   **Labyrinth**

255   **Vestibular apparatus. Equilibrium. Spatial orientation**
         Classify works on motion sickness in WD 630.

Labyrinth - Continued

258   Ménière's disease

265   Otosclerosis

270   Audiology. Hearing. Hearing disorders. Deafness

271   Deafness and other hearing disorders in children

272   Physiology of hearing. Auditory perception. Tinnitus. Function tests

274   Hearing aids

276   Treatment of deafness

280   Deaf–mutism

290   Neoplasms
         Classify works on neoplasms of specific parts of the ear with the part.

NOSE AND PARANASAL SINUSES

300   General works
         Classify works on nasopharyngeal diseases in WV 410.

301   Anatomy. Physiology. Olfaction

310   External nose

312   Plastic surgery

320   Nasal septum

335   Rhinitis. Hay fever
         Cf. WC 510 Common cold.

340   Paranasal sinuses

345   Maxillary

Paranasal sinuses - Continued

350   Frontal

355   Ethmoid

358   Sphenoid

PHARYNGEAL REGION

400   **General works**
       Classify works on nasopharyngeal diseases in WV 410.

401   **Anatomy.   Physiology**

410   **Pharynx.   Uvula.   Palate**
       Classify works relating to respiration and the pharynx in WF 490.

430   **Tonsils.   Adenoids**

440   **Cleft lip.   Cleft palate**

LARYNX

500   **General works on larynx, speech, and voice and their organic disorders**
       Classify works on neurological speech disorders in WL 340.2–340.6; on psychogenic speech disorders in WM 475–475.6.

501   **Anatomy.   Physiology.   Physiology of speech**

505   **Laryngoscopy**

510   **Inflammation**

520   **Neoplasms**

530   **Vocal cords**

535   **Paralysis**

540   **Surgery. Laryngectomy. Alaryngeal voice production**
Classify works on artificial larynx here.

WW

OPHTHALMOLOGY

Classify works on ophthalmic nursing in WY 158.

GENERAL

* 1   **Societies (Cutter from name of agency)**
           Includes ephemeral membership lists issued serially or separately. Classify substantial lists with directories. Classify annual reports, journals, etc., in W1.

           Collections (General)
5   **By several authors**
7   **By individual authors**

9   **Addresses. Essays. Lectures (General)**

11   **History of ophthalmology and optometry (Table G)**
11.1   **General coverage (Not Table G)**

* 13   **Dictionaries. Encyclopedias**

* 15   **Classification. Nomenclature. Terminology**

* 16   **Tables. Statistics**
           Classify tables used in optical dispensing calculations in WW 352.

17   **Atlases. Pictorial works**
           Classify here also atlases on a specific part of the eye.

18   **Education**
Classify here works about education.

* 18.2   **Educational materials**
Classify here educational materials, e.g., outlines, questions and answers, programmed instruction, catalogs, computer–assisted instruction, etc., regardless of format. Classify textbooks, regardless of format, by subject.

* 19   **Schools and colleges**
Classify courses of study, catalogs, etc., in W 19.5.

20   **Research (General)**
Classify here works about research in general. Classify works about research on a particular subject by subject.

21   **Ophthalmology as a profession. Ethics. Peer review**
Classify works on optometry and opticianry in WW 721.

21.5   **Ophthalmic assistants**

* 22   **Directories (Table G)**
Classify directories of optometrists and/or opticians in WW 722.
* 22.1   **General coverage (Not Table G)**

    Laboratories, institutes, eye banks, etc.
23   **Collective**
24   **Individual (Cutter from name of agency)**

25   **Laboratory manuals. Technique**

26   **Equipment and supplies**
Classify catalogs in W 26.

26.5   **Medical informatics. Automatic data processing. Computers (General)**
Classify works on use for special subjects by subject.

    Hospitals, clinics, dispensaries, etc.
27   **Collective (Table G)**
27.1   **General coverage (Not Table G)**
28   **Individual (Table G)**

* 32   **Laws. Estimation of disability for compensation (Table G)**
* 32.1   **General coverage (Not Table G)**

* 33   **Discussion of law (Table G)**
* 33.1   **General coverage (Not Table G)**

*NUMBER CAN BE USED FOR BOTH MONOGRAPHS AND SERIALS.

* 39   **Handbooks**

80   **Popular works (General)**

100   **General works**
         Classify works on specialty and on the specialty and diseases here. Classify works on diseases alone in WW 140.

EYE

101   **Anatomy. Histology. Embryology. Biochemistry. Abnormalities**

103   **Physiology of the eye. Vision (General)**

105   **Visual perception. Space perception**
         Cf. WW 150 Color perception.

109   **Ocular accommodation. Ocular adaptation**

113   **Hygiene. Conservation of vision**
         Cf. WW 80 Popular works.

140   **Eye diseases. Vision disorders (General or not elsewhere classified)**

141   **Examination. Diagnostic methods**
         Classify works on the examination of a part with the part.

143   **Objective methods**
         e.g., Ophthalmoscopy. Slit lamp microscopy. Tonometry
         Classify works on electronystagmography in WW 410; on electroretinography in WW 270; on gonioscopy in WW 210; on retinography in WW 300.

145   **Subjective methods. Evaluation of function**
         e.g., Visual acuity testing. Perimetry

149   **Neoplasms**
         Classify works on neoplasms of parts of the eye with the part.

150   **Color perception. Color blindness**
         Cf. WW 105 Visual perception

160   **Diseases due to infection, hypersensitivity, etc. (General or not elsewhere classified)**

166   **Ocular therapeutics (Medical)**

168   **Ophthalmological surgery (General)**

170   **Eye bank procedures (including those for specific parts of the eye)**
           Classify material on eye banks in WW 23–24.

PARTS OF THE EYE

202   **Orbit**

205   **Eyelids. Eyebrows**
           Cf. WR 390–465 Skin appendage diseases.

208   **Lacrimal apparatus**

210   **Anterior chamber. Posterior chamber. Aqueous humor (Eyeball)**

212   **Conjunctiva**

215   **Trachoma**

220   **Cornea**

230   **Sclera**

240   **Uvea. Iris. Ciliary body**

245   **Choroid**

250   **Vitreous body**

260   **Crystalline lens. Cataract**

270   **Retina**

276   Blindness. Amblyopia

280   Optic nerve

290   Glaucoma

REFRACTION AND ERRORS OF REFRACTION

300   General works

310   Astigmatism

320   Myopia

CORRECTIVE DEVICES

350   Optical dispensing. Spectacle fitting. Opticianry
       Classify works on optometry and opticianry as specialties in WW 704–722.1.

352   Principles. Calculations. Tables

354   Frames. Eyeglasses
         Classify works on intraocular lenses in WW 358 or if exclusively for cataract therapy, in WW 260.

355   Contact lenses

358   Prosthesis

NEUROMUSCULAR MECHANISM

400   General works

405   Orthoptics (General)

410   Disorders of ocular motility

Disorders of ocular motility - Continued

415   **Strabismus**

460   **Disorders due to diseases of the central nervous system. Neurologic manifestations of eye diseases (General)**

PROBLEMS ASSOCIATED WITH EYE DISEASES

475   **Eye manifestations of general disease**
          Classify works on eye manifestations of specific diseases with disease.

480   **Medical aspects of reading problems associated with poor vision.**

OCCUPATIONAL AND TRAUMATIC OPHTHALMOLOGY

505   **Occupational ophthalmology**

525   **Foreign bodies. Injuries. Toxic injuries**

AGE GROUPS

600   **Pediatric ophthalmology and optometry**
          Classify works on particular disorders with the disorder.

620   **Geriatric ophthalmology and optometry**
          Classify works on particular disorders with the disorder.

OPTOMETRY

704   **General works. Office management**
          Classify works on the specific functions of the optometrist in the WW number for the function; on functions of the optician in WW 350–355.

721   **Optometry and opticianry as professions. Ethics. Peer review**
          Classify works on history of the professions in WW 11–11.1.

* 722   **Directories (Table G)**
* 722.1   **General coverage (Not Table G)**

WX

HOSPITALS AND OTHER HEALTH FACILITIES

WX 1–147   General
WX 150–190   Hospital Administration
WX 200–225   Clinical Departments and Units

GENERAL

* 1   **Societies (Cutter from name of society)**
Includes ephemeral membership lists issued serially or separately. Classify substantial lists with directories. Classify annual reports, journals, etc., in W1.

* 2   **Serial hospital reports (Table G)**
Classify here hospital administrative reports and statistics. Classify clinical material (e.g., Bulletin of the Johns Hopkins Hospital, Guy's Hospital Reports, etc.) in W1. Cf. W2 Serials documents for administrative reports and statistics on several hospitals under governmental administration.

    Collections (General)
5   **By several authors**
7   **By individual authors**

9   **Addresses. Essays. Lectures (General)**

11   **General history of hospitals and the hospital movement (Table G)**
Cf. WX 27–28 History of individual hospitals or groups of individual hospitals. Classify history of emergency or ambulance services in WX 215.
11.1   **General coverage (Not Table G)**

* 13   **Dictionaries. Encyclopedias**

* 15   **Classification. Nomenclature. Terminology. Standardization. Accreditation**

* 16   **Tables. Statistics**

17   **Atlases. Pictorial works**

18   **Education**
            Classify here works about education.

* 18.2   **Educational materials**
            Classify here educational materials, e.g., outlines, questions and answers, programmed instruction, catalogs, computer–assisted instruction, etc., regardless of format. Classify textbooks, regardless of format, by subject.

* 19   **Schools, departments, and faculties of hospital administration**

20   **Research (General)**
            Classify here works about research in general. Classify works about research on a particular subject by subject.

[21]   **[This number not used]**
            Classify hospital administration as a career in WX 155.

* 22   **Directories (Table G)**
* 22.1   **General coverage (Not Table G)**

[26]   **[This number not used]**
            Classify works on equipment and supplies in WX 147. Classify catalogs in W 26.

26.5   **Medical informatics. Automatic data processing. Computers (General)**
            Classify works on use for special subjects by subject.

            Hospitals and medical centers. Health facilities (General)
            Classify here non–serial hospital reports. Classify serial reports in WX 2; reports of army hospitals in UH 470–475; on those of naval hospitals in VG 410–450. Classify works on special types of hospitals or of specialized departments of general hospitals in the appropriate schedule for the field, e.g., isolation hospitals in WC 27–28; on psychiatric departments of general hospitals in WM 27–28, etc.
27   **Collective (Table G)**
27.1   **General coverage (Not Table G)**
28   **Individual (Table G)**

            Hospices and hospice care programs
28.6   **Collective (Table G)**
28.61   **General coverage (Not Table G)**
28.62   **Individual (Table G)**

29   **Day care centers and programs (Table G)**
29.1   **General coverage (Not Table G)**
                Cf. WA 310–320 Child day care centers; WT 29–29.1 Geriatric day care centers; WX 205 Hospital outpatient clinics.

* 32   **Laws (Table G)**
* 32.1   **General coverage (Not Table G)**

* 33   **Discussion of law. Jurisprudence (Table G)**
* 33.1   **General coverage (Not Table G)**

* 39   **Handbooks**

100   **General works**

140   **Health facility planning and construction**
Classify works on special facilities with the specialty.

147   **Equipment and supplies**
Classify catalogs in W 26.

HOSPITAL ADMINISTRATION

150   **General works**

153   **Utilization review. Quality of service. Medical audit**

155   **Hospital administration as a career, e.g., Educational requirements.
Professional opportunities**

157   **Financial administration. Business management. Cost accounting**

157.4   **Multi-institutional systems**

157.8   **Diagnosis–related groups**

158   **Hospitalization**
*Include here narrative reports on admissions and discharges; also on patient
readmissions. Classify works that are largely statistical in WX 16. Classify works
on hospitalization insurance in W 160.*

158.5   **Hospital patients. Attitude and compliance. Satisfaction**

159   **Hospital personnel administration. Staff manuals. Career literature**
Classify manuals for professional staff only in WX 203.

Hospital personnel administration. Staff manuals. Career literature - Continued

159.5   **Volunteers**
Classify works on professional hospital social work in W 322.

159.8   **Collective bargaining (Hospitals and hospital personnel)**

160   **Public relations. Interinstitutional relations. Staff relations. Staff attitudes**

161   **Hospital shops**

162   **Patient care planning. Progressive patient care. Long term care**
Classify here works on hospital care only. For general comprehensive works on patient care planning, use W 84.7–84.8. Classify works limited to nursing care in WY; on long term care of geriatric patients in WT 30.

162.5   **Patient care team**

165   **General housekeeping. Maintenance. Laundries. Environmental control**

167   **Cross infection prevention and control**
Cf. WC 195 for general works on infection.

168   **Hospital food service**

173   **Medical records. Medical record administrators**
Cf. WB 290 for works on medical history taking in general.

179   **Hospital pharmacy service. Hospital medication systems**

185   **Safety, fire and disaster programs**

187   **Chaplaincy service**

190   **Mobile health units**

CLINICAL DEPARTMENTS AND UNITS

Classify works on specialty departments in the hospital number for the specialty, e.g., psychiatric wards in WM 27–28.

200   **General works**
Include works on services not indexed elsewhere.

203   **Medical personnel. Interns. Staff manuals. Ward manuals and precedent books**
Classify general staff manuals and those for non-professional personnel in WX 159.

205   **Hospital outpatient clinics. Ambulatory care facilities**
Cf. WB 101 for works on general ambulatory care.

207   **Clinical and pathological laboratories**
Classify works on laboratories not connected with hospitals in QY 23–24.

215   **Emergency service. Ambulance service**
Include here works on ambulance and general emergency health services not indexed elsewhere even if they are not connected with hospitals. Classify those connected with occupational medicine in WA 400–495.

218   **Intensive care units. Critical care (General)**
Cf. WB 105 Medical emergencies; WY 154 for works on nursing care. Classify works on critical care in the specialty fields with the specialty, e.g., Cardiac emergencies WG 205; Coronary care units WG 27–28.

223   **Physical therapy department**

225   **Occupational therapy department**

WY

NURSING

GENERAL

* 1   **Societies (Cutter from name of society)**
Includes ephemeral membership lists issued serially or separately. Classify substantial lists with directories. Classify annual reports, journals, etc., in W1.

    Collections (General)
5   **By several authors**
7   **By individual authors**

9   **Addresses. Essays. Lectures (General)**

11   **History (Table G)**
11.1   **General coverage (Not Table G)**

* 13   **Dictionaries. Encyclopedias**

* 15   **Classification. Nomenclature. Terminology**

16   **Nursing as a profession. Peer review**
Classify works on specific types of nursing in WY 101–200.

17   **Atlases. Pictorial works**

18   **Education**
Classify here works about education.

* 18.2   **Educational materials**
Classify here educational materials, e.g., outlines, questions and answers, programmed instruction, catalogs, computer-assisted instruction, etc., regardless of format. Classify textbooks, regardless of format, by subject.

*NUMBER CAN BE USED FOR BOTH MONOGRAPHS AND SERIALS.

18.5   Graduate and continuing nursing education (including fellowships, internships, residencies, etc.)

18.8   Practical nursing education

* 19   Schools of nursing
        Classify courses of study, catalogs, etc., in W 19.5. Include here works on the history of nursing schools.

20   Organization and administration of nursing schools

20.5   Research (General)
        Classify here works about research in general. Classify works about research on a particular subject by subject.

* 21   Licensure. Certification. Registration (Table G)
* 21.1   General coverage (Not Table G)

* 22   Directories (Table G)
* 22.1   General coverage (Not Table G)

26.5   Medical informatics. Automatic data processing. Computers (General)
        Classify works on use for special subjects by subject.

29   Employment. Placement agencies
30   Personnel management. Collective bargaining

31   Statistics. Surveys

* 32   Laws (Table G)
* 32.1   General coverage (Not Table G)

* 33   Discussion of law. Jurisprudence (Table G)
* 33.1   General coverage (Not Table G)

44   Malpractice. Liability. Liability insurance (Table G)
44.1   General coverage (Not Table G)

* 49   Handbooks

77   Economics of nursing

85   Nursing ethics

*NUMBER CAN BE USED FOR BOTH MONOGRAPHS AND SERIALS.

86   Nursing philosophy. Nursing theory

87   Psychology applied to nursing. Psychological aspects of nursing. Relations to patients, physicians, public

90   Referral and consultation (General)

100   General works on nursing procedures
           Classify works on nursing techniques in special fields of medicine in WY 150–164.

100.4   Nursing assessment. Nursing diagnosis

100.5   Nursing records. Nursing audit

SPECIAL FIELDS IN NURSING

101   General works. Primary nursing care
           e.g., Special nursing as a career; types of specialized fields in nursing
           Cf. WY 150 General works on nursing techniques in special fields of medicine.

105   Administrative work. Supervisory nursing. Teaching

106   Community health nursing
           Classify works on a particular kind of community nursing with the more specific type, e.g., Public health nursing WY 108.

107   Transcultural nursing

108   Public health nursing
           e.g., Federal, state, etc.
           Cf. WY 130 Governmental nursing services.

109   Office nursing

113   School nursing

115   Home care services (including visiting nursing and visiting nurse associations, and respite care)

125   **Institutional nursing. Team nursing**
> e.g., In hospitals, sanatoriums, etc.
> *Cf. WY 105 Administrative work.*

127   **Private nursing**

128   **Nurse practitioners. Nurse clinicians**

130   **Governmental nursing services**
> e.g., Armed Forces. Veterans Administration. Indian Health Service, etc.
> *Cf. WY 108 Public health nursing; UH 490–495 Army nursing.*

137   **Red Cross nursing**

141   **Occupational health nursing**

143   **Transportation nursing**
> e.g., On airplanes, ships, trains

145   **Nursing by religious orders**

NURSING TECHNIQUES IN SPECIAL FIELDS OF MEDICINE

Classify background materials on specific subjects prepared for a nursing audience by subject, e.g. surgery for nurses, WO 100; bacteriology for nurses, QW 50.

150   **General works**

151   **Nurse anesthetists**

152   **Geriatric and chronic disease nursing. Life support care. Long term care. Terminal care**

152.5   **Cardiovascular nursing. Hemic and lymphatic disease nursing**

153   **Communicable disease nursing**

153.5   **AIDS/HIV nursing**

154   **Emergency nursing. Critical care. Intensive care. Recovery room care. Postanesthesia nuring**

154.5   Dermatological nursing

155   Endocrine disease nursing

156   Oncologic nursing

156.5   Gastroenterologic nursing

156.7   Gynecological nursing

157   Obstetrical nursing

157.3   Maternity nursing. Maternal–child nursing. Neonatal nursing. Perinatal nursing
> *Classify here works on care of the mother and child shortly before and after the child is born.*

157.6   Nursing of diseases of the musculoskeletal system. Orthopedic nursing

158   Ophthalmic nursing

158.5   Otolaryngological nursing

159   Pediatric nursing. Adolescent nursing
> *Classify works on pediatric and adolescent nursing in special fields by type, e.g., on pediatric surgical nursing in WY 161.*

160   Psychiatric nursing
> *Include works on psychiatric aides and ward attendants here. Classify works on supervision of ward attendance in WM 35.*

160.5   Neurological nursing

161   Surgical nursing

162   Operating room techniques

163   Nursing of diseases of the respiratory system

164   Urologic nursing

OTHER NURSING SERVICES

191   **Male nurses**

193   **Nurses' aides, ward attendants and orderlies**
              Classify ward attendants for psychiatric institutions in WY 160.

195   **Practical nursing**

200   **Home nursing**

BY COUNTRY

300   **Nursing by country (Table G)**

WZ

HISTORY OF MEDICINE

Classify history of a particular subject with the subject, e.g., History of surgery WO 11.

GENERAL

* 1   **Societies (Cutter from name of society)**
Includes ephemeral membership lists issued serially or separately. Classify substantial lists with directories. Classify annual reports, journals, etc. in W1.

Collections (General)
5   **By several authors**
7   **By individual authors**

9   **Addresses. Essays. Lectures (General)**

[11]   **[This number not used]**

* 13   **Dictionaries. Encyclopedias**

17   **Atlases. Pictorial works**

18   **Education**
Classify here works about education.

* 18.2   **Educational materials**
Classify here educational materials, e.g., outlines, questions and answers, programmed instruction, catalogs, computer-assisted instruction, etc., regardless of format. Classify textbooks, regardless of format, by subject.

*NUMBER CAN BE USED FOR BOTH MONOGRAPHS AND SERIALS.

* 22		Directories (Table G)
* 22.1		General coverage (Not Table G)
23		Institutes (Cutter from name of institute)
		Museums
	27	Collective
	28	Individual (Cutter from name of museum)
30		Chronologies
* 39		Handbooks
40		General works

HISTORY, BY PERIOD, LOCALITY, ETC.

Except in WZ 51 (which see) prefer classification by locality if applicable.

51	**Ancient (to 476 A.D.)**
	Include works on countries of the western world. Classify those on history of medicine in other countries by locality in WZ 70.
54	**Medieval (to 1453 A.D.)**
55	**Modern (1454 A.D.–)**
56	**Early modern (to 1800 A.D.)**
59	**Late modern (1801 A.D.–)**
60	**19th century**
64	**20th century**
70	**History (By locality) (Table G)**
80	**History (Special groups, general or not elsewhere classified)**

80.5	Specific groups, A–Z

.A8	Arabic and Islamic groups
.B5	Blacks
.H6	Hindu
.I3	Indians, North American
.J3	Jews
.O6	Asian
.W5	Women

BIOGRAPHY

100   **Individual biography (Cutter from name of biographee)**
Classify here biographies and bibliographies of persons in the medical field, the preclinical sciences and other related fields. Cf. WZ 294 Modern criticism and bibliographies of early works. Include here works about two persons or a family, e.g., the Mayos.

* 112   **Collective biography (General or not specified below)**
Classify here collective biographies in the field of medicine and the preclinical sciences. Classify collective biographies of persons in other fields in the appropriate LC schedule.

* 112.5   **By specialty, A–Z**
Classify biography of individuals in WZ 100 regardless of specialty.

.C2	Cardiologists
.D3	Dentists
.I5	Immunologists
.M4	Military physicians and surgeons
.N4	Neurologists, neurosurgeons, etc.
.N8	Nurses
.O5	Oncologists
.O7	Ophthalmologists, optometrists, etc.
.O8	Otolaryngologists
.P2	Pathologists
.P4	Pharmacists
.P5	Physiologists
.P6	Psychiatrists
.S8	Surgeons
	Cf. WZ 112.5.M4 above.

Collective biography (By period)
Prefer specialty numbers above or if not applicable locality number below.

* 121	Ancient (to 476 A.D.)
* 124	Medieval (to 1453 A.D.)
* 126	Early modern (to 1800 A.D.)

*NUMBER CAN BE USED FOR BOTH MONOGRAPHS AND SERIALS.

* 129	Late modern (1801 A.D.–)	
* 132	19th century	
* 134	20th century	

* 140   Collective biography (By locality) (Table G)

* 150   Collective biography (Special groups)
              e.g., Women

MANUSCRIPTS

220   Early Western manuscripts
Note that at NLM western manuscripts produced before 1601 are classified in WZ 220, those produced after 1601 are classified as MS B (Manuscripts Books), MS C (Manuscripts Collections), or MS F (Manuscripts Oversize books).

225   Other early manuscripts

EARLY PRINTED BOOKS

Works published before 1801 (or later if considered Americana) are not classed by subject; instead, they are arranged alphabetically by author under classification number for period during which they were printed.

230   Incunabula
pre–1501

240   XVI century

250   XVII century

260   XVIII century

For 19th century publications see separate schedule below.

AMERICANA

270 **Americana**
The closing dates given in the following table (based on the American Imprints Inventory for the U.S.) will be used to determine inclusion in this class.

North and South America (except U.S.), 1820

United States

Alabama, 1840

Alaska, 1890

Arizona, 1890

Arkansas, 1870

California, 1875

Colorado, 1876

Connecticut, 1820

Delaware, 1820

District of Columbia, 1820

Florida, 1860

Georgia, 1820

Hawaii, 1860

Idaho, 1890

Illinois (except Chicago), 1850

Chicago, 1871

Indiana, 1850

Iowa, 1860

Kansas, 1875

Kentucky, 1830

Louisiana, 1820

Maine, 1820

Maryland, 1820

Massachusetts, 1820

Michigan, 1850

Minnesota, 1865

Mississippi, 1840

Missouri, 1850

Montana, 1890

Nebraska, 1875

Nevada, 1890

New Hampshire, 1820

New Jersey, 1820

New Mexico, 1875

New York (except N.Y. City, Brooklyn, and Hudson River towns), 1850

New York City, 1820

Brooklyn, 1825

Hudson River towns, e.g., Poughkeepsie, Hudson, Troy, Albany, 1830

North Carolina, 1820

North Dakota, 1890

Ohio, 1840

Oklahoma, 1870

Oregon, 1875

Pennsylvania (except Philadelphia), 1830

Philadelphia, 1820

Rhode Island, 1820

South Carolina, 1820

South Dakota, 1890

Tennessee, 1840

Texas, 1860

Utah, 1890

Vermont, 1820

Virginia, 1820

Washington, 1875

West Virginia, 1830

Wisconsin, 1850

Wyoming, 1890

MODERN EDITIONS AND CRITICISM OF EARLY WORKS

290   **Modern editions of early works**
Classify here 1801–   editions of works originally published before 1801, except for Americana (Cf. WZ 270). Classify by subject editions of Americana published after the closing date for the particular area, e.g., an 1825 edition of a work with a New York City imprint, originally published before 1820.

* 292   **Modern collections of early works**
Classify here collections (including those serially issued) which contain pre–1801 works of three or more authors. Classify works of only two authors in WZ 290 with the first author.

294   **Modern criticism of early works and bibliographies of single titles**
Classify here studies, commentaries, etc, of pre–1801 works including Americana unless they are largely the biography of one or two authors, in which case classify them in WZ 100. Classify in WZ 290 works that include the original text unless it is decidedly subordinate to the commentary. Classify here a bibliography of a single work. Cf. WZ 100 for bibliography of a single author's works.

MISCELLANY RELATING TO MEDICINE

305   **Anecdotes. Humor. Light verse**

305.5   **Surgery. Hospitalization**

308   **Curiosities**

309   **Folklore. Proverbs. Superstitions**

310   **Quacks. Quackery**
Classify here works the subject of which the author considers quackery. Works on special systems of therapeutics are classed in WB 890–962.

313   **Biographical clinics (Diagnosis of diseases of famous persons, derived from records, memoirs, letters, portraits, etc.)**

320   **Body snatching. Resurrectionists**

330   **Medicine etc., as depicted in art and literature (critical studies) e.g., Medicine in the works of Rabelais**
          Cf. WM 49   Art and literature as related to psychiatry.

332   **Anniversaries and special events**
          Classify here general works only.   Classify material on specific events by subject.

334   **Emblems, insignia, etc.**

336   **Caricatures.   Cartoons**

340   **Numismatics, philately, bookplates, etc.**

345   **Medical writing and publishing.   Historiography**

348   **Medical illustration (General)**

350   **Literary and artistic works by physicians and other association items**
          Cf. WZ 330 Medicine in art and literature.

19TH CENTURY SCHEDULE

Classify here works published between 1801–1913.

QS   **Anatomy**

QS 22   **Directories (Table G)**

QSA   **Histology**

QSB   **Embryology**

QT   **Physiology**

QT 22   **Directories (Table G)**

QTA   **Hygiene**

QU   **Biochemistry**

QU 22   **Directories (Table G)**

QV   **Pharmacology. Pharmacy. Materia medica**

QV 22   **Directories (Table G)**

QVA   **Pharmacopoeias (Official)**

QVB   **Toxicology**

QW   **Microbiology**

QW 22   **Directories (Table G)**

QWA   **Immunology**

QX   Parasitology

QX 22   Directories (Table G)

QY   Clinical pathology

[QY 22]   [Directories. Use QZ 22]

QZ   Pathology

QZ 22   Directories (Table G)

QZA   Neoplasms

W   Medicine (General)

W1   Serials. Periodicals

W2   Documents

W3   Congresses
              NLM no longer assigns W3 to newly acquired publications.

W4   Dissertations

W4A   American dissertations

W5   Collections by several authors

W6   Pamphlet volumes

W 22   Directories (Table G)

W 600   Medical jurisprudence

WA   Public health

WA 22   Directories (Table G)

WAA   Sanitation and sanitary control

WB   Practice of medicine

WB 22   Directories (Table G)

WBA   Popular medicine

WBB   Diagnosis

WBC   Therapeutics (General)

WBD   Dietetics

WBE   Electric stimulation therapy

WBF   Hydrotherapy

WBG   Massage

WBH   Climatology. Geography of disease

WBI   Health resorts

WBJ   Special systems (General)

WBK   Homeopathy

WBL   Osteopathic medicine

WC   Communicable diseases (General)

WC 22   Directories (Table G)

WCA   Sexually transmitted diseases

WCB   Cholera

WCC   Diphtheria

WCD   Influenza

WCE	Leprosy
WCF	Malaria
WCG	Plague
WCH	Smallpox
WCI	Typhoid fever
WCJ	Typhus fever
WCK	Yellow fever
WDA	Deficiency diseases. Metabolic diseases (including obesity and disorders of acid-base balance)
WDB	Hypersensitivity
WDC	Animal poisons. Plant poisons
WDD	Diseases due to physical agents
WE	Musculoskeletal system
WE 22	Directories (Table G)
WEA	Fractures. Dislocations. Sprains
WF	Respiratory system
WF 22	Directories (Table G)
WFA	Tuberculosis
WG	Cardiovascular system
WG 22	Directories (Table G)

WH   Hemic and lymphatic systems

WH 22   Directories (Table G)

WI   Digestive system

WI 22   Directories (Table G)

WIA   Stomach

WIB   Anus and rectum

WIC   Liver

WJ   Urogenital system

WJ 22   Directories (Table G)

WJA   Male genitalia

WK   Endocrine system

WK 22   Directories (Table G)

WKA   Diabetes

WL   Nervous system

WL 22   Directories (Table G)

WLA   Epilepsies

WM   Psychiatry

WM 22   Directories (Table G)

WMA   Substance dependence

WN   Radiology

WN 22   Directories (Table G)

WO   Surgery

WO 22   Directories (Table G)

WOA   Anesthesia

WP   Gynecology

WP 22   Directories (Table G)

WPA   Breast

WQ   Obstetrics

WQ 22   Directories (Table G)

WR   Dermatology

WR 22   Directories (Table G)

WS   Pediatrics

WS 22   Directories (Table G)

WT   Geriatrics. Chronic disease

WT 22   Directories (Table G)

WU   Dentistry. Oral surgery

WU 22   Directories (Table G)

WV   Otolaryngology. Nose

WV 22   Directories (Table G)

WVA   Ear

WVB   Throat.   Larynx

WW   Ophthalmology

WW 22   Directories (Table G)

WX   Hospitals

WX 2   Serial reports of hospitals (Table G)

WX 22   Directories (Table G)

WY   Nursing

WY 22   Directories (Table G)

History of medicine
Use schedule in full, as for twentieth century.

INTRODUCTION TO THE
INDEX TO THE CLASSIFICATION

The Index to the *National Library of Medicine Classification* consists primarily of entries from the current *Medical Subject Headings* (MeSH) and some non-MeSH terms when no appropriate MeSH term is available to express a concept. All MeSH entries in the Index were updated to be consistent with the 1995 edition of MeSH. The index terms are arranged in alphabetical order with Roman numerals filed as letters in this arrangement. Arabic numerals are found at the end of the Index following the letter Z.

The classification numbers assigned to the index terms are usually general numbers for the concept represented or numbers reflecting a medical view when that is more appropriate. In this edition see references no longer contain a classification notation.

Indented terms represent more specific aspects of the subject or aspects of the subject to which a number different from the general number has been assigned. The indented terms are often elliptical and should be interpreted broadly. For example, when "Organic chemistry" is used as a term indented under the name of a chemical, the number following is to be selected if the principal focus of the work being classified is the organic chemistry of the chemical. Some subheadings refer the user to another heading. General references or see also references are listed at the end of the alphabetical sequence of the indented terms under the index term.

Example:

Electrodes   QD 571
    Biomedical engineering   QT 36
    In electric stimulation therapy   WB 495
    Used for special purposes, by subjects, e.g., in
        Urinalysis   QY 185
    See also Microelectrodes   QT 36, etc.

Library of Congress numbers are assigned to subjects that fall outside the scope of the *NLM Classification*. When a concept represented in MeSH has no exact equivalent in LC's schedules a number was selected that fitted the concept most closely. Since NLM rarely uses LC's K (Law) schedules the numbers provided for index terms relating to laws are for the subject rather than the law.

How to use the Index

1. The Index is not a substitute for the main schedules. A user should always refer to the schedules for confirmation of the proper application of the number and its relationship to other numbers.

2. Many headings are assigned a range of numbers rather than a specific number. The schedules of the *NLM Classification* or the *Library of Congress Classification* are the only source of the meaning of specific numbers within the range.

3. The number assigned to a heading in this Index should not be used unless it represents the principal subject of the material being cataloged.

4. The Index represents only those MeSH terms that are linked to an NLM or LC classification notation. The Index does not include all MeSH headings found in the *Medical Subject Headings Annotated Alphabetic List* and it is not a substitute for the *Annotated Alphabetic List*.

When assigning MeSH headings to a work the *Annotated Alphabetic List* must always be consulted. The Index does not provide annotations nor does it show relationships between headings, these are found in the *Annotated Alphabetic List* and the *Tree Structures*, respectively.

5. The number of indented terms under an index term varies greatly. The choice was dependent upon the needs that arose in the past. Therefore, the list is in no way exhaustive of the possibilities that can occur.

6. The Index contains over ten thousand index terms to which classification notations are assigned. Many terms are found only in the index and will not appear in the schedules. They refer to a number in the schedule where only a broader term or a related term appears.

7. **Cross References:** There are several types of cross references used in the index.
   7.1 "See" References Pointing to a Single Index Term
   A see reference points to a single index term or concept when any or all numbers assigned to the index term or concept apply also to the reference term.

   Acquired Immunity see Immunity

   7.2 "See" References Pointing to Multiple Index Terms
   A see reference points to multiple index terms or concepts when no one index term or concept represents the entire concept of the reference term.

   Abrasions see Dermabrasion; Tooth Abrasion; Wounds and Injuries

   7.3 "See" References Under Index Terms
   See references that are indented under index terms link the concept to a more specific index term.

   Health
   > **Developing countries   WA 395**
   > **[etc.]**
   > **Mental see Mental Health   WM 105, etc.**
   > **Oral see Oral Health   WU 113**
   > **Public see Public Health   WA, etc.**
   > **[etc.]**

   7.4 General References Under Index Terms
   General references following all indented terms or concepts relate to the main index term or concept. Examples of general references are: "Used for special purposes, by subject ...," " Specific types of [topic], by subject," etc.

   Disasters   HC 79.D45
   > **First aid   WA 292**
   > **Hospital programs see Disaster Planning   WX 185**
   > **[etc.]**
   > **Specific types of disaster, by subject**
   > **See also Civil Defense   UA 926-929, etc.**

   7.5 "See also" References Under Indented Terms
   A see also reference provided under an indented term relates only to the indented term. When the see also reference is related to the main index term only it follows all indented terms and general references. The latter is represented in the Disasters example above (See also Civil Defense   UA 926-929, etc.). The former is represented here.

Advertising
    Alcoholic beverages   HF 6161.L46
    [etc.]
    Pharmaceutical   QV 736
        See also Drug Labeling   QV 835
    Tobacco   HF 6161.T6
    Other special subjects, by business in HF 6161
        or other appropriate number

7.6 See also References to General Terms

See also references lead the user from one index term to a more general index term under which are listed indented terms that apply equally to both headings.

Accidents, Home   WA 288
    See also special topics under Accidents

Accidents
    First aid   WA 292
    In anesthesia   WO 288
    Medicolegal aspects
        Cause of death   W 843
        Disability evaluation   W 900-925
    See also Insurance, Accident   W 100-250, etc.

Note when "etc." follows a number in any type of reference, it indicates that in addition to the numbers given in the reference, there are other numbers which also represent the index term. The user will find these other numbers listed under the main entry for the index term.

8. **Drugs, etc.**: The numbers provided after index terms for drugs, chemicals and biological agents represent their biochemical, pharmacological or chemical properties. The index rarely gives a number for these agents when the material being cataloged discusses their use in the therapy of a particular disease or in a particular study. In such cases the material is classified with the disease or the subject of the study.

A

A Fibers see Nerve Fibers, Myelinated
Abate
    Agriculture   SB 952.P5
    Public health   WA 240
Abattoirs   WA 707
Abbreviations
    Chemistry   QD 7
    General   P 365–365.5
    Library symbols (U.S.)   Z 881
    Medical   W 13
        By specialties (Form number 13 in any NLM
           schedule where applicable)
    Organizations (General)   AS 8
    Periodical titles   Z 6945.A2
    Science (General)   Q 179
    Particular languages, by language in appropriate
        LC schedule
Abdomen   WI 900–970
    Surgery   WI 900–970
Abdomen, Acute   WI 900
    In infancy & childhood   WI 900
Abdominal Cramps see Colic
Abdominal Injuries   WI 900
Abdominal Muscles   WI 900
Abdominal Neoplasms   WI 970
Abdominal Pain   WI 147
Abdominal Wall see Abdominal Muscles
Abducens Nerve   WL 330
Abiogenesis see Biogenesis
Abnormal Reflex see Reflex, Abnormal
Abnormalities
    Congenital   QS 675–681
        Autosome see Autosome Abnormalities   QS
           677
        Bone   WE 250
        Brain   WL 350
        Cardiovascular   WG 220
        Chromosome see Chromosome Abnormalities
           QS 677
        Embryological   QS 675–681
        Etiology   QS 675
        Foot   WE 883
        Gynecological
           General   WP 150
           Pelvic   WQ 320
        Heart see Heart Defects, Congenital   WG 220
        Intestines   WI 412
        Jaw see Jaw Abnormalities   WU 101.5
        Medical curiosities   WZ 308
        Mouth see Mouth Abnormalities   WU 101.5
        Nervous system   WL 101
        Otolaryngology   WV 101
        Respiratory system   WF 101
        Sex chromosome see Sex Chromosome
           Abnormalities   QS 677
        Tooth see Tooth Abnormalities   WU 101.5
        Urogenital system   WJ 101
        Vertebrae   WE 730–735
        Veterinary   SF 769
    Developmental   QZ 45
    See also names of other organs affected or of

specific abnormalities
Abnormalities, Drug–Induced   QS 679
Abnormalities, Multiple   QS 675
Abnormalities, Radiation–Induced   QS 681
Abomasum   QL 862
Aborigines
    Indians   E 51–99
    Eskimos   E 99.E7
    Special topics, by subject
    See also Australoid Race   GN 662–671
Abortifacient Agents   QV 175
Abortifacient Agents, Non–Steroidal   QV 175
Abortifacient Agents, Steroidal   QV 175
Abortion   WQ 225
    Drugs provoking see Abortifacient Agents   QV
        175
    Medicolegal aspects   W 867
    Religious and social aspects   HQ 767–767.52
Abortion, Criminal   W 867
Abortion, Habitual   WQ 225
Abortion, Illegal see Abortion, Criminal
Abortion, Incomplete   WQ 225
Abortion, Induced
    Religious and social aspects   HQ 767–767.52
    Technique   WQ 440
Abortion, Legal   WQ 440
    See also Family Planning   HQ 763.5–767.7
Abortion, Missed   WQ 225
Abortion on Demand see Abortion, Legal
Abortion, Septic   WQ 256
    Veterinary   SF 887
Abortion, Spontaneous see Abortion
Abortion, Therapeutic   WQ 440
Abortion, Threatened   WQ 225
Abortion, Veterinary   SF 887
Abrasions see Dermabrasion; Tooth Abrasion;
   Wounds and Injuries
Abreaction   WM 420.5.A2
Abruptio Placentae   WQ 212
Abscess   WC 195
    Bone   WE 251
    Cerebral see Brain Abscess   WL 351
    General (requiring surgery)   WO 140
    Liver see Liver Abscess   WI 730
    Lung see Lung Abscess   WF 651
    Pelvic   WP 155
    Periapical see Periapical Abscess   WU 230
    Puerperal   WQ 505
    Subphrenic see Subphrenic Abscess   WI 575
    Surgery   WO 140
    Other localities, by site
Abscess, Amebic, Hepatic see Liver Abscess,
   Amebic
Abscess, Cerebral see Brain Abscess
Abscess, Hepatic see Liver Abscess
Abscess, Hepatic, Amebic see Liver Abscess,
   Amebic
Abscess, Liver, Amebic see Liver Abscess, Amebic
Abscess, Periapical see Periapical Abscess
Abscess, Pulmonary see Lung Abscess
Abscess, Subphrenic see Subphrenic Abscess
Absence Seizures see Epilepsy, Absence

Absenteeism
    Workplace   HD 5115–5115.2
    School   WA 350
Absorption
    Immunochemistry   QW 504.5
    Intestinal see Intestinal Absorption   WI 402
    Of drugs   QV 38
    Of foods   WI 102
    Of gases   QC 162
    Skin see Skin Absorption   WR 102
    Of other substances, with the substance
Absorption, Intestinal see Intestinal Absorption
Absorption, Skin see Skin Absorption
Abstinence Syndrome, Neonatal see Neonatal
    Abstinence Syndrome
Abstracting and Indexing   Z 695.9–695.92
Abstracts
    Of subjects represented in NLM's classification,
        appropriate classification number preceded by
        the letter Z
    Of other subjects, LC's Z schedule
Abuse of Health Services see Health Services Misuse
Academies and Institutes   AS
    (Form numbers 23–24 in any NLM schedule
        where applicable)
    For other particular purposes, by subject
Acanthocephala   QX 200
Acantholysis Bullosa see Epidermolysis Bullosa
Acanthosis Nigricans   WR 265
Acari   QX 473
Acariasis see Mite Infestations
Acarina see Acari
Acarus see Mites
Acceleration   WD 720
Accelography see Kinetocardiography
Acceptability of Health Care see Patient Acceptance
    of Health Care
Access to Health Care see Health Services
    Accessibility
Accessibility of Health Services see Health Services
    Accessibility
Accessory Cells, Immunologic see
    Antigen–Presenting Cells
Accessory Nerve   WL 330
Accident Insurance see Insurance, Accident
Accident Prevention   WA 250–288
    In hospitals   WX 185
    In workplace see Accidents, Occupational   WA
      485–491
    Radiation injuries   WN 650
    See also specific types of accidents, e.g.,
        Prevention & control under Accidents, Traffic
        WA 275; Protective devices   WA 260, etc.
Accident Services see Ambulances; Emergency
    Health Services; Insurance, Accident;
    Occupational Health Services
Accidental Falls
    In the home   WA 288
Accidents
    First aid   WA 292
    In anesthesia   WO 245
    Medicolegal aspects
        Cause of death   W 843

    Disability evaluation   W 900–925
    See also Insurance, Accident   W 100–250, etc.
Accidents, Aviation   WD 740
    See also special topics under Accidents
Accidents, Home   WA 288
    See also special topics under Accidents
Accidents, Industrial see Accidents, Occupational
Accidents, Occupational   WA 485–491, etc.
    Of the eye   WW 505–525
    See also special topics under Accidents
Accidents, Traffic   WA 275
    Prevention & control   WA 275
    See also special topics under Accidents
Acclimatization   QT 145
    Cold climate   QT 160
    Hot climate   QT 150
    See also Desert climate   QT 150, etc.; Tropical
      climate   QT 150, etc.
Accommodation, Ocular   WW 109
Accounting
    Dental administration   WU 77
    Hospital administration   WX 157
    Medical administration   W 80
    Nursing administration   WY 77
    Pharmacy administration   QV 736
    In other specific fields, by subject
Accounts Payable and Receivable see Accounting
    λ .
Accreditation
    Dentists   WU 40
    Hospitals   WX 15
        Special (Form numbers 27–28 in any NLM
          schedule where applicable)
    Physicians   W 40
    Schools (Form numbers 18 or other appropriate
        education number in any NLM schedule where
        applicable)
    Other institutes, etc. (Form numbers 23–24 in any
        NLM schedule where applicable)
    Other professionals (Form number 21 in any
        NLM schedule where applicable)
Acculturation   GN 366–367
    Of particular customs, by subject
    Of particular peoples, by race or country
ACE Inhibitors see Angiotensin–Converting
    Enzyme Inhibitors
Acephen see Meclofenoxate
Acetabularia   QK 569.D33
Acetabulum   WE 750
Acetaldehyde   QU 99
    In alcohol metabolism   QV 84
    Organic chemistry   QD 305.A6
    Special topics, by subject, e.g., in experiments
      on muscle contraction   WE 500
Acetanilides   QV 95
Acetarsone see Arsenic
Acetates   QU 90
    Organic chemistry   QD 305.A2
Acetic Acids   QU 90
    Organic chemistry   QD 305.A2
Acetoacetates   QU 90
    Organic chemistry   QD 305.A2
Acetobacter   QW 131

**ALWAYS CONSULT MAIN SCHEDULES. USE NUMBER ASSIGNED ONLY WHEN
SUBJECT REPRESENTS MAJOR EMPHASIS OF WORK BEING CLASSIFIED**

Acetonchloroform see Chlorobutanol
Acetone
    In urine   QY 185
    Organic chemistry   QD 305.K2
Acetone Bodies see Ketone Bodies
Acetophenetidin see Phenacetin
Acetyl Carnitine see Acetylcarnitine
Acetyl Glyceryl Ether Phosphorylcholine see
    Platelet Activating Factor
Acetylbenzoylaconine see Aconitine
Acetylcarnitine   QU 187
Acetylcholine   QV 122
Acetylcholine Antagonists see Cholinergic
    Antagonists
Acetylcholine Receptors see Receptors, Cholinergic
Acetylcholinesterase   QU 136
Acetylcholinesterase Inhibitors see Cholinesterase
    Inhibitors
Acetylene
    Organic chemistry   QD 305.H8
    Plant and soil microbiology   QW 60
    Toxicology   QV 633
Acetylformaldehyde see Pyruvaldehyde
Acetylmuramyl-Alanyl-Isoglutamine   QW 800
    Biochemistry   QU 68
Acetylsalicylic Acid see Aspirin
Achalasia, Esophageal see Esophageal Achalasia
Achievement   BF 637.S8
    In infancy & childhood
        Measurement   WS 105.5.E8
        Motivation   WS 105.5.M5
    Motivation   BF 501-505
    Personality development   BF 698.9.A3
    Success   BJ 1611-1618
    See also Educational Measurement   LB
        3050-3060.87
Achilles Tendon   WE 880
Achlorhydria   WI 308
Achondroplasia   WE 250
Achromobacter see Alcaligenes
Achromobacteriaceae see Gram-Negative Aerobic
    Bacteria
Achylia Gastrica see Achlorhydria
Acid Aspiration Syndrome see Pneumonia,
    Aspiration
Acid-Base Equilibrium   QU 105
Acid-Base Imbalance   WD 220
Acid Etching, Dental   WU 190
Acid Phosphatase   QU 136
Acid Seromucoid see Orosomucoid
Acidosis   WD 222
    Veterinary   SF 910.W38
Acidosis, Diabetic see Diabetic Ketoacidosis
Acidosis, Renal Tubular   WJ 301
Acidosis, Respiratory   WF 140
Acids
    Inorganic chemistry   QD 167
    Organic chemistry
        Aliphatic compounds   QD 305.A2
        Aromatic compounds   QD 341.A2
    Toxicology
        Inorganic   QV 612
        Organic   QV 632

    See also names of specific acids
Aciphenochinolium see Cinchophen
Aclacinomycin A see Aclarubicin
Aclarubicin   QV 269
Acne see Acne Vulgaris
Acne Rosacea   WR 430
Acne Vulgaris   WR 430
Acneform lesions see Acne
Acomys see Muridae
Aconite
    Toxicology   QV 628
Aconitine
    Toxicology   QV 628
Acosta's Disease see Altitude Sickness
Acoustic Evoked Brain Stem Potentials see Evoked
    Potentials, Auditory, Brain Stem
Acoustic Impedance Tests   WV 272
Acoustic Nerve   WL 330
    Physiology of hearing   WV 272
    See also Cochlear Nerve   WL 330; Vestibular
        Nerve   WL 330
Acoustic Nerve Diseases   WL 330
    See also Neuroma, Acoustic   WV 250
Acoustic Neuroma see Neuroma, Acoustic
Acoustic Sense see Hearing
Acoustic Trauma see Hearing Loss, Noise-Induced
Acoustics
    Noise abatement
        General   WA 776
        Housing   WA 795
        Industrial   WA 470
        Public buildings   WA 799
    Physics   QC 221-246
    Sound recording industry   TS 2301.S6
    See also Hearing   WV 270-280
        Noise   WA 776, etc.
Acoustics, Speech see Speech Acoustics
Acquired Immunity see Immunity
Acquired Immunodeficiency Syndrome   WC
    503-503.7
    General works   WC 503
    Complications   WC 503.5
    Diagnosis   WC 503.1
    Epidemiology   WC 503.4
    Etiology. Transmission   WC 503.3
    Nursing   WY 153.5
    Prevention & control   WC 503.6
    Psychosocial aspects   WC 503.7
    Therapy   WC 503.2
Acridines
    Dyes
        As a disinfectant   QV 235
        As a stain, etc.   QV 240
    In amino acid biochemistry   QU 65
    Organic chemistry   QD 401
Acrocephalosyndactylia   WE 250
Acrocephaly see Craniosynostoses
Acrodermatitis   WR 218
Acrolein
    Toxicology   QV 627
Acromegaly   WK 550
Acromelalgia see Erythromelalgia
Acromioclavicular Joint   WE 810

Acronine   QV 269
Acronycine see Acronine
Acronyms
   Medical   W 13
     By specialties (Form number 13 in any NLM
      schedule where applicable)
Acrosin   QU 136
Acrosomal proteinase see Acrosin
Acrylamides   QU 62
   Organic chemistry   QD 305.A7
Acrylates
   Chemical technology   TP 1180.A35
   In dentistry   WU 90
   In orthopedics   WE 190
   Pharmacology   QV 50
   Used in particular procedure, with the procedure
Acrylic Resins
   Chemical technology   TP 1180.A35
   In dentistry   WU 190
   Pharmacology   QV 50
   Used for special purposes, by subject, e.g., in
     orthopedic surgery   WE 190
   See also Bone Cements   WE 190
ACTH see Corticotropin
ACTH-Releasing Factor see
   Corticotropin-Releasing Hormone
Actihaemyl   QV 370
Actin-Binding Proteins see Microfilament Proteins
Acting Out   WM 193.5.A2
   In Adolescence   WS 463
   In infancy & childhood   WS 350.8.D3
Actinic Rays see Ultraviolet Rays
Actinides see Metals, Actinoid
Actinium   WN 420
   Nuclear physics   QC 796.A2
Actinoids see Metals, Actinoid
Actinomyces   QW 125.5.A2
Actinomyces Infections see Actinomycosis
Actinomycetaceae   QW 125.5.A2
Actinomycetales   QW 125-125.5
Actinomycetales Infections   WC 302
Actinomycete Infections see Actinomycetales
   Infections
Actinomycetes see Bacteria; names of specific
   organisms or groups, e.g., Coryneform group
Actinomycin   QV 269
Actinomycosis   WC 302
Actinomycosis, Cervicofacial   WC 302
Actinon see Radon
Actinotherapy see Ultraviolet Therapy
Action Potentials   WL 102
   Muscles   WE 102
   Other sites: classify in physiology number for the
     site or the general number if no physiology
     number exists.
Activation Analysis   QD 606
Activator Appliances   WU 426
Active Immunity see Immunity, Active
Active Site see Binding Sites
Active Transport see Biological Transport, Active
Activities of Daily Living
   Disabled   HV 3011
     Homemaking   HV 3011
   Old Age   WT 120
   Orthopedic devices for   WE 172
     Catalogs for   WE 26
   Special disabilities or diseases, by subject
   Special types of activity not limited to a special
     group of people, by activity
Activity Cycles   QT 167
Activity Therapy
   In psychotherapy   WM 450
   In therapy of physical diseases   WB 555
Actuarial Analysis   HG 8779-8793
   Related to specific service plans, by subject, e.g.,
     Psychiatric insurance   W 270
Acuity, Visual see Visual Acuity
Acupoints see Acupuncture Points
Acupuncture   WB 369
Acupuncture Anesthesia   WB 369
Acupuncture Points   WB 369
Acupuncture Therapy   WB 369
Acute Abdomen see Abdomen, Acute
Acute Disease   WB 105
   In infancy & childhood   WS 200
Acute Phase Proteins   WH 400
Acute Phase Reactants see Acute Phase Proteins
Acute-Phase Reaction   QZ 150
   Localized, by site
Acute-Phase State see Acute-Phase Reaction
Acycloguanosine see Acyclovir
Acyclovir   QV 268.5
Acyltransferases   QU 141
   Deficiency   WD 105
Adamantinoma see Ameloblastoma
Adams-Stokes Syndrome   WG 330
Adaptation, Biological   QH 546
Adaptation, Ocular   WW 109
Adaptation, Physiological   QT 140
   Aviation   WD 710
   Space flight   WD 752
Adaptation, Psychological   BF 335
   Aviation   WD 730
   In adolescence   WS 462
   In infancy & childhood   WS 105.5.A8
   Space flight   WD 754
   Other specific subjects, by subject
Adaptation Syndrome see Stress
Addictive Behavior see Behavior, Addictive
Addison's Anemia see Anemia, Pernicious
Addison's Disease   WK 765
Addresses see Form number 9 in any NLM schedule
   where applicable
Adenine
   In nucleic acids   QU 58
   Organic chemistry   QD 401
Adenine Arabinoside see Vidarabine
Adenine Nucleotides
   Biochemistry   QU 57
   Pharmacology   QV 185
Adenitis see Lymphadenitis
Adenocarcinoma   QZ 365
   Localized, by site
Adenocarcinoma, Bronchiolo-Alveolar   WF 658
Adenocarcinoma, Renal Cell see Carcinoma, Renal
   Cell

**ALWAYS CONSULT MAIN SCHEDULES. USE NUMBER ASSIGNED ONLY WHEN
SUBJECT REPRESENTS MAJOR EMPHASIS OF WORK BEING CLASSIFIED**

Adenofibroma   QZ 310
   Localized, by site
Adenohypophysis see Pituitary Gland, Anterior
Adenoidectomy   WV 430
Adenoids   WV 430
Adenolymphoma   WI 230
Adenoma   QZ 365
Adenoma, Acidophil   WK 585
Adenoma, Chromophobe   WK 585
Adenoma, Eosinophilic see Adenoma, Acidophil
Adenoma, Islet Cell   WK 885
Adenoma, Prolactin-Secreting, Pituitary see
   Prolactinoma
Adenoma, Prostatic see Prostatic Hypertrophy
Adenoma, Sweat Gland   WR 500
   Localized, by site
Adenoma, Virilizing   WK 780
Adenomatous Polyposis Coli   WI 520
Adenomyosis see Endometriosis
Adenosine   QU 57
   Pharmacology   QV 185
Adenosine Aminohydrolase see Adenosine
   Deaminase
Adenosine Cyclic Monophosphate see Cyclic AMP
Adenosine Cyclic 2',3'-Monophosphate see Cyclic
   AMP
Adenosine Cyclic 3',5'-Monophosphate see Cyclic
   AMP
Adenosine Deaminase   QU 136
Adenosine Diphosphate   QU 57
   Pharmacology   QV 185
Adenosine Diphosphate Ribose   QU 57
Adenosine Diphosphoribose see Adenosine
   Diphosphate Ribose
Adenosine Phosphates see Adenine Nucleotides
Adenosine Pyrophosphate see Adenosine
   Diphosphate
Adenosine Receptors see Receptors, Purinergic P1
Adenosine Triphosphate   QU 57
   In general metabolism   QU 120
   Pharmacology   QV 185
Adenosinetriphosphatase   QU 136
Adenosinetriphosphatase, Calcium see
   Ca(2+)-Transporting ATPase
Adenosinetriphosphatase, Calcium, Magnesium see
   Ca(2+) Mg(2+)-ATPase
Adenosinetriphosphatase F1 see H(+)-Transporting
   ATP Synthase
Adenosinetriphosphatase, Magnesium see Ca(2+)
   Mg(2+)-ATPase
Adenosinetriphosphatase, Sodium, Potassium see
   Na(+)-K(+)-Exchanging ATPase
Adenosis of Breast see Fibrocystic Disease of Breast
Adenoviridae   QW 165.5.A3
Adenoviridae Infections   WC 500
Adenovirus Infections see Adenoviridae Infections
Adenyl Cyclase   QU 139
Adenylate Cyclase see Adenyl Cyclase
Adenylpyrophosphate see Adenosine Triphosphate
Adhesion, Bacterial see Bacterial Adhesion
Adhesions
   Abdominal   WI 900
   Gynecologic   WP 140

   Localized, by site
Adhesive Plaster see Bandages
Adhesiveness   QC 183
   Chemical technology   TP 967-970
Adhesives   TP 967-970
Adipocere see Postmortem Changes
Adipose Tissue   QS 532.5.A3
Adiposis Dolorosa   WD 214
Adjustment Disorders   WM 171
   Psychotic see Affective Disorders, Psychotic
   WM 207
Adjustment, Social see Social Adjustment
Adjuvants, Anesthesia see Anesthesia Adjuvants
Adjuvants, Immunologic   QW 800
Adjuvants, Pharmaceutic   QV 38
ADL see Activities of Daily Living
Administration see Organization and Administration
Administration, Cutaneous   WB 340
Administration, Health see Public Health
   Administration
Administration, Inhalation   WB 342
Administration, Intranasal   WB 342
Administration, Intravesical   WB 340
Administration of Medicine see Administrative
   methods   WB 340-356 under Drugs
Administration, Oral   WB 350
Administration, Rectal   WB 344
Administration Research, Nursing see Nursing
   Administration Research
Administration Schedule, Drug see Drug
   Administration Schedule
Administration, Topical   WB 340
Administrative Personnel
   Business administration   HF 5549-5549.5
   Hospital administration   WX 155
   Industrial management   HD 28-70
   Nursing administration   WY 105
   Public health administration   WA 525-546
   See also names of particular types of
     administrators, e.g., Medical record
     administrators   WX 173
Administrative Work see Organization and
   Administration
Administrators see Administrative Personnel
Admission Tests, Routine see Diagnostic Tests,
   Routine
Admitting Department, Hospital   WX 158
   Of specialty hospitals (Form number 27-28 in any
     NLM schedule where applicable)
Adnexa Uteri   WP 275-322
Adnexal Diseases   WP 275-322
Adnexitis   WP 275
   Pelvic inflammations   WP 155-157
Adolescence   WS 460-463
   Pregnancy see Pregnancy in Adolescence   WS
     462, etc.
Adolescent Behavior   WS 462
Adolescent, Hospitalized   WS 460-463
Adolescent, Institutionalized   WS 460-463
Adolescent Medicine   WS 460
Adolescent Pregnancy see Pregnancy in
   Adolescence
Adolescent Psychiatry   WS 463

ALWAYS CONSULT MAIN SCHEDULES. USE NUMBER ASSIGNED ONLY WHEN
SUBJECT REPRESENTS MAJOR EMPHASIS OF WORK BEING CLASSIFIED

As a career   WS 463
Adolescent Psychology   WS 462
Adoption
    Psychological aspects   WS 105.5.F2
    Sociological aspects   HV 874.8–875.7
Adoptive Cell Transfer see Immunotherapy,
    Adoptive
Adoptive Cellular Immunotherapy see
    Immunotherapy, Adoptive
ADP see Adenosine Diphosphate
ADP Receptors see Receptors, Purinergic P2
ADP Ribose see Adenosine Diphosphate Ribose
ADP-Ribosyltransferase (Polymerizing) see NAD+
    ADP-Ribosyltransferase
Adrenal Cortex   WK 750–770
Adrenal Cortex Diseases   WK 760
Adrenal Cortex Function Tests   WK 750
Adrenal Cortex Hormones   WK 755
    Synthetic   WK 757
Adrenal Cortex Hyperfunction see Adrenal Gland
    Hyperfunction
Adrenal Cortex Hypofunction see Adrenal Gland
    Hypofunction
Adrenal Cortex Neoplasms   WK 780
Adrenal Gland Diseases   WK 700–790
Adrenal Gland Hyperfunction   WK 770
Adrenal Gland Hypofunction   WK 765
Adrenal Gland Neoplasms   WK 780
Adrenal Glands   WK 700–790
Adrenal Hyperplasia, Congenital   WK 700
Adrenal Insufficiency see Adrenal Gland
    Hypofunction
Adrenal Medulla   WK 725
Adrenalectomy   WK 790
Adrenalin see Epinephrine
Adrenaline see Epinephrine
Adrenergic Agents   QV 129–132
Adrenergic Agonists   QV 129
Adrenergic alpha-Agonists   QV 129
Adrenergic alpha-Antagonists   QV 132
Adrenergic alpha-Receptor Agonists see Adrenergic
    alpha-Agonists
Adrenergic alpha Receptor Blockaders see
    Adrenergic alpha-Antagonists
Adrenergic alpha-Receptors see Receptors,
    Adrenergic, alpha
Adrenergic Antagonists   QV 132
Adrenergic beta-Agonists   QV 129
Adrenergic beta-Antagonists   QV 132
Adrenergic beta-Receptor Agonists see Adrenergic
    beta-Agonists
Adrenergic beta-Receptor Blockaders see
    Adrenergic beta-Antagonists
Adrenergic beta-Receptors see Receptors,
    Adrenergic, beta
Adrenergic-Blocking Agents see Adrenergic
    Antagonists
Adrenergic Receptor Agonists see Adrenergic
    Agonists
Adrenergic Receptors see Receptors, Adrenergic
Adrenoceptors see Receptors, Adrenergic
Adrenochrome   QV 77.7
Adrenocorticotropic Hormone see Corticotropin

Adrenocorticotropin see Corticotropin
Adrenogenital Syndrome see Adrenal Hyperplasia,
    Congenital
Adrenoleukodystrophy   WD 205.5.L5
Adrenolytics see Adrenergic Agents
Adrenomimetics see Adrenergic Agents
Adrenomyeloneuropathy see Adrenoleukodystrophy
Adriamycin see Doxorubicin
Adsorbents see Dermatologic Agents;
    Gastrointestinal Agents; Powders
Adsorption
    Immunochemistry   QW 504.5
    Of drugs   QV 38
    Of gases   QC 162
        Chemical engineering   TP 156.A35
    Of matter   QC 182
    Of solutions   QD 547
    Virology   QW 160
    Of other substances, with the substance
Adult
    Developmental psychology   BF 724.5–724.85
        Middle age   BF 724.6–724.65
    Other particular topics, by subject
    See also Aging   WT 104
Adult Respiratory Distress Syndrome see
    Respiratory Distress Syndrome, Adult
Adult T-Cell Leukemia-Lymphoma Virus I see
    HTLV-I
Adulteration of Drugs see Drug Contamination;
    Legislation, Drug
Adulteration of food see Food Contamination
Advance Directives   W 85.5
Advertising
    Alcoholic beverages   HF 6161.L46
    Cigarette   HF 6161.T6
    Dental   WU 58
    Medical   W 58
    Pharmaceutical   QV 736
        See also Drug Labeling   QV 835
    Tobacco   HF 6161.T6
    Other special subjects, by business in HF 6161
    or other appropriate number
Aedes   QX 525
Aerobacter see Enterobacter
Aerobic Exercise see Exercise
Aerobiosis   QU 120
Aeroembolism see Embolism, Air
Aerophagy   WI 150
Aerophobia see Phobic Disorders
Aeroplanes see Aircraft
Aerosols
    Disinfectant   QV 220
    Dosage form   QV 785
    Pollutant see Air Pollutants   WA 450; WA 754
    Used in inhalation therapy   WB 342
Aerospace Medicine   WD 700–758
    Aviation medicine   WD 700–745
        Psychological aspects   WD 730
        General   WD 700–745
    Space medicine   WD 750–758
        Psychological aspects   WD 754
Aerotherapy see Therapy   WB 460 under Air
AET   WN 650

Affect   BF 511–568
    In adolescence   WS 462
    In infancy & childhood   WS 105.5.E5
Affective Disorders   WM 171
    In adolescence   WS 463
    In infancy & childhood   WS 350.6
Affective Disorders, Psychotic   WM 207
Affective Disturbances see Affective Symptoms
Affective Psychosis, Bipolar see Bipolar Disorder
Affective Symptoms
    In adolescence   WS 463
    In infancy & childhood   WS 350.6
    Neurotic   WM 171
    Psychotic   WM 207
Affinity, Antibody see Antibody Affinity
Afibrinogenemia   WH 322
Aflatoxins   QW 630
AFP see alpha Fetoproteins
African Americans see Blacks
African Green Monkey see Cercopithecus aethiops
African Lymphoma see Burkitt's Lymphoma
African Swine Fever   SF 977.A4
African Swine Fever Virus   QW 165.5.I6
Afterbirth see Fetal Membranes; Placenta
Afterbrain see Cerebellum; Pons
Aftercare
    In infancy & childhood   WS 366
    Of the mentally ill   WM 29
    Of the physically ill and disabled   WB 325
    Of particular diseases, with the disease
    See also Nursing Care   WY 100; Postoperative
      Care   WO 183; Surgical Nursing   WY 161
Afterimage   WW 105
Agammaglobulinemia   WH 400
Agar   QU 83
    Cathartic   QV 75
    Culture medium   QY 26
Agaric, Fly see Mushrooms
Agaricaceae see Agaricales
Agaricales   QW 180.5.B2
    Poisoning   WD 520
Age Determination by Skeleton   GN 70
Age Determination by Teeth   GN 209
    Animal   SF 869
Age Factors
    As a cause of disease   QZ 53
    Demography   HB 1531–1737
    Related to other particular subjects, by subject
    See also Gestational Age   WQ 210.5
Age-Related Osteoporosis see Osteoporosis
Aged   WT
    Anesthesia   WO 445
    Dentistry see Geriatric Dentistry   WU 490
    Mental health   WT 145
    Nursing see Geriatric Nursing   WY 152
    Nutritional requirements; Nutrition Disorders
    WT 115
    Physical examination and diagnosis   WT 141
    Psychiatry see Geriatric Psychiatry   WT 150
    See also Dementia, Senile   WT 155
    Psychology   WT 145
    Social problems; Surveys   WT 30
    Surgery   WO 950

    Therapeutics (General)   WT 166
    See also Geriatrics
Aged Abuse see Elder Abuse
Aged, 80 and over   WT
    See special topics under Aged
AGEPC see Platelet Activating Factor
Agglutination   QW 640
    Diagnostic reactions   QY 265
    See also Hemagglutination   QW 640
Agglutination Tests   QY 265
Agglutinins   QW 640
    Plant   QW 640
Agglutinins, Plant see Lectins
Aggression
    Animals   QL 758.5
    Psychology
      In adolescence   WS 462
      In adulthood   BF 575.A3
      In infancy & childhood   WS 105.5.S6
    Social behavior disorder
      In adolescence   WS 463
      In adulthood   WM 600
      In infancy & childhood   WS 350.8.A4
      See also Violence   HM 281–283
Aggressiveness see Aggression
Aging   WT 104
    Psychological changes   WT 145
Agkistrodon rhodostoma Venom Protease see
    Ancrod
Agkistrodon Serine Proteinase see Ancrod
Agnosia   WL 340
Agonistic Behavior   QL 758.5
Agoraphobia   WM 178
Agrammatism see Aphasia, Broca
Agranulocytosis   WH 200
Agraphia   WL 340
Agricultural Chemistry see Chemistry, Agricultural
Agricultural Workers' Diseases   WA 400
    See also Farmer's Lung   WF 652
Agriculture   S
    General works   S 491–494.5
AH 5158 see Labetalol
AHG–CDC Tests see Cytotoxicity Tests,
    Immunologic
Aid to Families with Dependent Children   HV
    697–700
    Public health aspects   WA 320
Aid to the Blind see Social Security
Aid to the Totally Disabled see Social Security
AIDS see Acquired Immunodeficiency Syndrome
AIDS Antibodies see HIV Antibodies
AIDS–Associated Nephropathy   WC 503.5
AIDS Dementia Complex   WC 503.5
AIDS Encephalopathy see AIDS Dementia
    Complex
AIDS–Related Complex   WC 503–503.7
AIDS–Related Opportunistic Infections
    General   WC 503.5
    See also names of specific infections
AIDS Seroconversion see HIV Seropositivity
AIDS Serodiagnosis   QY 265
AIDS Serology see AIDS Serodiagnosis
AIDS Seropositivity see HIV Seropositivity

AIDS Virus see HIV–1

Ainhum   WE 835

Air
    Industrial hygiene   WA 450
    Public health aspects   WA 750–776
    Relation to personal health   QT 230
    Therapy
        Pharmacology   QV 310
        Physical medicine   WB 460
    See also Atmosphere   WA 750–776, etc.

Air Bladder see Air Sacs

Air Conditioning   WA 774

Air Defense see Aviation; Civil Defense; Military
    Science

Air Ionization
    Physics
        Electricity   QC 702
        Meteorology   QC 969
    Physiology   QT 162.A5
    Public health hazard   WA 750
    Therapeutic use   WB 460
    For other uses, by subject

Air Microbiology   QW 82

Air Movements   QC 880.4.A8
    Clinical aspects of disease caused by
        Aviation problems   WD 720
        Extraterritorial environment   WD 758
        General works   WD 600
        Motion sickness   WD 630
        Vibration disorders   WD 640
    Etiology of disease   QZ 57
    Spread of pesticides   WA 240
    Wind (General)   QC 930.5–959

Air Pollutants   WA 754
    See also names of specific pollutants

Air Pollutants, Environmental   WA 754

Air Pollutants, Occupational   WA 450

Air Pollutants, Radioactive   WN 615

Air Pollution   WA 754
    In industry   WA 450
    Legislation   WA 32–33

Air Pollution, Indoor   WA 754

Air Pollution, Radioactive   WN 615
    See also Air Pollutants, Radioactive   WN 615;
        Radioactive Pollutants   WN 615, etc.; names
        of specific pollutants

Air Pollution, Tobacco Smoke see Tobacco Smoke
    Pollution

Air Pressure
    High altitude   WD 710
    Underwater   WD 650

Air Quality, Indoor see Air Pollution, Indoor

Air Radiography see Pneumoradiography

Air raid protection see Civil Defense

Air Sacs   QL 855

Air Swallowing see Aerophagy

Air Travel, Accidents see Accidents, Aviation

Aircraft
    As ambulances   WX 215
    Industrial diseases of aircraft construction and
        maintenance workers   WA 400–495
    Noise effects
        On aviators and passengers   WD 735

    On animals and humans on the ground   WA
        776
    Nursing service   WY 143
    Pollution   WA 754
    Relation to aviation and space medicine   WD
        700–758
    Sanitation   WA 810
    Speed effects   WD 720
    See also Aviation   WD 705, etc.

Airsickness see Motion Sickness

Airway Obstruction   WF 140
    In anesthesia   WO 250

Airway Resistance   WF 102
    Tests   WF 141

Akamushi Disease see Scrub Typhus

Akinetic Mutism   WL 348

Akinetic Petit Mal see Epilepsy, Absence

Alalia see Speech Disorders

Alanine Aminotransferase   QU 141

Alarm Reaction see Stress

Alaryngeal Speech see Speech, Alaryngeal

Albers–Schoenberg Disease see Osteopetrosis

Albinism   WR 267

Albright's Disease see Fibrous Dysplasia of Bone

Albumins   QU 55
    Serum see Serum Albumin   WH 400, etc.

Albuminuria   WJ 343

Alcaligenes   QW 131

Alchemy   QD 23.3–26.5
    Therapeutics   WB 890

Alcohol Abuse see Alcoholism

Alcohol Amnestic Disorder   WM 274

Alcohol Consumption see Alcohol Drinking

Alcohol Dehydrogenase   QU 140

Alcohol Drinking   WM 274
    Adolescents and children
        Psychiatric problem   WM 274
        School problem   WA 352
    Sociological problem   HV 5006–5722
    Traffic accidents   WA 275

Alcohol, Ethyl
    Organic chemistry   QD 305.A4
    Pharmacology   QV 84

Alcohol, Methyl   QV 83

Alcohol Oxidoreductases   QU 140

Alcohol, Propyl
    Organic chemistry   QD 305.A4
    Pharmacology   QV 82

Alcohol Withdrawal Delirium   WM 274

Alcoholic Beverages
    As dietary supplement in health or disease   WB
        444
    Chemical technology   TP 500–617
    See also Alcoholism   WM 274; Alcohol, Ethyl
        QV 84, etc.

Alcoholic Cardiomyopathy see Cardiomyopathy,
    Alcoholic

Alcoholic Cirrhosis see Liver Cirrhosis, Alcoholic

Alcoholic Fatty Liver see Fatty Liver, Alcoholic

Alcoholic Hepatitis see Hepatitis, Alcoholic

Alcoholic Intoxication   QV 84
    Associated with traffic accidents   WA 275
    In forensic medicine   W 780

Alcoholic Liver Diseases see Liver Diseases, Alcoholic
Alcoholism   WM 274
   Classify like material on Alcohol drinking
   See also Fatty liver, Alcoholic   WI 700;
      Hepatitis, Alcoholic   WI 700; Liver Cirrhosis,
      Alcoholic   WI 725; Psychoses, Alcoholic
      WM 274; Skid row alcoholics   WM 274, etc.
Alcohols   QV 82–84
   Organic chemistry
      Aliphatic compounds   QD 305.A4
      Aromatic compounds   QD 341.A4
Alcohols, Sugar see Sugar Alcohols
Aldehyde Dehydrogenase   QU 140
Aldehyde Reductase   QU 140
Aldehydes   QU 99
   In alcohol metabolism   QV 84
   Organic chemistry
      Aliphatic compounds   QD 305.A6
      Aromatic compounds   QD 341.A6
   Used for particular experiments, by main topic
      of the work, e.g. as a fixative in histological
      experiments   QS 525–530
Aldicarb
   Agriculture   SB 952.C3
   Public health   WA 240
Aldolase see Fructosediphosphate Aldolase
Aldose Reductase see Aldehyde Reductase
Aldosterone   WK 755
   Deficiency   WK 760
      As a cause of a particular disorder, with the
      disorder
Aldosterone Antagonists   WK 755
Aldosteronism see Hyperaldosteronism
Aleutian Disease Virus see Aleutian Mink Disease Parvovirus
Aleutian Mink Disease   SF 997.5.M5
Aleutian Mink Disease Parvovirus   QW 165.5.P3
Aleuts see Eskimos
Alexia see Dyslexia, Acquired
Alexin see Complement
Alexithymia see Affective Symptoms
Algae   QK 564–580.5
Algae, Blue-Green see Cyanobacteria
Alginates
   Biochemistry   QU 83
   Phytochemistry   QK 898.A3
   Used in dentistry   WU 190
   Used in surgical dressings   WO 167
Algodystrophic Syndrome see Reflex Sympathetic Dystrophy
Algolagnia see Paraphilias
Algor Mortis see Postmortem Changes
Algorithms
   For computers (General)   QA 76.9.A43
   In particular fields (Form number 26.5 in any
      NLM schedule where applicable)
   Applied to special topics, by subject
Alienation, Social see Social Alienation
Alienists see Biography   WZ 112.5.P6, etc. under
   Psychiatry; Directories   WM 22 under
   Psychiatry
Alimentary Tract see Digestive System

Alimentation (Therapeutics) see Diet Therapy
Aliphatic Compounds see Anti-Infective Agents,
   Local; Formaldehyde; Nitrofurans; Hydrocarbons
   or Aliphatic compounds under Chemistry,
   Organic
Alkalemia see Alkalosis
Alkali Disease see Tularemia
Alkalies
   Pharmacology   QV 275
   Toxicology   QV 612
Alkaline Earth Metals see Metals, Alkaline earth
Alkaline Phosphatase   QU 136
Alkaloids
   As a therapeutic system   WB 890
   Organic Chemistry   QD 421.A1–421.7
   Toxicology   QV 628
Alkalosis   WD 226
Alkalosis, Respiratory   WF 140
Alkanes
   Microbial chemistry   QW 52
   Organic chemistry   QD 305.H6
Alkanesulfonates   QU 98
   Organic chemistry   QD 305.S3
Alkenes
   Microbial chemistry   QW 52
   Organic chemistry   QD 305.H7
Alkyl Sulfonates see Alkanesulfonates
Alkylating Agents   QV 269
Alkylation   QD 281.A5
Alkynes
   Organic chemistry   QD 305.H8
ALL, Childhood see Leukemia, Lymphocytic, Acute, L1
Allantiasis see Botulism
Allantoin
   In amino acid metabolism   QU 65
Allantois
   Embryology   QS 645
Alleles   QH 447
Allergen Bronchial Provocation Tests see Bronchial
   Provocation Tests
Allergen Immunotherapy see Desensitization, Immunologic
Allergens   QW 900
Allergic Angiitis see Churg-Strauss Syndrome
Allergic Conjunctivitis see Conjunctivitis, Allergic
Allergic Cutaneous Angiitis see Vasculitis, Allergic Cutaneous
Allergic Cutaneous Vasculitis see Vasculitis, Allergic Cutaneous
Allergic Diseases see Hypersensitivity
Allergic Granulomatous Angiitis see Churg-Strauss Syndrome
Allergy see Hypersensitivity
Allergy and Immunology   QW 501–949
   Animals   SF 757.2
      Individual, by animal in   QL or SF
   Biography of immunologists
      Collective   WZ 112.5.I5
      Individual   WZ 100
   Directories   QW 522
   Military bacteriology, etc.   UH 450–455
   Nursing texts   QW 504, etc.

Transplantation see Transplantation Immunology
WO 680
Associated with a particular disease, with the
disease
Allergy (Specialty) see Allergy and Immunology
Allied Health Occupations   W 21.5
Allied Health Personnel   W 21.5
Directories
General   W 22
Special types of personnel, in the directory
number for the specialty involved
Education   W 18
Alligators and Crocodiles   QL 666.C925
Diseases   SF 997.5.R4
Allium
As a medicinal plant   QV 766
Botany   QK 495.L72
As a dietary supplement in health and disease
WB 430
Allium sativum see Garlic
Alloantibodies see Isoantibodies
Alloantigens see Isoantigens
Allograft see Transplantation, Homologous
Allograft Dressings see Biological Dressings
Allosteric Regulation   QU 34
Special topics, by subject
Allosteric Site   QU 34
Allotypes, Immunoglobulin see Immunoglobulin
Allotypes
Allotypic Antibodies see Immunoglobulin Allotypes
Allowing to Die see Euthanasia, Passive
Alloxan Diabetes see Diabetes Mellitus,
Experimental
Alloys
Analysis   QD 133–137
Dental applications   WU 180
Particular applications, by subject, e.g. used in
orthopedics,   WE 26, WE 172, etc.
Almanacs   AY 30–1730
Aloe
As a medicinal plant   QV 766
As a cathartic   QV 75
Alopecia   WR 460
Alopecia, Androgenetic see Alopecia
Alopecia, Male Pattern see Alopecia
Alpacas see Camelids, New World
Alpers Syndrome see Cerebral Sclerosis, Diffuse
alpha-Adrenergic Blocking Agents see Adrenergic
alpha-Antagonists
alpha Adrenergic Receptor Agonists see Adrenergic
alpha-Agonists
alpha-Adrenergic Receptor Blockaders see
Adrenergic alpha-Antagonists
alpha-Adrenergic Receptors see Receptors,
Adrenergic, alpha
alpha-Aminotoluene see Benzylamines
alpha-Blockers, Adrenergic see Adrenergic
alpha-Antagonists
alpha-Cell Tumor see Glucagonoma
alpha Fetoproteins   WQ 210.5
alpha-Glucosidases   QU 136
alpha-Heparin see Heparin
alpha-Hypophamine see Oxytocin

alpha Immunoglobulins see Immunoglobulins,
alpha-Chain
Alpha Particles   WN 110
In nuclear physics (General)   QC
793.5.A22–793.5.A229
Specific topics, by subject, e.g., of radioisotopes
WN 420
Alpha Rays see Alpha Particles
Alpha Rhythm   WL 150
alpha-Trichosanthin see Trichosanthin
alpha 1-Acid Glycoprotein see Orosomucoid
alpha 1-Acid Seromucoid see Orosomucoid
alpha 1-Antitrypsin   WH 400
As an enzyme inhibitor   QU 143
alpha 1-Protease Inhibitor see alpha 1-Antitrypsin
alpha 1-Proteinase Inhibitor see alpha 1-Antitrypsin
Alphamethyldopa see Methyldopa
Alport's Syndrome see Nephritis, Hereditary
Alprenolol   QV 132
Alprostadil   QU 90
Alteplase   QU 142
Alternative Medicine   WB 890–962
Cupping   WB 371
Directories   WB 22
Alternatives to Animal Testing see Animal Testing
Alternatives
Altitude
Physiological effects   WD 710–715
Altitude Sickness   WD 715
Altruism   BJ 1474
Special topics, by subject
Aluminosis see Pneumoconiosis
Aluminum
Inorganic chemistry   QD 181.A4
Pharmacology   QV 65
Aluminum Hydroxide
As an antacid   QV 69
Aluminum Hydroxide Gel see Aluminum Hydroxide
Aluminum Silicates
Inorganic chemistry   QD 181.S6
Pharmacology   QV 65
Aluminum Sucrose Sulfate see Sucralfate
Alveolar Abscess, Apical see Periapical Abscess
Alveolar Bone Loss   WU 240
Alveolar Echinococcis, Hepatic see Echinococcosis,
Hepatic
Alveolar Lavage Fluid see Bronchoalveolar Lavage
Fluid
Alveolar Nerve, Inferior see Mandibular Nerve
Alveolar Process   WU 240
Alveolar Resorption see Alveolar Bone Loss
Alveolar Ridge Augmentation   WU 600
Alveolitis, Fibrosing see Pulmonary Fibrosis
Alzheimer's Disease   WT 155
Amalgam Filling see Dental Amalgam
Amanita   QW 180.5.B2
Amanitz see Agaricales
Amaurosis see Blindness
Amaurotic Familial Idiocy see Lipoidosis
Ambidexterity see Laterality
Amblyopia   WW 276
Toxic   WW 276
Amblystoma see Ambystoma

Amboceptor see Bacteriolysis; Hemolysins
Ambulances   WX 215
    Military   UH 500-505
Ambulatory Care
    General   WB 101
    In hospitals   WX 205
    In infancy & childhood   WS 200
        Clinics   WS 27-28
    Nursing   WY 150
        Pediatric nursing   WY 159
    Of a patient with a particular disease, with the
      disease
Ambulatory Care Facilities   WX 205
Ambulatory Care Facilities, Hospital see Outpatient
    Clinics, Hospital
Ambulatory Care Information Systems   WX 26.5
Ambulatory Electrocardiography see
    Electrocardiography, Ambulatory
Ambulatory Surgery   WO 192
    Of particular parts, by subject
Ambystoma   QL 668.C23
    As laboratory animals   QY 60.A6
Ambystoma mexicanum   QL 668.C23
    As laboratory animals   QY 60.A6
    Diseases   SF 997.5.A45
Ameba see Amoeba
Amebiasis   WC 285
Amebiasis, Hepatic see Liver Abscess, Amebic
Amebiasis, Intestinal see Dysentery, Amebic
Amebic Dysentery see Dysentery, Amebic
Amebicides   QV 255
Ameboma see Amebiasis
Ameloblastoma   WU 280
Amenorrhea   WP 552
Americana see Books
Americium   WN 420
    Nuclear physics   QC 796.A5
    See also special topics under Radioisotopes
Amerinds, Central American see Indians, Central
    American
Amerinds, North American see Indians, North
    American
Amerinds, South American see Indians, South
    American
Amethocaine see Tetracaine
Amethopterin see Methotrexate
Ametropia see Refractive Errors
Amidases see Amidohydrolases
Amidazine see Ethionamide
Amides   QU 62
    Organic chemistry
        Aliphatic compounds   QD 305.A7
        Aromatic compounds   QD 341.A7
Amidines   QU 61
    Organic chemistry   QD 305.A8
Amidohydrolases   QU 136
Amidone see Methadone
Amidophenazon see Aminopyrine
Amidotrezoate see Diatrizoate
Amifostine
    As a radiation-protective agent   WN 650
Amiloride   QV 160
Amine Oxidase (Copper-Containing)   QU 140

Amines   QU 61
    Organic chemistry
        Aliphatic compounds   QD 305.A8
        Aromatic compounds   QD 341.A8
Amines, Biogenic see Biogenic Amines
Amines, Sympathomimetic see Sympathomimetics
Amino Acid Decarboxylases, Aromatic see
    Aromatic Amino Acid Decarboxylases
Amino Acid Metabolism, Inborn Errors   WD
    205.5.A5
Amino Acid Oxidoreductases   QU 140
Amino Acid Sequence   QU 60
Amino Acids   QU 60
Amino Acids, Branched-Chain   QU 60
Amino Acids, Essential   QU 60
Amino Acids, Sulfur   QU 60
Amino Acyl tRNA see RNA, Transfer, Amino Acyl
Amino Alcohols
    Organic chemistry   QD 305.A4
    Pharmacology   QV 82
Amino Sugars   QU 75
Aminoaciduria, Renal   WJ 343
Aminobenzoic Acids   QU 195
Aminobutyrate Aminotransferase   QU 141
Aminobutyric Acids   QU 60
Aminocaproic Acids   QU 60
Aminocaproic Lactam see Caprolactam
Aminoethanols see Ethanolamines
Aminoform see Methenamine
Aminoglycoside Antibiotics see Antibiotics,
    Aminoglycoside
Aminoglycosides   QU 75
Aminohippuric Acids   QU 62
    Organic chemistry   QD 341.A7
Aminohydrolases   QU 136
Aminophenazone see Aminopyrine
Aminophenurobutane see Carbutamide
Aminopropanols see Propanolamines
Aminopropionitrile
    Organic chemistry
        Aliphatic compounds   QD 305.N7
    In plant poisoning   WD 500
Aminopyrine   QV 95
Aminosalicylic Acids   QV 268
Aminotransferases   QU 141
Amiodarone   QV 150
Ammoidin see Methoxsalen
Ammonia
    Detergent use   QV 233
    In nitrogen fixation
        Biochemistry (General)   QU 70
        Phytochemistry   QK 898.N6
        Plant and soil   QW 60
    Inorganic chemistry   QD 181.N1
Ammonia-Lyases   QU 139
Ammonium Chloride
    Inorganic chemistry   QD 181.N1
    Pharmacology   QV 280
Ammonium Compounds
    Chemical technology   TP 223
    Detergent use   QV 233
    Organic chemistry   QD 305.A8
    Quaternary see Tetraethylammonium Compounds

QV 132
See also names of specific compounds
Ammotherapy   WB 525
Amnesia   WM 173.7
Amniocentesis   WQ 209
Amnion
   Animal embryology   QL 975
   Human embryology   QS 645
   Obstetrics   WQ 210.5
Amniotic Fluid
   Animal embryology   QL 975
   Human embryology   QS 645
   Obstetrics   WQ 210.5
   See also Embolism, Amniotic Fluid   WQ 244
Amniotic Membrane Dressings see Biological
  Dressings
Amoeba   QX 55
Amoebiasis see Amebiasis
Amoxapine   QV 77.5
Amoxicillin   QV 354
Amphetamines   QV 102
   Dependence   WM 270
Amphibia   QL 640–669.3
   As laboratory animals   QY 60.A6
Amphibian Venoms   WD 400
Amphiuma see Urodela
Ampholines see Ampholyte Mixtures
Ampholyte Mixtures   QV 786
Ampicillin   QV 354
Ampicillin Pivaloyl Ester see Pivampicillin
Ampulla of Vater see Vater's Ampulla
Amputation   WE 170
Amputation Stumps   WE 172
Amputees   WE 172
   Psychology   BF 727.P57
     Child psychology   WS 105.5.H2
   Rehabilitation
     General and medical aspects   WE 172
     Of children   WS 368
     Of disabled soldiers   UB 360–366
     Sociological aspects
       Disabled workers   HD 7255–7256
       Vocational rehabilitation   HV 3018–3019
Amygdala see Amygdaloid Body
Amygdalin   QV 269
Amygdaloid Body   WL 314
Amygdaloside see Amygdalin
Amyl Nitrate   QV 156
Amylases   QU 136
   Pancreatic   WI 802
Amyloid P Component   WH 400
Amyloidosis   WD 205.5.A6
Amyoplasia Congenita see Arthrogryposis
Amyotonia Congenita   WE 550
Amyotrophic Lateral Sclerosis   WE 550
Anabolic Steroids   WK 150
   See also Metabolism   QU 120, etc.; names of
    anabolic steroids that are also synthetic
    androgens, e.g. Methandrostenolone   WJ 875
Anabolism see Metabolism
Anaerobic Bacteria see Bacteria, Anaerobic
Anaerobiosis   QU 120
Anal Drug Administration see Administration,

Rectal
Anal Fissure see Fissure in Ano
Anal Fistula see Rectal Fistula
Anal Gland see Anus
Anal Sphincter see Anus
Anal Stage   WS 105.5.P3
Anal Ulcer see Fissure in Ano
Analeptics   QV 101–107
Analgesia   WO 200
   In labor see Anesthesia Obstetrical   WO 450
   Muscle relaxants with   WO 297
   Preanesthetic medication   WO 234
   Veterinary   SF 914
Analgesia, Epidural   WO 305
Analgesia in Labor see Anesthesia, Obstetrical
Analgesia Tests see Pain Measurement
Analgesic Cutaneous Electrostimulation see
  Transcutaneous Electric Nerve Stimulation
Analgesics   QV 95
Analgesics, Addictive see Analgesics, Opioid
Analgesics, Anti–Inflammatory see
  Anti–Inflammatory Agents, Non–Steroidal
Analgesics, Narcotic see Analgesics, Opioid
Analgesics, Non–Narcotic   QV 95
Analgesics, Opioid   QV 89–92
   In preanesthetic medication   WO 234
Analgin see Dipyrone
Analogue Pain Scale see Pain Measurement
Analysis see Chemistry, Analytical; names of
  substances being analyzed
Analysis of Variance   QA 279
   Particular variables, by subject
Analytical Psychology see Psychoanalysis
Analyzers, Neural see Neural Analyzers
Anankastic Personality see Compulsive Personality
  Disorder
Anaphylatoxins   QU 68
   In complement activation   QW 680
Anaphylaxis   QW 900
Anaplasma   QW 150
Anaplasmosis   WC 600
   Veterinary   SF 967.A6
Anarthria see Speech Disorders
Anastomosis, Arteriovenous see Arteriovenous
  Anastomosis
Anastomosis, Surgical
   In surgery for a particular condition, with the
   condition
Anatomic Models see Models, Anatomic
Anatomists see Biography   WZ 112, etc., and
  Directories   QS 22 under Anatomy
Anatomy   QS
   Adrenal glands   WK 701
   Bacterial   QW 51
   Cardiovascular system   WG 101
   Directories   QS 22
   Domestic animals   SF 761–767
   Ear   WV 201
   Eye   WW 101
   Fetus   WQ 210.5
   Gastrointestinal system   WI 101
   Gynecology   WP 101
   Heart   WG 201

**ALWAYS CONSULT MAIN SCHEDULES. USE NUMBER ASSIGNED ONLY WHEN
SUBJECT REPRESENTS MAJOR EMPHASIS OF WORK BEING CLASSIFIED**

Islands of Langerhans   WK 801
Kidney   WI 301
Larynx   WV 501
Male genitalia   WJ 701
Musculoskeletal system   WE 101
Nervous system   WL 101
Nose   WV 301
Nursing texts   QS 4, etc.
Otolaryngology   WV 101
Pathological (General)   QZ
Pharyngeal region   WV 401
Pituitary gland   WK 501
Respiratory system   WF 101
Skin   WR 101
Stomach   WI 301
Surgical   WO 101
Tooth   WU 101
Thyroid gland   WK 201
Urogenital system   WJ 101
Wild animals   QL 801–950.9
    See also names of specific animals
Other organs or systems, in the general number
    for the organ or system
Anatomy, Artistic   NC 760–783.8
Anatomy, Comparative
    Animals only   QL 801–950.9
    Human and animals   QS 124
Anatomy, Regional   QS 4
    For surgeons   WO 101
Anatomy, Veterinary   SF 761–767
    See also Anatomy, Comparative   QL 801–950.9,
    etc.
Anatoxins see Toxoids
Anavar see Oxandrolone
Anchored PCR see Polymerase Chain Reaction
Ancillary Information Systems see Information
    Systems
Ancillary Services, Hospital   WX 162
    Specific topics, by subject
Ancrod
    As an anticoagulant   QV 193
    Biochemistry   QU 136
Ancylostoma   QX 243
Ancylostoma caninum see Ancylostoma
Ancylostoma duodenale see Ancylostoma
Ancylostomatoidea   QX 243
Ancylostomiasis   WC 890
Andresen Appliance see Activator Appliances
Androblastoma   WP 322
Androgen Analogs see Androgens, Synthetic
Androgen Antagonists   WJ 875
Androgens   WJ 875
Androgens, Synthetic   WJ 875
Andrology see Urology
Androstenedione   WJ 875
Anecdotes   PN 6259–6268
    Medicine, medical specialties and related fields
    WZ 305–305.5
Anemia   WH 155–175
    Cooley's see Thalassemia   WH 170
    Erythroblastic see Thalassemia   WH 170
    In pregnancy   WQ 252
    Megaloblastic see Anemia, Macrocytic   WH 165

    Miners' see Hookworm Infections   WC 890, etc.
    Osteosclerotic see Anemia, Myelophthisic   WH
    175
    Tunnel see Ancylostomiasis   WC 890
    Specific named types not listed here, see for
    example: Hemoglobinuria   WJ 344
    Veterinary (General)   SF 769.5
Anemia, Addison's see Anemia, Pernicious
Anemia, Aplastic   WH 175
Anemia, Diamond-Blackfan see Fanconi's Anemia
Anemia, Fanconi see Fanconi's Anemia
Anemia, Hemolytic   WH 170
    See also Favism   WD 515; Hemoglobinuria
    WJ 344 and other special topics
Anemia, Hemolytic, Acquired see Anemia,
    Hemolytic
Anemia, Hemolytic, Autoimmune   WH 170
Anemia, Hemolytic, Congenital   WH 170
Anemia, Hemolytic, Idiopathic Acquired see
    Anemia, Hemolytic, Autoimmune
Anemia, Hypochromic   WH 160
Anemia, Hypoplastic see Anemia, Aplastic
Anemia, Hypoplastic, Congenital see Fanconi's
    Anemia
Anemia, Iron-Deficiency   WH 160
Anemia, Leukoerythroblastic see Anemia,
    Myelophthisic
Anemia, Macrocytic   WH 165
Anemia, Megaloblastic   WH 165
Anemia, Microangiopathic see Anemia, Hemolytic
Anemia, Myelophthisic   WH 175
Anemia, Neonatal   WS 421
Anemia, Pernicious   WH 165
Anemia, Sickle Cell   WH 170
Anemia, Splenic see Hypersplenism
Anencephaly   QS 675
Anesthesia   WO 200–460
    Adverse effects   WO 245
    Cardiac problems   WG 460
        Written for the anesthesiologist   WO 245
    Choice of   WO 235
    Drugs producing see Anesthetics   QV 81, etc.;
        Anesthetics, Local   QV 110–115
    In old age   WO 445
    In infancy & childhood   WO 440
    In pregnancy see Anesthesia, Obstetrical   WO
    450
    Nurses administering see Nurse anesthetists   WY
    151
    Of laboratory animals   QY 58
    Veterinary   SF 914
    See also the specialty Anesthesiology   WO
    200–222
Anesthesia Adjuvants   QV 81
Anesthesia Assistants see Physician Assistants
Anesthesia, Caudal   WO 305
Anesthesia, Closed-Circuit   WO 277
Anesthesia, Conduction   WO 300–340
Anesthesia, Dental   WO 460
Anesthesia Department, Hospital   WO 27–28
Anesthesia, Electric see Electronarcosis
Anesthesia, Epidural   WO 305
Anesthesia, Extradural see Anesthesia, Epidural

Anesthesia, General   WO 275
Anesthesia, Inhalation   WO 277
Anesthesia, Intratracheal   WO 280
Anesthesia, Intravenous   WO 285
Anesthesia, Local   WO 300
    Infiltration anesthesia   WO 340
    Surface anesthesia   WO 340
    Topical anesthesia   WO 340
Anesthesia, Obstetrical   WO 450
Anesthesia, Peridural see Anesthesia, Epidural
Anesthesia, Rebreathing see Anesthesia,
    Closed–Circuit
Anesthesia Recovery Period   WO 183
Anesthesia, Rectal   WO 290
Anesthesia, Refrigeration see Hypothermia, Induced
Anesthesia, Regional see Anesthesia, Conduction
Anesthesia, Sacral Epidural see Anesthesia, Caudal
Anesthesia, Spinal   WO 305
Anesthesiology   WO 200–460
    Children and other special groups see In infancy
      & childhood, etc. under Anesthesia
Anesthetics   QV 81
    Diagnostic use   WO 375
    Therapeutic use   WO 375
    Topical see Anesthetics, Local   QV 115
    See also Analgesics   QV 95, etc.
Anesthetics, Conduction Blocking see Anesthetics,
    Local
Anesthetics, Local   QV 110–115
    Synthetic   QV 115
Anestrus   SF 105
Aneuploidy   QH 461
Aneurin see Thiamine
Aneurysm   WG 580
    Aortic see Aortic Aneurysm   WG 410
    Arteriovenous see Arteriovenous Fistula   WG
      590
    Cardiac see Heart Aneurysm   WG 300
    Cerebral see Cerebral Aneurysm   WL 354–355
    See also Bone Cyst
Aneurysm, Arteriovenous see Arteriovenous Fistula
Aneurysm, Bacterial see Aneurysm, Infected
Aneurysm, Infected   WG 580
Aneurysm, Mycotic see Aneurysm, Infected
ANF see Atrial Natriuretic Factor
Angel Dust Abuse see Phencyclidine Abuse
Anger   BF 575.A5
    In adolescence   WS 462
    In infancy & childhood   WS 105.5.E5
Angiitis see Vasculitis
Angiitis, Allergic Cutaneous see Vasculitis, Allergic
    Cutaneous
Angiitis, Allergic Granulomatous see Churg–Strauss
    Syndrome
Angina Pectoris   WG 298
Angina Pectoris, Variant   WG 298
Angina, Preinfarction see Angina, Unstable
Angina, Unstable   WG 298
Angiocardiography   WG 141.5.A3
Angioedema see Angioneurotic Edema
Angiogenesis see Neovascularization
Angiogenesis Factor
    As a growth substance   QU 107

    In mitosis   QH 605.2
Angiography   WG 500
    Cerebral   WL 141
    Veterinary   SF 757.8
    Other specific organ or system, by site
Angiography, Cerebral see Cerebral Angiography
Angiohemophilia see von Willebrand's Disease
Angioid Streaks   WW 270
    As a manifestation of diseases   WW 475
Angioimmunoblastic Lymphadenopathy see
    Immunoblastic Lymphadenopathy
Angiokeratoma   WR 500
Angioma see Hemangioma
Angiomatosis   QZ 340
    Localized, by site, in the neoplasm number if
      available
Angioneurotic Edema   WR 170
Angioplasty, Balloon   WG 166.5.B2
    In the treatment of arterial occlusive diseases
      WG 510
Angioplasty, Balloon, Coronary see Angioplasty,
    Transluminal, Percutaneous Coronary
Angioplasty, Coronary Balloon see Angioplasty,
    Transluminal, Percutaneous Coronary
Angioplasty, Laser   WG 166.5.A5
Angioplasty, Transluminal see Angioplasty, Balloon
Angioplasty, Transluminal, Percutaneous Coronary
    WG 300
Angiotensin see Angiotensin II
Angiotensin Binding Sites see Receptors,
    Angiotensin
Angiotensin–Converting Enzyme Inhibitors
    As antihypertensive agents   QV 150
    As protease inhitors   QU 136
Angiotensin–Forming Enzyme see Renin
Angiotensin II   QU 68
Angiotensin Receptors see Receptors, Angiotensin
Angiotensinogen   QU 68
Angiotensinogenase see Renin
Angiotensins   QU 68
Angor Pectoris see Angina Pectoris
Anguilluliasis see Strongyloidiasis
Anhidrosis see Hypohidrosis
Anhidrotic Ectodermal Dysplasia see Ectodermal
    Dysplasia
Anhydrides
    Organic chemistry
      Aliphatic compounds   QD 305.A2
      Aromatic compounds   QD 341.A2
    Used for special purposes, by subject, e.g., for
      radiolabeling of proteins   QU 55
Aniline Compounds
    Organic chemistry   QD 341.A8
    Toxicology   QV 632
Animal–Borne Diseases see Zoonoses
Animal Care Committees see Animal Welfare
Animal Communication
    General   QL 776
Animal Culture see Animal Husbandry
Animal Diseases   SF 600–1100
    See also Zoonoses   WC 950
Animal Feed   SF 95–99
Animal Hospitals see Hospitals, Animal

Animal–Human Bonding see Bonding, Human–Pet
Animal Husbandry   SF 1–597
   Waste disposal   WA 778–785
Animal Identification Systems   QL 60.5
Animal Magnetism see Hypnosis; Mental Healing
Animal Nutrition   SF 95–99
Animal Parasites see Parasites
Animal Poisons see Animals, Poisonous; Fishes, Poisonous
Animal Testing Alternatives   W 20.55.A5
   Special topics, by subject
Animal Viruses see Viruses
Animal Vocalization see Vocalization, Animal
Animal Welfare
   Laboratory animals   QY 54
   Other Animals   HV 4701–4959
Animals
   Bites see Bites and stings and entries under it WD 400–430, etc.
   Clinical use see Animals, Laboratory   QY 50–60, etc.
   Inoculation see Veterinary   SF 757.2 under Vaccination
   Laboratory see Animals, Laboratory   QY 50–60, etc.
   Microbiology   QW 70
   Quarantine   SF 740
     General works   SF 740
     By country   SF 621–723
   Wounds by   WO 700
Animals, Domestic   SF
   Anatomy and physiology   SF 761–768.2
   Culture   SF 1–597
   Diseases   SF 600–1100
   Laboratory see Animals, Laboratory   QY 50–60
   See also Animals
Animals, Infancy of see Animals, Newborn
Animals, Laboratory   QY 50–60
   Domestic
     Anatomy and physiology   SF 761–768.2
     Care and breeding   QY 54
     Diseases   SF 996.5
     See also names of specific animals or groups of animals
   Wild
     Anatomy   QL 801–950.9
     Care and breeding   QY 54
     Diseases   SF 996.5
     Physiology   QP
     See also names of specific animals or groups of animals
Animals, Newborn
   Animal behavior   QL 751
   Developmental behavior   QL 763–763.2
   Popular works   QL 50
Animals, Nondomestic see Animals, Wild
Animals, Poisonous   WD 400–430
Animals, Suckling
   As laboratory animals   QY 60.M2
   Diseases   SF 600–1100
   Domestic   SF
   Wild   QL 700–739.8

Animals, Transgenic
   As laboratory animals   QY 50
   Genetics   QH 442.6
Animals, Wild
   Anatomy   QL 801–950.9
   Diseases   SF 996.35–996.45
   Laboratory see Animals, Laboratory
   Physiology   QP
Animals, Zoo   QL 77.5
   Diseases   SF 996
   See also names of individual animals
Anion Gap see Acid–Base Equilibrium
Anion Transport Protein, Erythrocyte see Band 3 Protein
Anions   QV 280–285
Aniseikonia   WW 300
Anisoles
   Organic chemistry   QD 341.E7
   Toxicology   QV 632
Anisometropia   WW 300
Ankle   WE 880–883
Ankle Injuries   WE 880
Ankle Joint   WE 880
Ankylosis   WE 346
   Veterinary   SF 901
   Localized, by site
Annelida   QX 451
Anniversaries and Special Events
   Medical, dental, pharmaceutical, etc. (General)   WZ 332
   Specific occasions, by subject
Anniversary Reaction see Adjustment Disorders
Annual Implementation Plans see Regional Health Planning
Anoci–Association see Preanesthetic Medication
Anode see Electrodes
Anodontia   WU 101.5
Anodynes see Analgesics
Anomalies see Abnormalities
Anomie   HM 291
Anonyms and Pseudonyms   Z 1041–1121
Anopheles   QX 515
Anoplura   QX 502
Anorectics see Appetite Depressants
Anorexia   WI 143
   See also Anorexia Nervosa
Anorexia Nervosa   WM 175
Anosmia   WV 301
ANOVA see Analysis of Variance
Anovulation   WP 540
Anoxemia   WF 143
   Associated with high altitude   WD 715
   Associated with high atmospheric pressure   WD 655
Anoxia   WF 143
   Altitude see Altitude Sickness   WD 715
   Cerebral see Cerebral Anoxia   WL 355
   Fetal see Fetal Anoxia   WQ 211
   Submarine medicine   WD 655
Anoxia, Cellular see Cell Hypoxia
Anoxia, Fetal see Fetal Anoxia
ANP see Atrial Natriuretic Factor
Ant Venoms   WD 430

Antacids   QV 69
Antagonism of Drugs see Drug Antagonism
Antagonists see Names of substances affected, e.g.,
    Hormone Antagonists
Anterior Chamber   WW 210
Anterior Chamber Epithelium see Endothelium,
    Corneal
Anterior Cruciate Ligament   WE 870
Anterior Eye Segment   WW 210
Anterior Lobe Hormones see Pituitary Hormones,
    Anterior
Anterior Perforated Substance see Olfactory
    Pathways
Anthelmintics   QV 253
Anthemorrhagics see Hemostatics
Anthocyanins   QU 75
Anthracenediones see Anthraquinones
Anthracenes
    As carcinogens   QZ 202
    As cathartics   QV 75
Anthracosilicosis   WF 654
Anthracosis see Anthracosilicosis; Pneumoconiosis
Anthracycline Antibiotics see Antibiotics,
    Anthracycline
Anthralin
    Pharmacology   QV 60
Anthraquinones   QV 240
    Organic chemistry   QD 393
Anthrax   WC 305
    Veterinary   SF 787
Anthropoidea see Haplorhini
Anthropology   GN
    Criminal   HV 6035-6197
    Parapsychology   BF 1045.A65
    Psychological   GN 502-517
Anthropology, Cultural   GN 307-673
    See also Ethnopsychology   GN 270-279
Anthropology, Physical   GN 50.2-298
    Miscegenation   GN 254
    In marriage   HQ 1031
Anthropometry   GN 51-59
    Criminal see Anthropology   HV 6035-6197, etc.
Anthroposophy
    Philosophy   BP 595-597
    Alternative medicine   WB 903
Anti-Antibodies see Antibodies, Anti-Idiotypic
Anti-Anxiety Agents   QV 77.9
Anti-Anxiety Agents, Benzodiazepine   QV 77.9
Anti-Arrhythmia Agents   QV 150
Anti-DNA Antibodies see Antibodies, Antinuclear
Anti-HIV Positive see HIV Seropositivity
Anti-Human Globulin Complement-Dependent
    Cytotoxicity Tests see Cytotoxicity Tests,
    Immunologic
Anti-Human Globulin Consumption Test see
    Coombs' Test
Anti-Idiotype Antibodies see Antibodies,
    Anti-Idiotypic
Anti-Infective Agents   QV 250-268.5
Anti-Infective Agents, Local   QV 220-239
    Oxidizing antiseptics   QV 229
Anti-Infective Agents, Quinolone   QV 250
Anti-Infective Agents, Urinary   QV 243

Anti-Inflammatory Agents   QV 247
Anti-Inflammatory Agents, Gold see Antirheumatic
    Agents, Gold
Anti-Inflammatory Agents, Non-Steroidal   QV 95
Anti-Inflammatory Agents, Steroidal   QV 247
Anti-Inflammatory Agents, Topical   QV 60
Anti-Rheumatic Agents, Non-Steroidal see
    Anti-Inflammatory Agents, Non-Steroidal
Anti-Rheumatic Agents, Steroidal see
    Anti-Inflammatory Agents, Steroidal
Anti-Ulcer Agents   QV 69
Antiadrenergic Agents see Adrenergic Antagonists
Antiaggregants, Platelet see Platelet Aggregation
    Inhibitors
Antiandrogens see Androgen Antagonists
Antibiotic Resistance see Drug Resistance, Microbial
Antibiotics   QV 350-360
    See also specific types of antibiotics
Antibiotics, Aminoglycoside   QV 350
Antibiotics, Anthracycline   QV 269
Antibiotics, Antifungal   QV 252
Antibiotics, Antineoplastic
    Pharmacology   QV 269
    Therapeutic use   QZ 267
Antibiotics, Antitubercular
    Pharmacology   QV 268
    Therapeutic use   WF 360
Antibiotics, beta-Lactam see Antibiotics, Lactam
Antibiotics, Glycoside see Antibiotics,
    Aminoglycoside
Antibiotics, Lactam   QV 350
Antibodies   QW 575
    See also Antigen-Antibody reactions   QW 570
Antibodies, Allotypic see Immunoglobulin Allotypes
Antibodies, Anti-DNA see Antibodies, Antinuclear
Antibodies, Anti-Idiotypic   QW 575
Antibodies, Antinuclear   QW 575
Antibodies, Bacterial   QW 575
Antibodies, Heterogenetic see Antibodies,
    Heterophile
Antibodies, Heterophile   QW 575
Antibodies, Heterotypic see Antibodies, Heterophile
Antibodies, Monoclonal   QW 575.5.A6
Antibodies, Neoplasm   QW 575
    Neoplastic pathogenesis   QZ 202
Antibodies, Viral   QW 575
Antibodies, Xenogeneic see Antibodies, Heterophile
Antibody Affinity   QW 570
Antibody Avidity see Antibody Affinity
Antibody Binding Sites see Binding Sites, Antibody
Antibody Deficiency Syndrome see Immunologic
    Deficiency Syndromes
Antibody-Dependent Cell Cytotoxicity   QW 568
Antibody Diversity   QW 575
    Immunogenetic aspects   QW 541
Antibody Enzyme Technique, Unlabeled see
    Immunoenzyme Techniques
Antibody Formation   QW 575
Antibody-Producing Cells   QW 575
Antibody-Secreting Cells see Antibody-Producing
    Cells
Antibody Specificity   QW 570
Antibody-Toxin Conjugates see Immunotoxins

**ALWAYS CONSULT MAIN SCHEDULES. USE NUMBER ASSIGNED ONLY WHEN
SUBJECT REPRESENTS MAJOR EMPHASIS OF WORK BEING CLASSIFIED**

I-16

Antibody-Toxin Hybrids see Immunotoxins
Anticancer Drug Combinations see Antineoplastic
  Agents, Combined
Anticancer Drug Sensitivity Tests see Drug
  Screening Assays, Antitumor
Anticestodal Agents QV 253
Anticholesteremic Agents QU 95
Anticholinergic Agents see Cholinergic Antagonists
Anticholinesterase Agents see Cholinesterase
  Inhibitors
Anticoagulants QV 193
Anticonvulsants QV 85
Antidepressants see Antidepressive Agents
Antidepressive Agents QV 77.5
Antidiabetics see Hypoglycemic Agents; Insulin
Antidiarrheals QV 71
Antidiuretic Hormones see Vasopressins
Antidiuretics see Vasopressins
Antidotes QV 601
    Lists QV 605
    For a particular poison, with the poison
Antidromic Potentials see Evoked Potentials
Antiemetics QV 73
Antiepileptic Agents see Anticonvulsants
Antiestrogens see Estrogen Antagonists
Antifibrillatory Agents see Anti-Arrhythmia Agents
Antifibrinolysins see Antifibrinolytic Agents
Antifibrinolytic Agents QV 195
Antifungal Agents QV 252
    See also Antibiotics, Antifungal QV 252;
    Fungicides, Industrial SB 951.3
Antigamma Globulin Antibodies see Antibodies,
  Anti-Idiotypic
Antigen-Antibody Reactions QW 570
Antigen Bronchial Provocation Tests see Bronchial
  Provocation Tests
Antigen-Presenting Cells QW 568
Antigen Receptors see Receptors, Antigen
Antigen Receptors, T-Cell see Receptors, Antigen,
  T-Cell
Antigenic Determinants QW 573
    Special topics, by subject
Antigenic Specificity see Antigenic Determinants
Antigens QW 573
    In histocompatibility WO 680
Antigens, Bacterial QW 573
Antigens, Carbohydrate, Tumor-Associated see
  Antigens, Tumor-Associated, Carbohydrate
Antigens, CD QW 573
Antigens, CD25 see Receptors, Interleukin-2
Antigens, CD4 QW 573
Antigens, Differentiation QW 573
Antigens, Differentiation, B-Cell see Antigens,
  Differentiation, B-Lymphocyte
Antigens, Differentiation, B-Lymphocyte QW 573
Antigens, Fungal QW 573
Antigens, Helminth QW 573
Antigens, HLA-D see HLA-D Antigens
Antigens, Immune Response see Histocompatibility
  Antigens Class II
Antigens, Neoplasm QW 573
    Neoplasm etiology QZ 202
    Neoplasm research QZ 206

Antigens, Neoplasm, Viral see Antigens, Viral,
  Tumor
Antigens, Surface QW 573
Antigens, Synthetic see Vaccines, Synthetic
Antigens, Tumor-Associated, Carbohydrate QW
  573
Antigens, Viral QW 573
Antigens, Viral, Tumor QW 573
    Neoplasm etiology QZ 202
Antiglobulin Consumption Test see Coombs' Test
Antiglobulin Test see Coombs' Test
Antiglobulins see Antibodies, Anti-Idiotypic
Antigout Agents see Gout Suppressants
Antihistamines, Classical see Histamine H1
  Antagonists
Antihistaminics, Classical see Histamine H1
  Antagonists
Antihistaminics, H1 see Histamine H1 Antagonists
Antihistaminics, H2 see Histamine H2 Antagonists
Antihypertensive Agents QV 150
Antileprotic Agents see Leprostatic Agents
Antilipemic Agents QU 85
Antiluetics see Syphilis
Antilymphoblast Globulins see Antilymphocyte
  Serum
Antilymphocyte Antibodies see Antilymphocyte
  Serum
Antilymphocyte Globulin see Antilymphocyte
  Serum
Antilymphocyte Serum QW 815
    Immunosuppressive agent QW 920
Antimalarials QV 256-258
Antimetabolites QV 38
    See also names of specific antimetabolites
Antimetabolites, Antineoplastic QV 269
    Therapeutic use QZ 267
Antimitotic Agents see Antineoplastic Agents
Antimony QV 295
Antimony Potassium Tartrate QV 253
    As an emetic QV 73
Antimuscarinic Agents see Muscarinic Antagonists
Antimycin A QV 252
Antineoplastic Agents QV 269
    Therapeutic use QZ 267
    See also Antibiotics, Antineoplastic QV 269
Antineoplastic Agents, Combined QV 269
    Therapeutic use QZ 267
Antineoplastic Agents, Phytogenic QV 269
    Therapeutic use QZ 267
Antineoplastic Drug Combinations see
  Antineoplastic Agents, Combined
Antineoplastics, Botanical see Antineoplastic Agents,
  Phytogenic
Antinociceptive Agents see Analgesics
Antinuclear Antibodies see Antibodies, Antinuclear
Antinuclear Antibody Test, Fluorescent see
  Fluorescent Antibody Technique
Antinuclear Factors see Antibodies, Antinuclear
Antioncogenes see Genes, Suppressor, Tumor
Antioxidants
    As a pharmaceutic aid QV 800
    In food preservation WA 710-712
Antiparkinson Agents QV 80

See also Levodopa   WK 725
Antiperspirants see Astringents
Antiplasmins see Antifibrinolytic Agents
Antiplatelet Agents see Platelet Aggregation
    Inhibitors
Antiprotozoal Agents   QV 254–258
Antipruritics   QV 60
Antipsychotic Agents   QV 77.9
Antipsychotic Agents, Butyrophenone   QV 77.9
Antipsychotic Agents, Phenothiazine   QV 77.9
Antipyretics see Analgesics, Non–Narcotic
Antirejection Therapy see Immunosuppression
Antireticular Cytotoxic Serum   QW 815
Antirheumatic Agents   QV 247
Antirheumatic Agents, Gold   QV 247
Antisense DNA see DNA, Antisense
Antisense Elements (Genetics)   QU 57
Antisense Oligodeoxyribonucleotides see
    Oligonucleotides, Antisense
Antisense Oligonucleotides see Oligonucleotides,
    Antisense
Antisense Oligoribonucleotides see Oligonucleotides,
    Antisense
Antisense Probes see Antisense Elements (Genetics)
Antisense RNA see RNA, Antisense
Antisepsis
    Dental   WU 300
    In labor   WQ 400
    Public health aspects   WA 240
    Surgical   WO 113
Antiseptics see Anti–infective Agents, Local
Antiseptics, Urinary see Anti–Infective Agents,
    Urinary
Antisera see Immune Sera
Antiserotonergic Agents see Serotonin Antagonists
Antisickling Agents   QV 180
Antisocial Personality Disorder   WM 190
    In infancy & childhood   WS 350.8.P3
Antispasmodics see Parasympatholytics
Antisyphilitics see Syphilis
Antithrombin II see Antithrombin III
Antithrombin III   QV 193
Antithrombins   QV 193
Antithrombotic Agents see Fibrinolytic Agents
Antithyroid Drugs see Thyroid Antagonists
Antitoxins
    Immunology
        Immunizing agent   QW 805
        Pharmacology   QW 630
    Used for particular diseases, with the disease
    See also names of specific antitoxins
Antitrichomonal Agents   QV 254
Antitrust Laws
    (Form number 32–33 in any NLM schedule where
    applicable)
Antitrust Liability see Antitrust Laws
Antitubercular Agents
    Pharmacology   QV 268
    Therapeutic use   WF 360
    See also Antibiotics, Antitubercular   QV 268
Antitumor Drug Screening Assays see Drug
    Screening Assays, Antitumor
Antitussive Agents   QV 76

Antivenins
    Immunology
        Immunizing agent   QW 805
        Pharmacology   QW 630
    Therapy   WD 400–430
Antiviral Agents   QV 268.5
Antivivisection see Vivisection
Antrum of Highmore see Maxillary Sinus
Antrum, Pyloric see Pyloric Antrum
Ants   QX 565
Anura   QL 668.E2–668.E275
    As laboratory animals   QY 60.A6
    Diseases   SF 997.5.A45
Anuria   WJ 303
Anus   WI 600–650
Anus, Artificial see Colostomy
Anus Diseases   WI 600
Anus Neoplasms   WI 610
Anus Prolapse see Rectal Prolapse
Anxiety   WM 172
    In adolescence   WS 463
    In infancy & childhood   WS 350.6
    Neuroses see Neuroses, Anxiety   WM 172
Anxiety Disorders   WM 172
Anxiety Neuroses see Anxiety Disorders
Anxiety States, Neurotic see Anxiety Disorders
Anxiolytic Agents see Anti–Anxiety Agents
Anxiolytics, Benzodiazepine see Anti–Anxiety
    Agents, Benzodiazepine
Aorta   WG 410
Aorta, Abdominal   WG 410
Aorta, Ascending see Aorta
Aorta, Descending see Aorta, Thoracic
Aorta, Thoracic   WG 410
Aortic Aneurysm   WG 410
Aortic Arch see Aorta, Thoracic
Aortic Arch Syndromes   WG 410
Aortic Bodies   WL 600
Aortic Coarctation   WG 220
Aortic Incompetence see Aortic Valve Insufficiency
Aortic Regurgitation see Aortic Valve Insufficiency
Aortic Stenosis see Aortic Valve Stenosis
Aortic Stenosis, Supravalvular see Aortic Valve
    Stenosis
Aortic Valve   WG 265
Aortic Valve Incompetence see Aortic Valve
    Insufficiency
Aortic Valve Insufficiency   WG 265
Aortic Valve Stenosis   WG 265
Aorticopulmonary Septal Defect see
    Aortopulmonary Septal Defect
Aortitis   WG 410
Aortitis Syndrome see Aortic Arch Syndromes
Aortitis, Syphilitic see Syphilis, Cardiovascular
Aortocoronary Bypass see Coronary Artery Bypass
Aortography   WG 410
Aortopulmonary Septal Defect   WG 220
Aotus trivirgatus   QL 737.P925
    Diseases   SF 997.5.P7
    As laboratory animals   QY 60.P7
Apazone   QV 95
Ape, Barbary see Macaca
Ape, Black see Macaca

Ape, Celebes see Macaca
Apert Syndrome see Acrocephalosyndactylia
Apes see Pongidae
Apex Cardiography see Kinetocardiography
Aphakia   WW 260
Aphakia, Postcataract   WW 260
Aphaniptera see Fleas
Aphasia
    Neurologic   WL 340.5
    Psychogenic   WM 475.5
Aphasia, Acquired   WL 340.5
    Psychogenic   WM 475.5
Aphasia, Broca   WL 340.5
    Psychogenic   WM 475.5
Aphasia, Childhood   WL 340.5
    Psychogenic   WM 475.5
Aphasia, Expressive see Aphasia, Broca
Aphasia, Motor see Aphasia, Broca
Aphasia, Nonfluent see Aphasia, Broca
Aphasia Tests see Neuropsychological Tests
Aphemia see Aphasia
Apheresis see Blood Component Removal
Aphids   QX 503
    As vectors of plant virus diseases   SB 736
Aphonia
    Neurologic origin   WL 340.2
    Psychogenic origin   WM 475
Aphorisms and Proverbs   PN 6269–6278
    Medicine and related fields   WZ 309
Aphrodisiacs   QV 170
Aphthae see Stomatitis, Aphthous; Moniliasis, Oral
Aphthovirus   QW 168.5.P4
Apicoectomy   WU 230
Apis see Bees
Apis Venoms see Bee Venoms
Aplastic Anemia see Anemia, Aplastic
Aplysia   QX 675
Apnea   WF 143
Apnea, Central see Sleep Apnea Syndromes
Apnea, Obstructive see Sleep Apnea Syndromes
Apnea, Sleep see Sleep Apnea Syndromes
Apocrine Glands   WR 400
Apodemus see Muridae
Apomorphine   QV 73
Apoplexy see Cerebrovascular Disorders
Apothecaries see Pharmacies
Apparatus see Equipment and Supplies
Apparatus and Instruments see Equipment and Supplies
Appendectomy   WI 535
Appendiceal Neoplasms   WI 535
Appendicitis   WI 535
Appendix   WI 535
Appetite   WI 102
Appetite Depressants   QV 129
Appetite Disorders see Eating Disorders
Appetite Regulation   WI 102
Appetite Suppressants see Appetite Depressants
Appetitive Behavior   BF 685
    Animal aspects   QL 758–785
    Sex psychology   BF 692
Apple see Fruit

Appointments and Schedules
    In hospitals   WX 159
    Practice management
        Dental   WU 77
        Medical   W 80
        Nursing, by type, e.g. Private duty nursing   WY 127
Appropriateness Review see Regional Health Planning
Apraxia   WL 340
Apricot see Fruit
Aprotinin   QU 143
Aptitude Tests   BF 431–433
    In special fields, in the career number for the field, e.g., for dentistry   WU 21
APUD Cells   WL 102
Apudoma   QZ 200–380
    Localized, by site
Aqueous Humor   WW 210
Ara-A see Vidarabine
Ara-C see Cytarabine
Arabic Physicians see Physicians
Arabinofuranosyladenine see Vidarabine
Arabinofuranosylcytosine see Cytarabine
Arabinofuranosylnucleotides see Arabinonucleotides
Arabinonucleotides   QU 57
Arabinosyladenine see Vidarabine
Arabinosylcytosine see Cytarabine
Arachis see Peanuts
Arachnid Venoms see Spider Venoms
Arachnida   QX 467–483
Arachnidism   WD 420
Arachnoid   WL 200
Arachnoiditis   WL 200
Araneid Venoms see Spider Venoms
Arbovirus, Group B see Flavivirus
Arbovirus Infections   WC 524–532
    General works   WC 524
    See also Encephalitis, Epidemic   WC 542
Arboviruses   QW 168.5.A7
Archaebacteria see Archaeobacteria
Archaeobacteria   QW 50
Archaeology
    General   CC (entire schedule)
    Individual countries   D–F
    Prehistoric   GN 700–890
Architectural Accessibility
    In health facilities   WX 140
    Public health aspects   WA 795–799
    See also specific types of buildings, e.g., Drug Treatment Centers   WM 29–29.1, etc.
Architecture   NA
    Public health aspects   WA 795–799
    See also Design and Construction, Hospital   WX 140; Housing   WA 795, etc; types of particular buildings, e.g., Laboratories, Dental   WU 23–24
Archives   CD 931–4280
    Cataloging   Z 695.2
Arctic Regions
    Physiological effects and adaptation   QT 160
Arcus Senilis   WW 220
ARDS, Human see Respiratory Distress Syndrome,

Adult

Area Health Education Centers   W 19

Areawide Planning see Regional Health Planning

Areca
    As medicinal plant   QV 766
    Botany   QK 495.P17
    Culture   SB 317.P3

Arenaviridae   QW 168.5.A8

Arenaviridae Infections   WC 501

Arenavirus Infections see Arenaviridae Infections

Argentaffin Cells see Enterochromaffin Cells

Argentaffin System see Chromaffin System

Argentaffinoma see Carcinoid Tumor

Arginase   QU 136

Arginine   QU 60

Arginine Vasopressin see Argipressin

Argipressin   WK 520
    As an antidiuretic   QV 160

Argon
    Inorganic chemistry   QD 181.A6
    Pharmacology   QV 310

Argyria   WR 265

Arizona Bacteria see Salmonella arizonae

Arm   WE 805
    Artificial see Artificial Limbs   WE 172
    Upper arm   WE 810
    See also Forearm   WE 820

Arm Ergometry Test see Exercise Test

Arm Injuries   WE 805
    See also Forearm Injuries   WE 820

Armadillos   QL 737.E23
    As laboratory animals   QY 60.M2

Armed Forces Personnel see Military Personnel

Armpit see Axilla

Arnold–Chiari Deformity   WL 101

Aroclors
    As air pollutants   WA 754, etc.
    As water pollutants   WA 689
    Organic chemistry   QD 341.H9
    Toxicology (General)   QV 633

Aromatase   QU 140

Aromatic Amino Acid Decarboxylases   QU 139

Aromatic Compounds see Anti–Infective Agents,
    Local; Cresols; Phenols   QV 223, etc. and other
    compounds by name; Hydrocarbons; Polycyclic
    Hydrocarbons; Aromatic Compounds   QD
    330–341 under Chemistry, Organic

Arousal   WL 103
    Behaviorism   BF 199
    In infancy & childhood   WS 105.5.C7

Arrhenoblastoma see Androblastoma

Arrhythmia   WG 330

Arrhythmia, Sinus   WG 330

Arsenic   QV 294

Arsenicals   QU 143
    As amebicides   QV 255
    As antisyphilitic agents   QV 262

Arson see Firesetting Behavior

Arsphenamine   QV 262

Art   N
    Accidents in professional work   WA 487.5.A78
    Anatomy see Anatomy, Artistic   NC 760–783.8
    By physicians   WZ 350

Child study   WS 105.5.E8
    In psychotherapy see Art Therapy   WM
    450.5.A8
    Related to medicine see Medicine in Art   WZ
    330, etc.
    Related to psychiatry   WM 49
    See also Medical Illustration   WZ 348

Art Therapy   WM 450.5.A8
    In adolescence   WS 463
    In infancy & childhood   WS 350.2

Artemia   QX 463

Arterenol see Norepinephrine

Arterial Catheterization, Peripheral see
    Catheterization, Peripheral

Arterial Lines see Catheters, Indwelling

Arterial Obstructive Diseases see Arterial Occlusive
    Diseases

Arterial Occlusive Diseases   WG 510

Arteries   WG 510–595
    Coronary see Coronary Vessels   WG 300
    See also Aorta   WG 410

Arteriography see Angiography

Arteriosclerosis   WG 550
    Cerebral see Cerebral Arteriosclerosis   WL 355
    Veterinary   SF 811

Arteriosclerosis, Coronary see Coronary
    Arteriosclerosis

Arteriosclerosis Obliterans   WG 550

Arteriosclerotic Dementia see Dementia, Vascular

Arteriosclerotic Heart Disease see Coronary Disease

Arteriovenous Anastomosis   WG 590

Arteriovenous Aneurysm see Arteriovenous Fistula

Arteriovenous Fistula   WG 590
    Congenital see Arteriovenous Malformations
    WG 500

Arteriovenous Hemofiltration see Hemofiltration

Arteriovenous Malformations   WG 500
    Cerebral see Cerebral Arteriovenous
    malformations   WL 355

Arteriovenous Malformations, Cerebral see Cerebral
    Arteriovenous Malformations

Arteriovenous Shunt, Surgical   WG 170

Arteritis   WG 515
    Coronary   WG 300
    See also Endarteritis   WG 515; Periarteritis
    Nodossa   WG 518; Temporal Arteritis   WG
    510

Arteritis, Temporal see Temporal Arteritis

Arthritis   WE 344–348

Arthritis, Bacterial see Arthritis, Infectious

Arthritis, Degenerative see Osteoarthritis

Arthritis, Infectious   WE 344

Arthritis, Juvenile Chronic see Arthritis, Juvenile
    Rheumatoid

Arthritis, Juvenile Rheumatoid   WE 346

Arthritis, Rheumatic, Acute see Rheumatic Fever

Arthritis, Rheumatoid   WE 346

Arthritis, Septic see Arthritis, Infectious

Arthritis, Viral see Arthritis, Infectious

Arthroderma see Ascomycetes

Arthrodesis   WE 312
    Localized, by site

Arthrography   WE 300

Arthrogryposis   WE 300
Arthromyodysplasia, Congenital see Arthrogryposis
Arthropathy, Neurogenic   WE 344
Arthroplasty   WE 312
    Localized, by site
Arthroplasty, Replacement see Joint Prosthesis
Arthroplasty, Replacement, Hip see Hip Prosthesis
Arthroplasty, Replacement, Knee see Knee
    Prosthesis
Arthropod–Borne Viruses see Arboviruses
Arthropod Vectors   QX 460
    See also Insect vectors   QX 650
Arthropod Venoms   WD 400–430
Arthropods   QX 460–570
    Bites, stings and poisoning   WD 400–430
    Cause of skin diseases   WR 360–375
    Non–medical
        Paleozoology   QE 815–832
        Zoology   QL 434–599.82
    See also specific arthropods
Arthroscopy   WE 304
Arthus Phenomenon see Arthus Reaction
Arthus Reaction   QW 900
Artic Regions see Cold Climate
Articulation see Speech
Articulation Disorders
    Neurologic   WL 340.2
    Psychologic   WM 475
Articulators see Dental Articulators
Artificial Eye see Eye, Artificial
Artificial Fever see Hyperthermia, Induced
Artificial Heart see Heart, Artificial
Artificial Hibernation see Hibernation, Artificial
Artificial Insemination see Insemination, Artificial
Artificial Intelligence   Q 334–341
    In medicine (General)   W 26.55.A7
    In other special fields (Form number 26.5 in any
        NLM schedule where applicable)
    Used for special purposes, by subject
Artificial Kidney see Kidney, Artificial
Artificial Limbs   WE 172
Artificial Organs   WO 176
    Banks   WO 23–24
    See also names of specific artificial organs
Artificial Pneumothorax see Pneumothorax,
    Artificial
Artificial Respiration see Respiration, Artificial
Artificial Sweeteners see Sweetening Agents
Artificial Tears see Ophthalmic Solutions
Artificial Teeth see Dental Prosthesis; Denture,
    Partial; Denture, Complete; Tooth, Artificial
Artificial Ventricle see Heart–Assist Devices
Artiodactyla
    Diseases   SF 997.5.U5
    Wild   QL 737.U5–737.U595
Artistic Anatomy see Anatomy, Artistic
Arvicolinae see Microtinae
Arvicolines see Microtinae
Arvin see Ancrod
Arylsulfonates   QU 98
    Organic chemistry   QD 341.S3
As If Personality see Personality Disorders

Asbestos
    As a mineral   TN 930
    As air pollutant   WA 754
        In industry   WA 450
    Industrial wastes   WA 788
    Toxicology   QV 610
Asbestosis   WF 654
Ascariasis   WC 870
    Veterinary   SF 810.A5
Ascaridiasis   WC 870
Ascaridoidea   QX 277
Ascaris   QX 277
Ascaroidea see Ascaridoidea
Aschelminthes see Helminths
Ascites   WI 575
Ascites Shunt, Peritoneovenous see Peritoneovenous
    Shunt
Ascitic Fluid   WI 575
    Clinical analysis   QY 210
Ascomycetes   QW 180.5.A8
Ascorbic Acid   QU 210
Ascorbic Acid Deficiency   WD 140
Asepsis
    Dental   WU 300
    Surgical   WO 113
Asialia see Xerostomia
Asialoglycoproteins   QU 55
Asian Americans   E 184.O6
    Specific topics, by subject
    See also special topics under Ethnic Groups
Asiatic Race see Mongoloid Race
Asjike see Beriberi
ASPA Cement see Glass Ionomer Cements
Asparaginase   QV 269
    Enzymology   QU 136
Asparagine   QU 60
Aspartame   WA 712
    Peptides   QU 68
Aspartate Aminotransferase   QU 141
Aspartate Aminotransferase Isoenzymes see
    Aspartate Aminotransferase
Aspartate Aminotransferase Isozymes see Aspartate
    Aminotransferase
Aspartic Acid   QU 60
Aspartic Proteinases   QU 136
Aspartyl Proteinases see Aspartic Proteinases
Aspartylphenylalanine Methyl Ester see Aspartame
Aspergillosis   WC 450
    Veterinary   SF 809.A86
Aspergillus   QW 180.5.D38
Aspergillus flavus   QW 180.5.D38
Asphyxia   WO 250
    First aid   WA 292
Asphyxia Neonatorum   WQ 450
Aspiculariasis see Oxyuriasis
Aspidium   QV 253
Aspiration Biopsy see Biopsy, Needle
Aspiration Lipectomy see Lipectomy
Aspiration, Mechanical see Suction
Aspiration of Gastric Contents see Pneumonia,
    Aspiration
Aspiration, Pneumatic see Suction
Aspiration Pneumonia see Pneumonia, Aspiration

Aspirin   QV 95
Aspirin-Like Agents see Anti-Inflammatory Agents,
     Non-Steroidal
Asporogenous Rods, Gram-Positive see Bacteria
Assay see Biological Assay
Assertiveness
     Psychology
          In adolescence   WS 462
          In adulthood   BF 575.A85
          In infancy & childhood   WS 105.5.S6
     Social behavior disorders
          In adolescence   WS 463
          In adulthood   WM 600
          In infancy & childhood   WS 350.8.S6
Assessment, Educational see Educational
     Measurement
Assessment of Health Care Needs see Health
     Services Needs and Demand
Assimilation see Acculturation
Assimilation of Food see Metabolism
Assisted Circulation   WG 168
Associateship Practice, Dental see Partnership
     Practice, Dental
Association
     Free see Free Association   WM 460.5.F8
     Of ideas (psychology)   BF 365-395
     Word tests see Word Association Tests   WM
          145.5.W9, etc.
Association, Free see Free Association
Association Learning   BF 319.5.P34
Astasia-Abasia see Conversion Disorder
Asthenia   WB 146
     Neurocirculatory see Neurocirculatory Asthenia
          WG 320
     See also Neurasthenia   WM 174
Asthma
     Bronchial   WF 553
     Cardiac see Dyspnea, Paroxysmal   WG 370
Asthma, Bronchial see Asthma
Asthma, Cardiac see Dyspnea, Paroxysmal
Asthma, Exercise-Induced   WF 553
Asthmatic Crisis see Status Asthmaticus
Asthmatic Shock see Status Asthmaticus
Astigmatism   WW 310
Astringents   QV 65
Astrocytes   WL 102.5
Astrocytoma   QZ 380
     Localized, by site
Astrology   BF 1651-1729
     And birth control   BF 1729.B4
     And medicine   BF 1718
     And sex   BF 1729.S4
Astronauts, Physical Standards see Standards   WD
     752 under Space flight
Astronomy   QB
     General works   QB 42-43.2
Asylums, Insane see Hospitals, Psychiatric
Asystole see Heart Arrest
Atabrine see Quinacrine
Ataractics see Tranquilizing Agents
Ataxia   WL 390
     See also Cerebellar Ataxia   WL 320
Ataxia, Cerebellar see Cerebellar Ataxia

Ataxia, Locomotor see Tables Dorsalis
Atelectasis   WF 645
Atelectasis, Congestive see Respiratory Distress
     Syndrome, Adult
Ateles see Cebidae
Atelinae see Cebidae
Atenolol   QV 132
Atheroma see Atherosclerosis
Atherosclerosis   WG 550
Atherosclerosis, Coronary see Coronary
     Arteriosclerosis
Athetosis   WL 390
Athlete's Foot see Tinea Pedis
Athletic Injuries   QT 261
     First aid   WA 292
Athletics see Sports
Athymic Mice see Mice, Nude
Atlanto-Axial Joint   WE 725
Atlanto-Occipital Joint   WE 708
Atlas   WE 725
Atlases   G
     (Form number 17 in any NLM schedule where
          applicable)
     Embryology   QS 617
     Forensic medicine and dentistry   W 617
     Histology   QS 517
     Immunology   QW 517
     Operative dentistry   WU 317
     Oral surgery   WU 600.7
     Orthodontics   WU 417
     Pharmacy and pharmaceutics   QV 717
     Prosthodontics   WU 507
     Surgery   WO 517
Atloido-Occipital Joint see Atlanto-Occipital Joint
ATLV see HTLV-I
Atmosphere   QC 851-999
     Control   WA 750-776
          In industry   WA 450
          See also Environment, Controlled   WA 750,
               etc.
     Pollutants see Air pollutants   WA 754, etc.
     Relation to disease see Climate   WB 700
Atmospheric Pressure
     High altitude   WD 710
     In industry   WA 450
     Meteorology   QC 885-896
     Underwater   WD 650
Atomic Absorption see Spectrophotometry, Atomic
     Absorption
Atomic Energy see Nuclear Energy
Atomic Medicine see Nuclear Medicine
Atomic Warfare see Nuclear Warfare
Atomizers see Nebulizers and Vaporizers
Atopic Hypersensitivity see Hypersensitivity,
     Immediate
Atopy see Hypersensitivity, Immediate
ATP see Adenosine Triphosphate
ATP Receptors see Receptors, Purinergic P2
ATPase see Adenosinetriphosphatase
ATPase, Calcium see Ca(2+)-Transporting ATPase
ATPase, Calcium Magnesium see Ca(2+)
     Mg(2+)-ATPase
ATPase, F0 see H(+)-Transporting ATP Synthase

**ALWAYS CONSULT MAIN SCHEDULES. USE NUMBER ASSIGNED ONLY WHEN
SUBJECT REPRESENTS MAJOR EMPHASIS OF WORK BEING CLASSIFIED**

ATPase, F1 see H(+)-Transporting ATP Synthase
ATPase, Magnesium see Ca(2+) Mg(2+)-ATPase
ATPase, Sodium, Potassium see
   Na(+)-K(+)-Exchanging ATPase
Atractylic Acid see Atractyloside
Atractyloside   QU 75
Atracurium   QV 140
Atracurium Besylate see Atracurium
Atracurium Dibesylate see Atracurium
Atrial Fibrillation   WG 330
Atrial Flutter   WG 330
Atrial Natriuretic Factor   QU 68
Atrial Natriuretic Peptides see Atrial Natriuretic
   Factor
Atriopeptins see Atrial Natriuretic Factor
Atrioventricular Block see Heart Block
Atrioventricular Bundle see Bundle of His
Atrioventricular Node   WG 201-202
Atrocities see Violence
Atropa Belladonna see Belladonna
Atrophy
   Manifestation of disease   QZ 180
Atropine   QV 134
Atropine Derivatives   QV 134
Attendants see Nurses' Aides; Psychiatric Aides;
   Allied Health Personnel
Attention   BF 321-323
   Children   WS 105.5.C7
   Vigilance   BF 323.V5
Attention Deficit Disorder with Hyperactivity   WS
350.8.A8
   In adulthood   WL 354
Attention Deficit Hyperactivity Disorder see
Attention Deficit Disorder with Hyperactivity
Attitude   BF 327
   In adolescence   WS 462
   In infancy & childhood   WS 105.5.A8
   Of patients   W 85
      In hospitals   WX 158.5
      In mental hospitals   WM 29.5
   Toward health insurance   W 275
   To specific topics, by subject
Attitude of Health Personnel
   Allied health personnel   W 21.5
   Dentists   WU 61
   Hospital staff   WX 160
   Nurses   WY 87
   Physicians   W 62
   Psychiatrists   WM 62
   Special areas, with the area
Attitude to Computers   QA 76.9.P75
Attitude to Death   BF 789.D4
   In infancy & childhood   WS 105.5.A8
   Pastoral care   WM 61
   Speculative philosophy   BD 443.8-445
Attitude to Health   W 85
   Other specific subjects, by subject
Audio-Visual Aids
   (Form number 18.2 in any NLM schedule where
      applicable)
   Special topics, by subject
Audiology   WV 270-280
   See also Hearing   WV 270-280

Audiometry   WV 272
Audiometry, Electroencephalic Response see
   Audiometry, Evoked Response
Audiometry, Evoked Response   WV 272
Audiometry, Impedance see Acoustic Impedance
   Tests
Audiometry, Speech   WV 272
Audition, Limits of see Auditory Threshold
Auditory Brain Stem Evoked Responses see Evoked
   Potentials, Auditory, Brain Stem
Auditory Canal, External see Ear Canal
Auditory Cortex   WL 307
Auditory Diseases, Central   WV 270
Auditory Evoked Potentials see Evoked Potentials,
   Auditory
Auditory Evoked Response see Evoked Potentials,
   Auditory
Auditory Fatigue   WV 272
Auditory Localization see Sound Localization
Auditory Nerve see Acoustic Nerve
Auditory Ossicles see Ear Ossicles
Auditory Pathways   WV 272
Auditory Perception   WV 272
   In infancy & childhood and other groups   WV
   272
   Paracusis   WV 272
Auditory Perceptual Disorders   WV 270
Auditory Prosthesis see Cochlear Implant
Auditory Threshold   WV 272
   In infancy & childhood and other groups   WV
   272
Auditory Tube see Eustachian Tube
Auerbach's Plexus see Myenteric Plexus
Aujeszky's Disease see Pseudorabies
Aujeszky's Disease Virus see Herpesvirus 1, Suid
Aural Vertigo see Ménière's Disease
Auramine O see Benzophenoneidum
Auranofin   QV 247
Aureolic Acid see Plicamycin
Aureomycin see Chlortetracycline
Auricle, Ear see Ear, External
Auricular Fibrillation see Atrial Fibrillation
Auricular Flutter see Atrial Flutter
Auriculin see Atrial Natriuretic Factor
Auriculo-Ventricular Dissociation see Heart Block
Auriculoventricular Bundle see Heart Conduction
   System
Aurothioglucose   QV 247
Auscultation   WB 278
   Heart see Heart Auscultation   WG 141.5.A9
   Used for special purposes, by subject
Australia Antigen see Hepatitis B Antigens
Australoid Race
   Anthropology   GN 662-671
   See also applicable special topics under Ethnic
      groups
Authoritarianism
   Psychology   BF 698.35.A87
   Social psychology   HM 271
Autism   WM 203.5
Autism, Infantile   WM 203.5
Autoanalysis   Q 183.9
   Analysis in a special field, in the technique number

**ALWAYS CONSULT MAIN SCHEDULES. USE NUMBER ASSIGNED ONLY WHEN
SUBJECT REPRESENTS MAJOR EMPHASIS OF WORK BEING CLASSIFIED**

for the field, e.g. QY 25 for clinical analysis
Special topics, by subject
Autoantibodies   QW 575
   As a cause of autoimmune diseases   WD 305
Autobiography   CT
   As a literary form   CT 25
   Of mentally ill   WM 40
   Of physicians   WZ 100
   Of specialists in dentistry, nursing, pharmacy,
     psychology, science, etc.   WZ 100
   Of patients with a particular disease, with the
     disease
Autoeroticism see Paraphilias
Autogenic Training
   Parapsychology   BF 1156.S8
   Psychiatry   WM 415
Autograft see Transplantation, Autologous
Autohemolysis see Hemolysis
Autoimmune Diseases   WD 305
Autoimmunity   QW 545
Autolysis   QZ 180
Automated Multiphasic Health Testing see
   Multiphasic Screening
Automatic Data Processing
   In medicine (General)   W 26.55.A9
   In other special fields (Form number 26.5 in any
     NLM schedule where applicable)
   Used for special purposes, by subject
Automation   T 59.5
   Used for special purposes, by subject, e.g., of
     clinical laboratory procedures   QY 23
Automation, Office see Office Automation
Automatism
   Parapsychology (General)   BF 1321
   Psychiatry   WM 197
   Other special topics by subject, e.g., Automatic
     writing   BF 1343
Automobile Accidents see Accidents, Traffic
Automobile Driver Examination   WA 275
Automobile Driving
   Public health aspects   WA 275
Automobile Exhaust   WA 754
Automobiles   TL 1–390
   Human engineering in design   TL 250
   Noise hazard   WA 776
   Sanitary conditions of buses and other public
     carriers   WA 810
   Sanitary disposal   WA 778
Autonomic Agents   QV 120–137
Autonomic Denervation   WL 600
Autonomic Ganglia see Ganglia, Autonomic
Autonomic Nerve Block   WO 375
Autonomic Nervous System   WL 600–610
Autonomic Nervous System Diseases   WL 600
Autonomous Replication see DNA Replication
Autopsy   QZ 35
   Medicolegal   W 825
   Veterinary   SF 769
   See also names of particular conditions requiring
     autopsy, e.g., Substance Abuse   WM 270–290
Autoradiography
   Biochemistry
     General   QU 4

     Techniques   QU 25
   Biology   QH 324.9.A9
   Cytological techniques   QH 585–585.5
     Clinical pathology   QY 95
   Diagnosis (General)   WN 445
   Histological technique   QS 525
   Used for special purposes, by subject
Autoregulation see Homeostasis
Autosexuality see Narcissism
Autosome Abnormalities see Chromosome
   Abnormalities
Autosuggestion
   Parapsychology   BF 1156.S8
   Psychiatry   WM 415
Autotransplant see Transplantation, Autologous
AV Node see Atrioventricular Node
Availability Equivalency see Biological Availability
Availability of Health Services see Health Services
   Accessibility
Aversive Therapy   WM 425.5.A9
Avertin see Alcohol, Ethyl
Avian Hypersensitivity Pneumonitis see Bird
   Fancier's Lung
Avian Infectious Bronchitis Virus see Infectious
   Bronchitis Virus, Avian
Avian Leukosis   SF 995.6.L4
Avian Orthomyxovirus Type A see Orthomyxovirus
   Type A, Avian
Avian Sarcoma Virus B77 see Sarcoma Viruses,
   Avian
Aviation   TL
   Air defense   UG 730, etc.
   Standards
     Physical   WD 705
     Psychological   WD 730
   See also Aircraft   WD 700, etc.; Space Flight
     WD 750–758
Aviation Accidents see Accidents, Aviation
Aviation Dentistry see Dentistry; Aerospace
   Medicine; Military Dentistry
Aviation Medicine see Aerospace Medicine
Aviation Nursing see Aviation   WY 143 under
   Nursing
Aviation, Physical Standards see Standards   WD
   705 under Aviation
Avidin   QU 55
Avidity, Antibody see Antibody Affinity
Avitaminosis   WD 105–155
   Pathogenesis of disease in general   QZ 109
   Veterinary   SF 855.V58
   See also names of specific vitamin deficiencies
Avoidance Learning   BF 319.5.A9
Awareness   BF 321
Axenic Animals see Germ-Free Life
Axilla   WE 812
Axillary Artery   WG 595.A9
Axillary Vein   WG 625.A9
Axis   WE 725
Axolotl see Ambystoma
Axolotl, Mexican see Ambystoma mexicanum
Axons   WL 102.5
Ayerza's Syndrome see Hypertension, Pulmonary
Ayurvedic Medicine see Medicine, Ayurvedic

**ALWAYS CONSULT MAIN SCHEDULES. USE NUMBER ASSIGNED ONLY WHEN
SUBJECT REPRESENTS MAJOR EMPHASIS OF WORK BEING CLASSIFIED**

Azacyclopropanes see Aziridines
Azapropazone see Apazone
Azaserine   QU 60
   As antifungal agent   QV 252
   Cancer chemotherapy   QZ 267
   Immunosuppression   QW 920
Azathioprine   QV 269
   Cancer chemotherapy   QZ 267
   Immunosuppression   QW 920
Azeserine see Azaserine
Azides   QU 54
   Organic chemistry
      Aliphatic compounds   QD 305.N84
Azidothymidine see Zidovudine
Aziridines
   Organic chemistry   QD 401
      As carcinogens   QZ 202
Azirines
   Organic chemistry   QD 401
Azo Compounds   QV 235
   Organic chemistry
      Aliphatic compounds   QD 305.A9
      Aromatic compounds   QD 341.A9
Azoles
   Organic chemistry   QD 401
Azotemia see Uremia
Azotobacter   QW 131
AZT (Antiviral) see Zidovudine
Aztreonam   QV 350
Azygos Vein   WG 625.A99

B

B-Cell Differentiation Antigens see Antigens, Differentiation, B-Lymphocyte
B-Cells see B-Lymphocytes
B-K Mole Syndrome see Dysplastic Nevus Syndrome
B-Lymphocyte Differentiation Antigens see Antigens, Differentiation, B-Lymphocyte
B-Lymphocytes   WH 200
Babesiasis see Babesiosis
Babesiosis   SF 791
Baboon, Gelada see Theropithecus gelada
Baboons see Papio
Baboons, Savanna see Papio
Bacillaceae   QW 127
Bacillary Dysentery see Dysentery, Bacillary
Bacillus   QW 127.5.B2
Bacillus anthracis   QW 127.5.B2
Bacillus megaterium   QW 127.5.B2
Bacillus stearothermophilus   QW 127.5.B2
Bacillus subtilis   QW 127.5.B2
Bacillus thuringiensis   QW 127.5.B2
Bacitracin   QV 350
Back   WE 720-755
Back Pain   WE 720
   See also Low back pain   WE 755
Backache see Back Pain
Background Radiation   WN 105
Baclofen
   Biochemistry   QU 60
   As a central muscle relaxant   QV 140

Baclophen see Baclofen
Bacteremia see Septicemia   WC 240
Bacteria   QW
   Actinomycetes   QW 115, etc.
   Anatomy and morphology   QW 51
   As cause of disease   QZ 65
   Budding and/or appendaged   QW 153
   General works   QW 50
   Gliding   QW 128
   Gram-negative facultatively anaerobic rods   QW 137-141
   Gram-positive bacteria   QW 142-142.5
      Asporogenous rods   QW 142.5.A8
      Cocci   QW 142.5.C6
   Invasiveness   QW 730
   Metabolism   QW 52
   Sheathed   QW 153
   Spiral and curved   QW 154
Bacteria, Anaerobic   QW 52
Bacterial Adhesion   QW 52
Bacterial Antibodies see Antibodies, Bacterial
Bacterial Antigens see Antigens, Bacterial
Bacterial Conjugation see Conjugation, Genetic
Bacterial DNA see DNA, Bacterial
Bacterial Drug Resistance see Drug Resistance, Microbial
Bacterial Gene Expression Regulation see Gene Expression Regulation, Bacterial
Bacterial Gene Products see Bacterial Proteins
Bacterial Gene Proteins see Bacterial Proteins
Bacterial Genetics see Genetics, Microbial
Bacterial Infections   WC 200-425
   Enteric   WC 260-290
   In infancy & childhood   WC 200-425
   In plants   SB 734
   Of the kidney   WJ 351
   Veterinary   SF 780.3
   Specific infection see name of infection
   Other particular organ affected, by organ or region
Bacterial Outer Membrane Proteins   QW 52
Bacterial Pili see Pili, Sex
Bacterial Polysaccharides see Polysaccharides, Bacterial
Bacterial Proteins   QW 52
   Therapeutic use, with the disease being treated
Bacterial RNA see RNA, Bacterial
Bacterial Sensitivity Tests see Microbial Sensitivity Tests
Bacterial Spores see Spores, Bacterial
Bacterial Toxins   QW 630.5.B2
Bacterial Vaccines   WC 200
   Pyrogenic   WB 469 or with disease being treated
   For specific diseases, with the diseases
Bacterial Warfare see Biological Warfare
Bactericidal Action of Antibodies see Bacteriolysis
Bacteriocins   QV 350
Bacteriodaceae   QW 133
Bacteriological Techniques   QW 25
   Clinical pathology   QY 100
   Veterinary   QW 70
Bacteriologists, Directories see Directories   QW 22 under Bacteriology

Bacteriology   QW 1-155
   General works   QW 50
   Clinical see Bacteriological Techniques   QY 100
   Dental   QW 65
   Directories   QW 22
   Industrial   QW 75
   Nursing texts   QW 50, etc.
   Of air see Air Microbiology   QW 82
   Of food see Food Microbiology   QW 85
   Of milk   QW 85
   Of plants   QW 60
   Of sewage   QW 80
   Of soil see Soil Microbiology   QW 60
   Of water see Water Microbiology   QW 80
   Veterinary science   QW 70
Bacteriolysis   QW 660
Bacteriophage lambda   QW 161.5.C6
Bacteriophage Typing   QW 25
Bacteriophages   QW 161
Bacteriophages T see T-Phages
Bacteriorhodopsin   QW 52
Bacteriuria   WJ 351
   In urine analysis   QY 185
Bacteroides   QW 133
Bacteroides Infections   WC 200
Bagassosis see Pneumoconiosis
Balance see Equilibrium
Balantidiasis   WC 735
Balantidium   QX 151
Baldness see Alopecia
Balint Psychoanalytic Therapy see Psychoanalytic
   Therapy
Ballistics, Wound see Wounds, Gunshot
Ballistocardiography   WG 141.5.B2
Balloon Angioplasty see Angioplasty, Balloon
Balloon Catheterization see Balloon Dilatation
Balloon Dilatation   WB 365
   In cardiovascular diseases   WG 166.5.B2
   In other diseases, with the disease
Balloon Dilatation, Coronary Artery see
   Angioplasty, Transluminal, Percutaneous
   Coronary
Balloon Tamponade see Balloon Dilatation
Balloon Valvotomy see Balloon Dilatation
Balloon Valvuloplasty see Balloon Dilatation
Balneology   WB 525
Balneotherapy see Balneology
Balsams   QV 241
Banana see Fruit
Bancroftian Elephantiasis see Elephantiasis, Filarial
Band 3 Protein   WH 400
Bandages
   First aid   WA 292
   Surgical   WO 167
   See also Occlusive Dressings   WO 167
Bandages, Occlusive see Occlusive Dressings
Bandicoot Rats see Muridae
Bandicota see Muridae
Banding, Chromosome see Chromosome Banding
Bang's Disease see Brucellosis, Bovine
Banks see Blood Banks; Eye Banks; Tissue Banks
   (Form number 23-24 in any NLM schedule where
   applicable)

Bar Codes see Automatic Data Processing
Barany's Test see Caloric Tests
Barbary Ape see Macaca
Barber Surgeons see Surgery
Barbering
   Care of hair   WR 465
   Public health aspects of barber shops   WA 744
   Registration of barbers   WA 32
Barbital   QV 88
Barbitone see Barbital
Barbiturates   QV 88
Barbituric Acid Derivatives see Barbiturates
Barefoot Doctors see Community Health Aides
Barium   QV 618
   As a contrast medium in radiology   WN 160
Barlow's Disease see Scurvy
Barnacles   QX 463
Baroreceptors see Pressoreceptors
Barotrauma
   In high altitude   WD 710
   Underwater   WD 650
   See also Atmospheric Pressure
Barr Bodies see Sex Chromatin
Barrett Esophagus   WI 250
Barriers, Architectural see Architectural
   Accessibility
Bartholin's Glands   WP 200
Bartonella Infections   WC 640
Bartonellaceae Infections   WC 640
Bartonellosis see Bartonella Infections
Bartter's Disease   WK 770
Basal Anesthesia see Preanesthetic Medication
Basal Ganglia   WL 307
Basal Ganglia Diseases   WL 307
   See also names of specific disorders, e.g.,
    Parkinson Disease   WL 359
Basal Metabolism   QU 125
Basal Nuclei see Basal Ganglia
Basal Vein see Cerebral Veins
Base Composition   QU 58
Base Pairs see Base Composition
Base Ratio see Base Composition
Base Sequence   QU 58
Base Sequence Homology see Sequence Homology,
   Nucleic Acid
Baseball   QT 260.5.B2
Basedow's Disease see Goiter, Exophthalmic
Basic Life Support see Cardiopulmonary
   Resuscitation
Basic Pancreatic Trypsin Inhibitor see Aprotinin
Basidiomycetes   QW 180.5.B2
Basilar Artery   WG 595.B2
Basilar Artery Insufficiency see Vertebrobasilar
   Insufficiency
Basilar Impression see Platybasia
Basilar Membrane   WV 250
Basketball   QT 260.5.B3
Basophilism, Pituitary see Cushing's Syndrome
Basophils   WH 200
Basophils, Tissue see Mast Cells
Bathing Beaches   WA 820
Baths
   Hygiene   QT 240

**ALWAYS CONSULT MAIN SCHEDULES. USE NUMBER ASSIGNED ONLY WHEN
SUBJECT REPRESENTS MAJOR EMPHASIS OF WORK BEING CLASSIFIED**

Mud see Mud Therapy   WB 525
Public   WA 820
Sand see Ammotherapy   WB 525
See also Balneology   WB 525; Thalassotherapy
   WB 750
Baths, Finnish   WB 525
Baths, Sand see Ammotherapy
Bats see Chiroptera
Batten–Spielmeyer–Vogt Disease see Neuronal
   Ceroid–Lipofuscinosis
Battered Child Syndrome   WA 320
Battle Fatigue see Combat Disorders
Baunscheidtism see Acupuncture
Bayer 39 see Inproquone
BCG see Mycobacterium bovis
BCG Vaccine   WF 250
Beaches, Bathing see Bathing Beaches
Beans see Legumes
Beard see Hair
Beauty   BH
   Women   HQ 1219–1220
   Plastic surgery   WO 600
Beauty Culture
   Hygienic aspects   QT 275
   Public health aspects   WA 744
   Registration of beauticians and cosmeticians
      WA 32
Beauty Salons see Beauty Culture
Beavers see Rodentia
Bechterew's Disease see Spondylitis, Ankylosing
Becker Muscular Dystrophy see Muscular
   Dystrophy
Beclomethasone   WK 757
Beclomethasone Dipropionate see Beclomethasone
Bed Capacity, Hospital see Hospital Bed Capacity
Bed Conversion   WX 140
   In special type of facilities, with the facility
Bed Occupancy   WX 16
Bed Size, Hospital see Hospital Bed Capacity
Bedbugs   QX 503
Bedding and Linens   WX 165
   Home Care of Sick   W 26
Beds
   Home Care of Sick   W 26
   Hospitals   WX 147
Beds, Swing see Bed Conversion
Bedsore see Decubitus Ulcer
Bedsores see Decubitus Ulcer
Bee Venoms   WD 430
Beer
   As a dietary supplement in health or disease
      WB 444
   Chemical technology   TP 577
   Microorganisms of fermentation   QW 85
   See also Alcoholism   WM 274; Alcohol, Ethyl
      QV 84, etc.
Bees   QX 565
Beetles   QX 555
Beggiatoales see Cytophagales   QW 128
Beginning of Life see Biogenesis
Behavior
   Drug effects   WM; QV
   In adolescence   WS 462

In infancy & childhood   WS 105
Psychology (General)   BF 11–32
Sex see Sex behavior   HQ 12–30.7, etc
Special topics, by subject
Behavior, Adaptive see Adaptation, Psychological
Behavior, Addictive   WM 176
Behavior, Adolescent see Adolescent Behavior
Behavior, Animal   QL 750–785.3
Behavior, Compulsive see Compulsive Behavior
Behavior, Dangerous see Dangerous Behavior
Behavior Disorders see Affective Symptoms; Child
   Behavior Disorders; Social Behavior Disorders;
   names of specific disorders
Behavior, Exploratory see Exploratory Behavior
Behavior Modification see Behavior Therapy
Behavior Modifiers see Psychotropic Drugs
Behavior Therapy   WM 425
   In adolescence   WS 463
   In infancy & childhood   WS 350.6
   Nursing texts   WY 160
      See also Counseling   WY 87, etc.;
         Nurse–patient relations   WY 87
Behavior Therapy, Cognitive see Cognitive Therapy
Behavioral Medicine   WB 103
   Special topics, by subject
Behavioral Sciences
   Animals see Ethology   QL 750–785.3
   Educational aspects   LB–LC
   Psychiatric aspects   WM
   Psychological aspects   BF
   Sociological aspects   HM
   Other special topics, by subject, e.g., statistics
   for the behavioral sciences   HA 29
Behaviorism   BF 199
Behcet's Syndrome   WW 240
Bejel   WC 422
Belching see Eructation
Belgian Hare see Rabbits
Belladonna
   As a medicinal plant   QV 766
   As a sympatholytic   QV 134
   Culture   SB 295.B4
   Poisoning   WD 500
Bell's Palsy see Facial Paralysis
Benactyzine   QV 77.9
Bence Jones Protein   WH 540
Bender–Gestalt Test   WM 145.5.B4
Bends see Decompression Sickness
Beneckea see Vibrio
Benhydramin see Diphenhydramine
Benign Intracranial Hypertension see Pseudotumor
   Cerebri
Benign Monoclonal Gammopathies see Monoclonal
   Gammopathies, Benign
Bensokain see Benzocaine
Benzalacetophenone see Chalcone
Benzalkonium see Benzalkonium Compounds
Benzalkonium Compounds   QV 233
Benzamides   QU 62
   Organic chemistry   QD 341.A7
Benzanthracenes   QZ 202
Benzathine Penicillin see Penicillin G, Benzathine

Benzene
    Organic chemistry   QD 341.H9
    Toxicology   QV 633
Benzene Derivatives
    Organic chemistry   QD 341.H9
    Toxicology   QV 633
Benzene Hexachloride
    As an insecticide   WA 240
    Toxicology   QV 633
Benzimidazoles
    As anthelmintics   QV 253
    Organic chemistry   QD 401
    Veterinary pharmacology   SF 918.A45
Benzo(a)pyrene   QZ 202
Benzoates   QU 98
    Organic chemistry   QD 341.A2
Benzocaine   QV 115
Benzodiazepine Tranquilizers see Anti-Anxiety
    Agents, Benzodiazepine
Benzoin   QV 241
Benzol see Benzene
Benzophenoneidum
    Toxicology   QV 632
    As a disinfectant   QV 235
Benzopyrans
    Organic chemistry   QD 405
Benzopyrenes
    As carcinogens   QZ 202
Benzothiadiazines
    Organic chemistry   QD 401
Benzoyl Peroxide
    As a dermatological agent   QV 60
Benzoyl Superoxide see Benzoyl Peroxide
Benzylamines
    Biochemistry   QU 61
Benzylideneacetophenone see Chalcone
Benzylpenicillin see Penicillin G
Bereavement   BF 575.G7
    In adolescence   WS 462
    In infancy & childhood   WS 105.5.E5
Bereavement Care see Hospice Care
Berger's Disease see Glomerulonephritis, IGA
Beriberi   WD 122
Berries see Fruit
Berry Aneurysm see Cerebral Aneurysm
Bertielliasis see Cestode Infections
Berylliosis   WF 654
Beryllium   QV 275
Beryllium Disease see Berylliosis
Besnier-Boeck Disease see Sarcoidosis
Besnoitiasis see Protozoan Infections
Bestiality see Paraphilias
beta-Adrenergic Blocking Agents see Adrenergic
    beta-Antagonists
beta-Adrenergic Receptor Agonists see Adrenergic
    beta-Agonists
beta-Adrenergic Receptor Blockaders see
    Adrenergic beta-Antagonists
beta-Adrenergic Receptors see Receptors,
    Adrenergic, beta
beta-Alanine Ketoglutarate Aminotransferase see
    Aminobutyrate Aminotransferase
beta,beta-Dimethylcysteine see Penicillamine

beta-Blockers, Adrenergic see Adrenergic
    beta-Antagonists
Beta Cell, Artificial see Insulin Infusion Systems
beta-Cell Tumor see Insulinoma
Beta Globulins   WH 400
    Clinical analysis   QY 455
beta-Hydroxyphenethylamine see
    2-Hydroxyphenethylamine
beta-Hypophamine see Vasopressins
beta-Lactam Antibiotics see Antibiotics, Lactam
beta-Lactamase I see Penicillinase
beta-Lactamases   QU 136
Beta-naphthol see Naphthols
Beta Particles see Beta Rays
beta-Phenylethanolamine see
    2-Hydroxyphenethylamine
Beta Rays   WN 105
beta 2-Microglobulin   WH 400
    Clinical analysis   QY 455
Betadexamethasone see Betamethasone
Betaine   QV 87
Betamethasone   WK 757
Betatrons see Particle Accelerators
Betel see Areca
Beverages
    As a dietary supplement in health or disease
        WB 433-444
    Chemical technology   TP 500-659
    Microbiology   QW 85
    Public health (General)   WA 695
        Legislation (General)   WA 697
    See also names of specific beverages, e.g.
        Alcoholic beverages   WB 444, etc.
Bezoars   WI 300
    Of the intestines   WI 400
    Veterinary   SF 851
Bhang see Cannabis
Bible   BS
    Medicine depicted in   WZ 330
    Special topics, by subject, e.g., medical properties
        of Biblical plants   QV 766
Bibliography
    Of subjects represented in NLM's classification,
        appropriate classification number preceded by
        the letter Z
    Of other subjects, LC's Z schedule
    See bibliography section of Introduction for
        further instructions
Bibliography, Descriptive   Z 1001
Bibliography, National   Z 1201-4980
Bibliography of Medicine
    General works including monographs and serials
        Issued as monograph   ZWB 100
        Issued as serial   ZW 1
    Of monographs   ZWB 100
        Issued serially   ZW 1
    Of serials   ZW 1
    On specific subject, NLM number for the subject
        preceded by Z
Bibliography, Statistical see Bibliometrics
Bibliometrics   Z 669.8
    Special topics, by subject
Bibliotherapy   WM 450.5.B5

**ALWAYS CONSULT MAIN SCHEDULES. USE NUMBER ASSIGNED ONLY WHEN
SUBJECT REPRESENTS MAJOR EMPHASIS OF WORK BEING CLASSIFIED**

Bicarbonates
    Inorganic chemistry   QD 181.C1
    Pharmacology   QV 138.C1
Bicuculline   QV 103
Bicycle Ergometry Test see Exercise Test
Bicycling   QT 260.5.B5
Bifidobacterium   QW 125.5.A2
Bifocal Lenses see Eyeglasses
Bifunctional Reagents see Cross–Linking Reagents
Biguanides   QU 61
    Organic chemistry   QD 305.A8
Bilayer Fluidity see Membrane Fluidity
Bilayers, Lipid see Lipid Bilayers
Bile   WI 703
Bile Acids and Salts   WI 703
Bile Duct Diseases   WI 750
Bile Duct Neoplasms   WI 765
Bile Duct Obstruction see Cholestasis
Bile Duct Obstruction, Extrahepatic   WI 750
Bile Ducts   WI 750
    See also Common Bile Duct   WI 750; Cystic
    Duct   WI 750; Hepatic Duct   WI 750
Bile Ducts, Intrahepatic   WI 750
Bile Pigments   WI 703
    Clinical pathology   QY 143
Bile Reflux   WI 703
Bile Salts see Bile Acids and Salts
Bilharzia see Schistosoma
Bilharziasis see Schistosomiasis
Biliary Atresia   WI 750
Biliary Calculi see Cholelithiasis
Biliary Calculi, Common Bile Duct see Common Bile
    Duct Calculi
Biliary Fistula   WI 750
Biliary Stasis see Cholestasis
Biliary Stasis, Extrahepatic see Bile Duct
    Obstruction, Extrahepatic
Biliary Surgery see Biliary Tract Surgery
Biliary Tract   WI 700–770
Biliary Tract Diseases   WI 700–770
    General works   WI 700
Biliary Tract Neoplasms   WI 735
Biliary Tract Surgery   WI 770
Bilirubin   WI 703
    Clinical pathology   QY 143
Bilirubin Encephalopathy see Kernicterus
Bilirubinemia see Hyperbilirubinemia
Binding, Competitive
    Bacteriology   QW 570
    Biochemistry (General)   QU 34
    Pharmacology   QV 38
Binding Proteins see Carrier Proteins
Binding Sites
    Antigen–antibody reactions   QW 570
    Biochemistry (General)   QU 34
    Immunochemistry   QW 504.5
    Pharmacology   QV 38
Binding Sites, Antibody   QW 575
    See also Agglutination   QW 640
Binocular Vision see Depth Perception; Eye
    Movements; Accommodation, Ocular; Vision
Bioassay see Biological assay
Bioavailability see Biological Availability

Biobibliography
    General Z 1010
    Individual   WZ 100
    Of individuals in fields largely unrelated to the
    biological sciences, in the appropriate LC
    number
    Of groups of persons in special fields   WZ
    112–112.5 or in appropriate LC number
Biochemic Medicine see Alternative Medicine
Biochemical Genetics see Genetics, Biochemical
Biochemical Markers see Biological Markers
Biochemical Phenomena see Biochemistry
Biochemistry   QU
    Biochemical phenomena (General)   QU 34
    Biography
        Collective   WZ 112
        Individual   WZ 100
    Cryobiochemistry   QU 25
    Directories   QU 22
    Fetus   WQ 210.5
    Inorganic substances   QU 130
    Nursing texts   QU 4, etc.
    Of respiration   WF 110
    Technique   QU 25
    See also names of specialties and systems
Biochemists see Biography; Directories   QU 22
    under Biochemistry
Biocompatible Materials   QT 37
    Used for special purposes, by subject, e.g., for
    artificial organs (General)   WO 176
Biocompatible Materials Testing see Materials
    Testing
Biodegradation   WA 671
    Waste disposal   WA 778–788
    Special topics, by subject
Bioelectric Energy Sources   QT 34
    Used for special purposes, by subject, e.g. for
    pacemakers   WG 26
Bioenergetics see Energy Metabolism
Bioequivalence see Therapeutic Equivalency
Bioethics   QH 332
    Special topics, by subject
    See also Ethics, Medical   W 50
Biofeedback (Psychology)   WL 103
    Behavior therapy   WM 425.5.B6
Bioflavonoids   QU 220
Biogenesis   QH 325
    Legal establishment of beginning of life   W 789
Biogenic Amines   QU 61
    Special topics, by subject
Biographical Accounts of Disease see Name of
    diseases, e.g. Mental Retardation
Biographical Clinics see Famous Persons;
    Psychoanalytic Interpretation; names of particular
    persons
Biography   CT
    As a form of literature   CT 21
    Of mentally ill   WM 40
    Of other persons with particular diseases, with
    the disease
    Physicians and specialists of medically related
    fields
        Collective   WZ 112–150

**ALWAYS CONSULT MAIN SCHEDULES. USE NUMBER ASSIGNED ONLY WHEN
SUBJECT REPRESENTS MAJOR EMPHASIS OF WORK BEING CLASSIFIED**

Individual   WZ 100
Scientists and behavioral scientists
    Collective in appropriate LC number
    Individual   WZ 100
Other professions, in appropriate LC number
See also names of other groups of persons, e.g.,
    Pharmacists   WZ 112.5.P4
Biohazards Containment see Containment of
    Biohazards
Biological Assay   QV 771
    Of hormones   QY 330
    Of vitamins   QY 350
Biological Availability   QV 38
    Special topics, by subject
Biological Availability, Nutritional see Nutritive
    Value
Biological Chemistry see Biochemistry
Biological Clocks   QT 167
    See also special topics under Circadian Rhythm
Biological Dressings   WO 167
Biological Energy Sources see Bioelectric Energy
    Sources
Biological Markers
    Genetics   QH 438.4.B55
    In the diagnosis of a particular disease, with the
    disease
Biological Monitoring see Environmental
    Monitoring
Biological Oscillators see Biological Clocks
Biological Pest Control see Pest Control, Biological
Biological Products   QW 800
    Refrigeration   WA 730
    Tissue extracts   QV 370
    Veterinary   SF 918.B5
    See also Hormones, Synthetic   WK 187
Biological Psychiatry   WM 102
    Special topics, by subject
Biological Pump see Biological Transport, Active
Biological Response Modifiers   QW 800
Biological Transport   QH 509
    Cytology   QH 601
    Metabolism   QU 120
    See also Osmosis   QH 615, etc.
Biological Transport, Active   QH 509
    Cytology   QH 601
    Metabolism   QU 120
Biological Warfare
    Bacteriological aspects   QW 300
    Military aspects   UG 447.8
Biological Waste Disposal see Medical Waste
    Disposal
Biologics see Biological Products
Biology   QH 301–705
    General works   QH 307–307.2
    History   QH 305–305.2
    In art   N 72.B5
Bioluminescence see Luminescence
Bioluminescent Proteins see Luminescent Proteins
Biomass see Ecology
Biomaterials see Biocompatible Materials
Biomathematics see Mathematics
Biomechanics   WE 103
Biomedical Engineering   QT 36

Special topics, by subject
Biomedical Research see Research
Biomedical Technology see Technology, Medical
Biometry   QH 323.5
    Medical   WA 950
Biomodulators see Biological Response Modifiers
Bionator see Activator Appliances
Bionics   Q 317–321
    Used for special purposes, by subject, e.g. in
    biophysics   QT 34
Bionomics see Ecology
Bioperiodicity see Periodicity
Biopharmaceutics   QV 38
Biophysics   QT 34
    Radiation   WN 110
Biopolymers
    Organic chemistry   QD 380–388
Bioprobes see Biosensors
Bioprosthesis
    For heart valve   WG 169
    See also Heart valve prosthesis
Biopsy
    Clinical diagnosis   WB 379
    Surgical diagnosis   WO 142
    Veterinary   SF 772
    Specific area, by organ; in specific diseases, with
    the disease
Biopsy, Chorionic Villi see Chorionic Villi Sampling
Biopsy, Needle
    Clinical diagnosis   WB 379
    Surgical diagnosis   WO 142
    Specific area, by organ; in specific diseases, with
    the disease
Biopterin
    As a pteridines   QU 188
    As a growth substance   QU 107
Biorhythms see Biological Clocks; Circadian
    Rhythm; Periodicity
Biosensors   QT 36
Biostatistics see Statistics
Biosynthetic Proteins see Recombinant Proteins
Biotechnology   TP 248.13–248.65
    Applied to specific topics, by subject
Biotin   QU 195
Biotransformation
    Metabolism   QU 120
    Pharmacology   QV 38
Biphenyl Compounds
    As carcinogens   QZ 202
    As insecticides   WA 240
    Organic chemistry   QD 341.H9
    Toxicology   QV 633
Bipolar Disorder   WM 207
Bird Diseases   SF 994–995.6
Bird Fancier's Lung   WF 150
Birds
    As laboratory animals   QY 60.B4
    Domestic (Breeding)   SF 460–473
    Wild   QL 671–699
Birth see Delivery; Biogenesis
Birth Certificates   HA 38–39
Birth Control see Contraception; Family Planning
Birth Defects see Abnormalities

Birth Injuries   WS 405
Birth, Multiple see Pregnancy Multiple; named
   groups, e.g., Twins
Birth Order
   Psychological aspects in children   WS 105.5.F2
Birth Rate   HB 901–1108
Birth Registration see Birth Certificates
Birth Statistics see Birth Rate; Vital Statistics
Birth Weight
   Newborn   WS 420
   Premature infant   WS 410
   Tables   WS 16
Birthmark see Hemangioma; Nevus; Nevus,
   Pigmented
Bis(Chloromethyl) Ether
   As a carcinogen   QZ 202
Bisexuality
   As a life style   HQ 74
   Psychiatric aspects   WM 611
Bishydroxycoumarin   QV 193
Bismuth   QV 290
Bisnorephedrine see 2-Hydroxyphenethylamine
Bite Force   WU 440
Bites and Stings   WD 400–430
   Insects see Insect Bites and Stings   WD 430
   Snake see Snake Bites   WD 410
   Spider and scorpion see Arachnidism   WD 420
   Surgical treatment   WO 700
Bitters see Flavoring Agents; Gastrointestinal Agents
Biundulant Meningo-Encephalitis Virus see
   Encephalitis Viruses, Tick-Borne
Biureas
   Organic chemistry   QD 315
BK Virus see Polyomavirus hominis 1
Black Ape see Macaca
Black Flies see Simuliidae
Black Tongue see Tongue, Hairy
Blacks
   American   E 184.6–185.97
   As physicians
      Collective biography   WZ 150
      History   WZ 80.5.B5
      Individual biography   WZ 100
   In other countries, see name of country in LC
      schedules   D–F
   See also special topics under Ethnic groups
Blackwater Fever   WC 750–770
Bladder   WJ 500–504
Bladder Calculi   WJ 500
Bladder Diseases   WJ 500–504
   General   WJ 500
   See also Vesicovaginal Fistula   WP 180
Bladder Drug Administration see Administration,
   Intravesical
Bladder Exstrophy   WJ 500
Bladder Fistula   WJ 500
Bladder Neck Obstruction   WJ 500
Bladder Neoplasms   WJ 504
Bladder, Neurogenic   WJ 500
Bladder Stones see Bladder Calculi
Bladder Worm see Taenia
Blast Injuries   WO 820
Blast Transformation see Lymphocyte

Transformation
Blast-2 Antigen, B-Cell see Antigens,
   Differentiation, B-Lymphocyte
Blastocladiella   QW 180.5.P4
Blastocyst Transfer see Embryo Transfer
Blastogenesis see Lymphocyte Transformation
Blastomyces   QW 180.5.A8
Blastomycosis   WC 450
Blastomycosis, North American see Blastomycosis
Blastomycosis, South American see
   Paracoccidioidomycosis
Bleeding see Hemorrhage
Blennorrhea, Inclusion see Conjunctivitis, Inclusion
Bleomycins
   Pharmacology   QV 269
   Therapeutic use   QZ 267
Blepharitis   WW 205
Blepharoptosis   WW 205
Blepharospasm   WW 205
Blindness   WW 276
   Color see Color Blindness   WW 150
   Education of blind   HV 1618–2349
   Hysterical   WM 173.5
   In infancy & childhood   WW 276
   Libraries for the blind   Z 675.B6
   Library operations   Z 729–871
   Night see Night Blindness   WD 110
   Rehabilitation
      Physical & medical   WW 276
      Social   HV 1573–2349
      Veterinary   SF 891
Blister   WR 143
   Localized, by site
Block Anesthesia see Anesthesia, Conduction
Blood   WH
   Chemistry see Blood chemical analysis   QY
      450–490, etc.
   Children   WS 300
   Clinical examination   QY 400–490
   Corpuscles see Blood Cells   WH 140, etc.;
      Erythrocytes   WH 150–180; Leukocytes   WH
      200
   Derivatives   WH 450
   Fluid elements   WH 400
   Flukes see Schistosoma   QX 355
   Medicolegal examination   W 750
   Substitutes see Plasma Substitutes   WH 450
   Typing see Blood Grouping and Crossmatching
      QY 415
   Velocity see Blood Flow Velocity   WG 106
   See also Anticoagulants   QV 193; Lipids   QU
      85–95; Plasma   WH 400, etc.
Blood, Artificial see Blood Substitutes
Blood Bactericidal Activity   QW 541
   Special topics, by subject
Blood Banks   WH 23–24
   Procedures   WH 460
Blood-Borne Pathogens   WA 790
Blood-Brain Barrier   WL 200
Blood Cell Count   QY 402
   Veterinary   SF 772.67
Blood Cell Count, Red see Erythrocyte Count
Blood Cell Count, White see Leukocyte Count

Blood Cell Number see Blood Cell Count
Blood Cells   WH 140
    Clinical examination   QY 402
    Drugs affecting   QV 180–185
Blood Cells, Red see Erythrocytes
Blood Cells, White see Leukocytes
Blood Chemical Analysis   QY 450–490
    In infancy & childhood   QY 450–490
    Medicolegal   W 750
    Veterinary   SF 772.67
Blood Circulation   WG 103
    Disorders as a manifestation of disease   QZ 170
    In infancy & childhood   WG 103
    Tests   WG 103
    See also names of specific types of circulation,
      e.g., Pulmonary Circulation   WF 600
Blood Circulation, Collateral see Collateral
    Circulation
Blood Circulation Time   WG 103
Blood Coagulation
    Clinical examination   QY 410
    Drugs affecting   QV 190–195
    Physiology   WH 310
Blood Coagulation Disorders   WH 322
    Hemophilia   WH 325
    Veterinary   SF 769.5
    See also names of specific disorders
Blood Coagulation Factors   WH 310
    Clinical examination   QY 410
    Pharmacology   QV 195
Blood Coagulation Tests   QY 410
Blood Component Removal   WH 460
Blood Component Transfusion   WB 356
Blood Count, Complete see Blood Cell Count
Blood Diseases see Hematologic Diseases
Blood Donors   WH 460
Blood Doping see Doping in Sports
Blood Expanders see Plasma Substitutes
Blood Flow see Rheology
Blood Flow Velocity   WG 106
Blood Gas Analysis   QY 450
    Veterinary   SF 774
Blood Gas Monitoring, Transcutaneous   QY 450
Blood Glucose   QU 75
    Clinical analysis   QY 470
Blood Glucose Self-Monitoring
    In diabetes   WK 850
Blood Group Incompatibility   WH 420
Blood Grouping and Crossmatching   QY 415
    Special topics, by subject
Blood Groups   WH 420–425
    Medicolegal examination   W 791
    Typing see Blood Grouping and Crossmatching
      QY 415
Blood Loss, Surgical
    During surgery for a particular condition, with
      the condition
Blood Plasma see Plasma
Blood Plasma Volume see Plasma Volume
Blood Platelet Disorders   WH 300
    See also Purpura, Thrombopenic   WH 315
Blood Platelet Transfusion see Platelet Transfusion
Blood Plateletpheresis see Plateletpheresis

Blood Platelets   WH 300
    Count   QY 402
Blood Poisoning see Septicemia
Blood Preservation   WH 460
Blood Pressure   WG 106
    General physical examination   WB 280
    High see Hypertension   WG 340
    Low see Hypotension   WG 340
Blood Pressure Determination   WG 106
    Physical examination   WB 280
Blood Pressure, High see Hypertension
Blood Pressure, Low see Hypotension
Blood Pressure Monitors   WG 26
Blood Pressure, Venous see Venous Pressure
Blood Protein Disorders   WH 400
    Clinical pathology   QY 455
    Specific disorders involving various blood
      elements, with the element
    See other specific disorders under their names
      in the index
Blood Protein Electrophoresis   QY 455
Blood Proteins   WH 400
    Clinical analysis   QY 455
    Coagulation factors   WH 310
      Clinical pathology   QY 410
Blood Sedimentation   QY 408
Blood Serum see Blood
Blood Specimen Collection   QY 26
Blood Substitutes   WH 450
Blood Sugar see Blood Glucose
Blood Sugar Self-Monitoring see Blood Glucose
    Self-Monitoring
Blood Tests see Hematologic Tests
Blood Transfusion   WB 356
    Veterinary   SF 919.5.B55
    See also Blood Banks   WH 23–24, etc.; Blood
      Donors   WH 460
Blood Transfusion, Intrauterine   WQ 210
Blood Typing see Blood Grouping and
    Crossmatching
Blood Vessel Prosthesis   WG 170
Blood Vessels
    Peripheral   WG 500–700
    Surgery   WG 170
    Of a particular region or organ, with the region
      or organ
Blood Viscosity   WG 106
    Clinical analysis   QY 408
Blood Volume   WG 106
    Volume index   QY 408
Bloodletting   WB 381
Blotting, Northern   QH 441
Blotting, Southern   QH 441
Blotting, Western   QW 525.5.I32
    Proteins   QU 55
    Peptides   QU 68
Blue-Green Bacteria see Cyanobacteria
Blue Sclera see Abnormalities   WW 230 under
    Sclera
Bluetongue Virus   QW 168.5.R15
BLV Infections see HTLV-BLV Infections
Board, Governing see Governing Board
Boats see Ships

Bodies, Dead see Cadaver
Body Buffer Zone see Personal Space
Body Build see Somatotypes
Body Burden   WN 660
Body Composition   QU 100–110
Body Constitution
   Anthropology   GN 62
   As a cause of disease   QZ 50
Body Fluid Compartments   QU 105
Body Fluids   QU 105
Body Height
   Adults   GN 66
   In infancy & childhood   WS 103
     Tables   WS 16
Body Image   BF 697.5.B63
   In adolescence   WS 462
   In infancy & childhood   WS 105.5.S3
Body Language see Kinesics
Body Lice see Lice
Body Rocking see Stereotyped Behavior
Body Size see Body Constitution
Body Snatching see Cadaver
Body Surface Area   GN 66
   Veterinary
     Domestic animals   SF 761
     Wild animals   QL 363
Body Temperature   WB 270
   High see Fever   WB 152
   In antibody production   QW 570
   In infancy & childhood   WS 141
     Newborn   WS 420
   In ovulation   WP 540
   In physical examination   WB 270
     Veterinary   SF 772.5
   See also Skin Temperature   WR 102
Body Temperature Regulation   QT 165
   Skin as a factor   WR 102
Body Types see Somatotypes
Body vermin see Lice; Bedbugs
Body Water   QU 105
Body Weight
   In adulthood   GN 66
   In infancy & childhood   WS 103
     Tables   WS 16
   Infant, Premature see Birth Weight   WS 410, etc.
   Newborn see Birth Weight   WS 420, etc.
Boeck's Sarcoid see Sarcoidosis
Boils see Furunculosis
Bombesin   QU 68
Bombina see Anura
Bond Issues, Construction see Financing, Construction
Bonding, Dental see Dental Bonding
Bonding, Human–Pet   WM 460.5.B7
Bonding (Psychology) see Object Attachment
Bonds, Emotional see Object Attachment
Bone Age Measurement see Age Determination by Skeleton
Bone and Bones   WE 200–259
   Physiology   WE 200
   Surgery   WE 168–190
   Transplantation   WE 190

   See also Skeleton   WE 100–102
Bone Cements   WE 190
   Used for special purposes, by subject
Bone Conduction   WV 272
Bone Cysts   WE 258
   Localized, by site
Bone Density   WE 200
Bone–Derived Transforming Growth Factor see Transforming Growth Factor beta
Bone Development   WE 200
Bone Diseases   WE 225–259
   In infancy & childhood   WS 270
   Infectious   WE 251
   Veterinary   SF 901
Bone Diseases, Developmental   WE 250
Bone Diseases, Infectious see Infectious   WE 251 under Bone Diseases
Bone Diseases, Metabolic   WE 250
Bone Dysplasias see Bone Diseases, Developmental
Bone Lengthening   WE 168
   Localized, by site
Bone Loss, Age–Related see Osteoporosis
Bone Loss, Osteoclastic see Bone Resorption
Bone Loss, Perimenopausal see Osteoporosis, Postmenopausal
Bone Loss, Periodontal see Alveolar Bone Loss
Bone Loss, Postmenopausal see Osteoporosis, Postmenopausal
Bone Marrow   WH 380
Bone Marrow Diseases   WH 380
   See also Anemia, Aplastic   WH 175; Anemia, Myelophthisic   WH 175; Leukemoid reaction   WH 200; Polycythemia vera   WH 180
Bone Marrow Examination   WH 380
Bone Marrow Fibrosis see Myelofibrosis
Bone Marrow Transplantation   WH 380
Bone Mineral Content see Bone Density
Bone Mineral Density see Bone Density
Bone Mineralization see Calcification, Physiologic
Bone Neoplasms   WE 258
   Veterinary   SF 910.T8
Bone Plates   WE 185
Bone Regeneration   WE 200
Bone Resorption   WE 200
   See also Ainhum   WE 835
Bone Screws   WE 185
Bone Transplantation   WE 190
Bone Tuberculosis see Tuberculosis, Osteoarticular
Book Circulation see Library Services
Book Classification   Z 696–697
   Medicine   Z 697.M4
Book Collecting   Z 987–997
   See also Libraries   Z 662–1000; names of specific types of libraries
Book Illustration see Books, Illustrated
Book Imprints   Z 242.I3
Book Industry   Z 116.A2–656
Book Ornamentation   Z 276
   See also Medical Illustration   WZ 348
Book Prices   Z 1000
Book Reviews   Z 1035.A1
   Criticism of early works (pre–1801)   WZ 294
   Of books on specific subjects in the bibliography

ALWAYS CONSULT MAIN SCHEDULES. USE NUMBER ASSIGNED ONLY WHEN SUBJECT REPRESENTS MAJOR EMPHASIS OF WORK BEING CLASSIFIED

number for the subject
See also Bibliography
Book Selection   Z 689–689.8
Bookbinding   Z 266–276
Booklets see Pamphlets
Bookplates   Z 993–996
   Medical   WZ 340
Books
   History   Z 4–8
   Medicine and related fields
      Americana   WZ 270
      Early imprints   WZ 240–270
         Criticism   WZ 294
         Modern editions   WZ 290
         Modern collections   WZ 292
      See also Incunabula   WZ 230, etc.
Books, Illustrated
   Bibliography   Z 1023
   Techniques   NC
   Special types of books, by subject
   See also Medical Illustration   WZ 348, etc.
Booksellers' Catalogs see Catalogs, Booksellers'
Bookselling   Z 278–549
Boranes   QD 181.B1
   Pharmacology   QV 239
Borates   QD 181.B1
   Pharmacology   QV 239
Borderline Personality Disorder   WM 190
Bordetella   QW 131
Bordetella Infections   WC 340
Bordetella pertussis   QW 131
Bordetella Pertussis Toxins see Pertussis Toxins
Boredom
   In adolescence   WS 462
   In infancy & childhood   WS 105.5.E5
   Psychology   BF 575.B67
Boric Acids   QV 239
Bornholm Disease see Pleurodynia, Epidemic
Borohydrides   QD 181.B1
   Pharmacology   QV 239
Boron   QD 181.B1
   Metabolism   QU 130.5
Boron Compounds   QD 181.B1
   As antiseptics   QV 239
   Dental use   WU 190
Borrelia   QW 155
Borrelia Infections   WC 406
   Veterinary   SF 809.B67
Botany   QK
   Economic   SB 107–109
   Medical see Pharmacognosy   QV 752; Plants,
      Medicinal   QV 766, etc.
Botrytis see Hyphomycetes
Bottle Feeding   WS 120
Botulism   WC 268
Bouillaud's Disease see Rheumatic Heart Disease
Bourneville's Disease see Tuberous Sclerosis
Bovine Herpesvirus 1 see Herpesvirus 1, Bovine
Bovine Kunitz Pancreatic Trypsin Inhibitor see
   Aprotinin
Bovine Leukemia Virus see Leukemia Virus, Bovine
Bovine Virus Diarrhea–Mucosal Disease   SF
   967.M78

Boxing   QT 260.5.B7
Braces   WE 172
   Catalogs   W 26
Brachial Artery   WG 595.B7
Brachial–Basilar Insufficiency Syndrome see
   Subclavian Steal Syndrome
Brachial Neuralgia see Cervico–Brachial Neuralgia
Brachial Plexus   WL 400
Brachiocephalic Trunk   WG 595.B72
Brachiocephalic Veins   WG 625.B7
Brachytherapy   WN 250.5.B7
Bracyteles see Cebidae
Bradyarrhythmia see Bradycardia
Bradycardia   WG 330
Bradykinin   QU 68
Brain   WL 300–385
   Blood supply   WL 302
      See also Cerebral arteries   WG 595.C37
   Cerebral hemispheres   WL 307
   Cerebrum   WL 307
   Embryology   WL 300
   Hemorrhage see Cerebral hemorrhage   WL 355
   Injury   WL 354
   Intracranial complications of ENT diseases   WV
   180
   Radiography   WL 141
   Surgery   WL 368
Brain Abscess   WL 351
Brain Chemistry   WL 300
Brain Concussion   WL 354
Brain Damage, Chronic   WL 354
   In infancy & childhood   WS 340
Brain Death   W 820
Brain Diseases   WL 348–362
   In infancy & childhood   WS 340
   Veterinary   SF 895
   See also specific Brain Diseases
Brain Dysfunction, Minimal see Attention Deficit
   Disorder with Hyperactivity
Brain Edema   WL 348
Brain Electrical Activity Mapping see Brain
   Mapping
Brain Injuries   WL 354
   In infancy & childhood   WS 340
Brain Mapping   WL 335
Brain Neoplasms   WL 358
   Localized, by site
Brain Revascularization see Cerebral
   Revascularization
Brain Stem   WL 310
Brain Stem Auditory Evoked Potentials see Evoked
   Potentials, Auditory, Brain Stem
Brain Tissue Transplantation   WL 368
Brainwashing see Persuasive Communication
Branched–Chain Ketoaciduria see Maple Syrup
   Urine Disease
Branchial Arches see Branchial Region
Branchial Clefts see Branchial Region
Branchial Cyst see Branchioma
Branchial Region   WE 101
Branchioma   QZ 310
Brassica
   Botany   QK 495.C9

ALWAYS CONSULT MAIN SCHEDULES.   USE NUMBER ASSIGNED ONLY WHEN
SUBJECT REPRESENTS MAJOR EMPHASIS OF WORK BEING CLASSIFIED

Culture   SB 317.B65
   As a dietary supplement in health and disease
   WB 430
Bread
   As a dietary supplement in health or disease
   WB 431
   Baking   TX 769
Breakbone Fever see Dengue
Breast   WP 800–910
Breast Cysts see Fibrocystic Disease of Breast
Breast Diseases   WP 840–910
Breast Dysplasia see Fibrocystic Disease of Breast
Breast Feeding   WS 125
   See also Lactation Disorders   WP 825
Breast Neoplasms   WP 870
   Male   WP 870
Breast Xeroradiography see Xeromammography
Breath Tests
   For alcoholic intoxication in traffic accidents
   WA 275
   Forensic medicine   W 780
   In general physical examination   WB 205
   Manifestation of gastroenterological diseases
   WI 143
Breathalyzer Tests see Breath Tests
Breathing see Respiration
Breathing Exercises   WB 541
Breech Presentation   WQ 307
Breeding
   Animal   SF 105–109
   Of laboratory animals   QY 54
   Of plants   SB 123–123.5
   Of individual animals or plants, with animal or
   plant
Brevibacterium   QW 118
Bridged Compounds
   Organic chemistry   QD 341.H9
   Toxicity   QV 633
   Used for special purposes, by subject
Bridges, Dental see Denture, Partial; Tooth,
   Artificial
Brief Psychotherapy see Psychotherapy, Brief
Bright Disease see Glomerulonephritis
Bright's Disease see Nephritis
Brill–Symmers Disease see Lymphoma, Follicular
Brill–Zinsser Disease see Brill's Disease
Brill's Disease   WC 605
   Epidemics   WC 610
Brine Shrimp see Artemia
Briquet Syndrome see Somatoform Disorders
Bristle–Coated Pits see Coated Pits, Cell–Membrane
BRL 2288 see Ticarcillin
Broad Ligament   WP 275
Broadsides   Z 240.4
Broca Area see Frontal Lobe
Brochures see Pamphlets
Bromchlortrifluorethane see Halothane
Bromhexine   QV 76
Bromides   QV 87
Bromine   QV 231
   Metabolism   QU 130
Bromocriptine   QV 174
Bromocryptin see Bromocriptine

Bromosuccinimide   QV 85
Bromsulphalein see Sulfobromophthalein
Bronchi   WF 500–553
   Blood supply   WF 500
   Calculi   WF 500
   Children   WS 280
   Drugs affecting see names of specific agents
Bronchial Arteries   WG 595.B76
   See also Blood supply   WF 500 under Bronchi
Bronchial Asthma see Asthma
Bronchial Constriction see Bronchoconstriction
Bronchial Diseases   WF 500–553
   In infancy & childhood   WS 280
   Veterinary   SF 831
Bronchial Fistula   WF 500
Bronchial Lavage Fluid see Bronchoalveolar Lavage
   Fluid
Bronchial Neoplasms   WF 500
   See also Adenocarcinoma, Bronchiolo–Alveolar
     WF 658; Carcinoma, Bronchogenic   WF
   658
Bronchial Provocation Tests   WF 141.5.B8
Bronchial Spasm   WF 500
Bronchiectasis   WF 544
Bronchiolar Carcinoma see Adenocarcinoma,
   Bronchiolo–Alveolar
Bronchioles see Bronchi
Bronchitis   WF 546
   Veterinary   SF 831
Bronchoalveolar Lavage Fluid   WF 600
Bronchoconstriction   WF 102
Bronchodilator Agents   QV 120
Bronchography   WF 500
Broncholithiasis see Bronchial Diseases
Bronchopneumonia   WC 202
   Veterinary   SF 831
Bronchopulmonary Dysplasia   WS 410
Bronchoscopy   WF 500
Bronchospasm see Bronchial Spasm
Bronchospasm, Exercise–Induced see Asthma,
   Exercise–Induced
Bronchospirometry   WB 284
Bronze Diabetes see Hemochromatosis
Browning Reaction see Maillard Reaction
Brucella abortus   QW 131
Brucella Vaccine   WC 310
Brucellosis   WC 310
   Veterinary   SF 809.B8
Brucellosis, Bovine   SF 967.B7
Brucine see Strychnine
Brucite see Magnesium Hydroxide
Brugia   QX 301
Bruises see Contusions
Brunhilde Virus see Polioviruses, Human 1–3
Brunner's Gland see Duodenum
Brush Border see Microvilli
Bubo, Climatic or Tropical see Lymphogranuloma
   Venereum
Bubo, Venereal see Sexually Transmitted Diseases
Bubonic Plague see Plague
Bucca see Cheek
Buckthorn see Rhamnus
Buddhism   BQ

And medical philosophy   W 61
And psychology   BQ 4570.P76
   See also Religion and Psychology   WM 61,
   etc.
And psychoanalysis   WM 460.5.R3
Medicine in religious works   WZ 330
Budding and/or Appendaged Bacteria see Bacteria
Budgerigar Fancier's Lung see Bird Fancier's Lung
Budgetary Control see Budgets
Budgets
   Hospitals   WX 157
   General
      Public finance   HJ 2005+
      U.S.   HJ 2050–2053
   For other topics, class by subject if specific; if
   general, in economics number where available
Buerger's Disease see Thromboangiitis Obliterans
Buffaloes   QL 737.U5
   Diseases   SF 997.5.B8
   European bison   QL 737.U53
Buffers   QV 786
   In acid base equilibrium   QU 105
   See also Preservation, Biological   QH 324
Bufo see Bufonidae
Bufonidae   QL 668.E227
   As laboratory animals   QY 60.A6
Bugs see Hemiptera
Buildings, Public Health Aspects see Housing; Public
   Housing; Restaurants; and names of other types
   of buildings; also Architecture; Environment,
   Controlled; Sanitation
Bulbar Palsy see Paralysis, Bulbar
Bulbourethral Glands   WJ 600
Bulimia   WM 175
Bulla see Blister
Bullous Skin Diseases see Skin Diseases,
   Vesiculobullous
Bumetanide   QV 160
Bundle–Branch Block   WG 330
Bundle of His   WG 201–202
Bundle of Kent see Heart Conduction System
Bunion see Hallux Valgus
Bunostomiasis see Hookworm Infections
Bunostomum see Ancylostomatoidea
Bunyaviridae   QW 168.5.B9
Bunyaviridae Infections   WC 501
Bunyavirus Infections see Bunyaviridae Infections
Buphthalmos see Hydrophthalmos
Bupivacaine   QV 115
Bupranolol   QV 132
Buprenorphine   QV 92
Burial   WA 846
Burial Grounds see Mortuary Practice
Burkitt Herpesvirus see Herpesvirus 4, Human
Burkitt's Lymphoma   WH 525
   Localized by site
   Veterinary in the appropriate LC SF number,
   by site
Burkitt's Lymphoma Virus see Herpesvirus 4,
   Human
Burkitt's Tumor see Burkitt's Lymphoma
Burning Mouth Syndrome   WU 140
Burnout, Professional   WM 172

Burns   WO 704
   Death from (medicolegal aspects)   W 843
   Localized, by site
   See also Sunburn   WR 150
Burns, Chemical   WO 704
Burns, Electric   WO 704
Burns, Inhalation   WO 704
Bursa–Dependent Lymphocytes see B–Lymphocytes
Bursa, Synovial   WE 400
Bursine see Choline
Bursitis   WE 400
Burst–Promoting Factor, Erythrocyte see
   Interleukin–3
Buserelin   WK 515
   Used for treatment of particular disorders, with
   the disorder
Buses see Automobiles
Bush Babies see Galago
Business see Commerce
Business Administration see Hospital Administration;
   Organization and Administration; Practice
   Management, Dental; Practice Management,
   Medical
Business Coalitions (Health Care) see Health Care
   Coalitions
Buspirone   QV 77.9
Busulfan   QV 269
   Cancer chemotherapy   QZ 267
Busulphan see Busulfan
Butacaine   QV 115
Butanoic Acids see Butyric Acids
Butesin Picrate see Butylamines
Butorphanol   QV 92
Butter
   As a dietary supplement in health or disease
      WB 425
   Biochemistry   QU 86
   Manufacture   SF 263
   Public health aspects   WA 715
Butter Yellow see p–Dimethylaminoazobenzene
Butterflies   QX 560
Buttermilk see Milk
Buttocks   WE 750
Butylamines   QU 61
   As local anesthetics   QV 115
Butylated Hydroxyanisole
   Toxicology   QV 632
   As a food preservative   WA 712
Butylated Hydroxytoluene
   As a food preservative   WA 712
Butylcarbamide see Carbutamide
Butylhydroxyanisole see Butylated Hydroxyanisole
Butylhydroxytoluene see Butylated Hydroxytoluene
Butyn see Butacaine
Butyribacterium see Eubacterium
Butyric Acids   QU 90
Butyrophenone Antipsychotic Agents see
   Antipsychotic Agents, Butyrophenone
Butyrophenone Tranquilizers see Antipsychotic
   Agents, Butyrophenone
Butyrophenones   QV 77.9
By–Products, Industrial see Industrial Waste; names
   of specific products

**ALWAYS CONSULT MAIN SCHEDULES. USE NUMBER ASSIGNED ONLY WHEN
SUBJECT REPRESENTS MAJOR EMPHASIS OF WORK BEING CLASSIFIED**

Bylaws see Constitution and Bylaws
Bypass, Coronary Artery see Coronary Artery Bypass
Byssinosis   WF 654
B16 Melanoma see Melanoma, Experimental

C

C Fibers see Nerve Fibers
c–Ha–ras Genes see Genes, ras
c–Ki–ras Genes see Genes, ras
c–N–ras Genes see Genes, ras
C–Peptide   WK 820
CA Antigens see Antigens, Tumor–Associated, Carbohydrate
CA–125 Antigen see Antigens, Tumor–Associated, Carbohydrate
CA–15–3 Antigen see Antigens, Tumor–Associated, Carbohydrate
CA–19–9 Antigen see Antigens, Tumor–Associated, Carbohydrate
Ca(2+) Mg(2+)–ATPase   QU 136
Ca(2+)–Transporting ATPase   QU 136
CA–50 Antigen see Antigens, Tumor–Associated, Carbohydrate
Cabbage see Brassica
Cacajao see Cebidae
Cacao
    As a dietary supplement in health or disease   WB 438
    Chemical technology   TP 640
    Cultivation   SB 267
    Diseases of   SB 608.C17
    Pharmacology   QV 107
    See also Beverages   WB 438, etc.; Candy   WU 113.7, etc.
Cachectin see Tumor Necrosis Factor
Cachexia   WB 146
    Associated with malnutrition   WD 100
    Pituitary see Hypopituitarism   WK 550
Cacodylic Acid   QU 143
    As amebicides   QV 255
    As antisyphilitic agents   QV 262
Cadaver   WA 840–847
    Body snatching   WZ 320
    Destruction of human body   W 822
    Identification   W 800
    Resurrectionists   WZ 320
    See also Autopsy   QZ 35, etc.; Coroners and Medical Examiners   W 800; Death Certificates WA 54; Dissection   QS 130, etc.; Embalming   WA 844; Mortuary Practice WA 840–847
Cadmium   QV 290
Caduceus see Emblems and Insignia
Caenorhabditis   QX 203
Caerulein Receptors see Receptors, Cholecystokinin
Caeruloplasmin see Ceruloplasmin
Caesarean Section see Cesarean Section
Cafeterias see Restaurants
Caffea see Coffee
Caffeine   QV 107
Caffeine Receptors see Receptors, Purinergic

Caimans see Alligators and Crocodiles
Caisson Disease see Decompression Sickness
Calcaneus   WE 880
Calciferols see Ergocalciferols
Calcification, Pathologic see Calcinosis
Calcification, Physiologic   WE 200
    See also Ossification, Physiologic   WE 200
Calcinosis   WD 200.5.C2
    Intervertebralis   WE 740
    See also Ossification, Pathologic   QZ 180
Calciphylaxis   WD 200.5.C2
Calcitonin   WK 202
Calcium   QV 276
    Inorganic chemistry   QD 181.C2
Calcium–Activated Neutral Protease see Calpain
Calcium Adenosinetriphosphatase see Ca(2+)–Transporting ATPase
Calcium Antagonists, Exogenous see Calcium Channel Blockers
Calcium ATPase see Ca(2+)–Transporting ATPase
Calcium–Binding Proteins
Calcium Blockaders, Exogenous see Calcium Channel Blockers
Calcium Carbimide see Cyanamide
Calcium Channel Blockers   QV 150
Calcium Channels   QH 603.I54
Calcium Cyanamide see Cyanamide
Calcium–Dependent Activator Protein see Calmodulin
Calcium–Dependent Neutral Proteinase see Calpain
Calcium–Dependent Regulator see Calmodulin
Calcium, Dietary   QU 130
    As a supplement in health or disease   WB 428
Calcium Diphosphate see Calcium Pyrophosphate
Calcium Hydroxide
    Dentistry   WU 190
    Inorganic chemistry   QD 181.C2
    Pharmacology   QV 276
Calcium Inhibitors, Exogenous see Calcium Channel Blockers
Calcium Isotopes
    Inorganic chemistry   QD 181.C2
    Pharmacology   QV 276
Calcium Leucovorin see Leucovorin
Calcium Magnesium Adenosinetriphosphatase see Ca(2+) Mg(2+)–ATPase
Calcium Magnesium ATPase see Ca(2+) Mg(2+)–ATPase
Calcium Metabolism Disorders   WD 200.5.C2
    Decalcification, Pathologic   WE 250
Calcium Oxalate
    Biochemistry   QU 98
Calcium Phosphates
    Inorganic chemistry   QD 181.C2
    Of bone in general   WE 200
    Of teeth   WU 101
Calcium Pyrophosphate   QV 285
Calcium Sulfate
    In density   WU 190
    In casting models   QY 35
    In surgical casts   WO 170
Calcium Transport Proteins see Calcium–Binding Proteins

Calculators, Programmable see Computers
Calculi   QZ 180
   Biliary see Cholelithiasis   WI 755
   Bladder see Bladder Calculi   WJ 500
   Common bile duct see Common Bile Duct Calculi
     WI 755
   Kidney see Kidney Calculi   WJ 356
   Salivary duct see Salivary Duct Calculi   WI
     230
   Ureteral see Ureteral Calculi   WJ 400
   Urinary see Urinary Calculi   WJ 140
Caldesmon see Calmodulin-Binding Proteins
Calibration
   Special topics, by subject
California Encephalitis Virus see California Group
   Viruses
California Group Viruses   QW 168.5.B9
Californium   WN 420
   Nuclear physics   QC 796.C45
   For other specific aspects use numbers listed in
     this index under Radioisotopes
Calisthenics see Gymnastics
Callicebinae see Cebidae
Callithricidae see Callitrichinae
Callitrichinae   QL 737.P92
   As laboratory animals   QY 60.P7
   Diseases   SF 997.5.P7
Callosities   WR 500
   Foot   WE 880
   Toes   WE 835
   Other locations, by site
Calmette-Guerin Bacillus see Mycobacterium bovis
Calmette-Guerin Immunization see BCG Vaccine
Calmodulin   QU 55
Calmodulin-Binding Proteins   QU 55
Caloric Intake
   In normal diet   QT 235
   Nutritional requirements   QU 145
Caloric Tests   WV 255
Caloric Value of Foods see Nutrition
Calorie Deficiency see Deficiency Diseases;
   Protein-Energy Malnutrition
Calorimetry   QU 125
Calpain   QU 136
Calspectin see Calmodulin-Binding Proteins
Camelids, New World   QL 737.U54
   Diseases   SF 997.5.C3
Camellia see Tea
Camels   QL 737.U54
   Diseases   SF 997.5.C3
Camphor   QV 65
Campimetry see Perimetry
Camping   QT 250
   Special topics, by subject, e.g., discussion of camp
     safety act   WA 33
Campylobacter fetus   QW 154
Campylobacter pylori see Helicobacter pylori
Cancer see Neoplasms
Cancer-Associated Carbohydrate Antigens see
   Antigens, Tumor-Associated, Carbohydrate
Cancer Care Facilities   QZ 23-24
Cancer Chemotherapy see Drug therapy   QZ 267
   under Neoplasms or names of specific types of

neoplasm
Cancer Genes see Oncogenes
Cancer Research see Neoplasms, Experimental   QZ
   206 or names of specific types of neoplasm
Cancer Staging see Neoplasm Staging
Candida   QW 180.5.D38
Candidiasis   WC 470
Candidiasis, Cutaneous   WR 300
Candidiasis, Oral   WC 470
Candy
   As a dietary supplement in health or disease
     WB 400
   In dental health   WU 113.7
Canine Tooth see Cuspid
Canker Sore see Stomatitis, Aphthous
Cannabidiol
   As an anticonvulsant   QV 85
   As a hallucinogen   QV 77.7
Cannabinoids   QV 77.7
Cannabis
   Abuse see Marijuana Abuse   WM 276
   Associated with hallucinogens   QV 77.7
Cannabis Abuse see Marijuana Abuse
Cannabis Smoking see Marijuana Smoking
Canned Foods see Food Preservation;
   Food-Processing Industry
Canned Milk see Milk
Cannulation see Catheterization
Cantharides see Cantharidin
Cantharidin   QV 65
Caoutchouc see Rubber
CAPD see Peritoneal Dialysis, Continuous
   Ambulatory
Capgras Syndrome   WM 202
Capillaries   WG 700
Capillaries, Lymphatic see Lymphatic System
Capillarity   QC 183
Capillary Endothelium see Endothelium, Vascular
Capillary Fragility   WG 700
Capillary Permeability   WG 700
Capillary Resistance   WG 106
Capillary Resistance, Hematologic see Capillary
   Fragility
Capital Expenditures
   Medicine   W 74
   Other fields, by subject, in the number for
     economics when available
Capital Financing
   Hospitals   WX 157
   For other specific subject, class in economics
     number where applicalble
Capitalism see Political Systems
Capitation Fee
   Dental   WU 77
   Hospital   WX 157
   Medical   W 74
   Nursing   WY 77
   With other specialties, class in economics number
     where applicable
Caprines see Goats
Caproates   QU 90
Caprolactam
   As an industrial poison   WA 465

Special topics, by subject
Capsaicin   QU 90
Capsules   QV 785
Captopril
    As an antihypertensive agent   QV 150
    As an enzyme inhibitor   QU 143
Carassius auratus see Goldfish
Carassius carassius see Carp
Carbachol   QV 122
Carbamates   QU 98
    As insecticides   WA 240
    Organic chemistry
        Aliphatic compounds   QD 305.A2
Carbamazepine   QV 85
Carbamylcholine see Carbachol
Carbarsone see Arsenicals
Carbenicillin   QV 354
Carbenicillin Phenyl Sodium see Carfecillin
Carbenoxalone see Carbenoxolone
Carbenoxolone   QV 66
Carbocaine see Mepivacaine
Carbocysteine
    Biochemistry   QU 60
    Pharmacology   QV 76
Carbofuran
    Agriculture   SB 952.C3
    Public health   WA 240
Carbohydrate Antigens, Tumor-Associated see
    Antigens, Tumor-Associated, Carbohydrate
Carbohydrate Conformation   QU 75
Carbohydrate Linkage see Carbohydrate
    Conformation
Carbohydrate Metabolism, Inborn Errors   WD
    205.5.C2
Carbohydrates   QU 75
    Clinical analysis   QY 470
    See also Dietary Carbohydrates   WB 427, etc.
Carbolic Acid see Phenols
Carbolines
    As tranquilizing agents   QV 77.9
    Organic chemistry   QD 401
Carbon   QD 181.C1
    Pharmacology   QV 138.C1
Carbon Dioxide   QV 314
Carbon Dioxide Partial Pressure Determination,
    Transcutaneous see Blood Gas Monitoring,
    Transcutaneous
Carbon Disulfide   QD 181.C1
    Toxicological effects   QV 633
Carbon Isotopes
    Inorganic chemistry   QD 181.C1
    Pharmacology   QV 138.C1
Carbon Monoxide   QV 662
Carbon Monoxide Poisoning   QV 662
Carbon Tetrachloride
    As an anthelmintic   QV 253
    Organic chemistry   QD 305.H5
Carbon Tetrachloride Poisoning   QV 633
Carbonate Dehydratase   QU 139
Carbonate Dehydratase Inhibitors see Carbonic
    Anhydrase Inhibitors
Carbonate Dehydratase Isoenzymes see Carbonate
    Dehydratase

Carbonates
    Inorganic chemistry   QD 181.C1
    Organic chemistry   QD 305.A2
    Pharmacology   QV 138.C1
Carbonic Acid   QV 138.C1
Carbonic Anhydrase see Carbonate Dehydratase
Carbonic Anhydrase Inhibitors   QV 160
    Enzymology   QU 143
Carbonic Anhydrase Isoenzymes see Carbonate
    Dehydratase
Carbonic Anhydride see Carbon Dioxide
Carbonization see Drug Compounding
Carbonyl Chloride see Phosgene
Carboxy-Lyases   QU 139
Carboxybenzyl Penicillin see Carbenicillin
Carboxyl (Acid) Proteinases see Aspartic Proteinases
Carboxylic Acids   QU 98
    Organic chemistry
        Aliphatic compounds   QD 305.A2
        Aromatic compounds   QD 341.A2
Carboxymethylcysteine see Carbocysteine
Carbuncle   WR 235
Carbutamide   WK 825
Carcinoembryonic Antigen   QW 570
    Neoplasm immunology   QZ 310
Carcinogen Markers see Tumor Markers, Biological
Carcinogenesis see Neoplasms
Carcinogenicity Tests   QZ 202
Carcinogens   QZ 202
Carcinogens, Environmental   QZ 202
Carcinoid Heart Disease   WG 210
Carcinoid Tumor   WI 435
    Localized, by site
Carcinoma   QZ 365
    Localized, by site
Carcinoma, Adenoid Cystic   QZ 365
    Localized, by site
Carcinoma, Alveolar see Adenocarcinoma,
    Bronchiolo-Alveolar
Carcinoma, Bronchial see Carcinoma, Bronchogenic
Carcinoma, Bronchiolo-Alveolar see
    Adenocarcinoma, Bronchiolo-Alveolar
Carcinoma, Bronchogenic   WF 658
Carcinoma, Hepatocellular   WI 735
Carcinoma, Hypernephroid see Carcinoma, Renal
    Cell
Carcinoma, Renal Cell   WJ 358
Carcinosarcoma   QZ 310
Cardia   WI 300
    Neoplasms   WI 320
Cardiac Arrest see Heart Arrest
Cardiac Depressants see Anti-Arrhythmia Agents
Cardiac Electroversion see Electric Countershock
Cardiac Emergencies   WG 205
Cardiac Failure see Heart Failure, Congestive
Cardiac Glycosides   QV 153
Cardiac Hypertrophy see Heart Hypertrophy
Cardiac Neurosis see Neurocirculatory Asthenia
Cardiac Output   WG 106
Cardiac Output, Low   WG 210
Cardiac Pacemaker, Artificial see Pacemaker,
    Artificial
Cardiac Pacing, Artificial   WG 168

**ALWAYS CONSULT MAIN SCHEDULES. USE NUMBER ASSIGNED ONLY WHEN
SUBJECT REPRESENTS MAJOR EMPHASIS OF WORK BEING CLASSIFIED**

See also Pacemaker, Artificial   WG 26
Cardiac Rupture, Traumatic see Heart Injuries
Cardiac Stimulants see Cardiotonic Agents
Cardiac Transplantation see Heart Transplantation
Cardiac Volume   WG 106
Cardiography, Impedance   WG 141.5.C15
   Special topics, by subject, e.g., in the diagnosis
     of Tachycardia   WG 330
Cardiologists, Directories see Directories   WG 22
   under Cardiology
Cardiology   WG
   Directories   WG 22
   Experimental studies   WG 110
   General works   WG 100
   In infancy & childhood   WS 290
   Nursing   WY 152.5
Cardiomyopathies see Myocardial Diseases
Cardiomyopathy, Alcoholic   WG 280
Cardiomyopathy, Chagas see Chagas
   Cardiomyopathy
Cardiomyopathy, Congestive   WG 280
Cardiomyopathy, Dilated see Cardiomyopathy,
   Congestive
Cardiomyopathy, Restrictive   WG 280
Cardiopulmonary Arrest see Heart Arrest
Cardiopulmonary Resuscitation
   First Aid   WA 292
Cardiospasm see Esophageal Achalasia
Cardiotocography   WQ 209
Cardiotonic Agents   QV 150
Cardiotonic Steroids see Cardiac Glycosides
Cardiovascular Agents   QV 150–156
Cardiovascular Disease (Specialty) see Cardiology
Cardiovascular Diseases   WG
   General works   WG 120
   In infancy & childhood   WS 290
   In pregnancy see Pregnancy Complications,
     Cardiovascular   WQ 244
   Neoplasms (General)   WG 120
     See also Neoplasms, Vascular Tissue   QZ 340
   Nursing   WY 152.5
   Veterinary   SF 811
Cardiovascular System   WG
   Abnormalities   WG 220
   Children   WS 290
   Drugs affecting   QV 150–156
   Experimental studies   WG 110
   Radiography (General)   WG 141.5.R2
   Radionuclide imaging   WG 141.5.R3
   Surgery   WG 168–169.5
   Tomography   WG 141.5.T6
Cardioversion see Electric Countershock
Carditis, Bacterial see Endocarditis, Bacterial
Care, Surgical see Postoperative Care; Preoperative
   Care; Surgical Nursing
Career Choice
   Dentistry   WU 21
   Nursing   WY 16
   Ophthalmology   WW 21
   Pharmacy   QV 21
   Physicians   W 21
   Psychiatry   WM 21
   Surgery   WO 21

   In other fields, by subject
Career Counseling see Vocational Guidance
Career Ladders see Career Mobility
Career Mobility
   Social conditions   HN
   Vocational guidance   HF 5381–5382.5
   Specific careers, by subject, e.g. Nursing   WY
    16
Caregivers
   In particular fields, by subjects
   See also names of specific caregivers
Carfecillin   QV 354
Caricatures   NC 1300–1763
   Medical   WZ 336
   See also Medical Illustration   WZ 348
Caries see Dental Caries
Caries, Dental see Dental Caries
Cariogenic Agents   WU 270
   See also Diet, Cariogenic   WU 113.7
Carnitine   QU 187
Carnitine Palmitoyltransferase   QU 141
Carnivora   QL 737.C2–737.C28
   Diseases   SF 600–1100
   Specific carnivora or groups, by animal or group
Carnosine   QU 68
Carotene   QU 110
   Animal biochemistry wild   QP 671.C3
   Plants   QK 898.C35
   Vitamin A related   QU 167
Carotenoids   QU 110
   Animal biochemistry wild   QP 671.C35
   Plants   QK 898.C35
   Vitamin A related   QU 167
Carotid Arteries   WG 595.C2
Carotid Artery Diseases   WL 355
Carotid Artery, External   WG 595.5.C2
Carotid Artery, Internal   WG 595.5.C2
Carotid Artery Thrombosis   WL 355
Carotid Body   WL 102.9
Carotid Body Tumor   WL 102.9
Carotid Sinus   WG 595.5.C2
   Carotid sinus syndrome   WG 560
Carp   QL 638.C94
   Diseases   SH 179.C3
   As laboratory animals   QY 60.F4
Carpal Bones   WE 830
Carpal Tunnel Syndrome   WL 500
Carphenazine see Phenothiazine Tranquilizers
Carpus see Wrist
Carrageenan   QU 83
Carrier Ampholytes see Ampholyte Mixtures
Carrier Proteins   QU 55
   In immunochemistry   QW 504.5
   Special topics, by subject
   See also names of specific proteins, e.g.,
    Ferrodoxins   QW 52, etc.
Carrier State   QW 700
   Veterinary   SF 757.2
Carriers, Genetic see Heterozygote
Carriers, Genetic, Detection see Heterozygote
   Detection
Carriers of Infection see Carrier State; Disease
   Vectors; Insect Vectors

**ALWAYS CONSULT MAIN SCHEDULES. USE NUMBER ASSIGNED ONLY WHEN
SUBJECT REPRESENTS MAJOR EMPHASIS OF WORK BEING CLASSIFIED**

Carriers, Public see Railroads WA 810, etc. and names of other forms of transportation
Carrion's Disease see Bartonella Infections
Carsickness see Motion Sickness
Cartilage WE 300
Cartilage, Articular WE 300
Cartilage Diseases WE 300
   In infancy & childhood WS 270
Cartilage, Epiphyseal see Growth Plate
Cartoons WZ 336
Caryophanales see Bacteria
Casanthranol see Cascara
Cascara QV 75
Case-Base Studies see Case-Control Studies
Case-Comparison Studies see Case-Control Studies
Case-Control Studies WA 950
   Of particular disorders, with the disorder
Case Management, Insurance see Managed Care Programs
Case Mix see Diagnosis-Related Groups
Case-Referent Studies see Case-Control Studies
Case reports see Case studies
Case studies
   Medicine WB 293
   Psychiatry WM 40-49
   Surgery WO 16
   Special topics, by subject
Case Taking see Medical History Taking
Caseins WA 716
   Dairy science SF 253
   Food and milk microbiology QW 85
Cassava
   As a dietary supplement in health or disease WB 431
   Cultivation SB 211.C3
   Poisoning WD 500
Caste see Social Class
Castor see Rodentia
Castor Bean Lectin see Ricin
Castor Oil QV 75
Castration
   Female WP 660
   Male WJ 868
   Veterinary SF 889
Castration, Male see Orchiectomy
Casts see Models, Structural; Dental Casting Investment
Casts, Surgical WO 170
Cat Diseases SF 985-986
CAT Scan, Radionuclide see Tomography, Emission-Computed
CAT Scan, X-Ray see Tomography, X-Ray Computed
CAT Scanners, X-Ray see Tomography Scanners, X-Ray Computed
Cat-Scratch Disease WC 593
Catabolism see Metabolism
Catalase QU 140
Catalepsy WM 197
   Catatonic WM 203
   Hysterical neurosis WM 173
   Neurologic manifestation WL 390
Cataloging Z 693-695.83

Catalogs see Types of catalogs or product being announced, e.g., Catalogs, Drug QV 772
Catalogs, Booksellers' Z 998-1000.5
   General catalogs of modern books Z 1036
   On particular subjects, in bibliography number for the subject
Catalogs, Commercial HF 5861-5862
   Embryology QS 626
   Medical supplies W 26
   Non-book materials (Form number 18.2 in any NLM schedule where applicable)
      Embryology QS 618.2
      Histology QS 518.2
   Specialty catalogs W 26
   See also names of specific types of catalogs
Catalogs, Drug QV 772
Catalogs, Library Z 881-980
   Private libraries Z 997-997.2
   Other particular classes of libraries (not LC practice) Z 675.A-Z
Catalogs, Publishers' Z 1217-4980
   Booksellers Z 998-1000.5
   General catalogs of modern books Z 1036
   On particular subjects, in bibliography number for the subject
Catalogs, Union
   Books or general Z 695.83
   Serials Z 6945
   On particular subjects, in bibliography number for the subject
Catalysis
   Enzymatic QU 135
   Organic chemistry QD 281.C3
   Pharmaceutical chemistry QV 25
   Physical chemistry QD 505
   Therapeutics see Alternative Medicine WB 890
   Applications in other areas, by subject
Cataphoresis see Electrophoresis
Cataplexy WM 197
   Associated with narcolepsy WM 188
Cataract WW 260
Cataract Extraction WW 260
Catarrhina see Cercopithecidae
Catastrophic Health Insurance see Insurance, Major Medical
Catastrophic Illness
   Special topics, by subject
   See also Disease
Catatonia WM 197
   Associated with schizophrenia WM 203
Catatonic Schizophrenia see Schizophrenia, Catatonic
Catchment Area (Health) WA 541
   Geriatrics WT 30
Catechin
   In dyeing and tanning TP 925.C38
   Special topics by subject
Catechinic Acid see Catechin
Catechol Estrogens see Estrogens, Catechol
Catecholamines WK 725
Catechols
   Organic chemistry QD 341.P5
Catechu see Catechin

Catechuic Acid see Catechin
Caterpillars see Lepidoptera
Catharsis   WM 420.5.A2
Cathartics   QV 75
Cathepsins   QU 136
Catheterization
    General   WB 365
    Heart see Heart Catheterization   WG 141.5.C2
    Surgical technique   WO 500
    Urinary see Urinary Catheterization   WJ 500
Catheterization, Balloon see Balloon Dilatation
Catheterization, Bronchial see Catheterization,
    Peripheral
Catheterization, Cardiac see Heart Catheterization
Catheterization, Heart see Heart Catheterization
Catheterization, Peripheral
    General   WB 365
Catheterization, Peripheral Arterial see
    Catheterization, Peripheral
Catheterization, Peripheral Venous see
    Catheterization, Peripheral
Catheterization, Ureteral see Urinary Catheterization
Catheterization, Urethral see Urinary Catheterization
Catheterization, Urinary see Urinary Catheterization
Catheters, Indwelling
    (Form number 26 in any NLM schedule where
    applicable)
    See also names of various types of catheterization
Cathode see Electrodes
Cathode Ray Tube Display see Data Display
Cathode Rays see Beta Rays
Catholicism   BX 800–4795
    And birth control   HQ 766.3
    And psychiatry   WM 61
    Medical ethics   W 50
    Other special topics, by subject, e.g., nursing
    ethics according to Catholic standards   WY
    85
    See also Religion and Medicine   WB 885, etc.;
    other headings beginning with Religion
Cations   QV 275–278
Cations, Divalent   QV 275
Cations, Monovalent   QV 275
Cats
    As laboratory animals   QY 60.C2
    Anatomy   QL 813.C38
    Culture   SF 441–450
    Diseases see Cat Diseases   SF 985–986
    Wild   QL 737.C23
Cattell Personality Factor Questionnaire   WM
145.5.C3
    In psychology   BF 698.8.S5
Cattle
    Anatomy   SF 767.C3
    Culture   SF 191–219
    Physiology   SF 768.2.C3
Cattle Diseases   SF 961–967
Cattle Leukemia Virus see Leukemia Virus, Bovine
Cattle Plague see Rinderpest
Caucasoid Race
    Anthropology   GN 537
    See also special topics under Ethnic Groups
Caudal Anesthesia see Anesthesia, Epidural

Caudata see Urodela
Caudate Nucleus   WL 307
Causalgia   WL 544
Cause of Death   WA 900
    Special topics, by subject
Causes of Disease see Pathogenesis   QZ 40–109
    under Disease
Caustics   QV 612
Cautery   WO 198
Cavernous Sinus   WG 625.C7
CAVH see Hemofiltration
Cavia see Guinea Pigs
Caviidae see Guinea Pigs
Cavities, Dental see Dental Cavity Preparation
Cavus Deformity see Foot Deformities
Cazenave's Lupus see Lupus Erythematosus, Discoid
CD-ROM
    Catalogs and works about (Form number 18.2
    in any NLM schedules where applicable)
    Special topics, by subject
CDP Choline see Cytidine Diphosphate Choline
CD25 Antigens see Receptors, Interleukin-2
CD4 Antigens see Antigens, CD4
CD4 Molecule see Antigens, CD4
CD4 Receptors see Antigens, CD4
Cebidae   QL 737.P925
    Diseases   SF 997.5.P7
    As laboratory animals   QY 60.P7
Cebuella see Callitrichinae
Cebus   QL 737.P925
    Diseases   SF 997.5.P7
    As laboratory animals   QY 60.P7
Cecal Diseases   WI 530
Cecal Neoplasms   WI 530
Cecum   WI 530
Cefacler see Cephalexin
Cefaclor   QV 350.5.C3
Cefalotin see Cephalothin
Cefamandole   QV 350.5.C3
Cefotaxime   QV 350.5.C3
Cefoxitin   QV 350.5.C3
Ceftazidime   QV 350.5.C3
Ceftriaxone   QV 350.5.C3
Cefuroxime   QV 350.5.C3
Celebes Ape see Macaca
Celiac Artery   WG 595.C3
Celiac Disease   WD 175
Celiac Ganglia see Ganglia, Sympathetic
Celioscopy see Laparoscopy
Cell Adhesion Molecules
    Biochemistry   QU 55
Cell Aggregation   QH 604.2
Cell Anoxia see Cell Hypoxia
Cell Communication   QH 604.2
    Nerve cells   WL 102.8
Cell Compartmentation   QH 604.3
Cell Count   QH 585.5
    Of neoplasms   QZ 202
    Of particular organs, with the organ
Cell Cycle   QH 605–605.3
Cell Degranulation   QH 631
Cell Density see Cell Count

Cell Differentiation
  Animals
    Domestic   SF 767.5
    Wild   QL 963.5
  General and human   QH 607
Cell Division   QH 605–605.3
  Plants   QK 725
Cell Fractionation   QH 585.5.C43
  Special topics, by subject
Cell–Free System   QH 581–581.2
Cell Fusion   QH 451
Cell Growth see Cell Division
Cell Growth Inhibitors see Growth Inhibitors
Cell Hypoxia   QH 633
Cell Isolation see Cell Separation
Cell Line   QH 585.4–585.45
Cell Line, Tumor see Tumor Cells, Cultured
Cell–Mediated Immunity see Immunity, Cellular
Cell–Mediated Lympholytic Cells see
  T–Lymphocytes, Cytotoxic
Cell Membrane   QH 601–601.2
  Bacterial   QW 51–52
  See also Nuclear Membrane   QH 601.2
Cell–Membrane Coated Pits see Coated Pits,
  Cell–Membrane
Cell Membrane Permeability
  Cytology   QH 611
  Metabolism   QU 120
Cell Membrane Proteins see Membrane Proteins
Cell Movement   QH 647
Cell Nucleolus   QH 596
Cell Nucleus   QH 595
Cell Number see Cell Count
Cell Organelles see Organelles
Cell Segregation see Cell Separation
Cell Separation   QH 585.5.C44
Cell Surface Antigens see Antigens, Surface
Cell Surface Glycoproteins see Membrane
  Glycoproteins
Cell Surface Proteins see Membrane Proteins
Cell Surface Receptors see Receptors, Cell Surface
Cell Therapy see Tissue Therapy
Cell Transformation, Neoplastic   QZ 202
Cell Transformation, Viral   QH 604
  Of neoplasms   QZ 202
Cell Wall
  Bacterial   QW 51–52
  Plant   QK 725
Cellophane
  Plastics manufacture   TP 1180.C4
  Used for special purposes, by subject, e.g.; in
    hemodialysis   WJ 378
Cells
  Aging
    Animal   QH 608
    Human   WT 104
    Plants   QK 725
  Chromosome abnormalities   QS 675
  Eukaryotic   QH 603.E8
  Histology   QS 504–532
  Normal morphology and physiology   QH
    573–659
  Pathology

    Animal   QH 671
    Human   QZ 4, etc.
  Radiation effects   WN 620
  Of a specific tissue, with the tissue, e. g. Muscle
    cells   WE 500
Cells, Cultured   QH 585.2–585.45
  In histology   QS 530
    Techniques   QS 525
Cellular Immunity see Immunity, Cellular
Cellular Includions see Inclusion Bodies
Cellular Neurobiology see Neurobiology
Cellulitis   WR 220
  Phlegmon   WD 375
Cellulitis, Pelvic see Parametritis
Cellulose
  Biochemistry   QU 83
  Deficiency   WD 105
  Organic chemistry   QD 323
  Plastics manufacture   TP 1180.C6
  Therapeutic use by diet   WB 427
  Used for special purposes, by subject, e.g., in the
    treatment of kidney calculi   WJ 356
CELSS see Ecological Systems, Closed
Cement, Dental see Dental Cementum
Cement Fillings see Dental Cements; Silicate Cement
Cementation   WU 300
  Crowns   WU 515
  Inlays   WU 360
  See also Dental Cements   WU 190
Cementoblasts see Dental Cementum
Cementoma   WU 280
Cementoperiostitis see Periodontitis
Cementum see Dental Cementum
Cemeteries see Mortuary Practice
Census see Demography
Centenarian see Aged, 80 and over
Centers for Health Planning see Health Planning
  Organizations
Centipedes see Arthropods
Central Nervous System   WL 300–405
  Drugs affecting   QV 76.5–115
Central Nervous System Agents   QV 76.5
  Analeptics   QV 100–107
  Psychotropic drugs   QV 77.2–77.9
Central Nervous System Depressants   QV 80–98
  Local anesthetics   QV 110–115
  See also specific depressants and specific types
    of depressants
Central Nervous System Diseases   WL 300–405
  Associated eye diseases   WW 460
  General works   WL 300
  In infancy & childhood   WS 340–342
  Nursing   WY 160.5
  Veterinary   SF 895
Central Nervous System Neoplasms   WL 358
Central Nervous System Stimulants see Analeptics
Central Retinal Artery see Retinal Artery
Central Retinal Vein see Retinal Vein
Central Supply, Hospital   WX 165
Central Venous Pressure   WG 106
Centralized Hospital Services   WX 150
Centrally Acting Muscle Relaxants see Muscle
  Relaxants, Central

Centrifugation
    Biological research   QH 324.9.C4
    Chemical engineering   TP 159.C4
    Chemical techniques   QD 54.C4
    Clinical chemistry   QY 90
    See also Ultracentrifugation   QD 54.C4, etc.
Centrifugation, Density Gradient
    Clinical chemistry   QY 90
    Histochemistry   QS 531
    Other special topics, by subject
Centrioles   QH 597
Centrophenoxine see Meclofenoxate
Cenuriasis see Cestode Infections
Cephaelis see Ipecac (Syrup)
Cephalalgia see Headache
Cephalexin   QV 350.5.C3
Cephalins see Phosphatidylethanolamines
Cephalometry
    Anthropology (medieval and modern)   GN 71–131
    General dental diagnosis   WU 141.5.C3
    Used for diagnosis of particular disorders, with the disorder
Cephalopelvic Disproportion see Labor Complications
Cephalopelvic Proportion see Pelvimetry
Cephalopelvimetry see Pelvimetry
Cephalosporins   QV 350.5.C3
Cephalothin   QV 350.5.C3
Cephamycins   QV 350.5.C3
Cephradine   QV 350.5.C3
Ceramics
    Chemical technology   TP 785–842
    Dentistry   WU 190
    Medicine   QT 37.5.C4
    Used for special purposes, by subject
Ceratopogonidae   QX 505
Cercopithecidae   QL 737.P93
    Diseases   SF 997.5.P7
    As laboratory animals   QY 60.P7
Cercopithecus aethiops   QL 737.P93
    Diseases   SF 997.5.P7
    As laboratory animals   QY 60.P7
Cercopithecus pygerythrus see Cercopithecus aethiops
Cercopithecus sabeus see Cercopithecus aethiops
Cercopithecus tantalus see Cercopithecus aethiops
Cereals
    As a dietary supplement in health or disease WB 431
    Cultivation   SB 188–192
    Processing   TS 2120–2159
Cerebellar Ataxia   WL 320
Cerebellar Cortex   WL 320
Cerebellar Diseases   WL 320
Cerebellar Neoplasms   WL 320
Cerebellar Nuclei   WL 320
Cerebellopontile Angle see Cerebellopontine Angle
Cerebellopontine Angle   WL 320
Cerebellum   WL 320
Cerebral Aneurysm   WL 355
    Traumatic   WL 354
Cerebral Angiography   WL 141

Cerebral Anoxia   WL 355
Cerebral Arteries   WG 595.C37
    See also Blood supply   WL 302 under Brain
Cerebral Arteriosclerosis   WL 355
Cerebral Arteriovenous Malformations   WL 355
Cerebral Artery Diseases   WL 355
Cerebral Cortex   WL 307
Cerebral Decortication   WL 307
Cerebral Dominance see Dominance, Cerebral
Cerebral Edema see Brain Edema
Cerebral Embolism and Thrombosis   WL 355
Cerebral Hemispheres see Brain
Cerebral Hemorrhage   WL 355
    Localized, by site
Cerebral Infarction   WL 355
Cerebral Ischemia   WL 355
Cerebral Ischemia, Transient   WL 355
Cerebral Meningitis see Meningitis
Cerebral Palsy   WS 342
    In adulthood   WL 354
Cerebral Peduncle see Mesencephalon
Cerebral Revascularization   WL 355
Cerebral Sclerosis, Diffuse   WL 348
Cerebral Thrombosis see Cerebral Embolism and Thrombosis
Cerebral Vasospasm see Cerebral Ischemia, Transient
Cerebral Veins   WG 625.C3
Cerebral Ventricle Neoplasms   WL 358
Cerebral Ventricles   WL 307
Cerebral Ventriculography   WL 141
    In infancy & childhood   WS 340
Cerebrospinal Fluid   WL 203
    Clinical analysis   QY 220
    General diagnosis   WB 377
Cerebrospinal Fluid Pressure   WL 203
Cerebrospinal Fluid Proteins   WL 203
    Clinical examination   QY 220
Cerebrospinal Meningitis, Epidemic see Meningitis, Meningococcic
Cerebrovascular Circulation   WL 302
    Disorders   WL 355
Cerebrovascular Disorders   WL 355
Cerebrum see Brain
Ceremonial
    Coming of age (Primitive customs)   GN 483.3
    Religious (Primitive customs)   GN 473–473.6
    Royalty and nobility   GT 5010–5090
Cerium
    Inorganic chemistry   QD 181.C4
    Pharmacology   QV 290
Cerium Isotopes
    Inorganic chemistry   QD 181.C4
    Pharmacology   QV 290
Ceroid–Lipofuscinosis, Neuronal see Neuronal Ceroid–Lipofuscinosis
Certificate of Need
    Relating to health facilities   WX 157
    Relating to regional health planning   WA 541
    For other special purposes, by subject
Certification
    (Form number 21 in any NLM schedule where applicable)

Of paraprofessionals, with the general number for the type
Certification of the Dead see Death Certificates
Ceruloplasmin   WH 400
   Clinical examination   QY 455
Cerumen   WV 222
   Impacted   WV 222
Cervical Rib Syndrome   WL 500
Cervical Smears see Vaginal Smears
Cervical Vertebrae   WE 725
Cervicitis   WP 475
Cervico-Brachial Neuralgia   WL 400
Cervix Diseases   WP 470
   Veterinary   SF 871
Cervix Dysplasia   WP 480
Cervix Erosion   WP 470
Cervix Mucus   WP 470
Cervix Neoplasms   WP 480
Cervix Uteri   WP 470-480
   Dilatation (in labor)
      Obstetrical surgery   WQ 400
      Physiology   WQ 305
Cesarean Section   WQ 430
   Veterinary   SF 887
Cesium
   Inorganic chemistry   QD 181.C8
   Pharmacology   QV 275
Cesium Isotopes
   Inorganic chemistry   QD 181.C8
   Pharmacology   QV 275
Cesium Radioisotopes   WN 420
   Nuclear physics   QC 796.C8
   See also special topics under Radioisotopes
Cestoda   QX 400
Cestode Infections   WC 830-840
   Veterinary   SF 810.C5
Cetacea   QL 737.C4
   Paleozoology   QE 882.C5
Chagas Cardiomyopathy   WC 705
Chagas' Disease see Trypanosomiasis, South American
Chagas Disease   WC 705
Chalazion see Eyelid Diseases   WW 205
Chalcone
   Pharmacology   QV 150
Chalicosis see Pneumoconiosis
Chalones see Growth Inhibitors
CHAMPUS see Health Benefit Plans, Employee
Chancroid   WC 155
Channel Blockers, Calcium see Calcium Channel Blockers
Chaplaincy Service, Hospital   WX 187
Character   BF 818-839
   Disorders see Antisocial Personality   WM 190; Personality Disorders   WM 190
Charbon see Anthrax
Charcoal   QV 601
Charcot-Marie Disease   WE 550
Charcot-Marie-Tooth Disease see Charcot-Marie Disease
Charcot's Joint see Arthropathy, Neurogenic
Charge Nurses see Nursing, Supervisory
Charges see Fees and Charges

Charlatanry see Quackery
Charting, Clinical see Medical Records
Charts
   Statistical (Form number 16 in any NLM schedule where applicable)
Chaulmoogra Oil   QV 259
Chediak-Higashi Syndrome   WD 308
Cheek   WE 705
Cheese
   As a dietary supplement in health or disease   WB 428
   Dairying   SF 270-274
   Home economics   TX 382
   Sanitary processing   WA 715
Cheilitis   WI 200
Cheilosis see Riboflavin Deficiency
Chelating Agents   QV 290
Chelidonium see Plants, Medicinal
Chemexfoliation   WO 600
Chemical Analysis see Chemistry, Analytical
Chemical Elements see Elements; Isotopes; Radioisotopes
Chemical Engineering   TP 155-156
Chemical Face Peeling see Chemexfoliation
Chemical Genetics see Genetics, Biochemical
Chemical Industry   HD 9650-9663
   Occupational medicine   WA 400, etc.
   Industrial waste   WA 788
Chemical Models see Models, Chemical
Chemical Technology see Technology
Chemical Toxicology see Toxicology
Chemical Vaccines see Vaccines, Synthetic
Chemical Warfare Agents   QV 663-667
Chemical Water Pollution see Water Pollution, Chemical
Chemicals see Chemistry; Drugs; and names of particular chemicals and groups of chemicals, e.g. Poisons
Chemistry   QD
   Bacterial   QW 52
   Biological see Biochemistry   QU
   Chemicals as a cause of disease   QZ 59
   Dental   WU 170
   Forensic   W 750
   Industrial   TP
   Industrial protection   WA 465
   Milk, Public health aspects   WA 716
   Physiological   QU
   Water analysis   WA 686
   See also Blood Chemical Analysis   QY 450-490; Histocytochemistry   QS 531
Chemistry, Agricultural   S 583-587.7
Chemistry, Analytical
   Inorganic   QD 71-142
   Methods in clinical pathology   QY 90
   Of air   WA 750
   Of food see Food Analysis   QU 50, etc.
   Of milk   WA 716
   Of water   WA 686
Chemistry, Clinical   QY 90
   Animal   SF 772.66
Chemistry, Inorganic   QD 146-197
Chemistry, Organic   QD 241-441

Aliphatic compounds   QD 300–315
Aromatic compounds   QD 330–341
Physical   QD 476
Chemistry, Pharmaceutical   QV 744
Chemistry, Physical   QD 450–731
Chemodectoma see Paraganglioma, Extra–Adrenal
Chemolysis, Intervertebral Disk see Intervertebral Disk Chemolysis
Chemonucleolysis see Intervertebral Disk Chemolysis
Chemoreceptors   WL 102.9
Chemosterilants   WA 240
Chemotactic Factor, Macrophage–Derived see Interleukin–8
Chemotactic Factor, Neutrophil, Monocyte–Derived see Interleukin–8
Chemotactic Factors
  In immune reaction   QW 700
  In phagocytosis   QW 690
Chemotaxins see Chemotactic Factors
Chemotaxis
  Cells (General)   QH 647
  In phagocytosis   QW 690
  Special topics, by subject
Chemotaxis, Leukocyte
  In phagocytosis   QW 690
Chemotherapy see Drug Therapy
Chenic Acid see Chenodeoxycholic Acid
Chenodeoxycholate see Chenodeoxycholic Acid
Chenodeoxycholic Acid   WI 703
Chenodiol see Chenodeoxycholic Acid
Chenopodium   QV 766
  As an anthelmintic   QV 253
Chest see Thorax
Chest Injuries see Thoracic Injuries
Chest Pain   WF 970
Chest X–Ray see Mass Chest X–Ray; Thoracic Radiography
Chewing see Mastication
Chewing Tobacco see Tobacco, Smokeless
Chick Embryo
  General works   QL 959
Chicken Sarcoma Virus B77 see Sarcoma Viruses, Avian
Chicken Tumor 1 Virus see Sarcoma Viruses, Avian
Chickenpox   WC 572
Chickenpox Virus see Herpesvirus 3, Human
Chickens
  Anatomy   SF 767.P6
  Culture   SF 481–503.52
  Diseases   SF 995–995.6
  Physiology   SF 768.2.P6
Chiggers see Mites
Chilblains   WG 530
Child   WS
  Abnormal see Child, Exceptional   WS 105.5.C3, etc.
  Adopted see Adoption   WS 105.5.F2, etc.
  Anesthesia   WO 440
  Care and training see Child Care   WS 113
  Dentistry see Pedodontics   WU 480
  Labor   HD 6228–6250.5
  Nursing see Pediatric Nursing   WY 159

Radiography   WN 240
School child see School Health Services   WA 350–352
Surgery   WO 925
Tuberculosis see Tuberculosis in Childhood   WF 415
Child Abuse   WA 320
Child Abuse, Sexual   WA 320
  Abuser's psychological aspect   WM 610
Child Advocacy   WA 320
  Special topics, by subject
Child Behavior   WS 105
Child Behavior Disorders   WS 350.6
Child Care   WS 113
Child Custody
  Special topics, by subject
Child Day Care Centers
  Public health   WA 310–320
  Sociology   HV 851–861
Child Development   WS 105
  Educational measurement   LB 3051–3060.87
  Evaluation (General)   WS 105.5.E8
  External influences   WS 105.5.E9
  Intelligence tests   BF 432.C48
  Of the mentally retarded child   WS 107.5.D3
  Physical see Growth   WS 103, etc.
Child Development Deviations see Child Development Disorders
Child Development Disorders   WS 350.6
Child Development Disorders, Pervasive   WS 350
Child Development Disorders, Specific see Child Development Disorders
Child, Exceptional
  Education   LC 3951–4000
  Rearing (General)   WS 105.5.C3
  See also Child Gifted   LC 3991–4000, etc.; Education of Mentally Retarded   LC 4601–4640.4; Mental Retardation   WS 107–107.5, etc.
Child, Gifted
  Care   WS 113
  Education   LC 3991–4000
  Guidance   WS 350
  Mental development   WS 105
Child Guidance   WS 350–350.8
Child Guidance Clinics   WS 27–28
  Directories   WS 22
Child Health see Child Welfare
Child Health Services   WA 320
  Mother and child   WA 310
  In school   WA 350
    See also School Health   WA 350
Child, Hospitalized   WS 105.5.H7
Child, Institutionalized
  Public health aspects   WA 310–320
  Retarded child   WS 107.5.I4
  Sociological aspects   HV 959–1420.5
  See also Child, Hospitalized   WS 105.5.H7
Child Language   WS 105.5.C8
Child Molestation, Sexual see Child Abuse, Sexual
Child Neglect see Child Abuse
Child Nutrition
  Feeding   WS 130

ALWAYS CONSULT MAIN SCHEDULES. USE NUMBER ASSIGNED ONLY WHEN SUBJECT REPRESENTS MAJOR EMPHASIS OF WORK BEING CLASSIFIED

Requirements   WS 115
Child Nutrition Disorders   WS 115
Child of Impaired Parents   WS 105.5.F2
    Special topics, by subject
Child, Preschool
    General works   WS 440
    Other topics, by subject within the WS or other
        schedules
Child Psychiatry   WS 350-350.8
    As a career   WS 350
    Case studies in mental retardation   WS 107.5.C2
Child Psychology   WS 105
Child Reactive Disorders   WS 350.6
Child Rearing   WS 105.5.C3
    Physiological needs see Child Care   WS 113
Child, Unwanted   HV 873
    Effect on pregnancy   WQ 240
    Parent-child relations   WS 105.5.F2
    See also Child Welfare   WA 310, etc.
Child Welfare
    Public health aspects   WA 310-320
    Sociology   HV 701-1420.5
Childbirth see Labor; Popular works   WQ 150
    under Pregnancy; Natural Childbirth
Childbirth at Home see Home Childbirth
Childbirth Injuries see Birth Injuries; Labor
    Complications
Childhood Schizophrenia see Schizophrenia,
    Childhood
Children of Impaired Parents see Child of Impaired
    Parents
Chills see Shivering; Hypothermia; Freezing;
    Frostbite
Chimera   QH 445.7
Chimeric Toxins see Immunotoxins
Chimpansee troglodytes   QL 737.P9
    As laboratory animals   QY 60.P7
    Diseases   SF 997.5.P7
Chimpanzee see Chimpansee troglodytes
Chimpanzee Coryza Agent see Respiratory Syncytial
    Viruses
Chin   WE 705
    See also Mandible   WU 101, etc.
Chinacrin see Quinacrine
Chinchilla   QL 737.R636
    Culture   SF 405.C45
    Diseases   SF 997.5.C5
Chinese see Mongoloid Race
Chinese Americans see Asian Americans
Chinese Herbal Drugs see Drugs, Chinese Herbal
Chinese Liver Fluke see Opisthorchis
Chinese Medicine, Traditional see Medicine, Chinese
    Traditional
Chiniofon see Hydroxyquinolines
Chipmunks see Sciuridae
Chironex Venoms see Coelenterate Venoms
Chironomidae   QX 505
Chironomus see Chironomidae
Chiropody see Podiatry
Chiropotes see Cebidae
Chiropractic   WB 905-905.9
Chiroptera   QL 737.C5
    Diseases   SF 997.5.B38

Chitin   QU 83
Chitinase   QU 136
Chlamydia   QW 152
Chlamydia Infections   WC 600
    Veterinary   SF 809.C45
    Specific infection, by type
Chlamydiales   QW 152
Chloral Hydrate   QV 85
Chlorambucil   QV 269
Chloramiphene see Clomiphene
Chloramphenicol   QV 350.5.C5
Chlorbutol see Chlorobutanol
Chlordecone see Kepone
Chlordiazepoxide   QV 77.9
Chlorella   QK 569.C49
Chlorethazine see Mechlorethamine
Chlorhexidine   QV 220
Chlorides
    Inorganic chemistry   QD 181.C5
    Pharmacology   QV 280
    Water purification   WA 690
Chlorimipramine see Clomipramine
Chlorinated Hydrocarbons see Hydrocarbons,
    Chlorinated
Chlorine   QV 231
    Toxicology   QV 663
Chlormequat
    As a plant growth regulator   QK 745
    Organic chemistry   QD 305.A8
Chlormerodrin   QV 160
Chlormeroprin see Chlormerodrin
Chlormethine see Mechlorethamine
Chlorobutanol   QV 115
Chlorodinitrobenzene see Dinitrochlorobenzene
Chloroethylene see Vinyl Chloride
Chloroethylene Polymer see Polyvinyl Chloride
Chloroform   QV 81
Chloroiodoquine see Clioquinol
Chloromethyl Ether see Bis(Chloromethyl) Ether
Chlorophenols   QV 223
Chlorophenyl GABA see Baclofen
Chlorophyll   QK 898.C5
Chloropicrin   QV 664
Chloroplast Coupling Factor see H(+)-Transporting
    ATP Synthase
Chloroplasts   QK 898.C5
Chloroprene
    As a carcinogen   QZ 202
    Toxicology   QV 633
Chloroquine   QV 256
Chlorosis see Anemia, Hypochromic
Chlorosis, Egyptian see Hookworm Infections
Chlorphenamine see Chlorpheniramine
Chlorpheniramine   QV 157
Chlorpromazine   QV 77.9
Chlorprophenpyridamine see Chlorpheniramine
Chlorprothixene   QV 77.9
Chlortetracycline   QV 360
Chocolate see Cacao
Choice Behavior   BF 608-618
    Special topics, by subject
Choked Disk see Papilledema
Choking see Airway Obstruction

**ALWAYS CONSULT MAIN SCHEDULES. USE NUMBER ASSIGNED ONLY WHEN
SUBJECT REPRESENTS MAJOR EMPHASIS OF WORK BEING CLASSIFIED**

Cholagogues and Choleretics   QV 66
Cholalic Acids see Cholic Acids
Cholangiography   WI 750
Cholangiopancreatography, Endoscopic Retrograde
  WI 750
Cholates see Cholic Acids
Cholecalciferol   QU 173
Cholecystectomy   WI 750
Cholecystitis   WI 755
Cholecystography   WI 750
Cholecystokinin   WK 170
Cholecystokinin Octapeptide Receptors see
  Receptors, Cholecystokinin
Cholecystokinin–Pancreozymin Receptors see
  Receptors, Cholecystokinin
Cholecystokinin Receptors see Receptors,
  Cholecystokinin
Cholecystostomy   WI 750
Choledocholithiasis see Common Bile Duct Calculi
Choledochus see Common Bile Duct
Cholelithiasis   WI 755
Cholelithiasis, Common Bile Duct see Common Bile
  Duct Calculi
Cholera   WC 262–264
Cholera Toxin   WC 262
Cholera Vaccine   WC 262
Choleragen see Cholera Toxin
Choleragenoid see Cholera Toxin
Choleretics see Cholagogues and Choleretics
Cholestasis   WI 703
Cholestasis, Extrahepatic see Bile Duct Obstruction,
  Extrahepatic
Cholesteatoma   QZ 365
  Localized, by site
Cholesterol   QU 95
Cholesterol, Dietary   QU 95
  Control in sickness or health   WB 425
  Cookbooks   WB 425
Cholesterol HDL see Lipoproteins, HDL
  Cholesterol
Cholesterol Inhibitors see Anticholesteremic Agents
Cholesterol LDL see Lipoproteins, LDL Cholesterol
Cholesterol-7-Hydroxylase   QU 140
Cholic Acids   WI 703
Choline   QU 87
  Esters   QV 122
Choline Acetylase see Choline Acetyltransferase
Choline Acetyltransferase   QU 141
Choline Deficiency   WD 120
Choline Phosphoglycerides see Phosphatidylcholines
Cholinergic Agents   QV 122
Cholinergic Antagonists   QV 124
Cholinergic-Blocking Agents see Cholinergic
  Antagonists
Cholinergic Receptors see Receptors, Cholinergic
Cholinesterase Inhibitors   QV 124
Cholinesterase Reactivators   QV 124
Cholinesterases   QU 136
Cholinoceptive Sites see Receptors, Cholinergic
Cholinoceptors see Receptors, Cholinergic
Cholinolytics see Cholinergic Antagonists
Cholinomimetics see Cholinergic Agents
Chondroblastoma   QZ 340

Chondrodysplasia, Hereditary Deforming see
  Exostoses, Multiple Hereditary
Chondrodysplasia Punctata   WE 250
Chondrodystrophia Calcificans Congenita see
  Chondrodysplasia Punctata
Chondrodystrophia Fetalis see Achondroplasia
Chondroitin   QU 83
Chondroma   QZ 340
Chorda Tympani Nerve   WL 330
Chordata   QL 605–739.8
  See also special aspects, e.g., Embryology   QL
  958, etc.
Chordoma   QZ 310
  Localized, by site
Chorea   WL 390
  Associated with rheumatic fever   WC 220
Chorea, Hereditary see Huntington Chorea
Chorioadenoma see Hydatidiform Mole, Invasive
Choriocarcinoma   WP 465
  Pathology   QZ 310
Chorioepithelioma see Choriocarcinoma
Chorion   WQ 210
  Animal   QL 977
  Embryology   QS 645
Chorionic Somatomammotropin, Human see
  Placental Lactogen
Chorionic Villi   WQ 210
  Animal   QL 977
  Embryology   QS 645
Chorionic Villi Sampling   WQ 209
Chorioretinitis   WW 270
Choroid   WW 245
  Edema   WW 245
Choroid Diseases   WW 245
Choroid Neoplasms   WW 245
Choroid Plexus   WL 307
Choroiditis   WW 245
Christ-Siemens-Touraine Syndrome see Ectodermal
  Dysplasia
Christian Science   BX 6903–6997
  Healing   WB 885
  See also Mental Healing   WB 885, etc.
Christianity   BR
  And medicine   W 61
    See also Religion and Medicine   BL 65.M4,
    etc.
  And psychiatry   WM 61
    See also Religion and Psychology   BL 53,
    etc
  And psychoanalysis   WM 460.5.R3
  General works   BR 120–126
  Medical ethics   W 50
  Other special topics, by subject
Chromaffin System
  Endocrinology   WK 102
  Of particular glands or other organs, by gland
  or organ
Chromatin   QU 56
  Cytology   QH 599
Chromatin, Sex see Sex Chromatin
Chromatium   QW 145
Chromatography
  Analytical chemistry (General)   QD 79.C4

ALWAYS CONSULT MAIN SCHEDULES. USE NUMBER ASSIGNED ONLY WHEN
SUBJECT REPRESENTS MAJOR EMPHASIS OF WORK BEING CLASSIFIED

Organic analysis (General)   QD 272.C4
Qualitative analysis   QD 98.C4
Quantitative analysis   QD 117.C5
Used for special purposes, by subject, e.g., in
   Assay of Hormones   QY 330
Chromatography, Affinity
   Biochemistry   QU 25
Chromatography, Gas
   Analytical chemistry   QD 79.C45
   Organic analysis   QD 272.C44
Chromatography, Gas–Liquid see Chromatography,
   Gas
Chromatography, High Performance Liquid see
   Chromatography, High Pressure Liquid
Chromatography, High Pressure Liquid
   Analytical chemistry   QD 79.C454
Chromatography, High Speed Liquid see
   Chromatography, High Pressure Liquid
Chromatography, Paper
   Analytical chemistry   QD 79.C46
Chromatography, Thin Layer
   Analytical chemistry   QD 79.C8
   Organic analysis   QD 272.C45
Chromatophores   QS 532.5.E7
Chromium   QV 290
   Metabolism   QU 130.5
Chromium Isotopes
   Inorganic chemistry   QD 181.C7
   Pharmacology   QV 290
Chromogenic Compounds
   Analytical chemistry   QD 77
   Pharmaceutical chemistry   QV 744
   Used for special purposes, by subject
Chromogenic Substrates see Chromogenic
   Compounds
Chromomycins   QV 269
Chromophobe Adenoma see Adenoma,
   Chromophobe
Chromosomal Probes see DNA Probes
Chromosomal Translocation see Translocation
   (Genetics)
Chromosome Aberrations   QH 462.A1
   See also Chromosome Deletion   QH 462.D4;
      Inversion (Genetics)   QH 462.I5;
      Translocation (Genetics)   QH 462.T7
Chromosome Abnormalities   QS 677
   See also Trisomy   QH 461, etc.
Chromosome Banding   QH 600
Chromosome Deletion   QH 462.D4
Chromosome Fragile Sites   QH 461.A1
Chromosome Mapping   QH 445.2
Chromosome Markers see Genetic Markers
Chromosome 21 see Chromosomes, Human, Pair 21
Chromosomes   QH 600
   See also Sex Chromosomes   QH 600.5
Chromosomes A see Chromosomes, Human, 1–3
Chromosomes, Bacterial   QW 51–52
Chromosomes D see Chromosomes, Human, 13–15
Chromosomes, Human   QH 600
Chromosomes, Human, Pair 21   QH 600
Chromosomes, Human, 1–3   QH 600
Chromosomes, Human, 13–15   QH 600
Chronic Disease   WT 500

In infancy & childhood   WS 200
   Nursing   WY 152
   Social problems   WT 30
Chronic Fatigue Syndrome see Fatigue Syndrome,
   Chronic
Chronic Illness see Chronic Disease
Chronic Limitation of Activity see Activities of
   Daily Living
Chronic Obstructive Pulmonary Disease see Lung
   Diseases, Obstructive
Chronobiology   QT 167
Chronologies, Medicine see Chronologies   WZ 30
   under Medicine; Chronology
Chronology   CE
   Historical   D–F
   Medical   WZ 30
Chronotropism, Cardiac see Heart Rate
Chrysanthemum see Pyrethrum
Chrysenes   QV 138.C1
   Organic chemistry   QD 395
Chrysotherapeutic Agents see Antirheumatic
   Agents, Gold
Church see Catholicism; Religion
Churg–Strauss Syndrome   WG 515
Chyle   WI 402
Chylomicrons   QU 85
Chylothorax   WF 700
Chymopapain   QU 136
Chymosin   QU 136
   In milk analysis   WA 716
CI–581 see Ketamine
Cicatrix   WR 143
   Wound healing   WO 185
   Localized, by site
Ciguatera see Ciguatoxin
Ciguatoxin   QW 630
Cilastatin   QU 90
   As a protease inhibitor   QU 136
Cilia   QS 532.5.E7
   In animals   QP 310.C5
   Specific to an organ, with the organ
Ciliary Body   WW 240
Ciliary Dyskinesia see Ciliary Motility Disorders
Ciliary Motility Disorders   WF 140
   Cilia of specific organs, with the organ
Ciliata see Ciliophora
Ciliate Infections see Balantidiasis   WC 735 or
   names of other parasitic diseases caused by Ciliata
Ciliophora   QX 151
Cimetidine   QV 157
   As an anti-ulcer agent   QV 69
Cimex see Bedbugs
Cincain see Dibucaine
Cinchocain see Dibucaine
Cinchona   QV 257
Cinchophen   QV 95
Cine–CT see Tomography, X–Ray Computed
Cineangiography   WG 500
Cinefluorography see Cineradiography
Cineradiography   WN 220
   Heart   WG 141.5.R2
   Diagnosis of specific disease with the disease or
      organ

Ciprofloxacin   QV 250
Circadian Rhythm   QT 167
    Animals   QP 84.6
    Biology (General)   QH 527
Circular Dichroism   QD 473
Circulation see Blood Circulation; Cerebrovascular
    Circulation; Collateral Circulation; Coronary
    Circulation; Liver Circulation; Microcirculation;
    Pulmonary Circulation
Circulation of Books see Circulation   Z 712–714
    under Library Services
Circulatory Disorders see Blood Circulation;
    Cerebrovascular Circulation; Disorders   WI 720
    under Liver Circulation
Circulatory Function Tests see Blood Circulation
Circulatory System see Cardiovascular System
Circumcision
    Anthropology   GN 484
    Judaism   BM 705
    Medical procedure   WJ 790
Cirrhosis see Liver Cirrhosis; Pulmonary Fibrosis
Cirrhosis, Liver see Liver Cirrhosis
cis-Diamminedichloroplatinum(II) see Cisplatin
cis-Dichlorodiammineplatinum(II) see Cisplatin
Cisplatin   QV 269
    Therapeutic use for neoplasms   QZ 267
Cisterna Chyli see Thoracic Duct
Cisterna Magna   WL 200
Cisternal Puncture see Punctures
Cisternography, Myelographic see Myelography
Cisternography, Pneumoencephalographic see
    Pneumoencephalography
Citellus see Sciuridae
Citicoline see Cytidine Diphosphate Choline
Citizen Participation see Consumer Participation
Citrated Calcium Cyanamide see Cyanamide
Citrates   QU 98
    Organic chemistry
        Aliphatic compounds   QD 305.A2
Citric Acid Cycle   QU 98
Citrin see Bioflavonoids
Citrovorum Factor see Leucovorin
Citrus Fruits
    As a dietary supplement in health or disease
    WB 430
    Sanitary control   WA 703
City Planning   HT 165.5–169.9
    Architecture and engineering   NA 9000–9428
    Public health aspects in   WA
    See also Urban Renewal   HT 170–178, etc.
Civil Defense   UA 926–929
    Psychological aspects   UA 926.5
Civil Rights   JC 571–628
    Constitutional law (U.S.)   KF 4741–4785
        Control of individual rights   KF 4791–4856
    Mentally disabled   WM 30–32
    Political rights   JF 800–1191
    Other special topics, by subject, e.g., Medical
        records and privacy rights   WX 173, etc.
Civilian Protection see Civil Defense
Civilization   CB
    General works   CB 23–161
    Sociological aspects   HM 101–121

Other special topics, by subject, e.g. civilization
    and disease   WA 30
Claims Review see Insurance Claim Review
Clairvoyance see Parapsychology
Clams   QX 675
    Food poisoning   WC 268
    Food sanitation   WA 703; WA 710
Clarification, Pharmaceutical see Drug
    Compounding
Class I Genes see Genes, MHC Class I
Class II Antigens see Histocompatibility Antigens
    Class II
Class II Genes see Genes, MHC Class II
Class II Human Antigens see HLA–D Antigens
Classical Complement Pathway see Complement
    Pathway, Classical
Classification
    (Form number 15 in any NLM schedule where
        applicable)
    See also Book Classification   Z 696–697 and
        subjects or objects being classified
Clastogens see Mutagens
Claustrophobia see Phobic Disorders
Claustrum see Basal Ganglia
Clavicle   WE 810
Clavulanic Acids   QV 350
Claw see Hoof and Claw
Cleanliness, Personal see Cleanliness   QT 240 under
    Hygiene
Cleansing Agents see Detergents
Cleavage, Cell see Cell Division
Cleft Lip   WV 440
Cleft Palate   WV 440
Cleft Palate Prosthesis see Palatal Obturators
Clemastine   QV 157
Clerambault Syndrome see Organic Mental
    Disorders, Psychotic
Clergy   BV 659–683
    See also Psychology, Pastoral   WM 61
Clerical Medicine see Pastoral Care
Clethrionomys see Microtinae
Client–Centered Therapy see Nondirective Therapy
Climacteric
    Female   WP 580
        See also Menopause   WP 580
    Male   WJ 702
    Postmenopausal see Menopause   WP 580
Climate
    Climatology (Physics)   QC 980–999
    Prescribed for health   WB 750
    Prescribed for tuberculosis   WF 330
    Relation to disease   WB 700–710
    See also Acclimatization   QT 145, etc.; Cold
        Climate   QT 160, etc.; Desert Climate   QT
        150, etc.; Environment   QT 230, etc.;
        Meteorological Factors   WA 30, etc.; Tropical
        Climate   QT 150, etc.; Weather   WB
        700–710, etc.
Climatology, Medical see Climate; Weather
Climatotherapy see Climate; Health Resorts;
    Thalassotherapy
Clinical Charting see Medical Records
Clinical Chemistry see Chemistry, Clinical

Clinical Competence   W 21
  As an educational measurement
    Works about (Form number 18 in any NLM
      schedule where applicable)
    Actual tests (Form number 18.2 in any NLM
      schedule where applicable)
Clinical Departments see Hospital Departments
Clinical Engineering see Biomedical Engineering
Clinical Equivalency see Therapeutic Equivalency
Clinical Ethics see Ethics, Medical
Clinical Informatics see Medical Informatics
Clinical Investigators see Research Personnel
Clinical Laboratory Information Systems   QY 26.5
Clinical Ladders see Career Mobility
Clinical Markers see Biological Markers
Clinical Medicine   WB 102
Clinical Nurse Specialists see Nurse Clinicians
Clinical Nursing Research   WY 20.5
Clinical Pathology see Pathology, Clinical
Clinical Pharmacology see Pharmacology, Clinical
Clinical Pharmacy Service see Pharmacy Service,
  Hospital
Clinical Practice Nursing Research see Clinical
  Nursing Research
Clinical Practice Patterns see Physician's Practice
  Patterns
Clinical Practice Variations see Physician's Practice
  Patterns
Clinical Protocols
  Used for special purposes, by subject
Clinical Psychology see Psychology, Clinical
Clinical Refraction see Refraction, Ocular
Clinical Skills see Clinical Competence
Clinical Trials
  Drugs   QV 771
  Vision research   WW 20
  For other purposes, by subject or specific drug
    or procedure
Clinical Trials, Controlled see Controlled Clinical
  Trials
Clinical Trials, Randomized see Randomized
  Controlled Trials
Clinics, Dental see Dental Clinics
Clinics, Free–Standing see Ambulatory Care
  Facilities
Clinics, Outpatient see Outpatient Clinics, Hospital
Clioquinol   QV 255
Clitoris   WP 200
Cloaca   WJ 101
Clofibric Acid
  As an anticholesteremic agent   QU 95
Clofibrinic Acid see Clofibric Acid
Clomifene see Clomiphene
Clomiphene   QV 170
Clomipramine   QV 77.5
Clone Cells   QH 585
  Nuclear cloning   QH 442.2
Cloning, Molecular   QH 442.2
Cloning Vectors see Genetic Vectors
Clonogenic Cell Assay see Colony–Forming Units
  Assay
Clonogenic Cell Assay, Tumor see Tumor Stem Cell
  Assay

Clonorchis sinensis   QX 353
Cloranfenicol see Chloramphenicol
Closed–Circuit Anesthesia see Anesthesia,
  Closed–Circuit
Closed Cohort Studies see Cohort Studies
Closed Ecologic Life Support Systems see
  Ecological Systems, Closed
Clostridiopeptidase A see Microbial Collagenase
Clostridium   QW 127.5.C5
Clostridium botulinum   QW 127.5.C5
Clostridium histolyticum Collagenase see Microbial
  Collagenase
Clostridium Infections   WC 368–375
  See also Botulism   WC 268; Hemoglobinuria,
    Bacillary   WJ 344; Wound Infection   WC
    255
Clostridium perfringens   QW 127.5.C5
Clostridium welchii see Clostridium perfringens
Closure of Wounds see Wounds and Injuries
Clothing   QT 245
  See also Protective Clothing   WA 260, etc.
Clouston's Syndrome see Ectodermal Dysplasia
Clubfoot   WE 883
  Veterinary   SF 901
Clumping see Agglutination
Clumping, Erythrocytic see Hemagglutination
Cluster Headache   WL 344
Clysis see Enema
Clyster see Enema
CMHC see Community Mental Health Centers
Cnidaria   QX 195
CoA see Coenzyme A
Coagulants   QV 195
Coagulase   WH 310
  Special topics, by subject
Coagulation see Blood Coagulation; Laser
  Coagulation; Light Coagulation
Coagulation Factors see Blood Coagulation Factors
Coal   TP 325–326
  Poisoning   QV 633
  See also Pneumoconiosis   WF 654 and related
    disorders
Coal Mining
  Occupational accidents   WA 485
  Occupational medicine   WA 400–495
  Industrial waste   WA 788
Coal Tar   QV 60
  Anti–infective dyes derived from   QV 235
  Toxicology   QV 633
  See also Cresols   QV 223, etc.; Phenols   QV
    223, etc.
Coated Pits, Cell–Membrane   QH 603.C63
Cobalamin see Vitamin B 12
Cobalt
  Inorganic chemistry   QD 181.C6
  Metabolism   QU 130.5
  Pharmacology   QV 290
Cobalt Isotopes
  Inorganic chemistry   QD 181.C6
  Pharmacology   QV 290
Cobalt Radioisotopes   WN 420
  Nuclear physics   QC 796.C6
  See also special topics under Radioisotopes

Coca   QV 113
Cocaine   QV 113
    Dependence   WM 280
Cocarboxylase see Thiamine Pyrophosphate
Cocarcinogenesis   QZ 202
Cocci, Gram–Positive see Gram–Positive Cocci
Coccidia   QX 123
Coccidioides   QW 180.5.P4
Coccidioidomycosis   WC 460
Coccidiosis   WC 730
    Veterinary   SF 792
        Avian diseases   SF 995.6.C6
Coccygeal Region see Sacrococcygeal Region
Coccyx   WE 725
Cochlea   WV 250
Cochlear Aqueduct   WV 250
Cochlear Diseases   WV 250
Cochlear Implant   WV 274
Cochlear Microphonic Potentials   WV 270
Cochlear Nerve   WL 330
    Physiology of hearing   WV 272
Cochlear Prosthesis see Cochlear Implant
Cochliobolus see Ascomycetes
Cockroaches   QX 570
Cocoa see Cacao
Coconut
    Diets for control of fats   WB 425
    Diets for control of proteins   WB 426
    Plant culture   SB 401.C6
Cocos see Coconut
Cod Liver Oil   QU 86
Codeine   QV 92
    Dependence   WM 286
Codes of Ethics see Bioethics; Ethics; Ethics,
    Medical; ethics in other specialties
Codes, Sanitary see Legislation   WA 32–33 under
    Sanitation
Codon   QU 58.7
Coelenterata see Cnidaria
Coelenterate Venoms   WD 405
Coendou see Rodentia
Coenuriasis see Cestode Infections
Coenzyme A   QU 135
Coenzyme I see NAD
Coenzyme II see NADP
Coenzyme M see Mesna
Coenzyme Q see Ubiquinone
Coenzymes   QU 135
Coercion
    Special topics, by subject
Coffea see Coffee
Coffee
    As a dietary supplement in health or disease
    WB 438
    Cultivation   SB 269
    See also Caffeine   QV 107
Coformycin
    As an antineoplastic agent   QV 269
    As an immunosuppressant   QW 920
Cognition   BF 311–499
    Cognition & age (adulthood)   BF 724.55.C63
    In adolescence   WS 462
    In infancy & childhood   WS 105.5.C7

    In old age   WT 145
Cognition Disorders
    General and psychotic   WM 204–205
    Other special topics by subject, e.g.,   Amnesia
    WM 173.7
Cognitive Dissonance   BF 337.C63
Cognitive Therapy   WM 425.5.C6
    In infancy & childhood   WS 350.6
Cohort Analysis see Cohort Studies
Cohort Studies
    In epidemiology   WA 105
    Special topics, by subject
Coin Lesion, Pulmonary   WF 658
Coins see Numismatics
Coinsurance see Deductibles and Coinsurance
Coitus
    Animal (General) see Copulation   QL 761
    Human   HQ 19–30.7
    Psychophysiologic problems   WM 611
        Female   WP 610
        Male   WJ 709
Cola see Beverages
Colchicine   QV 98
Colchicum   QV 98
Cold
    Adverse effects   QZ 57
    In anesthesia see Anesthesia, Refrigeration   WO
    350
    Therapeutic use   WB 473
Cold Agglutinin Disease see Anemia, Hemolytic,
    Autoimmune
Cold Climate
    Physiological effects   QT 160
    Winter temperatures (meteorology)   QC 905
Cold, Common see Common Cold
Cold–Insoluble Globulins see Fibronectins
Cold Therapy see Cryotherapy
Colectomy   WI 520
Coleonol see Forskolin
Coleoptera   QX 555
Colic   WI 147
Colicines see Colicins
Colicins   QV 350
Coliform Bacilli see Enterobacteriaceae
Coliphage lambda see Bacteriophage lambda
Coliphages   QW 161.5.C6
Coliphages T see T–Phages
Colistin   QV 350
Colitis   WI 522
    Amebic see Dysentery, Amebic   WC 285
Colitis, Amebic see Dysentery, Amebic
Colitis, Granulomatous see Crohn Disease
Colitis, Mucous see Colonic Diseases, Functional
Colitis, Ulcerative   WI 522
Collagen   QU 55
Collagen Diseases   WD 375
    See also names of specific diseases
Collagen Type I see Collagen
Collagen Type II see Collagen
Collagen Type III see Collagen
Collagen Type IV see Collagen
Collagen Type IX see Collagen
Collagen Type V see Collagen

Collagen Type VI see Collagen
Collagen Type VII see Collagen
Collagen Type VIII see Collagen
Collagen Type X see Collagen
Collagen Type XI see Collagen
Collagen Type XII see Collagen
Collagen Type XIII see Collagen
Collagenase, Microbial see Microbial Collagenase
Collapse Therapy   WF 350
Collateral Circulation   WG 103
Collected works
    By several authors (Form number 5 in any NLM schedule where applicable)
    By individual authors (Form number 7 in any NLM schedule where applicable)
Collection of Fees see Fees and Charges; Fees, Dental; Fees, Medical; Fees, Pharmaceutical
Collections see Form numbers 5-7 in any NLM schedule where applicable
Collective Bargaining   HD 6971.5-6971.6
    Hospitals and hospital personnel   WX 159.8
    Industry and health services   WA 412
        Mental health services   WA 495
    Industry and health insurance   W 125-270

    Nurses   WY 30
        With hospital staff   WX 159.8
    Special topics, by subject
College Admission Test   LB 2353-2353.8
    Works about (Form number 18 in any NLM schedule where applicable)
    Actual tests (Form number 18.2 in any NLM schedule where applicable)
    See also Educational Measurement   LB 3051-3059, etc.
College Students, Health see Student Health Services
Colleges, Medical see Schools, Medical
Collodion
    Pharmaceutic aids   QV 800
    Photographic processing   TR 390
Colloids
    As dosage form   QV 785
    Biochemistry   QU 133
Colobus   QL 737.P93
    Diseases   SF 997.5.P7
    As laboratory animals   QY 60.P7
Colocynth   QV 75
Colon   WI 520-529
Colon and Rectal Surgery (Specialty)   WI 650
    Colon only   WI 520
Colon, Irritable see Colonic Diseases, Functional
Colonialism see Political Systems
Colonic Diseases   WI 520-529
Colonic Diseases, Functional   WI 520
Colonic Neoplasms   WI 529
Colonic Polyps   WI 529
Colonoscopy   WI 520
Colony-Forming Units see Stem Cells
Colony-Forming Units Assay   QH 585
Colony-Forming Units Assay, Tumor see Tumor Stem Cell Assay
Colony-Forming Units, Hematopoietic see Hematopoietic Stem Cells

Colony-Forming Units, Neoplastic see Tumor Stem Cells
Colony-Stimulating Factor, Mast-Cell see Interleukin-3
Colony-Stimulating Factor, Multipotential see Interleukin-3
Colony-Stimulating Factor 2 Alpha see Interleukin-3
Colony-Stimulating Factors
    In hematopoiesis   WH 140
Color   QC 494-496.9
    Psychology   BF 789.C7
    Therapeutics see Alternative Medicine   WB 890, etc.
    See also Eye Color   WW 101; Food Additives   WA 712; Hair Color   WR 450; Pigmentation   WR 102, etc.
Color Blindness see Color Vision Defects
Color Perception   WW 150
Color Vision see Color Perception
Color Vision Defects   WW 150
Colorectal Neoplasms   WI 529
Colorectal Neoplasms, Hereditary Nonpolyposis   WI 529
Colorimetry   QD 113
    Clinical pathology   QY 90
Coloring Agents see Dyes
Coloring Agents, Food see Food Coloring Agents
Coloring Agents, Hair see Hair Dyes
Colostomy   WI 520
Colostrum   WP 825
Colpohysterectomy see Hysterectomy, Vaginal
Colposcopy   WP 250
Coma   WB 182
    Diabetic see Diabetic Coma   WK 830
    Hepatic see Hepatic Encephalopathy   WI 700
Coma, Hyperglycemic Hyperosmolar Nonketotic see Hyperglycemic Hyperosmolar Nonketotic Coma
Combat Disorders   WM 184
Combat Psychiatry see Psychiatry, Military
Combination Chemotherapy see Drug Therapy, Combination
Combined Modality Therapy
    General   WB 300
    For neoplasms   QZ 266
Combining Site see Binding Sites
Comfort Stations see Toilet Facilities
Commerce   HF
    General works   HF 1003-1008
Commercial Oils see Industrial Oils
Commercial Preparations see Drugs, Non-prescription
Comminution, Pharmaceutical see Drug Compounding
Commitment of Mentally Ill   WM 32-33
Common Bile Duct   WI 750
Common Bile Duct Calculi   WI 755
Common Bile Duct Diseases   WI 750
Common Bile Duct Neoplasms   WI 765
Common Cold   WC 510
Common Cold Virus see Rhinovirus
Common Hepatic Duct see Hepatic Duct, Common
Communicable Disease Contact Tracing see Contact

Tracing

Communicable Disease Control   WA 110–240
   Disinfestation   WA 240
   Notifiable disease registration   WA 55
   See also Quarantine   WA 230, etc.; names of
    various types of control, e.g., Pest control
    WA 240

Communicable Diseases   WC
   Drugs used in   QV 250–268.5
   General works   WC 100
   In infancy & childhood   WC
   In pregnancy see Pregnancy, Complications,
    Infectious   WQ 256
   Nursing   WY 153
   Prevention see Communicable Disease Control
    WA 110, etc.; Insect Control   QX 600;
    Quarantine   WA 230, etc.
   Transmission
     Epidemiological aspects   WA 110
     Insect vectors   QX 650
     Mechanisms   QW 700
   Veterinary   SF 781–809

Communication
   In adolescence   WS 462
   In infancy & childhood   WS 105.5.C8
   In mentally retarded   WM 307.C6
    In infancy & childhood   WS 107.5.C6
   In psychoanalysis   WM 460.5.C5
   Information systems   Z 699, etc.
   Manual   HV 2474–2480
   Medical writing and publishing   WZ 345
   Nonverbal see Nonverbal communication   HM
    258
   Philosophy and linguistics   P 87–96
   Physician's interpersonal relations   W 62
   Psychology   BF 637.C45
   Social psychology   HM 258
   Telecommunication (General)   TK 5101–5105.9

Communication Aids for Disabled
   For communicative disorders   WL 340.2
   See also specific types of aids

Communication Aids for Handicapped see
  Communication Aids for Disabled

Communication, Animal see Animal Communication

Communication Barriers
   In adolescence   WS 462
   In infancy & childhood   WS 105.5.C8
   In mentally retarded   WM 307.C6
   Physician's interpersonal relations   W 62
   Psychological aspects   BF 637.C45
   Social psychology aspects   HM 258

Communication Boards see Communication Aids for
  Disabled

Communication Methods, Total   HV 2497

Communicative Disorders
   General   WL 340.2
   Psychogenic   WM 475
   Neurologic   WL 340.2

Communism   HX 72–73, 626–780.7
   As practiced in special countries in JN or in the
    history number for the country
   Special topics, by subject, e.g. State medicine in
    a Communist country   W 275

Community Action see Consumer Participation

Community Dentistry   WU 113

Community Health Aides   W 21.5

Community Health Care see Community Health
  Services

Community Health Education see Health Education

Community Health Nursing   WY 106

Community Health Services   WA 546

Community-Institutional Relations
   Hospital   WX 160
   Other types of institutions, by subject

Community Medicine   W 84.5

Community Mental Health Centers   WM 29

Community Mental Health Services   WM 30
   In infancy & childhood and other age groups
    WM 30
   Special population groups   WA 305
   See also Hospitals, Psychiatric   WM 27–28, etc.;
    Social Work, Psychiatric   WM 30.5

Community Pharmacies see Pharmacies

Community Pharmacy Services   QV 737

Community Psychiatry   WM 30.6–31.5
   Etiological factors in mental disorders   WM 31
   Preventive measures   WM 31.5
   Social psychiatry   WM 30.6–31.5

Comorbidity
   Of particular disorders, with the disorder

Compact Disk Read–Only Memory see CD-ROM

Comparative Anatomy see Anatomy, Comparative

Comparative Pathology see Pathology

Comparative Physiology see Physiology,
  Comparative

Comparative Psychology see Psychology,
  Comparative

Compartment Syndromes   WE 550

Compensation, Disability see Veterans Disability
  Claims; Disability Evaluation; Workers'
  Compensation

Competence, Clinical see Clinical Competence

Competence, Immunologic see Immunocompetence

Competence, Professional see Professional
  Competence

Competency-Based Education
   General works   LC 1031–1034.5
   In a particular field (Form number 18 in any NLM
    schedule where applicable)

Competition, Economic see Economic Competition

Competitive Behavior   HM 136

Competitive Bidding
   Medical work   W 74
   Other fields, in economics number by subject

Competitive Binding see Binding, Competitive

Complement   QW 680

Complement Activating Enzymes   QW 680
   Biochemistry   QU 135

Complement Activation   QW 680

Complement Fixation Tests   QY 265

Complement Pathway, Classical   QW 680

Complement Proteins see Complement

Complement Receptors see Receptors, Complement

Complement 1   QW 680

Complement 1 Esterase Inhibitors see Complement
  1 Inactivators

Complement 1 Inactivators   QW 680
　　Biochemistry   QU 136
Complement 1 Inhibitors see Complement 1
　　Inactivators
Complement 3   QW 680
Complement 3 Convertase   QW 680
Complement 5 Convertase see Complement 3
　　Convertase
Complexons see Chelating Agents
Compliant Behavior see Cooperative Behavior
Composite Resins   WU 190
Compound Fractures see Fractures, Open
Compound Q see Trichosanthin
Comprehensive Dental Care   WU 29
Comprehensive Health Care   W 84.5
Comprehensive Health Insurance see Insurance,
　　Major Medical
Comprehensive Health Planning see Regional Health
　　Planning
Comprehensive Health Planning Agencies see Health
　　Systems Agencies
Comprehensive Health Plans, Local see Health
　　Systems Plans
Comprehensive Health Plans, State see State Health
　　Plans
Compressed Air Disease see Decompression Sickness
Compression of the Brain see Brain Injuries, Acute
Compression of the Spinal Cord see Spinal Cord
　　Compression
Compulsive Behavior   WM 176
　　See also Obsessive–Compulsive Disorder   WM
　　176
Compulsive Personality see Compulsive Personality
　　Disorder
Compulsive Personality Disorder   WM 190
Compulsory Health Insurance see Insurance, Health
Computed Tomography Scanners, X–Ray see
　　Tomography Scanners, X–Ray Computed
Computer Architecture see Computer Systems
Computer–Assisted Decision Making see Decision
　　Making, Computer–Assisted
Computer–Assisted Diagnosis see Diagnosis,
　　Computer–Assisted
Computer–Assisted Image Processing see Image
　　Processing, Computer–Assisted
Computer–Assisted Instruction
　　(Form number 18.2 in any NLM schedule where
　　applicable)
　　Embryology   QS 618.2
　　General works   LB 1028.5
　　Histology   QS 518.2
Computer–Assisted Radiotherapy see Radiotherapy,
　　Computer–Assisted
Computer–Assisted Radiotherapy Planning see
　　Radiotherapy Planning, Computer–Assisted
Computer–Assisted Therapy see Therapy,
　　Computer–Assisted
Computer Communication Networks   TK
　　5105.5–5105.9
Computer Data Processing see Automatic Data
　　Processing
Computer Graphics   T 385
Computer Hardware see Computers

Computer Literacy   QA 76.9.C64
Computer Models see Computer Simulation
Computer Network Management see Computer
　　Communication Networks
Computer Programs see Software
Computer Reasoning see Artificial Intelligence
Computer Simulation   QA 76.9.C65
　　Used for special purposes, by subject
Computer Software see Software
Computer Systems
　　As equipment in special fields (Form number 26.5
　　in any NLM schedule where applicable)
　　Used for particular fields, by subject
Computer Systems Development see Computer
　　Systems
Computer Systems Evaluation see Computer
　　Systems
Computer Systems Organization see Computer
　　Systems
Computer Terminals   TK 7887.8.T4
Computer User Training   QA 76.27
　　In form number 26.5 in any NLM schedule where
　　applicable
Computer Vision Systems see Artificial Intelligence
Computerized Emission Tomography see
　　Tomography, Emission–Computed
Computerized Tomography, X–Ray see
　　Tomography, X–Ray Computed
Computers   QA 75–76.95
　　As equipment in special fields
　　　In medicine (General)   W 26.55.C7
　　　(Form number 26.5 in any other NLM schedule
　　　where applicable)
　　Computer engineering   TK 7885–7895
　　Digital   QA 76.5–76.73
　　Machine theory   QA 267–268.5
　　See also Automatic Data Processing   W
　　26.55.A9, etc.; Information Systems   Z 699,
　　etc.
Computers, Analog   QA 76.4
　　As equipment in special fields
　　　In medicine (General)   W 26.55.C7
　　　(Form number 26.5 in any other NLM schedule
　　　where applicable)
　　Computer engineering   TK 7885–7985
　　See also Automatic Data Processing   W
　　26.55.A9, etc.; Information Systems   Z 699,
　　etc.
Computers, Digital see Computers
Computers, Personal see Microcomputers
Concanavalin A
　　As antibodies   QW 575
　　Diagnostic use, with disease being diagnosed, e.g.,
　　in nephritis   WJ 353
　　Other special topics, by subject
Concentration see Attention
Concentration Camps   HV 8963–8964
Concept Formation   BF 443
　　In infancy & childhood   WS 105.5.D2
Conception see Fertilization
Conchae Nasales see Turbinates
Concurrent Review   WX 153
Concurrent Studies see Cohort Studies

**ALWAYS CONSULT MAIN SCHEDULES. USE NUMBER ASSIGNED ONLY WHEN
SUBJECT REPRESENTS MAJOR EMPHASIS OF WORK BEING CLASSIFIED**

Concussion see Brain Concussion   WL 354 and
   other localized injuries, e.g. of the spinal cord
Condiments
   As a dietary supplement in health or disease
      WB 447
   Cookery   TX 819
Conditioned Reflexes see Conditioning, Classical
Conditioning, Classical   BF 319
Conditioning, Operant   BF 319.5.O6
Conditioning (Psychology)   BF 319
Conditioning Therapy see Behavior Therapy
Conduct Disorders, Child see Child Behavior
   Disorders
Conduction Anesthesia see Anesthesia, Conduction
Conduction Blocking Anesthetics see Anesthetics,
   Local
Conduction of Nerve Impulses see Neural
   Conduction
Conductometry   QD 116.C65
   Clinical chemistry   QY 90
Condurango see Gastrointestinal Agents
Conferences see Congresses
Confidentiality
   Dentistry, Forensic   W 705
   United States   KF 8958-8959.5
   Medicolegal (General)   W 700
   Psychiatry, Forensic   W 740
Conflict of Interest   W 50
   Economic aspects   W 58
Conflict (Psychology)
   In infancy & childhood   WS 105.5.M5
   Interpersonal   BF 637.I48
   Psychoanalysis   WM 460.5.M6
   Social psychology   HM 136
Conformity, Social see Social Conformity
Confusion
   In old age   WT 150
   Related to psychoses   WM 204
Congenital Anomalies see Abnormalities
Congenital Defects see Abnormalities
Congestive Cardiomyopathy see Cardiomyopathy,
   Congestive
Congestive Heart Failure see Heart Failure,
   Congestive
Congo Red   QV 240
Congo Virus Infection see Hemorrhagic Fever,
   Crimean
Congresses   W3
   Directories   W 3.5
   See also NLM Classification Practices, preceding
      the Schedules
Conjoined Twins see Twins, Conjoined
Conjugation, Genetic   QW 51
Conjugative Pili see Pili, Sex
Conjunctiva   WW 212-215
Conjunctival Diseases   WW 212
Conjunctivitis   WW 212
   Contagious granular see Trachoma   WW 215
Conjunctivitis, Acute Hemorrhagic   WW 212
Conjunctivitis, Allergic   WW 212
Conjunctivitis, Atopic see Conjunctivitis, Allergic
Conjunctivitis, Giant Papillary see Conjunctivitis,
   Allergic

Conjunctivitis, Inclusion   WW 212
Conjunctivitis, Vernal see Conjunctivitis, Allergic
Connecting Peptide see C-Peptide
Connective Tissue   QS 532.5.C7
   Aging   WT 104
Connective Tissue Disease, Mixed see Mixed
   Connective Tissue Disease
Connective Tissue Diseases   WD 375
   See also names of specific diseases, e.g., Cellulitis
      WR 220
Conn's Disease see Hyperaldosteronism
Conradi-Hunermann Syndrome see
   Chondrodysplasia Punctata
Consanguinity
   Forensic medicine   W 791
   Marriage   HQ 1026
   Primitive customs   GN 480
   See also Inbreeding   SF 105, etc.
Conscience   BJ 1471
   Psychoanalysis   WM 460.5.R3
Conscious Sedation
   In dentistry   WO 460
Consciousness
   General diagnosis   WB 182
   In infancy & childhood   WS 105.5.C7
   Neurologic manifestation of disease   WL 341
   Physiological aspects   WL 705
   Psychology   BF 309-499
   See also Unconsciousness   WB 182 etc.
Consciousness Disorders   WL 341
Consensus Development Conferences
   On specific topics, by subject
Consensus Development Conferences, NIH
   On specific topics, by subject
Consensus Sequence   QU 58
Consensus Workshops see Consensus Development
   Conferences
Conservation of Energy Resources   TJ 163.3-163.5
   In hospitals   WX 140
   Other special topics, by subject
Conservation of Natural Resources   S 900-954
   Forestry   SD 411-428
   Game and bird conservation and protection   SK
      351-579
   Nature   QH 75-77
   Wildlife   QL 81.5-84.77
   See also Ecology   QH 540-549, etc.
Constipation   WI 409
   In pregnancy   WQ 240
Constitution and Bylaws
   Special topics, by subject, e.g. in Hospital
      Administration   WX 150
Constitution, Body see Body Constitution
Constitutional Psychopathic Personality see
   Antisocial Personality Disorder
Constriction, Pathologic
   Of blood vessels   WG 560
   Of duodenum   WI 505
   Special topics, by subject
Constrictive Pericarditis see Pericarditis,
   Constrictive
Construction Loans see Financing, Construction
Construction Materials   TA 401-492

ALWAYS CONSULT MAIN SCHEDULES. USE NUMBER ASSIGNED ONLY WHEN
SUBJECT REPRESENTS MAJOR EMPHASIS OF WORK BEING CLASSIFIED

Industrial wastes   WA 788
Consultants
    Medical   W 64
    Nursing   WY 90
    Psychiatric   WM 64
    Surgical   WO 64
    In other specific specialties in the number for
        interpersonal relationships or lacking that, in
        the general works number
Consultation see Referral and Consultation
Consumer Advocacy   WA 288
    Environmental control   WA 670–847
    General   HC 79.C63
    In special areas, by subject
Consumer Involvement see Consumer Participation
Consumer Organizations   HC 79.C6–79.C63
    By country   HC 94–1085 (with topical
        breakdown as given in HC 79, etc.)
    Consumer protection   HC 79.C63
        By country (as above)
    For community health planning   WA 546
    For special purposes, by subject
Consumer Participation
    In mental health planning   WM 30
    In special areas, in the administrative number for
        the area or lacking that, in the general number,
        e.g., in community health organizations   WA
        546
    See also Patient Participation   WX 158.5
Consumer Preference see Consumer Satisfaction
Consumer Price Index see Economics
Consumer Product Safety   WA 288
    Special topics, by subject
Consumer Protection see Accident Prevention;
    Consumer Organizations
Consumer Satisfaction
    General works   HF 5415.3–5415.5
    With hospitals   WX 158.5
    With health services, medical treatment, etc.
        W 85
    With mental hospitals   WM 29.5
    With other services or products, by subject
Consumption Coagulopathy see Disseminated
    Intravascular Coagulation
Contact Dermatitis see Dermatitis, Contact
Contact Lenses   WW 355
Contact Lenses, Extended–Wear   WW 355
Contact Lenses, Hydrophilic   WW 355
Contact Prevention in Illness see Communicable
    Disease Control; Patient Isolation; Quarantine
Contact Tracing
    Of particular disorders, with the disorder
Contactants as Allergens see Allergens
Contagious Diseases see Communicable Diseases
Contagious Pustular Dermatitis see Ecthyma,
    Contagious
Containment of Biohazards
    In the environment   WA 671
    In genetic engineering   QH 442
    In other areas, by subject
Contingent Negative Variation   WL 102
Continued Stay Review see Concurrent Review
Continuing Care Retirement Centers see Housing for

the Elderly
Continuity of Patient Care   W 84.6
Continuum of Care see Continuity of Patient Care
Contour Perception see Form Perception
Contraception   WP 630
    By prevention of ovulation   WP 630
    Male   WJ 710
    Religious aspects   HQ 766.2
        Catholicism   HQ 766.3
        Protestantism   HQ 766.35
        Islam   HQ 766.374
        Other   HQ 766.4, A–Z
    Sociological aspects   HQ 763–766
        See also Abortion   WQ 225, etc.
Contraception, Immunologic   WP 630
Contraceptive Agents   QV 177
    See also specific topics under Contraception
Contraceptive Agents, Female   QV 177
Contraceptive Agents, Male   QV 177
Contraceptive Devices   WP 640
Contraceptive Devices, Female   WP 640
    See also Intrauterine devices   WP 640
Contraceptive Devices, Intrauterine see Intrauterine
    Devices
Contraceptive Devices, Male   WJ 710
Contraceptives, Oral   QV 177
Contraceptives, Oral, Combined   QV 177
Contraceptives, Oral, Hormonal   QV 177
Contraceptives, Oral, Sequential   QV 177
Contraceptives, Oral, Synthetic   QV 177
Contraceptives, Postcoital   QV 177
Contract Services
    Medical work   W 74
    Other topics, class by subject if specific; if general,
        in economics number where available
Contracture
    Fingers, wrist see Volkmann's Contracture   WE
        835
    Hand see Dupuytren's Contracture   WE 830
    Hip see Hip Contracture   WE 855
    Joint   WE 300
    Muscle (General)   WE 545
Contrast Media
    In radiology
        Supplies   WN 150
        Technique of use   WN 160
    Used for special purposes, by subject
Contrast Sensitivity   WW 105
    As a measure of visual acuity   WW 145
Controlled Clinical Trials
    Drugs   QV 771
    For other purposes, by subject or specific drug
        or procedure
Controlled Clinical Trials, Randomized see
    Randomized Controlled Trials
Controlled Hypotension see Hypotension,
    Controlled
Contusions   WO 192
    First aid   WA 292
    Localized, by site
Convalescence   WB 545
    After surgery   WO 183
    Convalescence from particular disorder, by the

disorder
    Particular forms of convalescence, by subject
Convallaria   QV 153
Convergence, Ocular   WW 410
Convergent Strabismus see Esotropia
Conversion Disorder   WM 173.5
Convulsants   QV 103
Convulsions   WL 340
    Drugs checking see Anticonvulsants   QV 85
    In epilepsy   WL 385
    In infancy & childhood   WL 340
    In pregnancy see Eclampsia   WQ 215
    Veterinary   SF 895
Convulsions, Febrile   WL 340
Convulsive Disorders see Chorea; Epilepsy
Convulsive Therapy   WM 410–412
    With pentylenetetrazole   WM 410
Convulsive Therapy, Electric see Electroconvulsive
   Therapy
Cookery
    Army   UC 720–735, UH 487
    Diabetic diet   WK 819
    For hospitals   WX 168
    Institutional (General)   TX 820
    Navy   VC 370–375
    Obesity diet see Diet, Reducing   WD 210, etc.
    Therapeutic diet (General)   WB 405
    See also names of specific diets and diseases for
      which diet is being administered
Cooley's Anemia see Thalassemia
Coombs' Test   QY 265
    Diagnosis of erythroblastosis fetalis   WH 425
    Used for other special purposes, by subject
Coon's Technique see Fluorescent Antibody
   Technique
Cooperative Behavior   HM 131–134
COPD see Lung Diseases, Obstructive
Coping Behavior see Adaptation, Psychological
Copper   QV 65
    Metabolism   QU 130.5
Copulation   QL 761
    Human see Coitus
    Particular animals, in QL or SF number for the
      animal
Copying Processes   Z 265–265.5
Copyright   Z 551–656
Cor Pulmonale see Pulmonary Heart Disease
Coramine see 1 Nikethamide
Cord, Umbilical see Umbilical Cord
Cordials see Alcoholic Beverages
Corethamid see Nikethamide
Corn
    As a dietary supplement in health or disease
      WB 430
    Cultivation   SB 191.M2, 351.C7
Cornea   WW 220
    Eye bank procedures   WW 170
    Transplantation   WW 220
Corneal Arcus see Arcus Senilis
Corneal Diseases   WW 220
Corneal Endothelium see Endothelium, Corneal
Corneal Opacity   WW 220
Corneal Transplantation   WW 220

Corneal Ulcer   WW 220
Corns see Callosities
Coronary Angioplasty, Transluminal Balloon see
   Angioplasty, Transluminal, Percutaneous
   Coronary
Coronary Arteries see Coronary Vessels
Coronary Arteriosclerosis   WG 300
Coronary Arteritis see Coronary   WG 300 under
   Arteritis
Coronary Artery Bypass   WG 169
Coronary Artery Disease see Coronary Disease
Coronary Artery Vasospasm see Coronary
   Vasospasm
Coronary Atherosclerosis see Coronary
   Arteriosclerosis
Coronary Care Units   WG 27–28
Coronary Circulation   WG 300
Coronary Disease   WG 300
    Popular works   WG 113
Coronary Embolism see Embolism
Coronary Heart Disease see Coronary Disease
Coronary Infarction see Myocardial Infarction
Coronary-Prone Personality see Type A Personality
Coronary Reperfusion see Myocardial Reperfusion
Coronary Thrombosis   WG 300
Coronary Vasospasm   WG 300
Coronary Vessel Anomalies   WG 220
Coronary Vessels   WG 300
Coronaviridae   QW 168.5.C8
Coroners and Medical Examiners   W 800
Coronoid Fossa see Humerus
Corpora Bigemina see Optic Lobe
Corpora Quadrigemina   WL 310
Corporate Practice see Professional Corporations
Corpses see Cadaver
Corpulence see Obesity
Corpus Callosum   WL 307
Corpus Cardiacum see Neurosecretory Systems
Corpus Luteum   WP 320
    Endocrine functions   WP 530
      See also Corpus Luteum Hormones   WP 530
Corpus Luteum Cyst see Ovarian Cysts
Corpus Luteum Hormones   WP 530
Corpus Pineale see Pineal Body
Corpus Striatum   WL 307
Corpuscles, Blood see Blood Cells; Erythrocytes;
   Leukocytes
Correspondence
    Physicians and specialists of medically related
      fields
      Collective   WZ 112–150
      Individual   WZ 100
    Special topics, by subject
Correspondence Courses see Education
Corridor Disease see Theileriasis
Corrosion   TA 462
    In dentistry   WU 180
    In orthopedics   WE 26
    In other areas, by subject
Corrosion Casting   QS 525
Corrosive Poisons see Poisons
Corset see Braces; Clothing
Cortex see Adrenal Cortex; Auditory Cortex;

Cerebellar Cortex; Cerebral Cortex; Kidney Cortex; Motor Cortex; Somatosensory Cortex; Visual Cortex
Cortexone see Desoxycorticosterone
Cortical Depression, Spreading see Spreading Cortical Depression
Cortical Hormones see Adrenal Cortex Hormones
Corticoids see Adrenal Cortex Hormones
Corticospinal Tracts see Pyramidal Tracts
Corticosteroid Receptors see Receptors, Glucocorticoid
Corticosteroids see Adrenal Cortex Hormones
Corticosterone   WK 755
Corticotropin   WK 515
Corticotropin–Releasing Factor see Corticotropin–Releasing Hormone
Corticotropin–Releasing Hormone   WK 515
Corticotropin–Releasing Hormone–41 see Corticotropin–Releasing Hormone
Corti's Organ see Organ of Corti
Cortisol see Hydrocortisone
Cortisone   WK 755
Corynebacteriaceae see Actinomycetales
Corynebacterium   QW 118
Corynebacterium diphtheriae   QW 118
Corynebacterium Diphtheriae Toxin see Diphtheria Toxin
Corynebacterium Infections   WC 318–320
Coryneform Group   QW 118
Coryza, Acute see Common Cold
Coryza Viruses see Rhinovirus
Cosmetic Surgery see Surgery, Plastic
Cosmetics
   Chemical technology   TP 983
   Public health aspects   WA 744
   See also Beauty Culture   QT 275, etc.
Cosmetics, Hair see Hair Preparations
Cosmetology see Beauty Culture
Cosmic Radiation   WN 415
   Adverse effects   WN 610–650
   Biophysics   QT 34
   Cosmic physics   QC 809.R3
   Medical safety measures   WN 650
   Radiation physics   QC 484.8–485.9
Cosmids   QW 51
   As genetic vectors   QH 442.2
Cost Allocation
   Medicine   W 74
   Other topics, class by subject if specific; if general, in economics number where applicable
Cost Apportionment see Cost Allocation
Cost–Benefit Analysis   HD 47.4
   Of particular procedures, by subject if specific, e.g., value of a diagnostic test   WB 141; if general, in economics number for the specialty, e.g., economics of medical practice   W 74; lacking an economics number, in the general number
Cost–Benefit Data see Cost–Benefit Analysis
Cost Containment see Cost Control
Cost Control
   General   HD 47.3
   Dentistry   WU 77

Hospitals   WX 157
Medicine   W 74
Nursing   WY 77
Pharmacy   QV 736
Cost Effectiveness see Cost–Benefit Analysis
Cost Shifting see Cost Allocation
Costen's Syndrome see Temporomandibular Joint Syndrome
Costs and Cost Analysis
   Dentistry   WU 77
   Hospitals   WX 157
   Medicine   W 74
   Nursing   WY 77
   Pharmacy   QV 736
Costs, Direct Service see Direct Service Costs
Cot Death see Sudden Infant Death
Cotton
   Agriculture   SB 245–251.5
   Diseases from dust   WF 654
   Industrial wastes   WA 788
      Control in work atmosphere   WA 450
   Used for special purposes, by subject
Cottonseed see Cottonseed Oil
Cottonseed Oil   WB 431
   As dietary protein
      In animal feed   SF 99.C6
      In human nutrition   WB 426
   Biochemistry   QU 86
Cough   WF 143
Coumaphos
   Agriculture   SB 952.P5
   Public health   WA 240
Coumarins   QV 193
Counseling   WM 55
   By nurses   WY 87
   Divorce   WM 55
   Genetic see Genetic Counseling   QZ 50, etc.;
   In adolescence   WS 462
   In infancy & childhood   WS 105.5.C3
   Marriage   WM 55
   Pastoral care   WM 61
   Sex   WM 55
   Special population groups   WA 305, etc.
   Students   LB 1027.5–1027.9
      Extension. Adult education   LC 5225.C68
      Secondary education   LB 1620.4–1620.53
      Higher education   LB 2343
      (Form number 18 or other appropriate education number in any NLM schedule where applicable)
      See also Mental Health Services   WA 352–353, etc.
   Vocational   HF 5381–5382.5
   Workers   HD 5549.5.C8
      Mental health   WA 495
Counseling, Sex see Sex Counseling
Counterimmunoelectrophoresis   QY 250–275
   Used for diagnostic monitoring, or evaluation tests in special fields, with the field
Counterirritants see Irritants
Counterirritation see Therapeutic Use under Irritants
Countertransference (Psychology)   WM 62
Coupling Factor 1 see H(+)–Transporting ATP

ALWAYS CONSULT MAIN SCHEDULES. USE NUMBER ASSIGNED ONLY WHEN SUBJECT REPRESENTS MAJOR EMPHASIS OF WORK BEING CLASSIFIED

Synthase
Court Plaster see Bandages
Courtship   HQ 801-801.5
   Animal   QL 761
Cowper's Glands see Bulbourethral Glands
Coxa see Hip
Coxa Plana see Legg-Perthes Disease
Coxarthrosis see Osteoarthritis, Hip
Coxiella   QW 150
Coxsackievirus Infections   WC 500
Coxsackieviruses   QW 168.5.P4
CPR see Cardiopulmonary Resuscitation
Crabs, Horseshoe see Horseshoe Crabs
Crackles see Respiratory Sounds
Cramp see Muscle Cramp
Cranial Fossa, Posterior   WE 705
Cranial Nerve Diseases   WL 330
Cranial Nerve Neoplasms   WL 330
Cranial Nerves   WL 330
   See individual nerves under name of nerve
Cranial Sinus Thrombosis see Sinus Thrombosis
Cranial Sinuses   WG 625.C7
Cranial Sutures   WE 705
Craniofacial Dysostosis   WE 705
Craniology   GN 71-131
Craniometry   GN 71-131
Craniopharyngioma   QZ 310
Craniosynostoses   WE 705
Craniotomy   WL 368
Cranium see Skull
Crataegus   QV 150
Crayfish   QX 463
CRD-401 see Diltiazem
Creatine   QU 61
Creatine Kinase   QU 141
Creatine Kinase Isoenzymes   QU 141
   Used for special purposes, by subject
Creatine Kinase Isozymes see Creatine Kinase
   Isoenzymes
Creatine Phosphate see Phosphocreatine
Creatine Phosphokinase see Creatine Kinase
Creatinine   QU 65
Creativeness   BF 408-426
   In adolescence   WS 462
   In infancy & childhood   WS 105.5.C7
   In psychoanalysis   WM 460.5.C7
Credentialing
   (Form number 21 in any NLM schedule where
     applicable)
   Nursing   WY 16
   See also specific methods, e.g., Licensure,
     Medical   W 40
Credit and Collection, Patient see Patient Credit and
   Collection
Cremation see Mortuary Practice
Crenothrix see Bacteria
Creosote
   As an anti-infective agent   QV 223
   Toxicology   QV 627
Cresols
   As an anti-infective agent   QV 223
   Organic chemisty   QD 341.P5
Cresylic Acid see Cresols

Cretinism   WK 252
CRF-41 see Corticotropin-Releasing Hormone
Crib Death see Sudden Infant Death
Cribriform Plate see Ethmoid Bone
Cricetidae see Microtinae
Cricetinae see Hamsters
Cricetulus   QL 737.R666
   As laboratory animals   QY 60.R6
   As pets   SF 459.H3
Cricetus see Hamsters
Crigler-Najjar Syndrome   WD 205.5.H9
Crime   HV 6251-7220.5
   Compensation to victims   W 910
   Therapy for victims   WM 401
   Specific types, by subject
Criminal Justice see Criminal Law
Criminal Law
   Psychiatric aspects   W 740
Criminal Psychology   HV 6080-6113
Criminal Violence Victims see Crime
Criminology   HV 6001-9960
Crippled see Disabled
Crisis Intervention
   Community programs   WM 30
   General   WM 401
   In adolescence   WS 463
   In infancy & childhood   WS 350.2
   In preventing suicide   HV 6545
   See also Emergency Services, Psychiatric   WM
     401
Critical Care   WX 218
   In emergencies (not in hospital)   WB 105
   In infancy & childhood   WS 366
     Administration of hospital unit   WS 27-28
   Nursing   WY 154
     Pediatric   WY 159
   Of a particular disease or in a particular field
     General, with the disease or field
     Nursing, with the nursing specialty
Criticism see Book Reviews
Crocodiles see Alligators and Crocodiles
Crohn Disease   WI 512
   Affecting the colon only   WI 522
Cromolyn Sodium   QV 120
Cronkhite-Canada Syndrome see Churg-Strauss
   Syndrome
Cross-Cultural Comparison
   Comparative civilization   CB 151
   Ethnology   GN 378
   Ethnopsychology   GN 270-279
   Mental development   WS 105
   Special topics by subject, e.g., Cross-National
     MMPI Research   WM 145
Cross-Eye see Strabismus
Cross Infection   WC 195
   Prevention and control in hospitals   WX 167
Cross-Linking Reagents
   Analytical chemistry   QD 77
   Pharmaceutical chemistry   QV 744
   Used for special purposes, by subject
Cross-Sectional Studies   WA 950
   Special topics, by subject
Crossing Over (Genetics)   QH 445

**ALWAYS CONSULT MAIN SCHEDULES.   USE NUMBER ASSIGNED ONLY WHEN
SUBJECT REPRESENTS MAJOR EMPHASIS OF WORK BEING CLASSIFIED**

Crossmatching, Blood see Blood Grouping and Crossmatching
Crossmatching, Tissue see Histocompatibility Testing
Crotalid Venoms   WD 410
Croton Oil   QV 75
Croup   WV 510
Crouzon's Disease see Craniofacial Dysostosis
Crowding
    Animal population   QL 752
    Housing   WA 795
    Human population   HB 871
Crown Compounds see Ethers, Cyclic
Crowns   WU 515
Crude Oil see Petroleum
Cruor see Postmortem Changes
Crush Injuries see Wounds and Injuries
Crush Syndrome   WJ 342
Crustacea   QX 463
Crutches   WE 26
Crying
    Children   WS 105.5.E5
    Emotions   BF 575.C88
    Grief   BF 575.G7
    Neuroses   WM 170–184, etc.
Cryoanesthesia see Hypothermia, Induced
Cryobiochemistry see Biochemistry; Freezing
Cryobiology see Freezing
Cryofixation see Cryopreservation
Cryogenic Surgery   WO 510
    Localized, by site
    See also Freezing
Cryoglobulinemia   WH 400
Cryopreservation   QH 324.9.C7
Cryoprotective Agents
    In blood preservation   WH 460
    In microbiology   QW 25–26
    See also Freezing
Cryosurgery   WB 473
    Used for special purposes, by subject
    See also Freezing
Cryotherapy   WB 473
    Used for special purposes, by subject
Cryptococcosis   WC 475
Cryptococcus   QW 180.5.D3
Cryptorchidism   WJ 840
    Veterinary   SF 871
Cryptorchism see Cryptorchidism
Cryptosporidiosis   WC 730
    Veterinary   SF 792
Cryptosporidium   QX 123
Crystal Violet see Gentian Violet
Crystalline Lens see Lens, Crystalline
Crystallins   WW 101
Crystallization
    Crystal structure and growth   QD 921
    Pharmaceutical chemistry   QV 744
    Physical and theoretical chemistry   QD 548
    Other special topics, by subject
Crystallography   QD 901–999
CTG, Antepartum see Cardiotocography
Cu–Zn Superoxide Dismutase see Superoxide Dismutase

Cuban Americans see Hispanic Americans
Cubital Fossa see Elbow; Humerus
Cues
    Conditioned response   BF 319
    Prediction (Logic)   BC 181
Culdoscopy   WP 141
Culex   QX 530
Culicidae   QX 510–530
    See also Aedes   QX 525; Anopheles   QX 515;
        Culex   QX 530
Culicoides see Ceratopogonidae
Cults, Medical see Alternative Medicine
Cultural Characteristics
    Special topics, by subject
Cultural Deprivation
    Adolescents   WS 462
    Children   WS 105.5.D3
    Education   LC 4051–4100.4
Cultural Disadvantagement see Cultural Deprivation
Cultural Evolution   HM 106+
    Special topics, by subject
Culture   CB
    Anthropology   GN 301–499
    General works   CB 23–113
    Sociology   HM 101–121
Culture Media   QW 25–26
Cultured Cells see Cells, Cultured
Cultured Tumor Cells see Tumor Cells, Cultured
Cumulative Survival Rate see Survival Rate
Cupping see Alternative Medicine
Curare   QV 140
Curare–Like Agents see Neuromuscular Nondepolarizing Agents
Curariform Drugs see Neuromuscular Nondepolarizing Agents
Cures, Special see Alternative Medicine
Curettage   WO 500
    Localized, by site
    See also Dilatation and Curettage   WP 470, etc.
Curietherapy see Brachytherapy
Curiosities, Medical see Folklore; Superstitions
Curiosity see Exploratory Behavior
Curium   WN 420
    Nuclear physics   QC 796.C55
    See also special topics under Radioisotopes
Curriculum
    (Form number 18 in any NLM schedule where applicable)
    Education extension   LC 5219
    Elementary schools   LB 1570–1571
    Secondary schools   LB 1628–1629.8
    Universities and colleges   LB 2361–2365
    University extension   LC 6223
Curvatures, Spinal see Kyphosis; Lordosis; Scoliosis
Cushing's Syndrome   WK 770
Cushion Liners see Denture Liners
Cuspid   WU 101
Custody, Child see Child Custody
Customized Drugs see Designer Drugs
Customs see Culture
Cutaneous Drug Administration see Administration, Cutaneous
Cutaneous Leishmaniasis see Leishmaniasis

ALWAYS CONSULT MAIN SCHEDULES.   USE NUMBER ASSIGNED ONLY WHEN SUBJECT REPRESENTS MAJOR EMPHASIS OF WORK BEING CLASSIFIED

Cutaneous Oximetry see Blood Gas Monitoring, Transcutaneous
Cutis Elastica see Ehlers–Danlos Syndrome
Cutting Wounds see Wounds, Penetrating
Cyanamide   QV 610
Cyanates   QV 280
Cyanidanol–3 see Catechin
Cyanides   QV 610
Cyanobacteria   QW 131
Cyanocobalamin see Vitamin B 12
Cyanophyceae see Cyanobacteria
Cyanosis   WG 142
Cybernetics   Q 300–390
    Used for special purposes, by subject
    See also Information Theory   Q 350–390
Cyclamates   WA 712
Cyclandelate   QV 243
Cyclic AMP   QU 57
    Pharmacology   QV 185
Cyclic GMP   QU 58
    Pharmacology   QV 185
Cyclic N–Oxides
    Organic chemistry   QD 401
Cyclicity see Periodicity
Cyclitis, Heterochromic see Iridocyclitis
Cycloamylose see Cyclodextrins
Cyclodextrins   QU 83
Cycloheptaamylose see Cyclodextrins
Cyclohexanes
    Organic chemistry   QD 305.H9
Cyclohexanones
    As carcinogens   QZ 202
    Toxicology   QV 633
Cycloheximide   QV 252
Cyclopentanes
    Organic chemistry   QD 305.H9
Cyclophosphamide   QV 269
    Cancer chemotherapy   QZ 267
    Immunosuppression   QW 920
Cycloplegics see Mydriatics
Cyclopropanes   QV 81
Cycloserine   QV 268
Cyclosporins   QW 920
Cyclostomes   QL 638.12–638.25
Cyclothymic Disorder   WM 171
Cyclothymic Personality see Cyclothymic Disorder
Cyclothymic Psychoses see Psychoses, Manic–Depressive
Cylindroma see Carcinoma, Adenoid Cystic
Cyprinidae   SH 167.C3
    Anatomy and physiology   QL 638.C94
    Diseases   SH 179.C3
Cyprinus see Carp
Cyproheptadine   QV 157
Cyproterone   WJ 875
Cyprus Fever see Brucellosis
Cystadenocarcinoma   QZ 365
    Localized, by site
Cystadenoma   QZ 365
    Localized, by site
Cystadenoma Lymphomatosum, Papillary see Adenolymphoma
Cysteamine   QU 61

As a radiation–protective agent   WN 650
    Organic chemistry   QD 305.A8
Cysteinamine see Cysteamine
Cysteine   QU 60
Cysteinyldopa   WK 725
    As a disease marker, class with the specific disease
Cystic Disease of Breast see Fibrocystic Disease of Breast
Cystic Duct   WI 750
Cystic Fibrosis   WI 820
Cysticercosis   WC 838
    Localized, by site
    Veterinary   SF 810.C5
Cysticercus   QX 400
Cystine   QU 60
Cystinosis   WJ 301
Cystitis   WJ 500
Cystocele see Bladder Diseases
Cystosarcoma Phyllodes see Phyllodes Tumor
Cystoscopy   WJ 500
Cysts   QZ 200
    Bone see Bone Cyst   WE 258
    Breast   WP 840
    Dermoid see Dermoid Cyst   QZ 310
    Kidney see Kidney, Cystic   WJ 358
    Mediastinum see Mediastinal Cyst   WF 900
    Mesentery see Mesenteric Cyst   WI 500
    Nonodontogenic see Nonodontogenic Cysts WU 280
    Odontogenic see Odontogenic Cysts   WU 280
    Ovary see Ovarian Cysts   WP 322
    Pancreatic see Pancreatic Cyst   WI 810
    Periodontal see Periodontal Cyst   WU 240
    Pilonidal see Pilonidal Cyst   WE 750
    Radicular see Radicular Cyst   WU 240
    Sebaceous see Epidermal Cyst   WR 420
    Thyroglossal see Thyroglossal Cyst   WK 270
    Vaginal   WP 250
    Vulval   WP 200
    Other localities, by site
Cysts, Hydatid see Echinococcosis
Cytarabine   QV 269
Cytidine Diphosphate Choline   QU 87
Cytidine Phosphates see Cytosine Nucleotides
Cytochemistry see Histocytochemistry
Cytochrome aa3 see Cytochrome–c Oxidase
Cytochrome–c Oxidase   QU 140
Cytochrome Oxidase see Cytochrome–c Oxidase
Cytochrome P–450(arom) see Aromatase
Cytochromes   WH 190
    Clinical examination   QY 455
Cytodiagnosis   QY 95
    Neoplasms   QZ 241
    Gynecology   WP 141
    Used for diagnosis of particular disorders, with the disorder or system
Cytofluorometry, Flow see Flow Cytometry
Cytogenetics   QH 441.5
    General   QH 441.5
    Human   QH 431
        Blood analysis   QY 402
        Predisposition to disease   QZ 50
Cytokeratin see Keratin

Cytokines   QW 568
Cytokinesis see Cell Division
Cytokinetics see Cell Cycle
Cytological Techniques   QH 585
   Clinical pathology   QY 95
Cytology   QH 573–671
   Cell pathology, with specific subject in NLM schedules
   See also Cells   QH 573–659, etc. and related headings
Cytolysins see Cytotoxins
Cytomegalic Inclusion Disease see Cytomegalovirus Infections
Cytomegalovirus   QW 165.5.H3
Cytomegalovirus Infections   WC 500
Cytometry, Flow see Flow Cytometry
Cytopathic Effect, Viral see Cytopathogenic Effect, Viral
Cytopathogenic Effect, Viral   QW 160
Cytophagales   QW 128
Cytophotometry   QH 585.5.C984
   Clinical pathology   QY 95
Cytoplasm   QH 591
Cytoplasmic Filaments see Cytoskeleton
Cytoplasmic Granules   QH 603.M35
Cytoplasmic Inclusions see Inclusion Bodies
Cytosine
   In nucleic acids   QU 58
Cytosine Arabinoside see Cytarabine
Cytosine Nucleotides   QU 57
Cytoskeletal Filaments see Cytoskeleton
Cytoskeletal Proteins   QU 55
Cytoskeleton   QH 603.C96
Cytosol Aminopeptidase see Leucine Aminopeptidase
Cytostatic Agents see Antineoplastic Agents
Cytotaxinogens see Chemotactic Factors
Cytotaxins see Chemotactic Factors
Cytotoxic Antibiotics see Antibiotics, Antineoplastic
Cytotoxic Drugs see Antineoplastic Agents
Cytotoxic T-Lymphocytes see T-Lymphocytes, Cytotoxic
Cytotoxicity, Antibody-Dependent Cell see Antibody-Dependent Cell Cytotoxicity
Cytotoxicity, Immunologic   QW 568
Cytotoxicity Tests, Immunologic   QW 568
   Used for special purposes, by subject
Cytotoxin-Antibody Conjugates see Immunotoxins
Cytotoxins   QW 630.5.C9
   See also Antibiotics, Antineoplastic   QV 269; names of toxins specific to particular cells, e.g., Enterotoxins   QW 630.5.E6
C1 Esterase Inhibitors see Complement 1 Inactivators
C1 Inactivators see Complement 1 Inactivators
C3 Activator see Complement 3 Convertase
C3 Convertase see Complement 3 Convertase
C5 Cleaving Enzyme see Complement 3 Convertase

D

D-Amino-Acid Oxidase   QU 140
D-Glucuronolactone Dehydrogenase see Aldehyde Dehydrogenase
D 600 see Gallopamil
DAB see p-Dimethylaminoazobenzene
Dacryocystitis   WW 208
Dacryocystorhinostomy   WW 208
Dacryocystostomy see Dacryocystorhinostomy
Dactylolysis Spontanea see Ainhum
Dairy Products   SF 250.5–275
   As dietary supplement in health or disease   WB 428
   Bacteriology   QW 85
   Home Economics   TX 759–759.5
   Sanitation   WA 715
Dairying   SF 221–250
   Public health aspects   WA 715–719
   Pasteurization   WA 719
Danazol   WP 522
Dance Therapy   WM 450.5.D2
Dancing
   Injuries   WA 487.5.D4
   Physiological aspects   QT 255
Dandruff see Scalp Dermatoses
Dandy-Walker Syndrome   WL 350
Dane Particle see Hepatitis B Virus
Dangerous Behavior
   As a social behavior disorder   WM 600
   In adolescence   WS 463
   In infancy & childhood   WS 350.8.A4
Dantrolene   QV 140
Dapsone   QV 259
Dark Adaptation   WW 109
Darkness
   Physiological effects   QT 162.L5
   See also Nyctalopia   WD 110; Visual Perception   WW 105
Data Analysis, Statistical see Data Interpretation, Statistical
Data Collection   WA 950
   For particular purposes, by subject
Data Display   TK 7882.I6
   (Form number 26.5 in any NLM schedule where applicable)
   Special topics, by subject
Data Interpretation, Statistical
   Special topics, by subject
Data Processing, Automatic see Automatic Data Processing
Data Systems see Information Systems
Database Management Systems   W 26.5
   Used for special purposes, by subject
Databases see Databases, Bibliographic
Databases, Bibliographic   Z 699–699.5
   By subject   Z 699.5.A–Z
   In medicine (General)   W 26.55.I4
   In other special fields (Form number 26.5 in any NLM schedule where applicable)
Databases, Distributed see Computer Communication Networks
Datura see Stramonium
Day Blindness see Vision Disorders
Day Care
   In old age   WT 29
   Of the mentally ill   WM 29

Of the physically ill and disabled   WX 29
See also Child Day Care Centers   WA 310–320, etc.
Day Dreams see Fantasy
DDAVP see Desmopressin
DDD   WA 240
DDE   WA 240
DDT   WA 240
DDX see DDE
De Lange's Syndrome   QS 675
Dead Bodies see Cadaver
Deadly Nightshade see Belladonna
DEAE–Dextran   QU 83
Deaf–Mutism see Deafness; Mutism
Deafness   WV 270–280
  In infancy & childhood   WV 271
    Education see Education, Special   HV 2417–2990.5
    Rehabilitation
      Physical and medical   WV 270–280
      Social   HV 2353–2990.5
Deafness, Conductive see Hearing Loss, Conductive
Deafness, Partial see Hearing Loss, Partial
Deafness, Sensorineural see Deafness
Deafness, Sudden   WV 270
Deamination   QD 281.A6
  Biochemistry   QU 25
Deamino Arginine Vasopressin see Desmopressin
Death
  Attitude see Attitude to Death   BF 789.D4
  In infancy & childhood   WS 200
  Legal establishment of   W 820
    See also Death certificates   WA 54
  Medicolegal aspects   W 800–867
  In old age   WT 116
  Registration   WA 54
  Speculative philosophy   BD 443.8–445
  Statistics see Mortality   HB 1321–1528, etc.
  See also Brain death   W 820; Fetal death   WQ 225
Death Certificates   WA 54
Death Rate see Mortality
Death, Sudden   W 820
  Special topics, by subject, e.g., when associated with coronary disease   WG 300
  See also Sudden Infant Death   WS 430
Death with Dignity see Right to Die
Debridement   WO 700–820
  Localized, by site
Decalcification, Pathologic   WE 250
Decalcification Technique   QS 525
Decamethonium Compounds   QV 140
Decarboxylases see Carboxy–Lyases
Decay, Dental see Dental Caries
Decayed, Missing, and Filled Teeth see DMF Index
Deceleration   WD 720
Deception see Lying
Decerebrate State   WL 340
Decidua   WQ 210
  Embryology   QS 645
Decidual Cell Reaction see Ovum Implantation
Decision Analysis see Decision Support Techniques
Decision Making   BF 448

In adolescence   WS 462
In infancy & childhood   WS 105.5.D2
Special topics, by subject, e.g., in local health administration   WA 546
Decision Making, Computer–Assisted
  In medicine (General)   W 26.55.D2
  In other special fields (Form number 26.5 in any NLM schedule where applicable)
  Used for special purpose, by subject
Decision Making, Organizational
  Management   HD 30.23
  Psychology   BF 448
  Special topics, by subject
Decision Modeling see Decision Support Techniques
Decision Support Systems, Management   W 26.5
  In other areas, by subject
Decision Support Techniques
  Special topics, by subject, e.g., Diagnosis   WB 141
Decision Theory
  In mathematical statistics   QA 279.4–279.7
  In special topics, by subject
Decision Trees
  In mathematical statistics   QA 279.4
  In special topics, by subject
Decoctions see Solutions
Decoloration, Drug see Drug Compounding
Decompression
  Aerospace medicine   WD 710
  Submarine medicine   WD 650
  Other special topics, by subject
Decompression, Explosive see Atmospheric Pressure
Decompression Sickness
  Altitude effects   WD 712
  Aviation medicine   WD 712
  Diving problem   WD 650
  Submarine medicine   WD 650
Decontamination
  Chemical warfare agents   QV 663
  Radiation   WN 650
Decortication, Cerebral Cortex see Cerebral Decortication
Decubitus Ulcer   WR 598
Decussation, Pyramidal see Pyramidal Tracts
Dedications see Anniversaries and Special Events
Deductibles and Coinsurance
  Medical insurance   W 100–275
  See also specific types of insurance, e.g.
    Insurance, Health   W 100–275
Deer Fly Fever see Tularemia
Defecation   WI 600
  See also Encopresis   WI 600; Fecal incontinence   WI 600
Defectives, Mental see Mental Retardation
Defects, Equipment see Equipment Failure
Defense Mechanisms   WM 193–193.5
  In infancy & childhood   WS 350.8.D3
Defensive Medicine   W 44
  Dentistry   WU 44
  Nursing   WY 44
  (Form number 33 in any other NLM schedule where applicable)
Defensive Practice see Defensive Medicine

Deferoxamine   QV 183
Defibrillation, Electric see Electric Countershock
Deficiency Diseases   WD 105-155
   Veterinary   SF 854-855
Defoliants, Chemical
   Plant culture   SB 951.4
   Public health aspects   WA 240
Deformities see Abnormalities
Degeneration see Atrophy; Hepatolenticular
   Degeneration; Lipoidosis; Nerve Degeneration;
   Retinal Degeneration
Degeneration, Social see Skid Row Alcoholics;
   Social Alienation; Social Behavior Disorders
Degenerative Processes in Disease see Disease
Deglutition   WI 102
Deglutition Disorders   WI 250
Degus see Rodentia
Dehydration
   Diagnostic significance   WB 158
   In water-electrolyte imbalance   WD 220
Dehydrocholesterol see Cholecalciferol
Dehydrocortisone see Prednisone
Dehydrogenases see Oxidoreductases
Dehydromethyltestosterone see Methandrostenolone
Deinstitutionalization   W 84.7
   See also Home Care Services   WY 115, etc.
Deja Vu   WM 173.7
Delayed-Action Preparations   QV 785
Delayed Effects, Prenatal Exposure see Prenatal
   Exposure Delayed Effects
Deletion (Genetics) see Chromosome Deletion
Delhi Sore see Leishmaniasis
Delirium
   Neurologic manifestations   WL 340
   Psychotic   WM 204
   Specific disease associations, with the disease
Delirium Tremens see Alcohol Withdrawal Delirium
Delivery   WQ 415
   Drugs affecting see Oxytocics   QV 173
   Methods   WQ 415-430
      Forceps   WQ 425
      See also Cesarean section   WQ 430
   Version   WQ 415
   Veterinary   SF 887
   See also Natural Childbirth   WQ 152; Home
      Childbirth   WQ 155
Delivery, Abdominal see Cesarean Section
Delivery, Home see Home Childbirth
Delivery of Dental Care see Delivery of Health Care
Delivery of Health Care   W 84
   In developing countries   WA 395
   In rural areas   WA 390
Delphi Technique
   Research (Form number 20 or 20.5 in any NLM
      schedule where applicable)
   Used for particular purposes, by subject
Delta Agent   QW 170
Delta Hepatitis see Delta Infection
Delta Infection   WC 536
Delta Sleep-Inducing Peptide   WL 104
   Biochemistry   QU 68
Delta Superinfection see Delta Infection
delta(9)-THC see Tetrahydrocannabinol

Delusions   WM 204
Dementia   WM 220
Dementia, Multi-Infarct   WM 220
Dementia Paralytica see Paresis
Dementia Praecox see Schizophrenia
Dementia, Presenile   WM 220
Dementia, Primary Degenerative, Presenile see
   Dementia, Presenile
Dementia, Primary Degenerative, Senile see
   Dementia, Senile
Dementia, Senile   WT 155
Dementia, Vascular   WM 220
Demethyl Epipodophyllotoxin Ethylidine Glucoside
see Etoposide
Demography   HB 848-3697
Demulcents see Dermatologic Agents
Demyelinating Diseases
   General works   WL 140
   Manifestation of disease, with the disease
Demyelination see Demyelinating Diseases
Dendrites   WL 102.5
Dendritic Cells   QW 568
Dendritic Cells, Follicular see Dendritic Cells
Denervation   WL 368
Denervation, Autonomic see Autonomic
   Denervation
Denervation, Sympathetic see Sympathectomy
Dengue   WC 528
Denial (Psychology)   WM 193.5.D3
   In adolescence   WS 463
   In infancy & childhood   WS 350.8.D3
Densitometry
   Photometry (Optics)   QC 391
   Radiography   WN 160
      Technique in radiography of special systems
      with the radiography number for the system
      or disease being diagnosed
Dental Abrasion see Tooth Abrasion
Dental Acid Etching see Acid Etching, Dental
Dental Alloys   WU 180
Dental Amalgam   WU 180
Dental Anesthesia see Anesthesia, Dental
Dental Arch   WU 101
Dental Articulators   WU 26
Dental Assistants   WU 90
Dental Attrition see Tooth Abrasion
Dental Auxiliaries   WU 90
Dental Bonding   WU 190
Dental Bridgework see Denture, Partial
Dental Calculus   WU 250
Dental Care   WU 29
   School clinics see School Dentistry   WA
      350-351, etc.
Dental Care for Aged   WU 490
Dental Care for Disabled   WU 470
Dental Care for Handicapped see Dental Care for
   Disabled
Dental Care Plans see Insurance, Dental
Dental Caries   WU 270
Dental Casting Investment   WU 180
Dental Casting Technique   WU 25
Dental Cavity Preparation   WU 350
Dental Cements   WU 190

See also Silicate Cement   WU 190
Dental Cementum   WU 230
Dental Chemistry see Chemistry
Dental Clinics   WU 27–28
    School Dental Clinics   WA 350–351
Dental Crowns see Crowns
Dental Decay see Dental Caries
Dental Deposits   WU 250
Dental Economics see Economics, Dental
Dental Education see Education, Dental
Dental Education, Continuing see Education, Dental, Continuing
Dental Education, Graduate see Education, Dental, Graduate
Dental Enamel   WU 220
    See also Mottled Enamel   WU 220
Dental Enamel Solubility   WU 220
Dental Equipment   WU 26
Dental Facilities   WU 27–28
Dental Fillings, Permanent see Dental Restoration, Permanent
Dental Fillings, Temporary see Dental Restoration, Temporary
Dental Focal Infection see Focal Infection, Dental
Dental Granuloma see Periapical Granuloma
Dental Health Education see Health Education, Dental
Dental Health Services   WU 29
Dental Health Surveys   WU 30
Dental High–Speed Equipment   WU 26
Dental High–Speed Technique   WU 25
Dental Hygiene see Oral Hygiene
Dental Hygienists   WU 90
Dental Implantation   WU 640
Dental Implants   WU 640
Dental Impression Materials   WU 190
Dental Impression Technique   WU 25
Dental Inlays see Inlays
Dental Instruments   WU 26
Dental Materials   WU 190
    See also Equipment and Supplies   WU 26 under Dentistry.
Dental Medicaid Program see Medicaid
Dental Medicine see Dentistry; Jaw Diseases; Mouth Diseases; Tooth Diseases
Dental microbiology see Microbiology   QW 65 under Mouth or Tooth
Dental Models   WU 26
Dental Nurses see Dental Assistants
Dental Occlusion   WU 440
Dental Occlusion, Balanced   WU 440
Dental Occlusion, Centric   WU 440
Dental Occlusion, Traumatic   WU 440
Dental Offices   WU 77
Dental Onlays see Inlays
Dental Pharmacology see Pharmacology
Dental Pins   WU 26
Dental Plaque   WU 250
Dental Porcelain   WU 190
Dental Prophylaxis   WU 113
Dental Prosthesis   WU 500–530
    See also Prosthodontics   WU 500
Dental Prosthesis Design   WU 500

Dental Prosthesis, Surgical see Dental Implants
Dental Pulp   WU 230
Dental Pulp Calcification   WU 230
Dental Pulp Capping   WU 230
Dental Pulp Cavity   WU 230
Dental Pulp Devitalization   WU 230
Dental Pulp Diseases   WU 230
Dental Pulp Stones see Dental Pulp Calcification
Dental Radiography see Radiography, Dental
Dental Receptionists see Dental Auxiliaries
Dental Records   WU 95
Dental Restoration, Permanent   WU 300–360
Dental Restoration, Temporary   WU 350
Dental Scaling   WU 113
Dental Schools see Schools, Dental
Dental Sealants see Pit and Fissure Sealants
Dental Service, Hospital   WU 27–28
Dental Staff, Hospital   WU 27–28
Dental Stone, Artificial see Calcium Sulfate
Dental Stress Analysis
    Dental materials   WU 190
    Occlusion etiology   WU 150
Dental Technicians   WU 150
Dental Veneers   WU 515
Dental Waste   WA 790
Dental White Spots see Dental Caries
Dentate Nucleus see Cerebellar Nuclei
Denticaid see Medicaid
Denticle see Dental Pulp Calcification
Dentifrices   WU 113
Dentigerous Cyst   WU 280
Dentin   WU 220
Dentin Sensitivity   WU 220
Dentist–Patient Relations   WU 61
    Children   WU 480
Dentistry   WU
    Anesthesia see Anesthesia, Dental   WO 460
    Army see Military Dentistry   UH 430–435
    Assistants see Dental Assistants   WU 90
    Aviation   WD 745
    Cardiac Problems   WG 460
    Equipment and supplies   WU 26
    Ethics see Ethics, Dental   WU 50
    Forensic see Forensic Dentistry   W 705
    Geriatric see Geriatric Dentistry   WU 490
    Hygienists see Dental Hygienists   WU 90
    In infancy & childhood see Pedodontics   WU 480
    Occupational see Occupational Dentistry   WA 412
    Insurance see Insurance, Dental   W 260, etc.
    Manpower   WU 77
        See also supply & distribution   WU 77 under Dentists
    Microbiology see Microbiology   QW 65 under Mouth
    Navy   VG 280–285
    Pathology   WU 140
    Pharmacology   QV 50
    Roentgen diagnosis see Radiography, Dental   WN 230
    School clinics see School Dentistry   WA 350, etc.; Dental clinics   WU 27–28

ALWAYS CONSULT MAIN SCHEDULES. USE NUMBER ASSIGNED ONLY WHEN SUBJECT REPRESENTS MAJOR EMPHASIS OF WORK BEING CLASSIFIED

Social relations see Dentist–Patient Relations
WU 61, etc.; Interprofessional Relations (with
specialty emphasized); Public Relations   WU
61
Technicians see Dental Technicians   WU 90
Dentistry for Aged see Dental Care for Aged
Dentistry for Disabled see Dental Care for Disabled
Dentistry for Handicapped see Dental Care for
Disabled
Dentistry, Geriatric see Geriatric Dentistry
Dentistry, Operative   WU 300–360
In infancy & childhood   WU 480
In old age   WU 490
Dentistry, Pediatric see Pediatric Dentistry
Dentists
Attitudes see Attitude of Health Personnel   WU
61, etc.
Biography
Collective   WZ 112.5.D3
Individual   WZ 100
Directories   WU 22
Interprofessional and public relations   WU 61
Licensure see Licensure, Dental   WU 40
Supply & distribution   WU 77
Dentists, Women   WU 21
See also special topics under Dentistry where
applicable
Dentition   WU 210
Dentoalveolar Abscess, Apical see Periapical
Abscess
Dentoalveolar Cyst see Periodontal Cyst
Denture Bases   WU 500
Denture, Complete   WU 530
Denture, Complete, Immediate   WU 530
Denture Liners   WU 500
Denture, Overlay   WU 515
Denture, Partial   WU 515
Denture, Partial, Fixed   WU 515
Denture, Partial, Immediate   WU 515
Denture, Partial, Removable   WU 515
Denture, Precision Attachment   WU 515
Denture Retention   WU 500
Denture Stability see Denture Retention
Dentures see Dental Prosthesis   WU 500–530; types
of dentures
Denturists   WU 150
Deodorants   WA 744
Deontological Ethics see Ethics
Deoxycorticosterone see Desoxycorticosterone
Deoxyephedrine see Methamphetamine
Deoxyglucose   QU 75
Deoxyribonucleases   QU 136
Deoxyribonucleic Acid see DNA
Deoxythymidine Kinase see Thymidine Kinase
Deoxyursocholic Acid see Ursodeoxycholic Acid
Dependency (Psychology)   BF 575.D34
Dependent Personality Disorder   WM 190
Depersonalization see Depersonalization Disorder
Depersonalization Disorder   WM 171
Depilation see Hair Removal
Depolarizing Muscle Relaxants see Neuromuscular
Depolarizing Agents
Depot Preparations see Delayed-Action

Preparations
Depreciation
Hospital administration   WX 157
Other topics, class by subject if specific; if general,
in economics number where available
Deprenalin see Selegiline
Deprenil see Selegiline
Deprenyl see Selegiline
Depressants see Alcohols; Analgesics; Anesthetics;
Anticonvulsants; Hypnotics and Sedatives; names
of specific depressants
Depression   WM 171
Bipolar see Psychoses, Manic Depressive   WM
207
Neuroses see Depression, Reactive   WM 171
Depression, Bipolar see Bipolar Disorder
Depression, Chemical   QV 38
Depression, Endogenous see Depressive Disorder
Depression, Involutional   WM 207
Depression, Neurotic see Depressive Disorder
Depression, Reactive see Adjustment Disorders
Depression, Unipolar see Depressive Disorder
Depressive Disorder   WM 171
Psychotic   WM 207
Depressive Symptoms see Depression
Depressive Syndrome see Depressive Disorder
Deprivation see Names of types of deprivation, e.g.,
Maternal Deprivation, Psychosocial Deprivation,
Sleep Deprivation, etc.
Deprivation Diseases see Deficiency Diseases
Depth Intoxication see Inert Gas Narcosis
Depth Perception   WW 105
Dercum's disease see Adiposis Dolorosa
Dermabrasion   WO 600
Dermal Drug Administration see Administration,
Cutaneous
Dermal Sinus see Spina Bifida Occulta
Dermatalgia see Skin Diseases
Dermatitis   WR 160–190
General works   WR 160
Occupational see Occupational Dermatitis   WR
600
Dermatitis, Adverse Drug Reaction see Drug
Eruptions
Dermatitis, Atopic   WR 160
Veterinary   SF 901
Dermatitis, Contact   WR 175
Dermatitis, Contagious Pustular see Ecthyma,
Contagious
Dermatitis, Eczematous see Eczema
Dermatitis, Exfoliative   WR 180
Dermatitis Herpetiformis   WR 200
Dermatitis Medicamentosa see Drug Eruptions
Dermatitis, Occupational   WR 600
Dermatitis, Radiation-Induced see Radiodermatitis
Dermatitis, Seborrheic   WR 415
Dermatitis Seborrheica see Dermatitis, Seborrheic
Dermatitis, Toxicodendron   WR 175
Dermatitis Venenata see Dermatitis, Contact
Dermato-neuroses see Neurodermatitis
Dermatoglyphics
Anatomical structure   WR 101
Criminal anthropometry   HV 6074–6078

Physiological anthropology   GN 191–192
Used for diagnosis of particular disorders, with the disorder, or system, e.g., of chromosome abnormalities   QS 677
Dermatologic Agents   QV 60–65
   Adsorbents   QV 63
   Demulcents   QV 63
   Emollients   QV 63
   Protectives   QV 63
   See also Astringents   QV 65; Irritants   QV 65, etc.; Anti-Infective Agents, Local   QV 220–239
Dermatologists, Directories see Directories   WR 22 under Dermatology
Dermatology   WR
   Children   WS 260
   Directories   WR 22
   Nursing texts   WY 154.5
Dermatomycoses   WR 300–340
   General works   WR 300
   Veterinary   SF 901
Dermatomyositis   WE 544
Dermatophytes   QW 180.5.D3
Dermatophytoses see Dermatomycoses
Dermatoplasty see Skin Transplantation
Dermatosclerosis see Scleroderma, Circumscribed
Dermatoses see Skin Diseases
Dermatotoxins see Dermotoxins
Dermatotropic Virus Infections see Skin Diseases, Infectious
Dermoid see Dermoid Cyst
Dermoid Cyst   QZ 310
Dermotoxins   QW 630
Desensitization, Immunologic   QW 900
   For particular diseases of hypersensitivity, with the disease
Desensitization, Psychologic   WM 425.5.D4
   In adolescence   WS 463
   In infancy & childhood   WS 350.6
Desert Climate   QC 993.7
   Diseases of geographic areas   WB 710
   Physiological effects   QT 150
Desferrioxamine see Deferoxamine
Desiccated Stomach see Tissue Extracts
Desickling Agents see Antisickling Agents
Design and Construction, Hospital see Hospital Design and Construction
Design, Equipment see Equipment Design
Designer Drugs
   Abuse   WM 270
   General works   QV 55
   Pharmacology   QV 38
Desipramine   QV 77.5
Desmethylimipramine see Desipramine
Desmoid see Fibromatosis, Aggressive
Desmolases see Lyases
Desmopressin   WK 520
Desoxycorticosterone   WK 755
Desoxycortone see Desoxycorticosterone
Desoxyribonucleases see Deoxyribonucleases
Desoxyribonucleic Acid see DNA
Detachment, Choroid see Choroid
Detachment, Retinal see Retinal Detachment

Detergents   QV 233
Determination of Health Care Needs see Health Services Needs and Demand
Detoxication, Drug, Metabolic see Metabolic Detoxication, Drug
Deuterium   QV 275
   Inorganic chemistry   QD 181.H1
Deuteromycetes   QW 180.5.D38
Deuterons see Deuterium
Developing Countries
   Economics   HC 59.69–59.72
   Public health   WA 395
   Other special topics, by subject
Development see Bone Development; Child Development; Growth; Language Development; Maxillofacial Development; Personality Development; Psychosexual Development
Development, Urban see Urban Renewal
Developmental Biology   QH 491
   Genetics   QH 453
Developmental Bone Diseases see Bone Diseases, Developmental
Developmental Conditions as a Cause of Disease see Pathogenesis   QZ 45 under Growth Disorders
Developmental Delay Disorders see Child Development Disorders
Deviant Behavior, Social see Social Behavior Disorders
Deviants, Sexual see Paraphilias
Device Design see Equipment Design
Device Failure see Equipment Failure
Device Safety see Equipment Safety
Devices see Equipment and Supplies
Dexamethasone   QV 60
Dexpropranolol see Propranolol
Dextranase   QU 136
Dextrans   WH 450
Dextrins   QU 83
dextro-Amino Acid Oxidase see D-Amino-Acid Oxidase
Dextrose see Glucose
Dextrosulfenidol see Thiamphenicol
DFP see Isoflurophate
Diabetes, Autoimmune see Diabetes Mellitus, Insulin-Dependent
Diabetes, Bronze see Hemochromatosis
Diabetes Insipidus   WK 550
Diabetes Mellitus   WK 810–850
   See also Obesity in Diabetes   WK 835; Pregnancy in Diabetes   WQ 248; Prediabetic State   WK 810
Diabetes Mellitus, Adult-Onset see Diabetes Mellitus, Non-Insulin-Dependent
Diabetes Mellitus, Brittle see Diabetes Mellitus, Insulin-Dependent
Diabetes Mellitus, Experimental   WK 810
Diabetes Mellitus, Insulin-Dependent   WK 810
Diabetes Mellitus, Juvenile-Onset see Diabetes Mellitus, Insulin-Dependent
Diabetes Mellitus, Ketosis-Prone see Diabetes Mellitus, Insulin-Dependent
Diabetes Mellitus, Ketosis-Resistant see Diabetes Mellitus, Non-Insulin-Dependent

Diabetes Mellitus, Non–Insulin–Dependent WK 810
Diabetes Mellitus, Stable see Diabetes Mellitus, Non–Insulin–Dependent
Diabetes Mellitus, Type 1 see Diabetes Mellitus, Insulin–Dependent
Diabetes Mellitus, Type 2 see Diabetes Mellitus, Non–Insulin–Dependent
Diabetic Acidosis see Acidosis, Diabetic
Diabetic Angiopathies WK 835
Diabetic Coma WK 830
Diabetic Diet WK 818–819
Diabetic Foot WK 835
Diabetic Ketoacidosis WK 830
Diabetic Ketosis see Diabetic Ketoacidosis
Diabetic Nephropathies WK 835
Diabetic Neuropathies WK 835
Diabetic Retinopathy WK 835
Diacetylmorphine QV 92
    Dependence see Heroin Dependence WM 288
Diagnosis WB 141–293
    Breast diseases WP 815
    Cardiovascular diseases WG 141
    Ear diseases WV 210
    Eye diseases WW 141–145
    Gastrointestinal diseases WI 141
    Gynecologic diseases WP 141
    In infancy & childhood WS 141
    Mental disorders WM 141
    Musculoskeletal system WE 141
    Neoplasms QZ 241
    Nervous system diseases WL 141
    Otorhinolaryngologic diseases WV 150
    Physical WB 200–288
        See also Physical Examination WB 205, etc.
    Pregnancy WQ 202
        See also Pregnancy Complications WQ 240; Pregnancy Tests QY 335; Sex Determination WQ 206, etc.
    Prenatal see Prenatal diagnosis WQ 209
    Radioisotope WN 445
    Radioscopic see Fluoroscopy WN 220
    Skin diseases WR 141
    Symptomatology WB 143
    Thoracic diseases WF 975
    Tooth diseases WU 141
    Tuberculosis WF 220–225
    Urologic WJ 141
    For diagnosis of other diseases see specific headings below or general works number for disease, organ or system
Diagnosis, Computer–Assisted
    General WB 141
    Used for diagnosis of particular disorders, with the disorder or system
Diagnosis, Differential WB 141.5
    In infancy & childhood WS 141
Diagnosis, Immunological see Immunologic Tests
Diagnosis, Laboratory QY
    In adolescence WS 141
    In infancy & childhood WS 141
    In old age WT 100
    Of other age groups QY

    Veterinary SF 772.6–773
Diagnosis, Nursing see Nursing Diagnosis
Diagnosis, Oral WU 141
Diagnosis, Prenatal see Prenatal Diagnosis
Diagnosis–Related Groups WX 157.8
Diagnosis, Surgical WO 141
Diagnostic Errors WB 141
    In special fields, in the diagnosis number for the field
Diagnostic Imaging WN 180
Diagnostic Reagent Kits see Reagent Kits, Diagnostic
Diagnostic Services WA 243
Diagnostic Skin Tests see Skin Tests
Diagnostic Tests, Routine WB 200
    Used for specific purposes, by subject
Diagnosticians, Directories see Directories W 22 under Medicine
Dialysis
    Biochemical technique QU 25
    Organic chemistry (General) QD 281.D47
    See also Hemodialysis WJ 378, etc.
Dialysis, Extracorporeal see Hemodialysis
Diamine Oxidase see Amine Oxidase (Copper–Containing)
Diaminodiphenylsulfone see Dapsone
Diammonium Chloroplatinum Compounds
    Inorganic chemistry QD 181.P8
    Pharmacology QV 290
Diamond–Blackfan Anemia see Fanconi's Anemia
Diamorphine see Diacetylmorphine
Diaper Pins see Infant Care
Diaper Rash WS 420–430
Diapers, Infant see Infant Care
Diaphanography see Transillumination
Diaphanoscopy see Transillumination
Diaphorase see Lipoamide Dehydrogenase
Diaphoretics see Drugs for QV 122 under Hypohidrosis
Diaphragm WF 800–810
Diaphragmatic Eventration WF 800
Diaphragmatic Hernia see Hernia, Diaphragmatic
Diaphragmatic Hernia, Traumatic see Hernia, Diaphragmatic, Traumatic
Diaphragmatic Paralysis see Respiratory Paralysis
Diaphyseal Aclasis see Exostoses, Multiple Hereditary
Diarrhea WI 407
    In infancy & childhood WS 312
    Veterinary SF 851
Diarrhea, Infantile WS 312
Diarsenol see Arsphenamine
Diastase see Amylase
Diastematomyelia see Spina Bifida Occulta
Diastole WG 280
Diathermy WB 510
    Surgical see Electrocoagulation WO 198
Diathermy, Surgical see Electrocoagulation
Diathesis see Disease Susceptibility
Diathetic Disease see Disease Susceptibility
Diatrizoate
    As contrast medium WN 160
    Organic chemistry QD 341.A2

Diazepam   QV 77.9
Diazinon
    Public health   WA 240
Diazonium Compounds   QU 54
    Organic chemistry
        Aliphatic compounds   QD 305.A9
        Aromatic compounds   QD 341.A9
Diazoxide   QV 150
Dibekacin   QV 268
Dibenzazepines
    As antidepressive agents   QV 77.5
    Organic chemistry   QD 401
Dibothriocephalus see Diphyllobothrium
Dibucaine   QV 115
Dichlorodiethyl Sulfide see Mustard Gas   QV 666
    under Mustard Compounds
Dichlorodiphenyldichloroethane see DDD
Dichloroethanes see Ethylene Dichlorides
Dichloroethylenes
    Toxicology   QV 633
Dichloromethane see Methylene Chloride
Dichloromethyl Ether see Bis(Chloromethyl) Ether
Dichotic Listening Tests   WV 272
Diclofenac
    As an analgesic   QV 95
    Biochemistry   QU 98
Diclophenac see Diclofenac
Dicoumarin see Bishydroxycoumarin
Dicrostonyx see Microtinae
Dictionaries
    (Form number 13 in any NLM schedule where
      applicable)
    Others, in appropriate LC number
Dictionaries, Chemical   QD 5
Dictionaries, Classical   DE 5
Dictionaries, Dental   WU 13
Dictionaries, Medical   W 13
Dictionaries, Pharmaceutic   QV 13
Dictionaries, Polyglot   P 361
    Of a specific subject, with the subject
Dictyocaulus   QX 248
Dictyoptera see Orthoptera
Dictyostelium   QW 180.5.M9
Dictyostelium discoideum see Dictyostelium
Dicumarol see Bishydroxycoumarin
Didelphis see Opossums
Dideoxykanamycin B see Dibekacin
Dieldrin   WA 240
Diemal see Barbital
Diencephalon   WL 312
Diet   QT 235
    And oral health   WU 113.7
    Diabetic see Diabetic Diet   WK 818–819
    In disease see Diet Therapy   WB 400–449
    In infancy & childhood   WS 115–130
    Low sodium see Diet, Salt–Free   WB 424
    Raw food   WB 432
    See also Nutrition   QU 145; Vegetarianism
      WB 430; names of particular foods used in
      special diets; particular diseases for which diet
      is prescribed
Diet, Atherogenic   WG 550
Diet, Cariogenic   WU 113.7

Diet, Chemically Defined see Food, Formulated
Diet, Diabetic see Diabetic Diet
Diet, Elemental see Food, Formulated
Diet Fads   WB 449
Diet, Formula see Food, Formulated
Diet, Low–Salt see Diet, Sodium–Restricted
Diet, Macrobiotic   WB 422
Diet, Reducing   WD 210–212
    Popular works   WD 212
Diet, Salt–Free see Diet, Sodium–Restricted
Diet, Sodium–Restricted   WB 424
    Cookery   WB 424
Diet Surveys   QU 146
Diet, Synthetic see Food, Formulated
Diet Therapy   WB 400–449
    In infancy & childhood   WS 366
Dietary Calcium see Calcium, Dietary
Dietary Carbohydrates   QU 75
    As a supplement in health or disease   WB 427
    Cookery for carbohydrate control   WB 427
      See also Diet, Reducing   WD 210–212
Dietary Cholesterol see Cholesterol, Dietary
Dietary Fats   QU 86
    As a supplement in health or disease   WB 425
    Cookery for fat control   WB 425
    See also Butter   QU 86, etc.; Cholesterol,
      Dietary   QU 95, etc.; Diet, Reducing   WD
      210–212; Margarine   QU 86, etc.
Dietary Fats, Unsaturated   QU 86
    As a supplement in health or disease   WB 425
    Cookery for fat control   WB 425
Dietary Fiber   QU 83
    As a supplement in health or disease   WB 427
Dietary Formulations see Food, Formulated
Dietary Habits see Food Habits
Dietary Modification see Food Habits
Dietary Oils see Dietary Fats, Unsaturated
Dietary Proteins   QU 55
    As a supplement in health or disease   WB 426
    Cookery for protein control   WB 426
Dietary Services
    Hospitals   WX 168
      See also Food Service, Hospital   WX 168
    Public health aspects   WA 695–722
    See also Dietetics   WB 400; Food Services
      WA 350, etc.
Dietary Sodium see Sodium, Dietary
Dietetic Departments in Hospitals see Dietary
    Services; Food Service, Hospital
Dietetics   WB 400
    In infancy & childhood   WS 115
Diethyl Ether see Ether, Ethyl
Diethyldithiocarbamate see Ditiocarb
Diethylmalonylurea see Barbital
Diethylnicotinamid see Nikethamide
Diethylnitrosamine
    As a carcinogen   QZ 202
Diethylstilbestrol   WP 522
    Animal Feed   SF 98.H67
    Organic chemistry   QD 341.H9
Dietotherapy see Diet Therapy
Differential Diagnosis see Diagnosis, Differential
Differential Leukocyte Count see Leukocyte Count

Differential Thermal Analysis   QD 79.T38
    Of a particular substance, with the substance
Differentiation Antigens see Antigens,
    Differentiation
Differentiation Antigens, B-Cell see Antigens,
    Differentiation, B-Lymphocyte
Differentiation Antigens, B-Lymphocyte see
    Antigens, Differentiation, B-Lymphocyte
Differentiation Antigens, Hairy Cell Leukemia see
    Antigens, Differentiation
Differentiation Antigens, Leukocyte, Human see
    Antigens, CD
Differentiation Markers see Antigens, Differentiation
Difficult Labor see Dystocia
Diffuse Lewy Body Disease see Parkinson Disease
Diffusion
    Biochemistry   QU 34
    Biophysics   QT 34
    Solution chemistry   QD 543
Diffusion of Innovation
    Special topics, by subject
Diflucortolone
    As a dermatologic agent   QV 60
Diflunisal   QV 95
    As a dermatological agent   QV 60
Digenic Acid see Kainic Acid
Digestants see Gastrointestinal Agents
Digestion   WI 102
    Liver function in   WJ 704
Digestive System   WI
    Animal   SF 851
    Children   WS 310
Digestive System Diseases   WI 140
    Diagnosis   WI 141
    Surgery   WI 900
    In infancy & childhood   WS 310
Digestive System Neoplasms   WI 149
Digital Radiography see Radiographic Image
    Enhancement
Digital Signal Processing see Signal Processing,
    Computer-Assisted
Digitalis   QV 153
Dihydrodiethylstilbestrol see Hexestrol
Dihydrofolate Dehydrogenase see Tetrahydrofolate
    Dehydrogenase
Dihydrofolate Reductase see Tetrahydrofolate
    Dehydrogenase
Dihydrolipoamide Dehydrogenase see Lipoamide
    Dehydrogenase
Dihydrotachysterol   QU 95
Dihydroxycholecalciferols   QU 173
Dihydroxyphenylalanine see Dopa
Dihydroxyvitamins D see Dihydroxycholecalciferols
Diiodohydroxyquin see Iodoquinol
Diiodotyrosine Receptors see Receptors, Thyroid
    Hormone
Diisocyanatotoluene see Toluene 2,4-Diisocyanate
Diisopropylfluorophosphate see Isoflurophate
Dilatation
    Of the cervix
        Obstetrical surgery   WQ 400
        Physiology   WQ 305
    Of the pupil   WW 240

Dilatation and Curettage   WP 470
    Used for special purposes, by subject
Dilatation, Balloon see Balloon Dilatation
Dilatation, Pathologic
    Of the blood vessels   WG 578
    Of the colon see Megacolon   WI 528
    Of the heart see Heart Hypertrophy   WG 210
    Of the pupil   WW 240
    Of the stomach see Stomach Dilatation   WI 300
    Of other specific parts, with the part
Dilatation, Transluminal Arterial see Angioplasty,
    Balloon
Dilated Cardiomyopathy see Cardiomyopathy,
    Congestive
Diltiazem   QV 150
Dilution Techniques see Indicator Dilution
    Techniques
Dimenhydrinate   QV 73
Dimethoxystrychnine see Brucine
Dimethyl Sulfoxide   QV 60
Dimethylaminoazobenzene see
    p-Dimethylaminoazobenzene
Dimethylaminophenazone see Aminopyrine
Dimethylcysteine see Penicillamine
Dimethylguanylguanidine see Metformin
Dimexide see Dimethyl Sulfoxide
Dinitrochlorobenzene
    Toxicology   QV 633
Dinitrophenols
    As fungicides   WA 240, etc.
    Pharmaceutical indicators or reagents   QV 744
    Toxicology   QV 632
Dinoflagellida   QX 70
Dinoprost   QU 90
    As an abortifacient agent   QV 175
Diodone see Iodopyracet
Diodoquin see Diiodohydroxyquin
Diodoxyquinoline see Iodoquinol
Diosgenin
    Biochemistry   QU 85
Diothane Hydrochloride see Anesthetics, Local
Dioxanes   WA 240
    As a carcinogen   QZ 202
Dioxins
    Organic chemistry   QD 405
Dioxoles
    As pesticides   WA 240
    Organic chemistry   QD 405
Dipeptidyl Aminopeptidases see Dipeptidyl
    Peptidases
Dipeptidyl Peptidases   QU 136
Diphasic Milk Fever Virus see Encephalitis Viruses,
    Tick-Borne
Diphenhydramine   QV 157
Diphenhydramine Theoclate see Dimenhydrinate
Diphenyl Oxides see Phenyl Ethers
Diphenylamine
    Toxicology   QV 632
Diphenylbutazone see Phenylbutazone
Diphenylhydantoin see Phenytoin
Diphenylhydramin see Diphenhydramine
Diphosgene see Phosgene
Diphosphates   QV 285

Diphosphopyridine Nucleotide see NAD
Diphtheria   WC 320
Diphtheria Antitoxin   WC 320
Diphtheria Toxin   WC 320
Diphtheria Toxoid   WC 320
Diphtheria Vaccine see Diphtheria Toxoid
Diphyllobothrium   QX 400
Diploidy   QH 461
Diplopia   WW 410
Dipropyl Acetate see Valproic Acid
Diptera   QX 505
Dipylidiasis see Cestode Infections
Dipyridamole   QV 150
Dipyrine see Aminopyrine
Dipyrone   QV 95
Direct Service Costs
    By subject, in economics number where
        applicable
Directories
    (Form number 22 in any NLM schedule where
        applicable)
    Embryology   QS 622
    Forensic medicine   W 622
    Optometry   WW 722
    Toxicology   QV 605
Dirofilaria immitis   QX 301
Dirofilariasis   WC 880
Disability Compensation see Veterans Disability
    Claims; Workers' Compensation
Disability Evaluation
    Medicolegal aspects of insurance   W 900
    Medicolegal aspects of occupational disease and
        injury   W 925
    Other special topics, by subject, e.g., in epilepsy
        WL 385; in ophthalmology   WW 32; in
        otolaryngology   WV 32
Disability Insurance see Medicare
Disabled
    Consumer rights   HD 7255-7256
    Education   LC 4001-4824
        In adulthood   LC 4815-4824
            Mentally disabled   LC 4815
            Socially disabled   LC 4822-4824
        In infancy & childhood   LC 4001-4806.5
    Psychological problems
        Group psychotherapy   WM 430.5.H2
        In adulthood
            Counseling   WM 55
            Special problems, by subject, e.g., Neuroses
                WM 170
        In infancy & childhood   WS 105.5.H2
    Readers for disabled children   PE 1126.D4
    Rehabilitation
        In adulthood   WB 320
        In infancy & childhood   WS 368
        Sociological aspects only   HD 7255-7256
        See also other entries under Rehabilitation;
            names of disabilities
    Sociological aspects   HV 1551-3024
        Transportation
            Mentally disabled   HV 3005.5
            Physically disabled   HV 3022
        Vocational guidance

    Mentally disabled   HV 3005
    Physically disabled   HV 3018-3019
Disaccharides   QU 83
Disaster Planning   WX 185
    See also special topics under Disasters
Disasters   HC 79.D45
    First aid   WA 292
    Hospital emergency service   WX 215
    Hospital programs see Disaster Planning   WX
        185
    Medical emergencies   WB 105
    Relief (General)   HV 553-555
    Nursing   WY 154
    Specific types of disaster, by subject
    See also Civil Defense   UA 926-929, etc.
Discharge Planning see Patient Discharge
Disclosure, Truth see Truth Disclosure
Discolysis see Intervertebral Disk Chemolysis
Discrete Subaortic Stenosis see Aortic Valve
    Stenosis
Discretionary Adjustment Factor see Prospective
    Payment System
Discriminant Analysis   QA 278.65
    Special topics, by subject
Discrimination Learning
    Animal   QL 785
    Educational psychology   LB 1059
    General psychology   BF 318
Discrimination (Psychology)   BF 697
    Racial see Prejudice   BF 575.P9
    Sex see Women's Rights   HQ 1154, etc.
    See also Race Relations   HT 1503-1595, etc.
Disease
    General manifestations   QZ 140-190
        Degenerative processes   QZ 180
    Pathogenesis   QZ 40-109
        Bacterial   QZ 65
    Special topics, by subject, e.g., endocrine aspects
        of disease processes   WK 140
Disease Frequency Surveys see Cross-Sectional
    Studies
Disease Models, Animal   QY 58
Disease Outbreaks   WA 105
    Cholera   WC 264
    History   WA 11
    Plague   WC 350-355
    Smallpox   WC 590
    Statistics and surveys   WA 900
    Typhus   WC 610
    Veterinary   SF 781
    Yellow fever   WC 532
Disease Reservoirs   WA 106
    Endemic to a particular locality   WB 710
    Pathogenesis   QZ 40
    Veterinary   SF 780.9
    See also names of particular diseases
Disease Resistance see Immunity, Natural
Disease Susceptibility   QZ 50
Disease Vectors
    Bacteriology   QW 700
    Parasitology
        Arthropod Vectors   QX 460, etc.
        Insect Vectors   QX 650

**ALWAYS CONSULT MAIN SCHEDULES. USE NUMBER ASSIGNED ONLY WHEN
SUBJECT REPRESENTS MAJOR EMPHASIS OF WORK BEING CLASSIFIED**

Public health aspects   WA 110
   See also Insect Control   QX 600
Diseases in Twins   QZ 50
   Particular deseases, with the disease
Disgerminoma see Dysgerminoma
Disinfectants   QV 220–239
Disinfection
   In hospitals   WX 165
   In preventive medicine   WA 240
   In surgery   WO 113
Disinfection, Hand see Handwashing
Disinfestation see Communicable Disease Control;
   Ectoparasitic Infestations; Mite Infestations; Tick
   Infestations
Disk, Herniated see Intervertebral Disk
   Displacement
Disk, Intervertebral see Intervertebral Disk
Dislocation, Tooth see Tooth Luxation
Dislocations   WE 175
   Hip see Hip Dislocation   WE 860
   Jaw   WU 610
   Shoulder see Shoulder Dislocation   WE 810
   Tooth see Tooth Luxation   WU 158
   Of other specific bones or joints, with the bone
   or joint
Disodium Cromoglycate see Cromolyn Sodium
Disopyramide   QV 150
Dispensaries, Outpatient see Outpatient Clinics,
   Hospital
Dispensatories   QV 740
Dispensing Fees see Prescription Fees
Dispensing, Pharmaceutical see Drug Compounding;
   Pharmacy Service, Hospital; Pharmaceutical
   Services
Displacement (Psychology)   WM 193.5.D5
   In adolescence   WS 463
   In infancy & childhood   WS 350.8.D3
Disposable Equipment   W 26
Disposal of the Dead see Cadaver; Mortuary
   Practice
Dissection   QS 130–132
   Veterinary   SF 762
Disseminated Intravascular Coagulation   WH 322
Dissertations, Academic
   General   Z 5053
   Presented to medical, dental, pharmacy, nursing,
   public health and veterinary schools or
   departments.
      American schools   W 4A
      Foreign schools   W4
Dissociation see Dissociative Disorders
Dissociative Disorders   WM 173.6
Distance Perception   WW 105
Distemper Virus, Canine   QW 168.5.P2
Distributed Systems see Computer Communication
   Networks
Disulfides   QV 280
Disulfiram
   Organic chemistry   QD 305.S3
   Used in treatment of alcoholism   WM 274
   Used for other particular purposes, by subject.
Dithranol see Anthralin

Ditiocarb
   As a chelating agent   QV 290
Diuresis   WJ 303
Diuretics   QV 160
Diuretics, Mercurial   QV 160
Diuretics, Osmotic   QV 160
Diuretics, Sulfamyl   QV 160
Diurnal Rhythm see Circadian Rhythm
Divalproex see Valproic Acid
Divers' Paralysis see Decompression Sickness
Diverticulitis   WI 425
Diverticulitis, Colonic   WI 425
Diverticulosis see Diverticulum
Diverticulosis, Colonic   WI 425
Diverticulosis, Esophageal see Esophageal
   Diverticulum
Diverticulum   WI 425
Diving   QT 260.5.D6
   Accidents   QT 260.5.D6
   Anoxia associated with   WD 650
   Industrial accidents   WA 485
   Submarine and deep–water   VM 975–989
Divorce   HQ 811–960.7
   Counseling   WM 55
   Effect on adolescents   WS 462
   Effect on children   WS 105.5.F2
      See also Maternal Deprivation   WS 105.5.D3;
      Paternal Deprivation   WS 105.5.D3
Dixamon Bromide see Methantheline
Dizziness   WL 340
DMF Index   WU 30
DMSO see Dimethyl Sulfoxide
DNA   QU 58.5
DNA, Antisense   QU 58.5
DNA, Bacterial   QW 52
DNA–Binding Proteins   QU 58.5
DNA Cytosine–5–Methylase see DNA
   (Cytosine–5–)–Methyltransferase
DNA (Cytosine–5–)–Methyltransferase   QU 141
DNA Damage   QH 465
   By specific agent, A–Z, e.g., Chemicals   QH
   465.C5
DNA–Dependent RNA Polymerases see RNA
   Polymerases
DNA, Double–Stranded see DNA
DNA Fingerprinting
   As a genetic technique   QH 441
   In forensic medicine   W 700–791
DNA–Gyrase see DNA Topoisomerase
   (ATP–Hydrolysing)
DNA Helix Destabilizing Proteins see
   DNA–Binding Proteins
DNA Injury see DNA Damage
DNA Insertion Elements   QH 462.I48
DNA Joinases see Polydeoxyribonucleotide
   Synthetases
DNA Ligases see Polydeoxyribonucleotide
   Synthetases
DNA Markers see Genetic Markers
DNA Mutational Analysis   QU 58.5
DNA, Neoplasm   QZ 200
DNA Nicking–Closing Protein see DNA
   Topoisomerase

DNA Nucleotidylexotransferase   QU 141
DNA Probes   QU 58.5
DNA Rearrangement see Gene Rearrangement
DNA, Recombinant   QU 58.5
   Genetic and ethical emphasis   QH 438.7
DNA Recombinant Proteins see Recombinant
   Proteins
DNA Relaxing Enzyme see DNA Topoisomerase
DNA Repair   QH 467
   Biochemistry   QU 58.5
DNA Repair Enzymes see Polydeoxyribonucleotide
   Synthetases
DNA Replication   QH 462.D8
   Biochemistry   QU 58.5
DNA Restriction Enzymes   QU 136
DNA, Satellite   QU 58.5
DNA Sequence see Base Sequence
DNA Sequence Analysis see Sequence Analysis,
   DNA
DNA, Single-Stranded   QU 58.5
   Phages   QW 161
DNA Topoisomerase   QU 58.5
DNA Topoisomerase (ATP-Hydrolysing)   QU 137
DNA Topoisomerase I see DNA Topoisomerase
DNA Topoisomerase II see DNA Topoisomerase
   (ATP-Hydrolysing)
DNA Tumor Viruses   QW 166
   Directory of research   QW 22
DNA Untwisting Enzyme see DNA Topoisomerase
DNA Untwisting Protein see DNA Topoisomerase
DNA, Viral   QW 165
DNA Viruses
   General works   QW 165
   Specific viruses   QW 165.5A–Z
DNAase see Deoxyribonucleases
DNase see Deoxyribonucleases
DNCB see Dinitrochlorobenzene
Do-Not-Resuscitate Orders see Resuscitation
   Orders
Dobutamine
DOCA see Desoxycorticosterone
Docimasia, Pulmonary see Autopsy; Biogenesis
Docosenoic Acids see Erucic Acids
Doctor-Patient Relations see Physician-Patient
   Relations
Doctors see Physicians
Documentation   Z 1001
Documents, Serial see Periodicals
Dog Diseases   SF 991–992
Dog Heartworm see Dirofilaria immitis
Dogfish   QL 638.95.S84
Dogs
   As laboratory animals   QY 60.D6
   Domestic   SF 421–440.2
   Anatomy   SF 767.D6
   Wild   QL 737.C22
Dolphins   QL 737.C432
Domestic Medicine see Popular works   WB 120
   under Medicine; Self-Medication
Domestic Violence   HQ 809–809.3
   Criminal   W 860
Domiciliary Care see Home Care Services
Dominance, Cerebral   WL 335

Dominance, Social see Social Dominance
Dominance-Subordination
   In animals   QL 775
   Sociology   HM 132
Donovanosis see Granuloma Inguinale
Dopa   WK 725
Dopa Decarboxylase   QU 139
Dopamine   WK 725
Dopamine Agents   QV 76.5
Dopamine Agonists   QV 76.5
Dopamine Antagonists   QV 76.5
Dopamine Receptor Agonists see Dopamine
   Agonists
Dopamine Receptor Antagonists see Dopamine
   Antagonists
Dopamine Receptors see Receptors, Dopamine
Dopaminergic Agonists see Dopamine Agonists
Dopaminergic Antagonists see Dopamine
   Antagonists
Doping in Sports   QT 261
Doppler Echocardiography see Echocardiography,
   Doppler
Doppler Effect
   Biophysics   QT 34
   Health physics   WN 110
   Special topics, by subject
Doppler Shift see Doppler Effect
Doppler Ultrasound see Ultrasonics
Dormice see Rodentia
Dosage see Drug Administration Schedule; Drug
   Therapy; Prescriptions, Drug; Radiation Dosage;
   Radiotherapy Dosage
Dosage Forms   QV 785
   See also names of specific forms
Dose-Response Relationship, Drug   QV 38
Dose-Response Relationship, Radiation
   Non-ionizing radiation   WB 460
   Radioisotopes   WN 450
   Radium   WN 340
   X-rays   WN 250.5X7
   Ultraviolet rays   WB 480
   Other specific types of radiation, by type
   Specific disease treated, with the disease
Dosimetric System of Therapeutics see Alternative
   Medicine
Dosimetry Calculations, Computer-Assisted see
   Radiotherapy Planning, Computer-Assisted
Dot Immunoblotting see Immunoblotting
Double Bind Theory
   In parent-child communication   WS 105.5.F2
   In psychotherapy   WM 420
   Other applications, by subject
Double-Stranded RNA see RNA, Double-Stranded
Double Vision see Diplopia
Down Syndrome   WS 107
   Adult   WM 300
Doxorubicin   QV 269
Doxylamine   QV 157
   As enzyme inhibitors   QU 143
   Organic chemistry   QD 401
   As sedatives   QV 85
DPN see NAD
Dracunculus   QX 203

Dracunculus medinensis see Dracunculus
Dragon Worm see Dracunculus
Drainage   WO 188
   Localized, by site
Drainage, Sanitary   WA 670
Drainage, Suction see Suction
Drama
   Related to medicine   WZ 330
   Related to psychiatry   WM 49
Drama Therapy in Psychiatry see Psychodrama
Drawings
   (Form number 17 in any NLM schedule where
    applicable)
Dreams
   In infancy & childhood   WS 105.5.D8
   Parapsychology   BF 1074–1099
   Psychoanalysis   WM 460.5.D8
   Sleep, Normal   WL 108
Dress see Clothing; Protective Clothing
Dressings see Bandages
Dressings, Biological see Biological Dressings
Dressings, Occlusive see Occlusive Dressings
Dressings, Surgical see Bandages; Occlusive
   Dressings
DRG see Diagnosis–Related Groups
Dried Milk see Dairy Products; Milk
Drill see Papio
Drinking   WI 102
   See also Alcohol Drinking   WM 274, etc.; Water
    Supply   WA 675–690
Drinking, Alcohol see Alcohol Drinking
Drinking Behavior
   Customs   GT 2850–2930
Drinks see Beverages
Drip Infusions see Infusions, Intravenous
Drive   BF 501–505
   In adolescence   WS 462
   In infancy & childhood   WS 105.5.M5
   Psychoanalysis   WM 460.5.M6
Dromedary see Camels
Dropsy see Edema
Drosophila   QX 505
Drought see Natural Disasters
Drowning
   Resuscitation   WA 292
   Statistics   HB 1323.D7
   Swimming, accidents   QT 260.5.S9
Drowsiness see Sleep Stages
Drug Abuse see Substance Abuse
Drug Abuse, Intravenous see Substance Abuse,
   Intravenous
Drug Abuse, Parenteral see Substance Abuse,
   Intravenous
Drug Abuse, Sports see Doping in Sports
Drug Abuse Testing see Substance Abuse Detection
Drug Action see Pharmacology; Drug interactions;
   Dose-response relationships, Drug   QV 38 and
   other specific actions
Drug Addiction see Substance Dependence
Drug Administration, Bladder see Administration,
   Intravesical
Drug Administration, Dermal see Administration,
   Cutaneous

Drug Administration, Inhalation see Administration,
   Inhalation
Drug Administration, Intranasal see Administration,
   Intranasal
Drug Administration, Oral see Administration, Oral
Drug Administration, Rectal see Administration,
   Rectal
Drug Administration, Respiratory see
   Administration, Inhalation
Drug Administration Routes   WB 340–356
Drug Administration Schedule   WB 340
Drug Administration, Topical see Administration,
   Topical
Drug Adulteration see Drug Contamination
Drug Aerosol Therapy see Administration,
   Inhalation
Drug and Narcotic Control
   Laws (sales)   QV 32–33
   Laws (use)   WM 32–33
   Sociological aspects   HV 5800–5840
   Special topics, by subject
Drug Antagonism   QV 38
Drug Benefit Plans see Insurance, Pharmaceutical
   Services
Drug Carriers   QV 785
Drug Catalogs see Catalogs, Drug
Drug Combinations   QV 785
   See also Drug Therapy, Combination   WB 330
   and names of specific drugs, or diseases for
   which the drug combinations are prescribed
Drug Combinations, Antineoplastic see
   Antineoplastic Agents, Combined
Drug Compounding   QV 778
Drug Containers and Closures see Drug Packaging
Drug Contamination
   Fraud   QV 773
   Legislation and jurisprudence   QV 32–33
   Public health aspects   WA 730
Drug Counterfeiting see Drug Contamination
Drug Delivery Systems, Implantable see Infusion
   Pumps, Implantable
Drug Dependence see Substance Dependence
Drug Design   QV 744
Drug Detoxication, Metabolic see Metabolic
   Detoxication, Drug
Drug Eruptions   WR 165
Drug Evaluation   QV 771
   See also Drug Screening   QV 771
Drug Evaluation, Preclinical see Drug Screening
Drug Exanthems see Drug Eruptions
Drug Habituation see Substance Dependence
Drug Hypersensitivity   WD 320
Drug Incompatibility   QV 746
Drug Industry   QV 736
   Fraud   QV 773
   See also Ethics, Pharmacy   QV 21
   Occupational medicine   WA 400–495
   Industrial waste   WA 788
Drug Information Services
   Computerized   QV 26.5
   Services in particular fields, by subject
Drug Infusion Systems see Infusion Pumps
Drug Insurance see Insurance, Pharmaceutical

Services
Drug Interactions   QV 38
Drug Kinetics see Pharmacokinetics
Drug Labeling   QV 835
Drug Laws see Legislation, Drug
Drug Modeling see Drug Design
Drug Packaging   QV 825
Drug Potentiation see Drug Synergism
Drug Precursors see Prodrugs
Drug Recall see Drug and Narcotic Control
Drug Receptors see Receptors, Drug
Drug Regulations see Drug and Narcotic Control
Drug Residues
   Food contamination   WA 701
   Public health   WA 730
Drug Resistance   WB 330
   In particular diseases, with the disease
Drug Resistance, Microbial   QW 52
   In drug therapy   WB 330
   Of particular organisms, with the organism
   To particular drugs, with the drug
Drug Screening   QV 771
   See also Drug Evaluation   QV 771
Drug Screening Assays, Antitumor
   Used in testing antineoplastic agents   QV 269
Drug Screening Tests, Tumor-Specific see Drug
   Screening Assays, Antitumor
Drug Sensitivity Assay, Microbial see Microbial
   Sensitivity Tests
Drug Stability   QV 754
Drug Storage   QV 754
   Public health aspects   WA 730
Drug Stores see Pharmacies
Drug Surveillance, Postmarketing see Product
   Surveillance, Postmarketing
Drug Synergism   QV 38
Drug Therapy   WB 330
   Adverse effects   QZ 42
   In infancy & childhood   WS 366
   In old age   WT 166
   In pregnancy   WQ 200
   Mental Disorders   WM 402
    In infancy & childhood   WS 350.2
   Neoplasms   QZ 267
   Veterinary   SF 915-919.5
   For particular diseases, with the disease
Drug Therapy, Combination   WB 330
   Anti-neoplastic   QZ 267
   For other particular diseases, with the disease
   See also Drug Combinations   QV 785
Drug Tolerance   QV 38
Drug Use Disorders see Substance Use Disorders
Drug Utilization   WB 330
Drug Withdrawal Symptoms see Substance
   Withdrawal Syndrome
Drugs
   Administration & dosage   QV 748
   Administrative methods   WB 340-356
    See also Administration, Intranasal   WB 342;
     Administration, Oral   WB 350;
     Administration, Topical   WB 340; Dosage
     Forms   QV 785; Drug Administration
     Schedule   WB 340; Injections   WB 354;

    Perfusion, Regional   QZ 267; Respiratory
    Therapy   WF 145, etc., and particular
    diseases being treated
   Adverse effects   QZ 42
   Analysis   QV 25
   Autonomic see Autonomic Agents   QV 120
   Catalogs see Catalogs, Drug   QV 772
   General works   QV 55
   Legislation see Legislation, Drug   QV 32-33
   Metabolism   QV 38
   Military supplies   UH 420-425
   Mucopolysaccharidosis IV   WD 205.5.C2
   Packaging   QV 825
   Patent medicines see Drugs, Non-Prescription
   QV 772
   Preservation   QV 754
    Public health aspects   WA 730
   Proprietary   QV 772
   Public health aspects   WA 730
   Quack see Nostrums   QV 722
   Receptors see Receptors, Drug   QV 38
   Standards   QV 771
   See also Iatrogenic Disease   QZ 42; names of
    specific drugs and types of drugs
Drugs, Chinese Herbal   QV 767
   See also Medicine, Herbal   WB 925
Drugs, Investigational   QV 771
Drugs, Non-Prescription   QV 772
Drugs of Abuse see Street Drugs
Dry Eye Syndromes   WW 208
DSIP see Delta Sleep-Inducing Peptide
Dual Personality see Multiple-Personality Disorder
Dubin-Johnson Syndrome see Jaundice, Chronic
   Idiopathic
Duchenne Muscular Dystrophy see Muscular
   Dystrophy
Ducks
   Anatomy   SF 767.P6
   Culture   SF 504.7-505.63
   Diseases
    Domestic and wild   SF 995.2
   Wild   SF 510.D8
Ductless Glands see Endocrine Glands
Ductus Arteriosus   WQ 210.5
Ductus Arteriosus, Patent   WG 220
Ductus Deferens see Vas Deferens
Due Process see Jurisprudence
Duffy Blood-Group System   WH 420
Duhring's Disease see Dermatitis Herpetiformis
Dumbness, Hysteric see Mutism
Dumping Syndrome   WI 380
Duncan's Syndrome see Lymphoproliferative
   Disorders
Duodenal Contents see Analysis   QY 130 under
   Duodenum
Duodenal Diseases   WI 505
Duodenal Neoplasms   WI 505
Duodenal Obstruction   WI 505
Duodenal Papilla, Major see Vater's Ampulla
Duodenal Papilla, Minor see Pancreatic Ducts
Duodenal Ulcer   WI 370
Duodenitis   WI 505
Duodenogastric Reflux   WI 302

**ALWAYS CONSULT MAIN SCHEDULES. USE NUMBER ASSIGNED ONLY WHEN
SUBJECT REPRESENTS MAJOR EMPHASIS OF WORK BEING CLASSIFIED**

Duodenoscopy   WI 505
Duodenum   WI 505
    Analysis   QY 130
    Feeding by see Tube Feeding   WB 410
Duplicating Processes see Copying Processes
Dupuytren's Contracture   WE 830
Dura Mater   WL 200
Durable Power of Attorney see Living Wills
Dwarfism   WE 250
    See also Cretinism   WK 252
Dwarfism, Pituitary   WK 550
Dwellings see Housing
Dye Dilution Technique   WG 141
    In hemodynamics   WG 106
Dye Exclusion Assays, Antitumor see Drug
    Screening Assays, Antitumor
Dyes
    As anti–infective agents   QV 235
    As reagents, indicators, etc.   QV 240
    Used in particular procedures, with the procedure
    See also Stains and Staining   QW 25, etc.
Dyes, Hair see Hair Dyes
Dynorphins   QU 68
Dysarthria   WL 340.2
    Psychogenic   WM 475
Dysautonomia see Autonomic Nervous System
    Diseases
Dysautonomia, Familial   WL 600
Dyschondroplasias see Osteochondrodysplasias
Dysembryoma see Teratoma
Dysentery   WC 280–285
    Veterinary   SF 809.D87
Dysentery, Amebic   WC 285
Dysentery, Bacillary   WC 282
Dysgammaglobulinemia   WD 308
Dysgerminoma   QZ 310
    Localized, by site
Dyskinesia see Movement Disorders
Dyskinesia, Drug–Induced   WL 390
Dyskinesia, Tardive see Dyskinesia, Drug–Induced
Dyslexia
    Neurologic   WL 340.6
    Psychogenic   WM 475.6
    Remedial teaching   LB 1050.5
Dyslexia, Acquired
    Neurologic   WL 340.6
    Psychogenic   WM 475.6
    Remedial teaching   LB 1050.5
Dyslexia, Congenital see Dyslexia
Dyslexia, Developmental see Dyslexia
Dysmenorrhea   WP 560
Dysmyelopoietic Syndromes see Myelodysplastic
    Syndromes
Dysostosis, Craniofacial see Craniofacial Dysostosis
Dyspareunia   WP 610
Dyspepsia   WI 145
Dysphagia see Deglutition Disorders
Dysphasia see Aphasia
Dysphonia see Voice Disorders
Dyspituitarism see Hyperpituitarism;
    Hypopituitarism
Dysplasia Epiphysialis Punctata see
    Chondrodysplasia Punctata

Dysplastic Nevus Syndrome   WR 500
    Pathology   QZ 310
Dyspnea   WF 143
Dyspnea, Paroxysmal   WG 370
Dyssocial Behavior see Antisocial Personality
    Disorder
Dysthymic Disorder see Depressive Disorder
Dystocia   WQ 310
Dystonia   WL 390
Dystonia Musculorum Deformans   WE 550
Dystrophic Skin Disorders see Skin Diseases   WR
    140, etc. or name of specific disorders, e.g.,
    Scleroderma, Circumscribed
Dystrophy, Progressive Muscular see Muscular
    Dystrophy

E

E Antigens see Hepatitis B e Antigens
E–B Virus see Herpesvirus 4, Human
E. coli Infections see Escherichia coli Infections
EAC142 see Complement 3 Convertase
Ear   WV 200–290
    Surgery   WV 200
Ear Canal   WV 222
Ear Deformities, Acquired   WV 220
    Deformities of other than the external ear, by
    part
Ear Diseases   WV 200–290
    General works   WV 200
    In infancy & childhood   WV 200–290
    Nursing   WY 158.5
Ear Drum see Tympanic Membrane
Ear, External   WV 220–222
Ear, Inner see Labyrinth
Ear, Internal see Labyrinth
Ear, Middle   WV 230–233
Ear Molds see Hearing Aids
Ear Neoplasms   WV 290
    Localized, by site
Ear Ossicles   WV 230
Ear Protective Devices   WV 26
Ear Trumpets see Hearing Aids
Ear Wax see Cerumen
Early Gene Transcription see Transcription, Genetic
Earthquakes see Natural Disasters
Earthworms see Oligochaeta
East Coast Fever see Theileriasis
Eating Behavior see Feeding Behavior
Eating Disorders
    In infancy & childhood
        Children   WS 130
        Infants   WS 120
    Manifestation of disease   WI 143
    Psychophysiological   WM 175
Ebstein's Anomaly   WG 220
EBV see Herpesvirus 4, Human
EC Cells see Tumor Stem Cells
EC–IC Arterial Bypass see Cerebral
    Revascularization
Eccentro–Osteochondrodysplasia see
    Mucopolysaccharidosis IV
Eccrine Glands   WR 400

Ecdysone   SF 768.3
    Zoology   QL 868
ECG see Electrocardiography
Echinococcosis   WC 840
    Veterinary   SF 810.H8
Echinococcosis, Hepatic   WI 700
Echinococcosis, Hepatic Alveolar see
    Echinococcosis, Hepatic
Echinococcosis, Pulmonary   WF 600
Echinococcus   QX 442
Echinopanax see Ginseng
Echo Viruses see Echoviruses
Echocardiography   WG 141.5.E2
Echocardiography, Continuous Doppler see
    Echocardiography, Doppler
Echocardiography, Contrast see Echocardiography
Echocardiography, Cross-Sectional see
    Echocardiography
Echocardiography, Doppler   WG 141.5.E2
Echocardiography, Doppler, Color   WG 141.5.E2
Echocardiography, Doppler, Pulsed   WG 141.5.E2
Echocardiography, M-Mode see Echocardiography
Echocardiography, Two-Dimensional see
    Echocardiography
Echocardiography, Two-Dimensional Doppler see
    Echocardiography, Doppler
Echoencephalography   WL 154
Echography see Ultrasonography
Echolalia   WM 475
Echolocation   QL 782.5
Echothiophate Iodide   QV 124
Echoviruses   QW 168.5.P4
Eck Fistula see Portacaval Shunt, Surgical
Eclampsia   WQ 215
Eclecticism   WB 920
Eco DNA Topoisomerase II see DNA
    Topoisomerase (ATP-Hydrolysing)
Ecological Monitoring see Environmental
    Monitoring
Ecological Systems, Closed   WD 756
Ecology
    General and animal   QH 540-549.5
    Human   GF
        General works   GF 31-48
    Plant   QK 901-938
Economic Competition
    By subject, in economics number where
    applicable
Economic Factors see Socioeconomic Factors
Economic Inflation see Inflation, Economic
Economics
    Land, agriculture, industry   HD
        General works   HD 31-37
    National production   HC
        General works   HC 21
    Pharmacy   QV 736
    Theory   HB
        General works   HB 151-181
Economics, Dental   WU 77-79
Economics, Hospital   WX 157
Economics, Medical   W 74-80
Economics, Nursing   WY 77
Ecosystem see Ecology

Ecothiopate Iodide see Echothiophate Iodide
ECT (Psychotherapy) see Electroconvulsive
    Therapy
Ectasia, Alveolar see Pulmonary Emphysema
Ecthyma   WR 225
Ecthyma, Contagious   WC 584
Ectodermal Defect, Congenital see Ectodermal
    Dysplasia
Ectodermal Dysplasia   WR 218
Ectogenesis   WQ 205
Ectohormones see Pheromones
Ectoparasitic Infestations   WC 900
    Disinfestation   WC 900
    Veterinary   SF 810
Ectopia Cordis see Heart Defects, Congenital
Ectopic Hormone Syndromes see Neoplastic
    Endocrine-Like Syndromes
Ectopic Pregnancy see Pregnancy, Ectopic
Ectropion   WW 205
Eczema   WR 190
    Veterinary   SF 901
Eczema, Atopic see Dermatitis, Atopic
Eczema, Contact see Dermatitis, Contact
Eczema, Dyshidrotic   WR 200
Eczema, Infantile see Dermatitis, Atopic
Eczema, Vesicular Palmoplantar see Eczema,
    Dyshidrotic
Edathamil see Edetic Acid
Edema
    Angioneurotic see Angioneurotic Edema   WR
    170
    Brain see Brain Edema   WL 348
    Bronchial   WF 500
    Diagnostic significance   WB 158
    Drugs affecting   QV 160
    Laryngeal see Laryngeal Edema   WV 500
    Lymph see Lymphedema   WH 700, etc.
    Manifestation of Disease   QZ 170
    Optic papilla see Papilledema   WW 280
    Pulmonary see Pulmonary Edema   WF 600
    See also names of body parts with which the
    edema is associated
Edema, Cardiac   WG 370
Edema-Proteinuria-Hypertension Gestosis see
    Gestosis, EPH
Edentata   QL 737.E2
Edetates see Edetic Acid
Edetic Acid   QV 276
EDTA see Edetic Acid
Education
    (Form number 18 in any NLM schedule where
    applicable)
    Elementary   LB 1555-1602
    Health see Health Education   WA 590, etc.;
        Health Education, Dental   WU 113
    Higher   LB 2300-2430
    Physical see Physical Education and Training
    QT 255
    Safety   WA 250
    Secondary   LB 1603-1696.6
    Sex see Sex Education   QT 225, etc.
    Vocational see Vocational Education   LC
    1041-1048

ALWAYS CONSULT MAIN SCHEDULES. USE NUMBER ASSIGNED ONLY WHEN
SUBJECT REPRESENTS MAJOR EMPHASIS OF WORK BEING CLASSIFIED

See also subheading Education under names of
disabilities, specialties, etc.
Education, Competency-Based see
Competency-Based Education
Education, Continuing   LC 5201-6660.4
See also specific continuing education terms, e.g.,
Education, Dental, Continuing; Education,
Medical, Continuing; Education, Pharmacy,
Continuing; etc.
Education, Dental   WU 18
Education, Dental, Continuing   WU 20
Education, Dental, Graduate   WU 20
Education, Dental Health see Health Education,
Dental
Education, Graduate   LB 2371-2372
Education, Health see Health Education
Education, Medical   W 18
Education, Medical, Continuing   W 20
In psychiatry   WM 19.5
Education, Medical, Graduate   W 20
In psychiatry   WM 19.5
Education, Medical, Undergraduate   W 18
Education, Nursing   WY 18
See also Education   WY 18.8 under Nursing,
Practical
Education, Nursing, Associate   WY 18
Education, Nursing, Baccalaureate   WY 18
Education, Nursing, Continuing   WY 18.5
Education, Nursing, Diploma Programs   WY 18
Education, Nursing, Graduate   WY 18.5
Education of Mentally Defective see Education of
Mentally Retarded
Education of Mentally Retarded   LC 4601-4640.4
Sex education   HQ 54.3
Health education   LC 4613
Education of Patients see Patient Education
Education, Pharmacy   QV 18
Education, Pharmacy, Continuing   QV 20
Education, Pharmacy, Graduate   QV 20
Education, Predental   WU 18
Education, Premedical   W 18
Education Research, Nursing see Nursing Education
Research
Education, Sex see Sex Education
Education, Special
Blind children   HV 1618-2349
Children with behavior disorders   LC
4801-4803
Deaf children   HV 2417-2990.5
Disabled adults   LC 4812-4824
Disabled children   LC 4001-4043
Mentally ill children   LC 4165-4184
Mentally retarded children see Education of
Mentally Retarded   LC 4601-4640.4
Other ill children   LC 4580-4599
Physically disabled children   LC 4201-4243
Slow learning or under achieving children   LC
4661-4700.4
Socially disabled children   LC 4051-4100.4
See also subheading Education under names of
disabilities, specialties, etc.
Education, Veterinary   SF 756.3-756.37
Educational Achievement see Educational Status

Educational Measurement   LB 3051-3060.87
In a particular field
Works about (Form number 18 in any NLM
schedule where applicable)
Actual tests (Form number 18.2 in any NLM
schedule where applicable)
Other special topics, by subject
Educational Status
General official reports, by country   L 111-791
School surveys   LB 2823
Relation to special topics, by subject
Special classes of people   LC 1390-5160.3
Educational Therapy in Psychiatry see Occupational
Therapy; Education of Mentally Retarded
EEG see Electroencephalography
Eel, Congo see Urodela
Efficiency
Industrial   T 58.8
Use of time   BF 637.T5
Effort see Exertion
Effort Syndrome see Neurocirculatory Asthenia
EGF-URO Receptors see Receptors, Epidermal
Growth Factor-Urogastrone
Egg see Ovum
Egg Proteins   QU 55
In diet therapy   WB 426
Egg Shell Proteins see Egg Proteins
Egg White Proteins see Egg Proteins
Egg Yolk Proteins see Egg Proteins
Eggs
As a dietary supplement in health and disease
Cholesterol content   WB 425
Protein content   WB 426
See also Egg Proteins   QU 55
Sanitary handling   WA 703
Ego
Child psychology   WS 105.5.S3
Psychoanalysis   WM 460.5.E3
See also Self Concept   BF 697, etc.
Ehlers-Danlos Syndrome   WR 218
Ehrlichia   QW 150
Eicosanoids   QU 90
Eidetic Imagery   WL 705
Eigenmannia see Electric Fish
Ejaculation
Physiology   WJ 750
Psychological disorders   WM 611
Ejaculatory Ducts   WJ 750
Ejection Seats   WD 740
EKG see Electrocardiography
Elaeophoriasis see Filariasis
Elastic Stockings see Bandages
Elastic Tissue   QS 532.5.E5
Elastica see Rubber
Elasticity   QC 191
Of arteries, bones, etc. in general   QT 34
Of specific organs or parts, by subject
Of a particular material, with material
Elastin   QU 55
Elastomers see Rubber
Elastomers, Silicone see Silicone Elastomers
Elbow   WE 820
Elbow Joint   WE 820

Elder Abuse   HV 6626.3
    For the aged being abused   WT 30
    For the abusers' aggressive behavior   WM 600
Elderly see Aged
Elderly, Frail see Frail Elderly
Electric Anesthesia see Electronarcosis
Electric Burns see Burns, Electric
Electric Conductance, Skin see Galvanic Skin
    Response
Electric Conductivity
    Human   QT 34
    Physics   QC 610.3–612
Electric Countershock   WG 330
Electric Fish   QL 639.1
    As laboratory animals   QY 60.F4
Electric Injuries   WD 602
    Industrial   WA 485
    See also Burns, Electric   WO 704
Electric Organ
    In fishes   QL 639.1
Electric Power Plants see Power Plants
Electric Shock see Electric Injuries;
    Electroconvulsive Therapy; Electroshock
Electric Stimulation
    Neurophysiology   WL 102
    Therapeutic use see Electric Stimulation Therapy
        WB 495
    Diagnostic use see Electrodiagnosis   WB 141
Electric Stimulation Therapy   WB 495
    See also Electroconvulsive Therapy   WM 412
Electric Stimulation, Transcutaneous see
    Transcutaneous Electric Nerve Stimulation
Electricity
    Adverse effects   WD 602
        See also Electric Injuries   WD 602
    Atmospheric   QC 960.5–969
        See also Lightning   WD 602, etc.
    Death by (Medicolegal aspects)   W 843
    Physics   QC 501–718.8
        Electric currents   QC 601–625
Electroacoustic Impedance Tests see Acoustic
    Impedance Tests
Electroacupuncture   WB 369
Electroanalgesia see Transcutaneous Electric Nerve
    Stimulation
Electroanesthesia see Electronarcosis
Electrocardiography   WG 140
    In infancy & childhood   WS 290
    Veterinary   SF 811
Electrocardiography, Ambulatory   WG 140
Electrocardiography, Dynamic see
    Electrocardiography, Ambulatory
Electrocardiography, Holter see
    Electrocardiography, Ambulatory
Electrocautery see Electrocoagulation
Electrochemistry   QD 551–575
    Electrochemical analysis   QD 115
    Industrial   TP 250–261
    Organic compounds   QD 273
Electrocoagulation   WO 198
Electrocochleography see Audiometry, Evoked
    Response
Electroconvulsive Therapy   WM 412

See also Electroshock   WM 25
Electrocution, Accidental see Electric Injuries
Electrodeposition see Electroplating
Electrodermal Response see Galvanic Skin Response
Electrodes   QD 571
    Biomedical engineering   QT 36
    In electric stimulation therapy   WB 495
    Used for special purposes, by subject, e.g., in
        Urinalysis   QY 185
    See also Microelectrodes   QT 36, etc.
Electrodes, Enzyme see Biosensors
Electrodes, Miniaturized see Microelectrodes
Electrodiagnosis   WB 141
    Used for diagnosis of particular disorders, with
        the disorder or system
Electroencephalography   WL 150
Electroencephalography, Alpha Rhythm see Alpha
    Rhythm
Electrofocusing see Isoelectric Focusing
Electrogalvanism, Intraoral   WU 180
Electrohydraulic Shockwave Lithotripsy see
    Lithotripsy
Electroimmunoblotting see Immunoblotting
Electroimmunodiffusion Test see Immunodiffusion
Electrokymography   WN 100
    Cardiovascular   WG 141.5.K9
    Used for diagnosis of particular disorders, with
        the disorder or system
Electrolysis   QD 551–575
    In electrotherapy   WB 495
    In hair removal   WR 450
    Special topics, by subject
Electrolytes   QV 270
    Analytical chemistry   QD 139.E4
    Bacteriology   QW 52
    Electrochemistry   QD 565
    Physiological effects (General)   QT 162.E4
    See also Water–Electrolyte Balance   QU 105;
        Water–Electrolyte Imbalance   WD 220
Electrolytic Depilation see Hair Removal
Electromagnetic Energy see Radiation
Electromagnetic Fields
    Biophysics   QT 34
    Physics   QC 665.E4
Electromagnetic Radiation see Radiation
Electromagnetic Radiation, Ionizing see Radiation,
    Ionizing
Electromagnetic Radiation, Non–Ionizing see
    Radiation, Non–Ionizing
Electromagnetic Waves see Radiation
Electromagnetics
    Biophysics   QT 34
    Electromyography   WE 500
Electromyography   WE 500
    Special topics, by subject
Electron Microscope see Microscopy, Electron
Electron Microscopy see Microscopy, Electron
Electron Microscopy, Transmission see Microscopy,
    Electron
Electron Nuclear Double Resonance see Electron
    Spin Resonance Spectroscopy
Electron Paramagnetic Resonance see Electron Spin
    Resonance Spectroscopy

**ALWAYS CONSULT MAIN SCHEDULES. USE NUMBER ASSIGNED ONLY WHEN
SUBJECT REPRESENTS MAJOR EMPHASIS OF WORK BEING CLASSIFIED**

Electron Probe Microanalysis
    Qualitative analysis   QD 98.E4
    Quantitative analysis   QD 117.E42
    Special topics, by subject
Electron Spin Resonance Spectroscopy
    Biological research
       General   QH 324.9.E36
       Medically oriented   QT 34
    Chemistry   QD 455.2
    Used for special purposes, by subject
Electron Theory, Roentgenographic see Health
    Physics
Electron Transport   QU 125
Electronarcosis
    Anesthesiology   WO 275
    Psychiatry   WM 412
Electronic Data Processing see Automatic Data
    Processing
Electronic Mail see Office Automation
Electronics   TK 7800-8360
Electronics, Medical   QT 34
    See also Biomedical Engineering   QT 36
Electrons   WN 415-450
    In general nuclear physics   QC
    793.5.E62-793.5.E629
    In health physics   WN 110
Electronystagmography   WW 410
Electrooculography   WW 143
Electrophoresis
    Analytical chemistry (General)   QD 79.E44
    Biology   QH 324.9.E4
       Medically oriented   QU 25
    Microbiology   QW 25
    Organic chemistry (General)   QD 272.E43
    Quantitative analysis   QD 117.E45
    Used for other special purposes, by subject
    See also Blood Protein Electrophoresis   QY 455;
       Isoelectric focusing   QW 25, etc.
Electrophoresis, Agar Gel   QU 25
    Special topics, by subject
Electrophoresis, Agarose Gel see Electrophoresis,
    Agar Gel
Electrophoresis, Gel, Two-Dimensional   QU 25
    Special topics, by subject
Electrophysiology   QT 34
    Animals (General)   QP 341
       Domestic   SF 768
       Wild   QP 341
    Biology (General)   QH 517
    Nervous system   WL 102
    Plants   QK 845
    Other systems involved, in physiology number
    for the system or part
Electroplating   TS 670-693
Electroretinography   WW 270
Electroshock   WM 25
    See also Electric injuries   WD 602;
       Electroconvulsive therapy   WM 412
Electroshock Therapy see Electroconvulsive
    Therapy
Electrosleep see Electronarcosis
Electrosurgery   WO 198
    Dental   WU 600

Electrosyneresis see Counterimmunoelectrophoresis
Electrotherapy see Electric Stimulation Therapy
Electroversion, Cardiac see Electric Countershock
Elements
    Biochemistry   QU 130
    Inorganic chemistry   QD 181
    Non-metallic (pharmacology)   QV 138
    Physical chemistry   QD 466-469
    See also Isotopes   QD 181, etc.; Radioisotopes
       WN 420, etc. and specific chemical elements
Elephantiasis   WH 700
Elephantiasis, Bancroftian see Elephantiasis, Filarial
Elephantiasis, Filarial   WC 880
Elephants   QL 737.P98
    Diseases   SF 997.5.E4
Eligibility Determination
    For Medicaid   W 250
    For Medicare   WT 31
    Medicolegal aspects
       Of insurance   W 900
       Of occupational disease & injury   W 925
    Eligibility for other benefits and services, by
    subject
    See also Disability Evaluation, W 900, etc.
ELISA see Enzyme-Linked Immunosorbent Assay
Elixirs, Pharmacy see Pharmaceutic Aids
Emaciation   WB 146
    Malnutrition   WD 100, etc.
    Metabolic diseases   WD 200
Emasculation see Castration
Embalming   WA 844
Emblems and Insignia
    In medicine and related fields   WZ 334
    Seals   CD 5005-6471
Embolic Tumor Cells see Neoplasm Circulating
    Cells
Embolism   QZ 170
    Arterial   WG 540
    Cerebral see Cerebral Embolism and Thrombosis
       WL 355
    Coronary   WG 300
    Pulmonary see Pulmonary Embolism   WG 420
    Venous   WG 610
Embolism, Air   QZ 170
    As an effect of high altitude   WD 710
    In decompression sickness   WD 712
    In other disorders, with the disorder
Embolism, Amniotic Fluid   WQ 244
Embolism, Fat   QZ 170
Embolism, Gas see Embolism, Air
Embolism, Tumor see Neoplasm Circulating Cells
Embolus see Embolism
Embryo   QS 604
    Animals
       Domestic   SF 767.5
       Wild animals   QL 971
       Specific animals, with the animal
Embryo, Chick see Chick Embryo
Embryo Development see Fetal Development
Embryo Transfer
    Human   WQ 205
Embryologists, Directories see Directories   QS 622
    under Embryology

**ALWAYS CONSULT MAIN SCHEDULES. USE NUMBER ASSIGNED ONLY WHEN
SUBJECT REPRESENTS MAJOR EMPHASIS OF WORK BEING CLASSIFIED**

I-81

Embryology   QS 604–681
　Directories   QS 622
　Domestic animals   SF 767.5
　Experimental   QS 604
　Gynecology   WP 150
　Twinning   QS 642
　　See also Twins   WQ 235, etc.; Pregnancy,
　　　Multiple   WQ 235
　Zoology   QL 951–991
　　See also special topics under Anatomy
　Localized, by site
Embryonal Carcinoma Cells see Tumor Stem Cells
Embryonic Induction   QH 607
Embryopathies see Fetal Diseases
Embryos, Plant see Seeds
Embryotomy   WQ 435
Embryotoxins see Teratogens
Emergencies
　Cardiac   WG 205
　Dental (General)   WU 105
　First aid   WA 292
　General   WB 105
　In infancy & childhood   WS 205
　Medical see Emergency Medicine   WB 105
　Surgical   WO 700–820
　Veterinary (General)   SF 778
　Veterinary surgery   SF 914.3–914.4
　　See also Crisis Intervention   WM 401, etc.
Emergency Care see Emergency Medical Services
Emergency Care Information Systems see
　Information Systems
Emergency Health Services see Emergency Medical
　Services
Emergency Medical Service Communication
　Systems see Emergency Medical Services   WX
　215, etc.
Emergency Medical Services   WX 215
　Occupational   WA 412
　　See also Emergency Services, Psychiatric   WM
　　　401; Emergency Service, Hospital   WX 215;
　　　names of particular types of service, e.g., Mobile
　　　Health Units   WX 190
Emergency Medical Tags   W 26
Emergency Medical Technicians   W 21.5
Emergency Medicine   WB 105
　In infancy & childhood   WS 205
Emergency Mobile Units see Ambulances
Emergency Nursing   WY 154
Emergency Outpatient Unit see Emergency Service,
　Hospital
Emergency Service, Hospital   WX 215
Emergency Services, Psychiatric   WM 401
Emergency Surgery see Surgery
Emergicenters see Emergency Medical Services
Emerogenes see Genes, Suppressor, Tumor
Emetics   QV 73
Emetine   QV 255
Emigration and Immigration   JV 6008–6348
　Emigration   JV 6061–6149
　General works   JV 6008–6049
　Immigration   JV 6201–6348
　Of health manpower   W 76
　　See also Transients and Migrants   WA 300, etc.

Emmenagogues see Menstruation-Inducing Agents
Emollients   QV 63
Emotional Bonds see Object Attachment
Emotional Disturbances see Affective Symptoms
Emotional Maladjustment see Affective Symptoms
Emotional Stress see Stress, Psychological
Emotions   BF 531–593
　Disorders see Affective Symptoms   WS 350.6,
　　etc.
　In adolescence   WS 462
　In infancy & childhood   WS 105.5.E5
　Physiology   WL 103
Empathy   BF 575.E55
　In adolescence   WS 462
　In infancy & childhood   WS 105.5.E5
Emphysema   QZ 140
　Mediastinal see Mediastinal Emphysema   WF
　　900
　Pulmonary see Pulmonary Emphysema   WF 648
Emphysema, Mediastinal see Mediastinal
　Emphysema
Emphysema, Pulmonary see Pulmonary Emphysema
Employee Assistance Programs (Health Care) see
　Occupational Health Services
Employee Discipline
　Hospital   WX 159
　Nursing   WY 30
　Psychiatry   WM 30
　In other areas, by subject
Employee Grievances
　Hospital   WX 159
　Nursing   WY 30
　Psychiatry   WM 30
　In other areas, by subject
Employee Health see Occupational Health
Employee Health Benefit Plans see Health Benefit
　Plans, Employee
Employee Health Services see Occupational Health
　Services
Employee Orientation Programs see Inservice
　Training
Employee Performance Appraisal
　Hospital Personnel   WX 159
　Nursing   WY 30
　Psychiatry   WM 30
Employee Strikes see Strikes, Employee
Employee Turnover see Personnel Turnover
Employment
　Children   HD 6228–6250.5
　Employment agencies   HD 5860–6000.7
　Health problems see Occupational Medicine
　　WA 400–495
　Labor market   HD 5701–5856
　Migrants see Transients and Migrants   WA 300,
　　etc.
　Nurses   WY 29
　Women   HD 6050–6223
　　See also Physicians, Women   W 21, etc.
　Other special topics, by subject
　　See also Rehabilitation, Vocational   HD
　　　7255–7256; Unemployment   HD 5707.5–5851;
　　　Vocational Guidance   HF 5381, etc.
Employment Application see Job Application

Employment Termination see Employment
Emporiatrics see Travel
Empyema   WF 745
Empyema, Gallbladder see Cholecystitis
Empyema, Tuberculous   WF 745
EMS Communication Systems see Emergency
   Medical Service Communication Systems
Emulsifying Agents see Excipients
Emulsions   QV 785
EN–1639A see Naltrexone
Enalapril   QV 150
Enalapril Maleate see Enalapril
Enallynymalum see Methohexital
Enamel see Dental Enamel
Encephalitis   WL 351
      Equine see Encephalomyelitis, Equine   SF
      959.E5, etc.
      Meningeal see Meningoencephalitis   WL 351,
      etc.
Encephalitis, Central European see Encephalitis,
   Tick-Borne
Encephalitis, Epidemic   WC 542
Encephalitis, Equine see Encephalomyelitis, Equine
Encephalitis, Japanese   WC 542
   Veterinary   SF 809.E62
Encephalitis, Japanese B see Encephalitis, Japanese
Encephalitis, Post-Vaccinal see Encephalomyelitis,
   Acute Disseminated
Encephalitis, St. Louis   WC 542
Encephalitis, Tick-Borne   WC 542
   Veterinary   SF 809.E62
Encephalitis Virus, California see California Group
   Viruses
Encephalitis Virus, Central European see
   Encephalitis Viruses, Tick-Borne
Encephalitis Virus, St. Louis   QW 168.5A7
   As arthropod-borne virus   QW 168.5.A7
Encephalitis Virus, Venezuelan Equine   QW
   168.5.A7
Encephalitis Viruses   QW 168.5.A7
Encephalitis Viruses, Tick-Borne   QW 168.5.A7
Encephalocele
   Congenital   WL 350
   Traumatic   WL 354
Encephalography see Cerebral Angiography;
   Electroencephalography; Radiography   WL 141
   under Brain; Cerebral Ventriculography
Encephalomalacia   WL 348
   Associated with cerebral infarction   WL 355
Encephalomyelitis   WL 351
   Equine see Encephalomyelitis, Equine   SF
   959.E5
      As a communicable disease   SF 809.E7
Encephalomyelitis, Acute Disseminated   WL 351
Encephalomyelitis, Allergic   WL 351
Encephalomyelitis, Equine   SF 959.E5
   In humans   WC 542
Encephalomyelitis, Experimental Allergic see
   Encephalomyelitis, Allergic
Encephalomyelitis, Myalgic see Fatigue Syndrome,
   Chronic
Encephalomyelitis Virus, Venezuelan Equine see
   Encephalitis Virus, Venezuelan Equine

Enchondroma see Chondroma
Enclomifene see Clomiphene
Encopresis   WI 600
   Toilet training   WS 113
   See also Defecation   WI 600; Fecal Incontinence
   WI 600
Encounter Groups
   In psychotherapy   WM 430.5.S3
   In sociology   HM 134
Encyclopedias   AE
   (Form number 13 in any NLM schedule where
   applicable)
   Science   Q 121
   On other topics, by subject
End-Stage Renal Disease see Kidney Failure,
   Chronic
Endamoeba see Entamoeba
Endarterectomy   WG 170
Endarteritis   WG 515
Endbrain see Telencephalon
Endemic Typhus see Typhus, Endemic Flea-Borne
Endocardial Cushion Defects   WG 220
Endocarditis   WG 285
Endocarditis, Bacterial   WG 285
Endocarditis Lenta see Endocarditis, Subacute
   Bacterial
Endocarditis, Subacute Bacterial   WG 285
Endocardium   WG 285
Endocavitary Fulguration see Electrocoagulation
Endocrine Diseases   WK
   General works   WK 140
   In infancy & childhood   WS 330
   Nursing   WY 155
Endocrine Drugs see Hormones; Hormones,
   Synthetic; Hypoglycemic Agents
Endocrine Glands   WK
   Of children   WS 330
   Of domestic animals   SF 768.3
   Of wild animals   QP 187
   See also Corpus Luteum   WP 530, etc.; Ovary
      WP 520–530, etc.; Testis   WJ 875, etc.;
   names of other specific glands
Endocrinologists, Directories see Directories   WK
22 under Endocrinology
Endocrinology   WK
   Directories   WK 22
   In infancy & childhood   WS 330
Endocrinology and Metabolism (Specialty) see
   Endocrinology
Endoderm   WQ 205
Endodermal Sinus Tumor
   In the ovary   WP 322
Endodontics   WU 230
Endolymph   WV 250
Endolymphatic Duct   WV 255
Endolymphatic Sac   WV 255
Endometrial Cycle see Menstrual Cycle
Endometriosis   WP 390
Endometritis   WP 451
Endometrium   WP 400
Endomycetales   QW 180.5.A8
Endomycopsis see Endomycetales
Endophthalmitis   WW 212

Endoplasmic Reticulum   QH 603.E6
ENDOR see Electron Spin Resonance Spectroscopy
Endorphins   QU 68
    Neurochemistry   WL 104
    Other special topics, by subject
Endoscopic Retrograde Cholangiopancreatography
    see Cholangiopancreatography, Endoscopic
    Retrograde
Endoscopy   WB 141
    Used for diagnosis of particular disorders, with
      the disorder or system
    See also specific types of endoscopy
Endoscopy, Digestive System   WI 141
Endoscopy, Gastrointestinal   WI 141
Endoscopy, Uterine see Hysteroscopy
Endosomes   QH 591
Endothelin-1 see Endothelins
Endothelin-2 see Endothelins
Endothelin-3 see Endothelins
Endothelins
    As vasoconstrictors   QV 150
    Biochemistry   QU 68
Endothelium
    Histology   QS 532.5.E7
    See also organ-specific terms, e.g., Endothelium,
      Corneal   WW 220
Endothelium, Anterior Chamber see Endothelium,
    Corneal
Endothelium, Corneal   WW 220
    Anterior chamber epithelium   WW 210
    Eyebank procedures   WW 170
Endothelium-Derived Relaxing Factor   QV 150
Endothelium-Derived Vasoconstrictor Factors see
    Endothelins
Endothelium, Vascular   WG 500-700
    Histology   QS 532.5.E7
Endotoxins   QW 630.5.E5
Endotracheal Anesthesia see Anesthesia,
    Intratracheal
Endowments see Financial Management
Enema   WB 344
Energy Expenditure see Energy Metabolism
Energy-Generating Resources
    Special topics, by subject, e.g. Environmental
      Health   WA 30
Energy Metabolism   QU 125
Energy Resources Conservation see Conservation of
    Energy Resources
Energy Transfer   QU 34
Enflurane   QV 81
Engineering   TA
    Biomedical see Biomedical Engineering   QT 36
    General works   TA 144-145
    Hospital maintenance   WX 165
    Sanitary see Sanitary Engineering   WA 671, etc.
Engineering, Hospital see Maintenance and
    Engineering, Hospital
Engineering Psychology see Human Engineering
English Literature see Literature   P, etc. and
    related headings
Enhancer Elements (Genetics)   QH 450.2
Enkephalins   QU 68
    Neurochemistry   WL 104

Other special topics, by subject
Enoxacin   QV 250
    As an urinary anti-infective agent   QV 243
Enoxaparin   QV 193
Enoxolone see Glycyrrhetinic Acid
Enriched Food see Food, Fortified
Entamoeba   QX 55
Entamoebiasis   WC 285
Entamoebiasis, Hepatic see Liver Abscess, Amebic
Entamoebiasis, Intestinal see Dysentery, Amebic
Enteral Feeding see Enteral Nutrition
Enteral Nutrition   WB 410
Enteric Fever see Typhoid
Enteric Hormones see Gastrointestinal Hormones
Enteric Infections see Enterobacteriaceae Infections;
    Enterovirus Infections; Intestinal Diseases,
    Parasitic; names of specific infections
Enterically-Transmitted Non-A, Non-B Hepatitis
    see Hepatitis E
Enteritis   WI 420
Enteritis, Granulomatous see Crohn Disease
Enteritis, Regional see Crohn Disease
Enterobacter   QW 138.5.E5
Enterobacteriaceae   QW 138
Enterobacteriaceae Infections   WC 260-290
    Veterinary   SF 809.E63
Enterobiasis see Oxyuriasis
Enterocele see Hernia
Enterochromaffin Cells   WI 400
    Physiology   WI 402
Enteroclysis see Enema
Enterocolitis   WI 420
Enterocolitis, Pseudomembranous   WI 420
Enteropathy, Exudative see Protein-Losing
    Enteropathies
Enterostomy   WI 480
Enterotoxins   QW 630.5.E6
Enterovirus   QW 168.5.P4
Enterovirus Infections   WC 500
    Veterinary   SF 809.E64
    See also names of specific infections, e.g.,
      Poliomyelitis   WC 555-556
Enterovirus 70 see Enterovirus
Entomology   QL 461-599.82
    Medical   QX 500-650
    See also Insects   QX 500-650, etc.
Entrapment Neuropathy see Nerve Compression
    Syndromes
Entropion   WW 205
Enuresis   WJ 146
    In infancy & childhood   WS 322
Environment
    Living space   QT 230
    Physical
      Adaptation to   QT 140-165
      As a cause of disease (Pathology)   QZ 57
      See also Climate   WB 750, etc. and related
        headings
    Relation to general public health see
      Environmental Health   WA 30, etc.
    Relation to mental health see Environmental
      Health   WM 31, etc.
    Social see Social Environment   HM 206

See also Ecology   QH 540–549.5
Environment, Controlled   WA 670–847
  General works   WA 671
  In hospitals
    General   WX 165
    Intensive care   WX 218
  In industry   WA 440–491
  Of laboratory animals   QY 56
  See also Extraterrestrial Environment   WD 758;
    Germ-Free Life   QY 56, etc.; Incubators
    QS 530, etc.; Ecological Systems, Closed   WD
    756, etc.; names of specific types of control, e.g.,
    Ventilation   WA 770, etc.
Environment Design   TA 170
  Government policy
    General   HC 79.E5
    By country   HC 94–1085
  See also City Planning   HT 165.5–169.9, etc.;
    Environment, Controlled   WA 670–847, etc.
Environmental Air Pollutants see Air Pollutants,
  Environmental
Environmental Exposure   QT 140–162
  In workplace   WA 400–495
  To air pollution (General)   WA 754
  To radiation   WN 415–650
  To other specific conditions, by subject
Environmental Factors see Environmental Exposure;
  Meteorological Factors; Socioeconomic Factors;
  names of physical agents, e.g., Heat
Environmental Health   WA 30
  Diseases of geographic areas   WB 710
  Psychiatric aspects   WM 31
  See also Environment, Controlled   WA 671, etc.
Environmental Microbiology   QW 55
Environmental Monitoring   QH 541.15.M64
  In occupational health   WA 400–495
  Of environmental pollutants   WA 671
  Of air pollutants   WA 754
  Of water pollutants   WA 689
  Of radioactive pollutants   WN 615
  Of other specific conditions, by subject
Environmental Pollutants   WA 671
Environmental Pollution   WA 670
  See also specific types of pollution; e.g., Water
  Pollution   WA 689
Environmental Pollution, Tobacco Smoke see
  Tobacco Smoke Pollution
Enzymatic Zonulolysis   WW 260
Enzyme Activation   QU 135
Enzyme Immunoassay see Immunoenzyme
  Techniques
Enzyme Induction   QU 135
Enzyme Inhibitors   QU 143
Enzyme-Labeled Antibody Technique see
  Immunoenzyme Techniques
Enzyme-Linked Immunosorbent Assay   QW
  525.5.E6
  Used for diagnostic, monitoring, or evaluation
  tests in special fields, with the field
Enzyme Precursors   QU 142
Enzyme Reactivators   QU 144
Enzyme Repression   QU 135
Enzyme Tests   QY 490

Enzymes   QU 135–141
  Blood chemistry   QY 490
Enzymes, Immobilized   QU 135–141
Enzymologic Gene Expression Regulation see Gene
  Expression Regulation, Enzymologic
Enzymology see Enzymes
EOG see Electrooculography
Eosinophilia   WH 200
Eosinophilic Granuloma   WH 650
  Localized, by site
Eosinophils   WH 200
Ependyma   WL 307
EPH Gestosis see Gestosis, EPH
Ephedrine   QV 129
Ephemeral Fever   SF 967.T47
Epidemic Non-A, Non-B Hepatitis see Hepatitis E
Epidemics see Disease Outbreaks
Epidemiologic Determinants see Epidemiologic
  Factors
Epidemiologic Factors
  In a particular subject, with the subject
Epidemiologic Methods   WA 950
Epidemiological Monitoring see Environmental
  Monitoring
Epidemiology   WA 105–106
  Statistics   WA 900
    See also Epidemiologic Methods   WA 950
  Of particular disorders with the disorder
  (Form number 16 in any NLM schedule where
  applicable)
Epidermal Cyst   WR 420
Epidermal Growth Factor see Epidermal Growth
  Factor-Urogastrone
Epidermal Growth Factor Receptors see Receptors,
  Epidermal Growth Factor-Urogastrone
Epidermal Growth Factor-Urogastrone   WK 170
  As a growth substance   QU 107
  As an antacid   QV 69
Epidermal Necrolysis, Toxic   WR 165
Epidermis   WR 101
Epidermoid Cyst see Epidermal Cyst
Epidermolysis Bullosa   WR 200
Epidermophytosis see Tinea
Epidermotoxins see Dermotoxins
Epididymis   WJ 800
Epidural Analgesia see Analgesia, Epidural
Epidural Anesthesia see Anesthesia, Epidural
Epidural Space   WE 725
Epiglottis   WV 500
Epilation see Hair Removal
Epilepsy   WL 385
  Experimental see Convulsions   WL 385, etc.
Epilepsy, Abdominal see Epilepsy, Temporal Lobe
Epilepsy, Absence   WL 385
Epilepsy, Cryptogenic see Epilepsy
Epilepsy, Focal see Epilepsy, Partial
Epilepsy, Generalized Secondary see Epilepsy,
  Partial
Epilepsy, Grand Mal see Epilepsy, Tonic-Clonic
Epilepsy, Localization-Related see Epilepsy, Partial
Epilepsy, Myoclonic   WL 385
Epilepsy, Myoclonus see Epilepsy, Myoclonic
Epilepsy, Partial   WL 385

Epilepsy, Petit Mal see Epilepsy, Absence
Epilepsy, Post-Traumatic   WL 385
Epilepsy, Simple Partial see Epilepsy, Partial
Epilepsy, Temporal Lobe   WL 385
Epilepsy, Tonic-Clonic   WL 385
Epilepsy, Traumatic see Epilepsy, Post-Traumatic
Epilepsy, Uncinate see Epilepsy, Temporal Lobe
Epinephrine   WK 725
Epiphyseal Cartilage see Growth Plate
Epiphyseal Plate see Growth Plate
Epiphyses   WE 200
Epiphyses, Slipped   WE 175
Epiphyses, Stippled see Chondrodysplasia Punctata
Epiphysiolysis see Epiphyses, Slipped
Epiphysis Cerebri see Pineal Body
Episiotomy   WQ 415
Episomes see Plasmids
Epispadias   WJ 600
Epistaxis   WV 320
Epistropheus see Axis
Epithalamus see Diencephalon
Epithelial Attachment   WU 240
Epithelioma see Carcinoma
Epithelium
    Dermatology   WR 101
    Histology   QS 532.5.E7
    Neoplasms   QZ 365
Epithelium, Anterior Chamber see Endothelium, Corneal
Epithelium, Retinal Pigment see Pigment Epithelium of Eye
Epitopes see Antigenic Determinants
Eponyms
    Disease (General)   WB 15
    In specialties (Form number 15 in NLM schedule or in appropriate LC number)
Epoprostenol   QV 180
    Biochemistry   QU 90
Epoxides see Epoxy Compounds
Epoxy Compounds
    Organic chemistry   QD 305.E7
Epoxy Resins
    Chemical technology   TP 1180.E6
    Dentistry   WU 190
    Used for special purposes, by subject
Epoxytrichothecenes see Trichothecenes
Epsom Salts see Magnesium Sulphate
Epstein-Barr Virus see Herpesvirus 4, Human
Epstein-Barr Virus Syndrome, Chronic see Fatigue Syndrome, Chronic
Epulis, Giant Cell see Granuloma, Giant Cell
Equilibrium   WV 255
    See also Acid-Base Equilibrium   QU 105; Water-Electrolyte Balance   QU 105
Equine Infectious Anemia   SF 959.A6
Equipment Alarm Systems see Equipment Failure
Equipment and Supplies
    Anesthetic   WO 240
    Catalogs (medical and surgical)   W 26
    Dental see Dental Equipment   WU 26; Dental High Speed Equipment   WU 26; Dental Instruments   WU 26
    Disposable see Disposable Equipment   W 26

    Immunology   QW 526
    Orthopedic see Orthopedic Equipment   WE 26
    Pharmaceutical   QV 26; QV 785-835
        Military   UH 420-425
    Radiological   WN 150
    Surgical see Surgical Equipment   WO 162, etc.
    (Form number 26 in any NLM schedule where applicable)
    See also particular types of equipment or supplies
Equipment and Supplies, Hospital   WX 147
    See also particular items, e.g., Beds   WX 147, etc.
Equipment Contamination
    Of particular equipment, with the equipment
    See also Equipment and Supplies
Equipment Design
    Of a specific equipment, with the equipment
Equipment Failure
    of a specific equipment, with the equipment
Equipment Safety
    Of a specific equipment, with the equipment
Equivalency, Therapeutic see Therapeutic Equivalency
ERCP see Cholangiopancreatography, Endoscopic Retrograde
Eremothecium see Endomycetales
Ergastoplasm see Endoplasmic Reticulum
Ergobasin see Ergonovine
Ergocalciferols   QU 173
Ergolines
    Pharmacology   QV 174
Ergometrin see Ergonovine
Ergometrine see Ergonovine
Ergonomics see Human Engineering
Ergonovine   QV 173
Ergot Alkaloids   QV 174
Ergot Poisoning see Ergotism
Ergotamine   QV 174
Ergotamine Derivatives   QV 174
Ergotamine Tartrate see Ergotamine
Ergotism   WD 505
Ergotoxine   QV 174
Erosion, Cervix see Cervix Erosion
Erotica   HQ 450-472
Erucic Acids   QU 90
Eructation   WI 143
Eruption, Skin see Exanthema; Exanthema Subitum
Erysipelas   WC 234
Erysipeloid   WC 234
Erysipelothrix Infections
    Swine   SF 977.E7
Erythema   WR 150
    Migrans see Glossitis, Benign Migratory   WI 210
Erythema Multiforme   WR 150
Erythema Nodosum   WR 150
Erythermalgia see Erythromelalgia
Erythremia see Polycythemia Vera
Erythrina   QV 140
Erythroblastic Anemia see Thalassemia
Erythroblastosis, Fetal   WH 425
Erythroblasts   WH 150

ALWAYS CONSULT MAIN SCHEDULES. USE NUMBER ASSIGNED ONLY WHEN SUBJECT REPRESENTS MAJOR EMPHASIS OF WORK BEING CLASSIFIED

Erythrocebus patas   QL 737.P93
   Diseases   SF 997.5.P7
      As laboratory animals   QY 60.P7
Erythrocyte Aggregation, Intravascular   WH 150
Erythrocyte Aging   WH 150
Erythrocyte Anion Transport Protein see Band 3
   Protein
Erythrocyte Aplasia see Red-Cell Aplasia, Pure
Erythrocyte Burst-Promoting Factor see
   Interleukin-3
Erythrocyte Count   QY 402
Erythrocyte Ghost see Erythrocyte Membrane
Erythrocyte Membrane   WH 150
Erythrocyte Membrane Band 3 Protein see Band 3
   Protein
Erythrocyte Number see Erythrocyte Count
Erythrocyte Sedimentation see Blood Sedimentation
Erythrocyte Sialoglycoprotein see Glycophorin
Erythrocyte Substitutes see Blood Substitutes
Erythrocyte Survival see Erythrocyte Aging
Erythrocyte Transfusion   WB 356
Erythrocyte Volume   WG 106
Erythrocyte Volume, Packed see Hematocrit
Erythrocytes   WH 150-180
   Clinical examination   QY 402
Erythrocytes, Abnormal   WH 150
Erythrocythemia see Polycythemia; Polycythemia
   Vera
Erythrocytosis see Polycythemia
Erythroderma see Dermatitis, Exfoliative
Erythroderma, Maculopapular see Parapsoriasis
Erythromelalgia   WG 578
Erythromycin   QV 350.5.E7
Erythropoiesis   WH 150
Erythropoietin   WH 150
   Special topics, by subject
Erythroxylon see Coca
Escape Reaction   BF 319.5.A9
Escharotics see Caustics
Escherichia coli   QW 138.5.E8
Escherichia coli Infections   WC 290
   Veterinary   SF 809.E82
      In swine   SF 977.E83
Escherichia coli Phages see Coliphages
Eserine see Physostigmine
Eskimos   E99.E7
   See also special topics under Ethnic Groups
Esophageal Achalasia   WI 250
Esophageal and Gastric Varices   WI 720
Esophageal Atresia   WI 250
Esophageal Diseases   WI 250
Esophageal Diverticulum   WI 250
Esophageal Dysmotility see Esophageal Motility
   Disorders
Esophageal Fistula   WI 250
Esophageal Motility Disorders   WI 250
Esophageal Neoplasms   WI 250
Esophageal Reflux see Gastroesophageal Reflux
Esophageal Stenosis   WI 250
Esophageal Stricture see Esophageal Stenosis
Esophageal Varices see Esophageal and Gastric
   Varices
Esophagitis   WI 250
Esophagogastroduodenoscopy see Endoscopy,

Digestive System
Esophagoplasty   WI 250
Esophagotracheal Fistula see Tracheoesophageal
   Fistula
Esophagus   WI 250
Esophagus, Barrett see Barrett Esophagus
Esotropia   WW 415
Esox see Salmonidae
ESRD see Kidney Failure, Chronic
Essays see Form number 9 in any NLM schedule
   where applicable
Essences see Solutions
Essential Amino Acids see Amino Acids, Essential
Essential Oils see Oils, Volatile
Essential Polyarteritis see Polyarteritis Nodosa
Esterases   QU 136
Esthetic Surgery see Surgery, Plastic
Esthetics   BH
   Plastic surgery   WO 600
   Transplantation   WO 660
   Women   HQ 1219-1220
Esthetics, Dental   WU 100
   Special methods, by subject, e.g. Orthodontics
      WU 400-440
Estradiol   WP 522
Estradiol-17 beta see Estradiol
Estramustine   QV 269
Estramustinphosphate see Estramustine
Estriol   WP 522
Estrogen Analogs see Estrogens, Synthetic
Estrogen Antagonists   WP 522
Estrogen Receptors see Receptors, Estrogen
Estrogen Replacement Therapy   WP 522
Estrogenic Substances, Conjugated see Estrogens,
   Conjugated
Estrogens   WP 522
Estrogens, Catechol   WP 522
Estrogens, Conjugated   WP 522
Estrogens, Synthetic   WP 522
   Used for special purposes, by subject
Estrone   WP 522
Estrous Cycle see Estrus
Estrus   SF 105
ESWL (Extracorporeal Shockwave Lithotripsy) see
   Lithotripsy
Etching, Dental see Acid Etching, Dental
Ethambutol   QV 268
Ethanol see Alcohol, Ethyl
Ethanolamine Phosphoglycerides see
   Phosphatidylethanolamines
Ethanolamines   QV 84
   Organic chemistry   QD 305.A4
Ether, Ethyl   QV 81
Ethers
   As anesthetics   QV 81
   Organic chemistry
      Aliphatic compounds   QD 305.E7
      Aromatic compounds   QD 341.E7
   Spectra   QC 463.E7
   Used for special purposes, by subject
Ethers, Cyclic
   Organic chemistry   QD 305.E7
   Used for special purposes, by subject

Ethics   BJ
    General works   BJ 991–1185
    Special applications, by subject
Ethics, Dental   WU 50
Ethics in Publishing see Scientific Misconduct
Ethics, Institutional
    Special topics, by subject, e.g., in hospitals   WX 150
Ethics, Medical   W 50
    In psychiatry   WM 62
Ethics, Nursing   WY 85
Ethics, Pharmacy   QV 21
Ethics, Professional   BJ 1725
    Of special groups, by name of group
Ethinyl Estradiol   WP 522
    As a contraceptive   QV 177
Ethinyl Estradiol 3–Methyl Ether see Mestranol
Ethinyl Trichloride see Trichloroethylene
Ethinylestrenol see Lynestrenol
Ethinylnortestosterone see Norethindrone
Ethiofos see Amifostine
Ethionamide   QV 268
Ethioniamide see Ethionamide
Ethmoid Bone   WE 705
Ethmoid Sinus   WV 355
Ethnic Groups
    Anthropology   GN 301–673
    Diseases   WB 720
    Education   LC 3701–3747
    General works   DA 125, E 184–185, F 1035, etc.
    Health surveys   WA 300
    Medical biography   WZ 150
    Medical history   WZ 80
    Mental ability assessment   BF 432
    Nutrition surveys   QU 146
    Psychology   GN 270–279
    Public health (including mental health)   WA 300–305
    Other special topics, by subject
    See also names of specific groups
Ethnography see Anthropology, Cultural
Ethnology   GN 307–673
    See also Anthropology, Cultural   GN 307–673
Ethnomedicine see Medicine, Traditional
Ethnopsychology   GN 270–279
Ethoform see Benzocaine
Ethology   QL 750–785.3
    Veterinary sciences   SF 756.7
Ethoxy Compounds see Ethyl Ethers
Ethyl Alcohol see Alcohol, Ethyl
Ethyl Aminobenzoate see Benzocaine
Ethyl Carbamate see Urethane
Ethyl Chloride   QV 81
Ethyl Ether see Ether, Ethyl
Ethyl Ethers   QV 81
    Organic chemistry   QD 305.E7
Ethyl Methanesulfonate
    As an antineoplastic agent   QV 269
Ethylamines   QU 61
    Organic chemistry   QD 305.A8
Ethylbarbital see Barbital
Ethyldithiourame see Disulfiram

Ethylene Chlorohydrin   QV 82
Ethylene Dibromide   QV 633
    Public health aspects   WA 240
Ethylene Dichlorides
    Toxicology   QV 633
Ethylene Oxide
    As a fungicide   SB 951.3
    Organic chemistry   QD 305.E7
Ethylene Polymers see Polyethylenes
Ethylenediaminetetraacetic Acid see Edetic Acid
Ethyleneimines see Aziridines
Ethylenes   QV 81
    Organic chemistry   QD 305.H7
Ethylenethiourea
    As a carcinogen   QZ 202
    Biochemistry   QU 65
Ethylestrenolone see Norethandrolone
Ethylnortestosterone see Norethandrolone
Ethynyl Estradiol see Ethinyl Estradiol
Etiology see Pathogenesis   QZ 40–109 under Disease; names of particular diseases
Etoposide   QV 269
Etretinate   QU 167
    Used in treating a particular skin disease, with the disease
Etryptamine see Indoles
Etymology see Dictionaries; Nomenclature
Eubacterium   QW 120
Eugenics   HQ 750–755.5
Euglena   QX 50
Euglobulins see Serum Globulins
Eukaryotic Cells   QH 581–581.2
Eunuchism   WJ 840
Euoticus see Galago
Euphausia see Crustacea
Euphoria   BF 575.E5
    In adolescence   WS 462
    In infancy & childhood   WS 105.5.E5
Europium
    Inorganic chemistry   QD 181.E8
    Pharmacology   QV 290
Eustachian Tube   WV 230
Eutamias see Sciuridae
Eutelegenesis see Insemination, Artificial
Euthanasia   W 50
Euthanasia, Passive   W 50
Evaluation, Program see Program Evaluation
Evaluation Research, Nursing see Nursing Evaluation Research
Evaluation Studies
    Health services   W 84
    Other special topics, by subject being evaluated
Evaluation Studies, Drug see Drug Evaluation
Evaluation Studies, Drug, Pre–Clinical see Drug Screening
Evaluation Studies, Postmarketing see Product Surveillance, Postmarketing
Evidential Material see Forensic Medicine
Evoked Potentials   WL 102
Evoked Potentials, Auditory   WV 270
Evoked Potentials, Auditory, Brain Stem   WV 270
Evoked Potentials, Somatosensory   WL 102
Evoked Potentials, Visual   WW 103

ALWAYS CONSULT MAIN SCHEDULES. USE NUMBER ASSIGNED ONLY WHEN
SUBJECT REPRESENTS MAJOR EMPHASIS OF WORK BEING CLASSIFIED

Evoked Response Audiometry see Audiometry,
Evoked Response
Evoked Responses, Auditory, Brain Stem see
Evoked Potentials, Auditory, Brain Stem
Evolution   QH 359-425
Darwin's works   QH 365
General works   QH 366-366.2
Periodicals, numbered congresses, serial
collections, yearbooks, in appropriate NLM
numbers
Single organs with the organ
See also Ontogeny   QH 359-425, etc.;
Phylogeny   QH 367.5
Ewing's Tumor see Sarcoma, Ewing's
Examination see Diagnosis; names of specific types
of examination, e.g., Neurologic Examination
Examination questions
(Form number 18.2 in any NLM schedule where
applicable)
Exanthema   WR 220
Veterinary   SF 901
Exanthema Subitum   WC 570
Exchange Transfusion, Whole Blood   WB 356
RH factor   WH 425
Excipients   QV 800
Excitotoxins see Neurotoxins
Excretion of Drugs see Metabolism   QV 38 under
Drugs
Exercise
Movement   WE 103
Physical education   QT 255
Sports   QT 260
Exercise, Aerobic see Exercise
Exercise-Induced Asthma see Asthma,
Exercise-Induced
Exercise-Induced Bronchospasm see Asthma,
Exercise-Induced
Exercise, Isometric see Exercise
Exercise, Physical see Exercise
Exercise Test   WG 141.5.F9
Exercise Therapy   WB 541
In water see Hydrotherapy   WB 520
Exertion
Movement   WE 103
Physical education   QT 255
Sports   QT 260
Exfoliative dermatitis see Dermatitis Exfoliativa
Exhaustion see Fatigue; Heat exhaustion;
Neurasthenia
Exhibitionism   WM 610
Exhibits   T 391-999
(Form numbers 27-28 in any NLM schedule
where applicable)
Existential Psychology see Existentialism
Existentialism
Philosophy
General   B 105.E8
Modern   B 819
Psychoanalysis   WM 460.5.E8
Psychology   BF 204.5
Exocrine Glands   QT 172
Skin glands   WR 101
Specific glands, with system where located, e.g.

Sebaceous glands   WR 410
Exodontia see Tooth Extraction
Exodontics see Tooth Extraction
Exomphalos see Hernia, Umbilical
Exophthalmic Goiter see Graves' Disease
Exophthalmos   WW 210
See also Goiter, Exophthalmic   WK 265
Exostoses   WE 250
Localized, by site
Exostoses, Familial see Exostoses, Multiple
Hereditary
Exostoses, Hereditary Multiple see Exostoses,
Multiple Hereditary
Exostoses, Multiple see Exostoses, Multiple
Hereditary
Exostoses, Multiple Cartilaginous see Exostoses,
Multiple Hereditary
Exostoses, Multiple Hereditary   WE 250
Exotoxins   QW 630
Expectation (Psychology)   BF 323.E8
Expectorants   QV 76
Expeditions
Medical   W 10
Scientific expeditions   Q 115-116
Expenditures, Health see Health Expenditures
Experimental Design see Research Design
Experimental Psychology see Psychology,
Experimental
Experimental works in specialties other than
psychology see Under the specialty
Expert Systems   QA 76.76.E95
In medicine (General)   W 26.55.A7
In other special fields (Form number 26.5 in any
NLM schedule where applicable)
Expert Testimony
Chemistry   W 750
Dentistry   W 705
Medicine   W 725
Psychiatry   W 740
Special topics, by subject
Expiratory Forced Flow Rates see Forced
Expiratory Flow Rates
Expiratory Peak Flow Rate see Peak Expiratory
Flow Rate
Exploratory Behavior   BF 323.C8
Children   WS 105.5.M5
Exploratory Surgery see Diagnosis, Surgical
Explosions
Hospital emergency service   WX 215
In industry   WA 485
Mining   WA 485
Nuclear explosions   WN 610
Nursing in emergency situations   WY 154
Prevention & control   WA 288
In industry   WA 485
Thermochemistry   QD 516
Explosive Decompression see Atmospheric Pressure
Exposure (Radiology) see Environmental Exposure;
conditions under which exposure takes place, e.g.,
Radiotherapy
Expression, Pharmacy see Drug Compounding
Extended Care Facilities see Skilled Nursing
Facilities

**ALWAYS CONSULT MAIN SCHEDULES. USE NUMBER ASSIGNED ONLY WHEN
SUBJECT REPRESENTS MAJOR EMPHASIS OF WORK BEING CLASSIFIED**

External Degree Programs, Nursing see Education,
Nursing, Baccalaureate
External Ear see Ear, External
External Influences on Child see Child Development;
Television; related topics
Extinction (Psychology)   BF 319.5.E9
Extracellular Fluid see Extracellular Space
Extracellular Matrix   QH 603.E93
    Body fluids   QU 105
Extracellular Matrix Proteins   QU 55
Extracellular Space   QU 105
Extrachromosomal Inheritance   QW 51
Extracorporeal Circulation   WG 168
Extracorporeal Dialysis see Hemodialysis
Extracorporeal Shockwave Lithotripsy see
    Lithotripsy
Extracranial–Intracranial Arterial Bypass see
    Cerebral Revascularization
Extraction, Obstetrical   WQ 415
Extraction of Teeth see Tooth Extraction
Extracts see Dosage Forms; Liver Extracts;
    Pancreatic Extracts; Placental Extracts; Thymus
    Extracts; Tissue Extracts
Extramarital Relations   HQ 806
Extraordinary Treatment see Life Support Care
Extrapyramidal Disorders see Basal Ganglia Diseases
Extrapyramidal Tracts   WL 400
Extrasensory Perception see Parapsychology
Extrasystole   WG 330
Extraterrestrial Environment   WD 758
Extraversion (Psychology)
    Personality   BF 698.35.E98
    Psychoanalysis   WM 460.5.E9
Extremities   WE 800–890
    Blood supply   WG 500–700
        Specific extremities, with the part, e.g. Blood
        supply to the leg   WE 850
    Lower extremities   WE 850–890
    Upper extremities   WE 805–835
Extremities, Artificial see Artificial Limbs
Extremity, Lower see Leg
Extremity, Upper see Arm
Exudates and Transudates   QU 105
    Clinical examination   QY 210
Eye   WW
    Blood supply   WW 101–103
        See also names of particular arteries and veins,
        e.g., Ophthalmic Artery   WG 595.O7
    Conservation   WW 113
    Innervation   WW 101–103
        See also Optic Nerves   WW 280, etc.
    Pathology due to diseases of central nervous
    system   WW 460
    Pathological eye conditions in other diseases
    WW 475
    Posterior chamber   WW 210
    Surgery   WW 168
Eye Abnormalities   WW 101
Eye, Artificial   WW 358
Eye Banks   WW 23–24
    Procedures   WW 170
Eye Burns   WW 100
Eye Color   WW 101

Eye Conservation see Eye
Eye Diseases   WW
    Disability evaluation   WW 32
    General works   WW 140
    In infancy & childhood   WW 600
    In old age   WW 620
    Neurologic manifestation   WW 460
    Nursing   WY 158
    Surgery   WW 168
    Therapy   WW 166
    Veterinary   SF 891
Eye Diseases, Hereditary   WW 140
Eye Enucleation   WW 168
Eye Foreign Bodies   WW 525
Eye Hemorrhage   WW 140
Eye Infections, Parasitic   WW 160
Eye Injuries   WW 525
    Disability evaluation   WW 32
Eye Injuries, Penetrating   WW 525
Eye Manifestations   WW 475
    Ocular disorders due to neurological disorders
    WW 460
    Of particular diseases, with the disease
Eye Motility Disorders see Ocular Motility
    Disorders
Eye Movements   WW 400–460
    General works   WW 400
Eye Neoplasms   WW 149
    Of parts of the eye, with the part
Eye Protective Devices   WW 113
Eye Proteins   WW 101
Eyeball see Eye
Eyebrows   WW 205
Eyedrops see Ophthalmic Solutions
Eyeglasses   WW 350–354
Eyelashes   WW 205
Eyelid Diseases   WW 205
Eyelids   WW 205

F

F Factor   QW 51
F–2 Toxin see Zearalenone
Face   WE 705–707
Facial Bones   WE 705
    Maxillofacial injuries   WU 610
    Physiological works for the dentist   WU 102
Facial Dermatoses   WR 140
Facial Expression   BF 592.F33
    In infancy & childhood   WS 105.5.C8
    Physical examination   WB 275
    Physiology   WE 705
    See also Nonverbal Communication   HM 258,
    etc.; Physiognomy   BF 840–861
Facial Injuries   WE 706
Facial Muscles   WE 705
Facial Neoplasms   WE 707
Facial Nerve   WL 330
Facial Nerve Diseases   WL 330
Facial Neuralgia   WL 544
Facial Pain   WE 705
    In dentistry   WU 140
Facial Paralysis   WL 330

Facility Access see Architectural Accessibility

Facility Construction see Facility Design and Construction

Facility Design and Construction
    Health facilities   WX 140
        For the specialties (Form number 27–29 in any NLM schedule where applicable)
    Hospital departments   WX 200–225
    Public health aspects of houses and public buildings   WA 795–799
    See also Design and Construction, Hospital   WX 140, etc.

Facility Regulation and Control   WX 153
    See also names of particular types of facility, e.g., Rehabilitation Centers   WM 29, etc.

Facteur Thymique Serique see Thymic Factor, Circulating

Factor Analysis, Statistical   QA 278.5
    In psychology   BF 39.2.F32
    Used in diagnosis, in the diagnosis number for the disease or specialty or lacking that in the general works number
    Used in other studies, by subject

Factor Construct Rating Scales (FCRS) see Psychiatric Status Rating Scales

Factor I see Fibrinogen

Factor II see Prothrombin

Factor III see Thromboplastin

Factor IV see Calcium

Factor, RH see RH–HR Blood Group System

Factor VII   WH 310
    Clinical examination   QY 410

Factor VIII-Related Antigen see von Willebrand Factor

Factor XIII, Activated see Protein–Glutamine gamma–Glutamyltransferase

Factor XIII Transamidase see Protein–Glutamine gamma–Glutamyltransferase

Factor XIIIa see Protein–Glutamine gamma–Glutamyltransferase

Faculty
    (Form number 19 in any NLM schedule where applicable)
    Superintendents and principals   LB 2831.7–2831.99
    Teaching personnel   LB 2832–2844.47

Faculty, Medical
    General   W 19
    Graduate   W 20
    Undergraduate   W 19

Faculty, Nursing
    General   WY 19
    Graduate   WY 18.5
    Undergraduate   WY 19

Faculty, Pharmacy see Faculty

FAD   QU 135

Fads, Food see Diet Fads

Fagine see Choline

Failure, Equipment see Equipment Failure

Failure to Thrive   WS 104

Fainting see Syncope

Faith Cures see Mental Healing

Faith Healing see Mental Healing

Fallopian Tube Diseases   WP 300

Fallopian Tube Neoplasms   WP 300

Fallopian Tubes   WP 300
    Neoplasms   WP 300
    Pregnancy see Pregnancy, Tubal   WQ 220
    Sterilization see Sterilization, Tubal   WP 660

Fallot's Tetralogy see Tetralogy of Fallot

Falls, Accidental see Accidental Falls

Familial Atypical Multiple Mole-Melanoma see Dysplastic Nevus Syndrome

Familial Erythroblastic Anemia see Thalassemia

Familial Jaundice see Spherocytosis, Hereditary

Familial Mediterranean Fever see Periodic Disease

Family   HQ 503–1057
    Adjustment to mentally retarded child   WS 107.5.R5
    Health   WA 308
    Relations   WS 105.5.F2
    See also Father-Child Relations   WS 105.5.F2; Mother-Child Relations   WS 105.5.F2; Parent-Child Relations   WS 105.5.F2; Sibling Relations   WS 105.5.F2

Family Caregivers see Caregivers

Family Characteristics   HQ 503–743

Family Health   WA 308

Family Leave
    General works   HD 6065–6065.5

Family Life Cycles see Family

Family-Patient Lodging see Housing

Family Physicians see Physicians, Family

Family Planning   HQ 763.5–767.7

Family Practice
    As a profession   W 89
    Texts and treatises   WB 110

Family Relationship see Family

Family, Single-Parent see Single Parent

Family Size see Family Characteristics

Family Therapy   WM 430.5.F2

Famotidine
    As an anti-ulcer agent   QV 69

Famous Persons
    Biography
        Collective
            In the field of medicine and related sciences   WZ 112–150
            In other fields, by subject in LC schedules
        Individual   WZ 100
    Illnesses   WZ 313

Fanconi's Anemia   WH 175

Fangotherapy see Mud Therapy

Fantasy   BF 408–411
    In adolescence   WS 462
    In infancy & childhood   WS 105.5.C7
    Psychiatry   WM 193.5.S8

Far Eastern Russian Encephalitis see Encephalitis, Tick-Borne

Faradic Currents see Electric Conductivity; Electric Stimulation Therapy; Electricity

Farcy see Glanders

Farm Animals see Animals, Domestic

Farmer's Lung   WF 652
    Veterinary   SF 831

Farsightedness see Hyperopia

ALWAYS CONSULT MAIN SCHEDULES. USE NUMBER ASSIGNED ONLY WHEN SUBJECT REPRESENTS MAJOR EMPHASIS OF WORK BEING CLASSIFIED

Fascia   WE 500
   Localized, by site
Fascicular Block see Bundle–Branch Block
Fasciola   QX 365
Fascioliasis   WC 805
   Veterinary   SF 810.F3
Fasciolopsiasis see Trematode Infections
Fast Electrons see Electrons
Fast Neutrons
   Nuclear physics   QC 793.5.F32–793.5.F329
   In health physics   WN 110
Fasting   WB 420
Fat Emulsions, Intravenous   QU 86
   In parenteral feeding   WB 410
Father–Child Relations   WS 105.5.F2
Fathers
   Popular works   HQ 756–756.7
   Special topics, by subject
Fatigue
   Aviation   WD 735
   Occupational
      General   WA 475
      Mental   WA 495
      Physical   WA 475
   Nervous see Fatigue, Mental   WM 174, etc.
   Physical (General)   WB 146
Fatigue Fractures see Fractures, Stress
Fatigue, Mental see Mental Fatigue
Fatigue Syndrome, Chronic
   As a virus disease   WC 500
   Etiology unknown   WB 146
Fatigue Syndrome, Postviral see Fatigue Syndrome, Chronic
Fats   QU 86
   Public health aspects   WA 722
   See also Dietary Fats   WB 425, etc.
Fats, Unsaturated   QU 86
Fatty Acids   QU 90
Fatty Acids, Essential   QU 90
Fatty Acids, Free see Fatty Acids, Nonesterified
Fatty Acids, Monounsaturated   QU 90
Fatty Acids, Nonesterified   QU 90
Fatty Acids, Omega–3   QU 90
   As a supplement in health or disease   WB 425
Fatty Acids, Polyunsaturated see Fatty Acids, Unsaturated
Fatty Acids, Unsaturated   QU 90
Fatty Acids, Volatile   QU 90
Fatty Liver   WI 700
   In chickens   SF 995.6.F3
Fatty Liver, Alcoholic   WI 700
Fatty Streak, Arterial see Atherosclerosis
Fatty Tissue see Adipose Tissue
Fatty Tumor see Lipoma
Favism   WD 515
Favus see Tinea Favosa
Fc Receptors see Receptors, Fc
Fear   WM 178
   In adolescence   WS 462
   In aviation & space flight   WD 730; WD 754
   In infancy & childhood   WS 105.5.E5
   See also Phobic Disorders   WM 178
Febrifuges see Anti–Inflammatory Agents,

Non–Steroidal
Fecal Incontinence   WI 600
   See also Defecation   WI 600; Encopresis   WI 600
Feces   QY 160
   Analysis   QY 160
      Veterinary diagnosis   SF 772.7
Feces, Impacted   WI 460
Fecundity see Fertility
Federal Health Insurance Plans, United States see National Health Insurance, United States
Federal Regulations see Names of Legislation; in products or specialties being regulated, e.g., Drug and Narcotic Control
Fee, Capitation see Capitation Fee
Fee for Service, Medical see Fees, Medical
Fee Schedules
   Dental   WU 77
   Hospital   WX 157
   Medical   W 74
   Nursing   WY 77
   Pharmaceutical   QV 736
   For other services, by subject
Fee–Splitting
   Dental   WU 58
   Medical   W 58
   See also Fees, Dental   WU 77; Fees, Medical   W 80; Fees and Charges   W 74, etc.
Feeble–Mindedness see Mental Retardation
Feedback
   Electronics   TK 7871.58.F4
   Mechanical engineering   TJ 216
   Psychophysiology   WL 103
   See also Biofeedback (Psychology)   WL 103, etc.
Feedback, Psychophysiologic see Biofeedback (Psychology)
Feeding see Child Nutrition; Food Supply; Infant Nutrition
Feeding Behavior
   Customs   GT 2850–2960
   Disorders (Neurosis)   WM 175
Feeding Methods (Non Mesh) see Bottle Feeding; Breast Feeding; Parenteral Feeding; Tube Feeding
Feeding Patterns see Feeding Behavior
Feelings see Emotions
Fees and Charges   W 74
   Fee–splitting
      Dental   WU 58
      Medical   W 58
   Hospitals   WX 157
   Nursing   WY 77
   See also Economics, Medical   W 74 and economics in other specialties
Fees, Dental   WU 77
   Fee–splitting   WU 58
Fees, Medical   W 80
   Fee–splitting   W 58
Fees, Pharmaceutical   QV 736
Fees, Prescription see Prescription Fees
Feigned Diseases see Malingering
Feldshers see Physician Assistants
Feline Fibrosarcoma Virus see Sarcoma Virus,

Feline
Feline Sarcoma Virus see Sarcoma Virus, Feline
Fellowships and Scholarships
  Dental   WU 20
  Medical   W 20
  Nursing   WY 18.5
  Pharmacy   QV 20
Female Genitalia see Genitalia, Female
Femoral Artery   WG 595.F3
Femoral Fractures   WE 865
Femoral Head Prosthesis see Hip Prosthesis
Femoral Hernia see Hernia, Femoral
Femoral Neck Fractures   WE 865
Femoral Nerve   WL 400
Femoral Vein   WG 625.F3
Femur   WE 865
Femur Head   WE 865
Femur Neck   WE 865
Fenazoxine see Nefopam
Fendiline   QV 150
Fenestration   WV 265
  See also Otosclerosis   WV 265
Fenfluramine   QV 129
Fenformin see Phenformin
Fenilbutazon see Phenylbutazone
Fenitoin see Phenytoin
Fenoterol
Fentanyl   QV 89
Fermentation   QU 34
  Industrial   QW 75
  Of beverages   QW 85
Ferments see Enzymes
Ferredoxins
  In bacteriological chemistry   QW 52
  In photosynthesis   QK 882
  Other special topics, by subject
Ferrets   QL 737.C25
  As laboratory animals   QY 60.M2
  As pets   SF 459.F47
  Diseases   SF 997.3
Ferrihemoglobin see Methemoglobin
Ferriprotoporphyrin see Hemin
Ferritin   QV 183
Ferrocyanides
  Inorganic chemistry   QD 181.F4
  Pharmacology   QV 183
Ferroprotoporphyrin see Heme
Ferrous Compounds   QV 183
Ferroxidase see Ceruloplasmin
Fertility   WP 565
  Animals
    Domestic   SF 871
    Wild   QP 273
  Drugs affecting   QV 170
  Drug effects   WP 565
  Male   WJ 702
  Radiation effects   WN 620
Fertility Agents   QV 170
Fertility Factor see F Factor
Fertilization   WQ 205
  Animals
    Domestic   SF 871
    Wild   QP 273

  Biology (General)   QH 485
  Plants   QK 828
Fertilization, Delayed see Fertilization
Fertilization in Vitro   WQ 205
Fertilization, Polyspermic see Fertilization
Fertilized Ovum see Zygote
Fertilizers   S 631–667
Festivals see Holidays
Fetal Alcohol Syndrome   WQ 211
Fetal Anoxia   WQ 211
Fetal Circulation, Persistent see Persistent Fetal
  Circulation Syndrome
Fetal Death   WQ 225
  Veterinary   SF 887
Fetal Development   WQ 210.5
Fetal Diseases   WQ 211
Fetal Distress   WQ 211
Fetal Growth Retardation   WQ 211
Fetal Heart   WQ 210.5
Fetal Heart Rate see Heart Rate, Fetal
Fetal Hemoglobin   WQ 210.5
Fetal Maturity, Chronologic see Gestational Age
Fetal Maturity, Functional see Fetal Organ Maturity
Fetal Membranes
  Embryology   QS 645
  Neoplasms   QZ 310
  Obstetrics   WQ 210
  See also Chorion   WQ 210 etc.
Fetal Monitoring   WQ 209
Fetal Organ Maturity   WQ 210.5
Fetal Presentation see Labor Presentation
Fetal Presentation, Breech see Breech Presentation
Fetal Transfusion see Blood Transfusion, Intrauterine
Fetal Ultrasonography see Ultrasonography,
  Prenatal
Fetal Viability   WQ 210.5
Fetishism (Psychiatric)   WM 610
Fetoplacental Function Tests see Placental Function
  Tests
Fetoscopy   WQ 209
Fetotoxins see Teratogens
Fetuins see alpha Fetoproteins
Fetus   WQ 210–211
  Disproportion   WQ 310
  Effect of labor on   WS 405
  Embryology   QS 645
  Experimentation   W 20.5
  Manipulation   WQ 415
  Monitoring   WQ 209
  Presentation see Labor Presentation   WQ 307,
    etc.
  Version see Delivery   WQ 415, etc.
Fever   WB 152
  Drugs relieving see Analgesics,
    Anti-Inflammatory   QV 95
  Therapeutic use see Hyperthermia, Induced
    WB 469, etc.
Fever Blister Virus see Simplexvirus
Fever Therapy see Hyperthermia, Induced
Fiber Optics   QC 447.9–448.2
  In endoscopy   WB 141
    See also use in specific types of endoscopy
Fiberglass Casts see Casts, Surgical

Fibrillation see Atrial Fibrillation; Ventricular
   Fibrillation
Fibrin   WH 310
   Clinical examination   QY 410
Fibrinogen   WH 310
   Clinical examination   QY 410
Fibrinogen Deficiency see Afibrinogenemia
Fibrinokinase see Streptodornase and Streptokinase
Fibrinoligase see Protein–Glutamine
   gamma–Glutamyltransferase
Fibrinolysis   WH 310
Fibrinolytic Agents   QV 190
Fibrinolytic Therapy see Thrombolytic Therapy
Fibroblast Growth Factor   QU 107
Fibrocystic Disease of Breast   WP 840
Fibrocystic Disease of Pancreas see Cystic Fibrosis
Fibrocystic Mastopathy see Fibrocystic Disease of
   Breast
Fibroid see Fibroma; Leiomyoma
Fibroid Tumor see Leiomyoma
Fibroids, Uterine see Uterine Neoplasms
Fibroma   QZ 340
Fibroma, Shope see Tumor Virus Infections
Fibromatosis, Aggressive   QZ 340
   Localized, by site
Fibromyalgia   WE 544
Fibronectins   QU 55
Fibrosarcoma Virus, Feline see Sarcoma Virus,
   Feline
Fibrosis   QZ 150
   Localized, by site
Fibrosis, Bone Marrow see Myelofibrosis
Fibrosis, Liver see Liver Cirrhosis
Fibrositis see Fibromyalgia
Fibrous Dysplasia of Bone   WE 250
Fibula   WE 870
Fiedler's Disease see Weil's Disease
Field–Block Anesthesia see Anesthesia, Conduction
Field Dependence–Independence   BF 323.F45
Figural Aftereffect   WW 105
Filaria see Filarioidea
Filarial Elephantiasis see Elephantiasis, Filarial
Filariasis   WC 880
Filariasis, Lymphatic see Elephantiasis, Filarial
Filarioidea   QX 301
Filarioidea Infections see Filariasis
Fillings, Dental see Inlays; Dental Materials; specific
   types of material used
Film, Radiographic see X-Ray Film
Film–Screen Systems, X-Ray see X-Ray
   Intensifying Screens
Film, X-Ray see X-Ray Film
Films see Motion Pictures
Filth, Epidemic Factor see Communicable Disease
   Control; Environmental Health
Filtration   QD 63.F5
Finances see Economics; headings beginning with
   Fee or Fees, etc.
Financial Audit
   Dental administration   WU 77
   Hospital administration   WX 157
   Medical administration   W 80
   Nursing administration   WY 77

   Pharmacy administration   QV 736
   In other specific fields, by subject
Financial Management
   Dentistry   WU 77
   Medicine   W 80
   Nursing   WY 77
   Pharmacy   QV 736
Financial Management, Hospital   WX 157
Financing, Capital see Capital Financing
Financing, Construction   WX 157
Financing, Government   HJ
   Education (Form number 18 in any NLM
     schedule where applicable)
   Health insurance   W 275, etc.
   Hospitals   WX 157
   Public health organizations   WA 540
   Other special topics, by subject
Financing, Organized
   Fund raising   HG 177
     Hospitals   WX 157
   Medical research (Form number 20 in any
     schedule where applicable)
   Voluntary health agencies (Form number 1 in
     any NLM schedule where applicable)
   See also Insurance, Health   W 100–275, etc. and
     names of other types of insurance
Financing, Personal   HG 179–195
   Medical costs   W 74
   Physicians' income   W 79
   See also Fees and charges   W 74, etc.; Insurance,
     Health   W 100–275; names of other types of
     insurance
Financing, Public see Financing, Government
Finger Injuries   WE 835
Finger Joint   WE 835
Fingernails see Nails
Fingerprints see Dermatoglyphics
Fingerprints, DNA see DNA Fingerprinting
Fingers   WE 835
   Abnormalities   WE 835
Fingersucking   WS 350.6
   Malocclusion etiology   WU 440
Fire Retardants see Flame Retardants
Fireflies see Beetles
Fireproofing Agents see Flame Retardants
Fires
   Accidents in firefighting   WA 487.5.F4
   Prevention   WA 250
     In hospitals   WX 185
Firesetting Behavior   WM 190
First Aid   WA 292
   Military   UH 396
   Naval   VG 466
   Veterinary   SF 778
Fischer Rats see Rats, Inbred F344
Fish Diseases   SH 171–179
   Aquarium fish diseases   SF 458.5
Fish Liver Oils see Fish Oils
Fish Oils   QU 86
   As a source of vitamins A and D   QU 165
Fish Poisoning see Fishes, Poisonous
Fish Products
   As a dietary supplement in health or disease

WB 426
Preservation   WA 710
Sanitation   WA 703
Supply   WA 703
Fish Skin Disease see Ichthyosis
Fish Venoms   WD 405
Fisheries   SH 201–399
Public health aspects   WA 703
Fishes   QL 614–639.8
Aquaculture   SH
As a dietary supplement see Fish Products   WB 426, etc.
As laboratory animals   QY 60.F4
Fishes, Poisonous   WD 405
Fission Yeast see Schizosaccharomyces
Fissure in Ano   WI 605
Fissure Sealants see Pit and Fissure Sealants
Fistula
Anal see Rectal Fistula   WI 605
Arteriovenous see Arteriovenous Fistula   WG 590
Biliary see Biliary Fistula   WI 750
Bladder see Bladder Fistula   WJ 500
Bronchial see Bronchial Fistula   WF 500
Esophagotracheal see Tracheoesophageal Fistula   WI 250
Esophagus see Esophageal Fistula   WI 250
Gastric see Gastric Fistula   WI 300
Genital see Rectovaginal Fistula   WP 180; Vaginal Fistula   WP 250; Vesicovaginal Fistula   WP 180
Intestinal see Intestinal Fistula   WI 400
Pancreatic see Pancreatic Fistula   WI 800
Rectal see Rectal Fistula   WI 605
Salivary see Salivary Gland Fistula   WI 230
Tracheoesophageal see Tracheoesophageal Fistula   WI 250
Urinary see Urinary Fistula   WJ 140
Fixation, Ocular   WW 400
Fixed Action Pattern see Instinct
Fixed Bridge see Denture, Partial, Fixed
Fixed Partial Denture see Denture, Partial, Fixed
Flagella   QW 51
Flagellata see Mastigophora
Flame Retardants
General   WA 250
In hospitals   WX 185
Flaps see Surgical Flaps
Flatfoot   WE 886
Flatulence   WI 150
Flatus see Flatulence
Flatworms see Platyhelminths
Flavin-Adenine Dinucleotide see FAD
Flavin Mononucleotide see FMN
Flavins   QU 110
Flavivirus   QW 168.5.A7
Flavoring Agents   WA 712
For drugs   QV 810
See also Food Additives   WA 712
Fleas   QX 550
Fletcher Factor see Prekallikrein
Flicker Fusion   WW 105
Flies see Diptera

Flies, True see Diptera
Flight, Animal
Birds   QL 698.7
General   QP 310.F5
Flight Reaction see Escape Reaction
Flocculation Tests   QY 265
Flood Fever see Scrub Typhus
Flooding see Implosive Therapy
Floods see Natural Disasters
Floor of Mouth see Mouth Floor
Floppy Mitral Valve see Mitral Valve Prolapse
Florafur see Tegafur
Flour
As a dietary supplement in health or disease   WB 431
Sanitary control   WA 695–701
Flow Cytometry   QH 585.5.F56
Clinical pathology   QY 95
Flow Microfluorimetry see Flow Cytometry
Flow, Pulsating see Pulsatile Flow
Flowmeters
Measuring blood flow velocity   WG 106
Measuring fluids   TJ 935
Measuring gases   TJ 1025
Measuring water   TC 177
Flowmetry see Rheology
Floxuridine   QV 268.5
Flubenisolone see Betamethasone
Flufenazin see Fluphenazine
Fluid Balance see Water-Electrolyte Balance
Fluid Therapy   WD 220
Flukes see Trematoda
Flumazenil   QV 77.9
Flumazepil see Flumazenil
Flunarizine   QV 150
Fluocortolone
As dermatologic agent   QV 60
Fluocortolone Caproate see Fluocortolone
Fluocortolone Pivalate see Fluocortolone
Fluoren-2-ylacetamide see 2-Acetylaminofluorene
Fluorenes   QZ 202
Fluorescein Angiography   WG 500
Ocular diagnosis   WW 141
Fluoresceins   QV 240
Fluorescence
Physics   QC 477–477.4
Qualitative and quantitative analysis (Fluorimetry)   QD 79.F4
Quantitative analysis   QD 117.F5
Special topics, by subject, e.g., in urinalysis   QY 185
Fluorescence-Activated Cell Sorting see Flow Cytometry
Fluorescence Angiography see Fluorescein Angiography
Fluorescence Microscopy see Microscopy, Fluorescence
Fluorescent Antibody Technique   QW 525.5.F6
In clinical pathology   QY 250
Used for special purposes, by subject
Fluorescent Antinuclear Antibodies see Antibodies, Antinuclear
Fluorescent Antinuclear Antibody Test see

**ALWAYS CONSULT MAIN SCHEDULES. USE NUMBER ASSIGNED ONLY WHEN
SUBJECT REPRESENTS MAJOR EMPHASIS OF WORK BEING CLASSIFIED**

Fluorescent Antibody Technique
Fluorescent Dyes   QV 240
Fluorescent Probes see Fluorescent Dyes
Fluorescent Protein Tracing see Fluorescent
    Antibody Technique
Fluoridation   WU 270
Fluoride Poisoning   QV 282
    Dentistry   WU 270
    Veterinary   SF 757.5
Fluoride Varnishes see Fluorides, Topical
Fluorides   QV 282
Fluorides, Topical   QV 282
    Dental pharmacology   QV 50
Fluorimetry see Fluorometry
Fluorinated Hydrocarbons see Hydrocarbons,
    Fluorinated
Fluorine   QV 282
    Metabolism   QU 130.5
    Toxicity in animals   SF 757.5
Fluormethyldehydrocorticosterone see
    Fluocortolone
Fluorochromes see Fluorescent Dyes
Fluorodeoxyuridine see Floxuridine
Fluorofur see Tegafur
Fluoroimmunoassay   QW 525.5.F6
    In clinical pathology   QY 250
    Used for special purposes, by subject
Fluorometry
    Analytical chemistry (General)   QD 79.F4
    Laboratory diagnosis   QY 25
    Quantitative analysis   QD 117.F5
    Used for particular purposes, by subject
Fluorophotometry   WW 143
Fluoroscopy   WN 220
    Used for diagnosis of particular disorders, with
        the disorder or system
Fluorosis see Mottled Enamel
Fluorosis, Dental see Mottled Enamel
Fluorouracil   QV 269
Fluostigmine see Isoflurophate
Fluoxetine   QV 126
    Biochemistry   QU 61
Fluphenazine   QV 77.9
Flurazepam   QV 77.9
Flurbiprofen   QV 95
    Biochemistry   QU 98
Flutter, Auricular see Auricular Flutter
FMN   QU 135
Focal Epilepsy see Epilepsy, Focal
Focal Infection   WC 230
Focal Infection, Dental   WU 290
Fogarty Balloon Catheterization see Balloon
    Dilatation
Folate Polyglutamates see Pteroylpolyglutamic
    Acids
Foley Balloon Catheterization see Balloon Dilatation
Folic Acid   QU 188
Folic Acid Deficiency   WD 120
Folic Acid Reductase see Tetrahydrofolate
    Dehydrogenase
Folie a Deux see Shared Paranoid Disorder
Folinic Acid see Leucovorin
Folk Medicine see Medicine, Traditional

Folklore   GR
    Curiosities   WZ 308
    Medical   WZ 309
    General works   GR 60–71
Follicle–Stimulating Hormone see FSH
Follicular Lymphoma see Lymphoma, Follicular
Folliculostatin see Inhibin
Follow–Up Studies
    (Form number 20 in any NLM schedule where
        applicable)
    In a particular area, with the subject of the
        original study, e.g., Heart Diseases   WG 210
Food
    Adulteration see Food Contamination   WA 701
    Allergy see Food Hypersensitivity   WD 310
    Assimilation   QU 120
    Chemical technology see Food Technology   TP
        368–465, etc.
    Chemistry   QU 50
    Deficiency diseases   WD 105–155
    Digestion   WI 102
    Fads see Diet Fads   WB 449
    For children   WS 115–130
    For infants see Infant Food   WS 115–125
    Fresh   WA 703
    Hospital service see Food Service, Hospital
        WX 168
    Laws see Legislation, Food   WA 697;
        subheading legislation under heading beginning
        with Food
    Nutritive value   QU 145.5
    Public health aspects   WA 695–722
    Therapeutic use see Diet Therapy   WB 400–449;
        names of specific foods
Food Additives   WA 712
Food Adulteration see Food Contamination
Food Allergy see Food Hypersensitivity
Food Analysis
    Bacteriology   QW 85
    Biochemistry   QU 50
    Home Economics   TX 501–597
    Nutrition   QU 145.5
    Sanitation   WA 695–722
    Analysis for specific nutritive agents   QU 50–98,
        etc.
Food, Artificial see Food, Formulated
Food–Borne Diseases see Communicable Diseases;
    Food Contamination; Food Poisoning
Food Browning see Maillard Reaction
Food, Canned see Food Preservation
Food Coloring Agents   WA 712
Food Contamination   WA 701
    Poisoning from see Food Poisoning   WC 268,
        etc.
Food Contamination, Radioactive   WN 612
Food Deprivation
    Experimental biochemistry   QU 34
    Experimental pharmacology   QV 34
    See also Hunger   QU 146, etc.
        Deficiency diseases   WD 105–155, etc.
Food, Dried see Food Preservation
Food, Drug and Cosmetic Act see Legislation, Drug
Food Fads see Diet Fads

ALWAYS CONSULT MAIN SCHEDULES. USE NUMBER ASSIGNED ONLY WHEN
SUBJECT REPRESENTS MAJOR EMPHASIS OF WORK BEING CLASSIFIED

Food, Formulated   WB 447
   Special types or for special purposes, by subject
Food, Fortified   QU 145.5
   Food processing (General)   TP 370
Food, Frozen see Frozen Foods
Food Habits   GT 2850–2960
Food Handling
   Restaurant sanitation   WA 799
   Sanitation   WA 695–722
   Technology   TP 368–684
Food Hypersensitivity   WD 310
Food, Infant see Infant Food
Food Inspection   WA 695
Food Intake Regulation see Appetite Regulation
Food, Irradiated see Food Irradiation
Food Irradiation   WA 710
Food Laws see Legislation, Food
Food Microbiology   QW 85
Food Parasitology   WA 701
Food Plants see Plants, Edible
Food Poisoning   WC 268
   Veterinary   SF 757.5
     See also Mushroom Poisoning   WD 520; Plant
     Poisoning   WD 500–530, etc.; Salmonella
     Food Poisoning   WC 268; Staphylococcal
     Food Poisoning   WC 268 and specific types
     of poisoning or poisoning agents
Food Preferences
   Health aspects   QT 235
   Institutional cooking   TX 820
Food Preservation   WA 710
Food Preservatives   WA 712
Food, Preserved see Food Preservation
Food Processing see Food Handling
Food–Processing Industry
   Chemical technology   TP 368–684
   Economic aspects   HD 9000–9440
   Occupational medicine   WA 400–495
   Industrial waste   WA 788
Food Selection see Food Preferences
Food Service, Hospital   WX 168
Food Services
   Public health aspects   WA 695–722
   Schools
     Elementary and Secondary   WA 350
     University and College   WA 351
   See also Dietary services   WX 168, etc.;
     Restaurants   WA 799
Food, Supplemented see Food, Fortified
Food Supply
   Home economics   TX 351–354.5
   Public health aspects   WA 695–722
Food Technology
   Chemical technology   TP 368–465
   Public health aspects   WA 695–722
   See also Meat   WA 707, etc.; names of other
     specific foods
Food Values see Nutritive value
Foot   WE 880–886
Foot–and–Mouth Disease   SF 793
Foot–and–Mouth Disease Virus see Aphthovirus
Foot Deformities   WE 883
Foot Deformities, Acquired   WE 883

Foot Deformities, Congenital   WE 883
Foot Dermatoses   WR 140
   See also Tinea pedis   WR 310
Foot Diseases   WE 880
   Veterinary (General)   SF 906
Foot Joint see Tarsal Joint
Foot Ulcer, Diabetic see Diabetic Foot
Football   QT 260.5.F6
Foramen of Monro see Cerebral Ventricles
Foramen Ovale, Patent see Heart Septal Defects,
   Atrial
Forced Expiratory Flow Rates   WF 102
   As a diagnostic test   WF 141
   General physical examination   WB 284
Forced Expiratory Flow 0.2–1.2 see Maximal
   Expiratory Flow Rate
Forced Expiratory Flow 200–1200 see Maximal
   Expiratory Flow Rate
Forceps Delivery see Methods   WQ 425 under
   Delivery; Obstetrical Forceps
Forearm   WE 820
Forearm Injuries   WE 820
Forebrain see Embryology   WL 300 under Brain
Forecasting   CB 158
   Agriculture   HD 1401–2210
   Business   HB 3730
   Civilization   CB 428–430
   Environment   HC 79.E5
   Health manpower   W 76
   Hospitals   WX 140
   Natural resources
     Conservation   S 900–954
     Economics   HC 55
     Land   HD 1635–1741; S 950–954
   Urban areas   HT 165.5–178
   Other special topics, by subject
Forefoot, Human   WE 880
Foreign Aid see International Cooperation
Foreign Bodies
   As a cause of disease   QZ 55
   In the ear   WV 222
   Localization by radiography   WN 210
   Removal   WO 700
   Localized, by site
   See also Bezoars   WI 300, etc.; Eye foreign
     bodies   WW 525
Foreign Medical Graduates
   Education   W 18–20
   Supply & distribution   W 76
Foreign Professional Personnel
   Health sciences (General)   W 76
   Science   Q 147–149
   See also Foreign Medical Graduates   W 76, etc.
Forelimb   QL 950.7
Forensic Chemistry see Chemistry
Forensic Dentistry   W 601–925
   General works   W 705
Forensic Examination of Blood see Blood Chemical
   Analysis
Forensic Medicine   W 601–925
   Directories   W 622
   Examination of evidential material   W 750
     Postmortem   W 825

Medical evidence for establishing responsibility
W 725
Medicolegal examination   W 775–867
Nineteenth century works   W 600
See also Jurisprudence   W 32.5–32.6
Forensic Psychiatry   W 740
As a career   W 740
Foreskin see Penis
Forestier–Certonciny Syndrome see Polymyalgia Rheumatica
Forests see Trees
Form Perception   WW 105
Formaldehyde
Organic chemistry   QD 305.A6
Pharmacology   QV 225
Formalin see Formaldehyde
Formalin Test see Pain Measurement
Formates   QU 98
Organic chemistry
Aliphatic compounds   QD 305.A2
Formicoidea Venoms see Ant Venoms
Forms and Records Control   W 80
Special field, by subject
Formularies   QV 740
Formularies, Dental   QV 50
Formularies, Homeopathic   WB 930
Formularies, Hospital   QV 740
Forskolin
Biochemistry   QU 85
Toxicology   QV 633
Fosfomycin   QV 350
Fossils   QE 701–996.5
Special topics, by subject
Foster Home Care   HV 875
Public health aspects   WA 310–320
Of persons with various disabilities, with the disability, e.g., of mental patients   WM 29; of the mentally retarded child   WS 107.5.F6
Fourier Analysis   QA 403.5–404.5
Biomedical mathematics   QT 35
Fowl Paralysis see Marek's Disease
Fowl Pest see Fowl Plague
Fowl Plague   SF 995.6.F59
Fowl Plague Virus see Orthomyxovirus Type A, Avian
Fowls, Domestic see Poultry
Foxes   QL 737.C22
Foxglove see Digitalis
Fractionation
Of a particular substance, with the substance, e.g., Blood protein fractionation   QY 455
See also Cell Fractionation   QH 585.5.C43
Fracture Fixation   WE 185
Veterinary   SF 914.4
Fracture Fixation, Internal   WE 185
Fracture Fixation, Intramedullary   WE 185
Fractures   WE 175–185
In infancy & childhood   WE 175–180
See also types of fracture by site, e.g., Skull Fractures   WL 354
Fractures, Compound see Fractures, Open
Fractures, Fatigue see Fractures, Stress
Fractures, March see Fractures, Stress

Fractures, Open   WE 182
Fractures, Pathological see Fractures, Spontaneous
Fractures, Spontaneous   WE 180
Fractures, Stress   WE 180
Fractures, Ununited   WE 180
Fragile Sites, Chromosome see Chromosome Fragile Sites
Fragile X Syndrome   QS 677
Fragilitas Ossium see Osteogenesis Imperfecta
Frail Elderly   WT
See special topics under Aged
Frail Older Adults see Frail Elderly
Frambesia see Yaws
Frames (Spectacles) see Eyeglasses
Frangula see Rhamnus
Fraternities see Societies; names of specialties
Fraud   HV 6691–6699
Special topics, by subject
Fraud, Drug Manufacture and Sales see Drug Industry
Fraud, Scientific see Scientific Misconduct
Fraudulent Data see Scientific Misconduct
Freckles see Lentigo
Free Association   WM 460.5.F8
Free Fatty Acids see Fatty Acids, Nonesterified
Free Radicals   QD 471
Freedom
Political theory   JC 585–599
Sociology   HM 271
Special topics, by subject
Freeze Drying
Blood   WH 460
Food   WA 710
Research techniques   QH 324.9.C7
Tissue   QS 525
See also Tissue Preservation   WO 665, etc.
Freeze Fracturing   QH 236.2
Freezing
Anesthesia see Hypothermia, Induced   WO 350
Biochemical technique   QU 25
Blood   WH 460
Food   WA 710
Normal effects on cells   QH 653
Research techniques   QH 324.9.C7
Special aspects, by subject
Tissue   WO 665
Frei's Disease see Lymphogranuloma Venereum
Frenum, Labial see Labial Frenum
Fresh Foods see Food
Fresh Frozen Plasma see Plasma
Fresh Water   WA 675–690
Freudian Theory   WM 460
Friedlaender's Pneumonia see Pneumonia
Friedreich's Ataxia   WL 390
Friedreich's Disease see Paramyoclonus Multiplex
Frigidity   WP 610
Fringe Benefits see Salaries and Fringe Benefits
Froehlich's Syndrome   WK 550
Frog Venoms see Amphibian Venoms
Frogs and Toads see Anura
Frontal Bone   WE 705
Frontal Lobe   WL 307
Frontal Sinus   WV 350

Frostbite   WG 530
Frottage see Paraphilias
Frozen Foods   WA 710
Frozen Sections   QH 233
Frozen Semen see Semen Preservation
Fructose   QU 75
Fructosediphosphate Aldolase   QU 139
Fructosediphosphates   QU 75
Fruit
    As a dietary supplement in health or disease
    WB 430
    Plant culture   SB 354–399
    Sanitation and other public health aspects   WA
    703
Fruit Flies see Drosophila
Frusemide see Furosemide
Frustration   BF 575.F7
    In adolescence   WS 462
    In infancy & childhood   WS 105.5.E5
FSH   WK 515
FSH–Releasing Hormone see Gonadorelin
Ftorafur see Tegafur
Fuchsin Dyes see Rosaniline Dyes
Fuchsins see Rosaniline Dyes
Fucidin see Fusidic Acid
Fucosyltransferases   QU 141
FUdR see Floxuridine
Fuel Oils
    Chemical technology   TP 345–359
    Toxicology   QV 633
Fuels
    Chemical technology   TP 315–360
    Energy conservation   TJ 163.3–163.5
    Heating   WA 770
    Pollution   WA 754
    See also Gas Poisoning   QV 662, etc. and names
    of other specific fuels
Fugue see Dissociative Disorders
Full Dentures see Denture, Complete
Fumigation see Sterilization
Function Tests see Heart Function Tests; Kidney
    Function Tests; Liver Function Tests; Ovarian
    Function Tests; Pituitary–Adrenal Function Tests;
    Pituitary Function Tests; Placental Function
    Tests; Respiratory Function Tests; Thyroid
    Function Tests; Vestibular Function Tests; See
    also names of specific tests
Functional Heart Disease see Neurocirculatory
    Asthenia and names of other functional disorders
Functional Psychoses see Psychotic Disorders
Functionally–Impaired Elderly see Frail Elderly
Fund Raising
    Hospitals   WX 157
    Other special topics, by subject
Funding, Capital see Capital Financing
Fundus Fluorescence Photography see Fluorescein
    Angiography
Fundus Oculi   WW 270
Funeral Directors see Mortuary Practice
Funeral Rites
    Ethnology   GN 486
    Manners and customs   GT 3150–3390.5
    Psychology   BF 789.F8

Fungal Antigens see Antigens, Fungal
Fungal Spores see Spores, Fungal
Fungal Toxins see Mycotoxins
Fungal Vaccines   WC 450
Fungi
    As a cause of disease   QZ 65
    Non–pathogenic   QK 600–635
    Pathogenic   QW 180–180.5
Fungi imperfecti see Deuteromycetes
Fungicides, Industrial
    Agriculture   SB 951.3
    Public health aspects   WA 240
    See also Antifungal Agents   QV 252
Fungicides, Therapeutic see Antifungal Agents
Fungus Diseases see Mycoses
Fungus Poisoning see Mycotoxicosis
Funnel Chest   WE 715
Furans
    Organic chemistry   QD 405
Furazosin see Prazosin
Furniture see Interior Design and Furnishings
Furocoumarins see Psoralens
Furosemide   QV 160
Furrow Keratitis see Keratitis, Dendritic
Fursemide see Furosemide
Furunculosis   WR 235
Fusarium   QW 180.5.D38
Fusidic Acid   QV 350
Fusobacterium   QW 133
Fusobacterium Infections   WC 200
    Veterinary   SF 809.F87
Futurology see Forecasting
F1 ATPase see H(+)–Transporting ATP Synthase
F1F0 ATPase Complex see H(+)–Transporting
    ATP Synthase

G

G Force see Gravitation
G Periods see Interphase
G Phases see Interphase
G–Proteins   QU 55
GABA   QU 60
GABA Receptors see Receptors, GABA
GABA Transaminase see Aminobutyrate
    Aminotransferase
Gagging   WI 143
Gait   WE 103
Galactokinase   QU 141
Galactose   QU 75
Galactosemia   WD 205.5.C2
Galactosidases   QU 136
Galago   QL 737.P955
    As laboratory animals   QY 60.P7
    Diseases   SF 997.5.P7
Galantamin see Galanthamine
Galanthamine   QV 124
Gallbladder   WI 750
Gallbladder Diseases   WI 750
Gallbladder Neoplasms   WI 765
Gallium
    Organic chemistry   QD 181.G2
    Pharmacology   QV 290

**ALWAYS CONSULT MAIN SCHEDULES. USE NUMBER ASSIGNED ONLY WHEN
SUBJECT REPRESENTS MAJOR EMPHASIS OF WORK BEING CLASSIFIED**

Gallodesoxycholic Acid see Chenodeoxycholic Acid
Gallopamil   QV 150
Gallstones see Cholelithiasis
Gallstones, Common Bile Duct see Common Bile
    Duct Calculi
Galvanic Skin Response
    Psychiatric test   WM 145
    Reflex test (general)   WL 106
Galvanism, Oral see Electrogalvanism, Intraoral
Galvanosurgery see Electrosurgery
Galvanotherapy see Electric Stimulation Therapy
Gamasoidiasis see Mite Infestations
Gambling
    As an impulse control disorder   WM 190
    See also Risk–Taking   BF 637.R57
Game Theory   QA 269–272
    In leadership development   HM 141
    Other uses with the area being studied, e.g.,
        doctor/nurse relations   WY 87
Games see Physical Education and Training; Play
    and Playthings; Sports; Recreation
Games, Experimental   QA 269
Gamete Intrafallopian Transfer
    Human   WQ 205
Gametogenesis   WQ 205
Gamma–Aminobutyric Acid see GABA
gamma–Aminobutyric Acid Receptors see
    Receptors, GABA
gamma–Benzene Hexachloride see Benzene
    Hexachloride
Gamma Camera Imaging see Radionuclide Imaging
Gamma Globulin, 7S see IgG
Gamma Globulins   WH 400
    Clinical examination   QY 455
    Prophylactic   QW 806
    Used for treatment of particular disorder, with
        the disorder or system
gamma–Interferon see Interferon Type II
Gamma Rays   WN 105
Gammaphos see Amifostine
Ganciclovir   QV 268.5
Ganglia   WL 500
Ganglia, Autonomic   WL 600
Ganglia, Basal see Basal Ganglia
Ganglia, Parasympathetic   WL 610
Ganglia, Sympathetic   WL 610
Ganglion of Corti see Spiral Ganglion
Ganglioneuroma   QZ 380
    Localized, by site
Ganglionic Blockers   QV 132
Ganglionic Blocking Agents see Ganglionic Blockers
Ganglioplegic Agents see Ganglionic Blockers
Gangliosides   QU 85
Gangliosidoses   WD 205.5.L5
Gangrene   QZ 180
    Gas see Gas Gangrene   WC 375
Ganja see Cannabis
Garbage Disposal see Refuse Disposal
Gargoylism see Mucopolysaccharidosis I
Garlic
    As a dietary supplement in health or disease
        WB 430
    As a medicinal plant   QV 766

Gas Gangrene   WC 375
Gas Masks see Respiratory Protective Devices
Gas Poisoning   QV 662
    In industry   WA 465
Gases
    Analysis   QD 121
    As anesthetics   QV 81
    Asphyxiating see Lung irritants   QV 664 under
        Irritants
    Chemical technology   TP 242–244
    Description and properties   QC 161–168.86
    In air pollution see Air Pollutants   WA 754,
        etc.
    Inorganic chemistry   QD 162
    Irritant see Irritants   QV 666, etc.
    Lacrimator see Tear Gases   QV 665
    Paralysants   QV 667
    Pharmacology   QV 310–318
    Poisonous see Gas Poisoning   QV 662, etc.
    Vesicant see Irritants   QV 666, etc.
    War see Chemical Warfare Agents   QV 663–667
Gasoline
    Chemical technology   TP 692.2
    Handling and storage   TP 692.5
    Toxicology   QV 633
Gastrectomy   WI 380
    In infancy & childhood   WS 310
Gastric Acid   WI 302
Gastric Acidity Determination   QY 130
Gastric Antacid Drugs see Antacids
Gastric Antrum see Pyloric Antrum
Gastric Contents see Analysis   QY 130 under
    Stomach
Gastric Emptying   WI 302
Gastric Fistula   WI 300
Gastric Fundus   WI 300
Gastric Hypothermia   WI 380
    Used for treatment of particular disorders, with
        the disorder
Gastric Juice   WI 302
    Clinical pathology   QY 130
Gastric Parietal Cells see Parietal Cells, Gastric
Gastric Ulcer see Stomach Ulcer
Gastric Varices see Esophageal and Gastric Varices
Gastrin Receptors see Receptors, Cholecystokinin
Gastrins   WK 170
Gastritis   WI 310
Gastroduodenal Ulcer see Peptic Ulcer
Gastroenteritis   WI 140
Gastroenteritis, Transmissible, of Swine   SF 977.T7
Gastroenterology   WI
    In infancy & childhood   WS 310–312
Gastroenterostomy   WI 900
Gastroesophageal Reflux   WI 250
Gastrointestinal Agents   QV 66
Gastrointestinal Diseases   WI 140
    In infancy & childhood   WS 310–312
    Nursing   WY 156.5
    Veterinary   SF 851
Gastrointestinal Hemorrhage   WI 143
    Particular types, by type
Gastrointestinal Hormone Receptors see Receptors,
    Gastrointestinal Hormone

Gastrointestinal Hormones   WK 170
Gastrointestinal Motility   WI 102
Gastrointestinal Neoplasms   WI 149
Gastrointestinal System   WI
   Children   WS 310-312
   Drugs acting on see Gastrointestinal Agents
   QV 66
   Hormones see Gastrointestinal Hormones   WK
   170
   Manifestations of Disease   WI 143
Gastroscopy   WI 300
Gatekeepers, Health Service see Referral and
  Consultation
Gaucher's Disease   WD 205.5.L5
Gays see Homosexuality, Male
Geese   QL 696.A52
   Culture   SF 505-505.63
   Diseases   SF 995.2
Gehrig's Disease see Amyotrophic Lateral Sclerosis
Geiger-Mueller Counters see Radiometry
Gel Diffusion Tests see Immunodiffusion
Gel Electrophoresis, Two-Dimensional see
  Electrophoresis, Gel, Two-Dimensional
Gel Precipitation Test see Immunodiffusion
Gelada Baboon see Theropithecus gelada
Gelatin   QU 55
Gels   QV 785
Gelsemium   QV 766
   Toxicology   QV 628
Gender see Sex
Gender Identity   HQ 1075
   In adolescence   WS 462
   In infancy & childhood   WS 105.5.P3
   Psychological aspects   BF 692.2
     In men   BF 692.5
     In women   HQ 1206, etc.
Gender Role see Gender Identity
Gene Action Regulation see Gene Expression
  Regulation
Gene Activation see Gene Expression Regulation
Gene Amplification   QH 450.3
Gene Bank see Gene Library
Gene Clusters see Genes, Reiterated
Gene Duplication see Genes, Reiterated
Gene Expression   QH 450
Gene Expression Regulation   QH 450
Gene Expression Regulation, Bacterial   QW 51
Gene Expression Regulation, Enzymologic   QU
  135
Gene Expression Regulation, Neoplastic   QZ 202
Gene Expression Regulation, Viral   QW 160
Gene Fusion see Cloning, Molecular
Gene Library   QH 442.4
Gene Mapping see Chromosome Mapping
Gene Pool   QH 455
Gene Probes, DNA see DNA Probes
Gene Products see Proteins
Gene Products, Bacterial see Bacterial Proteins
Gene Products, Viral see Viral Proteins
Gene Proteins see Proteins
Gene Rearrangement   QW 541
   In antibodies   QW 575
Gene Therapy   QZ 50

Genetic engineering aspects   QH 442
  Of a specific disease, with the disease
Gene Transfer see Transfection
General Adaptation Syndrome   QZ 160
General Paralysis see Paresis
General Practice see Family Practice
General Practice, Dental   WU 21
   Textbooks   WU 100
General Practitioners see Physicians, Family
General Systems Theory see Systems Theory
Generalists see Physicians, Family
Generalization (Psychology)   BD 235
   Stimulus   BF 319.5.S7
Generalized Radiation Sickness see Radiation
  Injuries
Generic Equivalency see Therapeutic Equivalency
Genes   QH 447-447.8
Genes, Bacterial   QW 51
Genes, Class I see Genes, MHC Class I
Genes, Class II see Genes, MHC Class II
Genes, H-2 Class I see Genes, MHC Class I
Genes, HLA Class I see Genes, MHC Class I
Genes, HLA Class II see Genes, MHC Class II
Genes, Ig see Genes, Immunoglobulin
Genes, Immune Response see Genes, MHC Class
  II
Genes, Immunoglobulin   QW 601
Genes, Immunoglobulin Heavy Chain see Genes,
  Immunoglobulin
Genes, Immunoglobulin Light Chain see Genes,
  Immunoglobulin
Genes, Immunoglobulin VH Germ Line see Genes,
  Immunoglobulin
Genes, MHC Class I
   In immunogenetics   QW 541
   Speical topics, by subject
Genes, MHC Class II
   In immunogenetics   QW 541
   Special topics, by subject
Genes, ras   QZ 202
Genes, Regulator   QH 450
   Genetic regulation   QH 450-450.6
Genes, Reiterated   QH 447
Genes, Spliced see DNA, Recombinant
Genes, Split see Genes
Genes, Suppressor, Tumor
Genes, Synthetic   QH 447
Genes, Viral   QW 160
Genetic...
   See also inverted headings, e.g., Transformation,
   Genetic QW 51
Genetic Carriers see Heterozygote
Genetic Carriers, Detection see Heterozygote
  Detection
Genetic Code   QH 450.2
Genetic Counseling   QZ 50
   In family planning   HQ 766
   Other special topics, by subject
Genetic Diversity see Variation (Genetics)
Genetic Engineering   QH 442-442.6
   Chemical technology   TP 248.6
   Special topics, by subject
Genetic Engineering of Proteins see Protein

**ALWAYS CONSULT MAIN SCHEDULES. USE NUMBER ASSIGNED ONLY WHEN
SUBJECT REPRESENTS MAJOR EMPHASIS OF WORK BEING CLASSIFIED**

Engineering
Genetic Induction see Gene Expression Regulation
Genetic Intervention see Genetic Engineering
Genetic Markers   QZ 50
Genetic Recombination see Recombination, Genetic
Genetic Screening   QZ 50
Genetic Skin Diseases see Genetic   WR 218 under
    Skin Diseases
Genetic Techniques   QH 441
    Medical   QZ 50
    Social and moral aspects   QH 438.7
Genetic Toxicity Tests see Mutagenicity Tests
Genetic Translation see Translation, Genetic
Genetic Vectors   QH 442.2
Genetics   QH 426–470
    Animal (General)   QH 432
        Domestic animal breeding   SF 105
    Developmental   QH 453
    Plant   QK 981–981.7
    Veterinary genetics   SF 756.5
    See also Cytogenetics   QH 605, etc.;
        Pharmacogenetics   QV 38
Genetics, Bacterial see Genetics, Microbial
Genetics, Behavioral   QH 457
Genetics, Biochemical
    For the biochemist   QU 4
    Genetic regulation   QH 450–450.6
    General works   QH 430
        Human   QH 431
    Works on the retarded child   WS 107.5.B4
    Special topics, by subject
Genetics, Human see Genetics; Genetics, Medical
Genetics, Medical   QZ 50
Genetics, Microbial   QW 51
Genetics, Molecular see Genetics, Biochemical
Genetics, Population   QH 455
    Physical anthropology   GN 289
Genetics, Radiation see Radiation Genetics
Geniculate Ganglion   WL 330
Genital Diseases, Female   WP
    General works   WP 140
    In infancy & childhood   WS 360
    Nursing   WY 156.7
    See also Obstetrical Nursing   WY 157, etc.
    Surgery   WP 660
    Therapy   WP 650
    Urologic   WJ 190
    Veterinary   SF 871
Genital Diseases, Male   WJ 700
    Veterinary   SF 871
Genital Neoplasms, Female   WP 145
Genital Neoplasms, Male   WJ 706
Genitalia
    Animals, Domestic   SF 871
    Children   WS 320
    Drugs affecting   QV 170–177
    General works (male and female, combined)
    WJ 700
        See also Gonads   WK 900
Genitalia, Female   WP
    Children   WS 360
    General works   WP 100
    See also specific organs

Genitalia, Male   WJ 700–875
Genitourinary Diseases see Urogenital Diseases
Genitourinary Neoplasms see Urogenital Neoplasms
Genitourinary System see Urogenital System
Genius see Child, Gifted; Creativeness; Intelligence
Genome, Human   QH 447
Genomic Library   QH 442.4
Genotype   QH 447
    Histocompatibility   WO 680
Gentamicins   QV 350.5.G3
Gentamycin see Gentamicins
Gentian see Plants, Medicinal
Gentian Violet
    As an anthelmintic   QV 253
    As an anti-infective agent   QV 235
Geographic Tongue see Glossitis, Benign Migratory
Geography
    Medical see Climate   WB 700–710;
        Epidemiology   WA 900, etc.; names of
        diseases in a particular area   WB 700–710, etc.
Geology   QE
    General works   QE 26–26.2
Geopathology see Climate; Disease Reservoirs;
    Environmental Health
Gerbillinae   QL 737.R666
    As laboratory animals   QY 60.R6
    As pets   SF 459.G4
Gerbils see Gerbillinae
Geriatric Assessment   WT 30
Geriatric Dentistry   WU 490
Geriatric Health Services see Health Services for
    the Aged
Geriatric Nursing   WY 152
Geriatric Ophthalmology see In Old Age   WW 620
    under Ophthalmology
Geriatric Psychiatry   WT 150
    As a career   WT 150
Geriatrics   WT
    See also Aged
Germ Cells   WQ 205
    Animal   QL 964–966
Germ-Free Life
    Experimentation   QY 56
        Particular experiments, by subject
    Laboratory animals   QY 56
Germ-Line Cells see Germ Cells
Germ Line Theory see Antibody Diversity
Germ Theory of Disease see Pathogenesis   QZ 65
    under Disease
German Measles see Rubella
Germanium
    Inorganic chemistry   QD 181.G5
    Pharmacology   QV 290
Germinoblastoma see Lymphoma
Gerontology see Geriatrics
Gestalt Theory   BF 203
Gestalt Therapy   WM 420.5.G3
Gestation see Pregnancy
Gestational Age   WQ 210.5
Gestosis, EPH   WQ 215
Gestures
    In adolescence   WS 462
    In infancy & childhood   WS 105.5.C8

Psychology   BF 637.N66
   Social psychology   HM 258
Ghettos see Poverty Areas
Giant Cell Arteritis see Temporal Arteritis
Giant Cell Granuloma see Granuloma, Giant Cell
Giant Cell Tumors   QZ 340
   Bone   WE 258
   Localized, by site
Giardia   QX 70
Giardiasis   WC 700
Gibbons see Hylobates
Gibraltar Fever see Brucellosis
GIFT see Gamete Intrafallopian Transfer
Gifted Child see Child, Gifted
Gifts, Financial see Fund Raising
Gigantism   WK 550
Gilbert's Disease   WD 205.5.H9
Gilles de la Tourette's Disease see Tourette
   Syndrome
Gingiva   WU 240
Gingival Crevicular Fluid   WU 240
Gingival Diseases   WU 240
Gingival Exudate see Gingival Crevicular Fluid
Gingival Index see Periodontal Index
Gingivectomy   WU 240
Gingivitis   WU 240
Gingivitis, Necrotizing Ulcerative
   For the dentist   WU 240
   For the gastroenterologist   WI 200
Gingivosis see Gingival Diseases
Gingivostomatitis, Herpetic see Stomatitis, Herpetic
Ginseng   QV 766
Glanders   WC 330
   Veterinary   SF 796
Glands see Endrocrine Glands; Exocrine Glands;
   names of specific glands
Glandula Carotica see Carotid Body
Glandular Fever see Infectious Mononucleosis
Glass
   Occupational medicine   WA 400–495
   Materials of engineering and construction   TA
   450
   Optical instruments   QC 375
Glass Ionomer Cements   WU 190
Glasses see Eyeglasses
Glaucoma   WW 290
Glaucoma, Angle–Closure   WW 290
Glaucoma, Closed–Angle see Glaucoma,
   Angle–Closure
Glaucoma, Open–Angle   WW 290
Glaucoma, Pigmentary see Glaucoma, Open–Angle
Glaucoma, Simple see Glaucoma, Open–Angle
Glaucoma Simplex see Glaucoma, Open–Angle
Glial Fibrillary Acidic Protein   QU 55
Glial Intermediate Filament Protein see Glial
   Fibrillary Acidic Protein
Gliclazide   WK 825
   Organic chemistry   QD 305.S6
Gliding Bacteria (Non Mesh) see Bacteria
Gliobastoma see Astrocytoma
Glioblastoma   QZ 380
   Localized, by site
Glioblastoma–Derived T–Cell Suppressor Factor see

Transforming Growth Factor beta
Glioblastoma Multiforme see Glioblastoma
Gliocladium see Hyphomycetes
Glioma   QZ 380
   Localized, by site
Global Warming see Greenhouse Effect
Globulins   QU 55
Globus Hystericus see Conversion Disorder
Globus Pallidus   WL 307
Glomangioma see Glomus Tumor
Glomerular Filtration Rate   QY 175
Glomerulonephritis   WJ 353
Glomerulonephritis, IGA   WJ 353
Glomerulonephritis, Lupus see Lupus Nephritis
Glomerulosclerosis, Diabetic see Diabetic
   Nephropathies
Glomus Caroticum see Carotid Body
Glomus Tumor   QZ 340
   Localized, by site
Glossalgia   WI 210
Glossectomy   WI 210
Glossina see Tsetse Flies
Glossitis   WI 210
Glossitis Areata Exfoliativa see Glossitis, Benign
   Migratory
Glossitis, Benign Migratory   WI 210
Glossodynia see Glossalgia
Glossopharyngeal Nerve   WL 330
Gloves, Surgical   WO 162
GLQ223 see Trichosanthin
Glucagon   WK 801
   Associated with hypoglycemia   WK 880
Glucagonoma   WK 885
Glucan Phosphorylase see Glycogen Phosphorylase
Glucans   QU 83
Glucitol see Sorbitol
Glucocorticoid Analogs see Glucocorticoids,
   Synthetic
Glucocorticoid Receptors see Receptors,
   Glucocorticoid
Glucocorticoids   WK 755
Glucocorticoids, Synthetic   WK 757
Glucocorticoids, Topical   QV 60
Glucokinase   QU 141
Gluconeogenesis   QU 75
Glucosamine   QU 75
Glucose   QU 75
   Dietary supplement   WB 427
   Infusion technique   WB 354
   Pharmacology   QU 75
Glucose, Blood see Blood Glucose
Glucose Infusion see Glucose; Infusions, Parenteral
Glucose Oxidase   QU 140
Glucose Solution, Hypertonic   QU 75
   Infusion   WB 354
Glucose Tolerance Test   QY 470
Glucose–6–Phosphatase   QU 136
Glucose–6–Phosphatase Deficiency see Glycogen
   Storage Disease Type I
Glucose–6–Phosphate Dehydrogenase see
   Glucosephosphate Dehydrogenase
Glucosephosphatase see Glucose–6–Phosphatase
Glucosephosphatase Deficiency see Glycogen

Storage Disease Type I
Glucosephosphate Dehydrogenase   QU 140
Glucosephosphate Dehydrogenase Deficiency
    WH 170
Glucosides   QU 75
Glucosiduronates see Glucuronates
Glucosyltransferases   QU 141
Glucuronates   QU 84
    Organic chemistry   QD 321
Glucuronidase   QU 136
Glucuronides see Glucuronates
Glue Sniffing see Substance Use Disorders
Glues see Adhesives
Glutamate–Ammonia Ligase   QU 138
Glutamate Dehydrogenase   QU 140
Glutamates   QU 60
Glutamic–Oxaloacetic Transaminase see Aspartate
    Aminotransferase
Glutamic–Pyruvic Transaminase see Alanine
    Aminotransferase
Glutaminase   QU 136
Glutamine   QU 60
Glutamine Synthetase see Glutamate–Ammonia
    Ligase
Glutaminyl–Peptide Gamma–Glutamyltransferase
    see Protein–Glutamine
    gamma–Glutamyltransferase
Glutaraldehyde–Stabilized Grafts see Bioprosthesis
Glutathione   QU 68
Glutathione Peroxidase   QU 140
Glutathione Reductase   QU 140
Gluteal Region see Buttocks
Gluten   QK 898.G49
Gluten Enteropathy see Celiac Disease
Glutethimide   QV 85
Glybutamide see Carbutamide
Glycans see Polysaccharides
Glycerides   QU 85
Glycerin
    Biochemistry   QU 75
    In blood preservation   WH 460
    In tissue culture   QS 525
    Organic chemistry   QD 305.A4
    Pharmacology   QV 82
Glycerites see Solutions
Glycerol see Glycerin
Glycerophosphates   QU 93
Glyceryl Trinitrate see Nitroglycerin
Glycine Max see Soybeans
Glycoconjugates   QU 75
Glycogen   QU 83
Glycogen Phosphorylase   QU 141
Glycogen Storage Disease   WD 205.5.C2
Glycogen Storage Disease Type I   WD 205.5.C2
Glycogen Synthase   QU 136
Glycogen Synthetase see Glycogen Synthase
Glycogenosis see Glycogen Storage Disease
Glycogenosis 1 see Glycogen Storage Disease Type
    I
Glycolates   QU 98
    Organic chemistry
        Aliphatic compounds   QD 305.A2
Glycolipids   QU 85

Glycols
    Organic chemistry   QD 305.A4
    Pharmacology   QV 82
Glycolysis   QU 75
Glyconeogenesis see Gluconeogenesis
Glycophorin
Glycoprotein Sialyltransferases see Sialyltransferases
Glycoproteins   QU 55
Glycosidases see Glycoside Hydrolases
Glycoside Antibiotics see Antibiotics,
    Aminoglycoside
Glycoside Hydrolases   QU 136
Glycosides   QU 75
    Cardiac see Cardiac Glycosides   QV 153
Glycosuria   WK 870
Glycosylation
    Of proteins   QU 55
Glycyrrhetic Acid see Glycyrrhetinic Acid
Glycyrrhetinic Acid
    As a dermatologic agent   QV 60
    As a gastrointestinal agent   QV 66
Glycyrrhiza   QV 766
Glyoxylates   QU 98
    Organic chemistry
        Aliphatic compounds   QD 305.A2
Gnathostoma   QX 203
Gnotobiotics see Germ–Free Life
GnRH see Gonadorelin
Goals   BF 505.G6
    As a philosopical concept   B 105.G63
Goat Diseases   SF 968–969
Goat Fever see Brucellosis
Goats
    Culture   SF 380–388
Goggles see Eye Protective Devices
Goiter   WK 259
    Veterinary   SF 768.3
Goiter, Endemic   WK 259
Goiter, Exophthalmic see Graves' Disease
Goiter, Intrathoracic see Goiter, Substernal
Goiter, Substernal   WK 259
Goitrogens see Thyroid Antagonists
Gold
    Dental application   WU 180
    In organic chemistry   QD 181.A9
    Pharmacology   QV 296
    Used for treatment of particular disorders, with
        the disorder or system
Gold Alloys
    Analytical chemistry   QD 137.G6
    Dentistry   WU 180
Gold Anti–Inflammatory Agents see Antirheumatic
    Agents, Gold
Gold Antiarthritic Agents see Antirheumatic Agents,
    Gold
Gold Colloid, Radioactive   WN 420
    Nuclear physics   QC 796.A9
    See also special topics under Radioisotopes
Gold Isotopes
    Inorganic chemistry   QD 181.A9
    Pharmacology   QV 296
Gold Salts, Anti–Rheumatic see Antirheumatic
    Agents, Gold

Gold Thioglucose see Aurothioglucose
Goldfish   SF 458.G6
   As laboratory animals   QY 60.F4
Golf   QT 260.5.G6
Golgi Apparatus   QH 603.G6
Gonadal Dysgenesis   QS 677
Gonadal Dysgenesis, 45,X see Turner's Syndrome
Gonadal Dysgenesis, 45,XO see Turner's Syndrome
Gonadoliberin see Gonadorelin
Gonadorelin   WK 515
Gonadotropin–Releasing Hormone see Gonadorelin
Gonadotropins   WK 900
Gonadotropins, Chorionic   WK 920
Gonadotropins, Chorionic, Human see
   Gonadotropins, Chorionic
Gonadotropins, Human Menopausal see Menotropins
Gonadotropins, Pituitary   WK 515
Gonads   WK 900
   See also Ovary   WP 320–322, etc.
   Testis   WJ 830, etc.; Castration   WJ 868, etc.
Gonioscopy   WW 210
Goniotomy see Trabeculectomy
Gonococcus see Neisseria gonorrhoeae
Gonorrhea   WC 150
   Female   WP 157
Gonosomes see Sex Chromosomes
Gonyaulax see Dinoflagellida
Gordius see Helminths
Gossypium see Cotton
Gout   WE 350
   Drugs for see Gout Suppressants   QV 98
Gout Suppressants   QV 98
Governing Board
   Hospitals   WX 150
   Of other organizations and institutions, in the administration number for the agency or lacking that, in the general number, e.g., governing board of the American Medical Association   WB 1
Government   J
   Agencies (General), with the country in J schedule
   Medical practice   W 94
     See also Institutional Practice   W 96, etc.; Veterinary Service, Military   UH 650–655
   Nursing service   WY 130
     See also Military Nursing   WY 130; Public Health Nursing   WY 108, etc.; Specialties, Nursing   WY 130, etc.
Government Agencies   JF 1501–1525
   Public health   WA 540–546
   See also Hospitals, Veterans   UH 460–485; names of particular types of agencies
Government Nursing Services see Military Nursing; Public Health Nursing
Government Publications
   Administrative serials   W2
   Bibliography   Z 7164.G7
   Of individual countries   Z 1201–4980
   Statistical serials   W2
   Subject oriented publications
     Monographs, by subject
     Serials (Medicine and related fields)   W1

Government Regulations see Legislation; names of products or specialties being regulated, e.g. Drug and Narcotic Control
Government, State see State Government
Graafian Follicle   WP 320
Graduate Education see Education, Medical, Graduate; names of other branches of graduate education
Graduate Records Examination see Educational Measurement
Graffi Virus see Leukemia Viruses, Murine
Graffi's Chloroleukemic Strain see Leukemia Viruses, Murine
Graft Rejection   WO 680
Graft–Versus–Host Disease see Graft vs Host Disease
Graft vs Host Disease   WD 300
   Transplantation complication   WO 680
Graft vs Host Reaction   WO 680
Grafting, Bone see Bone Transplantation
Grafting, Bone Marrow see Bone Marrow Transplantation
Grafting, Brain Tissue see Brain Tissue Transplantation
Grafting, Heart see Heart Transplantation
Grafting, Heart–Lung see Heart–Lung Transplantation
Grafting, Islets of Langerhans see Islets of Langerhans Transplantation
Grafting, Kidney see Kidney Transplantation
Grafting, Liver see Liver Transplantation
Grafting, Lung see Lung Transplantation
Grafting of Tissue see Transplantation
Grafting, Organ see Organ Transplantation
Grafting, Pancreas see Pancreas Transplantation
Grafting, Skin see Skin Transplantation
Grafting, Tissue see Tissue Transplantation
Grain see Cereals
Gram–Negative Aerobic Bacteria   QW 131
Gram–Negative Anaerobic Bacteria   QW 133
Gram–Negative Bacteria   QW 131
Gram–Negative Chemolithotrophic Bacteria   QW 135
Gram–Negative Facultatively Anaerobic Rods (Non Mesh) see Bacteria
Gram–Positive Bacteria   QW 142–142.5
Gram–Positive Cocci   QW 142.5.C6
Gram–Positive Organisms see Bacteria
Gramicidins   QV 350
Graminea see Grasses
Grammar see Philology; "phrase books" under specialties, e.g., Medicine
Grana see Chloroplasts
Grand Mal Attacks see Epilepsy, Tonic–Clonic
Grants and Subsidies, Educational see Training Support
Grants and Subsidies, Government see Financing, Government
Grants and Subsidies, Health Planning see Health Planning Support
Grants and Subsidies, Research see Research Support
Granulocytes   WH 200

Granulocytic Leukemia see Leukemia, Myeloid
Granulocytic Leukemia, Chronic see Leukemia,
  Myeloid, Chronic
Granulocytopenia see Agranulocytosis
Granuloma   QZ 140
    Eosinophilic see Eosinophilic Granuloma   WH
      650, etc.
    Fungoides see Mycosis Fungoides   WR 500
Granuloma, Eosinophilic see Eosinophilic
  Granuloma
Granuloma Gangraenescens see Granuloma, Lethal
  Midline
Granuloma, Giant Cell
    Gingiva   WU 240
    Jaws   WU 140.5
Granuloma, Giant Cell Reparative see Granuloma,
  Giant Cell
Granuloma, Hodgkin's see Hodgkin's Disease
Granuloma Inguinale   WC 180
Granuloma, Lethal Midline   WV 300
Granuloma, Malignant see Hodgkin's Disease
Granuloma, Periapical see Periapical Granuloma
Granuloma, Reparative Giant Cell see Granuloma,
  Giant Cell
Granuloma Sarcomatodes see Mycosis Fungoides
Granuloma Venereum see Granuloma Inguinale
Granulomatosis, Wegener's see Wegener's
  Granulomatosis
Granulomatous Disease, Chronic   QW 690
Granulosa Cell Tumor   WP 322
Grapes
    As a dietary supplement in health or disease
      WB 430
    Cultivation   SB 387–398
    See also Wine   WB 444, etc.
Graphite
    Pharmacology   QV 138.C1
    Inorganic chemistry   QD 181.C1
Grasses
    As allergens   QW 900
    Cultivation   SB 197–202
Graves' Disease   WK 265
Grave's Disease see Goiter, Exophthalmic
Gravitation   QC 178
    Aviation medicine   WD 720
    Physiological effects   QT 162.G7
    Space medicine   WD 752
Gravity see Gravitation
Grawitz Tumor see Carcinoma, Renal Cell
Graylings see Salmonidae
Green Monkey see Cercopithecus aethiops
Greenhouse Effect
    On environmental health   WA 30
    Physics   QC 912.3
      Global warming   QC 981.8.G56
    Special topics, by subject
Grenz Rays see X-Rays
Grief   BF 575.G7
    In adolescence   WS 462
    In infancy & childhood   WS 105.5.E5
Grievances, Employee see Employee Grievances
Grippe see Influenza
Grivet Monkey see Cercopithecus aethiops

Grommet Insertion see Middle Ear Ventilation
Groundnuts see Peanuts
Group Health Insurance see Insurance, Health
Group Health Organizations, Prepaid see Health
  Maintenance Organizations
Group Hospitalization see Insurance, Hospitalization
Group Identification see Social Identification
Group Practice   W 92
Group Practice, Dental   WU 79
Group Practice, Prepaid   W 92
Group Processes   HM 131–134
    Psychotherapy   WM 430
    Small groups   HM 133
    Sensitivity training groups   WM 430.5.S3 etc.
    Special topics, by subject
Group Psychotherapy see Psychotherapy, Group
Group Structure   HM 131–134
Group Therapy see Psychotherapy, Group
Growth
    General growth of child   WS 103
    Mental growth see Child Development   WS 105,
      etc.
    Physical   WS 103
    Tables   WS 16
Growth Disorders
    Congenital   WE 250
    Endocrine   WK 550
    In infancy & childhood   WS 104
    Manifestation of disease   QZ 190
    Pathogenesis   QZ 45
Growth Factor, Mast-Cell see Interleukin-3
Growth Factors see Growth Substances
Growth Hormone see Somatotropin
Growth Hormone, Pituitary see Somatotropin
Growth Hormone Receptors see Receptors,
  Somatotropin
Growth Inhibitors   QU 107
    See also Growth Disorders   WE 250, etc.
Growth Plate   WE 200
Growth Retardation, Intrauterine see Fetal Growth
  Retardation
Growth Substances   QU 107
    Plant see Plant Growth Regulators   QK 745
GTP-Binding Proteins see G-Proteins
GTP-Regulatory Proteins see G-Proteins
Guanacos see Camelids, New World
Guanidines   QU 61
    Organic chemistry   QD 305.A8
Guanine Nucleotide Regulatory Proteins see
  G-Proteins
Guanosine Cyclic Monophosphate see Cyclic GMP
Guanosine Cyclic 2',3'-Monophosphate see Cyclic
  GMP
Guanosine Cyclic 3',5'-Monophosphate see Cyclic
  GMP
Guanylyl Imidodiphosphate   QU 57
Guerin-Stern Syndrome see Arthrogryposis
Guest Relations see Hospital-Patient Relations
Guidelines for Health Planning see Health Planning
  Guidelines
Guillain-Barre Syndrome see Polyradiculoneuritis
Guilt   BF 575.G8
    In adolescence   WS 462

ALWAYS CONSULT MAIN SCHEDULES. USE NUMBER ASSIGNED ONLY WHEN
SUBJECT REPRESENTS MAJOR EMPHASIS OF WORK BEING CLASSIFIED

In infancy & childhood   WS 105.5.E5
Guinea Pigs   QL 737.R634
      As laboratory animals   QY 60.R6
Guinea Worm see Dracunculus
Gums see Gingiva
Gunshot Wounds see Wounds, Gunshot
Gymnastics   QT 255
      Medical   WB 541
Gymnodinium see Dinoflagellida
Gymnotid see Electric Fish
Gynecologic Diseases see Genital Diseases, Female
Gynecologic Neoplasms see Genital Neoplasms, Female
Gynecology   WP
      Pediatrics   WS 360
      Physiology   WP 505
      Urology   WJ 190
Gynecomastia   WP 840
Gypsies see Transients and Migrants   WA 300, etc.
Gypsum see Calcium Sulfate
Gypsum Dressings see Calcium Sulfate
Gyrectomy see Psychosurgery

H

H(+)ATPase Complex see H(+)-Transporting ATP Synthase
H-D Antibodies see Antibodies, Heterophile
H(+)-Transporting ATP Synthase   QU 136
H(+)-Transporting ATPase see H(+)-Transporting ATP Synthase
H-Y Antigen   WO 680
H-2 Antigens   WO 680
      See also Mice as laboratory animals   QY 60.R6
H 93-26 see Metoprolol
Ha-ras Genes see Genes, ras
Habilitation see Rehabilitation
Habit Disturbances see Habits
Habitations see Housing
Habits   BF 335
Habituation (Psychophysiology)   WL 103
Haem Oxygenase see Heme Oxygenase
Haemophilus   QW 139
Haemophilus ducreyi   QW 139
Haemophilus Infections   WC 200
      See also Chancroid   WC 155
Haemophilus influenzae   QW 139
Haemophilus pertussis see Bordetella pertussis
Hafnium
      Inorganic chemistry   QD 181.H5
      Pharmacology   QV 290
Hair   WR 450-465
Hair Balls see Bezoars
Hair Cells   WV 250
Hair Color   WR 450
Hair Colorants see Hair Dyes
Hair Diseases   WR 450
Hair Dyes   WR 465
      Pharmacology   QV 235
Hair Follicle Diseases see Hair Diseases
Hair Preparations   WR 465
      See also Barbering   WA 744, etc.
Hair Removal   WR 450

Hairy Cell Leukemia see Leukemia, Hairy Cell
Halfway Houses
      For criminal offenders   HV 9081-9920.5
      For psychiatric patients   WM 29
Halitosis   WI 143
Hallucinations   WM 204
Hallucinogens   QV 77.7
Hallucinosis, Organic see Organic Mental Disorders, Psychotic
Hallux   WE 835
Hallux Abductovalgus see Hallux Valgus
Hallux Valgus   WE 883
Halogenated Hydrocarbons see Hydrocarbons, Halogenated
Halogens   QV 280
      Antiseptics   QV 231
Haloperidol   QV 77.9
Halothane   QV 81
Halsted Mastectomy see Mastectomy, Radical
Hamadryas see Papio
Hamman-Rich Syndrome see Pulmonary Fibrosis
Hamsters
      As laboratory animals   QY 60.R6
Hamsters, Armenian see Cricetulus
Hamsters, Chinese see Cricetulus
Hamsters, Golden see Mesocricetus
Hamsters, Golden Syrian see Mesocricetus
Hamsters, Grey see Cricetulus
Hamsters, Syrian see Mesocricetus
Hand   WE 830
      Infections   WE 832
            See also Hand Dermatoses   WR 140
Hand Deformities   WE 830
Hand Deformities, Acquired   WE 830
Hand Deformities, Congenital   WE 830
Hand Dermatoses   WR 140
      See also Infections   WE 832 under Hand
Hand Injuries   WE 830
Hand-Schueller-Christian Syndrome   WH 650
Hand-Shoulder Syndrome see Reflex Sympathetic Dystrophy
Handbooks
      (Form number 39 in any NLM schedule where applicable)
      Anesthesiology   WO 231
      Animal poisoning   WD 401
      Aviation and space medicine   WD 701
      Dentistry   WU 49
      Diseases and injuries caused by physical agents   WD 601
      Embryology   QS 629
      Histology   QS 529
      History of medicine   WZ 39
      Immunologic diseases. Hypersensitivity. Collagen diseases   WD 301
      Medicine   W 49
      Metabolic diseases   WD 201
      Nursing   WY 49
      Nutrition disorders   WD 101
      Pharmacy   QV 735
      Physiology   QT 29
      Plant poisoning   WD 501
      Psychiatry   WM 34

Toxicology   QV 607
Handedness see Laterality
Handicapped see Disabled
Handwashing
   In hospitals   WX 165
   In preventive medicine   WA 240
Handwriting
   Graphology   BF 889–905
   Paleography   Z 105–115.5
   Used for diagnostic purposes, with the disorder
Hanganutziu–Deicher Antibodies see Antibodies,
   Heterophile
Hansen's Disease see Leprosy
Hantaan Virus   QW 168.5.B9
Hantavirus   QW 168.5.B9
Haplorhini   QL 737.P925–737.P965
   Diseases   SF 997.5.P7
   As laboratory animals   QY 60.P7
Happiness   BF 575.H27
   In adolescence   WS 462
   In infancy & childhood   WS 105.5.E5
Haptoglobins   WH 400
   Clinical examination   QY 455
Harassment, Non–Sexual see Social Behavior
Hardware, Computer see Computers
Harelip see Cleft Lip
Harvest Mites see Mites
Hashish see Cannabis
Hashish Abuse see Marijuana Abuse
Hashish Smoking see Marijuana Smoking
Hate   BF 575.H3
   In adolescence   WS 462
   In infancy & childhood   WS 105.5.E5
Haverhill Fever see Rat–Bite Fever
Hay Fever   WV 335
Hazardous Chemicals see Hazardous Substances
Hazardous Materials see Hazardous Substances
Hazardous Substances
   Environment   WA 670–788
   Occupational   WA 400–495
   Radioactive   WN 615
   Other specific conditions, by subject
Hazardous Waste   WA 788
Hazardous Waste, Radioactive see Radioactive
   Waste
Hazardous Waste Sites see Hazardous Waste
Hazards, Equipment see Equipment Safety
HBAg see Hepatitis B Antigens
HBeAg see Hepatitis B e Antigens
HBsAg see Hepatitis B Surface Antigens
HCB see Hexachlorobenzene
HCG see Gonadotropins, Chorionic
HDL Cholesterol see Lipoproteins, HDL
   Cholesterol
Head   WE 705–707
   See also Scalp   WR 450
Head and Neck Neoplasms   WE 707
Head Banging see Stereotyped Behavior
Head Injuries   WE 706
   See also Skull Fractures   WL 354
Head Nurses see Nursing, Supervisory
Head Protective Devices
   In industry   WA 485

Headache   WL 342
   See also Migraine   WL 344
Healing, Mental see Mental Healing
Healing of Wounds see Wound Healing
Healing, Religious see Mental Healing
Health
   Developing countries   WA 395
   Occupational see Occupational Health   WA 400–495
   Maintenance of personal health   QT 255
   Mental see Mental Health   WM 105, etc.
   Oral see Oral Health   WU 113
   Public see Public Health   WA, etc.
   Rural see Rural Health   WA 390
   Statistics   WA 900
   Students see School Health Services   WA 350, etc.; Student Health Services   WA 351, etc.
   Urban   WA 380
   See also Hygiene   QT 180–275, etc.; Physical Fitness   QT 255
Health Administration   WA 525–546
Health and Welfare Planning see Health Planning
Health Behavior   W 85
   Special topics, by subject
Health Benefit Plans, Employee   W 100–275
Health Benefits see Insurance Benefits
Health Care Coalitions   WA 525–546
   In special fields by subject
Health Care Costs
   General   W 74
   For providing particular types of care, by subject, if specific; if general, in economics number where applicable
Health Care Delivery see Delivery of Health Care
Health Care Rationing   WA 525–546
Health Care Reform   WA 525–546
Health Care Research see Health Services Research
Health Care Seeking Behavior see Patient Acceptance of Health Care
Health Care Systems see Delivery of Health Care
Health Care Team see Patient Care Team
Health Centers, Ambulatory see Ambulatory Care Facilities
Health Centers, Ambulatory, Non–Hospital see Ambulatory Care Facilities
Health Diaries see Medical Records
Health Education
   Informal   WA 590
   Physical see Physical Education and Training   QT 255
   School texts   QT 200–215
   See also education under Patients
Health Education, Dental   WU 113
Health Expenditures   W 74
Health Facilities   WX
   General works   WX 27
   Special types of facilities, with the specialty for which designed
   See also names of types of facilities, e.g., Maternal–Child Health Centers   WA 310; Rehabilitation Centers   WM 29, etc.
Health Facility Administrators   WX 155
   Directories   WX 22

ALWAYS CONSULT MAIN SCHEDULES. USE NUMBER ASSIGNED ONLY WHEN SUBJECT REPRESENTS MAJOR EMPHASIS OF WORK BEING CLASSIFIED

Health Facility Conversion see Health Facility
  Planning
Health Facility Planning   WX 140
    Facility planning in the specialties, with the
    specialty, e.g., Coronary Care Units   WG
    27–28
Health Facility Size   WX 140
    Special types of facility, with the specialty for
    which designed
Health Fairs   WA 590
    Special topics, by subject
Health Insurance see Insurance, Health
Health Insurance for Aged and Disabled, Title 18
  see Medicare
Health Insurance Reimbursement see Insurance,
  Health, Reimbursement
Health Insurance, Voluntary see Insurance, Health
Health Legislation see Legislation
Health Maintenance Organizations   W 132
Health Manpower   W 76
    Excluding physicians   W 21.5
    In specialties see Manpower in the economics
    number under the specialty, e.g., Dentistry
    WU 77, etc. or lacking that in the number for
    the career, e.g., manpower in otolaryngology
    WV 21
Health Occupations   W 21
    Specialties, with the field, e.g., Surgery   WO
    21
    Types of medical practice   W 87
    See also names of particular occupations, e.g.,
    Allied Health Occupations   W 21.5, etc.;
    Mortuary Practice   WA 840–847
Health Occupations Manpower see Health
  Manpower
Health Occupations Schools see Schools, Health
  Occupations
Health Physics   WN 110
Health Plan Implementation   WA 525–546
    Special topics, by subject
Health Planning
    Government   WA 525–546
    Of health services   W 84
    Of other special topics, by subject
Health Planning Councils   WA 525–546
    With special topics, class by subject
Health Planning Guidelines
    Government   WA 525–546
    Special topics, by subject
Health Planning Organizations   WA 23
    In special fields, by subject, e.g., WW 23 for
    ophthalmology institutes
Health Planning Support   WA 540
Health Policy
    Government   WA 525–546
    Special topics, by subject
Health Priorities   WA 525–546
    In special areas by subject
Health Professions see Health Occupations
Health Promotion
    Government   WA 525–546
    Through education   WA 590
    Special topics, by subject

Health Records, Personal see Medical Records
Health Resorts   WB 760
    History   WB 760
Health Resources   W 74
    Hospital financial management   WX 157
    Specific purposes, by subject
Health Risk Appraisal see Health Status Indicators
Health Service Area see Catchment Area (Health)
Health Services   W 84–84.8
    Community see Community Health Services
    WA 546
    Emergency see Emergency Medical Services
    WX 215, etc.
        See also Emergency Service, Hospital   WX
        215
    For children see Child Health Services   WA
    320, etc.
    For the aged   WT 31
    For the indigent   W 250
        See also Medical Indigency   W 250, etc.
    Occupational see Occupational Health Services
    WA 412
    Maternal see Maternal Health Services   WA 310
    Mental see Community Mental Health Services
    WM 30; Mental Health Services   WM 30,
    etc.
    Personal see Personal Health Services   W 84
    Private practice   WB 50
    Public see Preventive Health Services   WA 108;
    Public Health Administration   WA 525–590
    School see School Health Services   WA 350,
    etc.; Student Health Services   WA 351, etc.
    Supply & distribution   W 76
    See also names of specific services, e.g., Home
    Care Services   WY 115, etc.
Health Services Accessibility   W 76
    Special population groups   WA 300–395
Health Services for the Aged   WT 31
Health Services, Indigenous   W 250
Health Services Marketing see Marketing of Health
  Services
Health Services Misuse   W 84–84.8
    Special topics, by subject
Health Services Needs and Demand
    In a particular population or community, by
    subject
Health Services Research   W 84.3
    In special areas, by subject
Health Status   WB 141.4
Health Status Index see Health Status Indicators
Health Status Indicators   WA 900
    Special topics, by subject
Health Surveys   WA 900
    Chronic disease   WT 30
    Dental see Dental Health Surveys   WU 30
    Diet see Nutrition Surveys   QU 146
    Geriatric   WT 30
    Hospital surveys   WX 27
    Nursing surveys   WY 31
    Public health   WA 900
    Sanitary   WA 672
    Of special population groups   WA 300, etc.
Health Systems Agencies   WA 525–546

**ALWAYS CONSULT MAIN SCHEDULES. USE NUMBER ASSIGNED ONLY WHEN
SUBJECT REPRESENTS MAJOR EMPHASIS OF WORK BEING CLASSIFIED**

Health Systems Plans   WA 540–546
Health Visitors see Community Health Nursing
Hearing   WV 270–280
    Conservation   WV 276
Hearing Aids   WV 274
Hearing Disorders   WV 270
    In infancy & childhood   WV 271
Hearing Loss, Bilateral   WV 270
Hearing Loss, Conductive   WV 270
Hearing Loss, Extreme see Deafness
Hearing Loss, Functional   WV 270
Hearing Loss, Noise-Induced   WV 270
    Industrial   WA 470
    Veterinary   SF 891
Hearing Loss, Nonorganic see Hearing Loss,
    Functional
Hearing Loss, Partial   WV 270
Hearing Loss, Sensorineural   WV 270–276
Hearing Protective Devices see Ear Protective
    Devices
Hearing Tests   WV 272
    See also Acoustic Impedance Tests   WV 272;
    Audiometry   WV 272; names of other specific
    tests
Heart   WG
    Beat
        Disorders   WG 330
        Physiology   WG 202
        See also Heart Rate   WG 106; Pulse   WB
        282, etc.; Tachycardia   WG 330
    Children   WS 290
    Drugs affecting   QV 150
        See also specific drugs
    Fetal see Fetal heart   WQ 210.5
    Radiography   WG 141.5.R2
    Radionuclide imaging   WG 141.5.R3
    Sounds see Heart Auscultation   WG 141.5.A9;
        Phonocardiography   WG 141.5.P4
    Tomography   WG 141.5.T6
Heart Abnormalities see Heart Defects, Congenital
Heart Aneurysm   WG 300
Heart Arrest   WG 205
Heart, Artificial   WG 169.5
Heart-Assist Devices   WG 169.5
Heart Atrium   WG 201–202
Heart Auscultation   WG 141.5.A9
    See also Phonocardiography   WG 141.5.P4
Heart Block   WG 330
Heart Catheterization   WG 141.5.C2
    Veterinary   SF 811
Heart Conduction System   WG 201–202
Heart Contractility see Myocardial Contraction
Heart Defects, Congenital   WG 220
    Children   WS 290
Heart Diseases   WG 210
    In infancy & childhood   WS 290
    Ischemic see Coronary Disease   WG 300, etc.
    Pick's disease see Pericarditis, Constrictive   WG
    275
    Pulmonary see Pulmonary Heart Disease   WG
    420
    Rheumatic see Rheumatic Heart Disease   WG
    240

    Veterinary   SF 811
Heart Enlargement see Heart Hypertrophy
Heart Failure, Congestive   WG 370
    Popular works   WG 113
    See also Adverse effects   WO 245 under
    Anesthesia
Heart Function Tests   WG 141.5.F9
    See also names of specific tests
Heart Hypertrophy   WG 210
Heart Injuries   WG 210
    Surgery   WG 169
Heart-Lung Machine see Heart, Mechanical
Heart-Lung Transplantation   WG 169
Heart Massage   WG 205
Heart, Mechanical   WG 169.5
Heart Rate   WG 106
Heart Rate, Fetal   WQ 210.5
    Monitoring   WQ 209
Heart Rupture, Traumatic see Heart Injuries
Heart Septal Defects   WG 220
Heart Septal Defects, Atrial   WG 220
Heart Septal Defects, Ventricular   WG 220
Heart Sounds
    Physiology   WG 106
    See also Heart Auscultation   WG 141.5.A9;
        Phonocardiography   WG 141.5.P4
Heart Surgery   WG 169
    In infancy & childhood   WS 290
Heart Transplantation   WG 169
Heart Valve Diseases   WG 260–269
Heart Valve Prosthesis   WG 169
Heart Valves   WG 260–269
Heart Ventricle   WG 201–202
Heart Ventricle, Artificial see Heart-Assist Devices
Heart Volume see Cardiac Volume
Heartburn   WI 145
Heartworm Disease see Dirofilariasis
Heat
    As a cause of disease   QZ 57
    Body see Body Temperature   WB 270, etc.; Skin
        Temperature   WR 102
    Control in industry   WA 450
    Prostration see Heat Exhaustion   WD 610
    Therapeutic use   WB 469
    See also Desert Climate   QT 150, etc.;
        Temperature   WB 700, etc.
Heat Exhaustion   WD 610
    See also Sunstroke   WD 610
Heat Loss see Body Temperature Regulation
Heat Production see Body Temperature Regulation
Heat-Shock Protein 70 see Heat-Shock Proteins
Heat-Shock Protein 90 see Heat-Shock Proteins
Heat-Shock Proteins   QU 55
Heat Waves see Infrared Rays
Heating   WA 770
    In industry   WA 450
Heatstroke see Heat Exhaustion
Heavy Metals see Metals
Hebephrenic Schizophrenia see Schizophrenia,
    Disorganized
Hedgehogs   QL 737.I53
Hedonism see Philosophy
Heel   WE 880

Height see Body Height
Height–Weight–Growth Tables see Tables   WS 16
    under Birth Weight, Body Height, Body Weight,
    Growth
Hela Cells   QH 585
Helicobacter Infections   WC 200
    In specific diseases, with the disease
Helicobacter pylori   QW 154
Helicopters see Aircraft
Heliotherapy
    General medical   WB 480
    For treating pulmonary tuberculosis   WF 330
Heliotrope see Valerian
Helium   QV 318
    Inorganic chemistry   QD 181.H4
Hellebore see Veratrum
Helmets see Head Protective Devices
Helminth Antigens see Antigens, Helminth
Helminthiasis   WC 800–890
    Veterinary   SF 810.H44
Helminthiasis, Animal (Non Mesh) see Veterinary
    SF 810.H44 under Helminthiasis
Helminths   QX 200–442
    See also Anthelmintics   QV 253
Helping Behavior   BF 637.H4
Helplessness, Learned   WM 165
Hemadsorption Virus 2 see Parainfluenza Virus Type
    1
Hemagglutinating Virus of Japan see Parainfluenza
    Virus Type 1
Hemagglutination   QW 640
Hemagglutination Inhibition Tests   QY 265
    Used for special purposes by subject
Hemagglutination Tests
    Used for special purposes, by subject
Hemagglutinins, Plant see Lectins
Hemangioma   QZ 340
    Localized, by site
Hemangioma, Cavernous   QZ 340
    Localized, by site
Hemangiopericytoma   QZ 340
    Localized, by site
Hemarthrosis   WH 325
Hematemesis   WI 146
    Related to a particular disease, with the disease
Hematin see Heme
Hematinics   QV 181
Hemato–Encephalic Barrier see Blood–Brain Barrier
Hematoblast see Blood Cells
Hematochezia see Gastrointestinal Hemorrhage
Hematocrit   QY 408
    Apparatus   QY 26
Hematologic Diseases   WH
    General works   WH 120
    In infancy & childhood   WS 300
    In pregnancy see Pregnancy Complications,
        Hematologic   WQ 252, etc.
    Nursing   WY 152.5
    Veterinary   SF 769.5
Hematologic Tests   QY 400–415
    See also names of specific tests
Hematology   WH
    Blood (Clinical analysis)   QY 400–490

Children   WS 300
    In nursing   WY 152.5
Hematoma   WH 312
Hematoma, Epidural   WL 355
Hematoma, Subdural   WL 200
Hematopoiesis   WH 140
Hematopoietic Agents see Hematinics
Hematopoietic Cell Growth Factors   WH 140
Hematopoietic Stem Cells   WH 380
Hematopoietic System   WH 140
    Children   WS 300
    Drugs affecting   QV 180
Hematopoietins see Hematopoietic Cell Growth
    Factors
Hematoporphyria see Porphyria
Hematoporphyrin Photoradiation   WB 480
Hematuria   WJ 344
Heme   WH 190
Heme Oxygenase   QU 140
Hemeproteins   WH 190
    Clinical examination   QY 455
Hemeralopia see Vision Disorders
Hemianopsia   WW 276
Hemic System see Hematology
Hemicrania see Migraine
Hemin   WH 190
Hemiparesis see Hemiplegia
Hemiplegia   WL 346
    Specific etiological factors, by cause, e.g.,
        Cerebrovascular Disorders   WL 355
Hemiptera   QX 503
Hemispheres, Cerebral see Brain
Hemisporosis see Sporotrichosis
Hemochromatosis   WR 267
Hemocuprein see Superoxide Dismutase
Hemocyanin   WH 190
    Clinical examination   QY 455
Hemocytes   WH 140
Hemodialysis   WJ 378
    Nursing   WY 164
Hemodialysis, Home   WJ 378
Hemodilution   WG 166
    In blood transfusion   WB 356
    In hypothermia   WD 670
    In microculation   WG 104
    For other purposes, by subject
Hemodynamics   WG 106
Hemoencephalic Barrier see Blood–Brain Barrier
Hemofiltration
    Speicial topics, by subject
Hemofiltration, Continuous Arteriovenous see
    Hemofiltration
Hemoglobin A   WH 190
    Clinical examination   QY 455
Hemoglobin A, Glycosylated   WH 190
Hemoglobin C   WH 190
    Clinical examination   QY 455
Hemoglobin F see Fetal Hemoglobin
Hemoglobin Substitutes see Blood Substitutes
Hemoglobinopathies   WH 190
Hemoglobins   WH 190
    Clinical examination   QY 455
Hemoglobins, Abnormal   WH 190

ALWAYS CONSULT MAIN SCHEDULES. USE NUMBER ASSIGNED ONLY WHEN
SUBJECT REPRESENTS MAJOR EMPHASIS OF WORK BEING CLASSIFIED

Hemoglobinuria   WJ 344
Hemoglobinuria, Bacillary   WJ 344
Hemoglobinuria, Paroxysmal   WJ 344
Hemoglobinuric Fever see Malaria
Hemolymph   WH 400
Hemolysins   QW 660
Hemolysis
    Erythrocyte destruction   WH 150
    Immunology   QW 660
Hemolytic Anemias see Anemia, Hemolytic
Hemolytic Disease of Newborn see Erythroblastosis,
    Fetal
Hemoperfusion   WG 168
Hemopericardium see Pericardial Effusion
Hemoperitoneum   WI 575
Hemophilia   WH 325
Hemophilia A see Hemophilia
Hemophilia, Vascular see von Willebrand's Disease
Hemophilus see Haemophilus
Hemophilus Infections see Haemophilus Infections
Hemophthalmos see Eye Hemorrhage
Hemopneumothorax   WF 746
Hemoptysis   QY 120
    Associated with a particular disease, with the
    disease
Hemorrhage   WO 700
    Cerebral see Cerebral Hemorrhage   WL 355
    Drugs checking   QV 195
    In labor   WQ 330
    Nasal see Epistaxis   WV 320
    Ovarian   WP 320
    Peptic ulcer see Peptic Ulcer Hemorrhage   WI
    350
    Retinal see Retinal Hemorrhage   WW 270
    Subarachnoid see Subarachnoid Hemorrhage
    WL 200
    Uterine see Uterine Hemorrhage   WP 440
    Veterinary   SF 811
    Vulva   WP 200
    See also Menorrhagia   WP 555
Hemorrhage, Cerebral see Cerebral Hemorrhage
Hemorrhage, Eye see Eye Hemorrhage
Hemorrhage, Gastrointestinal see Gastrointestinal
    Hemorrhage
Hemorrhage, Oral see Oral Hemorrhage
Hemorrhage, Peptic Ulcer see Peptic Ulcer
    Hemorrhage
Hemorrhage, Postpartum see Postpartum
    Hemorrhage
Hemorrhage, Retinal see Retinal Hemorrhage
Hemorrhage, Subarachnoid see Subarachnoid
    Hemorrhage
Hemorrhage, Surgical see Blood Loss, Surgical
Hemorrhage, Uterine see Uterine Hemorrhage
Hemorrhagic Diathesis   WH 312–325
    See also names of specific disorders
Hemorrhagic Disease of Newborn   WS 421
Hemorrhagic Fever, American   WC 534
Hemorrhagic Fever, Argentinian see Hemorrhagic
    Fever, American
Hemorrhagic Fever, Bolivian see Hemorrhagic
    Fever, American
Hemorrhagic Fever, Crimean   WC 534

Hemorrhagic Fever, Dengue see Dengue
Hemorrhagic Fever, Epidemic see Hemorrhagic
    Fever with Renal Syndrome
Hemorrhagic Fever, Korean see Hemorrhagic Fever
    with Renal Syndrome
Hemorrhagic Fever, Omsk   WC 534
Hemorrhagic Fever Virus, Epidemic see Hantaan
    Virus
Hemorrhagic Fever Virus, Korean see Hantaan
    Virus
Hemorrhagic Fever Virus, Omsk see Encephalitis
    Viruses, Tick–Borne
Hemorrhagic Fever with Renal Syndrome   WC 534
    Veterinary   SF 809.H45
Hemorrhagic Fever with Renal Syndrome Virus see
    Hantaan Virus
Hemorrhagic Fevers, Viral   WC 534
Hemorrhagic Nephroso–Nephritis see Hemorrhagic
    Fever with Renal Syndrome
Hemorrhagic Nephroso–Nephritis Virus see Hantaan
    Virus
Hemorrhoids   WI 605
Hemosiderin   QV 183
Hemosiderosis   QU 130.5
    Localized, by site
Hemosorption see Hemoperfusion
Hemostasis   WH 310
Hemostasis, Surgical   WO 500
    Complications   WO 184
Hemostatics   QV 195
Hemothorax   WF 746
Hemotoxins see Hemolysins
Hemp see Cannabis
Heparin   QV 193
Heparin–Clearing Factor see Lipoprotein Lipase
Heparin Cofactor see Antithrombin III
Heparin, Low–Molecular–Weight   QV 193
Heparinic Acid see Heparin
Heparinoid   QV 193
Hepatectomy   WI 770
Hepatic Amebiasis see Liver Abscess, Amebic
Hepatic Artery   WG 595.H3
    See also Blood Supply   WI 702 under Liver;
    Liver Circulation   WI 702
Hepatic Cirrhosis see Liver Cirrhosis
Hepatic Coma see Hepatic Encephalopathy
Hepatic Duct, Common   WI 750
Hepatic Encephalopathy   WI 700
Hepatic Entamoebiasis see Liver Abscess, Amebic
Hepatic Failure, Fulminant see Hepatic
    Encephalopathy
Hepatic Transplantation see Liver Transplantation
Hepatic Veins   WG 625.H3
    See also Blood Supply   WI 702 under Liver;
    Liver Circulation   WI 702
Hepatitis   WI 700
    Veterinary see Hepatitis, Animal   SF 851
Hepatitis A   WC 536
Hepatitis A Virus see Hepatovirus
Hepatitis, Alcoholic   WI 700
Hepatitis, Animal   SF 851
Hepatitis B   WC 536
Hepatitis B Antigens   WC 536

Hepatitis B e Antigens   WC 536
Hepatitis B Surface Antigens   WC 536
Hepatitis B Virus   QW 170
Hepatitis C   WC 536
Hepatitis, Chronic Active   WC 536
Hepatitis D see Delta Infection
Hepatitis D Virus see Delta Agent
Hepatitis, Delta see Delta Infection
Hepatitis E   WC 536
Hepatitis, Homologous Serum see Hepatitis B
Hepatitis, Infectious see Hepatitis A
Hepatitis, Toxic   WI 700
Hepatitis, Viral, Human   WC 536
Hepatitis, Viral, Non–A, Non–B,
    Enterically–Transmitted see Hepatitis E
Hepatitis, Viral, Non–A, Non–B,
    Parenterally–Transmitted see Hepatitis C
Hepatitis, Viral, Vaccines see Viral Hepatitis
    Vaccines
Hepatitis Virus, Homologous Serum see Hepatitis B
    Virus
Hepatitis Virus, Infectious see Hepatovirus
Hepatitis Virus, Marmoset see Hepatitis Viruses
Hepatitis Viruses   QW 170
Hepatitis, Water–Borne see Hepatitis E
Hepatocellular Carcinoma see Carcinoma,
    Hepatocellular
Hepatolenticular Degeneration   WI 740
Hepatology see Gastroenterology
Hepatoma see Carcinoma, Hepatocellular
Hepatoma, Experimental see Liver Neoplasms,
    Experimental
Hepatoma, Morris see Liver Neoplasms,
    Experimental
Hepatoma, Novikoff see Liver Neoplasms,
    Experimental
Hepatomegaly   WI 700
Hepatorenal Glycogen Storage Disease see
    Glycogen Storage Disease Type I
Hepatovirus   QW 170
Herbal Teas see Beverages
Herbalism see Medicine, Herbal
Herbicides
    Plant culture   SB 951.4
    Public health aspects   WA 240
Herbs   QV 767
Herbs, Medicinal see Plants, Medicinal
Hereditary Diseases   QZ 50
    In infancy & childhood   WS 200
    Prenatal diagnosis   QZ 50
    Veterinary genetics   SF 756.5
    See also names of specific diseases
Hereditary Multiple Exostoses see Exostoses,
    Multiple Hereditary
Hereditary Nonpolyposis Colorectal Neoplasms see
    Colorectal Neoplasms, Hereditary Nonpolyposis
Hereditary Spinal Sclerosis see Friedreich's Ataxia
Hereditary Type I Motor and Sensory Neuropathy
see Charcot–Marie Disease
Heredity see Genetics
Hermaphroditism   WJ 712
Hernia   WI 950
    Vaginal   WP 250

See also names of specific hernias, e.g., Hernia,
    Diaphragmatic   WF 810, etc.
Hernia, Abdominal see Hernia, Ventral
Hernia, Cerebral see Encephalocele
Hernia, Diaphragmatic   WF 810
Hernia, Diaphragmatic, Traumatic   WF 810
Hernia, Femoral   WI 965
Hernia, Hiatal   WI 250
Hernia, Inguinal   WI 960
Hernia, Umbilical   WI 940
Hernia, Ventral   WI 955
Heroin see Diacetylmorphine
Heroin Dependence   WM 288
Herpes Genitalis   WC 578
Herpes labialis Virus see Simplexvirus
Herpes Simplex   WC 578
    Veterinary   SF 809.H47
Herpes Simplex, Genital see Herpes Genitalis
Herpes Simplex, Oral see Stomatitis, Herpetic
Herpes Simplex Virus see Simplexvirus
Herpes Zoster   WC 575
Herpes Zoster, Ocular see Herpes Zoster
    Ophthalmicus
Herpes Zoster Ophthalmicus   WW 160
Herpes zoster Virus see Herpesvirus 3, Human
Herpesviridae   QW 165.5.H3
Herpesviridae Infections   WC 571
    Veterinary   SF 809.H47
Herpesvirus hominis see Simplexvirus
Herpesvirus Infections see Herpesviridae Infections
Herpesvirus platyrhinae see Simplexvirus
Herpesvirus saimiri see Herpesvirus 2, Saimirine
Herpesvirus varicellae see Herpesvirus 3, Human
Herpesvirus 1, Bovine   QW 165.5.H3
Herpesvirus 1, Saimirine see Simplexvirus
Herpesvirus 1, Suid   QW 165.5.H3
Herpesvirus 2, Saimirine   QW 165.5.H3
Herpesvirus 3, Human   QW 165.5.H3
Herpesvirus 4, Human   QW 165.5.H3
Herpesvirus 5 (beta), Human see Cytomegalovirus
Herpesvirus 5, Human see Cytomegalovirus
Hertzian Waves see Radio Waves
HETE see Hydroxyeicosatetraenoic Acids
Heteroantibodies see Antibodies, Heterophile
Heterochromatin   QU 56
Heterochromic Cyclitis see Iridocyclitis
Heterocyclic Compounds
    Associated with amino acid biochemistry   QU
    65
    Organic chemistry   QD 399–406
    Used for special purposes, by subject
    See also names of specific compounds
Heterocyclic N–Oxides see Cyclic N–Oxides
Heterograft see Transplantation, Heterologous
Heterograft Bioprosthesis see Bioprosthesis
Heterograft Dressings see Biological Dressings
Heterologous Antibodies see Antibodies, Heterophile
Heterophile Antibodies see Antibodies, Heterophile
Heterophoria see Strabismus
Heterophyes see Heterophyidae
Heterophyidae   QX 353
Heteroptera see Hemiptera
Heterosexuality see Sex Behavior

Heterotropia see Strabismus
Heterozygote   QH 447
   Histocompatibility   WO 680
Heterozygote Detection
   Of a particular trait, with the trait
Hexachlorobenzene
   Toxicology   QV 633
Hexachlorocyclohexane see Benzene Hexachloride
Hexachlorophene   QV 233
Hexadecadrol see Dexamethasone
Hexadecanoic Acid see Palmitic Acids
Hexamethonium Compounds   QV 140
Hexamethylenamine see Methenamine
Hexamethylenetetramine see Methenamine
Hexamine see Methenamine
Hexanes
   Microbial chemistry   QW 52
   Toxicology   QV 633
Hexanoates see Caproates
Hexestrol   WP 522
Hexobarbital   QV 81
Hexokinase   QU 141
Hexose Monophosphate Shunt see Pentosephosphate
   Pathway
Hexosephosphates   QU 75
Hexoses   QU 75
Hexylresorcinol   QV 253
Heymann Nephritis see Glomerulonephritis
HFRS see Hemorrhagic Fever with Renal Syndrome
HFRS Virus see Hantaan Virus
Hiatal Hernia see Hernia, Hiatal
Hibernation   QL 755
Hibernation, Artificial see Hypothermia, Induced
Hiccup   WF 805
Hidradenoma see Adenoma, Sweat Gland
Hidrotic Ectodermal Dysplasia see Ectodermal
   Dysplasia
Hierarchy, Social   HM 132
   Special topics, by subject
High-Cost Technology see Technology, High-Cost
High-Frequency Currents see Electric Stimulation
   Therapy; Electricity
High-Frequency Jet Ventilation   WF 145
High Mobility Protein 20 see Ubiquitin
Higher Nervous Activity   WL 102
Highway Accidents see Accidents, Traffic
Hill-Burton Act see Financing, Government
Hindbrain see Cerebellum; Pons; Medulla Oblongata
Hindlimb   QL 950.7
Hip   WE 855
Hip Contracture   WE 855
Hip Dislocation   WE 860
Hip Dislocation, Congenital   WE 860
Hip Dysplasia, Canine   SF 992.H56
Hip Dysplasia, Congenital see Hip Dislocation,
   Congenital
Hip Fractures   WE 855
Hip Joint   WE 860
Hip Prosthesis   WE 860
Hippocampus   WL 314
Hippocratic Oath   W 50
Hippurates   QU 62
   Organic chemistry   QD 341.A7

   In human urine   WJ 303
   In urinalysis   QY 185
Hirschsprung Disease   WI 528
Hirsutism   WR 455
Hirudinea see Leeches
His-Werner Disease see Trench Fever
Hispanic Americans   E 184.S75
   Special topics, by subject
   See also special topics under Ethnic Groups
Histaminase see Amine Oxidase
   (Copper-Containing)
Histamine   QV 157
   Biochemistry   QU 61
Histamine Antagonists   QV 157
Histamine Binding Sites see Receptors, Histamine
Histamine H1 Antagonists   QV 157
Histamine H1 Receptor Antagonists see Histamine
   H1 Antagonists
Histamine H1 Receptor Blockaders see Histamine
   H1 Antagonists
Histamine H2 Antagonists   QV 157
Histamine H2 Receptor Antagonists see Histamine
   H2 Antagonists
Histamine H2 Receptor Blockaders see Histamine
   H2 Antagonists
Histamine H2 Receptors see Receptors, Histamine
   H2
Histamine Liberation
   In anaphylaxis and hypersensitivity   QW 900
   Special topics, by subject
Histamine Receptors see Receptors, Histamine
Histapyridamine see Pheniramine
Histidine   QU 60
Histiocytes   WH 650
   In phagocytosis   QW 690
Histiocytic Lymphoma see Lymphoma, Large-Cell
Histiocytosis, Langerhans-Cell   WH 650
Histiocytosis, Lipid see Niemann-Pick Disease
Histiocytosis X see Histiocytosis, Langerhans-Cell
Histochemistry see Histocytochemistry
Histocompatibility   WO 680
   Blood bank procedures   WH 460
Histocompatibility Antigens   QW 573.5.H6
   Transplantation immunology   WO 680
Histocompatibility Antigens Class II   QW 573.5.H6
   Transplantation immunology   WO 680
Histocompatibility Complex see Major
   Histocompatibility Complex
Histocompatibility Testing   WO 680
Histocytochemistry
   Cytology   QH 613
   Histology   QS 531
Histological Techniques   QS 525
Histologists, Directories see Directories   QS 22
   under Histology
Histology   QS 504-539
   Dental   WU 101
   Directories   QS 22
   Experimental   QS 530
   Pathological   QZ 4
   Veterinary medicine   SF 757.3
   See also special topics under Anatomy
Histology, Comparative   QS 504

Animal only   QL 807
Histomoniasis see Protozoan Infections
Histones   QU 56
Histopathology see Pathology   QZ 4 under
    Histology
Histoplasmosis   WC 465
Historical Cohort Studies see Cohort Studies
Historiography   D 13–15
    Medical   WZ 345
History of Dentistry   WU 11
History of Medicine   WZ
    By locality   WZ 70
    For special groups   WZ 80–80.5
    General works   WZ 40
    Symbols see Emblems and insignia   WZ 334
    See also form number 11 in any NLM schedule
        where applicable
History of Medicine, Ancient   WZ 51
History of Medicine, Medieval   WZ 54
History of Medicine, Modern   WZ 55
History of Medicine, 15th Cent.   WZ 56
History of Medicine, 16th Cent.   WZ 56
History of Medicine, 17th Cent.   WZ 56
History of Medicine, 18th Cent.   WZ 56
History of Medicine, 19th Cent.   WZ 60
History of Medicine, 20th Cent.   WZ 64
History of Nursing   WY 11
History Taking see Medical History Taking
Histrionic Personality Disorder   WM 173
HIV   QW 168.5.H6
HIV Antibodies   QW 575
HIV Antibody Positive see HIV Seropositivity
HIV–Associated Antibodies see HIV Antibodies
HIV–Associated Nephropathy see AIDS–Associated
    Nephropathy
HIV Dementia see AIDS Dementia Complex
HIV Encephalopathy see AIDS Dementia Complex
HIV Infections   WC 503–503.7
HIV Seroconversion see HIV Seropositivity
HIV Serodiagnosis see AIDS Serodiagnosis
HIV Seronegativity   WC 503–503.7
HIV Seropositivity   WC 503–503.7
HIV Seroprevalence   WC 503.4
HIV–1   QW 168.5.H6
HIV–2   QW 168.5.H6
Hives see Urticaria
HLA Antigens   QW 573.5.H7
    Transplantation immunology   WO 680
HLA–D Antigens   QW 573.5.H7
    Transplantation immunology   WO 680
HLA–Dw Antigens see HLA–D Antigens
HMG CoA Reductases see Hydroxymethylglutaryl
    CoA Reductases
HMG–20 see Ubiquitin
HMN Distal Type I see Charcot–Marie Disease
HMO see Health Maintenance Organizations
HMSN Type I see Charcot–Marie Disease
Hoarseness   WV 510
Hobbies   QT 250
Hockey   QT 260.5.H6
Hodgkin's Disease   WH 500
HOE 766 see Buserelin
Hog Cholera   SF 973

Holidays   GT 3925–4995
Holistic Health   W 61
    Medical ethics   W 50
    Medical philosophy   W 61
Holocaine Hydrochloride see Anesthetics, Local
Holography
    Acoustic (Physics)   QC 244.5
    Applied   TA 1540–1555
    Physical optics   QC 449–449.3
Holter Monitoring see Electrocardiography,
    Ambulatory
Home Accidents see Accidents, Home
Home Blood Glucose Monitoring see Blood Glucose
    Self–Monitoring
Home Care Agencies   WY 115
Home Care, Non–Professional see Home Nursing
Home Care Services   WY 115
    Mental patients   WM 35
    Tuberculous patients   WF 315
    See also Popular works   WB 120 under
        Medicine; Self Medication   WB 120
Home Childbirth   WQ 155
Home Health Agencies see Home Care Agencies
Home Health Care Agencies see Home Care
    Agencies
Home Hemodialysis see Hemodialysis, Home
Home Medicine see Popular works   WB 120 under
    Medicine; Self Medication
Home Nursing   WY 200
    See also Nursing, Practical   WY 195
    Home care services   WY 115, etc.
Home Range
    Animal behaviour   QL 751
    See also Territoriality   QL 756.2
Homeless Persons   HV 4480–4630
    Special topics, by subject, e.g., Health problems
        of homeless persons   WA 300–305
Homeopathy   WB 930
    History   WB 930
    In infancy & childhood   WS 366
    In treatment of particular diseases or system with
        the disease or system
    Veterinary medicine   SF 746
Homeostasis   QT 120
Homes for the Aged   WT 27–28
Homicide
    Criminology   HV 6499–6535
    Juvenile   HV 9067.H6
    Medicolegal aspects   W 860
Hominidae   GN 51–289
Hominids see Hominidae
Homo sapiens see Hominidae
Homocystinuria   WD 205.5.A5
Homograft see Transplantation, Homologous
Homograft Dressings see Biological Dressings
Homologous Sequences, Nucleic Acid see Sequence
    Homology, Nucleic Acid
Homologous Wasting Disease see Graft vs Host
    Disease
Homosexuality   HQ 75–76.8
    Psychiatric aspects   WM 611
Homosexuality, Ego–Dystonic   WM 611
Homosexuality, Female   HQ 75.3–75.6

**ALWAYS CONSULT MAIN SCHEDULES. USE NUMBER ASSIGNED ONLY WHEN
SUBJECT REPRESENTS MAJOR EMPHASIS OF WORK BEING CLASSIFIED**

Psychiatric aspects   WM 611
Homosexuality, Male   HQ 75.7–76.2
    Psychiatric aspects   WM 611
Homozygote   QH 447
    Histocompatibility   WO 680
Honey
    Dietary supplement in health or disease   WB 447
    Pharmaceutical preparation   QV 785
Hoof and Claw   QL 942
    Domestic animals   SF 761–768
Hookworm Infections   WC 890
    Veterinary   SF 810.N4
Hookworm, New World see Necator
Hookworm, Old World see Ancylostoma
Hookworms see Ancylostomatoidea
Hordeolum   WW 205
Hormone Analogs see Hormones, Synthetic
Hormone Antagonists   WK 102
    See also names of specific antagonists
Hormone-Dependent Neoplasms see Neoplasms, Hormone-Dependent
Hormone Replacement Therapy, Post-Menopausal see Estrogen Replacement Therapy
Hormones   WK
    Analysis   QY 330–335
    Female see Sex Hormones   WP 520–530, etc.; and names of specific hormones
    General works   WK 102
    Male see Sex Hormones   WJ 875, etc.; and names of specific hormones
    Renal   WK 180
    Secretion   WK 102
    Steroid   WK 150
    Therapeutic use   WK 190
    See also names of specific hormones
Hormones, Ectopic   WK 185
    Neoplastic etiology   QZ 202
Hormones, Invertebrate see Invertebrate Hormones
Hormones, Synthetic   WK 187
    See also names of specific hormones
Hornets see Wasps
Horse Diseases   SF 951–959
Horseradish Peroxidase   QU 140
Horses   SF 277–360.4
    Anatomy   SF 765
    Horseshoeing   SF 907
    Military   UC 600–695
Horseshoe Crabs   QX 460
Hospice Care   WB 310
Hospice Programs see Hospice Care
Hospices   WX 28.6–28.62
Hospital-Addiction Syndrome see Munchausen Syndrome
Hospital Administration   WX 150–190
    As a career   WX 155
    Of specialty hospitals (Form number 27–28 in any NLM schedule where applicable)
    Of wards
        General hospitals   WX 159
        Psychiatric hospitals   WM 30
Hospital Administrators   WX 155
Hospital Admission Tests see Diagnostic Tests,

Routine
Hospital Admissions Office see Admitting Department, Hospital
Hospital Admitting Department see Admitting Department, Hospital
Hospital Ancillary Services see Ancillary Services, Hospital
Hospital Anesthesia Department see Anesthesia Department, Hospital
Hospital Anesthesia-Resuscitation Department see Anesthesia Department, Hospital
Hospital Auxiliaries   WX 159.5
Hospital Bed Capacity   WX 140
Hospital Care see Hospitalization
Hospital Central Supply see Central Supply, Hospital
Hospital Chaplaincy Service see Chaplaincy Service, Hospital
Hospital Communication Systems   WX 150
    In disaster   WX 185
Hospital Dental Service see Dental Service, Hospital
Hospital Dental Staff see Dental Staff, Hospital
Hospital Departments   WX 200–225
    See also names of various hospital departments, e.g., Psychiatric Department, Hospital   WM 27–28
Hospital Design and Construction   WX 140
    In specialty fields (Form number 27–28 in any NLM schedule where applicable)
Hospital Distribution Systems   WX 165
Hospital Diversification see Hospital Restructuring
Hospital Drug Distribution Systems see Medication Systems, Hospital
Hospital Economics see Economics, Hospital
Hospital Emergency Service see Emergency Service, Hospital
Hospital Engineering see Maintenance and Engineering, Hospital
Hospital Equipment and Supplies see Equipment and Supplies, Hospital
Hospital Financial Management see Financial Management, Hospital
Hospital Food Service see Food Service, Hospital
Hospital Gift Shops see Hospital Shops
Hospital Groundskeeping see Maintenance and Engineering, Hospital
Hospital Housekeeping see Housekeeping, Hospital
Hospital Incident Reporting see Risk Management
Hospital Infection see Cross Infection
Hospital Infections see Cross Infection
Hospital Information Systems   WX 26.5
    In particular fields (Form number 26.5 in any NLM schedule where applicable)
Hospital Jurisprudence see Jurisprudence
Hospital Laboratories see Laboratories, Hospital
Hospital Laundry Service see Laundry Service, Hospital
Hospital Licensure see Licensure, Hospital
Hospital Maintenance see Maintenance and Engineering, Hospital
Hospital Materials Management see Materials Management, Hospital
Hospital Medical Records Department see Medical Records Department, Hospital

Hospital Medical Staff see Medical Staff, Hospital
Hospital Medication Systems see Medication Systems, Hospital
Hospital Nuclear Medicine Department see Nuclear Medicine Department, Hospital
Hospital Nurseries see Nurseries, Hospital
Hospital Nursing Service see Nursing Service, Hospital
Hospital Nursing Staff see Nursing Staff, Hospital
Hospital Obstetrics and Gynecology Department see Obstetrics and Gynecology Department, Hospital
Hospital Occupational Therapy Department see Occupational Therapy Department, Hospital
Hospital Organization and Administration see Hospital Administration
Hospital Outpatient Clinics see Outpatient Clinics, Hospital
Hospital–Patient Relations   WX 158.5
Hospital Personnel see Personnel, Hospital
Hospital Personnel Administration see Personnel Administration, Hospital
Hospital Pharmacy Service see Pharmacy Service, Hospital
Hospital Physical Therapy Department see Physical Therapy Department, Hospital
Hospital–Physician Joint Ventures   WX 150
Hospital Planning   WX 140
   Mental hospitals   WM 30
   Other special hospitals (Form number 27–28 in any NLM schedule where applicable)
Hospital Psychiatric Department see Psychiatric Department, Hospital
Hospital Purchasing see Purchasing, Hospital
Hospital Radiology Department see Radiology Department, Hospital
Hospital Readmission see Patient Readmission
Hospital Records   WX 173
Hospital Recovery Room see Recovery Room
Hospital Referral see Referral and Consultation
Hospital Renovation see Hospital Design and Construction
Hospital Reorganization see Hospital Restructuring
Hospital Respiratory Therapy Department see Respiratory Therapy Department, Hospital
Hospital Restructuring   WX 150
Hospital Services, Centralized see Centralized Hospital Services
Hospital Shared Services   WX 150
Hospital Shops   WX 161
Hospital Social Work Department see Social Work Department, Hospital
Hospital Surgery Department see Surgery Department, Hospital
Hospital Units   WX 200–218
   Self-care units   WX 200
   Wards   WX 200
Hospital Urology Department see Urology Department, Hospital
Hospital Volunteers   WX 159.5
   Mental hospitals   WM 30.5
   Nursing   WY 193
Hospitalization   WX 158–158.5
   Anecdotes about   WZ 305.5

   Children see Child, Hospitalized   WS 105.5.H7
   Insurance see Insurance, Hospitalization   W 160
   Tuberculosis   WF 330
Hospitalization Insurance see Insurance, Hospitalization
Hospitalized Child see Child, Hospitalized
Hospitals   WX
   Administrative serial reports (all types of hospitals)   WX 2
   Directories (Form number 22 in any NLM schedule where applicable)
   Disasters   WX 185
   Food service see Food Service, Hospital   WX 168
   Libraries see Libraries, Hospital   Z 675.H7
   Medical record libraries see Medical Records, Medical Record Administrators   WX 173, etc.
   Safety measures   WX 185
   Social service   W 322
   Standards   WX 15
   Surveys   WX 27
   Veterinary see Hospitals, Animal   SF 604.4–604.7
   See also Accreditation   WX 15, etc.; Hospitals, Military   UH 460–485; Utilization Review   WX 153
Hospitals, Air Force see Hospitals, Military
Hospitals, Animal   SF 604.5
Hospitals, Army see Hospitals, Military
Hospitals, Cancer see Cancer Care Facilities
Hospitals, Community   WX 27–28
   Administration and organization   WX 150–190
   Architectural planning and construction   WX 140
Hospitals, Convalescent   WX 27–28
   Administration and organization   WX 150–190
   Architectural planning and construction   WX 140
Hospitals, General   WX 27–28
   Administration and organization   WX 150–190
   Architectural planning and construction   WX 140
Hospitals, Maternity   WQ 27–28
Hospitals, Military   UH 460–485
   Naval   VG 410–450
Hospitals, Navy see Hospitals, Military
Hospitals, Private, Not-for-Profit see Hospitals, Voluntary
Hospitals, Psychiatric   WM 27–28
   Administration   WM 30
   Directories   WM 22
   For children only   WS 27–28
   Practices in care of mental patients   WM 35
   See also Psychiatric Department, Hospital   WM 27–28, etc.
Hospitals, Public   WX 27–28
   See also special topics under Hospitals
Hospitals, Special
   (Form number 27–28 in any NLM schedule where applicable)
   Cancer   QZ 23–24
   Hospices   WX 28.6–28.62

Isolation　WC 27–28
Leprosaria　WC 27–28
Maternity　WQ 27–28
Quarantine　WC 27–28
Tuberculosis　WF 27–28
Hospitals, Teaching　WX 27–28
　For specific curriculum, in hospital number of
　　appropriate schedule
Hospitals, Veterans　UH 460–485
　Administration　UH 460–465
　Nursing　WY 130
　Special topics, by subject
Hospitals, Veterinary see Hospitals, Animal
Hospitals, Voluntary see Hospitals　WX 27–28, etc.
Host-Parasite Relations　QX 45
Hostility　BF 575.H6
　In adolescence　WS 462
　In infancy & childhood　WS 105.5.E5
Hostility Catharsis see Abreaction
Hot Climate
　Physiological effect　QT 150
Hotlines
　Special topics, by subject, e.g., Emergency
　　Services, Psychiatric　WM 401
House Calls　WB 50
House Staff see Internship and Residency
Houseflies　QX 505
Household Articles
　Accidents from　WA 288
　Safety control
　　Home measures　WA 288
　　Regulatory measures　WA 288
Household Equipment see Household Articles
Household Medicine see Popular works　WB 120,
　etc. under Medicine
Household Products
　As a cause of accidents　WA 288
　Ocular toxicity　WW 100
　Safety control
　　Home measures　WA 288
　　Regulatory measures　WA 288
　See also names of specific products
Household Supplies see Household Products
Housekeeping
　Building operations and housekeeping　TX
　　955–985
　Home economics　TX 301–323
　Plant housekeeping　TS 193
　See also Self Help Devices　WB 320
Housekeeping, Hospital　WX 165
Housing
　Design for the disabled　WA 795
　　See also Architecture　WA 795, etc.
　　Architectural Accessibility　WA 795–799
　For the elderly　WT 30
　Real estate　HD 251–1395
　Repairs and maintenance　TH 4817
　Rural　HD 7289
　Sanitation　WA 795
　See also Public Housing　HD 7288–7288.78
Housing, Animal　SF 91
　Laboratory animals　QY 56
　Of particular animals, by animal

Housing for the Elderly　WT 30
HPLC see Chromatography, High Pressure Liquid
HSAN Type III see Dysautonomia, Familial
HTLV-BLV Infections　WC 502
HTLV-BLV Viruses　QW 168.5.R18
HTLV-I　QW 168.5.R18
HTLV-I Infections　WC 502
HTLV-III see HIV
HTLV-III Antibodies see HIV Antibodies
HTLV-III Infections see HIV Infections
HTLV-III-LAV Antibodies see HIV Antibodies
HTLV-III-LAV Infections see HIV Infections
HTLV-III Seroconversion see HIV Seropositivity
HTLV-III Serodiagnosis see AIDS Serodiagnosis
HTLV-III Serology see AIDS Serodiagnosis
HTLV-III Seronegativity see HIV Seronegativity
HTLV-III Seropositivity see HIV Seropositivity
HTLV Infections see HTLV-BLV Infections
HTLV-IV see HIV-2
HTLV Viruses see HTLV-BLV Viruses
Human Anatomy see Anatomy
Human Class II Antigens see HLA-D Antigens
Human Development　BF 713
　Aging process　WT 104
　Physical development　WS 103
Human Engineering　TA 166–167
　Special topics, by subject, e.g., Biomedical
　　Engineering　QT 36, etc.; Space Flight　WD
　　750–758
Human Experimentation　W 20.55.H9
　Special topics, by subject, e.g., in drug research
　　QV 20.5
Human Figure in Art see Anatomy, Artistic
Human Forefoot see Forefoot, Human
Human Genome see Genome, Human
Human Immunodeficiency Virus–Associated
　Nephropathy see AIDS–Associated Nephropathy
Human Immunodeficiency Virus Type 1 see HIV–1
Human Immunodeficiency Virus Type 2 see HIV–2
Human Immunodeficiency Viruses see HIV
Human-Pet Bonding see Bonding, Human-Pet
Human Physiology see Physiology
Human Reproduction see Reproduction
Human Resources Development see Staff
　Development
Human Rights
　Constitutional law (United States)　KF
　　4741–4786
　Right to education　KF 4151–4155
　Political theory　JC 571–628
　Special topic by subject, e.q., Advocacy of Child
　　Health Services　WA 320
　See also Civil Rights　WM 30–32, etc.; Women's
　　Rights　HQ 1236–1236.5
Human T-Cell Leukemia-Lymphoma Viruses see
　HTLV-BLV Viruses
Human T-Cell Leukemia Virus I see HTLV-I
Human T-Cell Leukemia Viruses see HTLV-BLV
　Viruses
Human T-Cell Lymphotropic Virus Type III see
　HIV
Human T-Lymphotropic Virus Type III see HIV
Human T-Lymphotropic Virus Type IV see HIV-2

Humanism
    In medical ethics   W 50
    In medical philosophy   W 61
    Modern   B 821
    Renaissance   B 778
    In other areas, by subject
Humanities   CB, AZ
    And religion   BL 65.H8
    And science   AZ 361, etc.
    Education (Humanistic)   LC 1001–1024
        Renaissance   LA 106–108
    Other special topics, by subject
Humeral Fractures   WE 810
Humeral Fractures, Proximal see Shoulder Fractures
Humerus   WE 810
Humic Acids
    Geochemistry   QE 516–516.5
    Soil acidity (agriculture)   S 592.57–592.575
Humidity
    Control   WA 774
        In industry   WA 450
    Hygienic aspects   QT 230
        Hot climates   QT 150
    Meteorology   QC 915–917
    Physiological effects (General)   QT 162.H8
Humor see Wit and Humor
Hunger
    Malnutrition   WD 100
    Nutrition surveys   QU 146
    Physiology   WI 102
    Prevention   WA 695
Huntington Chorea see Huntington's Disease
Huntington's Disease   WL 390
Hurler-Scheie Syndrome see Mucopolysaccharidosis I
Hurler's Syndrome see Mucopolysaccharidosis I
Hurricanes see Natural Disasters
Hutchinson's Teeth see Syphilis, Congenital
HY Antigen see H–Y Antigen
Hyaline Membrane Disease   WS 410
Hyaluronic Acid   QU 83
Hybrid Cells   QH 425
Hybridization   QH 421–425
    Animals   QH 425
    Plants   QK 982
        See also Animals   SF 105–109 and Plants
        under Breeding   SB 123–123.5
Hybridomas
    As fused cells   QH 451
    In the production of monoclonal antibodies   QW 575.5.A6
Hydantoins   QV 85
Hydatid see Echinococcus
Hydatid Cyst see Echinococcosis
Hydatid Cyst, Hepatic see Echinococcosis, Hepatic
Hydatid Cyst, Pulmonary see Echinococcosis, Pulmonary
Hydatidiform Mole   WP 465
    Malignant see Hydatidiform Mole, Invasive   WP 465, etc.
    Pathology   QZ 310
Hydatidiform Mole, Invasive   WP 465
    Pathology   QZ 310

Hydatidosis see Echinococcosis
Hydatidosis, Hepatic see Echinococcosis, Hepatic
Hydatidosis, Pulmonary see Echinococcosis, Pulmonary
Hydralazine   QV 150
Hydrallazin see Hydralazine
Hydrarthrosis   WE 304
Hydrated Alumina see Aluminum Hydroxide
Hydrazines
    As antiparkinson agents   QV 80
    Biochemistry   QU 60
    Organic chemistry
        Aliphatic compounds   QD 305.A8
    Neoplasm etiology   QZ 202
    See also Phenylhydrazines   QD 341.A8, etc.
Hydrocarbons
    Organic chemistry
        Aliphatic compounds   QD 305.H5–H9
        Aromatic compounds   QD 341.H9
    Toxicology   QV 633
Hydrocarbons, Chlorinated
    As anesthetics   QV 81
    Organic chemistry   QD 305.H5
        Aliphatic   QD 305.H5
        Aromatic   QD 341.H9
    Toxicology   QV 633
Hydrocarbons, Fluorinated
    Organic chemistry
        Aliphatic compounds   QD 305.H5
        Aromatic compounds   QD 341.H9
    Toxicology   QV 633
Hydrocarbons, Halogenated
    As anesthetics   QV 81
    As carcinogens   QZ 202
    Organic chemistry
        Aliphatic   QD 305.H5
        Aromatic   QD 341.H9
    Toxicology   QV 633
Hydrocarbons, Polycyclic see Polycyclic Hydrocarbons
Hydrocele   WJ 800
Hydrocephalus   WL 350
Hydrochloric Acid   QD 181.C5
    Gastric see Gastric Juice   WI 302, etc.
    Toxicology   QV 612
Hydrochloric Acid, Gastric see Gastric Acid
Hydrochlorothiazide   QV 160
Hydrocortisone   WK 755
    Deficiency   WK 760
        As a cause of a particular disorder, with the disorder
Hydrocortisone, Topical   QV 60
Hydrocyanic Acid see Hydrogen Cyanide
Hydroelectric Power Plants see Power Plants
Hydrogen
    Inorganic chemistry   QD 181.H1
    Pharmacology   QV 275
Hydrogen Acceptors see Oxidation–Reduction
Hydrogen Bonding   QD 464.H1
Hydrogen Chloride see Hydrochloric Acid
Hydrogen Cyanide   QV 632
Hydrogen-Ion Concentration
    Electrochemistry   QD 562.H93

**ALWAYS CONSULT MAIN SCHEDULES. USE NUMBER ASSIGNED ONLY WHEN
SUBJECT REPRESENTS MAJOR EMPHASIS OF WORK BEING CLASSIFIED**

Hypercholesterolemia   WD 200.5.H8
Hypercorticism see Adrenal Gland Hyperfunction
Hyperemesis Gravidarum   WQ 215
Hyperemia   QZ 170
    Localized, by site
Hyperesthesia   WL 710
    Of skin   WR 280
    Of the vagina   WP 250
    Other localities, by site
Hyperglycemia   WK 880
Hyperglycemic Hyperosmolar Nonketotic Coma
    WK 830
Hyperhidrosis   WR 400
Hyperinsulinism   WK 880
Hyperkeratosis Linguae see Tongue, Hairy
Hyperkeratosis Palmaris et Plantaris see
    Keratoderma, Palmoplantar
Hyperkinesis   WM 197
    In adolescence   WS 463
    In infancy & childhood   WS 350.8.H9
Hyperkinetic Heart Syndrome see Neurocirculatory
    Asthenia
Hyperkinetic Syndrome see Attention Deficit
    Disorder with Hyperactivity
Hyperlipemia see Hyperlipidemia
Hyperlipidemia   WD 200.5.H8
Hyperlipidemia, Essential Familial see
    Hyperlipidemia
Hyperlipoproteinemia   WD 205.5.L5
Hyperlipoproteinemia Type IV   WD 205.5.L5
Hypermenorrhea see Menorrhagia
Hypermetropia see Hyperopia
Hypermobility, Joint see Joint Instability
Hypernatremia   WD 220
Hypernephroma see Carcinoma, Renal Cell
Hyperopia   WW 300
Hyperostosis Corticalis Generalisata see
    Osteochondrodysplasias
Hyperostosis Frontalis Interna   WE 705
Hyperparathyroidism   WK 300
Hyperphagia   WM 175
Hyperpituitarism   WK 550
Hyperplasia   QZ 190
Hyperprebetalipoproteinemia see
    Hyperlipoproteinemia Type IV
Hyperprolactinemia   WD 200.5.H9
Hypersensitivity
    Allergenic substances see Allergens   QW 900
    Diseases (General)   WD 300–330
    Drug see Drug Hypersensitivity   WD 320
    Eye   WW 160
    Food see Food Hypersensitivity   WD 310
    Immunology   QW 900
    Light see Photosensitivity Disorders   WR 160
    Respiratory see Respiratory Hypersensitivity
    WF 150
    Skin   WR 160–190
    Veterinary   SF 757.2
    See also other specific diseases or disease groups
      associated with hypersensitivity, e.g., Collagen
      Diseases   WD 375
Hypersensitivity, Atopic see Hypersensitivity,
    Immediate

Hypersensitivity, Contact see Dermatitis, Contact
Hypersensitivity, Delayed   WD 300–330
    General works   WD 300
    Immunologic factors   QW 900
Hypersensitivity, Drug see Drug Hypersensitivity
Hypersensitivity, Food see Food Hypersensitivity
Hypersensitivity, Immediate   WD 300–305
    General works   WD 300
    Immunological factors   QW 900
Hypersensitivity Pneumonitis, Avian see Bird
    Fancier's Lung
Hypersensitivity, Respiratory see Respiratory
    Hypersensitivity
Hypersensitivity, Tuberculin–Type see
    Hypersensitivity, Delayed
Hypersensitivity, Type I see Hypersensitivity,
    Immediate
Hypersensitivity, Type III see Immune Complex
    Diseases
Hypersensitivity, Type IV see Hypersensitivity,
    Delayed
Hypersomnia   WM 188
Hypersomnia with Periodic Respiration see Sleep
    Apnea Syndromes
Hypersplenism   WH 600
Hypertelorism   WE 705
Hypertensinogen see Angiotensinogen
Hypertension   WG 340
Hypertension–Edema–Proteinuria Gestosis see
    Gestosis, EPH
Hypertension, Goldblatt see Hypertension,
    Renovascular
Hypertension, Malignant   WG 340
Hypertension, Portal   WI 720
Hypertension, Pulmonary   WG 340
Hypertension, Pulmonary, of Newborn, Persistent
    see Persistent Fetal Circulation Syndrome
Hypertension, Renal   WG 340
Hypertension, Renovascular   WG 340
Hyperthermia see Fever
Hyperthermia, Induced   WB 469
    In mental disorders   WM 405
Hyperthermia, Local see Hyperthermia, Induced
Hyperthermia, Therapeutic see Hyperthermia,
    Induced
Hyperthyroidism   WK 265
Hypertonic Glucose Solution see Glucose Solution,
    Hypertonic
Hypertonic Saline Solution see Saline Solution,
    Hypertonic
Hypertonic Solution, Glucose see Glucose Solution,
    Hypertonic
Hypertonic Solution, Saline see Saline Solution,
    Hypertonic
Hypertonic Solutions   QV 786
Hypertrichosis   WR 455
Hypertriglyceridemia   WD 200.5.H8
Hypertriglyceridemia, Familial see
    Hyperlipoproteinemia Type IV
Hypertrophic Arthritis see Osteoarthritis
Hypertrophy   QZ 190
    See also Cervix Hypertrophy   WP 470; Gingival
      Hypertrophy   WU 240; Heart Hypertrophy

WG 210; Myocardial Diseases, Primary   WG 280; Prostatic Hypertrophy   WJ 752
Hypertropia see Strabismus
Hyperventilation   WF 143
Hyphomycetes   QW 180.5.D3
Hypnosis
    Parapsychology   BF 1111–1156
    Psychiatric therapy   WM 415
    Self Hypnosis   WM 415
    Surgery see Hypnosis, Anesthetic   WO 200
Hypnosis, Anesthetic   WO 200
Hypnosis, Dental   WO 460
Hypnotics and Sedatives   QV 85–88
Hypobaropathy see Altitude Sickness
Hypocalcemia   WD 200.5.C2
    Veterinary   SF 910.H86
Hypochlorhydria see Achlorhydria
Hypocholesteremic Agents see Anticholesteremic Agents
Hypochondriasis   WM 178
Hypochromic Anemias see Anemia, Hypochromic
Hypodermic Medication see Infusions, Parenteral; Injections, Subcutaneous
Hypodermoclysis see Infusions, Parenteral; names of solutions or agents used, e.g., Sodium Chloride
Hypodermyiasis   WC 900
Hypodontia see Anodontia
Hypogalactia see Lactation Disorders
Hypogammaglobulinemia see Agammaglobulinemia
Hypogastric Plexus   WL 600
Hypoglossal Nerve   WL 330
Hypoglycemia   WK 880
Hypoglycemic Agents   WK 825
Hypogonadism   WK 900
Hypohidrosis   WR 400
    Drugs for   QV 122
Hypokalemia   WD 220
Hypokinesia see Immobilization
Hypomenorrhea see Menstruation Disorders
Hyponatremia   WD 220
Hypoparathyroidism   WK 300
Hypopharyngeal Neoplasms   WV 410
Hypophysectomy   WK 590
Hypophysectomy, Chemical   WK 590
Hypophysis see Pituitary Gland
Hypophysis Cerebri see Pituitary Gland
Hypopituitarism   WK 550
Hypopotassemia see Hypokalemia
Hypoprothrombinemias   WH 322
Hyposalivation see Xerostomia
Hyposensitization Therapy see Desensitization, Immunologic
Hyposomnia see Insomnia
Hypospadias   WJ 600
Hypotension   WG 340
Hypotension, Controlled   WO 350
Hypotension, Orthostatic   WG 340
Hypotension, Postural see Hypotension, Orthostatic
Hypothalamic Diseases   WL 312
Hypothalamic Hormones   WL 312
Hypothalamo–Hypophyseal System   WK 501–502
Hypothalamus   WL 312
Hypothalamus, Infundibular see Hypothalamus, Middle
Hypothalamus, Medial see Hypothalamus, Middle
Hypothalamus, Middle   WL 312
Hypothermia   WD 670
    Pathogenesis   QZ 57
    Physiological adaptation   QT 160
Hypothermia, Induced   WO 350
    For extending life for future therapy   WO 350
    Veterinary   SF 914
    See also Cryogenic Surgery   WO 510; Gastric Hypothermia   WI 380; Surgery of particular organs or systems, by part, e.g., Hypothermia in neurosurgery   WL 368
Hypothyroidism   WK 250
Hypoventilation, Central Alveolar see Sleep Apnea Syndromes
Hypovolemic Shock see Shock
Hypoxemia see Anoxemia
Hypoxia see Anoxia
Hypoxia, Cellular see Cell Hypoxia
Hypsarrhythmia see Spasms, Infantile
Hysterectomy, Vaginal   WP 468
Hysteria   WM 173–173.7
Hysteria, Conversion see Conversion Disorder
Hysteria, Dissociative see Dissociative Disorders
Hysterical Neuroses see Hysteria
Hysterical Personality see Histrionic Personality Disorder
Hysterosalpingography   WP 141
Hysteroscopy   WP 440
    Used in surgical interventions   WP 468
Hystrix see Rodentia

I

Ia Antigens see Histocompatibility Antigens Class II
Ia–Like Antigens see Histocompatibility Antigens Class II
Ia–Like Antigens, Human see HLA–D Antigens
IAP Pertussis Toxin see Pertussis Toxins
Iatrogenic Disease   QZ 42
IBR–IPV Virus see Herpesvirus 1, Bovine
Ibuprofen   QV 95
    As an enzyme inhibitor   QU 143
Ice
    Physical geography   GB 2401–2598
    Sanitation   WA 675
Ice Cream
    As a dietary supplement in health or disease   WB 428
    Sanitary control   WA 715
Ichthyosis   WR 500
ICI–46474 see Tamoxifen
ICI 66082 see Atenolol
ICSH see LH
Icterus see Jaundice
Icterus Gravis Neonatorum see Erythroblastosis, Fetal
Id   WM 460.5.U6
IDDM see Diabetes Mellitus, Insulin–Dependent
Identification of Persons see Forensic medicine   W 786, etc. and names of special means of

ALWAYS CONSULT MAIN SCHEDULES. USE NUMBER ASSIGNED ONLY WHEN SUBJECT REPRESENTS MAJOR EMPHASIS OF WORK BEING CLASSIFIED

I–122

identification, e.g., Dermatoglyphics
Identification (Psychology)
    In adolescence   WS 462
    In infancy & childhood   WS 105.5.P3
    Personality Development (General)   BF 698
    Psychoanalysis   WM 460.5.I4
Identification, Social see Social Identification
Identity Crisis   BF 697
    In adolescence   WS 463
    In infancy & childhood   WS 350.8.I3
    In psychoanalysis   WM 460.5.P3
Idiocy see Mental Retardation
Idiopathic Hypercatabolic Hypoproteinemia see
    Protein-Losing Enteropathies
Idiosyncrasy, Drug see Pharmacology
Idiotypes, Immunoglobulin see Immunoglobulin
    Idiotypes
Iditol Dehydrogenase   QU 140
Ifosfamide
    As an antineoplastic agent   QV 269
    As an immunosuppressive agent   QW 920
IGA Glomerulonephritis see Glomerulonephritis,
    IGA
IGA Nephropathy see Glomerulonephritis, IGA
IgE   QW 601
IGF-I see Insulin-Like Growth Factor I
IGF-II see Insulin-Like Growth Factor II
IgG   QW 601
IL-1 see Interleukin-1
IL-2 see Interleukin-2
IL-2 Receptors see Receptors, Interleukin-2
IL-3 see Interleukin-3
IL-8 see Interleukin-8
Ileal Neoplasms   WI 512
Ileitis   WI 512
Ileitis, Regional see Crohn Disease
Ileitis, Terminal see Crohn Disease
Ileocecal Valve   WI 512
Ileocolitis see Crohn Disease
Ileostomy   WI 512
Ileum   WI 512
Ileus see Intestinal Obstruction
Iliac Artery   WG 595.I5
Iliac Vein   WG 625.I5
Illegitimacy   HQ 998-999
    Adolescents   WS 462, etc.
    Child psychology   WS 105.5.A8
    Maternal welfare   WA 310
    Paternity   W 791
    Unwed parents
        Relationship to children   WS 105.5.F2
Illicit Drug Testing see Substance Abuse Detection
Illicit Drugs see Street Drugs
Illiteracy see Educational Status
Illness Behavior see Sick Role
Illuminating Gas Poisoning see Carbon Monoxide
    Poisoning
Illumination see Lighting
Illusions   BF 491-493
    Optical   WW 105
    Psychotic   WM 204
Illustrated Books see Books, Illustrated
Illustration, Medical see Medical Illustration

Illustrations, Surgical see Medical Illustration
Image Analysis, Computer-Assisted see Image
    Processing, Computer-Assisted
Image Enhancement
    Photoelectronic devices   TK 8316
    Photography
        Treatment of negatives   TR 299
        Treatment of positives   TR 335
    Specific objects, by subject
    See also Radiographic Image Enhancement
    WN 160
Image Intensifiers see Image Enhancement
Image Interpretation, Computer-Assisted
    General   WB 141
    For particular disorders, with the disorder
Image Processing, Computer-Assisted
    In particular fields (Form number 26.5 in any
        NLM schedule where applicable)
    Used for special purposes, by subject
Image Reconstruction see Image Processing,
    Computer-Assisted
Imagination
    In adolescence   WS 462
    In infancy & childhood   WS 105.5.C7
    Creative processes   BF 408-426
    Mental imagery (General)   BF 367
    See also Fantasy   BF 408-411, etc.
Imaging, Diagnostic see Diagnostic Imaging
Imaging, Medical see Diagnostic Imaging
Imaging Techniques see Diagnostic Imaging
Imbecility see Mental Retardation
Imidazoles   QU 65
    Organic chemistry   QD 401
Imidazolidinethione see Ethylenethiourea
Imidobenzyle see Imipramine
Imines   QU 54
    Organic chemistry
        Aliphatic compounds   QD 305.I6
        Aromatic compounds   QD 341.I6
Imipemide see Imipenem
Imipenem   QV 350
Imipramine   QV 77.5
Imitative Behavior   BF 357
    In infancy & childhood   WS 105.5.S6
Imizin see Imipramine
Immaturity Syndromes see Personality Disorders
Immediate Recall see Memory, Short-Term
Immersion
    As a cause of accident or disease   QZ 57
    Special conditions resulting, with the condition,
        e.g., Hypothermia   WD 670, etc.
Immersion Foot   WG 530
Immigration see Emigration and Immigration
Immobilization   WE 168
    Used for special purposes, by subject
Immobilized Enzymes see Enzymes, Immobilized
Immotile Cilia Syndrome see Ciliary Motility
    Disorders
Immune-Associated Antigens see Histocompatibility
    Antigens Class II
Immune-Associated Antigens, Human see HLA-D
    Antigens
Immune Body see Antibodies

Immune Complex Diseases   WD 308
Immune Monitoring see Monitoring, Immunologic
Immune Precipitates see Precipitins
Immune Response Antigens see Histocompatibility
    Antigens Class II
Immune-Response Antigens, Human see HLA-D
    Antigens
Immune-Response-Associated Antigens see
    Histocompatibility Antigens Class II
Immune Response-Associated Antigens, Human see
    HLA-D Antigens
Immune Response Genes see Genes, MHC Class II
Immune RNA Manipulation see Immunization,
    Passive
Immune Sera   QW 815
Immune System   QW 504
Immune Tolerance   QW 504
    Transplantation immunology   WO 680
Immunity   QW 540-949
    Acquired   QW 551
    Artificial   QW 551
    As affected by stress   QZ 160
    In infancy & childhood   WS 135
    Local   QW 563
    Preparations producing   QW 800-815
Immunity, Active   QW 552
Immunity, Cellular   QW 568
Immunity, Humoral see Antibody Formation
Immunity, Natural   QW 541
Immunity, Non-Specific see Immunity, Natural
Immunity, Passive   QW 553
Immunization   QW 800-815
    In infancy & childhood   WS 135
    Public health aspects   WA 110
    Veterinary   SF 757.2
    For a particular disease, with the disease
Immunization, Active see Vaccination
Immunization, Booster see Immunization, Secondary
Immunization, Passive   QW 945
    Of a particular disease, with the disease
Immunization Programs   WA 110
    In infancy & childhood   WS 135
    For prevention of specific diseases, by disease
Immunization Schedule   QW 800-815
    In infancy & childhood   WS 135
Immunization, Secondary   QW 800-815
    In infancy & childhood   WS 135
Immunoactivators see Adjuvants, Immunologic
Immunoadjuvants see Adjuvants, Immunologic
Immunoadsorbents see Immunosorbents
Immunoassay
    General   QW 525.5.I3
    Assay of hormones   QY 330
    Used for diagnostic, monitoring, or evaluation
        tests in special fields, with the field
Immunoassay, Enzyme see Immunoenzyme
    Techniques
Immunoblastic Lymphadenopathy   WH 700
Immunoblotting   QW 525.5.I32
    Used for diagnostic, monitoring, or evaluation
        tests in special fields, with the field
Immunoblotting, Western see Blotting, Western
Immunochemistry   QW 504.5

Immunocompetence   QW 568
Immunocompromised Host   QW 504
Immunocontraception see Contraception,
    Immunologic
Immunocytochemistry see Immunohistochemistry
Immunodeficiency Syndrome, Acquired see
    Acquired Immunodeficiency Syndrome
Immunodiagnosis see Immunologic Tests
Immunodiagnostic Tests see Immunologic Tests
Immunodiffusion   QY 265
Immunoelectroblotting see Immunoblotting
Immunoelectroosmophoresis see
    Counterimmunoelectrophoresis
Immunoelectrophoresis   QY 250-275
    Assay of hormones   QY 330
    Veterinary   SF 774
    Used for diagnostic monitoring, or evaluation
        tests in special fields, with the field
Immunoelectrophoresis, Countercurrent see
    Counterimmunoelectrophoresis
Immunoelectrophoresis, Crossover see
    Counterimmunoelectrophoresis
Immunoenzyme Techniques   QW 525.5.I34
    In immunodiagnostic tests   QY 250
Immunofluorescence Microscopy see Microscopy,
    Fluorescence
Immunofluorescence Technique see Fluorescent
    Antibody Technique
Immunofluorometric Assay see Fluoroimmunoassay
Immunogenetics   QW 541
Immunogens, Synthetic see Vaccines, Synthetic
Immunoglobulin Allotypes   QW 575
Immunoglobulin Genes see Genes, Immunoglobulin
Immunoglobulin Idiotypes   QW 601
Immunoglobulin-Producing Cells see
    Antibody-Producing Cells
Immunoglobulin-Secreting Cells see
    Antibody-Producing Cells
Immunoglobulin Therapy see Immunization, Passive
Immunoglobulins   QW 601
Immunoglobulins, alpha-Chain   QW 601
Immunoglobulins, mu-Chain   QW 601
Immunogold-Silver Techniques see
    Immunohistochemistry
Immunogold Techniques see Immunohistochemistry
Immunohistochemistry   QW 504.5
Immunohistocytochemistry see
    Immunohistochemistry
Immunolabeling Techniques see
    Immunohistochemistry
Immunologic Accessory Cells see
    Antigen-Presenting Cells
Immunologic Competence see Immunocompetence
Immunologic Deficiency Syndrome, Acquired see
    Acquired Immunodeficiency Syndrome
Immunologic Deficiency Syndromes   WD 308
Immunologic Diseases   WD 300-330
Immunologic Markers see Biological Markers
Immunologic Monitoring see Monitoring,
    Immunologic
Immunologic Receptors see Receptors, Immunologic
Immunologic Stimulation see Immunization
Immunologic Surveillance   QW 568

Immunologic Techniques   QW 525
   Immunodiagnostic tests   QY 250–275
   See also names of particular tests and procedures,
    e.g., Immunoassay   QW 525.5.I3, etc.
Immunologic Tests
   Used in diagnosis   QY 250–275
   Techniques   QW 525
   See also names of specific tests
Immunologists see Biography   WZ 112.5.I5 and
   Directories   QW 522 under Immunology
Immunology see Allergy and Immunology
Immunology, Transplantation see Transplantation
   Immunology
Immunomodulators see Adjuvants, Immunologic
Immunoperoxidase Techniques see Immunoenzyme
   Techniques
Immunopotentiators see Adjuvants, Immunologic
Immunoscintigraphy, Radiolabeled see
   Radioimmunodetection
Immunosorbents
   In antigen–antibody complex   QW 570
Immunostimulants see Adjuvants, Immunologic
Immunostimulation see Immunization
Immunosuppressed Host see Immunocompromised
   Host
Immunosuppression   QW 920
Immunosuppression (Physiology) see Immune
   Tolerance
Immunosuppressive Agents   QW 920
Immunosurveillance see Monitoring, Immunologic
Immunotherapy   QW 940–949
   Of a particular disease, with the disease
Immunotherapy, Active   QW 949
   Veterinary   SF 919
   Of a particular disease, with the disease
Immunotherapy, Adoptive   QW 940
Immunotherapy, Allergen see Desensitization,
   Immunologic
Immunotherapy, Passive see Immunotherapy,
   Adoptive
Immunotoxins   QW 630.5.I3
Impedance Tests, Acoustic see Acoustic Impedance
   Tests
Impedance, Transthoracic see Cardiography,
   Impedance
Impetigo   WR 225
Impetigo Contagiosa see Impetigo
Implant, Cochlear see Cochlear Implant
Implant Radiotherapy see Brachytherapy
Implantable Catheters see Catheters, Indwelling
Implantable Infusion Pumps see Infusion Pumps,
   Implantable
Implantation, Blastocyst see Ovum Implantation
Implantation, Dental see Dental Implantation
Implantation, Ovum see Nidation
Implantation, Ovum, Delayed see Ovum
   Implantation, Delayed
Implants, Artificial   WE 172
   See also Prosthesis
   See also names of specific artificial implants
Implants, Dental see Dental Implants
Implosive Therapy   WM 425.5.D4
Impotence   WJ 709

Impregnation, Artificial see Insemination, Artificial
Impulse Control Disorders   WM 190
Impulse–Ridden Personality see Personality
   Disorders
Impulsive Behavior   BF 575.I46
Inadequate Personality see Personality Disorders
Inanition see Deficiency Diseases
Inborn Errors of Metabolism see Metabolism, Inborn
   Errors
Inbreeding
   Animal   SF 105
   Physical anthropology   GN 252
   Social pathology   HV 4981
Incentive Reimbursement see Reimbursement,
   Incentive
Incentives see Motivation
Incest   WM 610
Incidence Studies see Cohort Studies
Incident Reporting, Hospital see Risk Management
Incipient Schizophrenia see Schizotypal Personality
   Disorder
Incisor   WU 101
Inclusion Bodies   QH 603.I49
Inclusion Disease see Cytomegalovirus Infections
Income
   Economic theory   HB 522–715
   Labor   HD 4906–5100.7
   Of dentists   WU 77
   Of nurses   WY 77
   Of physicians   W 79
   Of other specialties, by type
Income Tax   HJ 4621–4824
Incompatibility of Drugs see Drug Incompatibility
Incontinentia Pigmenti Achromians see Pigmentation
   Disorders
Incubation Period see Time Factors; Carrier State
Incubators
   (Form number 26 in any NLM schedule where
    applicable)
   Used in experimental histology   QS 530; in
    microbiology   QW 26
Incubators, Infant
   Catalogs   W 26
   Description   WS 26
   Usage   WS 410–421
Incunabula   Z 240–241
   Medical   WZ 230
Incus   WV 230
Indans
   Organic chemistry   QD 341.H9
   Special topics, by subject
Indapamide   QV 160
Indazoles   QV 95
   Organic chemistry   QD 401
Indenes
   As anti–arrhythmia agents   QV 150
   As anti–inflammatory analgesics   QV 95
   Organic chemistry   QD 341.H9
Independent Living see Activities of Daily Living
Independent Practice Associations   W 130
Index Medicus see MEDLARS
Indexes
   Of subjects represented in NLM's classification,

**ALWAYS CONSULT MAIN SCHEDULES. USE NUMBER ASSIGNED ONLY WHEN
SUBJECT REPRESENTS MAJOR EMPHASIS OF WORK BEING CLASSIFIED**

appropriate classification number preceded by the letter Z
Of other subjects, LC's Z schedule
Indexing see Abstracting and Indexing
Indian Nursing Service see Public Health Nursing
Indians, Central American   F 1434–1435
   See also special topics under Ethnic Groups
Indians, North American   E 75–99
   As physicians
      Collective biography   WZ 150
      History   WZ 80.5.I3
      Individual biography   WZ 100
   See also special topics under Ethnic Groups
   Mexico   F 1219–1220
Indians, South American   F 2229–2230.2 etc.
   As physicians
      Collective biography   WZ 150
      History   WZ 80.5.I3
      Individual biography   WZ 100
   See also special topics under Ethnic Groups
Indicator Dilution Techniques   WG 141
   Blood volume   WG 106
   See also Dye Dilution Technique   WG 141, etc.;
      Radioisotope Dilution Technique   WG 141, etc.
Indicators and Reagents
   Analytical chemistry   QD 77
   Pharmaceutical chemistry   QV 744
   See also Dyes   QV 240, etc.
Indigency see Poverty
Indigency, Medical see Medical Indigency
Indigent Care see Medical Indigency
Indigents, Medical Care see Medicaid; Medical Indigency
Indigestion see Dyspepsia; Heartburn
Indium
   Inorganic chemistry   QD 181.I5
   Pharmacology   QV 290
Indium Radioisotopes   WN 415–450
   Used for special purposes, by subject
Individual Differences see Individuality
Individual Practice Associations see Independent Practice Associations
Individuality
   Psychology   BF 697
   Sociology   HM 136
Individuation   WM 460.5.I5
   In personality development   BF 697
      In adolescence   WS 462
      In infancy & childhood   WS 105.5.P3
Indocyanine Green   QV 240
Indoleacetic Acids   QK 753.I5
   In amino acid metabolism   QU 65
Indoleamine 2,3-Dioxygenase see Tryptophan Oxygenase
Indoles
   As antidepressive agents   QV 77.5
   As hallucinogens   QV 77.7
   As tranquilizers   QV 77.9
   Organic chemistry   QD 401
Indolylethylamines see Tryptamines
Indomethacin   QV 95
Indoor Air Pollution see Air Pollution, Indoor

Indoor Air Quality see Air Pollution, Indoor
Indoprofen   QV 95
Indri see Strepsirhini
Indriidae see Strepsirhini
Induction of Labor see Labor, Induced
Industrial Accidents see Accidents, Occupational
Industrial Arts see Technology
Industrial Bacteriology see Bacteriology
Industrial By-Products in Air Pollution see Air Pollutants
Industrial Chemistry see Chemistry
Industrial Dentistry see Occupational Dentistry
Industrial Dermatoses see Dermatitis, Occupational
Industrial Diseases see Occupational Diseases
Industrial Health see Occupational Health
Industrial Hygiene see Occupational Health
Industrial Medical Departments see Occupational Health Services
Industrial Medicine see Occupational Medicine
Industrial Mental Health see Mental Health
Industrial Microbiology   QW 75
Industrial Nursing see Occupational Health Nursing
Industrial Oils
   Biochemistry   QU 86
   Chemical technology   TP 670–699
   Public health aspects   WA 722
Industrial Ophthalmology see Ophthalmology
Industrial Poisoning see Poisoning
Industrial Surgery see Surgery
Industrial Toxicology see Occupational Medicine; Poisons; Toxicology
Industrial Waste   WA 788
   See also names of specific types of waste, e.g.
      Air Pollutants   WA 450, etc.
Industry   HD 2321–4730.9
Inert Gas Narcosis
   Aviation and space medicine   WD 715
   Submarine medicine   WD 650
Infant   WS
   Anesthesia   WO 440
   General   WS 430
   Nursing see Pediatric Nursing   WY 159
   Radiography   WN 240
   Surgery   WO 925
   Welfare see Child Welfare   WA 310–320
   See also Birth Injuries   WS 405, other headings beginning with Birth.
Infant Care   WS 113
Infant Food   WS 115–125
Infant Health Services see Child Health Services
Infant, Low Birth Weight   WS 420
Infant Mortality   HB 1323.I4
   Including causes of death   WA 900
   See also Fetal Death   WQ 225, etc.
Infant, Newborn   WS 420
   Legal establishment of life   W 789
   Resuscitation   WQ 450
Infant, Newborn, Diseases   WS 421
Infant, Newborn, Intensive Care see Intensive Care, Neonatal
Infant, Newborn, Screening see Neonatal Screening
Infant Nutrition
   Feeding   WS 120–125

Requirements   WS 115
Infant Nutrition Disorders   WS 120
Infant, Premature   WS 410
Infant, Premature, Diseases   WS 410
Infant Psychology see Child Psychology
Infant Radiant Warmers see Incubators, Infant
Infant, Small for Gestational Age   WS 420
Infant Welfare
    Public health aspects   WA 310–320
    Social aspects   HV 697–700
Infanticide
    Criminology   HV 6537–6541
    Medicolegal aspects   W 867
Infantile Paralysis see Poliomyelitis
Infantilism   WK 900
    See also Dwarfism   WE 250
Infantilism, Genital see Hypogonadism
Infantilism, Sexual see Hypogonadism
Infanto Sexuality see Paraphilias
Infarction   QZ 170
    Coronary see Coronary Disease   WG 300, etc.;
        Myocardial Infarction   WG 300
    Pulmonary see Pulmonary Embolism   WG 420
Infection
    Bacteriological aspects   QW 700
    Eye   WW 160
    Disease process   WC 195
    Surgical see Surgical Wound Infection   WO 185
    Veterinary   SF 781
    Wound see Wound infection   WC 255
    Localized, by site
    See also Cross Infection   WC 195, Focal
        Infection   WC 230, etc.; Laboratory Infection
        WC 195; names of other specifc types of
        infection
Infection Control
    In hospitals   WX 167
Infectious Bovine Rhinotracheitis Virus see
    Herpesvirus 1, Bovine
Infectious Bronchitis Virus, Avian   QW 168.5.C8
Infectious Bronchitis Virus of Birds see Avian
    Infectious Bronchitis Virus
Infectious Disease Contact Tracing see Contact
    Tracing
Infectious Diseases see Communicable Diseases;
    names of particular infectious diseases
Infectious Human Wart Virus see Papillomavirus,
    Human
Infectious Keratoconjunctivitis see
    Keratoconjunctivitis, Infectious
Infectious Mononucleosis   WC 522
Infectious Mononucleosis–Like Syndrome, Chronic
    see Fatigue Syndrome, Chronic
Infectious Mononucleosis Virus see Herpesvirus 4,
    Human
Infectious Pustular Vulvovaginitis Virus see
    Herpesvirus 1, Bovine
Inferiority Complex see Personality Disorders
Inferiority, Constitutional Psychopathic see
    Antisocial Personality Disorder
Infertility   WP 570
    Veterinary   SF 871
Infertility, Female   WP 570

Infertility, Male   WJ 709
Infiltration anesthesia see Anesthesia, Local
Inflammation   QZ 150
    Immunological aspects   QW 700
    Localized, by site
Inflammatory Bowel Diseases   WI 420
Inflation, Economic
    By subject, in economics number where
        applicable
Influenza   WC 515
Influenza, Asian see Influenza
Influenza D Virus see Parainfluenza Virus Type 1
Influenza Vaccine   WC 515
Influenza Virus, Avian see Orthomyxovirus Type
    A, Avian
Influenza Virus, Porcine see Orthomyxovirus Type
    A, Porcine
Influenza Viruses see Orthomyxoviridae
Information Display see Data Display
Information Dissemination see Information Services
Information Processing, Automatic see Automatic
    Data Processing
Information Processing, Human see Mental
    Processes
Information Retrieval see Information Storage and
    Retrieval
Information Retrieval Systems see Information
    Systems
Information Science
    Information theory   Q 350–390
    Special topics, by subject
Information Services   Z 674.2–674.5
    Services in particular fields, by subject
Information Storage and Retrieval   Z 699
    By subject   Z 699.5.A–Z
    In medicine (General)   W 26.55.I4
    In other special fields (Form number 26.5 in any
        NLM schedule where applicable)
Information Systems   Z 699
    By subject   Z 699.5.A–Z
    In medicine (General)   W 26.55.I4
    In other special fields (Form number 26.5 in any
        NLM schedule where applicable)
    See also Automatic Data Processing   W
        26.55.A9, etc.; Computers   W 26.55.C7, etc.;
        MEDLARS   W 26.55.I4
Information Theory   Q 350–390
    Special applications, by subject
Informed Consent
    In human experimentation   W 20.5
    Legal aspects   W 32–33
    Other special topics, by subject, e.g., in drug
        research   QV 20.5
Infrared Detectors see Instrumentation   WB 26
    under Infrared Rays
Infrared Rays   QC 457
    Diagnostic use   WB 288
    General medical use   WB 117
    Instrumentation   WB 26
    Technology (Applied optics)   TA 1570
    Therapeutic use   WB 480
    See also Spectrophotometry, Infrared   QC 457,
        etc.

Infrared Spectroscopy see Spectrophotometry, Infrared
Infusion see Drug Compounding
Infusion Pumps   WB 354
Infusion Pumps, External see Infusion Pumps
Infusion Pumps, Implantable   WB 354
Infusions, Intra–Arterial   WB 354
Infusions, Intravenous   WB 354
Infusions, Parenteral   WB 354
    Glucose   WB 354
    Saline   WB 354
      See also Sodium Chloride   WB 354, etc.
Infusions, Regional Arterial see Infusions, Intra–Arterial
Infusors see Infusion Pumps
Inguinal Hernia see Hernia, Inguinal
Inhalation see Respiration
Inhalation Anesthesia see Anesthesia, Inhalation
Inhalation Burns see Burns, Inhalation
Inhalation Devices see Nebulizers and Vaporizers
Inhalation Drug Administration see Administration, Inhalation
Inhalation Injury, Smoke see Smoke Inhalation Injury
Inhalation of Drugs see Administration, Inhalation
Inhalation Provocation Tests see Bronchial Provocation Tests
Inhalation Therapy see Respiratory Therapy
Inhalators see Nebulizers and Vaporizers
Inhalers see Nebulizers and Vaporizers
Inhibin   WK 900
    Female   WP 520
    Male   WJ 875
Inhibition, Neural see Neural Inhibition
Inhibition (Psychology)   BF 335–337
    In infancy & childhood   WS 350.8.I4
Injections   WB 354
    Hypodermic   WB 354
    Saline   WB 354
    See also Enema   WB 344
Injections, Intra–Arterial   WB 354
Injections, Intradermal   WB 354
Injections, Intramuscular   WB 354
Injections, Intravenous   WB 354
Injections, Jet   WB 354
Injections, Sclerosing see Sclerosing Solutions
Injections, Subcutaneous   WB 354
Injured, Transportation see Transportation of Patients
Injuries see Wounds and Injuries
Injuries, Multiple see Multiple Trauma
Ink
    Paleography   Z 112
    Toxicology   QV 627
Ink Blot Tests   WM 145.5.I5
Inlays   WU 360
Innate Behavior see Instinct
Innominate Artery see Brachiocephalic Trunk
Innominate Veins see Brachiocephalic Veins
Innovation Diffusion see Diffusion of Innovation
Inoculation see Vaccination
Inoculation Lymphoreticulosis see Cat–Scratch Disease

Inorganic Chemistry see Chemistry, Inorganic
Inorganic Ions see Ions
Inorganic Poisons see Poisons
Inorganic Substances, Biochemistry see Biochemistry
Inosine
    Biochemistry   QU 57
    Pharmacology   QV 185
Inosine Phosphorylase see Purine–Nucleoside Phosphorylase
Inositol   QU 87
Inositol Hexaphosphate see Phytic Acid
Inositol Phosphates   QU 75
Inositol Phosphoglycerides see Phosphatidylinositols
Inotropic Agents, Positive Cardiac see Cardiotonic Agents
Inotropism see Muscle Contraction
Inotropism, Cardiac see Myocardial Contraction
Inpatients   WX 158.5
    With specific disabilities, with the disability
    See also Patients
Inproquone   QV 269
    Cancer chemotherapy   QZ 267
Insanity see Mental Disorders
Insanity Defense   W 740
    Legislation   WM 32–33
Insect Bites and Stings   WD 430
Insect Control   QX 600
Insect Growth Regulators see Juvenile Hormones
Insect Poisons see Insect Bites and Stings
Insect Repellents
    Pest control in agriculture   SB 951.5–951.54
    Public health aspects   WA 240
Insect Sterilization see Insect Control
Insect Vectors   QX 650
    Preventive medicine   WA 110
Insect Viruses   QW 162
Insecticide Resistance
    Agriculture   SB 957
    Chemically induced mutations   QH 465.C5
    Insect control (Parasitology)   QX 600
    Public health aspects   WA 240
Insecticides
    Agriculture   SB 951.5–951.54
    Public health   WA 240
Insecticides, Carbamate
    Agriculture   SB 952.C3
    Public health   WA 240
Insecticides, Organochlorine
    Agriculture   SB 952.C44
    Public health   WA 240
Insecticides, Organophosphate
    Agriculture   SB 952.P5
    Public health   WA 240
Insecticides, Organophosphate, Antagonists see Cholinesterase Reactivators
Insecticides, Organothiophosphate, Antagonists see Cholinesterase Reactivators
Insectivora   QL 737.I5–737.I58
Insects
    Diseases   SB 942
    Parasitology   QX 500–650
    Poisoning   WD 430

Insemination   WQ 205
Insemination, Artificial   WQ 208
    Sociological aspects   HQ 761
    Veterinary   SF 105.5
Insemination, Artificial, Heterologous   WQ 208
Insemination, Artificial, Homologous   WQ 208
Insemination, Artificial, Human Donor see
    Insemination, Artificial, Heterologous
Insemination, Artificial, Husband see Insemination,
    Artificial, Homologous
Insertion Elements, DNA see DNA Insertion
    Elements
Insertion Sequence see DNA Insertion Elements
Insertion Sequence Elements see DNA Insertion
    Elements
Inservice Training   HF 5549.5.T7
    In hospitals   WX 159
    For particular jobs, by subject, e.g. as a nurses'
        aide   WY 193
Insignia see Emblems and Insignia
Insomnia   WM 188
Inspection, Sanitary see Sanitation
Inspiratory Positive-Pressure Ventilation see
    Intermittent Positive-Pressure Ventilation
Instability, Joint see Joint Instability
Instillation, Bladder see Administration, Intravesical
Instillation, Rectal see Administration, Rectal
Instinct
    Animal   QL 781
    Psychology   BF 685
    Social psychology   HM 255
Institutes see Academies and institutes
Institutional Liability see Liability, Legal
Institutional Nursing see Nursing   WY 125 under
    Institutional Practice; Specialties, Nursing
Institutional Personnel Licensure see Licensure
Institutional Practice   W 96
    Nursing   WY 125
Institutional Review Board see Professional Staff
    Committees
Institutional Tax see Taxes
Institutionalization   W 84.7
    Geriatrics   WT 31
    See also Hospitals, Psychiatric   WM 27-28, etc.;
        Hospitalization   WX 158-158.5, etc.
Institutionalized Child see Child, Institutionalized
Institutions see Organizations
Instrumental Learning see Conditioning, Operant
Instruments see Equipment and Supplies; Surgical
    instruments; Catalogs, Commercial   W 26, etc.
    and names of particular instruments
Insufflation Anesthesia see Anesthesia, Inhalation
Insufflation Radiography see Pneumoradiography
Insula of Reil see Cerebral Cortex
Insular Tissue, Pancreas see Islets of Langerhans
Insulin   WK 820
    Shock see Hypoglycemia   WK 880
    Shock Therapy see Shock Therapy, Insulin
        WM 410
Insulin Antibodies   QW 575
Insulin Coma Therapy see Convulsive Therapy
Insulin Infusion Systems   WK 820
Insulin, Lente   WK 820

Insulin-Like Growth Factor I
    As a growth substance   QU 107
Insulin-Like Growth Factor II
    As a growth substance   QU 107
Insulinoma   WK 885
Insuloma see Insulinoma
Insurance   HG 8016-9999
Insurance, Accident   W 100-250

    Medicolegal aspects   W 900
Insurance Audit see Insurance Claim Review
Insurance Benefits
    Life insurance rates   HG 8751-9295
    Medical, etc. service plans   W 100-275
    For particular disabilities, by subject
Insurance Carriers
    Of health insurance   W 100-275
Insurance Case Management see Managed Care
    Programs
Insurance Claim Reporting
    Related to health insurance in gernal   W 100-275
    Special topics, by subject
Insurance Claim Review   W 100-275
    For particular disorder, by subject
Insurance Claims Processing see Insurance Claim
    Review
Insurance, Dental   W 260

Insurance, Disability see Medicare
Insurance, Health   W 100-275
    Medicolegal aspects   W 900
    Surgical   W 100-275
Insurance, Health, Catastrophic see Insurance, Major
    Medical
Insurance, Health, for Aged and Disabled see
    Medicare
Insurance, Health, Reimbursement   W 100-275
Insurance, Hospitalization   W 160
Insurance, Liability   HG 9990
    (Form number 33 or 33.1 in any NLM schedule
        where applicable and practical)
Insurance, Life   HG 8751-9271
Insurance, Long-Term Care   W 160
    For the aged   WT 31
Insurance, Major Medical   W 160
Insurance, Nursing Services   W 255
Insurance, Old Age see Medicare; Social Security
Insurance, Pharmaceutical Services   W 265
Insurance, Physician Services   W 100-275
Insurance, Psychiatric   W 270-275
Insurance, Surgical   W 100-275
Insurers see Insurance Carriers
Integral Membrane Proteins see Membrane Proteins
Integration, Prophage see Lysogeny
Integumentary System see Skin
Intelligence   BF 431-433
    Genius   BF 412-426
    In infancy & childhood   WS 105
    See also Educational Measurement   LB 3051;
        Psychological Tests   BF 176, etc.
Intelligence Tests   BF 431-433
    In infancy & childhood   BF 432.C48
Intensive Care   WX 218

In infancy & childhood   WS 366
Nursing   WY 154
   Pediatric   WY 159
Of a particular disease or in a particular field
   General, with the disease or field
   Nursing, with the nursing specialty
Intensive Care, Neonatal   WS 421
Intensive Care Nursing see Nursing   WY 154 under
   Intensive Care
Intensive Care, Surgical see Intensive Care
Intensive Care Units   WX 218
   Coronary see Coronary Care Units   WG 27-28
   Respiratory see Respiratory Care Units   WF
   27-28
   Special fields, form numbers 27-28 where
   applicable
   See also Critical Care   WX 218, etc.
Interagency Relations see Interinstitutional Relations
Interbrain see Diencephalon
Intercalated Neurons see Interneurons
Intercarotid Ganglion see Carotid Body
Intercellular Junctions   QH 603.C4
Intercellular Space see Extracellular Space
Intercostal Muscles   WE 715
Interdigitating Cells see Dendritic Cells
Interdisciplinary Health Team see Patient Care Team
Interface, User Computer see User-Computer
   Interface
Interferometry, Microscopic see Microscopy,
   Interference
Interferon Alfa, Recombinant
   Immunology   QW 800
   As an antiviral agent   QV 268.5
   As an antineoplastic agent   QV 269
Interferon Alfa-2c see Interferon Alfa, Recombinant
Interferon-gamma see Interferon Type II
Interferon, Immune see Interferon Type II
Interferon Inducers
   Immunology   QW 800
   Pharmacology   QV 268.5
Interferon Type I
   Immunology   QW 800
   As an antiviral agent   QV 268.5
   As an antineoplastic agent   QV 269
Interferon Type I, Recombinant see Interferon Alfa,
   Recombinant
Interferon Type II
   Immunology   QW 800
   As an antiviral agent   QV 268.5
   As an antineoplastic agent   QV 269
Interferons
   Immunology   QW 800
   Pharmacology   QV 268.5
Interinstitutional Relations
   Hospitals   WX 160
   Other types of institutions, by subject
Interior Design and Furnishings
   In health facilities   WX 140
    For the specialties (Form number 27-29 in any
    NLM schedule where applicable)
   Hospital departments   WX 200-225
   Public health aspects of houses and public
   buildings   WA 795-799

Interior Furnishings see Interior Design and
   Furnishings
Interleukin-1
   Cellular immunity   QW 568
   As a growth substance   QU 107
Interleukin-2
   Cellular immunity   QW 568
   As a growth substance   QU 107
Interleukin-2 Receptors see Receptors, Interleukin-2
Interleukin-3
   Cellular immunity   QW 568
   As a growth substance   QU 107
Interleukin-8
   Cellular immunity   QW 568
   As a growth substance   QU 107
Interleukins
   Cellular immunity   QW 568
   As growth substances   QU 107
Intermediary Body see Hemolysins
Intermediate Filaments   QH 603.C95
Intermedins see MSH
Intermetatarsal Joint see Tarsal Joint
Intermittent Claudication   WG 550
Intermittent Fever see Malaria
Intermittent Positive-Pressure Ventilation   WF 145
Internal Ear see Labyrinth
Internal-External Control
   Child development   WS 105.5.S6
   School management and discipline   LB 3011
   Training of will   BF 632
Internal Mammary-Coronary Artery Anastomosis
   WG 169
Internal Medicine   WB 115
   Directories   W 22
Internal Secretions see Body Fluids; Hormones;
   Intestinal Secretions   WI 400 and names of
   specific secretions
International Agencies   JX 1995
International Cooperation
   General works   JC 362
   Special area of cooperation, by subject
International Health Administration see World
   Health
International Health Problems see World Health
International System of Units   QC 90.8-94
   Pharmaceutical   QV 16
Interneurons   WL 102.5
Internists, Directories see Directories   W 22 under
   Internal Medicine
Internship and Residency
   Dental   WU 20
   Medical   W 20
    Hospital program   WX 203
   Nursing   WY 18.5
   Pharmacy   QV 20
Internship, Dental see Internship and Residency
Internship, Nonmedical
   Nursing   WY 18.5
   Pharmacy   QV 20
   Other fields, by subject
Interpersonal Relations   HM 132
   In adolescence   WS 462
   In infancy & childhood   WS 105.5.I5

Of the retarded child   WS 107.5.R4
In hospitals   WX 160
Of surgeons   WO 62
Specific relationships, by subject, e.g.,
Dentist–patient relations   WU 61, etc.; Family
WS 105.5.F2, etc.
Interphase   QH 605
Interprofessional Relations
Dentists   WU 61
In hospitals   WX 160
Nurses   WY 87
Physicians   W 62
Surgeons   WO 62
Others, with specialty primarily involved
Intersexuality see Hermaphroditism
Interstitial Cell–Stimulating Hormone see LH
Interstitial Fluid see Extracellular Space
Interstitial Lung Diseases see Lung Diseases,
Interstitial
Intertarsal Joint see Tarsal Joint
Intertrochanteric Fractures see Hip Fractures
Intervertebral Disk   WE 740
Of the lumbosacral region   WE 750
Intervertebral Disk Chemolysis   WE 740
Intervertebral Disk Displacement   WE 740
Veterinary   SF 901
Interview, Psychological
Applied psychology   BF 637.I5
In infancy & childhood   WS 105
Psychiatry   WM 141
Interviews
For admission to schools (Form number 19 or
20 in any NLM schedule where applicable)
For hospital jobs   WX 159
For nurses   WY 105
Of physicians and specialists of medically related
fields
Collective   WZ 112–150
Individual   WZ 100
Other special topics, by subject
Intestinal Absorption   WI 402
Intestinal Amebiasis see Dysentery, Amebic
Intestinal Atresia   WI 412
Intestinal Diseases   WI 400–650
General works   WI 400
In infancy & childhood   WS 310–312
Veterinary   SF 851
Intestinal Diseases, Parasitic   WC 698
Veterinary   SF 810.A3
Intestinal Fistula   WI 400
Intestinal Hormone Receptors see Receptors,
Gastrointestinal Hormone
Intestinal Hormones see Gastrointestinal Hormones
Intestinal Motility see Gastrointestinal Motility
Intestinal Neoplasms   WI 435
Localized, by site
Intestinal Obstruction   WI 460
Veterinary   SF 851
Volvulus   WI 450
See also Stomach Volvulus   WI 300
Intestinal Perforation
General   WI 400
Localized, by site

Intestinal Polyps   WI 430
Localized, by site
Intestinal Secretions   WI 400
Intestine, Large   WI 400
See–also names of specific organs, e.g., Colon
WI 520–529
Intestine, Small   WI 500–512
Intestines   WI 400–650
See also specific organs, e.g., Rectum   WI
600–650
Intoxication see Poisoning
Intoxication, Alcoholic see Alcoholic Intoxication
Intra–Abdominal Infusions see Infusions, Parenteral
Intra–Aortic Balloon Pumping   WG 168
Intra–Arterial Lines see Catheters, Indwelling
Intracaine see Benzocaine
Intracellular Adhesion Molecules see Cell Adhesion
Molecules
Intracellular Fluid   QU 105
Intracellular Membranes   QH 601
Intracellular Second Messengers see Second
Messenger Systems
Intracerebral Pressure see Intracranial Pressure
Intracoronal Attachment see Denture, Precision
Attachment
Intracranial Aneurysm see Cerebral Aneurysm
Intracranial Arteriovenous Malformations see
Cerebral Arteriovenous Malformations
Intracranial Hypertension, Benign see Pseudotumor
Cerebri
Intracranial Pressure   WL 203
Intraligamentous Pregnancy see Preganancy,
Ectopic
Intramedullary Nailing see Fracture Fixation,
Intramedullary
Intraocular Pressure   WW 103
In glaucoma   WW 290
Measurement   WW 143
Intraoperative Care   WO 181
Geriatric surgery   WO 950
Pediatric surgery   WO 925
Intraoperative Complications   WO 181
Special topics, by subject
Intraoperative Monitoring   WO 181
Intraoperative Period   WO 181
Intraperitoneal Infusions see Infusions, Parenteral
Intratracheal Anesthesia see Anesthesia,
Intratracheal
Intrauterine Devices   WP 640
Intrauterine Devices, Medicated   WP 640
Intrauterine Diagnosis see Prenatal Diagnosis
Intrauterine Growth Retardation see Fetal Growth
Retardation
Intrauterine Transfusion see Blood Transfusion,
Intrauterine
Intravascular Agglutination see Erythrocyte
Aggregation, Intravascular
Intravascular Erythrocyte Aggregation see
Erythrocyte Aggregation, Intravascular
Intravenous Anesthesia see Anesthesia, Intravenous
Intravenous Drip see Infusions, Intravenous
Intravenous Drug Abuse see Substance Abuse,
Intravenous

**ALWAYS CONSULT MAIN SCHEDULES. USE NUMBER ASSIGNED ONLY WHEN
SUBJECT REPRESENTS MAJOR EMPHASIS OF WORK BEING CLASSIFIED**

Intravenous Drug Delivery Systems see Infusion
   Pumps
Intravenous Feeding see Parenteral Nutrition
Intravenous Hyperalimentation see Parenteral
   Nutrition, Total
Intravenous Infusions see Infusions, Intravenous
Intravesical Drug Administration see
   Administration, Intravesical
Intrinsic Factor   QU 195
Introversion (Psychology)
   Personality   BF 698.35.I59
   Psychoanalysis   WM 460.5.E9
Intubation   WB 365
   Feeding   WB 410
Intubation, Endotracheal see Intubation,
   Intratracheal
Intubation, Gastrointestinal   WI 141
   Used for special purposes, by subject
Intubation, Intratracheal
   In anesthesia   WO 280
Intubation, Nasogastric see Intubation,
   Gastrointestinal
Intussusception   WI 450
Inuits see Eskimos
Inulin   QU 83
Invasive Mole see Hydatidiform Mole, Invasive
Invasiveness see Bacteria; Neoplasm Invasiveness
Invasiveness, Neoplasm see Neoplasm Invasiveness
Inventories, Hospital   WX 147
Inverse PCR see Polymerase Chain Reaction
Inversion (Genetics)   QH 462.I5
Inversion, Visceral see Situs Inversus
Invertebrate Hormones   QL 364
Investigational New Drugs see Drugs,
   Investigational
Investments   HG 4501-5993
Involuntary Commitment see Commitment of
   Mentally Ill
Involution of the Uterus see Puerperium; Anatomy
   & histology under Uterus
Iodamoebiasis see Amebiasis
Iodide Peroxidase   QU 140
Iodides   QV 283
   For syphilis   QV 261
Iodinase see Iodide Peroxidase
Iodine   QV 283
   As an antiseptic   QV 231
   Metabolism   WK 202
Iodine Isotopes   QV 231
   Inorganic chemistry   QD 181.I1
   Metabolism   WK 202
Iodine Radioisotopes   WN 420
   Nuclear physics   QC 796.I1
   See also special topics under Radioisotopes
Iodobenzoylglycine see Iodohippuric Acid
Iodochlorhydroxyquin see Clioquinol
Iodochloroxyquinoline see Clioquinol
Iodohippuric Acid   WN 160
   In kidney function tests   QY 175
   Organic chemistry   QD 341.A7
   Used for special purposes, by subject
Iodopanoic Acid see Iopanoic Acid
Iodopyracet   WJ 141

Iodoquinol   QV 255
Iodothyronine Deiodinase see Iodide Peroxidase
Iodothyronine 5'-Deiodinase see Iodide Peroxidase
Iodotyrosine Deiodase see Iodide Peroxidase
Ion Channels   QH 603.I54
Ion Channels, Calcium see Calcium Channels
Ion Channels, Potassium see Potassium Channels
Ion Channels, Sodium see Sodium Channels
Ion Exchange   QD 562.163
   See also Iontophoresis   WB 495
Ion Exchange Resins
   Anions   QV 280
   Cations   QV 275
Ionic Strength see Osmolar Concentration
Ionium see Thorium
Ions
   Electrochemistry   QD 561
   Inorganic
      Biochemistry   QU 130
      Pharmacology   QV 270
   Physics   QC 701.7-702.7
   See also Anions   QV 280-285; Cations   QV
   275-278
Iontophoresis   WB 495
Iopanoic Acid   WI 750
Iotalamic Acid see Iothalamic Acid
Iothalamic Acid
   As contrast medium   WN 160
   Organic chemistry   QD 341.A2
   Biochemistry   QU 98
IPA (Independent Practice Association) see
   Independent Practice Associations
Ipecac (Syrup)   QV 73
Ipecine see Emetine
IPPV see Intermittent Positive-Pressure Ventilation
Iproniazid   QV 77.5
Iproveratril see Verapamil
Ir Genes see Genes, MHC Class II
Iridium
   Inorganic chemistry   QD 181.I7
   Radioactive   WN 420
Iridocyclitis   WW 240
Iridodiagnosis see Eye Manifestations
Iridoviridae   QW 165.5.I6
Iridoviruses see Iridoviridae
Iris   WW 240
Iris Diseases   WW 240
Iritis   WW 240
Iron
   Pharmacology   QV 183
Iron Chelates
   Pharmacology   QV 183
   Physical chemistry   QD 474
Iron-Deficiency Anemia see Anemia,
   Iron-Deficiency
Iron Isotopes
   Inorganic chemistry   QD 181.F4
   Pharmacology   QV 183
Iron Lung see Ventilators, Mechanical
Iron Salts see Iron; names of specific salts
Iron-Sulfur Proteins   QU 55
Irritable Bowel Syndrome see Colonic Diseases,
   Functional

Irritable Heart see Neurocirculatory Asthenia
Irritants   QV 65
    Gases   QV 666
        Lung irritants   QV 664
      Poisons other than gases   QV 618
      Therapeutic use   WB 371
IS Elements see DNA Insertion Elements
Ischemia   QZ 170
    Localized, by site
Ischemia–Reperfusion Injury see Reperfusion Injury
Islam   BP 1–253
    Birth control   HQ 766.37
    Psychological aspects   BP 175
    Special topics, by subject
Islamic Physicians see Physicians
Island Fever see Scrub Typhus
Island Flaps see Surgical Flaps
Islands of Langerhans see Islets of Langerhans
Islet-Activating Protein see Pertussis Toxins
Islet Cell Tumor see Adenoma, Islet Cell
Islet Cell Tumor, Ulcerogenic see Zollinger–Ellison Syndrome
Islets of Langerhans   WK 800–885
    Neoplasms   WK 885
Islets of Langerhans Transplantation   WK 800
Isoantibodies   QW 575
Isoantigens   QW 573
Isoaspartic Acid see Aspartic Acid
Isocyanates see Cyanates
Isocyanides see Cyanides
Isoelectric Focusing
    Analytical chemistry (General)   QD 79.E44
    Biochemistry   QU 25
    Clinical pathology   QY 25
    Microbiology   QW 25
    Parasitology   QX 25
    Used for special purposes, by subject
Isoelectric Focusing Agents see Ampholyte Mixtures
Isoenzymes   QU 135–141
Isoephedrine see Ephedrine
Isoflurane   QV 81
Isoflurophate   QV 124
Isofosfamide see Ifosfamide
Isohexanes see Hexanes
Isoimmunization, Rhesus see Rh Isoimmunization
Isolation Hospitals see Hospitals, Special; Patient Isolation
Isolation, Patient see Patient Isolation
Isolation Perfusion see Perfusion, Regional
Isolation Perfusion Therapy see Perfusion, Regional
Isolation, Social see Social Isolation
Isoleucine   QU 60
Isoleucyl, Leucyl Vasopressin see Oxytocin
Isomerases   QU 137
Isomerism   QD 471
Isometric Contraction   WE 500
Isometric Exercise see Exercise
Isoniazid   QV 268
Isonicotinic Acid Hydrazide see Isoniazid
Isonipecain see Meperidine
Isophosphamide see Ifosfamide
Isoprenaline see Isoproterenol
Isoprenoid Phosphate Sugars see Polyisoprenyl

Phosphate Sugars
Isoprenoid Phosphates see Polyisoprenyl Phosphates
Isopropanol see Alcohol, Propyl
Isopropyl Alcohol see Alcohol, Propyl
Isopropylarterenol see Isoproterenol
Isoproterenol   WK 725
Isoquinolines
    As antihypertensive agents   QV 150
    In opium alkaloids   QV 90
    Organic chemistry   QD 401
Isotachophoresis see Electrophoresis
Isotonic Solutions   QV 786
Isotopes
    In organic chemistry   QD 181
    Physical chemistry   QD 466.5
    Radioactive see Radioisotopes   WN 420, etc.
    Research in medicine, etc., by subject
Isotretinoin   QU 167
Isozymes see Isoenzymes
Itch see Scabies
Itch Mites see Sarcoptes scabiei
Itching see Pruritus
Ito Syndrome see Pigmentation Disorders
IUGR see Fetal Growth Retardation
Ivermectin   SF 918.I83
Ivy, Poison see Toxicodendron
Ixodoidea see Ticks

J

Jackknife Seizures see Spasms, Infantile
Jacksonian Seizure see Epilepsy, Partial
Jamestown Canyon Virus see California Group Viruses
Jansky–Bielschowsky Disease see Neuronal Ceroid-Lipofuscinosis
Japanese see Mongoloid Race
Japanese Americans see Asian Americans
Japanese Monkey see Macaca
Japanese River Fever see Scrub Typhus
Jaundice   WI 703
    Of the newborn see Jaundice, Neonatal   WH 425
    Spirochetal see Weil's Disease   WC 420, etc.
Jaundice, Cholestatic see Cholestasis
Jaundice, Cholestatic, Extrahepatic see Bile Duct Obstruction, Extrahepatic
Jaundice, Chronic Idiopathic   WI 703
Jaundice, Hemolytic see Anemia, Hemolytic
Jaundice, Mechanical see Cholestasis
Jaundice, Neonatal   WH 425
    See also Erythroblastosis, Fetal   WH 425
Jaundice, Obstructive see Cholestasis
Jaundice, Obstructive, Extrahepatic see Bile Duct Obstruction, Extrahepatic
Jaundice, Spirochetal see Weil's Disease
Jaw
    Anatomy   WU 101
    Dislocation   WU 610
    Physiology   WU 102
Jaw Abnormalities   WU 101.5
Jaw Cysts   WU 140.5
Jaw Diseases   WU 140.5

ALWAYS CONSULT MAIN SCHEDULES. USE NUMBER ASSIGNED ONLY WHEN
SUBJECT REPRESENTS MAJOR EMPHASIS OF WORK BEING CLASSIFIED

Jaw, Edentulous, Partially   WU 140.5
Jaw Fractures   WU 610
Jaw Neoplasms   WU 280
Jealousy   BF 575.J4
    In adolescence   WS 462
    In infancy & childhood   WS 105.5.E5
Jehovah's Witnesses see Christianity
Jejunum   WI 510
Jellyfish Venoms see Coelenterate Venoms
Jervell-Lange Nielsen Syndrome see Long QT
   Syndrome
Jews
    Cookery for the sick   WB 405
    Dietary laws   BM 710
    Diseases   WB 720
    General works   DS 101-151
    In medicine
       Collective biography   WZ 150
       History   WZ 80.5.J3
    Religion see Judaism   BM
    See also special topics under Ethnic Groups
Jimsonweed see Stramonium
Jird see Gerbillinae
Job Application
    Hospitals   WX 159
    Nursing   WY 29
    Medicine as a career   W 21
    Special fields, by subject
Job Description
    Hospitals   WX 159
    Dentistry   WU 21
    Medicine   W 21
    Nursing   WY 29
    Special fields, by subject
Job Ladders see Career Mobility
Job Satisfaction   HF 5549.5.J63
Jogging   QT 260.5.J6
Johne's Disease see Paratuberculosis
Joint Contracture see Contracture
Joint Diseases   WE 304-350
    General works   WE 304
    In infancy & childhood   WS 270
    Veterinary   SF 901
Joint Instability   WE 304
Joint Prosthesis   WE 312
Joint Tuberculosis see Tuberculosis, Osteoarticular
Joint Ventures, Hospital-Physician see
   Hospital-Physician Joint Ventures
Joints   WE 300-350
    Localized, by site
Journals see Periodicals
Judaism   BM
    And medicine   WZ 80.5.J3
       See also Religion and Medicine   W 50, etc.
    Medical ethics   W 50
    See also Jews   WZ 150, etc.
Judgment   BF 447
    In infancy & childhood   WS 105.5.D2
Jugular Veins   WG 625.J8
    See also Blood Supply   WE 708 under Neck
Jungian Theory   WM 460
Juniper   QV 766

Jurisprudence
    Dental see Forensic Dentistry   W 705
    Hospital   WX 33
    Medical   W 32.5-32.6
    Nursing   WY 33
    Pharmaceutical   QV 33
    Psychiatric see Forensic Psychiatry   W 740, etc.
    Veterinary   K 3615-3617
    See also Forensic Medicine   W 601-925, etc.
Jurisprudence, Psychiatric see Forensic Psychiatry
Juvenile Delinquency
    Legal problem (non-medical) U.S.   KF 184
    Parent and physician   WS 463, etc.
    Society   HV 9051-9230.7
Juvenile Hormones   SF 768.3
    Zoology   QL 868
Juxtaglomerular Apparatus   WJ 301

K

K Cells see Killer Cells
Kahn Test see Syphilis Serodiagnosis
Kainic Acid   QV 253
Kakke see Beriberi
Kala-Azar see Leishmaniasis, Visceral
Kallidin   QU 68
Kallikrein   QU 136
Kallikrein-Kinin System
    Enzymology   QU 136
    In regulating blood pressure   WG 106
    In water-electrolyte balance   QU 105
Kallikrein-Trypsin Inactivator see Aprotinin
Kanamycin   QV 268
Kandinsky Syndrome see Organic Mental Disorders,
   Psychotic
Kangaroos   QL 737.M35
Kanner's Syndrome see Autism, Infantile
Kaolin   QV 71
Kaposi's Disease see Xeroderma Pigmentosum
Kaposi's Sarcoma see Sarcoma, Kaposi's
Kappa Allotypes see Immunoglobulin Allotypes
Karwinskia see Rhamnus
Karyokinesis see Mitosis
Karyometry   QH 595
    Neoplasm diagnosis   QZ 241
Kawasaki Disease see Mucocutaneous Lymph Node
   Syndrome
Kedani Disease see Scrub Typhus
Kell Blood-Group System   WH 420
Keloid   WR 143
    Localized, by site
Kepone
    Agriculture   SB 952.C44
    Public health   WA 240
Keratan Sulfate   QU 83
Keratin   QU 55
Keratitis   WW 220
Keratitis, Dendritic   WW 220
Keratitis, Furrow see Keratitis, Dendritic
Keratitis, Ulcerative see Corneal Ulcer
Keratoconjunctivitis, Infectious
    Veterinary (General)   SF 891
    In cattle   SF 967.K47

In sheep and goats   SF 969.K47
Keratoconjunctivitis, Vernal see Conjunctivitis,
   Allergic
Keratoconus   WW 220
Keratoderma, Palmoplantar   WR 500
Keratoma see Keratosis
Keratomalacia see Xerophthalmia
Keratomycosis Linguae see Tongue, Hairy
Keratosis   WR 500
Keratosis Palmaris et Plantaris see Keratoderma,
   Palmoplantar
Keratosis, Palmoplantar see Keratoderma,
   Palmoplantar
Keratosulfate see Keratan Sulfate
Keratotomy, Radial   WW 220
Kernicterus   WL 362
Kerosine
   Chemical technology   TP 692.4.K4
   Toxicology   QV 633
Ketamine   QV 81
Ketoacidosis, Diabetic see Diabetic Ketoacidosis
Ketoconazole   QV 252
Ketoglutaric Acids   QU 98
   Organic chemistry   QD 305.A2
Ketone Bodies
   Organic chemistry
      Aliphatic compounds   QD 305.K2
      Aromatic compounds   QD 341.K2
   Liver metabolism and physiology   WI 702
Ketones
   Organic chemistry
      Aliphatic compounds   QD 305.K2
      Aromatic compounds   QD 341.K2
   Used for special purposes, by subject
Ketoquinolines see Quinolones
Ketosis, Diabetic see Diabetic Ketoacidosis
Ketotifen   QV 157
Khellin   QV 150
Ki-ras Genes see Genes, ras
Kickbacks see Crime
Kidd Blood-Group System   WH 420
Kidnapping see Crime
Kidney   WJ 300-378
   Blood supply   WJ 301
      See also Renal Artery   WG 595.R3; Renal
         Veins   WG 625.R3
Kidney, Artificial   WJ 378
Kidney Bean Lectins see Phytohemagglutinins
Kidney Calculi   WJ 356
Kidney Calices   WJ 301
Kidney Circulation see Renal Circulation
Kidney Concentrating Ability   WJ 303
Kidney Cortex   WJ 301
Kidney, Cystic   WJ 358
Kidney Diseases   WJ 300-378
   General works   WJ 300
   In infancy & childhood   WS 320
   Veterinary   SF 871
Kidney Failure, Acute   WJ 342
Kidney Failure, Chronic   WJ 342
Kidney Function Tests   QY 175
Kidney Glomerulus   WJ 301
Kidney Insufficiency, Acute see Kidney Failure,

Acute
Kidney Insufficiency, Chronic see Kidney Failure,
   Chronic
Kidney Medulla   WJ 301
Kidney Neoplasms   WJ 358
Kidney Papilla see Kidney Medulla
Kidney Papillary Necrosis   WJ 351
Kidney Pelvis   WJ 301
Kidney, Polycystic   WJ 358
Kidney Stones see Kidney Calculi
Kidney Transplantation   WJ 368
Kidney Tubular Transport, Inborn Errors see Renal
   Tubular Transport, Inborn Errors
Kidney Tubules   WJ 301
Kienboeck's Disease see Osteochondritis
Killer Cells   WH 200
   Cytotoxicity   QW 568
Killer Cells, Lymphokine-Activated   WH 200
   In cellular immunity   QW 568
Killer Cells, Natural   WH 200
   In cellular immunity   QW 568
Killer Phenotype see Phenotype
Kimmelstiel-Wilson Syndrome see Diabetic
   Nephropathies
Kinases see Phosphotransferases
Kindling (Neurology)   WL 102
Kinesics
   In adolescence   WS 462
   In infancy & childhood   WS 105.5.C8
   Psychology   BF 637.N66
   Social psychology   HM 258
Kinesiology see Movement
Kinesitherapy see Exercise Therapy
Kinesthesis   WE 104
   See also Motion Perception   WW 105; Weight
      Perception   WE 104
Kinetics
   Biochemical techniques   QU 25
   Enzymology   QU 135
   Pharmacology   QV 38
   Physical chemistry   QD 502-502.2
   Special topics, by subject, e.g.; mechanokinetics
      in the nervous system   WL 102
Kinetics, Drug see Pharmacokinetics
Kinetocardiography   WG 141.5.K5
Kininase II Inhibitors see Angiotensin-Converting
   Enzyme Inhibitors
Kininogenase see Kallikrein
Kinins   QU 68
Kinship see Consanguinity
Kitchens, Hospital see Food Service, Hospital
Klebsiella   QW 138.5.K5
Klebsiella Infections   WC 260
   See also Pneumonia   WC 209, etc.
   Rhinoscleroma   WV 300
Kleptomania see Impulse Control Disorders
Klinefelter's Syndrome   QS 677
Kloramfenikol see Chloramphenicol
Knee   WE 870
   Blood supply   WE 870
      See also Popliteal Artery   WG 595.P6;
         Popliteal Vein   WG 625.P6
Knee Injuries   WE 870

Knee Prosthesis   WE 870
Knee Replacement, Total see Knee Prosthesis
Knowledge Acquisition (Computer) see Artificial
    Intelligence
Knowledge, Attitudes, Practice
    Related to specific topics, by subject
    See also Attitude to Health   W 85
Knowledge Bases (Computer) see Artificial
    Intelligence
Knowledge of Results (Psychology)
    Incentive (Educational psychology)   LB 1065
    See also Motivation   BF 501–505, etc.; Feedback
        WL 102, etc.
Knowledge Representation (Computer) see Artificial
    Intelligence
KO 1173 see Mexiletine
Koehler's Disease see Osteochondritis
Korsakoff Psychosis see Alcohol Amnestic Disorder
Korsakoff Syndrome see Alcohol Amnestic Disorder
Korsakoff's Syndrome see Alcohol Amnestic
    Disorder
Koumiss see Milk
Kraurosis Vulvae   WP 200
Krause's End Bulbs see Thermoreceptors
Krebiozen see Quackery
Krebs Cycle see Citric Acid Cycle
Krill see Crustacea
Krypton
    Inorganic chemistry   QD 181.K6
    Pharmacology   QV 310
    Radioactive   WN 420
Kufs Disease see Neuronal Ceroid-Lipofuscinosis
Kunitz Pancreatic Trypsin Inhibitor see Aprotinin
Kupffer Cells   WH 650
    Localized, by site
Kuru   WC 540
Kwashiorkor   WS 115
Kyasanur Forest Disease Virus see Encephalitis
    Viruses, Tick-Borne
Kyasanur Forest Disease Virus see Flaviviruses
Kymography
    In cardiology   WG 141.5.K9
    Radiographic see Electrokymography   WN 100,
        etc.
        Used for diagnosis of particular disorders, with
            the disorder or system
Kymography, Radiographic see Electrokymography
Kynurenine   QU 60
Kyphosis   WE 735

L

L Cells   QS 532.5.C7
L-Dopa see Levodopa
L Forms   QW 51
La Crosse Virus see California Group Viruses
Labeling, Drug see Drug Labeling
Labeling, Product see Product Labeling
Labels, Pharmaceutical see Drug Labeling
Labetalol   QV 150
Labia see Vulva
Labial Frenum   WI 200
Labor   WQ 300–330

Difficult see Dystocia   WQ 310
General   WQ 300
Labor Complications   WQ 330
    Lacerations   WP 170
    See also Injuries   WP 170 under Perineum; other
        parts injured; names of other injuries
Labor, Induced   WQ 440
    Drugs for see Oxytocics   QV 173
Labor Migration see Transients and Migrants
Labor Onset   WQ 305
Labor, Premature   WQ 330
    See also Infant, Premature   WS 410
Labor Presentation   WQ 307
    Animal   SF 887
Labor Presentation, Breech see Breech Presentation
Labor Unions   HD 6350–6940.7
    Hospitals and hospital personnel   WX 159.8
    Industry and health services   WA 412
        Mental health services   WA 495
    Industry and health insurance   W 125–270

    Nurses   WY 30
        Dealings with hospitals   WX 159.8
Laboratories
    Form numbers 23–24 in any NLM schedule where
        applicable
    In military hospitals   UH 470–475
    Military research   UH 399.5–399.7
Laboratories, Hospital   WX 207
Laboratory Animal Science   QY 50–60
Laboratory Animals see Animals, Laboratory
Laboratory Diagnosis see Diagnosis, Laboratory
Laboratory Infection   WC 195
    Infection in particular types of laboratory with
        the laboratory
    Prevention & control in laboratories   QY 23
    Special types of infection, with the infection
Laboratory Information Systems see Clinical
    Laboratory Information Systems
Laboratory Manuals
    (Form number 25 in any NLM schedule where
        applicable)
    Embryology   QS 625
    Forensic medicine   W 625
    Histology   QS 525
    Immunology   QW 525
    Toxicology   QV 602
Laboratory Markers see Biological Markers
Labyrinth   WV 250–258
Labyrinth Diseases   WV 250–258
    General works   WV 250
    See also Motion Sickness   WD 630
Labyrinthic Gases see Gases   QV 664, etc. under
    Irritants
Labyrinthine Fluids   WV 250
Labyrinthitis   WV 250
Lac Operon   QH 450.2
    Special topics, by subject
Laceration Therapy see Surgery, Minor; Wounds
    and Injuries
Lacerations see Wounds and Injuries; Labor
    Complications

**ALWAYS CONSULT MAIN SCHEDULES. USE NUMBER ASSIGNED ONLY WHEN
SUBJECT REPRESENTS MAJOR EMPHASIS OF WORK BEING CLASSIFIED**

I–136

Lacquer
    Chemical technology   TP 939
    Industrial toxicology   WA 465
Lacrimal Apparatus   WW 208
Lacrimal Apparatus Diseases   WW 208
Lacrimal Duct Obstruction   WW 208
Lacrimal Gland see Lacrimal Apparatus
Lacrimators see Tear Gases
Lactams   QU 62
    Antibiotics   QV 350
    Other special topics, by subject
Lactate Dehydrogenase   QU 140
Lactate Dehydrogenase Isoenzymes   QU 140
Lactate Dehydrogenase Isozymes see Lactate
    Dehydrogenase Isoenzymes
Lactates   QU 98
    Organic chemistry
        Aliphatic compounds   QD 305.A2
Lactation   WP 825
    Animal
        Domestic   SF 768
        Wild   QP 246
    See also Mammae   SF 890
Lactation Disorders   WP 825
    Veterinary   SF 890
Lactic Cytochrome Reductase see Lactate
    Dehydrogenase
Lactobacillus   QW 142.5.A8
Lactoflavin see Riboflavin
Lactogen Hormone, Placental see Placental
    Lactogen
Lactogenic Hormone, Pituitary see Prolactin
Lactoglobulins   QU 55
    Analysis
        Dairy science   SF 251
        Public health   QW 601
Lactones
    Organic chemistry   QD 305.A2
Lactoperoxidase   QU 140
Lactose   QU 83
    Analysis
        Dairy science   SF 251
        Public health   WA 716
Lactose Intolerance   WD 200.5.M2
    In infancy & childhood   WD 200.5.M2
Lactulose   QU 83
Lacunar Dementia see Dementia, Multi-Infarct
LacZ Genes see Lac Operon
Laetrile see Amygdalin
Lafora Disease see Epilepsy, Myoclonic
Lagomorpha   QY 60.L3
Lagothrix see Cebidae
LAK Cells see Killer Cells, Lymphokine-Activated
lambda Phage see Bacteriophage lambda
Lamblia see Giardia
Lambliasis see Giardiasis
Laminagraphy, X-Ray see Tomography, X-Ray
Laminar Air-Flow Areas see Environment,
    Controlled
Laminectomy   WE 725
Lampreys   QL 638.2-638.25
    As laboratory animals   QY 60.F4
LAN see Local Area Networks

Landscaping, Hospital see Maintenance and
    Engineering, Hospital
Langerhans-Cell Granulomatosis see Histiocytosis,
    Langerhans-Cell
Langerhans' Islands see Islets of Langerhans
Language   P 1-410
    Disorders   WL 340.2
    In psychoanalysis, psychoanalytic therapy, or
        psychoanalytic interpretation   WM 460.5.L2
    Psychology   BF 455-463
    Other special topics, by subject
    See also Communication   WM 460.5.C5, etc.
Language Comprehension Tests see Language Tests
Language Delay see Language Development
    Disorders
Language Development   WS 105.5.C8
    Formal education   LB 1139.L3
Language Development Disorders
    Neurologic   WL 340.2
    Psychogenic   WM 475
Language Disorders
    General   WL 340.2
    In infancy & childhood   WL 340.2, etc.
    Neurologic   WL 340.2
    Psychogenic   WM 475
    See also Speech Disorders   WM 475, etc.
Language Pathology see Speech-Language
    Pathology
Language Tests
    For aphasia of neurologic origin   WL 340.5
    For aphasia of psychogenic origin   WM 475.5
    For general and neurologic speech and language
        disorders   WL 340.2
    For psychogenic speech and language disorders
        WM 475
Language Therapy
    General   WL 340.2
    For disorders of neurologic origins   WL 340.2
    For disorders of psychogenic origins   WM 475
Language Training see Language Therapy
Langurs see Cercopithecidae
Lansing Virus see Polioviruses, Human 1-3
Lanthanides see Metals, Rare Earth
Lanthanum
    Inorganic chemistry   QD 181.L2
    Pharmacology   QV 290
Lanugo see Hair
Laparoscopy   WI 575
    Gynecologic   WP 141
    In infancy & childhood   WS 310
Laparotomy   WI 900
Laryngeal Cartilages   WV 500-501
Laryngeal Diseases   WV 500-540
    General works   WV 500
    In infancy & childhood   WV 500-540
    Nursing   WY 158.5
    Veterinary   SF 891
Laryngeal Edema   WV 500
Laryngeal Muscles   WV 500
Laryngeal Neoplasms   WV 520
Laryngeal Nerves   WL 330
    See also Innervation   WV 501 under Larynx
Laryngeal Paralysis see Vocal Cord Paralysis

Laryngeal Prosthesis see Larynx, Artificial
Laryngectomy   WV 540
Laryngismus   WV 500
    See also Adverse effects   WO 245 under
      Anesthesia
Laryngitis   WV 510
Laryngologists see Biography   WZ 112.5.08, etc.
   and Directories   WV 22 under Otolaryngology
Laryngology see Laryngeal Diseases;
    Otolaryngology
Laryngoscopy   WV 505
Laryngospasm see Laryngismus
Larynx   WV 500–540
    Innervation   WV 501
    Surgery   WV 540
Larynx, Artificial   WV 540
Laser Angioplasty see Angioplasty, Laser
Laser Coagulation   WO 198
    In ophthalmology   WW 168
    Used for treatment of a particular disorder, with
      the disorder or system
Laser Knife see Laser Surgery
Laser Scalpel see Laser Surgery
Laser Surgery   WO 511
Lasers
    Applied optics   TA 1671–1707
    Biomedical application   WB 117
    Diagnostic use   WB 288
    In dentistry (General)   WU 26
    In surgery (General)   WO 511
    Physics   QC 685–689.5
    Therapeutic use   WB 480
    Used for other purposes, by subject
    See also special topics under Radiation,
      Non–ionizing
Lassitude see Fatigue
Late Gene Transcription see Transcription, Genetic
Latency in Infection see Infection
Latency Period (Psychology)   WS 105.5.P3
Latent Schizophrenia see Schizotypal Personality
    Disorder
Lateral Cyst see Periodontal Cyst
Lateral Sclerosis see Amyotrophic Lateral Sclerosis
Laterality   WL 335
    Physical anthropology   GN 233
Latex
    Phytochemistry   QK 898.L3
    Used for special purposes, by subject, e.g., in
      scanning electron microscopy   QH 212.S3
Latex Rubber see Rubber
Lathyrism   WD 500
Lathyrus see Legumes
Latices see Latex
Latinos see Hispanic Americans
Latrines see Toilet Facilities
LATS Receptors see Receptors, Thyroid Hormone
Laughter   BF 575.L3
    In adolescence   WS 462
    In infancy & childhood   WS 105.5.E5
Laundering
    Hygiene   QT 240–245
    See also Laundry Service, Hospital   WX 165
Laundries, Hospital see Laundering; Housekeeping,

Hospital
Laundry Service, Hospital   WX 165
Laurence–Moon–Biedl Syndrome   QS 675
LAV Antibodies see HIV Antibodies
LAV–HTLV–III see HIV
LAV–2 see HIV–2
Law and Psychiatry see Forensic Psychiatry;
    Legislation & Jurisprudence   WM 32–33 under
    Psychiatry
Laws see Legislation
Laxatives see Cathartics
Laxity, Joint see Joint Instability
LDL Cholesterol see Lipoproteins, LDL Cholesterol
LDL Receptors see Receptors, LDL
LE Cells   WH 200
    In bone marrow   WH 380
    In lupus erythematosus   WR 152
Lead   QV 292
Lead Poisoning   QV 292
Leader Signal Peptides see Signal Peptides
Leadership   BF 637.L4
    Special topics, by subject
    See also Nursing, Supervisory   WY 105
Learned Helplessness see Helplessness, Learned
Learning
    In adolescence   LB 1603–1632
    In adulthood   LB 2300–2397
    In infancy & childhood
      Formal   LB 1051–1091
      Informal   WS 105.5.D2
    Kindergarten children   LB 1141–1489
      Informal   WS 105.5.D2
    Preschool children   L
      Formal   LB 1140–1140.5
      Informal   WS 105.5.D2 and WS 113
    Psychology of   LB 1051–1091
    Special topics, by subject
Learning Disorders
    Associated with poor vision   WW 480
    Educational aspects   LC 4704, etc.
    Medical aspects   WS 110
Lecithin Acyltransferase   QU 141
Lecithin Cholesterol Acyltransferase see Lecithin
    Acyltransferase
Lecithinase A1 see Phospholipases A
Lecithinase A2 see Phospholipases A
Lecithinases see Phospholipases
Lecithins see Phosphatidylcholines
Lectin, Castor Bean see Ricin
Lectin, Ricinus see Ricin
Lectins   QW 640
    See also Phytohemagglutinins   QW 640, etc.
Lectins, Kidney Bean see Phytohemagglutinins
Lectures see Form number 9 in any NLM schedule
    where applicable
Leeches   QX 451
    Poisoning   WD 420
Leeching see Bloodletting
Leg   WE 850
    Artificial see Artificial Limbs   WE 172
    Blood supply   WE 850
    Lower   WE 870
    Upper   WE 855

**ALWAYS CONSULT MAIN SCHEDULES. USE NUMBER ASSIGNED ONLY WHEN
SUBJECT REPRESENTS MAJOR EMPHASIS OF WORK BEING CLASSIFIED**

See also specific parts of the leg; Varicose Veins
WG 620, etc.
Leg Dermatoses   WR 140
Leg Injuries   WE 850
    Lower leg   WE 870
    Upper leg   WE 855
Leg Length Inequality   WE 850
Leg Ulcer   WE 850
Legal Guardians
    Special topics, by subject
Legal Medicine see Forensic Medicine
Legg–Perthes Disease   WE 865
Legionella
    QW 131
Legionella pneumophila Infections see Legionnaires'
    Disease
Legionellosis   WC 200
Legionnaires' Disease   WC 200
Legislation
    (Form number 32–33 in any NLM schedule where
        applicable)
    Non–medical subjects, in general works number
        for subject (avoiding K schedules when
        possible)
    See also specific legislation terms, i.e., Legislation,
        Dental; Legislation, Drug; Legislation, Food;
        etc.
Legislation, Dental   WU 32–44.1
Legislation, Drug   QV 32–33
    Food and drug laws   WA 697
Legislation, Food   WA 697
Legislation, Hospital   WX 32–33
Legislation, Medical   W 32–44
Legislation, Nursing   WY 32–44
Legislation, Pharmacy   QV 732–733
Legislation, Veterinary   K 3615–3617
Legumes
    As dietary supplement in health and disease
        WB 430
    As food plants   SB 177.L45
    As medicinal plants   QV 766
    Botany   QK 495.L52
    Poisoning   WD 500
Leiomyoblastoma see Leiomyoma, Epithelioid
Leiomyoma   QZ 340
    Localized, by site, e.g., of the uterus   WP 459
Leiomyoma, Epithelioid   QZ 340
    Localized, by site, e.g., of the stomach   WI 320
Leiomyosarcoma   QZ 340
    Localized, by site
Leishmania   QX 70
Leishmaniasis   WR 350
Leishmaniasis, Mucocutaneous   WR 350
Leishmaniasis, Visceral   WC 715
Leisure Activities   QT 250
    Special topics, by subject
Lemmings see Microtinae
Lemmus see Microtinae
Lemuriformes see Strepsirhini
Lemuroidea see Strepsirhini
Length of Life see Longevity
Length of Stay   WX 158
    At specialized hospitals (Form number 27–28 in

any NLM schedule where applicable)
Leninism see Communism
Lens, Crystalline   WW 260
Lens Diseases   WW 260
Lens Implantation, Intraocular see Lenses,
    Intraocular
Lens Opacities see Cataract
Lens Proteins see Crystallins
Lenses   QC 385–385.2
    Ophthalmic see Contact Lenses   WW 355;
        Eyeglasses   WW 350–354
    Prosthesis (Intraocular)   WW 358; For cataracts
        WW 260
Lenses, Contact see Contact Lenses
Lenses, Contact, Hydrophilic see Contact Lenses,
    Hydrophilic
Lenses, Intraocular   WW 358
    For cataracts   WW 260
Lenticular Nucleus see Corpus Striatum
Lentiform Nucleus see Corpus Striatum
Lentiginosis see Lentigo
Lentigo   WR 265
Lentils see Legumes
Lentinan   QU 83
Leon Virus see Polioviruses, Human 1–3
Leontiasis Ossium see Hyperostosis Frontalis Interna
Leontideus see Callitrichinae
Leontopithecus see Callitrichinae
Leper Colonies   WC 27–28
    See also Medical Missions, Official   W 323
Leper Hospitals see Hospitals, Special
Lepidoptera   QX 560
Leprosaria see Hospitals, Special; Leper Colonies
Leprostatic Agents   QV 259
Leprosy   WC 335
    Drugs affecting see Leprostatic Agents   QV 259
    Hospitals see Hospitals, Special   WC 27–28, etc.;
        Leper Colonies   WC 27–28, etc.
Leptazole see Pentylenetetrazole
Leptoconops see Ceratopogonidae
Leptomeninges see Arachnoid; Pia Mater
Leptophos see Phosvel
Leptospirosis   WC 420
    Icterohemorrhagic see Weil's Disease   WC 420
    Veterinary   SF 809.L4
Leptospirosis, Icterohemorrhagic see Weil's Disease
Leptothrix   QW 153
Leriche's Syndrome   WG 410
Lesbianism see Homosexuality, Female
Lesbianism, Ego–Dystonic see Homosexuality,
    Ego–Dystonic
Lesch–Nyhan Syndrome   WD 205.5.P8
LET see Energy Transfer
Lethal Midline Granuloma see Granuloma, Lethal
    Midline
Lethargy see Sleep Stages
LETS Proteins see Fibronectins
Leu Antigens see Antigens, Differentiation
Leu Antigens, B–Lymphocyte see Antigens,
    Differentiation, B–Lymphocyte
Leucine   QU 60
Leucine Aminopeptidase   QU 136
Leucokinin see Tuftsin

ALWAYS CONSULT MAIN SCHEDULES. USE NUMBER ASSIGNED ONLY WHEN
SUBJECT REPRESENTS MAJOR EMPHASIS OF WORK BEING CLASSIFIED

Leucosarcoma see Leukosarcoma
Leucotomy see Psychosurgery
Leucovorin   QU 195
Leukapheresis   WH 460
Leukemia   WH 250
  Clinical pathology   QZ 350
  Veterinary   SF 910.L4
Leukemia, Granulocytic see Leukemia, Myeloid
Leukemia, Granulocytic, Chronic see Leukemia,
  Myeloid, Chronic
Leukemia, Hairy Cell   WH 250
  Clinical pathology   QZ 350
Leukemia, Lymphoblastic see Leukemia,
  Lymphocytic
Leukemia, Lymphoblastic, Acute see Leukemia,
  Lymphocytic, Acute
Leukemia, Lymphoblastic, Acute, L1 see Leukemia,
  Lymphocytic, Acute, L1
Leukemia, Lymphoblastic, Chronic see Leukemia,
  Lymphocytic, Chronic
Leukemia, Lymphocytic   WH 250
  Clinical pathology   QZ 350
Leukemia, Lymphocytic, Acute   WH 250
  Clinical pathology   QZ 350
Leukemia, Lymphocytic, Acute, L1   WH 250
  Clinical pathology   QZ 350
Leukemia, Lymphocytic, Chronic   WH 250
  Clinical Pathology   QZ 350
Leukemia, Lymphoid see Leukemia, Lymphocytic
Leukemia, Monoblastic   WH 250
  Clinical pathology   QZ 350
Leukemia, Monocytic   WH 250
  Clinical pathology   QZ 350
Leukemia, Monocytic, Chronic   WH 250
  Clinical pathology   QZ 350
Leukemia, Myeloblastic   WH 250
  Clinical pathology   QZ 350
Leukemia, Myelocytic see Leukemia, Myeloid
Leukemia, Myelocytic, Chronic see Leukemia,
  Myeloid, Chronic
Leukemia, Myelogenous see Leukemia, Myeloid
Leukemia, Myelogenous, Chronic see Leukemia,
  Myeloid, Chronic
Leukemia, Myeloid   WH 250
  Clinical pathology   QZ 350
Leukemia, Myeloid, Chronic   WH 250
  Clinical Pathology   QZ 350
Leukemia, Radiation-Induced   WH 250
  Clinical pathology   QZ 350
Leukemia Virus, Avian see Avian Leukosis Viruses
Leukemia Virus, Bovine   QW 166
Leukemia Virus I, Human T-Cell see HTLV-I
Leukemia Viruses, Human T-Cell see HTLV-BLV
  Viruses
Leukemia Viruses, Murine   QW 166
Leukemic Reticuloendotheliosis see Leukemia, Hairy
  Cell
Leukemogenic Viruses see Leukoviruses
Leukemoid Reaction   WH 200
Leukocytapheresis see Leukapheresis
Leukocyte Adherence Inhibition Test   QW
  525.5.L6
Leukocyte Adhesion Inhibitor see Interleukin-8

Leukocyte Antigens see HLA Antigens
Leukocyte Count   QY 402
Leukocyte Count, Differential see Leukocyte Count
Leukocyte Differentiation Antigens, Human see
  Antigens, CD
Leukocyte Number see Leukocyte Count
Leukocyte Transfusion   WB 356
Leukocytes   WH 200
  In inflammation   QW 700
Leukocytes, Polymorphonuclear see Neutrophils
Leukocytopenia see Leukopenia
Leukocytosis   WH 200
  Veterinary   SF 769.5
Leukoderma see Vitiligo
Leukokeratosis see Leukoplakia
Leukokinin see Tuftsin
Leukokraurosis see Kraurosis Vulvae
Leukoma see Corneal Opacity; Leukoplakia, Oral
Leukopenia   WH 200
Leukopheresis see Leukapheresis
Leukoplakia   QZ 204
  Localized, by site, e.g., cervical   WP 470
Leukoplakia, Oral   WU 280
  For the gastroenterologist   WI 200
Leukorrhea   WP 255
Leukosarcoma   WH 525
  Clinical pathology   QZ 350
Leukosis, Avian see Avian Leukosis
Leukosis Virus, Avian   QW 166
Leukotaxis see Chemotaxis, Leukocyte
Leukotomy see Psychosurgery
Leukotriene B4   QU 90
Leukotrienes   QU 90
Leukotrienes B see Leukotriene B4
Leukoviruses see Retroviridae
Leurocristine see Vincristine
Levarterenol see Norepinephrine
LeVeen Shunt see Peritoneovenous Shunt
Level of Health see Health Status
Levodopa   WK 725
Levomycetin see Chloramphenicol
Levonorepinephrine see Norepinephrine
Levulose see Fructose
Lewisite   QV 666
Lewy Body Disease see Parkinson Disease
LH   WK 515
LH-FSH Releasing Hormone see Gonadorelin
LH-Releasing Hormone see Gonadorelin
LHRH see Gonadorelin
Liability see Insurance, Liability; Malpractice
Liability, Legal   W 44
  General   W 44
  Dentistry   WU 44
  Nursing   WY 44
  (Form number 33 in any other NLM schedule
  where applicable)
Libido
  Psychoanalysis   WM 460.5.S3
Libman-Sacks Disease see Lupus Erythematosus,
  Systemic
Librarianship see Library Science
Libraries   Z 665-997.2
Libraries, Dental   Z 675.D3

Libraries, Health Science see Libraries, Medical
Libraries, Hospital   Z 675.H7
   Patients' libraries   Z 675.P27
Libraries, Medical   Z 675.M4
Libraries, Medical Record see Medical Records
Libraries, Nursing   Z 675.N8
   Nursing school   Z 675.N8
Library Administration   Z 678–678.88
Library Associations   Z 673
Library Automation   Z 678.9
Library Schools   Z 668–669.5
Library Science   Z 665–718.8
Library Services   Z 665–997
   Circulation   Z 712–714
   Extension   Z 716
   Reference   Z 711–711.92
   Reports   Z 729–871
   See also special types of service and specific types of libraries, e.g., Library technical services Z 688.5; Libraries, Medical   Z 675.M4; also headings beginning with Book
Library Surveys   Z 721–871
Library Technical Services   Z 688.5
Lice   QX 501–502
   Body lice   QX 502
   Disinfestation   WA 240
   Infestation see Pediculosis   WR 375
   Plant lice see Aphids   QX 503, etc.
Lice, Plant see Aphids
Licenses see Licensure
Licensure
   Barbers, beauticians, etc.   WA 32
   Dental hygienists   WU 40
   Midwives   WQ 32
   Other specialties, not listed here or below, by specialty
Licensure, Dental   WU 40
Licensure, Hospital   WX 15
Licensure, Institutional, Personnel see Licensure
Licensure, Medical   W 40
Licensure, Nursing   WY 21
Licensure, Pharmacy   QV 29
Lichen Planus   WR 215
Lichen Ruber Planus see Lichen Planus
Lichen Simplex Chronicus see Neurodermatitis
Lichens   QK 580.7–597.7
Licorice see Glycyrrhiza
Lidocaine   QV 115
Lidoflazine   QV 150
Lie Detection   HV 8078
Life see Biogenesis; Biology; Philosophy
Life Care Centers, Retirement see Housing for the Elderly
Life Change Events
   In adolescence   WS 462
   In infancy & childhood   WS 105
   In old age   WT 104
   Special topics, by subject
Life Expectancy   WT 116
   Actuarial science   HG 8781–8793
   Tables   WT 16
Life Experiences see Life Change Events
Life Insurance see Insurance, Life

Life Islands see Patient Isolators
Life, Legal Establishment see Biogenesis; Birth Certificates; Infant, Newborn; Physical Examination
Life Style
   Adolescents   WS 462
   Aging   WT 30
   Other special topics, by subject, e.g., Anthropology, Cultural   GN 315, etc.; conduct of life   BJ 1545–1697
Life Support Care   WX 162
   Ethical questions   W 50
   In old age   WT 31
   Nursing   WY 152
Life Support Systems   WD 756
Life Support Systems, Regenerative see Ecological Systems, Closed
Life Table Analysis see Life Tables
Life Table Methods see Life Tables
Life Table Models see Life Tables
Life Tables
   Demography   HB 1322
   Specific topics, by subject
   See also Actuarial Analysis
Ligament, Broad see Adnexa Uteri
Ligaments   WE 300
   Localized, by site
Ligaments, Articular   WE 300
   Localized, by site
Ligases   QU 138
Ligation, Tubal see Sterilization, Tubal
Ligatures, Surgical see Sutures
Light
   Adverse effects (General)   WD 605
   As cause of disease   QZ 57
   Diagnostic use (General)   WB 288
   General medical use   WB 117
   Hygiene see Lighting   QT 230, etc.; Sunlight QT 230, etc.
   Perception   WW 105
   Photobiology   QH 515
   Phototherapy   WB 480
   Physics   QC 350–467
   Physiological effects (General)   QT 162.L5
Light Coagulation   WW 166
   Used for specific disorders, by subject
Light, Luminescent see Luminescence
Light Metals see Metals   QU 130, etc. and names of specific light metals; Aluminum; Magnesium
Light, Visible see Light
Lighting
   Industrial health   WA 470
   Private homes   QT 230
   School buildings   WA 350
   Vision conservation   WW 113
Lightning
   Electric injuries   WD 602
   Meteorology   QC 966–966.7
Lignin
   Animal feed   SF 98.L54
   Biochemistry   QU 83
   Phytochemistry   QK 898.L5
Lignocaine see Lidocaine

Limbic System   WL 314
Limbs see Extremities
Limbs, Artificial see Artificial Limbs
Limitation of Activity, Chronic see Activities of
   Daily Living
Limulus see Horseshoe Crabs
Limulus Test   QW 25
   Special topics, by subject
Lincolnensin see Lincomycin
Lincomycin   QV 350
Lindane see Benzene Hexachloride
Linear Accelerators see Particle Accelerators
Linear Energy Transfer see Energy Transfer
Linear Regression see Regression Analysis
Linens see Bedding and Linens
Lingua Geographica see Glossitis, Benign Migratory
Lingua Villosa Negra see Tongue, Hairy
Lingual Bone see Hyoid Bone
Linguistics   P 121–149
Liniments   QV 785
Linkage (Genetics)   QH 445.2–445.5
Linkage Mapping see Chromosome Mapping
Linseed Oil   QV 785
Liothyronine see Triiodothyronine
Lip   WI 200
   Cleft see Cleft Lip   WV 440
   For the dentist   WU 140
Lip Diseases   WI 200
   For the dentist   WU 140
Lip Neoplasms   WU 280
   For the gastroenterologist   WI 200
Lip Reading see Lipreading
Lipase   QU 136
Lipectomy   WO 600
Lipemia–Clearing Factor see Lipoprotein Lipase
Lipid Bilayers   QU 85
Lipid Emulsions, Intravenous see Fat Emulsions,
   Intravenous
Lipid Metabolism, Inborn Errors   WD 205.5.L5
   See also Xanthomatosis   WD 205.5.X2
Lipid Mobilization   QU 85
Lipid Peroxidation   QU 85
Lipid Peroxides
   Biochemistry   QU 85
Lipidosis see Lipoidosis
Lipids   QU 85–95
   Clinical analysis   QY 465
Lipoamide Dehydrogenase   QU 140
Lipocaic see Lipotropic Factors
Lipochondrodystrophy see Mucopolysaccharidosis
   I
Lipodystrophy
   Internal   WD 214
   Progressive   WD 214
Lipofuscin   QU 110
Lipoic Acid see Thioctic Acid
Lipoidosis   WD 205.5.L5
Lipoids   QU 85
Lipolysis   QU 85
Lipolysis, Suction see Lipectomy
Lipoma   QZ 340
   Localized, by site
Lipomatosis   WD 214

Lipopolysaccharides   QU 83
Lipoprotein LDL Receptors see Receptors, LDL
Lipoprotein Lipase   QU 136
Lipoproteins   QU 85
   In blood chemistry   QY 465
Lipoproteins, HDL Cholesterol   QU 95
Lipoproteins, LDL Cholesterol   QU 95
Liposarcoma   QZ 345
   Localized, by site
Liposuction see Lipectomy
Lipotropic Factors   QU 87
Lipreading   HV 2487
Liquid Paraffin see Mineral Oil
Liquors see Alcoholic Beverages
Listeria   QW 142.5.A8
Listeria Infections   WC 242
   Veterinary   SF 809.L5
Listeria monocytogenes   QW 142.5.A8
Lisuride   QV 174
Literacy Programs see Education
Literature   P
   By physicians   WZ 350
   Chinese   PL 2250–3190
   General works   PN
   Influence on children   WS 105.5.E9
   Medicine in see Medicine in Literature   WZ 330,
     etc.
   Physicians in   WZ 330
   Psychiatry and literature   WM 49
   Psychotherapeutic Use see Bibliotherapy   WM
     450.5.B5
   Other languages, in appropriate LC schedule
   Other special topics, by subject
     See also Psychoanalytic Interpretation   WM
     460.7
Literature, Medieval
   History   PN 661–694
   Special topics, by subject, e.g., Dante e le scienze
     mediche   WZ 330
Literature, Modern   PN 695–779
   Special topics, by subject
Lithium   QV 77.9
Litholapaxy see Lithotripsy
Lithospermum   QV 766
Lithotripsy
   For urinary calculi   WJ 166
   For special purposes, with subject
Litomosoides see Filarioidea
Little's Disease see Cerebral Palsy
Liver   WI 700–770
   Blood supply   WI 702
     See also Hepatic Artery   WG 595.H3;
     Hepatic Veins   WG 625.H3; Liver
     Circulation   WI 702
   Tests   QY 140–147
     See also Liver Function Tests   QY 147
Liver Abscess   WI 730
Liver Abscess, Amebic   WI 730
Liver Cell Adhesion Molecules see Cell Adhesion
   Molecules
Liver Circulation   WI 702
   Disorders   WI 720
Liver Cirrhosis   WI 725

Pigmentary   WR 267
   Veterinary   SF 851
   See also Hemochromatosis   WR 267
Liver Cirrhosis, Alcoholic   WI 725
Liver Diseases   WI 700–770
   General works   WI 700
   In infancy & childhood   WS 310
   Veterinary   SF 851
Liver Diseases, Alcoholic   WI 700
Liver Diseases, Parasitic   WI 700
   Veterinary   SF 851
Liver Extracts
   Pharmacology   QV 184
   Therapeutic use (General)   WB 391
   Used for treatment of particular disorders, with
      the disorder or system
Liver Failure, Fulminant see Hepatic
   Encephalopathy
Liver Fibrosis see Liver Cirrhosis
Liver Function Tests   QY 147
Liver Glycogen   WI 704
Liver Microsomes see Microsomes, Liver
Liver Mitochondria see Mitochondria, Liver
Liver Neoplasms   WI 735
Liver Neoplasms, Experimental   WI 735
Liver Regeneration   WI 702
Liver Transplantation   WI 770
Livestock see Animals, Domestic
Living Space see Environment
Living Wills   W 85.5
Livor Mortis see Postmortem Changes
Lizards   QL 666.L2–666.L295
   Diseases   SF 997.5.R4
Llamas see Camelids, New World
LMWH see Heparin, Low-Molecular-Weight
Loa   QX 301
Loa loa see Loa
Lobbying
   Special topics, by subject
Lobectomy see Pneumonectomy; Psychosurgery
Lobotomy see Psychosurgery
Lobstein's Disease see Osteogenesis Imperfecta
Lobsters   QX 463
Local Anesthesia see Anesthesia, Local
Local Area Networks   TK 5105.7–5105.8
Local Immunity see Immunity
Localization of Function see Brain Mapping;
   Dominance, Cerebral
Localization of Infection see Infection
Location Directories and Signs
   In health facilities   WX 140
      For the specialties (form number 27–29 in any
         NLM schedule where applicable)
   In hospital departments   WX 200–225
   Public health aspects in public buildings   WA
      799
Lochia see Leukorrhea
Locked-In Syndrome see Quadriplegia
Lockjaw see Tetanus; Trismus
Locomotion   WE 103
Locomotion, Cell see Cell Movement
Locomotor Ataxia see Tabes Dorsalis
Locomotor System see Musculoskeletal System

Locus Coeruleus   WL 310
Locus of Control see Internal–External Control
Lofepramine   QV 77.5
Logic   BC
   Adolescents   WS 462
   Children   WS 105.5.D2
   Medical   W 61
Logotherapy   WM 460.5.E8
Loneliness   BF 575.L7
   In adolescence   WS 462
   In infancy & childhood   WS 105.5.E5
Long QT Syndrome   WG 330
Long-Term Care   WX 162–162.5
   In old age   WT 31
   Nursing   WY 152
   Of mentally ill   WM 30
Long-Term Care Insurance see Insurance,
   Long-Term Care
Longevity   WT 116
   See also Life Expectancy   WT 116, etc.
Longitudinal Studies   WA 950
   Special topics, by subject, e.g., of characteristics,
      etc. of medical school graduates   W 76
Loop Ileostomy see Ileostomy
Loperamide   QV 71
Lopramine see Lofepramine
Lordosis   WE 735
Loris, Slow see Lorisidae
Lorisidae   QL 737.P955
   Diseases   SF 997.5.P7
   As laboratory animals   QY 60.P7
Lorr's Inpatient Multidimensional Psychiatric Rating
   Scale see Psychiatric Status Rating Scales
Lotions see Cosmetics; Dermatologic Agents;
   Suspensions; Sunscreening Agents
Lou Gehrig's Disease see Amyotrophic Lateral
   Sclerosis
Loudness Perception   WV 272
Louping Ill Virus see Encephalitis Viruses,
   Tick-Borne
Love
   Adolescent psychology   WS 462
   Child psychology   WS 105.5.E5
   Family   HQ 728–743
   Marriage   HQ 728–746
   Psychology (General)   BF 575.L8
   Sex behavior   HQ 19–25
Low Back Pain   WE 755
Low Cardiac Output see Cardiac Output, Low
Low-Income Population see Poverty
Low-Molecular-Weight Heparin see Heparin,
   Low-Molecular-Weight
Low Molecular Weight Nuclear RNA see RNA,
   Small Nuclear
Low Sodium Diets see Diet, Sodium-Restricted
Lower Extremities see Extremities; names of
   particular parts
Lower Extremity see Leg
LSD see Lysergic Acid Diethylamide
LTB4 see Leukotriene B4
Luciferase   QU 140
Ludwig's Angina   WI 200
Luliberin see Gonadorelin

ALWAYS CONSULT MAIN SCHEDULES. USE NUMBER ASSIGNED ONLY WHEN
SUBJECT REPRESENTS MAJOR EMPHASIS OF WORK BEING CLASSIFIED

Lumbago see Low Back Pain
Lumbar Puncture see Spinal Puncture
Lumbar Region see Lumbosacral Region
Lumbar Vertebrae   WE 750
Lumbosacral Plexus   WL 400
Lumbosacral Region   WE 750–755
Luminal see Phenobarbital
Luminescence
   Bioluminescence   QH 641
   Radiation physics (General)   QC 476.4–480.2
   Used for particular purposes, by subject, in the
   techniques number 25 in any NLM schedule
   where applicable, or comparable LC number
Luminescent Proteins   QU 55
Lumpy Skin Disease   WC 584
Lunar Cycle see Moon
Lunar Phases see Moon
Lundborg-Unverricht Syndrome see Epilepsy,
  Myoclonic
Lung   WF 600–668
   Blood supply   WF 600
   Irritants   QV 664
   Radiography   WF 600
   Surgery   WF 668
   See also Mass Chest X-Ray   WF 225
Lung Abscess   WF 651
Lung Capacities see Lung Volume Measurements
Lung Diseases   WF 600–668
   In infancy & childhood   WS 280
   Veterinary   SF 831
Lung Diseases, Fungal   WF 652
Lung Diseases, Interstitial   WF 600
Lung Diseases, Obstructive   WF 600
Lung Diseases, Parasitic   WF 600
Lung Function Tests see Respiratory Function Tests
Lung Irritants see Irritants
Lung Lavage Fluid see Bronchoalveolar Lavage
  Fluid
Lung Neoplasms   WF 658
Lung Transplantation   WF 668
Lung Volume Measurements
   General diagnosis   WB 284
   Respiratory diseases   WF 141
Lupus   WR 245
Lupus Erythematosus, Chronic Cutaneous see Lupus
  Erythematosus, Discoid
Lupus Erythematosus, Cutaneous   WR 152
Lupus Erythematosus, Cutaneous, Chronic see
  Lupus Erythematosus, Discoid
Lupus Erythematosus, Cutaneous, Subacute see
  Lupus Erythematosus, Cutaneous
Lupus Erythematosus, Discoid   WR 152
Lupus Erythematosus Disseminatus see Lupus
  Erythematosus, Systemic
Lupus Erythematosus, Subacute Cutaneous see
  Lupus Erythematosus, Cutaneous
Lupus Erythematosus, Systemic   WR 152
Lupus Glomerulonephritis see Lupus Nephritis
Lupus Nephritis   WJ 353
Lupus Vulgaris see Lupus
Lurcher Mice see Mice, Neurologic Mutants
Luteinizing Hormone see LH
Luteinizing Hormone-Releasing Hormone see

Gonadorelin
Luteinoma see Luteoma
Luteoma   WP 322
Luteotropin see Prolactin
Lutropin see LH
Lyases   QU 139
Lycine see Betaine
Lycoremine see Galanthamine
Lyell's Syndrome see Epidermal Necrolysis, Toxic
Lying   BJ 1420–1428
   In adolescence   WS 463
   In infancy & childhood   WS 350.8.L9
Lying-In Hospitals see Hospitals, Maternity
Lyme Borreliosis see Lyme Disease
Lyme Disease   WC 406
Lymph   WH 700
Lymph Node Excision   WH 700
   Localized, by site
Lymph Node Syndrome, Mucocutaneous see
  Mucocutaneous Lymph Node Syndrome
Lymph Nodes   WH 700
   Tuberculosis see Tuberculosis, Lymph node
   WF 290
Lymphadenectomy see Lymph Node Excision
Lymphadenitis   WH 700
Lymphadenitis, Tuberculous see Tuberculosis,
  Lymph Node
Lymphadenopathy-Associated Antibodies see HIV
  Antibodies
Lymphadenopathy-Associated Virus see HIV
Lymphadenopathy, Immunoblastic see
  Immunoblastic Lymphadenopathy
Lymphadenopathy Syndrome see AIDS-Related
  Complex
Lymphangioendothelioma see Lymphangioma
Lymphangiography see Lymphography
Lymphangioma   QZ 340
   Localized, by site
Lymphangitis   WH 700
Lymphapheresis see Leukapheresis
Lymphatic Capillaries see Lymphatic System
Lymphatic Diseases   WH 700
   In infancy & childhood   WS 300
   Nursing   WY 152.5
   Veterinary   SF 769.5
   Localized, by site
Lymphatic Filariasis see Elephantiasis, Filarial
Lymphatic Metastasis   WH 700
   Of particular types of neoplasms, by site, e.g.,
   of the stomach   WI 320
Lymphatic Sarcoma see Lymphoma, Diffuse
Lymphatic System   WH 700
   Children   WS 300
   Tuberculosis see Tuberculosis, Lymph Node
   WF 290
Lymphedema   WH 700
   Secondary to filariasis   WC 880
   Veterinary   SF 769.5
   Localized, by site
Lymphoblast Transformation see Lymphocyte
  Transformation
Lymphoblastic Leukemia see Leukemia,
  Lymphocytic

Lymphoblastic Leukemia, Acute see Leukemia, Lymphocytic, Acute
Lymphoblastic Leukemia, Acute, Childhood see Leukemia, Lymphocytic, Acute, L1
Lymphoblastic Leukemia, Acute, L1 see Leukemia, Lymphocytic, Acute, L1
Lymphoblastic Leukemia, Chronic see Leukemia, Lymphocytic, Chronic
Lymphocytapheresis see Leukapheresis
Lymphocyte-Activating Factor see Interleukin-1
Lymphocyte Activation see Lymphocyte Transformation
Lymphocyte Cooperation
    Cellular immunity   QW 568
Lymphocyte Mediators see Lymphokines
Lymphocyte Mitogenic Factor see Interleukin-2
Lymphocyte Stimulation see Lymphocyte Transformation
Lymphocyte Transformation
    Clinical pathology   QY 402
    Hematology   WH 200
    Transplantation immunology   WO 680
Lymphocyte Transfusion   WB 356
Lymphocytes   WH 200
    Cellular immunity   QW 568
Lymphocytic Choriomeningitis   WC 540
Lymphocytic Leukemia see Leukemia, Lymphocytic
Lymphocytic Leukemia, Acute see Leukemia, Lymphocytic, Acute
Lymphocytic Leukemia, Chronic see Leukemia, Lymphocytic, Chronic
Lymphocytic Leukemia, L1 see Leukemia, Lymphocytic, Acute, L1
Lymphocytopenia see Lymphopenia
Lymphocytosis   WH 200
Lymphocytotoxic Antibodies see Antilymphocyte Serum
Lymphogranuloma Inguinale see Lymphogranuloma Venereum
Lymphogranuloma, Malignant see Hodgkin's Disease
Lymphogranuloma Venereum   WC 185
Lymphogranulomatosis Inguinalis see Lymphogranuloma Venereum
Lymphography   WH 700
Lymphoid Cells see Lymphocytes
Lymphoid Leukemia see Leukemia, Lymphocytic
Lymphoid Tissue   WH 700
Lymphokine-Activated Killer Cells see Killer Cells, Lymphokine-Activated
Lymphokines
    Cellular immunity   QW 568
    Other special topics, by subject
Lymphoma   WH 525
    Clinical pathology   QZ 350
    See also Burkitt's Lymphoma   WH 525
Lymphoma, Burkitt's see Burkitt's Lymphoma
Lymphoma, Diffuse   WH 525
    Clinical pathology   QZ 350
Lymphoma, Follicular   WH 525
    Clinical pathology   QZ 350
Lymphoma, Giant Follicular see Lymphoma, Follicular

Lymphoma, Histiocytic see Lymphoma, Large-Cell
Lymphoma, Large-Cell   WH 525
    Clinical pathology   QZ 350
    Localized, by site
Lymphoma, Malignant see Lymphoma
Lymphoma, Nodular see Lymphoma, Follicular
Lymphoma, Non-Hodgkin's   WH 525
    Clinical pathology   QZ 350
Lymphomatosis Virus, Avian see Leukosis Virus, Avian
Lymphopathia Venerea see Lymphogranuloma Venereum
Lymphopenia   WH 200
Lymphoproliferative Disorders
    General works   WH 700
    In infancy & childhood   WS 300
    Nursing   WY 152.5
    Veterinary   SF 769.5
    See also names of specific disorders, e.g., Lymphoma   WH 525
Lymphosarcoma see Lymphoma, Diffuse
Lynch Syndrome see Colorectal Neoplasms, Hereditary Nonpolyposis
Lynestrenol   WP 530
    As a contraceptive   QV 177
Lyophilization see Freeze Drying
Lypressin   WK 520
Lysergic Acid Diethylamide   QV 77.7
Lysergide see Lysergic Acid Diethylamide
Lysine   QU 60
Lysine Vasopressin see Lypressin
Lysis see Bacteriolysis; Hemolysis; Lysogeny
Lysogeny   QW 660
Lysol see Cresols
Lysolecithins see Lysophosphatidylcholines
Lysophosphatidylcholines   QU 93
Lysosomes   QH 603.L9
Lysozyme see Muramidase
Lysuride Hydrogen Maleate see Lisuride
Lysyl Bradykinin see Kallidin

M

m-Dihydroxybenzenes see Resorcinols
M Phase see Mitosis
Macaca   QL 737.P93
    As laboratory animals   QY 60.P7
    Diseases   SF 997.5.P7
Macaca mulatta   QL 737.P93
    Diseases   SF 997.5.P7
    As laboratory animals   QY 60.P7
Macaca nemestrina   QL 737.P93
    Diseases   SF 997.5.P7
    As laboratory animals   QY 60.P7
Macaque see Macaca
Mace see omega-Chloroacetophenone
Maceration (Pharmacy) see Drug Compounding
Machiavellianism   BF 698.35.M34
Macrocytic Anemias see Anemia, Macrocytic
Macroglobulinemia see Waldenstrom's Macroglobulinemia
Macromolecular Systems
    Polymers (General)

Inorganic   QD 196
Organic   QD 380–QD 388
Polysaccharides   QU 83
Proteins   QU 55
Special topics, by subject
Macrophage Activation   QW 690
Macrophage–Granulocyte Inducer see
Colony-Stimulating Factors
Macrophages   WH 650
In phagocytosis   QW 690
Macula Lutea   WW 270
Macular Degeneration   WW 270
Madura Foot see Maduromycosis
Madurella see Hyphomycetes
Maduromycosis   WR 340
Maedi Virus see Visna–Maedi Virus
Maedi–Visna Virus see Visna–Maedi Virus
Magentas see Rosaniline Dyes
Maggot Infestations see Myiasis
Magic
Medical   WZ 309
Occult sciences   BF 1585–1628
Magnesium
Metabolism   QU 130
Pharmacology   QV 278
Toxicology   QV 278
Magnesium Adenosinetriphosphatase see Ca(2+)
Mg(2+)-ATPase
Magnesium ADP see Adenosine Diphosphate
Magnesium ATP see Adenosine Triphosphate
Magnesium ATPase see Ca(2+) Mg(2+)-ATPase
Magnesium Deficiency   WD 105
Veterinary   SF 855.M34
Magnesium Hydroxide
As an antacid   QV 69
Magnesium Sulfate   QV 75
Magnetic Fields see Magnetics
Magnetic Resonance see Nuclear Magnetic
Resonance
Magnetic Resonance Imaging   WN 185
Magnetic Resonance Spectroscopy see Nuclear
Magnetic Resonance
Magnetics
And electricity collectively   QC 501–718.8
Biophysics   QT 34
Effect on cells   QH 656
Physics   QC 750–766
Physiological effects   QT 162.M3
Magnetism see Magnetics
Magnetism, Animal see Mental Healing
Magnetoencephalography   WL 141
Magnetometry see Magnetics
Maillard Reaction
As pathogenesis of disease (General)   QZ 40
Food processing technology   TP 372.55.M35
Mainstreaming (Education)
General   LC 4015, LC 4031, etc.
Of children with specific disabilities, with the
disability
Maintenance
Housing   WA 795–799
Of special equipment, by subject
Maintenance and Engineering, Hospital   WX 165

Maize see Corn
Major Histocompatibility Complex   WO 680
Mal de Pinto see Pinta
Malabsorption Syndromes   WD 200.5.M2
For the gastroenterologist   WI 500
See also Celiac Disease   WD 175; Sprue   WD
175
Malacosteon see Osteomalacia
Maladjustment see Personality Disorders
Malaria   WC 750–770
Drugs for see Antimalarials   QV 256–258
Prevention and control   WC 765
Veterinary   SF 791
Malaria, Avian   SF 995.6.M3
Malaria, Hemolytic see Blackwater Fever
Malathion
Carcinogenicity research   QZ 202
Public health   WA 240
Male Fern see Plants, Medicinal
Male Genitalia see Genitalia, Male
Male Nurses see Nurses, Male
Male Pattern Baldness see Alopecia
Maleates   QU 98
Organic chemistry
Aliphatic compounds   QD 305.A2
Malformations, Congenital see Abnormalities;
Arteriovenous Malformations; names of other
specific malformations
Malfunction, Equipment see Equipment Failure
Malignant Carcinoid Syndrome   WI 435
Malignant Hypertension see Hypertension,
Malignant
Malingering   W 783
Malleus   WV 230
Malnutrition see Nutrition Disorders
Malocclusion   WU 440
Malpractice   W 44
General   W 44
Dentistry   WU 44
Gynecology   WP 34
Nursing   WY 44
Obstetrics   WQ 34
(Form number 33 or 33.1 in any other NLM
schedule where applicable and practical)
Malt
As a dietary supplement in health or disease
WB 431
For alcoholic beverages   TP 587
Malta Fever see Brucellosis
Maltases see alpha–Glucosidases
Malthusianism see Population Dynamics
Maltose   QU 75
Mammae
General   SF 890
Wild animals   QP 188.M3
Mammals
As laboratory animals   QY 60.M2
Diseases   SF 600–1100
Domestic   SF
Wild   QL 700–739.3
Mammary Arteries   WG 595.T4
Mammary Dysplasia see Fibrocystic Disease of
Breast

Mammary Glands see Breast; Mammae; Udder
Mammary Glands, Animal see Mammae
Mammary Neoplasms, Experimental   WP 870
Mammography   WP 815
Mammotropic Hormone, Pituitary see Prolactin
Mammotropic Hormone, Placental see Placental Lactogen
Mammotropin see Prolactin
Man-Machine Systems   TA 167
   Biomedical engineering   QT 36
   Special topics, by subject
Managed Care Programs   W 130
Managed Health Care Insurance Plans see Managed Care Programs
Management Information Systems   W 26.5
   Ambulatory Care Information Systems   WX 26.5
   Clinical Laboratory Information Systems   QY 26.5
   Database Management Systems   W 26.5
   Decision Support Systems, Management   W 26.5
   Hospital Information Systems   WX 26.5
   Office Automation   W 26.5
   Radiology Information Systems   WN 26.5
   In other areas, by subject
Management Quality Circles
   Hospitals   WX 159
   Nursing   WY 30
Mandelic Acids   QV 243
Mandelonitrile beta Gentiobioside see Amygdalin
Mandible   WU 101
   See also special topics under Jaw
Mandibular Condyle   WU 101
   See also special topics under Jaw
Mandibular Diseases   WU 140.5
Mandibular Fractures   WU 610
Mandibular Injuries   WU 610
Mandibular Neoplasms   WU 280
Mandibular Nerve   WL 330
Mandibular Prosthesis   WU 600
Mandibular Ridge Augmentation see Alveolar Ridge Augmentation
Mandibulofacial Dysostosis   WU 101.5
Mandragora   QV 85
Mandrake, American see Podophyllum
Mandrake, European see Mandragora
Mandrake Root see Podophyllum
Mandrill see Papio
Manganese   QV 290
   Metabolism   QU 130.5
Mange see Mite Infestations
Mange, Sarcoptic see Scabies
Mania see Manic Disorder
Manic-Depressive Psychoses see Psychoses, Manic-Depressive
Manic-Depressive Psychosis see Bipolar Disorder
Manic Disorder   WM 207
Manic State see Manic Disorder
Manifestations of Disease see Disease; Eye Manifestations; Gastrointestinal System; Neurologic Manifestations; Oral Manifestations; Skin Manifestations
Manihot see Cassava

Manikins   QY 35
Manioc see Cassava
Manipulation, Chiropractic see Chiropractic
Manipulation, Orthopedic   WB 535
   Used for treatment of particular disorders, with the disorder
Manipulation, Psychological see Machiavellianism
Mannequins see Manikins
Mannitol   QV 160
Manpower see Health Manpower
Manslaughter see Homicide
Mantids see Orthoptera
Manual Communication   HV 2477-2480
   See also Sign Language   HV 2474-2476
Manuals
   Hospital staff
      Non-professional   WX 159
      Nursing   WY 105
      Pediatric   WS 29
      Ward manual   WX 203
      Other professional   WX 203
   Psychiatric   WM 30
   Others, by subject
Manuscripts   Z 6601-6625
Manuscripts, Medical
   Bibliography   Z 6611.M5
   Early western   WZ 220
   Other early   WZ 225
   Others, by subject
Mapharsen see Oxophenarsine
Maple Syrup Urine Disease   WD 205.5.A5
Maprotiline   QV 77.5
Maps   G
   Of diseases   WA 900
   See also Atlases   G
Marasmus see Protein-Energy Malnutrition
Marble Bone Disease see Osteopetrosis
Marchiafava-Micheli Syndrome see Hemoglobinuria, Paroxysmal
Marek's Disease   SF 995.6.M33
Margarine
   As a dietary supplement in health or disease   WB 425
   Biochemistry   QU 86
   Public health aspects   WA 722
Marguerite see Pyrethrum
Marie-Struempell Disease see Spondylitis, Ankylosing
Marihuana see Cannabis
Marijuana see Cannabis
Marijuana Abuse   WM 276
Marijuana Smoking
   Dependence   WM 276
   Pharmacological effect   QV 77.7
   Social pathology   HV 5822.M3
Marine Biology   QH 91-95.9
Marine Toxins   QW 630.5.M3
   See also Fish Venoms   WD 405
Marital Relationship see Marriage
Marital Therapy   WM 430.5.M3
Maritime Quarantine see Quarantine
Marker Antigens see Antigens, Differentiation
Markers, Biological see Biological Markers

Markers, DNA see Genetic Markers
Markers, Genetic see Genetic Markers
Markers, Laboratory see Biological Markers
Markers, Serum see Biological Markers
Markers, Surrogate see Biological Markers
Markers, Tumor see Tumor Markers, Biological
Marketing of Health Services   W 74
    Special topics, by subject
Marmoset Virus see Simplexvirus
Marriage   HQ 503–1058
    Counseling   WM 55
    Miscegenation   GN 254
    Statistics   HB 1111–1317
    See also Marital Therapy   WM 430.5.M3
Marriage Therapy see Marital Therapy
Marrow see Bone Marrow
Marsh Gas see Methane
Marsupialia   QL 737.M3–737.M39
Martial Arts   QT 260.5.M3
Marxism see Communism
Masks   WA 260
    In industry   WA 485
    In surgery   WO 162
Masochism   WM 610
Mass Behavior   HM 281–291
Mass Chest X–Ray   WF 225
Mass Media   P 87–96
    Special topics, by subject
Mass Screening   WA 245
    In infancy & childhood   WS 141
Mass Spectrometry see Spectrum Analysis, Mass
Mass Spectroscopy see Spectrum Analysis, Mass
Massage   WB 537
Mast–Cell Colony–Stimulating Factor see
    Interleukin–3
Mast Cells   QS 532.5.C7
Mastectomy   WP 910
Mastectomy, Modified Radical   WP 910
Mastectomy, Radical   WP 910
Mastication   WU 102
Masticatory Force see Bite Force
Masticatory Muscles
    Anatomy   WU 101
    Physiology   WU 102
Mastigophora   QX 70
Mastitis   WP 840
Mastitis, Cystic see Fibrocystic Disease of Breast
Mastocytosis, Bullous see Urticaria Pigmentosa
Mastocytosis, Diffuse Cutaneous see Urticaria
    Pigmentosa
Mastoid   WE 705
    Region of the middle ear   WV 233
Mastoiditis   WV 233
Mastomys see Muridae
Masturbation   HQ 447
    Psychiatric aspects   WM 611
Matched Case–Control Studies see Case–Control
    Studies
Materia Alba see Dental Deposits
Materia Medica   QV 760
Materials Management, Hospital   WX 147
Materials Testing
    General and mechanical   TA 410, etc.

In special fields, with the field, i.e. in Dentistry
    WU 190
Of biocompatible materials   QT 37
Of specific materials, with the material
Of specific property, with the property (e.g.,
    testing of impact strength   TA 418.34)
Maternal Age 35 and over
    Normal pregnancy   WQ 200
        Pregnancy complications   WQ 240–260
Maternal and Child Welfare see Child Welfare;
    Maternal Welfare
Maternal Behavior   WS 105.5.F2
Maternal–Child Health Centers see Health Facilities
    WA 310
Maternal–Child Nursing   WY 157.3
Maternal Deprivation   WS 105.5.D3
Maternal–Fetal Exchange   WQ 210.5
    Immunological factor   QW 553
Maternal Health see Maternal Welfare
Maternal Health Services   WA 310
    See also Prenatal Care   WQ 175; Postnatal Care
        WQ 500
Maternal Mortality   HB 1322.5
    Including causes of death   WA 900
Maternal Patterns of Care see Maternal Behavior
Maternal Welfare   WA 310
Maternity see Illegitimacy; Mothers; Parents;
    Pregnancy
Maternity Leave see Parental Leave
Maternity Nursing see Obstetrical Nursing
Mathematical Computing
    Special topics, by subject, e.g. Biological Models
        QH 324.8
Mathematics   QA
    Biomathematics
        In general biological sciences   QH 323.5
        In medicine and related fields   QT 35
        In public health statistics   WA 950
    Concept formation in children   WS 105.5.D2
    Statistical methods (General)   QA 276–280
    Used in various specialties
        (Form number 25 in any NLM schedule where
        applicable)
Mating Behavior, Animal see Sex Behavior, Animal
Matrix, Extracellular see Extracellular Matrix
Mattresses see Beds
Maxilla   WU
Maxillary Antrum see Maxillary Sinus
Maxillary Artery   WG 595.M2
Maxillary Diseases   WU 140.5
Maxillary Fractures   WU 610
Maxillary Neoplasms   WU 280
Maxillary Prosthesis see Maxillofacial Prosthesis
Maxillary Ridge Augmentation see Alveolar Ridge
    Augmentation
Maxillary Sinus   WV 345
Maxillary Sinus Neoplasms   WV 345
Maxillary Sinusitis   WV 345
Maxillofacial Development   WE 705
    Dental aspects   WU 101
Maxillofacial Injuries   WU 610
Maxillofacial Prosthesis   WU 600
Maximal Expiratory Flow Rate   WF 102

As a diagnostic test   WF 141
General physical examination   WB 284
Maximal Expiratory Flow–Volume Curves   WF 102
Maximum Allowable Concentration see Maximum Permissible Exposure Level
Maximum Permissible Exposure Level
    To industrial pollutants   WA 400–495
    To other specific conditions, by subject
May Apple see Podophyllum
McGill Pain Questionnaire see Pain Measurement
McNaughton Rule see Insanity Defense
MDA see 3,4–Methylenedioxyamphetamine
Meals on Wheels see Food Services
Measles   WC 580
Measles, German see Rubella
Measles Vaccine   WC 580
Measles Virus   QW 168.5.P2
Measles Virus, German see Rubella Virus
Meat
    As a dietary supplement in health or disease   WB 426
        Butchering, packaging, etc.   TS 1960–1981
            Sanitation   WA 707
        Inspection   WA 707
Meat–Packing Industry   TS 1970–1973
    Occupational medicine   WA 400–495
    Industrial waste   WA 788
    Meat inspection   WA 707
Meat Products
    As dietary supplement in health or disease   WB 426
    Contamination   WA 701
    Preserved   WA 710
    Sanitation   WA 707
Meatus, External Auditory see Ear Canal
Meatus, Internal Auditory see Petrous Bone
Meballymal see Secobarbital
Mebubarbital see Pentobarbital
Mebumal see Pentobarbital
Mechanoreceptors   WL 102.9
Mechanotherapy see WB 535 for works including Exercise Therapy; Gymnastics; Manipulation, Orthopedic; Massage and/or other similar procedures treated together.
Mechlorethamine   QV 269
Mechlorethamine Oxide see Mechlorethamine
Meckel's Diverticulum   WI 412
Meclastine see Clemastine
Meclofenoxate
    Biochemistry   QU 98
    As an analeptic   QV 101
    As a plant growth regulator   QK 745
Mecloprodin see Clemastine
Meconium   WQ 210.5
Medex see Physician Assistants
Median Bar see Prostatic Diseases
Median Nerve   WL 400
    See also names of organs affected, e.g., Hand   WE 830
Mediastinal Cyst   WF 900
Mediastinal Diseases   WF 900
Mediastinal Emphysema   WF 900

Mediastinal Neoplasms   WF 900
Mediastinitis   WF 900
Mediastinoscopy   WF 900
Mediastinum   WF 900
Medicaid
    W 250
Medical Assistance   W 100–275
Medical Assistance, Title 19 see Medicaid
Medical Audit   W 84
    Of a hospital   WX 153
Medical Botany see Plants, Medicinal
Medical Care see Health Services
Medical Care Costs see Health Care Costs
Medical Care Research see Health Services Research
Medical Care Team see Patient Care Team
Medical Centers see Health Facilities   WX and names of specific types of facilities
Medical Climatology see Climate; Weather
Medical Computer Science see Medical Informatics
Medical Curiosities see Abnormalities; Medicine
Medical Decision Making, Computer–Assisted see Decision Making, Computer–Assisted
Medical Device Design see Equipment Design
Medical Device Failure see Equipment Failure
Medical Device Safety see Equipment Safety
Medical Devices see Equipment and Supplies
Medical Dissertations see Dissertations, Academic
Medical Economics see Economics, Medical
Medical Education see Education, Medical
Medical Education, Continuing see Education, Medical, Continuing
Medical Education, Graduate see Education, Medical, Graduate
Medical Education, Undergraduate see Education, Medical, Undergraduate
Medical Emergencies see Emergencies; Emergency Medicine
Medical Ethics see Ethics, Medical
Medical Evidence see Forensic Medicine
Medical Examiners see Coroners and Medical Examiners
Medical Geography see Climate; Epidemiology; Weather; names of diseases involved
Medical Gymnastics see Exercise Therapy
Medical History Taking   WB 290
    See also Medical Records   WX 173
Medical Illustration   WZ 348
    (Form number 17 in any NLM schedule where applicable)
    Surgery   WO 517
    See also Anatomy, Artistic   NC 760–783.8; Medicine in Art   WZ 330; Photography   TR 708, etc.
Medical Imaging see Diagnostic Imaging
Medical Indigency   W 250
    See also Medicaid   W 250
Medical Informatics
    In particular fields (Form number 26.5 in any NLM schedules where applicable)
    Space medicine   WD 751.6
    Used for special purpose, by subject
Medical Informatics Applications
    In particular fields (Form number 26.5 in any

NLM schedules where applicables)
Used for special purpose, by subject
Medical Informatics Computing   W 26.5
Medical Information Science see Medical Informatics
Medical Insurance see Insurance, Health
Medical Jurisprudence see Jurisprudence
Medical Literature Analysis and Retrieval System see MEDLARS
Medical Logic see Logic
Medical Missions, Official   W 323
   See also Missions and Missionaries   W 323, etc.
Medical Museums see Museums
Medical Oncology   QZ 200
Medical Philosophy see Philosophy, Medical
Medical Profession see Medicine
Medical Psychology see Psychology, Medical
Medical Publishing see Publishing
Medical Record Administrators   WX 173
Medical Record Linkage   WX 173
Medical Records
   Medical record libraries   WX 173
   See also Hospital Records   WX 173; Medical History Taking   WB 290
Medical Records Department, Hospital   WX 173
Medical Records Librarians see Medical Record Administrators
Medical Records, Problem-Oriented   WX 173
   Hospital records   WX 173
   Specific topics, by subject
Medical Research see Research
Medical Schools see Schools, Medical
Medical Secretaries   W 80
Medical Service Plans see Insurance, Health
Medical Sociology see Sociology, Medical
Medical Staff   W 84
   Of industry
      Medical and dental   WA 412
      Mental health services   WA 495
   Of schools, colleges, universities
      Medical and dental   WA 350
         Elementary and secondary   WA 350
         University and college   WA 351
      Mental health services   WA 352
         Elementary and secondary   WA 352
         University and college   WA 353
   See also Medical Staff, Hospital   WX 203; names of specific types of hospitals
   See also Nursing Staff, Hospital   WY 125, etc. and other medical personnel
   See also Personnel, Hospital   WX 159; names of specific types of hospitals
Medical Staff Privileges   WX 203
Medical Staff Privileges, Nonphysician see Medical Staff Privileges
Medical Symbols see Emblems and Insignia
Medical Technology see Technology, Medical
Medical Terminology see Nomenclature
Medical Waste   WA 790
Medical Waste Disposal   WA 790
Medical Writing see Writing
Medically Underserved Area   W 76
   Developing countries   WA 395

Rural areas   WA 390
Urban areas   WA 380
Medicare   WT 31
Medicare Assignment   WT 31
Medication see Drug Therapy; Preanesthetic Medication; Premedication; Self Medication
Medication Errors
   As a cause of disease   QZ 42
   Drug action   QV 38
Medication Systems, Hospital   WX 179
Medicinal Herbs see Plants, Medicinal
Medicine
   As a profession   W 21
   As practiced in given localities   WB 50
   Bibliography see Bibliography of Medicine   ZWB 100, etc.
   Case studies   WB 293
   Chronologies   WZ 30
   Curiosities   WZ 308
   Directories   W 22
   History see History of Medicine   WZ, etc.
   Military see Military Medicine   UH 201-630
   Phrase books   W 15
   Popular works   WB 120-130
      Home medicine   WB 120
         See also Self Medication   WB 120
   Veterinary see Veterinary Medicine   SF 600-1100
   See also Clinical Medicine   WB 102
Medicine, Alternative see Alternative Medicine
Medicine, Arabic   WZ 80.5.A8
   Currently practiced   WB 50
   Pharmacology   WZ 80.5.A8
      Currently practiced   QV 4
Medicine, Ayurvedic   WZ 80.5.H6
   Current practices by country   WB 50
Medicine, Chinese Traditional   WZ 80.5.O6
   Currently practiced   WB 50
   History by country   WZ 70
Medicine, Emporiatric see Travel
Medicine, Folk see Medicine, Traditional
Medicine, Herbal   WB 925
Medicine, Hindu see Medicine, Ayurvedic
Medicine in Art   WZ 330
   Related to psychiatry   WM 49
Medicine in Literature   WZ 330
   Psychiatric aspects   WM 49
   See also Psychoanalytic Interpretation   WM 460.7, etc.
Medicine, Indigenous see Medicine, Traditional
Medicine, Oriental Traditional   WZ 80.5.O6
   Currently practiced   WB 50
   History by country   WZ 70
Medicine, Primitive see Medicine, Traditional
Medicine, Traditional
   Current practices by country   WB 50
   History   WZ 309
Medicine, Veterinary see Veterinary Medicine
Medicolegal Chemistry see Chemistry
Medicolegal Dentistry see Forensic Dentistry
Medicolegal Examination see Autopsy; Forensic Medicine
Medicolegal Psychiatry see Forensic Psychiatry

Medicolegal Specialists, Directories see Directories
   W 622 under Forensic Medicine
Medina Worm see Dracunculus
Mediterranean Disease see Thalassemia
Mediterranean Fever, Familial see Periodic Disease
MEDLARS   W 26.55.I4
Medroxyprogesterone   WP 530
   As a contraceptive   QV 177
Medulla Oblongata   WL 310
Medulloblastoma   WL 358
Mefenamic Acid   QV 95
Megacolon   WI 528
Megacolon, Toxic   WI 522
Megaesophagus see Esophageal Achalasia
Megakaryocytes   WH 380
Megaloblastic Anemia see Anemia, Macrocytic
Megavitamin Therapy see Orthomolecular Therapy
Megavolt Radiotherapy see Radiotherapy,
   High–Energy
Meibomian Cyst see Chalazion
Meiosis   QH 605.3
Melancholia see Depressive Disorder
Melancholia, Involutional see Depression,
   Involutional
Melanins   QU 110
Melanocyte–Stimulating Hormones see MSH
Melanocytes   QS 532.5.E7
Melanoma   QZ 200
Melanoma, B16 see Melanoma, Experimental
Melanoma, Cloudman S91 see Melanoma,
   Experimental
Melanoma, Experimental   QZ 206
Melanoma, Harding–Passey see Melanoma,
   Experimental
Melanophores   QS 532.5.E7
Melanosomes see Melanocytes
Melanotrichia Linguae see Tongue, Hairy
Melanotropin see MSH
Meleda Disease see Keratoderma, Palmoplantar
Melena   QY 160
   Related to a particular disease, with the disease
Melioidosis   WC 330
Melitococcosis see Brucellosis
Melnick–Needles Syndrome see
   Osteochondrodysplasias
Membrane Channels see Ion Channels
Membrane Fluidity   QU 34
Membrane Fusion   QH 601
Membrane Glycoproteins   QU 55
Membrane Potentials
   Biophysics   QT 34
   Cytology   QH 601
   Metabolism   QU 120
   Physiology   QS 532.5.M3
Membrane Proteins   QU 55
Membrane Tympani see Tympanic Membrane
Membranes
   Cell see Cell Membrane   QH 601, etc.
   Fetal see Fetal Membranes   QS 645, etc.
   Histology   QS 532.5.M3
   Mucous see Mucous Membrane   QS 532.5.M8
   Periodontal   WU 240
   Synaptic see Synaptic Membranes   WL 102.8

   Synovial see Synovial Membrane   WE 300
Membranes, Artificial
   Chemical technology   TP 159.M4
   In dialysis (chemical engineering)   TP 156.D45
   In hemodialysis   WJ 378
   Saline water conversion   WA 687
   Used for other special purposes, by subject
Membranes, Intracellular see Intracellular
   Membranes
Memory   BF 370–387
   In infancy & childhood   WS 105.5.M2
   Physiology   WL 102
   In psychoanalysis, psychoanalytic therapy, or
     psychoanalytic interpretation   WM 460.5.M5
Memory Disorders   WM 173.7
Memory for Designs Test see Neuropsychological
   Tests
Memory, Immediate see Memory, Short–Term
Memory, Photographic see Eidetic Imagery
Memory, Short–Term   BF 378.S54
Men
   Sexual life   HQ 36
   Other special topics, by subject
Menadione see Vitamin K
Menaquinone see Vitamin K
Menarche   WP 540
Mendel's Law see Genetics; Hybridization
Meniere's Disease   WV 258
Meniere's Syndrome see Meniere's Disease
Meningeal Arteries   WG 595.M3
Meningeal Neoplasms   WL 200
   Clinical pathology   QZ 380
Meninges   WL 200
Meningioma   QZ 380
   Localized, by site
Meningism   WL 340
Meningitis   WL 200
   Cerebral   WL 200
   Epidemic cerebrospinal see Meningitis,
     Meningococcal   WC 245
   Tuberculous see Tuberculosis, Meningeal   WL
     200
Meningitis, Listeria   WC 242
Meningitis, Meningococcal   WC 245
Meningitis, Tuberculous see Tuberculosis, Meningeal
Meningitis, Viral   WC 540
Meningocele   WL 200
Meningococcal Infections   WC 245
Meningococcal Meningitis see Meningitis,
   Meningococcal
Meningoencephalitis   WL 351
   Epidemic   WC 542
   Syphilitic see Paresis   WC 165, etc.
Meningomyelitis   WL 400
Meningomyelocele   WE 730
Menisci, Tibial   WE 870
Menopause   WP 580
Menorrhagia   WP 555
Menotropins   WK 515
Menstrual Cycle   WP 540
Menstrual Proliferative Phase see Menstrual Cycle
Menstrual Secretory Phase see Menstrual Cycle
Menstruation   WP 550–560

Menstruation Disorders   WP 550–560
  Hypomenorrhea   WP 552
  Oligomenorrhea   WP 552
  See also names of other specific disorders
Menstruation–Inducing Agents   QV 170
Menstruation, Retrograde see Menstruation
  Disorders
Mental Deficiency see Mental Retardation
Mental Disorders   WM
  Case studies   WM 40
  Diagnosis   WM 141
  Drug therapy   WM 402
  Environmental factors   WM 31
  General works   WM 140
  In adolescence   WS 463
  In infancy & childhood   WS 350–350.8
  In mental retardation   WM 307.M5
  In old age   WT 150
  In pregnancy   WQ 240
  Jurisprudence see Forensic Psychiatry   W 740,
    etc.
  Nursing see Psychiatric Nursing   WY 160
  Rehabilitation   WM 29
  Socioeconomic factors   WM 31
  Therapy   WM 400, etc.
  See also names of specific disorders
Mental Disorders, Organic see Organic Mental
  Disorders
Mental Disorders, Organic, Psychotic see Organic
  Mental Disorders, Psychotic
Mental Fatigue   WM 174
  Industrial   WA 495
Mental Healing   WB 880–885
  Faith cure   WB 885
    See also Christian Science   WB 885, etc.
Mental Health   WM 105
  Environmental factors   WM 31
  In adolescence   WS 462
  In infancy & childhood   WS 105.5.M3
  In old age   WT 145
  Occupational   WA 495
  Military   UH 629–629.5
  Popular works   WM 75
  Rural   WA 390
  School   WA 352
  Socioeconomic factors   WM 31
  Special population groups   WA 305
  Women   WA 309
Mental Health Services   WM 30
  In industry   WA 495
  In infancy & childhood   WM 30
  Military   UH 629–629.5
  School programs
    Elementary and secondary   WA 352
    University and college   WA 353
  Special population groups   WA 305
Mental Health Services, Community see Community
  Mental Health Services
Mental Hospitals see Hospitals, Psychiatric
Mental Hygiene see Mental Health
Mental Hygiene Services see Mental Health Services
Mental Processes   BF 441–449
  In infancy & childhood   WS 105.5.D2

Mental Retardation   WM 300–308
  Complications   WM 300
    In infancy & childhood   WS 107
  In adolescence   WS 463
  In infancy & childhood   WS 107–107.5
    Biographical accounts   WS 107.5.C2
  Mental disorders   WM 307.M5
  Vocational guidance   HV 3005
  See also Child, Exceptional   WS 105.5.C3, etc.;
    Education of the Mentally Retarded   LC
    4601–4640.4
Mental Retardation, Psychosocial   WM 300
  In adolescence   WS 463
  In infancy & childhood   WS 107.5.P8
Mental Status Schedule   WM 141
Mental Tests see Intelligence Tests
Mentally Handicapped see Mental Retardation
Menthol
  Organic chemistry   QD 416
  Pharmacology   QV 60
Menthyl Mercury Compounds   QV 293
  As fungicides   WA 240, etc.
Mentors
  In nursing education   WY 18–18.8
  Special topics, by subject
Mentorships see Mentors
Menu Planning
  In hospitals   WX 168
  In schools
    Elementary and secondary   WA 350
    Universities and colleges   WA 351
  Public health aspects in restaurants   WA 799
Mepacrine see Quinacrine
Meperidine   QV 89
Mepivacaine   QV 115
Meprobamate   QV 77.9
MER–29 see Triparanol
Mercaptamine see Cysteamine
Mercapto Compounds see Sulfhydryl Compounds
Mercaptoethanol   QV 84
  Organic chemistry   QD 305.A4
  Pharmacology   QV 84
Mercaptoethylamines   QU 61
  Organic chemistry   QD 305.A8
Mercaptovaline see Penicillamine
Mercurial Diuretics see Diuretics, Mercurial
Mercuric Chloride
  As an anti–infective agent   QV 231
Mercury   QV 293
  For syphilis   QV 261
Mercury Dichloride see Mercuric Chloride
Mercury Isotopes
  Inorganic chemistry   QD 181.H6
  Pharmacology   QV 293
Mercury Poisoning   QV 293
Mercy Death see Euthanasia
Mercy Killing see Euthanasia
Meriones see Gerbillinae
Mescaline   QV 77.7
  Used in North American Indian religion   E
  98.R3
Mesencephalic Central Gray see Periaqueductal
  Gray

Mesencephalon   WL 310
Mesenchyma see Connective Tissue
Mesenchyme see Mesoderm
Mesenchymoma   QZ 310
   Localized, by site
Mesenteric Arteries   WG 595.M38
   See also Blood supply   WI 500 under Mesentery
Mesenteric Circulation see Splanchnic Circulation
Mesenteric Cyst   WI 500
Mesenteric Lymphadenitis   WI 500
Mesenteric Vascular Occlusion   WI 500
Mesenteric Veins   WI 720
Mesentery   WI 500
   Blood supply   WI 500
   Neoplasms   WI 500
      Pathology   QZ 340
Mesmerism see Hypnosis
Mesna   QV 76
Mesocolon   WI 500
Mesocricetus   QL 737.R666
   As laboratory animals   QY 60.R6
   As pets   SF 459.H3
Mesoderm   WQ 205
Mesonephroma   WP 322
Mesosigmoid see Mesocolon
Mesothelioma   QZ 340
Mesothelium see Epithelium
Messenger RNA see RNA, Messenger
Mestranol   WP 522
   As a contraceptive   QV 177
Mesylates   QU 98
   Organic chemistry   QD 305.S3
meta-Dihydroxybenzenes see Resorcinols
Metabolic Activation see Biotransformation
Metabolic Clearance Rate   QY 450
   Rate of particular substance, with the substance
Metabolic Detoxication, Drug   QV 38
Metabolic Diseases   WD 200-226
   General   WD 200
   Veterinary   SF 910.M48
   See also Calcium Metabolism Disorders   WD 200.5.C2; Metabolism, Inborn errors   WD 205 and other specific diseases
Metabolic Pump see Biological Transport, Active
Metabolism   QU
   Bacterial see Bacteria   QW 52
   Disorders as a manifestation of disease   QZ 180
   General works   QU 120
   In infancy & childhood   QU
   Radiation effects   WN 610
   Skin   WR 102
Metabolism and Endocrinology (Specialty) see Endocrinology
Metabolism, Basal see Basal Metabolism
Metabolism, Inborn Errors   WD 205-205.5
   See also names of specific disorders
Metabolite Markers, Neoplasm see Tumor Markers, Biological
Metaethics see Ethics
Metagonimiasis see Trematode Infections
Metagonimus see Heterophyidae
Metal Metabolism, Inborn Errors   WD 205.5.M3
Metal Plating see Electroplating

Metallo-Organic Compounds see Organometallic Compounds
Metalloproteases see Metalloproteinases
Metalloproteinases   QU 136
Metalloproteins   QU 55
Metallotherapy see Alternative Medicine
Metallothionein   QU 55
Metallurgy   TN 600-799
   Dental   WU 180
   Occupational medicine   WA 400-495
   Industrial waste   WA 788
Metals
   In dentistry   WU 180
   Inorganic chemistry   QD 171-172
   Metabolism   QU 130
     See also Metal Metabolism, Inborn Errors   WD 205.5.M3
   Pharmacology and toxicology
     Alkaline earth metals   QV 275-278
     Heavy metals   QV 290-298
   See also names of specific metals
Metals, Actinide see Metals, Actinoid
Metals, Actinoid   WN 420
Metals, Alkaline Earth
   Inorganic chemistry   QD 172.A42
   Pharmacology   QV 275
   Salts   QV 275
Metals, Rare Earth
   Inorganic chemistry   QD 172.R2
   Pharmacology   QV 290
Metamizole see Dipyrone
Metamorphosis, Biological   QL 981
   Insects   QL 494.5
Metaphysical Healing see Mental Healing
Metaphysics   BD 100-131
Metaplasia   QZ 190
Metaproterenol see Orciprenaline
Metasqualene see Triparanol
Metastasis see Neoplasm Metastasis
Metatarsal Deformity see Foot Deformities
Metatarsus   WE 880
Metencephalon see Cerebellum
Meteorological Factors
   Climate and disease   WB 700-710
   Mental health   WM 31
   Public health   WA 30
   Other topics, by subject
Meteorology see Meteorological Factors; Weather
Metformin   WK 825
Methacholine Compounds   QV 122
Methadone   QV 89
   Dependence   WM 270
Methalamic Acid see Iothalamic Acid
Methaminodiazepoxide see Chlordiazepoxide
Methamphetamine   QV 102
   Dependence   WM 270
Methampyrone see Dipyrone
Methandienone see Methandrostenolone
Methandrostenolone   WJ 875
Methane
   Microbial chemistry   QW 52
   Toxicology   QV 662
Methanesulfonates see Mesylates

Methanobacteria see Methanogens
Methanogens   QW 50
Methanol see Alcohol, Methyl
Methantheline   QV 132
Methaqualone   QV 85
Methemoglobin   WH 190
Methemoglobinemia   WH 190
Methenamine   QV 243
Methicillin Resistance
    Bacteriology   QW 51
    Drug therapy   WB 330
    Pharmacology   QV 354
Methionine   QU 87
Methodology Research, Nursing see Nursing
    Methodology Research
Methods   Q 180.55.M4
    In particular areas, by subject
Methofluranum see Methoxyflurane
Methohexital   QV 88
Methohexitone see Methohexital
Methotrexate
    Folic acid antagonist   QU 188
    In therapy of neoplasms   QZ 267
    Other special topics, by subject
Methoxsalen   QV 63
    Cosmetics   WA 744
Methoxyflurane   QV 81
Methoxyhydroxyphenylglycol   QV 82
Methoxyverapamil see Gallopamil
Methyl Alcohol see Alcohol, Methyl
Methyl Chloride
    As an anesthetic   QV 115
    Organic chemistry
        Aliphatic compounds   QD 305.H5
    Toxicology   QV 633
Methyl Ethers   QV 81
    Organic chemistry   QD 305.E7
Methyl Violet see Gentian Violet
Methyl Viologen see Paraquat
Methyladenine Receptors see Receptors, Purinergic
Methylamines   QU 61
    Organic chemistry   QD 305.A8
Methylation   QD 281.M48
Methylcellulose
    Cathartic   QV 75
    Suspension agent   QV 787
Methylcephaeline see Emetine
Methylcholanthrene   QZ 202
Methyldopa   QV 150
Methyldopate see Methyldopa
Methylene Bichloride see Methylene Chloride
Methylene Bis(chloroaniline) see
    Methylenebis(chloroaniline)
Methylene Chloride
    Toxicology   QV 633
Methylene Dichloride see Methylene Chloride
Methylenebis(chloroaniline)
    As a carcinogen   QZ 202
    Toxicology   QV 633
Methylenesulfonates see Mesylates
Methylergol Carbamide see Lisuride
Methylglyoxal see Pyruvaldehyde
Methylhistamines   QV 157

Methylhydrazines
    Biochemistry   QU 60
    Neoplasm etiology   QZ 202
Methylhydroxyprogesterone see
    Medroxyprogesterone
Methylphenyl Ethers see Anisoles
Methylprednisolone   WK 757
Methylprednisolone Hemisuccinate   WK 757
Methylprednisolone Succinate see
    Methylprednisolone Hemisuccinate
Methylrosaniline Chloride see Gentian Violet
Methylxanthine Receptors see Receptors, Purinergic
Methypregnone see Medroxyprogesterone
Metindamide see Indapamide
Metipranolol see Trimepranol
Metolquizolone see Methaqualone
Metoprolol   QV 132
Metrazol see Pentylenetetrazole
Metric System   QC 90.8-94
    Used for special purposes, by subject
Metritis see Endometritis
Metrizamide
    As a contrast medium   WN 160
    Used for special purposes, by subject
Metronidazole   QV 254
Metrorrhagia   WP 555
Mevalonic Acid   QU 98
    Organic chemistry
        Aliphatic compounds   QD 305.A2
Mexiletine   QV 150
Mezcalin see Mescaline
MgADP see Adenosine Diphosphate
MgATP see Adenosine Triphosphate
MGI-1 see Colony-Stimulating Factors
MHC Class I Genes see Genes, MHC Class I
MHC Class II Genes see Genes, MHC Class II
MHPG see Methoxyhydroxyphenylglycol
Mianserin
    As an antidepressant   QV 77.5
Mice
    As laboratory animals   QY 60.R6
    Diseases   SF 997.5.M4
Mice, Athymic see Mice, Nude
Mice, House see Mice
Mice, Inbred Strains
    As laboratory animals   QY 60.R6
Mice, Laboratory see Mice
Mice, Mutant Strains
    As laboratory animals   QY 60.R6
Mice, Neurologic Mutants
    As laboratory animals   QY 60.R6
Mice, Nude
    As laboratory animals   QY 60.R6
Mice, Red-Backed see Microtinae
Mice, Transgenic
    As laboratory animals   QY 60.R6
    Genetic aspects   QH 442.6
Micelles
    Biochemistry   QU 133
Miconazole   QV 252
Micro-Organisms see Bacteria, Fungi, Rickettsia,
    Viruses
Microangiopathy, Diabetic see Diabetic

Angiopathies
Microbial Collagenase   QU 136
Microbial Sensitivity Tests   QW 25.5.M6
Microbiological Techniques   QW 25
   See also names of specific techniques and tests
Microbiology   QW
   Air see Air Microbiology   QW 82
   Food see Food Microbiology   QW 85
   Industrial   QW 75
   Plant   QW 60
   Soil see Soil microbiology   QW 60
   Veterinary medicine   QW 70
   Water see Water Microbiology   QW 80
   See also Microbiology under names of animals,
     organs, plants, diseases, etc., e.g., under Mouth
      QW 65; Bacteriology   QW; Virology   QW
     160, etc.
Microbodies   QH 603.M35
Microcapsules see Capsules
Microcephaly   QS 675
Microchemistry
   Analytical chemistry (General)   QD 79.M5
   Organic analysis (General)   QD 272.M5
   Qualitative analysis   QD 98.M5
   Quantitative analysis   QD 117.M5
Microcirculation   WG 104
Microclimate
   Of a particular area, with the area
   See also Climate
Microcomputers   QA 75.5–76.95
   As equipment in special fields
     In medicine (General)   W 26.55.C7
     (Form number 26.5 in any other NLM schedule
      where applicable)
   Computer engineering   TK 7885–7895
   See also Computers
Microcytotoxicity Tests see Cytotoxicity Tests,
   Immunologic
Microelectrodes   QD 571
   Biomedical engineering   QT 36
   In electrotherapy   WB 495
   In electrosurgery   WO 198
Microencapsulation see Drug Compounding
Microfilament Proteins   QU 55
Microfilaria   QX 301
Microfilming   TR 835
   In library science   Z 681
   In printing   Z 265
Microfluorometry see Cytophotometry
Microfluorometry, Flow see Flow Cytometry
Micrographic Surgery, Mohs see Mohs Surgery
Microinjections   WB 354
   Special topics, by subject
Microinterferometry see Microscopy, Interference
Micrometry see Weights and Measures
Microprocessors see Microcomputers
Micropunctures see Punctures
Microradiography   WN 100
Microscopy   QH 201–278.5
   Histology   QS 525
   Micrometry   QC 101–114
   Pathology   QZ 25
   Slit–lamp   WW 143

Used for other special purposes, by subject
Microscopy, Electron   QH 212.E4
   In cytodiagnosis   QY 95
   Used for other special purposes, by subject
Microscopy, Electron, Scanning   QH 212.S3
   Used for special purposes, by subject, e.g., for
     examining dental pulp   WU 230
Microscopy, Electron, Transmission see Microscopy,
   Electron
Microscopy, Electron, X–Ray Microanalysis see
   Electron Probe Microanalysis
Microscopy, Fluorescence   QH 212.F55
   Used in diagnosis of pulmonary tuberculosis
     WF 300
   Used for other special purposes, by subject
Microscopy, Immunofluorescence see Microscopy,
   Fluorescence
Microscopy, Interference   QH 212.I5
   Experimental histology   QS 530
   Used for other special purposes, by subject
Microscopy, Phase–Contrast   QH 212.P5
   Used for special purposes, by subject, e.g., in
     cytoscopic examination of urine   QY 185
Microscopy, Polarization   QH 212.P6
   Used for special purposes, by subject, e.g. in
     clinical pathology   QY 95
Microscopy, Polarized Light see Microscopy,
   Polarization
Microscopy, Ultraviolet   QH 212.U48
Microsomes   QH 603.M4
Microsomes, Liver   WI 700
Microsurgery   WO 512
   Localized, by site
Microsurgery, Laser see Laser Surgery
Microsurgical Revascularization, Cerebral see
   Cerebral Revascularization
Microtinae   QL 737.R666
   Diseases   SF 997.5.R3
   As laboratory animals   QY 60.R6
Microtines see Microtinae
Microtomy   QH 233
Microtrabecular Lattice see Cytoskeleton
Microtubule–Associated Proteins   QU 55
Microtubule Proteins   QU 55
Microtubules   QH 603.M44
Microtus see Microtinae
Microvascular Permeability see Capillary
   Permeability
Microvilli   QH 601
Microwaves   TK 7876
   Diagnostic use   WB 141
   Therapeutic use   WB 510
Midazolam   QV 85
Midbrain see Mesencephalon
Midbrain Central Gray see Periaqueductal Gray
Middle Age
   Developmental psychology   BF 724.6
   Medical treatment   WT 100
   Special topics, by subject
Middle Ear see Ear, Middle
Middle Ear Ventilation   WV 232
Midges, Biting see Ceratopogonidae
Midges, Nonbiting see Chironomidae

Midwifery   WQ 160-165
   See also Nurse Midwives   WY 157
Mifepristone
   As an abortifacient agent   QV 175
   As a contraceptive agent   QV 177
   Special topics, by subject
Migraine   WL 344
Migrants see Transients and Migrants
Migration, Cell see Cell Movement
Migration, Internal see Transients and Migrants
Miliaria   WR 400
Miliaria Rubra see Miliaria
Miliary Tuberculosis see Tuberculosis, Miliary
Milieu Therapy   WM 440
   In adolescence   WS 463
   In infancy & childhood   WS 350.2
Military Dentistry   UH 430-435
   Aviation   WD 745
   Naval   VG 280-285
Military Hygiene   UH 600-629.5
Military Medicine   UH 201-570
   Biography
      Collective   WZ 112.5.M4
      Individual   WZ 100
   History   UH 215-324
   Surgery   WO 800
      History   WO 11
   Special topics, by subject
Military Nursing   WY 130
   Education   WY 18-18.5
   Veterans hospitals   WY 130
Military Personnel
   General topics   U 1-145
   Military life   U 750-773
   Veterans   UB 356-405
   See also special aspects of military life, e.g.
      Disabled Veterans   UB 360-366 under
      Rehabilitation
Military Physicians see Military Medicine; Physicians
Military Psychiatry   UH 629-629.5
   See also Combat Disorders   WM 184
Military Psychology see Psychology, Military
Military Science   U
   Air defense   UG 730
   Civil   UA 926-929
   Military
      Anti-aircraft guns   UF 625
      Military aeronautics   UG 623-1435
Military Surgeons see Military Medicine; Biography
   WZ 112.5.M4, etc. under Surgery
Military Surgery see Military Medicine; Military
   WO 800 under Surgery
Military Veterinary Service see Veterinary Service,
   Military
Milk
   Analysis
      Dairying   SF 251-262.5
      Public health   WA 716
   Bacteriology   QW 85
   Dairying (General)   SF 221-275
      Public health aspects   WA 715-719
   Diet (General)   WB 428
      In infancy & childhood   WS 120; WS 130

   Preparation for use   SF 259
   Public health aspects   WA 715-719
      Pasteurization   WA 719
Milk-Alkali Syndrome see Hypercalcemia
Milk Fever, Animal see Parturient Paresis
Milk, Human
   Infant feeding   WS 125
   Secretion   WP 825
Milk Of Magnesia see Magnesium Hydroxide
Milk Proteins   WA 716
   Dairy science   SF 251
Milk Sickness   WD 530
Millipedes see Arthropods
Milroy's Disease see Lymphedema
Miltown see Meprobamate
Milzbrand see Anthrax
Mimetic Muscles see Facial Muscles
Minamata Disease see Mercury Poisoning
Mineral Content of Food see Minerals
Mineral Oil   QV 75
Mineral Waters   WB 442
Mineralocorticoids   WK 755
Minerals
   Biochemistry   QU 130
   Mineralogy   QE 351-399.2
   Of bone   WE 200
Miner's Anemia see Hookworm Infections
Minimal Brain Dysfunction see Attention Deficit
   Disorder with Hyperactivity
Mining   TN
   Occupational accidents   WA 485
   Occupational medicine   WA 400-495
   See also Pneumoconiosis   WF 654 and other
   related disorders
Mink   QL 737.C25
   Culture   SF 405.M6
   Diseases   SF 997.5.M5
Mink Encephalopathy Virus see Prions
Minnesota Multiphasic Personality Inventory see
   MMPI
Minnows see Cyprinidae
Minocycline   QV 360
Minor Injuries see Wounds and Injuries
Minor Surgery see Surgery, Minor
Minority Groups
   Adolescents   WS 462
   Representation   JF 1061-1063
   Suffrage   JF 879
   Special topics, by subject
   See also Ethnic Groups   GN 301-673, etc. and
   specific ethnic groups
Minoxidil   QV 150
Miopithecus talapoin see Cercopithecidae
Miotics   QV 120
Mirex
   Agriculture   SB 952.C44
   Public health   WA 240
Mirror Writing see Dominance, Cerebral
Misarticulation see Articulation Disorders
Miscarriage see Abortion
Miscegenation see Anthropology, Physical;
   Marriage; Racial Stocks
Missions and Missionaries   W 323

Biography (if medically related)
    Collective   WZ 112-150
    Individual   WZ 100
    See also Medical missions, Official   W 323
Missions, Official Medical see Medical Missions,
    Official
Misuse, Equipment see Equipment Failure
Misuse of Health Services see Health Services
    Misuse
Mite-Borne Rickettsial Fevers see Rickettsia
    Infections; names of specific infections
Mite Control see Tick Control
Mite Infestations
    Disinfestation   WC 900
    General   WC 900
    Veterinary   SF 810.M5
    See also Scabies   WR 365, etc.
Mites
    General   QX 473
    Sarcoptoidea   QX 475
    See also names of specific mites, e.g., Sarcoptes
    Scabiei   QX 475
Mithramycin see Plicamycin
Mitochondria   QH 603.M5
Mitochondria, Liver   WI 700
Mitochondria, Muscle   WE 500
Mitogenic Factors, Lymphocyte see Interleukin-2
Mitogens   QH 605.2
Mitogens, Endogenous see Growth Substances
Mitomycins   QV 269
Mitosis   QH 605.2
Mitoxantrone   QV 269
Mitozantrone see Mitoxantrone
Mitral Click-Murmur Syndrome see Mitral Valve
    Prolapse
Mitral Incompetence see Mitral Valve Insufficiency
Mitral Regurgitation see Mitral Valve Insufficiency
Mitral Valve Incompetence see Mitral Valve
    Insufficiency
Mitral Valve Insufficiency   WG 262
Mitral Valve Prolapse   WG 262
Mitral Valve Stenosis   WG 262
Mixed Connective Tissue Disease   WD 375
Mixed Function Oxidases   QU 140
Mixed Function Oxygenases see Mixed Function
    Oxidases
Mixtures see Dosage Forms
MK-421 see Enalapril
MMPI   WM 145.5.M6
MN Sialoglycoprotein see Glycophorin
Mobile Emergency Units see Ambulances
Mobile Genetic Elements see DNA Insertion
    Elements
Mobile Health Units   WX 190
    In specialty fields (Form number 27-28 in any
    NLM schedule where applicable)
Models, Anatomic   QY 35
Models, Biological   QH 324.8
    Of a particular subject, by subject, e.g. of human
    gait   WE 103
Models, Cardiovascular   WG 20
    Of a particular subject, by subject
Models, Chemical   QD 480

Biochemistry   QU 25 or in number for the item
    represented
Models, Computer see Computer Simulation
Models, Decision Support see Decision Support
    Techniques
Models, Dental see Dental Models
Models, Genetic
    Medical   QZ 50
    Special topics, by subject
Models, Molecular   QD 480
    Used for special purposes, by subject
Models, Neurological
    Research   WL 20
    Study and teaching   WL 18.2
Models, Nursing   WY 20.5
    Specific topics, by subject
Models, Obstetrical see Models, Structural
Models, Psychological
    Experimental psychology   BF 181-188
    Psychiatric
        Used in research   WM 20
        Used in teaching   WM 18.2
    Of specific subjects, by subject
Models, Statistical
    Used for special purposes, by subject
Models, Structural
    Construction   QY 35
    Obstetrical   WQ 26
    Other specific types, with the subject being
    illustrated
    Used in teaching (Form number 18.2 in any NLM
    schedule where applicable)
Models, Theoretical
    As an educational tool (Form number 18.2 in any
    NLM schedule where applicable)
    Model theory   QA 9.7
    Used for special purposes, by subject
Mohammedanism see Islam
Mohs Surgery   WR 500
Moire Topography   TR 708
    Used for specific subjects, by subject
Molar   WU 101
Molar, Third   WU 101
    Abnormalities   WU 101.5
    Extraction   WU 605
Molasses
    As a dietary supplement in health or disease
    WB 447
Molds see Fungi
Molds (Casts) see Dental Models; Models, Structural
Molecular Biology   QH 506
Molecular Cloning see Cloning, Molecular
Molecular Configuration see Molecular
    Conformation
Molecular Conformation   QC 179
Molecular Genetics see Genetics, Biochemical
Molecular Models see Models, Molecular
Molecular Neurobiology see Neurobiology
Molecular Probes   QY 95
    Used for diagnosis of particular disorders, with
    the disorder or system
Molecular Radiobiology see Radiobiology

Molecular Sequence Data
    Of a specific substance, with the substance
Molecular Stereochemistry see Molecular
    Conformation
Molecular Structure   QD 461
Molecular Vaccines see Vaccines, Synthetic
Molecular Weight   QD 463–464
    Biochemistry   QU 25
Molestation, Sexual, Child see Child Abuse, Sexual
Mollities Ossium see Osteomalacia
Mollusca   QX 675
Molluscacides
    Agriculture   SB 951.65
    Public health   WA 240
Molluscum Contagiosum   WC 584
Molsidomine   QV 150
Molting Hormone see Ecdysone
Molybdenum
    Inorganic chemistry   QD 181.M7
    Metabolism   QU 130.5
    Pharmacology   QV 290
Mongolism see Down Syndrome
Mongoloid Race
    Anthropology   GN 548
    See also specific topics under Ethnic Groups
Monieziasis   SF 810.C5
Monilia see Candida
Moniliales see Hyphomycetes
Moniliasis see Candidiasis
Moniliasis, Cutaneous see Candidiasis, Cutaneous
Moniliasis, Oral see Candidiasis, Oral
Monitoring, Ambulatory Electrocardiographic see
    Electrocardiography, Ambulatory
Monitoring, Environmental see Environmental
    Monitoring
Monitoring, Fetal see Fetal Monitoring
Monitoring, Holter see Electrocardiography,
    Ambulatory
Monitoring, Home Blood Glucose see Blood
    Glucose Self-Monitoring
Monitoring, Immune see Monitoring, Immunologic
Monitoring, Immunologic   QW 525
Monitoring, Intraoperative see Intraoperative
    Monitoring
Monitoring, Physiologic   WB 142
    Cardiovascular system   WG 140
    Drug utilization   WB 330
    In intensive care   WX 218, etc.
    Of particular function, by subject
    Of other systems, in the examination number,
        usually 141, in the schedule for the system
    See also Radiation Monitoring   WN 650
Monitoring, Radioimmunologic see Monitoring,
    Immunologic
Monitors, Blood Pressure see Blood Pressure
    Monitors
Monkey, African Green see Cercopithecus aethiops
Monkey, Capuchin see Cebus
Monkey, Colobus see Colobus
Monkey Diseases   SF 997.5.P7
Monkey, Green see Cercopithecus aethiops
Monkey, Grivet see Cercopithecus aethiops
Monkey, Japanese see Macaca

Monkey, Northern Night see Aotus trivirgatus
Monkey, Patas see Erythrocebus patas
Monkey, Pig-Tailed see Macaca nemestrina
Monkey, Red see Erythrocebus patas
Monkey, Rhesus see Macaca mulatta
Monkey, Ring-Tail see Cebus
Monkey, Spider see Cebidae
Monkey, Squirrel see Saimiri
Monkey, Talapoin see Cercopithecidae
Monkey, Vervet see Cercopithecus aethiops
Monkey, Woolly see Cebidae
Monkeypoxvirus   QW 165.5.P6
Monkeys see Haplorhini
Monkeys, New World see Cebidae
Monkeys, Old World see Cercopithecidae
Monoacylglycerols see Glycerides
Monoamine Oxidase   QU 140
Monoamine Oxidase Inhibitors   QV 77.5
Monoblastic Leukemia see Leukemia, Monoblastic
Monoclonal Antibodies see Antibodies, Monoclonal
Monoclonal Gammopathies see Paraproteinemias
Monoclonal Gammopathies, Benign   WH 400
Monocytes   WH 200
    In phagocytosis   QW 690
Monocytic Angina see Infectious Mononucleosis
Monocytic Leukemia see Leukemia, Monocytic
Monocytic Leukemia, Chronic see Leukemia,
    Monocytic, Chronic
Mononucleosis, Infectious see Infectious
    Mononucleosis
Monorchidism see Abnormalities   WJ 840 under
    Testis
Monosaccharides   QU 75
Monosodium Glutamate see Sodium Glutamate
Monosomy, Partial see Chromosome Deletion
Monounsaturated Fatty Acids see Fatty Acids,
    Monounsaturated
Monsters   QS 675
Monte Carlo Method   QA 298
    Special topics, by subject
Mood see Affect
Moon
MOPEG see Methoxyhydroxyphenylglycol
Morale   BJ 45
    War   U 22
Morals
    In adolescence   WS 462
    In infancy & childhood   WS 105.5.M4
    Ethics   BJ 11–18
    Psychoanalysis   WM 460.5.R3
    Sex   HQ 32
    Sociology   HM 216
Moraxella   QW 131
Morbid Obesity see Obesity, Morbid
Morbidity   WA 900
Morbillivirus   QW 168.5.P2
Morgagni-Stewart-Morel Syndrome see
    Hyperostosis Frontalis Interna
Mormyrid see Electric Fish
Morning-After Pill see Contraceptives, Postcoital
Moronity see Mental Retardation
Morphea see Scleroderma, Circumscribed
Morphine   QV 92

Morphine Dependence   WM 286
Morphine Derivatives   QV 92
Morphogenesis
    General biology   QH 491
    Human embryology   QS 604
    Localized, by site
Morphology see Anatomy
Morquio's Disease see Mucopolysaccharidosis IV
Morsydomine see Molsidomine
Mortality   HB 1321–1528
    Children   HB 1323.C5
    Including causes of death   WA 900
    See also Fetal Death   WQ 225; Infant Mortality
        HB 1323.I4, etc.; Maternal Mortality   HB
        1322.5, etc.
Mortuary Customs see Funeral Rites
Mortuary Practice   WA 840–847
    Burial   WA 846
    Cemeteries   WA 846
    Cremation   WA 847
    General works   WA 840
Mosaicism   QH 445.7
Mosquito Control   QX 600
    Malaria control   WC 765
Mosquitoes see Culicidae
Mother Cells see Stem Cells
Mother–Child Relations   WS 105.5.F2
Mothers   HQ 759–759.5
    Special topics, by subject
Mothers, Surrogate see Surrogate Mothers
Moths   QX 560
Motilin   WK 170
Motility, Cell see Cell Movement
Motion
    Aviation medicine   WD 720
    Special effects, by subject
    See also Movement   WE 103
Motion Perception
    Visual   WW 105
    See also Kinesthesis   WE 104
Motion Pictures
    Catalogs and works about
        (Form number 18.2 in any NLM schedule
        where applicable)
    Influence on children   WS 105.5.E9
    Reels, etc., by subject
Motion Sickness   WD 630
Motivation   BF 501–504
    In adolescence   WS 462
    In infancy & childhood   WS 105.5.M5
    Psychoanalysis   WM 460.5.M6
Motor Activity   WE 103
    In infancy & childhood   WE 103
    Perceptual motor learning   LB 1067
Motor Cortex   WL 307
Motor Endplate   WL 102.9
Motor Epilepsy see Epilepsy
Motor Neurons   WL 102.7
Motor Neurons, Gamma   WL 102.7
Motor Skills   WE 103
    In infancy & childhood   WE 103
    Psychological aspects   WE 104
Motor Vehicle Accidents see Accidents, Traffic

Mottled Enamel   WU 220
Moulages see Models, Anatomic
Mountain Sickness see Altitude Sickness
Mountaineering
    Accidents and illness   QT 260.5.M9
    Altitude sickness   WD 715
    First aid   WA 292
    Sports   QT 260.5.M9
Mourning see Grief
Mouse Leukemia Viruses see Leukemia Viruses,
    Murine
Mouse Thymic Virus see Herpesviridae
Mouse Tumor Viruses see Tumor Viruses, Murine
Mouth   WU
    General works for the dentist   WU 140
    General works for the gastroenterologist   WI
        200
    Injuries   WU 158
    Microbiology   QW 65
    Pathology   WU 140
    Surgery   WU 600
    See also Administration, Oral   WB 350
Mouth Abnormalities   WU 101.5
Mouth Breathing   WF 143
    Special topics, by subject
Mouth Diseases
    General works for the dentist   WU 140
        Therapy   WU 166
    General works for the gastroenterologist   WI
        200
        Therapy   WI 200
Mouth Dryness see Xerostomia
Mouth, Edentulous   WU 140
    Dentures for   WU 530
Mouth Floor
    Dentistry   WU 140
    Gastroenterology   WI 200
Mouth Mucosa
    For the dentist   WU 101
    For the gastroenterologist   WI 200
Mouth Neoplasms   WU 280
    Works for the gastroenterologist   WI 200
Mouth Rehabilitation   WU 140
    Jaw injuries   WU 610
    Oral and dental injuries   WU 158
    Surgery   WU 600–640
Mouth-to-Mouth Resuscitation see
    Cardiopulmonary Resuscitation
Mouthwashes   WU 113
    Pharmacology   QV 50
Movement   WE 103
Movement, Cell see Cell Movement
Movement Disorders   WL 390
    In infancy & childhood   WS 340
    Neuromuscular see Neuromuscular Diseases
        WE 550–559
    Psychomotor see Psychomotor Disorders   WM
        197
    Veterinary   SF 901
    Localized, by site or disease involved
Moxalactam   QV 350
Moxibustion   WB 369
Moyamoya Disease   WL 355

**ALWAYS CONSULT MAIN SCHEDULES. USE NUMBER ASSIGNED ONLY WHEN
SUBJECT REPRESENTS MAJOR EMPHASIS OF WORK BEING CLASSIFIED**

MR Spectroscopy see Nuclear Magnetic Resonance
MR Tomography see Magnetic Resonance Imaging
MRI Scans see Magnetic Resonance Imaging
mRNA see RNA, Messenger
MSG see Sodium Glutamate
MSH   WK 515
mu Immunoglobulins see Immunoglobulins,
   mu–Chain
Mucins   QU 55
Mucociliary Clearance   WF 102
Mucociliary Transport see Mucociliary Clearance
Mucocutaneous Lymph Node Syndrome   WH 700
Mucolytic Agents see Expectorants
Mucopolysaccharidosis I   WD 205.5.C2
Mucopolysaccharidosis IV   WD 205.5.C2
Mucopolysaccharidosis V see
   Mucopolysaccharidosis I
Mucoproteins   QU 55
   In blood chemistry   QY 455
Mucorales   QW 180.5.P4
Mucous Membrane   QS 532.5.M8
   Drugs affecting   QV 60–65
Mucoviscidosis see Cystic Fibrosis
Mucus   QS 532.5.M8
Mud Baths see Mud Therapy
Mud Therapy   WB 525
Mudminnows see Salmonidae
Multi–Hospital Information Systems see Hospital
   Information Systems
Multi–Hospital Systems see Multi–Institutional
   Systems
Multi–Infarct Dementia see Dementia, Multi–Infarct
Multi–Institutional Systems
   Hospitals (General)   WX 157.4
   In specific fields, by subject
Multigene Family see Genes, Reiterated
Multimodal Treatment see Combined Modality
   Therapy
Multiphasic Screening   WA 245
Multiple Epiphyseal Dysplasia see
   Osteochondrodysplasias
Multiple Myeloma   WH 540
Multiple Organ Failure   QZ 140
   In specific diseases, with the disease
Multiple–Personality Disorder   WM 173.6
Multiple Pregnancy see Pregnancy, Multiple
Multiple Sclerosis   WL 360
Multiple Trauma   WO 700
Multiplication–Stimulating Activity see Insulin–Like
   Growth Factor II
Multipotential Colony–Stimulating Factor see
   Interleukin–3
Multivariate Analysis   QA 278
   Special topics, by subject
Mumps   WC 520
Mumps Vaccine   WC 520
Munchausen Syndrome   WM 178
Mur–NAc–L–Ala–D–isoGln see
   Acetylmuramyl–Alanyl–Isoglutamine
Muramidase   QU 136
Muramyl Dipeptide see
   Acetylmuramyl–Alanyl–Isoglutamine
Murder see Homicide

Muridae   QL 737.R666
   Diseases   SF 997.5.R64
   As laboratory animals   QY 60.R6
Murids see Muridae
Murine Leukemia Viruses see Leukemia Viruses,
   Murine
Murine Tumor Viruses see Tumor Viruses, Murine
Murine Typhus see Typhus, Endemic Flea–Borne
Murray Valley Encephalitis Virus see Flaviviruses
Mus see Muridae
Mus musculus see Mice
Musca domestica see Houseflies
Muscarinic Agents see Cholinergic Agents
Muscarinic Antagonists   QV 132
Muscarinic Receptors see Receptors, Muscarinic
Muscle Contraction   WE 500
Muscle Contracture see Contracture
Muscle Cramp   WE 550
Muscle Denervation   WE 500
Muscle Dystonia see Dystonia
Muscle Proteins   WE 500
Muscle Relaxants, Central   QV 140
   In anesthesia   WO 297
Muscle Relaxants, Depolarizing see Neuromuscular
   Depolarizing Agents
Muscle Relaxants, Non–Depolarizing see
   Neuromuscular Nondepolarizing Agents
Muscle Relaxants, Polarizing see Neuromuscular
   Nondepolarizing Agents
Muscle Relaxation   WE 500
Muscle Rigidity   WE 550
Muscle, Smooth   WE 500
   Localized, by site
Muscle, Smooth, Vascular   WE 500
Muscle Spasticity   WE 550
   In infancy & childhood   WS 270
Muscle Spindles   WL 102.9
Muscle Tonus   WE 500
Muscles   WE 500–559
   Anatomy   WE 500
   Physiology   WE 500
   Localized, by site
Muscular Atrophy   WE 550
   Veterinary   SF 901
Muscular Atrophy, Spinal   WE 550
Muscular Diseases   WE 544–559
   General works   WE 550
   In infancy & childhood   WS 270
Muscular Dystrophy   WE 559
Musculocutaneous Nerve   WL 400
   See also names of organs innervated, e.g. Forearm
      WE 820
Musculoskeletal Diseases   WE 140
   In infancy & childhood   WS 270
   Nursing   WY 157.6
Musculoskeletal System   WE
   Children   WS 270
   Neoplasms (General)   WE 140
      See also Neoplasms, Muscle tissue   QZ 340
   Nursing care   WY 157.6
   Trunk   WE 700
Museums
   (Form numbers 27–28 in QS–QT, QV–QZ, W,

WA and WZ schedules)
Art   N 405-3990
General   AM
Scientific   Q 105
Mushroom Poisoning   WD 520
Mushrooms
   Edible   QK 617
   Poisonous   QW 180.5.B2
Music   M
   Special topics, by subject, e.g., mouth instruments
      as a cause of malocclusion   WU 440
Music Therapy
   General   WB 550
   In psychiatry   WM 450.5.M8
Muskrats see Microtinae
Muslims see Islam
Mussels   QX 675
Mustard
   As a condiment plant   SB 307.M87
   As a skin irritant   QV 65
   Botany   QK 495.C9
Mustard Compounds
   As antineoplastics   QV 269
   Chemical warfare agent   QV 666
   Organic chemistry
      Aliphatic compounds   QD 305.H5
Mustard Gas
   As a carcinogen   QZ 202
   As a chemical warfare agent   QV 666
Mustard Plasters see Therapeutic use   WB 371
   under Irritants
Mustine see Mechlorethamine
Mutagen Screening see Mutagenicity Tests
Mutagenesis   QH 460-468
Mutagenesis, Oligonucleotide-Directed see
   Mutagenesis, Site-Directed
Mutagenesis, Site-Directed   QH 465.S5
Mutagenesis, Site-Specific see Mutagenesis,
   Site-Directed
Mutagenicity Tests   QH 465
Mutagens
   As a cause of congenital abnormalities   QS 679
   As air pollutants   WA 754
   General works on chemical mutagens   QH 460
   Industrial waste   WA 788
   Virology   QW 160
Mutases see Oxidoreductases
Mutation
   Evolution   QH 390
   Genetics   QH 460-468
   In specific organisms, with the organism
Mutational Analysis, DNA see DNA Mutational
   Analysis
Mutism
   Associated with deafness   WV 280
   Psychogenic   WM 475
   Hysterical   WM 173.5
   Other specific associations, by subject
   See also Akinetic Mutism   WL 348;
      Deaf-Mutism   WV 280
Mutism, Akinetic see Akinetic Mutism
Myalgia, Epidemic see Pleurodynia, Epidemic
Myasthenia Gravis   WE 555

Myatonia Congenita see Amyotonia Congenita
myb Genes see Oncogenes
Mycetoma see Maduromycosis
Mycetozoa see Myxomycota
Mycobacteriaceae   QW 125.5.M9
Mycobacteriophages   QW 161.5.M9
Mycobacterium   QW 125.5.M9
Mycobacterium bovis   QW 125.5.M9
Mycobacterium Infections   WC 302
   See also Leprosy   WC 335; Paratuberculosis
   SF 809.J6; Tuberculosis   WF, etc.
Mycobacterium Infections, Atypical   WC 302
Mycobacterium leprae   QW 125.5.M9
Mycobacterium tuberculosis   QW 125.5.M9
Mycology
   Botany   QK 600-635
   Fungus diseases see Mycoses   WC 450-475
   Medical (General)   QW 180
      Dictionaries   QW 13
      Laboratory manuals   QW 25
   Methods in medical mycology   QY 110
   See also Fungi   QW 180, etc.
Mycoplasma   QW 143
Mycoplasma Infections   WC 246
   Veterinary   SF 809.M9
Mycoplasma Pneumonia see Pneumonia,
   Mycoplasma
Mycoplasmatales   QW 143
Mycoplasmatales Infections   WC 246
Mycoses   WC 450-475
   Veterinary   SF 780.7
   See also Dermatomycosis   WR 300-340, etc.;
   Lung Diseases, Fungal   WF 652; and names
   of specific fungal diseases
Mycosis Fungoides   WR 500
Mycotic Aneurysm see Aneurysm, Infected
Mycotic Lung Infections see Lung Diseases, Fungal
Mycotic Skin Infections see Dermatomycosis
Mycotoxicosis   WD 520
Mycotoxins   QW 630.5.M9
Mydriasis see Pupil   WW 240; Dilatation,
   Pathologic   WW 240, etc.
Mydriatics   QV 134
Myelencephalon see Embryology   WL 300 under
   Brain
Myelin Sheath   WL 102.5
Myelitis   WL 400
Myeloblastic Leukemia see Leukemia, Myeloblastic
Myelocele see Meningomyelocele
Myelocytic Leukemia see Leukemia, Myelocytic
Myelocytic Leukemia, Chronic see Leukemia,
   Myeloid, Chronic
Myelodysplasia see Neural Tube Defects
Myelodysplastic Syndromes   WH 380
Myelofibrosis   WH 380
Myelogenous Leukemia see Leukemia, Myeloid
Myelogenous Leukemia, Chronic see Leukemia,
   Myeloid, Chronic
Myelography   WL 405
Myeloid Leukemia see Leukemia, Myeloid
Myeloid Leukemia, Chronic see Leukemia, Myeloid,
   Chronic
Myeloid Tissue see Bone Marrow

Myeloma, Plasma Cell see Multiple Myeloma
Myeloma Proteins   WH 540
Myelomeningocele see Meningomyelocele
Myelopathic Muscular Atrophy see Muscular
   Atrophy, Spinal
Myelophthisic Anemia see Anemia, Myelophthisic
Myeloproliferative Disorders   WH 380
   See also Anemia, Myelophthisic   WH 175;
      Leukemoid Reaction   WH 200; Polycythemia
      Vera   WH 180
Myelosclerosis see Myelofibrosis
Myenteric Plexus   WL 600
Myers–Briggs Type Indicator see Personality
   Inventory
Myiasis   WC 900
   Veterinary   SF 810.F5
Myoblastoma see Neoplasms, Muscle Tissue
Myocardial Contraction   WG 280
Myocardial Depressants see Anti–Arrhythmia
   Agents
Myocardial Diseases   WG 280
   Veterinary   SF 811
Myocardial Diseases, Primary see Myocardial
   Diseases
Myocardial Diseases, Secondary see Myocardial
   Diseases
Myocardial Infarction   WG 300
Myocardial Preinfarction Syndrome see Angina,
   Unstable
Myocardial Reperfusion   WG 280
Myocardial Reperfusion Injury   WG 280
Myocardial Revascularization   WG 169
Myocardial Stimulants see Cardiotonic Agents
Myocardiopathies see Myocardial Diseases
Myocarditis   WG 280
Myocardium   WG 280
   See also Myocardial Revascularization   WG 169
Myoclonia Epileptica see Epilepsy, Myoclonus
Myoclonic Epilepsy, Progressive see Epilepsy,
   Myoclonic
Myoclonic Jerking see Epilepsy, Myoclonic
Myoclonic Jerking, Massive see Spasms, Infantile
Myoclonus   WE 550
Myodystrophia Fetalis Deformans see
   Arthrogryposis
Myoepithelial Tumor see Myoepithelioma
Myoepithelioma   QZ 310
   Localized, by site
Myofascial Pain Dysfunction Syndrome,
   Temporomandibular Joint see
   Temporomandibular Joint Syndrome
Myofascial Pain Syndromes   WE 550
Myofibrils   WE 500
Myoglobin   WH 190
   Clinical analysis   QY 455
Myoglobinuria   WJ 344
Myoinositol see Inositol
Myoma   QZ 340
   Uterine see Leiomyoma   WP 459; Uterine
      Neoplasms   WP 459, etc.
Myometrium   WP 400–460, 468
Myoneural Junction see Neuromuscular Junction
Myopathies see Muscular Diseases

Myopia   WW 320
Myositis   WE 544
Myotonia   WE 550
Myoxidae see Rodentia
Myringoplasty   WV 225
Mysticism   BV 5070–5095
   And alchemy   QD 23.3–26.5
   And hallucinogens   QV 77.7
Mythology   BL 300–325
   In medicine and related fields   WZ 309
Mytilus see Mussels
Myxedema   WK 252
Myxobacterales see Myxococcales
Myxococcales   QW 128
Myxoma   QZ 340
   Localized, by site
Myxoma Virus   QW 165.5.P6
Myxomatosis, Infectious   SF 997.5.R2
Myxomatosis Virus see Myxoma Virus
Myxomycetes see Myxomycota
Myxomycota   QW 180.5.M9
Myxovirus Infections see Orthomyxoviridae
   Infections
Myxovirus influenzae–A suis see Orthomyxovirus
   Type A, Porcine
Myxovirus pestis galli see Orthomyxovirus Type A,
   Avian
Myxoviruses see Orthomyxoviridae

N

N–Formimidoylthienamycin see Imipenem
N–Methyl–D–Aspartate Receptors see Receptors,
   N–Methyl–D–Aspartate
N–ras Genes see Genes, ras
n–3 Fatty Acids see Fatty Acids, Omega–3
N(5)–Formyltetrahydrofolate see Leucovorin
Na(+)–K(+)–Exchanging ATPase   QU 136
Na(+)–K(+)–Transporting ATPase see
   NA(+)–K(+)–Exchanging ATPase
NAD   QU 135
NAD+ ADP–Ribosyltransferase   QU 141
NAD Diaphorase see Lipoamide Dehydrogenase
NADH Diaphorase see Lipoamide Dehydrogenase
Nadide see NAD
NADP   QU 135
Nail Biting   WM 172
   In adolescence   WS 463
   In infancy & childhood   WS 350.6
Nailing, Intramedullary see Fracture Fixation,
   Intramedullary
Nails   WR 475
Nails, Ingrown   WR 475
Nalbuphine   QV 92
Nalidixic Acid   QV 243
Nalidixin see Nalidixic Acid
Naltrexone   QV 89
Names
   Corporate names (cataloging)   Z 695.8
   Geographic names (General)   G 104–108
      Special country, in appropriate LC number
   Subject cataloging
      Personal names   Z 695.1.P4

Nanism see Dwarfism
Naphthalenediones see Naphthoquinones
Naphthalenes
    Organic chemistry   QD 391
    Pharmacology   QV 241
Naphthols   QV 241
Naphthoquinones
    As antiviral agents   QV 268.5
    Organic chemistry   QD 341.H9
Naproxen   QV 95
Narceine see Noscapine
Narcissism   WM 460.5.E3
Narcolepsy   WM 188
Narcosis, Therapeutic Use see Narcotherapy
Narcosynthesis see Narcotherapy
Narcotherapy   WM 402
Narcotic Addiction see Narcotic Dependence
Narcotic Analgesics see Analgesics, Opioid
Narcotic Antagonists   QV 89
Narcotic Control see Drug and Narcotic Control
Narcotic Dependence   WM 284
    See also names of specific narcotics
Narcotic Laws see Legislation, Drug
Narcotics   QV 89
    Control see Drug and Narcotic Control   QV 32, etc.
    Legislation see Legislation, Drug   QV 32–33
    Public health aspects   WA 730
    See also Analgesics, Opioid   QV 89–92, etc.
Narcotine see Noscapine
Nasal Accessory Sinuses see Paranasal Sinuses
Nasal Bone   WV 301
Nasal Cavity   WV 301
Nasal Decongestants see Vasoconstrictor Agents, Nasal
Nasal Fossae see Nasal Cavity
Nasal Polyps   WV 300
Nasal Provocation Tests
   Used in the diagnosis of nasal hypersensitivity WV 335
Nasal Septum   WV 320
Nasal Sinuses see Paranasal Sinuses
Nasopharyngeal Diseases   WV 410
Nasopharyngeal Neoplasms   WV 410
Nasopharynx   WV 410
   In respiration   WF 490
National Council on Health Planning and Development see Health Planning Councils
National Health Insurance, Non–U.S. see National Health Programs
National Health Insurance, United States   W 275
National Health Policy see Health Policy
National Health Programs   WA 540
   Programs in particular areas, by subject, e.g., Maternal Welfare   WA 310
National Health Service, British see State Medicine
National Health Service Corps see Medically Underserved Area
Nationality see Ethnic Groups
Native Americans see Indians, North American
Natriuresis   WJ 303
Natriuretic Factor see Natriuretic Hormone
Natriuretic Hormone   WK 185

Natriuretic Peptides, Atrial see Atrial Natriuretic Factor
Natural Childbirth   WQ 152
Natural Disasters
    Communicable disease control   WA 110
    Hospital emergency service   WX 215
    Medical emergencies   WB 105
    See also special topics under Disasters
Natural History of Drugs see Pharmacognosy
Natural Immunity see Immunity, Natural
Natural Killer Cells see Killer Cells, Natural
Natural Radiation see Background Radiation
Natural Resources see Conservation of Natural Resources   S 900–954, etc., and names of specific resources
Natural Selection   QH 375
Naturopathy   WB 935
Nausea   WI 146
Nautical Medicine see Naval Medicine
Naval Hygiene see Naval Medicine
Naval Medicine   VG 100–475
   Biography
      Collective   WZ 112.5.M4
      Individual   WZ 100
   Hygiene   VG 470–475
   Surgery   WO 800
Naval Nursing see Military Nursing
Naval Science   V
   General works   V 101–109
Naval Surgery see Naval Medicine; Naval   WO 800 under Surgery
Nazism see Political Systems
Neamin see Neomycin
Neapolitan Fever see Brucellosis
Nearsightedness see Myopia
Nebramycin Factor 6 see Tobramycin
Nebulizers and Vaporizers   WB 342
Necator   QX 243
Necatoriasis   WC 890
Neck   WE 708
    Blood supply   WE 708
    Neoplasms see Head and Neck Neoplasms   WE 707
Neck Muscles   WE 708
Neck Neoplasms see Head and Neck Neoplasms
Necrobacillosis see Fusobacterium Infections
Necrophilia see Paraphilias
Necrosis   QZ 180
    Veterinary   SF 769
    Localized, by site
Necrotizing Arteritis see Polyarteritis Nodosa
Necrotizing Pyelonephritis see Kidney Papillary Necrosis
Need Certification, Health Care see Certificate of Need
Needle Biopsy see Biopsy, Needle
Needle Sharing
   Special topics, by subject
NEFA see Fatty Acids, Nonesterified
Nefopam   QV 95
Negative Contrast Radiography see Pneumoradiography
Negative Reinforcement see Reinforcement

(Psychology)
Negatrons see Electrons
Negligence, Professional see Malpractice
Negroes see Blacks
Negroid Race
    Anthropology   GN 645
    See also specific topics under Ethnic groups
Neisseria   QW 131
Neisseria gonorrhoeae   QW 131
Neisseriaceae   QW 131
Nelavane see Trypanosomiasis, African
Nemathelminthes see Acanthocephala; Nematoda
Nematoda   QX 203-301
Nematode Infections   WC 850-890
    Veterinary   SF 810.N4
Nematomorpha see Helminths
Nematomorpha Infections see Helminthiasis
Neoarsphenamine   QV 262
Neocaine see Procaine
Neomalthusianism see Population Dynamics
Neomycin   QV 350
Neomycin A see Neomycin
Neon
    Inorganic chemistry   QD 181.N5
    Pharmacology   QV 310
Neonatal Abstinence Syndrome   WS 421
Neonatal Intensive Care see Intensive Care, Neonatal
Neonatal Mortality see Infant Mortality
Neonatal Nursing   WY 157.3
Neonatal Screening
    For specific diseases, with the disease
Neonate see Infant, Newborn
Neonatology   WS 420
    See also Infant, Newborn   WS 420, etc.;
       Perinatology   WQ 210
Neoplasm Antibodies see Antibodies, Neoplasm
Neoplasm Antigens see Antigens, Neoplasm
Neoplasm Antigens, Viral see Antigens, Viral, Tumor
Neoplasm Circulating Cells   QZ 202
Neoplasm DNA see DNA, Neoplasm
Neoplasm Invasiveness   QZ 202
Neoplasm Metastasis   QZ 202
Neoplasm Metastasis, Unknown Primary see Neoplasms, Unknown Primary
Neoplasm Proteins   QZ 200
Neoplasm Recurrence, Local   QZ 202
Neoplasm Regression, Spontaneous   QZ 202
Neoplasm Remission, Spontaneous see Neoplasm Regression, Spontaneous
Neoplasm RNA see RNA, Neoplasm
Neoplasm Staging   QZ 241
Neoplasm Stem Cell Assay see Tumor Stem Cell Assay
Neoplasm Transplantation   QZ 206
Neoplasms   QZ 200-380
    Drug therapy   QZ 267
       See also Antineoplastic Agents   QV 269
    In adolescence (General)   QZ 275
    In infancy & childhood (General)   QZ 275
    Nursing   WY 156
    Oncolysis   QZ 266
       Special topics, by subject

Radiotherapy   QZ 269
    Veterinary   SF 910.T8
    Localized, by site
Neoplasms, Connective Tissue   QZ 340
Neoplasms, Dental Tissue see Odontogenic Tumors
Neoplasms, Embryonal and Mixed see Neoplasms, Germ Cell and Embryonal
Neoplasms, Experimental   QZ 206
Neoplasms, Germ Cell and Embryonal   QZ 310
Neoplasms, Glandular and Epithelial   QZ 365
Neoplasms, Hormone-Dependent   QZ 200
    Localized, by site
Neoplasms, Mesenchymal see Neoplasms, Connective Tissue
Neoplasms, Multiple Primary   QZ 200
Neoplasms, Muscle Tissue   QZ 340
    Localized, by site
Neoplasms, Nerve Tissue   QZ 380
Neoplasms, Occult Primary see Neoplasms, Unknown Primary
Neoplasms, Radiation-Induced   QZ 200
Neoplasms, Unknown Primary   QZ 202
Neoplasms, Vascular Tissue   QZ 340
Neoplastic Cells, Cultured see Tumor Cells, Cultured
Neoplastic Endocrine-Like Syndromes   QZ 200
    See also Hormones, Ectopic   QZ 202, etc.
Neoplastic Gene Expression Regulation see Gene Expression Regulation, Neoplastic
Neoplastic Transformation, Cell see Cell Transformation, Neoplastic
Neorickettsia see Rickettsiaceae
Neostigmine   QV 124
Neovascularization   WG 500
Nephelometry and Turbidimetry
    Analytical chemistry   QD 79.P46
    Used for the diagnosis of particular disorder, with the disorder
Nephrectomy   WJ 368
    Veterinary   SF 871
Nephritis   WJ 353
    Veterinary   SF 871
Nephritis, Familial see Nephritis, Hereditary
Nephritis, Hereditary   WJ 353
    As a cause of deafness   WV 270
Nephritis, Lupus see Lupus Nephritis
Nephroblastoma   WJ 358
Nephrocalcinosis   WJ 356
Nephrolithiasis see Kidney Calculi
Nephrolithotomy, Percutaneous see Nephrostomy, Percutaneous
Nephrology   WJ 300-378
    Nursing   WY 164
Nephrons   WJ 301
Nephropathy, IGA see Glomerulonephritis, IGA
Nephrosis   WJ 340
Nephrostomy, Percutaneous   WJ 368
Nephrotic Syndrome   WJ 340
Neptunium   WN 420
    Nuclear physics   QC 796.N7
    See also special topics under Radioisotopes
Nerve Block
    Anesthetic uses   WO 300
    Diagnostic and therapeutic uses   WO 375

See also Autonomic Nerve Block   WO 375
Nerve Block anesthesia see Anesthesia, Conduction
Nerve Cells see Neurons
Nerve Centers see Neurons
Nerve Compression Syndromes   WL 500
Nerve Conduction see Neural Conduction
Nerve Degeneration   WL 102.5
 Of a particular part, by subject, e.g., in the cerebellum   WL 320
Nerve Endings   WL 102.9
Nerve Endings, Sensory see Receptors, Sensory
Nerve Fibers   WL 102.5
Nerve Fibers, Myelinated   WL 102.5
Nerve Growth Factors   WL 104
Nerve Impulses see Physiology   WL 102 under Nervous System
Nerve Net   WL 102
Nerve Regeneration   WL 102
Nerve Roots see Spinal Nerve Roots
Nerve Tissue   WL 101-102
 Analysis   WL 104
 Anatomy   WL 101
 Histology   QS 532.5.N3
 Neoplasms   QZ 380
 Physiology   WL 102
Nerve Tissue Proteins   WL 104
Nerve Transmission see Synaptic Transmission
Nerve Transmitter Substances see Neurotransmitters
Nerves see Autonomic Nervous System; Nervous System; Peripheral Nervous System; Sympathetic Nervous System; names of specific nerves
Nervous Exhaustion see Neurasthenia
Nervous Mice see Mice, Neurologic Mutants
Nervous System
 Anatomy   WL 101
 Autonomic see Autonomic Nervous System WL 600-610
 Children   WS 340-342
 Drugs affecting   QV 76.5
  See also Analeptics   QV 101-107; Analgesics, Anti-Inflammatory   QV 95-98; Anesthetics QV 81, etc.; Anticonvulsants   QV 85; Autonomic Drugs   QV 120; Hypnotics and Sedatives   QV 85-88; Narcotics   QV 89; Neuromuscular Blocking Agents   QV 140; Neuromuscular Depolarizing Agents   QV 140
 Neoplasms (General)   WL 160
 Parasympathetic see Parasympathetic Nervous System   WL 610
 Pathology   WL 140
 Physiology   WL 102
 Surgery   WL 368
 Sympathetic see Sympathetic Nervous System WL 610
 See also Neoplasms, Nervous Tissue   QZ 380; Neuroanatomy (specialty only)   WL 101; Neurophysiology (specialty only)   WL 102; Neurosurgery (specialty only)   WL 368; names of specific nerves
Nervous System Diseases   WL 140-710
 ENT complications   WV 180
 In infancy & childhood   WS 340

Nursing   WY 160.5
 Veterinary   SF 895
Nervous System Neoplasms   WL 160
Nesidioblastoma see Adenoma, Islet Cell
Nesidioblastosis see Pancreatic Diseases
Nesidioblasts see Islets of Langerhans
Nested Case-Control Studies see Case-Control Studies
Nesting Behavior   QL 756
 Bird   QL 675
Netilmicin   QV 350
Nettle Rash see Urticaria
Network Communication Protocols see Computer Communication Networks
Neural Analyzers   WL 101-102
Neural Conduction   WL 102.7-102.8
Neural Crest   WL 101
 Animal   QL 938.N48
Neural Inhibition   WL 102.7-102.8
Neural Interconnections see Neural Pathways
Neural Networks (Anatomic) see Nerve Net
Neural Pathways   WL 102
 See also Pyramidal Tracts   WL 400; names of specific pathways
Neural Transmission see Synaptic Transmission
Neural Tube Defects   WL 101
 See also names of specific defects, e.g., Spinal Dysraphism   WE 730
Neuralgia   WL 544
 Cervico-brachial see Cervico-Brachial Neuralgia WL 400
 Facial see Facial Neuralgia   WL 544
 Trigeminal see Trigeminal Neuralgia   WL 544
Neuralgic Amyotrophy see Cervico-Brachial Neuralgia
Neuraminic Acids   QU 84
 Organic chemistry   QD 321
Neuraminidase   QU 136
Neurasthenia   WM 174
Neurasthenic Neuroses see Neurasthenia
Neurenteric Cyst see Spina Bifida Occulta
Neurilemmoma   QZ 380
 Localized, by site
Neurilemmoma, Acoustic see Neuroma, Acoustic
Neurinoma see Neurilemmoma
Neurinoma, Acoustic see Neuroma, Acoustic
Neurite Outgrowth Factor see Nerve Growth Factors
Neuritis   WL 544
 Endemic multiple see Beriberi   WD 122
 Optic see Optic Neuritis   WW 280
Neuritis, Experimental Allergic   WL 544
Neuro-Ophthalmology see Innervation   WW 101-103 under Eye; Eye Movements; Oculomotor Muscles; Oculomotor Nerve; Optic Nerve
Neuroanatomy   WL 101
 See also Anatomy   WL 101 under Nervous System
Neurobiology   WL 100-102
Neuroblastoma   QZ 380
 Localized, by site
Neurochemistry   WL 104
 See also Analysis   WL 104 under Nerve Tissue

ALWAYS CONSULT MAIN SCHEDULES. USE NUMBER ASSIGNED ONLY WHEN
SUBJECT REPRESENTS MAJOR EMPHASIS OF WORK BEING CLASSIFIED

Neurocirculatory Asthenia   WG 320
Neurodermatitis   WR 280
Neurodermatitis, Atopic see Dermatitis, Atopic
Neurodermatitis, Circumscribed see Neurodermatitis
Neurodermatitis, Disseminated see Dermatitis,
    Atopic
Neurodermatitis, Localized see Neurodermatitis
Neuroeffector Junction   WL 102.9
Neuroendocrine System see Neurosecretory Systems
Neuroendocrinology   WL 105
Neurofibrils   WL 102.5
Neurofibroma   QZ 380
    Localized, by site
Neurofibromatosis   QZ 380
Neurofilaments see Intermediate Filaments
Neuroglia
    Anatomy   WL 101
    Histology   QS 532.5.N3
    Physiology   WL 102
Neurohemal Organ see Neurosecretory Systems
Neurohumor Receptors see Receptors,
    Neurotransmitter
Neurohumors see Neurotransmitters
Neurohypophysis see Pituitary Gland, Posterior
Neuroimmune Processes see
    Neuroimmunomodulation
Neuroimmunomodulation   WL 102
    Emphasis on immune system   QW 504
Neuroleptanalgesia   WO 297
Neuroleptic Malignant Syndrome   WL 307
Neuroleptics see Antipsychotic Agents
Neurologic Examination   WL 141
    In infancy & childhood   WS 340
Neurologic Manifestations   WL 340
    Of eye diseases   WW 460
    Of particular diseases, with the disease
    See also Movement Disorders   WL 390;
        Neuromuscular Diseases   WE 550–559, etc.;
        Psychomotor Disorders   WM 197; names of
        specific disorders
Neurologic Models see Models, Neurological
Neurology   WL
    In infancy & childhood   WS 340
Neurolymphomatosis see Marek's Disease
Neuroma   QZ 380
    Localized, by site
Neuroma, Acoustic   WV 250
Neuroma, Acoustic, Unilateral see Neuroma,
    Acoustic
Neuromediator Receptors see Receptors,
    Neurotransmitter
Neuromodulator Receptors see Receptors,
    Neurotransmitter
Neuromodulators see Neurotransmitters
Neuromuscular Agents   QV 140
Neuromuscular Blocking Agents   QV 140
Neuromuscular Blocking Agents, Competitive see
    Neuromuscular Nondepolarizing Agents
Neuromuscular Depolarizing Agents   QV 140
Neuromuscular Diseases   WE 550–559
    In infancy & childhood   WS 340
    Ophthalmological   WW 400–475
Neuromuscular Junction   WL 102.9

Neuromuscular Mechanisms of the Eye see Eye
    Movements
Neuromuscular Nondepolarizing Agents   QV 140
Neuromuscular Spindles see Muscle Spindles
Neuron Degeneration see Nerve Degeneration
Neuronal Ceroid-Lipofuscinosis   WD 205.5.L5
Neuronal Plasticity   WL 102
Neurons   WL 102.5
Neurons, Fusimotor see Motor Neurons, Gamma
Neurons, Gamma Motor see Motor Neurons,
    Gamma
Neuropathology see Pathology   WL 140 under
    Nervous System
Neuropathy, Type I Hereditary Motor and Sensory
    see Charcot-Marie Disease
Neuropeptide Y   WL 104
Neuropeptide Y-Like Immunoreactive Peptide see
    Neuropeptide Y
Neuropeptides   WL 104
Neuropharmacology   QV 76.5
Neurophysins   QU 55
    Endocrinology   WK 520
    Neurochemistry   WL 104
Neurophysiology   WL 102
    See also Physiology   WL 102 under Nervous
    System
Neuropsychological Tests
    In psychiatry   WM 145.5.N4
    In neurology   WL 141
    In infancy & childhood   WS 340
Neuropsychology   WL 103.5
Neuroradiography   WL 141
    In infancy & childhood   WS 340
Neuroreceptors see Receptors, Sensory
Neuroregulator Receptors see Receptors,
    Neurotransmitter
Neuroregulators see Neurotransmitters
Neurosciences   WL 100
Neurosecretion   WL 102
Neurosecretory Systems   WL 102
Neuroses see Neurotic Disorders
Neuroses, Anxiety see Anxiety Disorders
Neuroses, Neurasthenic see Neurasthenia
Neuroses, Phobic see Phobic Disorders
Neuroses, Post-Traumatic see Stress Disorders,
    Post-Traumatic
Neuroses, War see Combat Disorders
Neurosis, Depressive see Depressive Disorder
Neurosis, Hypochondriacal see Hypochondriasis
Neurosis, Obsessive-Compulsive see
    Obsessive-Compulsive Disorder
Neurospora   QW 180.5.A8
Neurosurgery   WL 368
    See also Surgery   WL 368 under Nervous
    System
Neurosyphilis   WC 165
Neurotensin   WL 104
Neurotic Disorders   WM 170–184
    In adolescence   WS 463
    In infancy & childhood   WS 350.6
    In old age   WT 150
Neurotoxins   QW 630.5.N4
    Of insecticides   WA 240

ALWAYS CONSULT MAIN SCHEDULES. USE NUMBER ASSIGNED ONLY WHEN
SUBJECT REPRESENTS MAJOR EMPHASIS OF WORK BEING CLASSIFIED

Neurotransmitter Uptake Inhibitors   QV 129
Neurotransmitters   QV 126
    See also names of specific neurotransmitters
Neurotropic Virus Infections see Virus Diseases
Neutron Activation Analysis   QD 606
    Of a particular substance, with the substance
Neutrons   WN 415–420
    In general nuclear physics   QC
    793.5.N462–793.5.N4629
    In health physics   WN 110
Neutropenia   WH 200
Neutrophil-Activating Peptide,
    Lymphocyte-Derived see Interleukin-8
Neutrophil-Activating Peptide, Monocyte-Derived
    see Interleukin-8
Neutrophil-Activating Peptides, Fibroblast-Derived
see Interleukin-8
Neutrophil-Derived Relaxant Factor see
    Endothelium-Derived Relaxing Factor
Neutrophils   WH 200
    In phagocytosis   QW 690
Nevus   WR 500
    Pathology   QZ 310
Nevus, Pigmented   WR 265
    Pathology   QZ 310
Nevus Syndrome, Dysplastic see Dysplastic Nevus
    Syndrome
Newborn see Infant, Newborn
Newborn Infant Screening see Neonatal Screening
Newcastle Disease   SF 995.6.N4
Newcastle Disease Virus   QW 168.5.P2
News Media Relations see Public Relations
Newsletters see Periodicals
Newspapers
    General bibliography   Z 6940–6967
    Medical and related areas   W1
      Bibliography   ZW 1
Niacin see Nicotinic Acids   QU 193
Niacinamide   QU 193
Nialamide   QV 77.5
Nicardipine   QV 150
Nickel
    Inorganic chemistry   QD 181.N6
    Pharmacology   QV 290
Nicolas-Favre Disease see Lymphogranuloma
    Venereum
Nicotiana see Tobacco
Nicotinamide see Niacinamide
Nicotinamide-Adenine Dinucleotide see NAD
Nicotinamide-Adenine Dinucleotide Phosphate see
    NADP
Nicotine   QV 137
    Dependence   WM 290
Nicotinic Acid see Niacin
Nicotinic Acids   QU 193
Nicotinic Agents see Cholinergic Agents
Nicotinic Receptors see Receptors, Nicotinic
Nidation see Ovum Implantation
Nidation, Delayed see Ovum Implantation, Delayed
NIDDM see Diabetes Mellitus,
    Non-Insulin-Dependent
Niemann-Pick Disease   WD 205.5.L5
Nifedipine   QV 150

Night Blindness   WD 110
Night Monkey, Northern see Aotus trivirgatus
Night Terrors see Sleep Disorders
Night Vision see Dark Adaptation
Nightmares see Dreams
NIH Consensus Development Conferences see
    Consensus Development Conferences, NIH
Nikethamide   QV 103
Nimodipine   QV 150
Niobium
    Inorganic chemistry   QD 181.N3
    Radioactive   WN 420
Nisoldipine   QV 150
Nitrates   QV 156
    As caustics (e.g. when nitrates are used for nitric
    acid)   QV 612
Nitric Acid see Nitrates
Nitric Oxide
    As an air pollutant   WA 754
    Inorganic chemistry   QD 181.N1
Nitriles
    As antineoplastic agents   QV 269
    Organic chemistry
      Aliphatic compounds   QD 305.N7
      Aromatic compounds   QD 341.N7
Nitrites   QV 156
Nitrobacter   QW 135
Nitrobacteraceae   QW 135
Nitrobenzenes
    Organic chemistry   QD 341.H9
    Toxicology   QV 632
Nitrocellulose see Collodion
Nitroferricyanide see Nitroprusside
Nitrofural see Nitrofurazone
Nitrofurans   QV 243
Nitrofurazone   QV 243
    As a local anti-infective agent   QV 225
Nitrogen   QU 54
    Blood chemistry   QY 455
Nitrogen Dioxide
    As an air pollutant   WA 754
    Inorganic chemistry   QD 181.N1
Nitrogen Fixation   QU 70
    Chemical technology   TP 245.N8
    In plants   QK 898.N6
    In soil   QW 60
Nitrogen Isotopes   QU 54
    Inorganic chemistry   QD 181.N1
Nitrogen Mustard see Mechlorethamine; Mustard
    Compounds; Thio-Tepa; Triethylene Melamine
Nitrogen Mustard Compounds   QV 269
    As war gases   QV 666
Nitrogen Mustard N-Oxide see Mechlorethamine
Nitrogen Narcosis see Inert Gas Narcosis
Nitrogen Oxides
    As air pollutants   WA 754
    Inorganic chemistry   QD 181.N1
    Mineralogy   QE 389.5
Nitroglycerin   QV 156
    Toxicology   QV 632
Nitroprusside
    As a vasodilator agent   QV 156
Nitrosamines   QZ 202

Nitrosation
    As a metabolic phenomenon   QU 120
    Organic chemistry   QD 281.N5
Nitroso Compounds
    As carcinogens   QZ 202
    Organic chemistry
        Aliphatic compounds   QD 305.N8
        Aromatic compounds   QD 341.N8
Nitrosodiethylamine see Diethylnitrosamine
Nitrosomonas   QW 135
Nitrous Oxide   QV 81
Nizethamid see Nikethamide
NK Cells see Killer Cells, Natural
NMDA Receptor-Ionophore Complex see
   Receptors, N-Methyl-D-Aspartate
NMR Imaging see Magnetic Resonance Imaging
NMR Tomography see Magnetic Resonance
   Imaging
No-Fault Insurance see Insurance, Liability
Nobel Prize   AS 911
    Collective biography of winners
        Chemists   QD 21
        General   AS 911
        Physicians   WZ 112
        Physicists   QC 15
        Physiologists   WZ 112.5.P5
Nocardia Infections   WC 302
    Veterinary   SF 809.N63
    See also Maduromycosis   WR 340
Nociception Tests see Pain Measurement
Nociceptors   WL 102.9
Nodding Spasm see Spasms, Infantile
Nodulus Intercaroticus see Carotid Body
Noise   WA 776
    Abatement   WA 776
        In industry   WA 470
    Adverse effects   WV 270
        In aviation   WD 735
    Prevention & control
        General public health   WA 776
        In industry   WA 470
Noise-Induced Hearing Loss see Hearing Loss,
   Noise-Induced
Noise, Occupational see Noise   WA 470, etc.
Noise, Transportation see Noise   WA 776, etc.
Nomascus see Hylobates
Nomenclature
    (Form number 15 in any NLM schedule where
    applicable)
Nomifensine
    As an antidepressant   QV 77.5
    As an antiparkinson agent   QV 80
Non-Hodgkin's Lymphoma see Lymphoma,
   Non-Hodgkin's
Non-Steroidal Anti-Inflammatory Agents see
   Anti-Inflammatory Agents, Non-Steroidal
Nonagenarian see Aged, 80 and over
Nondirective Therapy   WM 420.5.N8
Nondisjunction, Genetic   QH 462.N65
Noninvasive Litholapaxy see Lithotripsy
Nonodontogenic Cysts   WU 280
Nonopioid Analgesics see Analgesics, Non-Narcotic
Nonprofit Organizations see Organizations,

Nonprofit
Nonverbal Communication   HM 258
    In adolescence   WS 462
    In infancy & childhood   WS 105.5.C8
    In speech disorders   WM 475
    Psychology   BF 637.N66
    See also Kinesics   WS 462, etc.; Manual
    Communication   HV 2477, etc.
Nootropic Drugs see Psychotropic Drugs
Noradrenaline see Norepinephrine
Noramidopyrine Methanesulfonate see Dipyrone
Norepinephrine   WK 725
Norethandrolone   WJ 875
Norethindrone   WP 530
    As a contraceptive   QV 177
Norethisterone see Norethindrone
Norethynodrel   WP 530
    As a contraceptive   QV 177
Norfloxacin   QV 250
Norgestrel   WP 530
    As a contraceptive   QV 177
Normal Range see Reference Values
Normal Serum Globulin Therapy see Immunization,
   Passive
Normal Values see Reference Values
Normethandrolone   WP 530
Normoblasts see Erythroblasts
Norpregneninolone see Norethindrone
Northern Blotting see Blotting, Northern
Nortropanes
    Organic chemistry   QD 401
Noscapine   QV 76
Nose   WV 300-335
    Innervation   WV 301
    Surgery   WV 300
        Plastic   WV 312
Nose Bleed see Epistaxis
Nose Diseases   WV 300-335
    General works   WV 300
    In infancy & childhood   WV 300-335
    Nursing   WY 158.5
    Veterinary   SF 891
Nose Neoplasms   WV 300
Nosebleed see Epistaxis
Nosocomial Infections see Cross Infection
Nosology see Classification
Nostrums   QV 772
Notifiable Diseases, Registration see Communicable
   Disease Control; Registries
Novelty-Seeking Behavior see Exploratory
   Behavior
Novocaine see Procaine
Nuclear Energy   WN 415
    Meteorology   QC 913.2.A8
    Nuclear physics   QC 770-798
Nuclear Envelope see Nuclear Membrane
Nuclear Magnetic Resonance   QC 762
    In biochemistry   QU 25
    Spectroscopy   QD 96.N8
    Other special topics, by subject
    See also Magnetic Resonance Imaging   WN 185
Nuclear Medicine   WN 440-450
Nuclear Medicine Department, Hospital   WN

Transportation nursing   WY 143
Veterinary   SF 774.5
See also names of diseases being treated or the specialty involved
Nursing Administration Research   WY 105
Nursing Assessment   WY 100.4
Nursing Audit   WY 100.5
Nursing Care
General   WY 100
In special field   WY 150–164
Nursing Care Plans see Patient Care Planning
Nursing Diagnosis   WY 100.4
Nursing Economics see Economics, Nursing
Nursing Education see Education, Nursing
Nursing Education, Associate see Education, Nursing, Associate
Nursing Education, Baccalaureate see Education, Nursing, Baccalaureate
Nursing Education, Continuing see Education, Nursing, Continuing
Nursing Education, Diploma Programs see Education, Nursing, Diploma Programs
Nursing Education, Graduate see Education, Nursing, Graduate
Nursing Education Research   WY 18
Nursing Ethics see Ethics, Nursing
Nursing Evaluation Research   WY 20.5
Nursing Faculty see Faculty, Nursing
Nursing, Home see Home Nursing
Nursing Homes   WX 27–28
Administration   WX 150
Directories   WX 22
For the aged   WT 27–28
Directories   WT 22
For other purposes, by specialty
Nursing Libraries see Libraries, Nursing
Nursing, Maternal–Child see Maternal–Child Nursing
Nursing Methodology Research   WY 20.5
Nursing, Military and Naval see Military Nursing
Nursing Models see Models, Nursing
Nursing, Oncologic see Oncologic Nursing
Nursing Philosophy see Philosophy, Nursing
Nursing Pools see Employment; Nurses
Nursing, Practical   WY 195
Education   WY 18.8
Nursing, Private Duty   WY 127
Education   WY 18
Nursing Process   WY 100
Specific activities, by subject
Nursing Program Evaluation see Nursing Evaluation Research
Nursing Protocols see Nursing Assessment
Nursing Records   WY 100.5
See also Medical Records   WX 173, etc.
Nursing Research   WY 20.5
Nursing Research, Administrative see Nursing Administration Research
Nursing Research, Clinical see Clinical Nursing Research
Nursing Research, Educational see Nursing Education Research
Nursing Schools see Schools, Nursing

Nursing Service, Hospital   WY 125
Administration   WY 105
Nursing Services   WY 100
Nursing Staff
Of industry   WY 141
Of schools   WY 113
Nursing Staff, Hospital   WY 125
Administration   WY 105
Nursing, Supervisory   WY 105
Of wards   WY 105
Nursing, Team   WY 125
See also Patient Care Team   W 84.8, etc.
Nursing Theory   WY 86
Nursing, Transcultural see Transcultural Nursing
Nutcracker Esophagus see Esophageal Motility Disorders
Nutrition
And oral health   WU 113.7
General   QU 145
In animals see Animal Nutrition   SF 95–99
In children see Child Nutrition   WS 115, etc.
In infants see Infant Nutrition   WS 115–125
In old age   WT 115
In pregnancy   WQ 175
In sickness (General)   WB 400
Tables   QU 145
For children   WS 16
See also Diet   QT 235; Parenteral Feeding WB 410; other particular topics
Nutrition Assessment   QU 146
Nutrition Disorders   WD 100–175
As a cause of disease   QZ 105
In infancy & childhood   WS 115
Children   WS 115; WS 130
In old age   WT 115
Infant see Infant Nutrition Disorders   WS 120, etc.
Veterinary   SF 851
See also Obesity   WD 210–212
Nutrition Disorders, Child see Child Nutrition Disorders
Nutrition Disorders, Infant see Infant Nutrition Disorders
Nutrition, Enteral see Enteral Nutrition
Nutrition, Parenteral see Parenteral Nutrition
Nutrition Surveys   QU 146
Nutrition, Total Parenteral see Parenteral Nutrition, Total
Nutritional Availability see Nutritive Value
Nutritional Requirements   QU 145
In old age   WT 115
Nutritional Status   QU 145
Nutritive Value   QU 145.5
Tables   QU 145.5
Nuts
Diets for control of fats   WB 425
Diets for control of protein   WB 426
Nux Vomica see Strychnine
Nyctalopia see Night Blindness
Nycticebus see Lorisidae
Nyctiphanes see Crustacea
Nyctohemeral Rhythm see Circadian Rhythm

ALWAYS CONSULT MAIN SCHEDULES. USE NUMBER ASSIGNED ONLY WHEN
SUBJECT REPRESENTS MAJOR EMPHASIS OF WORK BEING CLASSIFIED

Nylons
    Chemical technology   TP 1180.P55
    Used for special purposes, by subject, e.g., in plastic surgery   WO 640
Nymphae see Vulva
Nymphomania see Paraphilias
Nystagmus   WW 410
Nystagmus, Barany's see Nystagmus, Physiologic
Nystagmus, Caloric see Nystagmus, Physiologic
Nystagmus, Physiologic   WW 410
Nystagmus, Thermal see Nystagmus, Physiologic

O

o–Dihydroxybenzenes see Catechols
Oath, Hippocratic see Hippocratic Oath
Oats
    As a dietary supplement in health or disease WB 431
    Cultivation   SB 191.O2
Obesity   WD 210–212
Obesity in Diabetes   WK 835
Obesity, Morbid   WD 210–212
Object Attachment   WM 460.5.O2
Object Relations see Object Attachment
Object Relationship see Object Attachment
Obligation, Social see Social Responsibility
Obsessive Behavior   WM 176
Obsessive–Compulsive Disorder   WM 176
Obsessive–Compulsive Personality see Compulsive Personality Disorder
Obstetrical Forceps   WQ 425
Obstetrical Nursing   WY 157
    Education   WY 18–18.5
    See also Postnatal Nursing   WY 157.3
Obstetricians, Directories see Directories   WQ 22 under Obstetrics
Obstetrics   WQ
    Anesthesia see Anesthesia, Obstetrical   WO 450
    Cardiac problems   WQ 244
    Directories   WQ 22
    Nursing see Obstetrical Nursing   WY 157, etc.
    Urology   WJ 190
        Complications   WQ 260.
Obstetrics and Gynecology Department, Hospital WQ 27–28
Obstruction, Intestinal see Intestinal Obstruction
Obturators, Palatal see Palatal Obturators
Occipital Lobe   WL 307
Occlusal Equilibration see Dental Occlusion, Balanced
Occlusal Force see Bite Force
Occlusion see Dental Occlusion
Occlusive Dressings   WO 167
Occult Blood   QY 160
Occult Primary Neoplasms see Neoplasms, Unknown Primary
Occult Spina Bifida see Spina Bifida Occulta
Occult Spinal Dysraphism see Spina Bifida Occulta
Occultism
    Medical superstitions   WZ 309
Occupational Accidents see Accidents, Occupational
Occupational Air Pollutants see Air Pollutants,

Occupational
Occupational Dentistry   WA 412
Occupational Dermatitis see Dermatitis, Occupational
Occupational Diseases   WA 400–495
    Medicolegal aspects   W 925
    Mental disorders (General)   WA 495
    Nursing see Occupational Health Nursing   WY 141
    Ophthalmological   WW 505
    Prevention & control   WA 412–495
    See also Disability Evaluation   W 925, etc.; Workers' Compensation   HD 7103.6–7103.65, etc.
Occupational Exposure   WA 400–495
    See also Environmental Exposure
Occupational Health   WA 400–495
    Special topics, by subject
Occupational Health Nursing   WY 141
    Education   WY 18–18.5
Occupational Health Services   WA 412
    Mental health   WA 495
        See also Mental Health Services   WM 30, etc.
Occupational Hygiene see Occupational Health
Occupational Medicine   WA 400–495
Occupational Mobility see Career Mobility
Occupational Neuroses see Occupational Diseases; Mental Health
Occupational Noise see Noise, Occupational
Occupational Nursing see Occupational Health Nursing
Occupational Safety see Occupational Health
Occupational Therapy   WB 555
    Hospital department   WX 225
    In adolescence   WS 463
    In infancy & childhood
        For mentally disabled   WS 350.2
        For physically disabled   WS 368
    In psychiatry   WM 450.5.O2
    See also Rehabilitation, Vocational   HD 7255–7256
Occupational Therapy Department, Hospital   WX 225
Occupational Toxicology see Poisons; Toxicology
Occupations
    Statistics and demographic discussions   HB 2581–2787
    Specific occupations, by type, e.g., Surgery   WO 21
    See also Vocational Guidance   HF 5381–5382.67, etc.
Oceanography   GC
    General works   GC 10.9–11.2
Ochronosis   WR 267
Octadecenoic Acids see Oleic Acids
Octodon see Rodentia
Octogenarian see Aged, 80 and over
Ocular Accommodation see Accommodation, Ocular
Ocular Adaptation see Adaptation, Ocular
Ocular Dominance see Vision
Ocular Fixation see Fixation, Ocular

Ocular Fluorophotometry see Fluorophotometry
Ocular Herpes zoster Virus see Herpesvirus 3, Human
Ocular Infections, Parasitic see Eye Infections, Parasitic
Ocular Motility see Eye Movements
Ocular Motility Disorders   WW 410
Ocular Prosthesis see Eye, Artificial
Ocular Refraction see Refraction, Ocular
Ocular Tension see Intraocular Pressure
Ocular Torticollis see Ocular Motility Disorders
Ocular Toxoplasmosis see Toxoplasmosis, Ocular
Ocular Tuberculosis see Tuberculosis, Ocular
Oculomotor Muscles   WW 400–460
   See also Eye Movements   WW 400–460
Oculomotor Nerve   WL 330
Oculomotor Paralysis see Ophthalmoplegia
Ocytocin see Oxytocin
Oddi's Sphincter   WI 750
Odontoblasts   WU 230
Odontogenic Cysts   WU 280
Odontogenic Tumors   WU 280
   Pathology of dental tissue   QZ 200
Odontometry   WU 141.5.O2
Odontostomatology see Mouth   WU, Tooth   WU and related headings
Odors
   Industrial control   WA 450
   Otolaryngology   WV 301
   Pollution   WA 754
Oedipus Complex   WM 460
Oesophagus see Esophagus
Offenses, Sexual see Sex Offenses
Office Automation   W 26.5
   In special areas, by subject
Office Management   W 80
   Dental   WU 77
   See also Dental Offices   WU 77 and names of specialties involved, e.g., Psychiatry   WM 30
Office Nursing   WY 109
Office Surgery see Ambulatory Surgery
Office Visits
   Made for special purpose, by subject
Offspring of Impaired Parents see Child of Impaired Parents
Ofloxacin   QV 250
Oils   QV 785
   Biochemistry   QU 86
   Public health aspects   WA 722
   See also names of specific oils
Oils, Essential see Oils, Volatile
Oils, Plant see Plant Oils
Oils, Unsaturated see Fats, Unsaturated
Oils, Vegetable see Plant Oils
Oils, Volatile   QV 785
   Biochemistry   QU 86
   Chemical technology   TP 958–959
Ointments   QV 785
OK–432 see Picibanil
Old Age see Aged   WT
Old Age Assistance   WT 30
   Social Security   HD 7090–7250
Old Age Homes see Homes for the Aged

Old Age Insurance see Medicare; Social Security
Oldest Old see Aged, 80 and over
Oleates see Oleic Acids
Olefins see Alkenes
Oleic Acids   QU 90
   Pharmaceutical agents   QV 785
Oleomargarine see Margarine
Oleoresins see Resins; specific resins or plants from which derived, e.g., Aspidium
Olfaction see Smell
Olfactory Cortex see Olfactory Pathways
Olfactory Mucosa   WV 301
Olfactory Nerve   WL 330
   See also Smell   WV 301
Olfactory Pathways   WL 314
Olfactory Sense see Smell
Olfactory Tract see Olfactory Pathways
Olfactory Tubercle see Olfactory Pathways
Oligemia see Anemia
Oligochaeta   QX 451
Oligochromemia see Anemia
Oligodeoxyribonucleotides, Antisense see Oligonucleotides, Antisense
Oligomenorrhea   WP 522
Oligonucleotide–Directed Mutagenesis see Mutagenesis, Site–Directed
Oligonucleotides   QU 57
Oligonucleotides, Antisense   QU 57
Oligoribonucleotides   QU 57
Oligoribonucleotides, Antisense see Oligonucleotides, Antisense
Oligosaccharides   QU 83
omega–Chloroacetophenone   QV 665
Omega Protein see DNA Topoisomerase
Omega-3 Fatty Acids see Fatty Acids, Omega-3
Omentum   WI 575
Omeprazole   QV 69
OMP Proteins see Bacterial Outer Membrane Proteins
Omphalocele see Hernia, Umbilical
On–Line Systems see Online Systems
Onchocerca   QX 301
Onchocerciasis   WC 885
Oncogenes   QZ 202
Oncogenic Viruses   QW 166
Oncogens see Carcinogens
Oncologic Nursing   WY 156
Oncology, Medical see Medical Oncology
Oncolysis see Neoplasms
Ondatra see Microtinae
Ondine's Curse see Sleep Apnea Syndromes
Onions see Allium
Onlays see Inlays
Online Systems   Z 699
   By subject   Z 699.5.A–Z
   In medicine (General)   W 26.55.I4
   In other special fields (Form number 26.5 in any NLM schedule where applicable)
Only Child   WS 105.5.F2
Ontogeny   QH 491
   Specific animal   QL
   Specific plant   QK
   See also names of organ or organism involved

Onychophagia see Nail Biting
Oocytes WQ 205
Oophoritis WP 320
Opacity, Vitreous see Vitreous Body
Opaque Media see Contrast Media
Open-Angle Glaucoma see Glaucoma, Open-Angle
Open Fractures see Fractures, Open
Operating Room Nursing WY 162
    Education WY 18-18.5
Operating Room Technicians WY 162
Operating Rooms WX 200
    Architectural planning and construction WX 140
Operations Research
    Industrial engineering T 57.6-57.97
    Special topics, by subject
Operative Dentistry see Dentistry, Operative
Operative Obstetrics see Abortion, Induced; Cesarean Section; Delivery; Embryotomy; and other specific subjects
Operative Surgery see Surgery, Operative
Operon QH 450.2
Ophthalmia see Endophthalmitis
Ophthalmia, Sympathetic WW 525
Ophthalmic Artery WG 595.07
    See also Blood supply WW 101-103 under Eye
Ophthalmic Assistants WW 21.5
Ophthalmic Nerve WL 330
Ophthalmic Solutions WW 166
Ophthalmologists see Biography WZ 100, etc, and Directories WW 22 under Ophthalmology
Ophthalmology WW
    Biography
        Collective WZ 112.5.07
        Individual WZ 100
    Directories WW 22
    In infancy & childhood WW 600
    In old age WW 620
    Occupational WW 505
    Instrumentation WW 26
    Traumatic see Eye Injuries WW 525
    See also Eye Diseases WW 140, etc.
Ophthalmoplegia WW 410
Ophthalmoscopy WW 143
    Veterinary SF 891
Opiate Dependence see Narcotic Dependence
Opiates see Narcotics
Opiates, Endogenous see Opioid Peptides
Opioid Analgesics see Analgesics, Opioid
Opioid Peptides QU 68
Opioids see Narcotics
Opisthorchiasis WC 805
Opisthorchis QX 353
Opisthorchis felineus see Opisthorchis
Opisthorchis sinensis see Clonorchis sinensis
Opisthorchis viverrini see Opisthorchis
Opium
    Dependence WM 286
        See also Heroin Dependence WM 288; Morphine Dependence WM 286
    Alkaloids QV 90
Opossums QL 737.M34
Oppenheim-Ziehen Disease see Dystonia

Musculorum Deformans
Oppenheim's Disease see Amyotonia Congenita
Opportunistic Infections
    General WC 195
    Parasitic WC 695
    Viral WC 500
Opportunistic Infections, AIDS-Related see AIDS-Related Opportunistic Infections
Opsonins
    Antibodies QW 601
    Clinical analysis QY 455
    Derived from complement QW 680
    See also Phagocytosis QW 690
Optic Atrophy WW 280
Optic Chiasm WW 280
    For the neurologist WL 330
Optic Lobe WL 310
Optic Nerve WW 280
    For the neurologist WL 330
    See also Innervation WW 101-103 under Eye; Vision WW 103, etc.
Optic Nerve Diseases WW 280
Optic Neuritis WW 280
Optical Dispensing see Optometry
Optical Illusions WW 105
Optical Instruments see Instrumentation WW 26 under Ophthalmology or Optometry; Instrumentation QC 370.5-379 under Optics; names of particular instruments or procedures
Optical Readers see Automatic Data Processing
Optical Rotatory Dispersion
    Physical chemistry QD 473
Opticians see Optometry
Optics QC 350-467
    Instrumentation QC 370.5-379
    Physiological see Optometry WW 704, etc.; Vision WW, etc.
    Stereoscopy WN 100
Optometrists see Biography WZ 112.5.07, etc., and Directories WW 722 under Optometry
Optometry WW 704-722
    Biography
        Collective WZ 122.5.O7
        Individual WZ 100
    Directories WW 722
    Instrumentation WW 26
    Optical dispensing WW 350-355
    Opticianry WW 350-358
    Opticians WW 704-722
    See also names of functions of the optometrist, e.g., Orthoptics WW 405
Oral Health WU 113
    Children WU 113.6
Oral Hemorrhage WU 140
Oral Hygiene WU 113
    Children WU 113.6
Oral Hygiene Index WU 30
Oral Manifestations WU 290
    Of particular diseases, with the disease
Oral Medicine see Dentistry
Oral Rehydration Therapy see Fluid Therapy
Oral Surgery see Surgery, Oral
Oral Tobacco see Tobacco, Smokeless

ALWAYS CONSULT MAIN SCHEDULES. USE NUMBER ASSIGNED ONLY WHEN
SUBJECT REPRESENTS MAJOR EMPHASIS OF WORK BEING CLASSIFIED

Orangutan see Pongo pygmaeus
Orbit   WW 202
Orbital Diseases   WW 202
Orbital Neoplasms   WW 202
Orchidectomy see Orchiectomy
Orchiectomy   WJ 868
Orchitis   WJ 830
Orciprenaline   QV 129
Orderlies see Personnel, Hospital
Ordiflazine see Lidoflazine
Orf see Ecthyma, Contagious
Organ Banks see Tissue Banks
Organ Donors see Tissue Donors
Organ Failure, Multiple see Multiple Organ Failure
Organ of Corti   WV 250
Organ Preservation   WO 665
    Of specific organs, with the organ
Organ regeneration see Regeneration
Organ Specificity   QW 700
    Special topics, by subject
Organ Temperature see Body Temperature
Organ Transplantation   WO 660-690
Organ Transplants see Organ Transplantation
Organelles   QH 591
Organic Brain Syndrome, Nonpsychotic see Organic
    Mental Disorders
Organic Brain Syndrome, Psychotic see Organic
    Mental Disorders, Psychotic
Organic Hallucinosis see Organic Mental Disorders,
    Psychotic
Organic Mental Disorders   WM 140
Organic Mental Disorders, Psychotic   WM 220
Organic Poisons see Poisons
Organic Psychoses see Psychoses, Organic
Organization and Administration
    Hospital see Hospital Administration   WX
        150-190
    Hospital Personnel see Personnel Administration,
        Hospital   WX 159-159.5
    Library see Library Administration   Z
        678-678.88
    Medicine   W 88
    Neurology   WL 30
    Nursing   WY 105
    Nursing schools   WY 20
    Pharmacy see Pharmacy Administration   QV
        737
    Psychiatry   WM 30
    Public health see Public Health Administration
        WA 525-590
Organization and Administration, Hospital see
    Hospital Administration
Organizational Change see Organizational
    Innovation
Organizational Decision Making see Decision
    Making, Organizational
Organizational Innovation
    Hospital Administration   WX 150-190
    Nursing Service   WY 105
    Public Health Administration   WA 525-590
    Specific types of organization, by organization
Organizations   HM 131
    See also names of specific types of organizations,

e.g. Voluntary Health Agencies   WA 1, etc.;
    names of specialties
Organizations, Nonprofit   WA 1, ETC.
    (Form number 1 in any NLM schedule where
    applicable)
    Non-medical   HD 2769.15-2769.2
Organochlorine Insecticides see Insecticides,
    Organochlorine
Organoids   QH 581-581.2
Organometallic Compounds
    Biochemistry   QU 131
    Organic chemistry   QD 410-412.5
    Pharmacology   QV 290
Organophosphorus Compounds
    Biochemistry   QU 131
    Organic chemistry   QD 305.P6; QD 406
    Toxicology   QV 627
    See also Insecticides, Organophosphate   WA
        240, etc.
Organoplatinum Compounds
    Biochemistry   QU 131
    Pharmacology   QV 290
Organotherapy   WB 391
Organothiophosphorus Compounds
    Biochemistry   QU 131
    Organic chemistry   QD 412.P1
    Toxicology   QV 627
    See also Insecticides, Organothiophosphate
        WA 240, etc.
Orgasm   HQ 19-25
Oriental Medicine, Traditional see Medicine,
    Oriental Traditional
Orientation
    Animal   QL 782.5
    Aviation   WD 730
    Bird navigation and migration   QL 698.8-698.9
    Outer space   WD 754
    Psychophysiology   WL 103
    Reflex   WL 106
    Spatial   WV 255
    Visual see Adaptation, Ocular   WW 109
    See also Adaption, Psychological   WD 730, etc.
Orientation Programs, Employee see Inservice
    Training
Origin of Life see Biogenesis
Ormond's Disease see Retroperitoneal Fibrosis
Ornithine   QU 60
Ornithine Carboxy-lyase see Ornithine
    Decarboxylase
Ornithine Decarboxylase   QU 139
Ornithosis   WC 660
Orosomucoid   WH 400
    Clinical examination   QY 455
Orotic Acid
    In nucleic acid biosynthesis and metabolism   QU
        58
    Organic chemistry   QD 401
Oroya Fever see Bartonella Infections
Orphan Drug Production   QV 736
ortho-Dihydroxybenzenes see Catechols
Orthodontia see Orthodontics
Orthodontic Appliances   WU 426
Orthodontic Appliances, Activator see Activator

Appliances
Orthodontic Wires   WU 426
Orthodontics   WU 400–440
   See also Dental Occlusion   WU 440;
    Malocclusion   WU 440
Orthodontics, Corrective   WU 400–440
Orthodontics, Preventive   WU 400
Orthomolecular Therapy   WB 330
   In psychiatry   WM 402
Orthomyxoviridae   QW 168.5.O7
Orthomyxoviridae Infections   WC 512
Orthomyxovirus Infections see Orthomyxoviridae
   Infections
Orthomyxovirus Type A, Avian   QW 168.5.O7
Orthomyxovirus Type A, Porcine   QW 168.5.O7
Orthopantomography see Radiography, Panoramic
Orthopedic Equipment   WE 26
   See also Prosthesis   WE 172, etc.; Specific types
    of equipment, e.g., Bone Plates   WE 185
Orthopedic Fixation Devices   WE 185
Orthopedic Nursing   WY 157.6
Orthopedic Surgery see Orthopedics
Orthopedics   WE 168–190
   Animals   SF 910.5
   General works   WE 168
   In infancy & childhood   WS 270
   Nursing   WY 157.6
   Reconstructive orthopedics   WE 190
   See also names of particular bones, joints, or
    procedures
Orthopsychiatry
   In adolescence   WS 463
   In infancy & childhood   WS 350.6
   Social Behavior Disorders   WM 600
    In infancy & childhood   WS 350.8.S6
Orthoptera   QX 570
Orthoptics   WW 405
Orthoses see Orthotic Devices
Orthotic Devices   WE 26
Ortonal see Methaqualone
Oryza see Rice
Oscillators, Endogenous see Biological Clocks
Oscillometry
   Biophysics   QT 34
   Circulation studies   WG 106
Osgood–Schlatter Disease see Osteochondritis
OSHA see Legislation   WA 32–33 under Accidents,
   Occupational, Occupational Medicine, or
   Occupational Diseases
Osler–Rendu Disease see Telangiectasia, Hereditary
   Hemorrhagic
Osler–Vaquez Disease see Polycythemia Vera
Osler's Disease see Polycythemia Vera;
   Telangiectasia, Hereditary Hemorrhagic
Osmium
   Inorganic chemistry   QD 181.O7
   Pharmacology   QV 290
Osmolality see Osmolar Concentration
Osmolar Concentration   QD 541
   Pharmaceutical chemistry   QV 744
Osmolarity see Osmolar Concentration
Osmoregulation see Water–Electrolyte Balance

Osmosis
   Biochemical phenomena   QU 34
   Cytology   QH 615
   Inorganic chemistry   QD 543
   Plant physiology   QK 871
Osmotic Diuretics see Diuretics, Osmotic
Osmotic Pressure   QD 543
Osseointegration   WE 200
Ossification, Heterotopic   QZ 180
Ossification, Pathologic see Ossification, Heterotopic
Ossification, Physiologic see Osteogenesis
Osteitis   WE 251
Osteitis Deformans   WE 250
Osteitis Fibrosa Cystica   WK 300
Osteitis Fibrosa Disseminata see Fibrous Dysplasia
   of Bone
Osteoarthritis   WE 348
   Localized, by site
   Veterinary   SF 901
Osteoarthritis, Hip   WE 860
Osteoarthrosis see Osteoarthritis
Osteoarthrosis Deformans see Osteoarthritis
Osteoblastoma   WE 258
   Localized, by site
Osteochondritis   WE 259
   Localized, by site
Osteochondrodysplasias   WE 250
Osteochondromas, Multiple see Exostoses, Multiple
   Hereditary
Osteochondromatosis   WE 250
Osteochondrosis see Osteochondritis
Osteoclastic Bone Loss see Bone Resorption
Osteocytes   WE 200
Osteogenesis   WE 200
Osteogenesis Imperfecta   WE 250
Osteology see Bone and Bones
Osteolysis   WE 200
Osteoma   QZ 340
   Localized, by site
Osteoma, Giant Osteoid see Osteoblastoma
Osteoma, Osteoid   WE 258
   Localized, by site
Osteomalacia   WD 145
Osteomyelitis   WE 251
Osteopathic Manipulation see Manipulation,
   Orthopedic
Osteopathic Medicine   WB 940
Osteopathy see Osteopathic Medicine
Osteopenia see Bone Diseases, Metabolic
Osteopetrosis   WE 250
Osteophytosis, Spinal see Spinal Osteophytosis
Osteoporosis   WE 250
Osteoporosis, Age–Related see Osteoporosis
Osteoporosis, Post–Traumatic see Sudeck's Atrophy
Osteoporosis, Postmenopausal   WE 250
Osteoporosis, Senile see Osteoporosis
Osteoradionecrosis   WE 250
Osteosarcoma   WE 258
   Localized, by site
Osteosclerosis   WE 250
Osteosclerosis Fragilis see Osteopetrosis
Osteosclerotic Anemia see Anemia, Myelophthisic
Osteosynthesis, Fracture see Fracture Fixation,
   Internal

Osteosynthesis, Fracture, Intramedullary see
    Fracture Fixation, Intramedullary
Osteotomy   WE 168
Ostomy
    General works   WI 900
    See also specific kind of ostomy, e.g.,
      Enterostomy, Gastrostomy, etc.
Otalgia see Ear Diseases
OTC Drugs see Drugs, Non-Prescription
Otitic Barotrauma see Otitis Media
Otitis   WV 200
Otitis Externa   WV 220
Otitis Interna see Labyrinthitis
Otitis Media   WV 232
Otitis Media, Purulent see Otitis Media, Suppurative
Otitis Media, Secretory see Otitis Media with
    Effusion
Otitis Media, Serous see Otitis Media
Otitis Media, Suppurative   WV 232
Otitis Media with Effusion   WV 232
Otolaryngologists see Biography   WZ 112.5.O8,
    etc., and Directories   WV 22 under
    Otolaryngology
Otolaryngology   WV
    Biography
      Collective   WZ 112.5.O8
      Individual   WZ 100
    Directories   WV 22
    In infancy & childhood   WV
Otology see Otolaryngology
Otorhinolaryngologic Diseases   WV 140
    Disability evaluation   WV 32
    In various age groups   WV 140
    Intracranial complications   WV 180
    Nursing   WY 158.5
    Surgery   WV 168
Otorhinolaryngologic Neoplasms   WV 190
Otorhinolaryngology see Otolaryngology
Otosclerosis   WV 265
Otospongiosis see Otosclerosis
Outbreaks see Disease Outbreaks
Outcome and Process Assessment (Health Care)
    W 84
    Of particular treatments, by subject, e.g.,
      Psychotherapy   WM 420
Outdoor Games see Recreation; Sports
Outer Membrane Proteins, Bacterial see Bacterial
    Outer Membrane Proteins
Outlines
    (Form number 18.2 in any NLM schedule where
    applicable)
Outpatient Care see Ambulatory Care
Outpatient Clinics see Ambulatory Care Facilities
Outpatient Clinics, Hospital   WX 205
    Specialty hospitals (Form numbers 27-28 in any
    NLM schedule where applicable)
Outpatient Health Services see Ambulatory Care
Outpatient Surgery see Ambulatory Surgery
Outpatients   WX 205
    Patient with a particular disease, with the disease
    See also Ambulatory Care
Ovarian Cycle see Menstrual Cycle

Ovarian Cysts   WP 322
Ovarian Diseases   WP 320-322
Ovarian Function Tests   WP 520
Ovarian Neoplasms   WP 322
Ovary   WP 320-322
    Endocrine function   WP 520-530
      General works   WP 520
      See also Corpus Lateum   WP 320, etc.;
      Graafian Follicle   WP 320; names of
      hormones produced
    Ovarian function   WP 540
    Pregnancy in see Pregnancy, Ectopic   WQ 220
Over-the-Counter Drugs see Drugs,
    Non-Prescription
Overdenture see Denture, Overlay
Overdose
    Adverse effects   QZ 42
    Drug action   QV 38
    Medication errors   QZ 42
    Particular drug, with the drug
Overeating see Hyperphagia
Overpopulation see Population Density
Overutilization of Health Services see Health
    Services Misuse
Oviducts
    Domestic animals   SF 871
    Human see Fallopian Tubes   WP 300, etc.
    Wild animals   QL 881
Oviducts, Mammalian see Fallopian Tubes
Ovine Catarrhal Fever Virus see Bluetongue Virus
Ovocytes see Oocytes
Ovulation   WP 540
    Animal   SF 871
    See also Contraception   WP 630, etc.
Ovulation Induction   WP 540
Ovum
    Animal   QL 965
    Development   WQ 205
Ovum Implantation   QS 645
Ovum Implantation, Delayed   WQ 205
Ovum Proteins see Egg Proteins
Ovum-Sperm Interactions see Sperm-Ovum
    Interactions
Oxalates
    As disinfectants   QV 220
    Biochemistry   QU 98
    Toxicology   QV 632
Oxandrolone   WJ 875
Oxazoles   QV 95
Oxidants, Photochemical   WA 754
Oxidases see Oxidoreductases
Oxidation see Metabolism
Oxidation-Reduction
    Organic chemistry   QD 281.O9
    Metabolism   QU 125
Oxidative Phosphorylation   QU 125
Oxides   QV 312
Oxidizing Antiseptics see Anti-Infective Agents,
    Local; Hydrogen Peroxide; Potassium
    Permanganate
Oxidoreductases   QU 140
Oximes   QV 124
Oximetry   QY 480

Oximetry, Transcutaneous see Blood Gas
   Monitoring, Transcutaneous
Oxine see Oxyquinoline
Oxoglutarates see Ketoglutaric Acids
Oxophenarsine   QV 254
Oxopropanal see Pyruvaldehyde
Oxoquinolines see Quinolones
Oxycephaly see Craniosynostoses
Oxychlorochin see Hydroxychloroquine
Oxychloroquine see Hydroxychloroquine
Oxygen   QV 312
   Deficiency see Anoxia   WD 715, etc.
Oxygen Consumption   WF 110
Oxygen Deficiency see Anoxia
Oxygen Inhalation Therapy   WF 145
Oxygen Partial Pressure Determination,
   Transcutaneous see Blood Gas Monitoring,
   Transcutaneous
Oxygenases   QU 140
Oxygenation, Hyperbaric see Hyperbaric
   Oxygenation
Oxygenators   WO 162
   Used for special purposes, by subject, e.g., during
      open heart surgery   WG 168
Oxygenators, Membrane   WO 162
   Used for special purposes, by subject, e.g., during
      postoperative care   WO 184, etc.
Oxyneurine see Betaine
Oxyntic Cells see Parietal Cells, Gastric
Oxyphenbutazone   QV 95
Oxyproline see Hydroxyproline
Oxyquinol see Oxyquinoline
Oxyquinoline
   As an anti-infective agent   QV 250
Oxytetracycline   QV 360
Oxytocics   QV 173-174
Oxytocin   QV 173
Oxyuriasis   WC 860
Oxyuroidea   QX 271
Oysters   QX 675
Ozena see Rhinitis, Atrophic
Ozone   QV 312

P

p-Aminohippuric Acid   QU 62
P-B Antibodies see Antibodies, Heterophile
P-Cell Stimulating Factor see Interleukin-3
p-Dihydroxybenzenes see Hydroquinones
p-Dimethylaminoazobenzene   QZ 202
P. P. Factor see Nicotinic Acids
Pacemaker, Artificial   WG 26
   See also Cardiac Pacing, Artificial   WG 168
Pacemakers, Biological see Biological Clocks
Pachymeninges see Dura Mater
Pacifiers see Infant Care
Pacing, Cardiac, Artificial see Cardiac Pacing,
   Artificial
Package Inserts see Product Labeling
Package Inserts, Drug see Drug Labeling
Packaging, Drug see Drug Packaging
Packaging of Drugs see Drug Packaging; Drug
   Labeling

Packed Red-Cell Volume see Hematocrit
PACS (Radiology) see Radiology Information
   Systems
Padutin see Kallikrein
PAF-Acether see Platelet Activating Factor
Paget's Disease of Bone see Osteitis Deformans
PAH see p-Aminohippuric Acid
PAI-3 see Protein C Inhibitor
Pain   WL 704
   Symptomatology   WB 176
   Localized, by site
   See also Abdominal Pain   WI 147
Pain Assessment see Pain Measurement
Pain, Facial see Facial Pain
Pain, Intractable   WL 704
Pain Measurement   WL 704
   In specific diseases, with the disease
Pain, Postoperative   WO 184
Pain Receptors see Nociceptors
Paint
   Chemical technology   TP 934-944
   Occupational health hazards, etc.   WA 400-495
   Lead poisoning   QV 292
Paintings
   Related to medicine   WZ 330
   Related to psychiatry   WM 49
Paired-Associate Learning   LB 1064
Palatal Neoplasms   WU 280
   For the otolaryngologist   WV 410
Palatal Obturators   WV 440
Palate   WV 410
   Cleft see Cleft Palate   WV 440
   Dentistry   WU 140
   Gastroenterology   WI 200
   Neoplasms see Palatal Neoplasms   WU 280, etc.
Palatine Tonsil see Tonsil
Palatopharyngeal Incompetence see Velopharyngeal
   Insufficiency
Paleodontology   GN 209
Paleography   Z 105-115.5
Paleontology
   Animal and plant   QE 701-996.5
   Human   GN 282-286.7
Paleopathology   QZ 11.5
   In veterinary medicine   SF 758
Paleostriatum see Globus Pallidus
Palladium
   Dental chemistry and metallurgy   WU 180
   Inorganic chemistry   QD 181.P4
   Pharmacology   QV 290
Palliative Treatment   WB 310
Palm of Hand see Hand
Palmitic Acids   QU 90
   Organic chemistry   QD 305.A2
Palmoplantar Keratoderma see Keratoderma,
   Palmoplantar
Palmoplantaris Pustulosis see Psoriasis
Palpation   WB 275
Palsy see Cerebral Palsy; Facial Paralysis; Paralysis
Palsy, Progressive Supranuclear see Supranuclear
   Palsy, Progressive
Paludism see Malaria

Pamphlets
    Collections   W6 P3
    Works about   Z 691
    Others, by subject
Pan see Chimpansee troglodytes
Panax see Ginseng
Pancoast's Syndrome   WF 658
Pancreas   WI 800–830
    Surgery (General)   WI 830
    See also Cystic Fibrosis   WI 820; Islets of
       Langerhans   WK 800–885
Pancreas, Artificial Endocrine see Insulin Infusion
   Systems
Pancreas, Endocrine see Islets of Langerhans
Pancreas Transplantation   WI 830
Pancreatectomy   WI 830
Pancreatic Alpha Cells see Islets of Langerhans
Pancreatic Beta Cells see Islets of Langerhans
Pancreatic Cyst   WI 810
Pancreatic Cystic Fibrosis see Cystic Fibrosis
Pancreatic Delta Cells see Islets of Langerhans
Pancreatic Diseases   WI 800–830
    General works   WI 800
Pancreatic Ducts   WI 802
Pancreatic Extracts
    Pharmacology   QV 370
    Therapeutic use (General)   WB 391
    Used for treatment of particular disorders, with
       the disorder or system
Pancreatic Fistula   WI 800
Pancreatic Function Tests   WI 802
Pancreatic Hormones   WK 801
    See also Glucagon   WK 801; Insulin   WK 820
Pancreatic Islets Transplantation see Islets of
   Langerhans Transplantation
Pancreatic Juice   WI 802
Pancreatic Neoplasms   WI 810
Pancreatitis   WI 805
Pancreozymin see Cholecystokinin
Pancreozymin Receptors see Receptors,
   Cholecystokinin
Panic   WM 172
Panic Attacks see Panic Disorder
Panic Disorder   WM 172
Panniculitis, Nodular Nonsuppurative   WR 140
Panophthalmitis   WW 140
Panoramic Radiography see Radiography,
   Panoramic
Panotitis see Otitis
Pantomography see Radiography, Panoramic
Pantothenic Acid   QU 195
Papain   QU 136
Papanicolaou Smear see Vaginal Smears
Papaver   QV 90
    As a medicinal plant   QV 766
    See also Opium   QV 90, etc.
Papaveretum see Opium
Paper
    Industrial waste   WA 778
    Printing   Z 237, Z 247
Papillary Muscles   WG 201–202
Papilledema   WW 280
Papilloma   QZ 365

    Localized, by site
Papilloma, Shope see Tumor Virus Infections
Papillomavirus   QW 165.5.P2
Papillomavirus, Human   QW 165.5.P2
Papio   QL 737.P93
    As laboratory animals   QY 60.P7
    Diseases   SF 997.5.P7
Papovaviridae   QW 165.5.P2
PAPP–D see Placental Lactogen
Pappataci Fever see Phlebotomus Fever
Papulosquamous Dermatoses see Skin Diseases
para–Aminohippuric Acid see p-Aminohippuric
   Acid
para–Dihydroxybenzenes see Hydroquinones
Parabiosis
    Immunology   QW 504
    Twins, Conjoined   QS 675
    Other special topics, by subject
Paracentesis see Punctures
Parachuting   WD 700
    Accidents   WD 740
Paracoccidioidomycosis   WC 460
Paracusis see Auditory Perception
Paradentium see Periodontium
Paradoxical Sleep see Sleep, REM
Paraffin   QV 800
    Plastic surgery   WO 640
Paraganglia, Chromaffin
    In sympathetic ganglia   WL 610
    In other organs, with the organ
Paraganglia, Nonchromaffin   WL 600
Paraganglioma   QZ 380
    Localized, by site
Paraganglioma, Extra–Adrenal   QZ 380
    Localized, by site
Paraganglioma, Nonchromaffin see Paraganglioma,
   Extra–Adrenal
Paragonimiasis   WC 805
Paragonimus   QX 353
Paraimmunoglobulinemias see Paraproteinemias
Parainfluenza   WC 518
Parainfluenza Virus Type 1   QW 168.5.P2
Parainfluenza Virus Type 4 see Parainfluenza Viruses
Parainfluenza Viruses   QW 168.5.P2
Parakeratosis Variegata see Parapsoriasis
Paralysants see Chemical Warfare Agents
Paralysins see Agglutinins
Paralysis   WL 346
    Agitans see Parkinsonism   WL 359
    Cervical sympathetic   WL 610
    Divers'   WD 712
    Facial see Facial paralysis   WL 330
    General see Paresis   WC 165, etc.
    Infantile see Poliomyelitis   WC 555, etc.
    Ocular muscles see Oculomotor paralysis   WW
    410
    Respiratory see Respiratory Paralysis   WF 140
    Vocal cord see Vocal Cord Paralysis   WV 535
    See also Hemiplegia   WL 346; Paraplegia
       WL 346; Quadriplegia   WL 346
Paralysis Agitans see Parkinson Disease
Paralysis, Bulbar   WL 310
Paralysis, Familial Periodic   WD 205.5.P2

Paralysis, General see Paresis
Paralysis, Obstetric   WS 405
Paralysis, Pseudobulbar see Paralysis
Paralysis, Spastic see Muscle Spasticity
Paramagnetic Resonance see Electron Spin
    Resonance Spectroscopy
Paramecium   QX 151
Paramedical Personnel see Allied Health Personnel
Paramedics see Allied Health Personnel
Paramedics, Emergency see Emergency Medical
    Technicians
Parametritis   WP 275
Paramyoclonus Multiplex   WE 550
Paramyxoviridae   QW 168.5.P2
Paramyxovirus Infections   WC 518-520
    Veterinary   SF 809.P37
    See also Measles   WC 580
Paranasal Sinuses   WV 340-358
    See also Ethmoid Sinus   WV 355; Frontal Sinus
        WV 350; Maxillary Sinus   WV 345;
        Sphenoid Sinus   WV 358
Paranoia see Paranoid Disorders
Paranoid Behavior   WM 205
Paranoid Disorder, Shared see Shared Paranoid
    Disorder
Paranoid Disorders   WM 205
Paranoid Psychoses see Paranoid Disorders
Paranoid Schizophrenia see Schizophrenia, Paranoid
Paraphilias   WM 610
Paraphimosis   WJ 790
Paraphrenia, Involutional see Depression,
    Involutional
Paraplegia   WL 346
Paraplegia, Spastic see Paraplegia
Paraproteinemias   WH 400
    See also Amyloidosis   WD 205.5.A6; Multiple
        Myeloma   WH 540
Paraproteins   QW 601
    See also Bence Jones Protein   WH 540;
        Myeloma Proteins   WH 540
Parapsoriasis   WR 204
Parapsoriasis en Plaques see Parapsoriasis
Parapsychology   BF 1009-1389
    Occult sciences   BF 1405-1999
Paraquat
    Public health aspects   WA 240
Parasite-Host Relations see Host-Parasite Relations
Parasites   QX
    Animal parasites
        As a cause of disease   QZ 85
        Zoology   QL 757
    Communicable disease control   WA 240
Parasitic Diseases   WC 695-900
    Veterinary   SF 810.A3
Parasitic Eye Infections see Eye Infections, Parasitic
Parasitic Skin Diseases see Skin Diseases, Parasitic
Parasitology   QX
    Nursing texts   QX 4
    Veterinary Medicine   SF 810.A3
Parasympathetic-Blocking Agents see
    Parasympatholytics
Parasympathetic Ganglia see Ganglia,
    Parasympathetic

Parasympathetic Nervous System   WL 610
    Children   WS 340
Parasympatholytics   QV 132
Parasympathomimetics   QV 122
Parathion
    Agriculture   SB 952.P3
    Public health   WA 240
Parathyroid Diseases   WK 300
Parathyroid Glands   WK 300
Parathyroid Hormones   WK 300
Parathyroid Neoplasms   WK 300
Paratopes see Binding Sites, Antibody
Paratuberculosis   SF 809.J6
Paratyphoid Fever   WC 266
    Veterinary   SF 809.S24
Paratyphoid Vaccine see Typhoid-Paratyphoid
    Vaccines
Paravertebral Anesthesia see Anesthesia,
    Conduction; Nerve Block
Parent-Child Relations   WS 105.5.F2
Parent, Single see Single Parent
Parental Leave
    General works   HD 6065-6065.5
Parenteral Feeding see Parenteral Nutrition
Parenteral Hyperalimentation see Parenteral
    Nutrition, Total
Parenteral Infusions see Infusions, Parenteral
Parenteral Nutrition   WB 410
Parenteral Nutrition, Total   WB 410
Parenterally-Transmitted Non-A, Non-B Hepatitis
    see Hepatitis C
Parents   HQ 755.7-759.92
    And illegitimacy   HQ 998-999
    Special topics, by subject
Paresis   WC 165
    Veterinary (Milk fever) see Parturient Paresis
        SF 967.M5
Paresthesia   WR 280
Parietal Cells, Gastric
    Cytology   WI 301
    Physiology   WI 302
Parietal Lobe   WL 307
Parkinson Disease   WL 359
    Drugs for see Antiparkinson agents   QV 80
Parodontitis see Periodontitis
Parodontosis see Periodontal Diseases
Paronychia   WR 475
Parotid Gland   WI 230
Parotid Neoplasms   WI 230
Parotitis   WI 230
    See also Mumps   WC 520
Parovarian Cyst   WP 275
Paroxysmal Dyspnea see Dyspnea, Paroxysmal
Paroxysmal Tachycardia see Tachycardia,
    Paroxysmal
Parrot Fever see Ornithosis
Parrots   QL 696.P7
    Diseases   SF 994.2.P37
    As laboratory animals   QY 60.B4
Parsonage-Turner Syndrome see Cervico-Brachial
    Neuralgia
Parthenogenesis   QH 487
Partial Denture see Denture, Partial

**ALWAYS CONSULT MAIN SCHEDULES. USE NUMBER ASSIGNED ONLY WHEN
SUBJECT REPRESENTS MAJOR EMPHASIS OF WORK BEING CLASSIFIED**

Partial Monosomy see Chromosome Deletion
Particle Accelerators   QC 787.P3
   In neoplasm radiotherapy   QZ 269
   Nuclear engineering   TK 9340
Particle-Induced X-Ray Emission Spectrometry see
  Spectrometry, X-Ray Emission
Particle Size
   Air pollutants   WA 754, etc.
   Determination   TA 418.8, etc.
   Dosage form   QV 785
   Particle technology (Chemical engineering)   TP
   156.P3
Partner Notification see Contact Tracing
Partnership Practice   W 92
Partnership Practice, Dental   WU 79
Parturient Paresis   SF 967.M5
Parturition see Labor
Parvoviridae   QW 165.5.P3
Parvoviridae Infections   WC 500
Parvovirus   QW 165.5.P3
Parvovirus Infections see Parvoviridae Infections
Passive Addiction, Neonatal see Neonatal
  Abstinence Syndrome
Passive-Aggressive Personality Disorder   WM 190
Passive Antibody Transfer see Immunization, Passive
Passive-Dependent Personality see Dependent
  Personality Disorder
Passive Immunity see Immunity, Passive
Passive Transfer of Immunity see Immunization,
  Passive
Pastes see Ointments
Pasteurella   QW 140
Pasteurella Infections   WC 200
   Veterinary   SF 809.P37
Pasteurellosis see Pasteurella Infections
Pastoral Care   WM 61
   See also Religion and Medicine   W 50, etc.;
     Religion and Psychology   WM 61, etc.;
     Chaplaincy Service, Hospital   WX 187
Pastoral Psychiatry see Pastoral Care
Pastoral Psychology see Pastoral Care
Patas Monkey see Erythrocebus patas
Patch Tests   QY 260
Patella   WE 870
Patent Medicines see Drugs, Non-prescription
Patents   T 201-342
   Chemicals   TP 210
   Drugs   QV 736
   Medical instruments (Form number 26 in any
   NLM schedule where applicable)
Paternal Behavior   WS 105.5.F2
Paternal Deprivation   WS 105.5.D3
Paternity
   Medicolegal aspects   W 791
   See also headings beginning with Father and
   Paternal
Paternity Leave see Parental Leave
Pathogenesis of Disease see Disease
Pathogenic Fungi see Fungi
Pathogens, Blood-Borne see Blood-Borne
  Pathogens
Pathological Waste see Medical Waste
Pathologists see Biography   WZ 112.5.P2, etc., and

Directories   QZ 22 under Pathology
Pathology   QZ
  Biography
    Collective   WZ 112.5.P2
    Individual   WZ 100
  Cardiovascular system   WG 142
  Clinical   QY
  Comparative   QZ 33
  Dental see Pathology, Oral   WU 140 and
    subheading Pathology   WU 140 under Tooth
  Dermatology   WR 105
  Directories   QZ 22
  In infancy & childhood   WS 200
  Nursing texts   QZ 4, etc.
    Clinical pathology   QY 4, etc.
  Physiological   QZ 140
  See also the general works numbers for parts of
   the body, diseases, or systems
Pathology, Clinical   QY
Pathology, Oral   WU 140
  See also Pathology under Mouth   WU 140 and
   Tooth   WU 140
Pathology, Surgical   WO 142
Pathology, Veterinary   SF 769
Pathomimesis see Malingering
Patient Acceptance of Health Care   W 85
  In the hospital   WX 158.5
  Special areas of health care, by area
Patient Admission   WX 158
Patient Advocacy   W 85
  Special topics, by subject
Patient Appointments see Appointments and
  Schedules
Patient Care Planning   W 84.7
  In nursing   WY 100
  Of hospital patients   WX 162-162.5
Patient Care Team   W 84.8
  Hospital team   WX 162.5
  See also Nursing, Team   WY 125
Patient Compliance   W 85
  In hospitals   WX 158.5
  In mental hospitals   WM 29.5
  Special areas of compliance, by subject
Patient Cooperation see Patient Compliance
Patient Credit and Collection
  Dental administration   WU 77
  Hospital administration   WX 157
  Medical administration   W 80
  Nursing administration   WY 77
  Pharmacy administration   QV 736
  In other specific fields, by subject
Patient Data Privacy see Confidentiality
Patient Discharge   WX 158
Patient Education
  General   W 85
    See also Health Education   WA 590, etc.
  In hospitals   WX 158.5
  In mental institutions   WM 29.5
  For specific conditions, with the condition
Patient-Family Lodging see Housing
Patient Isolation   WX 167
Patient Isolators   WX 147
Patient Monitoring see Monitoring, Physiologic

Patient Ombudsmen see Patient Advocacy
Patient Participation   WX 158.5
Patient Readmission   WX 158
Patient Representatives see Patient Advocacy
Patient Schedules see Appointments and Schedules
Patients   W 85
   In hospitals   WX 158.5
   In mental institutions   WM 29.5
   With specific disabilities, with the disability
Patients' Libraries see Libraries, Hospital
Patients' Rights see Patient Advocacy
Pattern Recognition
   Computer engineering   TK 7882.P3
   (Form number 26.5 in any NLM schedule where
     applicable)
Pattern Recognition, Visual   WW 105
Paul-Bunnell Antibodies see Antibodies, Heterophile
Pavor Nocturnus see Sleep Disorders
PCBs see Polychlorinated Biphenyls
PCP see Phencyclidine
PCP Abuse see Phencyclidine Abuse
PCR see Polymerase Chain Reaction
Peak Expiratory Flow Rate   WF 102
   As a diagnostic test   WF 141
   General physical examination   WB 284
Peanuts
   Diets for control of fats   WB 425
   Diets for control of protein   WB 426
Peas
   As dietary supplement in health and disease
     WB 430
   Cultivation   SB 343
Peat   S 592.85
   Soils   S 592.85
   See also Mud Therapy   WB 525; Soil
     Microbiology   QW 60
Peat Therapy see Mud Therapy
Pecten Oculi see Retinal Vessels
Pectins   QV 71
Pectoral Nerves see Thoracic Nerves
Pectoralis Muscles   WE 715
Pectus Excavatum see Funnel Chest
Pederasty see Paraphilias
Pediatric Dentistry   WU 480
   See also special topics, e.g., Children   WU 113.6
     under Oral hygiene
Pediatric Nursing   WY 159
   Education   WY 18-18.5
Pediatric Ophthalmology see In infancy & childhood
   WW 600 under Ophthalmology
Pediatric Psychology see Child Psychology
Pediatricians, Directories see Directories   WS 22
   under Pediatrics
Pediatrics   WS
   Anesthesia   WO 440
   Dentistry see Pediatric Dentistry   WU 480
   Directories   WS 22
   Nursing see Pediatric Nursing   WY 159
   Ophthalmology   WW 600
   Otolaryngology   WV
   Radiology   WN 240
   Surgery   WO 925
Pediculosis   WR 375

Pediculus   QX 502
Pedodontics see Pediatric Dentistry
Pedophilia   WM 610
PEEP see Positive-Pressure Respiration
Peer Group
   In adolescence   WS 462
   In infancy & childhood   WS 105.5.I5
   See also names of particular groups, e.g.
     Physicians   W 21; persons with diabetes under
     Diabetes mellitus   WK 810
Peer Review
   (Form number 21 in any NLM schedule where
     applicable, except Nursing   WY 16)
Peer Review Organizations see Professional Review
   Organizations
Pelizaeus-Merzbacher Disease see Cerebral
   Sclerosis, Diffuse
Pellagra   WD 126
Pelvic Bones   WE 750
Pelvic Exenteration   WE 750
Pelvic Infection see Adnexitis
Pelvic Inflammations see Adnexitis
Pelvic Inflammatory Disease see Adnexitis
Pelvic Neoplasms   WE 750
Pelvimetry   WQ 320
Pelvis
   Obstetrics   WQ 320
Pemphigus   WR 200
   Neonatorum see Impetigo   WR 225
Pemphigus Vulgaris see Pemphigus
Penicillamine   QV 354
Penicillanic Acid   QV 354
Penicillin, Aminobenzyl see Ampicillin
Penicillin G   QV 354
Penicillin G, Benzathine   QV 354
Penicillin Resistance
   Bacteriology   QW 51
   Drug therapy   WB 330
   Pharmacology   QV 354
Penicillinase   QU 136
Penicillins   QV 354
Penicillium   QW 180.5.D38
Penile Erection   WJ 790
Penile Neoplasms   WJ 790
Penis   WJ 790
Pensions   HD 7105-7105.45
   For particular groups of people, by group, e.g.,
     for occupational health nurses   WY 141; for
     nurses in general   WY 77
Pentachlorophenol
   As an anti-infective agent   QV 223
Pentamethylenetetrazole see Pentylenetetrazole
Pentanoates see Valerates
Pentazocine   QV 89
Pentetrazole see Pentylenetetrazole
Penthiobarbital see Thiopental
Pentobarbital   QV 88
Pentose Phosphate Shunt see Pentosephosphate
   Pathway
Pentose Shunt see Pentosephosphate Pathway
Pentosephosphate Pathway   QU 75
Pentoses   QU 75
Pentothal see Thiopental

Pentoxifylline   QV 107
Pentylenetetrazole   QV 103
   In shock therapy   WM 410
Pepsin see Pepsin A
Pepsin A
   Enzymology   QU 136
   Gastric physiology   WI 302
Pepsinogen
   Enzymology   QU 142
   Gastric physiology   WI 302
Peptic Ulcer   WI 350–370
Peptic Ulcer Hemorrhage   WI 350
Peptic Ulcer Perforation   WI 350
Peptidase Inhibitors see Protease Inhibitors
Peptide Hormones see Hormones
Peptide Hydrolase Inhibitors see Protease Inhibitors
Peptide Hydrolases   QU 136
Peptide Peptidohydrolase Inhibitors see Protease
   Inhibitors
Peptides   QU 68
   Peptide hormones   WK 185
   See also Oxytocin   QV 173
Peptococcus   QW 142.5.C6
Perception
   Auditory see Auditory Perception   WV 272
   Color see Color Perception   WW 150
   Depth see Depth Perception   WW 105
   Distance see Distance Perception   WW 105
   Form see Form Perception   WW 105
   In infancy & childhood   WS 105.5.D2
   Motion see Kinesthesis   WE 104; Motion
     Perception   WW 105
   Neurophysiology   WL 705
   Psychology   BF 311, etc.
   Self see Self Concept   BF 697, etc.
   Size see Size Perception   WW 105
   Social see Social Perception   HM 132
   Space see Space Perception   WW 105, etc.
   Speech see Speech Perception   WV 272
   Time see Time Perception   BF 468, etc.
   Visual see Visual Perception   WW 105
   Weight see Weight Perception   WE 104
Perception, Social see Social Perception
Perceptual Defense   WM 193.5.P3
   In adolescence   WS 463
   In infancy & childhood   WS 350.8.D3
Perceptual Disorders
   General and psychotic   WM 204
   Neurologic manifestation   WL 340
   Specific sensory disorder, with the organ
     involved
Perceptual Distortion   WL 705
Perceptual Motor Performance see Psychomotor
   Performance
Perchloroethylene see Tetrachloroethylene
Percussion   WB 278
Percutaneous Administration see Administration,
   Cutaneous
Percutaneous Electric Nerve Stimulation see
   Transcutaneous Electric Nerve Stimulation
Percutaneous Nephrolithotomy see Nephrostomy,
   Percutaneous
Percutaneous Nephrostomy see Nephrostomy,

Percutaneous
Percutaneous Transluminal Angioplasty see
   Angioplasty, Balloon
Percutaneous Transluminal Coronary Angioplasty
   see Angioplasty, Transluminal, Percutaneous
   Coronary
Percutaneous Ultrasonic Lithotripsy see Lithotripsy
Performance Appraisal, Employee see Employee
   Performance Appraisal
Perfume   WA 744
   Chemical technology   TP 983.A1–983.Z5
Perfusion
   Organ preservation   WO 665
   Specific organs, with the organ
Perfusion, Pulsatile see Pulsatile Flow
Perfusion Pumps see Infusion Pumps
Perfusion Pumps, Implantable see Infusion Pumps,
   Implantable
Perfusion, Regional   QZ 267
   Localized, by site
Perhexiline   QV 150
Periadenitis Mucosa Necrotica Recurrens see
   Stomatitis, Aphthous
Perianeurysmal Fibrosis, Inflammatory see
   Retroperitoneal Fibrosis
Periaortitis, Chronic see Retroperitoneal Fibrosis
Periapical Abscess   WU 230
Periapical Cyst see Radicular Cyst
Periapical Diseases   WU 230
Periapical Granuloma   WU 240
Periapical Periodontitis, Chronic Nonsuppurative see
   Periapical Granuloma
Periapical Periodontitis, Suppurative see Periapical
   Abscess
Periaqueductal Gray   WL 310
Periarteritis Nodosa see Polyarteritis Nodosa
Periarthritis   WE 344
Pericardial Cyst see Mediastinal Cyst
Pericardial Effusion   WG 275
   Clinical examination   QY 210
Pericardial Fluid see Secretion under Pericardium
Pericarditis   WG 275
Pericarditis, Constrictive   WG 275
Pericardium   WG 275
   Secretion
     Clinical examination   QY 210
     General   WG 275
     In general diagnosis   WB 373
Pericementitis see Periodontitis
Peridinium see Dinoflagellida
Perilymph   WV 250
Perilymphatic Duct see Cochlear Aqueduct
Perimenopausal Bone Loss see Osteoporosis,
   Postmenopausal
Perimetry   WW 145
Perinatal Medicine see Perinatology
Perinatal Mortality see Infant Mortality
Perinatal Nursing see Neonatal Nursing
Perinatology   WQ 210–211
   See also Neonatology   WS 420
Perineum   WE 750
   Injuries
     General   WE 750

In the female   WP 170
Periodic Acid   QV 180
    Inorganic chemistry   QD 181.I1
Periodic Disease   WB 720
Periodic Health Examination see Physical
    Examination
Periodicals   W1
    Bibliography of medical and medically related
    ZW 1
    Government administrative reports and statistics
    W2
    Hospital administrative reports and statitics   WX
    2
        See also Newspapers   W1, etc.
Periodicity
    Animal behavior   QL 753–755.5
    Animal physiology   QP 84.6
    General biology   QH 527
    Human physiology   QT 167
    Menstrual cycle   WP 540
    Plants   QK 761
Periodontal Bone Loss see Alveolar Bone Loss
Periodontal Cyst   WU 240
Periodontal Cyst, Apical see Radicular Cyst
Periodontal Diseases   WU 240–242
    Periodontoclasia   WU 242
    Periodontosis   WU 242
    Pyorrhea alveolaris   WU 242
Periodontal Index   WU 240
Periodontal Pocket   WU 242
Periodontal Prosthesis   WU 240
Periodontal Resorption see Alveolar Bone Loss
Periodontal Splints   WU 240
Periodontics   WU 240–242
Periodontitis   WU 242
Periodontitis, Apical, Chronic Nonsuppurative see
    Periapical Granuloma
Periodontitis, Apical, Suppurative see Periapical
    Abscess
Periodontium   WU 240–242
Perioperative Nursing see Operating Room Nursing
Peripheral Angiopathies see Peripheral Vascular
    Diseases
Peripheral Catheterization see Catheterization,
    Peripheral
Peripheral Nerve Diseases see Peripheral Nervous
    System Diseases
Peripheral Nerve Neoplasms   WL 500
    Localized, by site
Peripheral Nerves   WL 500–544
    See also Cranial Nerves   WL 330; Spinal Nerves
    WL 400
Peripheral Nervous System   WL 500–544
Peripheral Nervous System Diseases   WL 500–544
    In infancy & childhood   WS 340
    Localized, by site
    Veterinary   SF 895
Peripheral Resistance see Vascular Resistance
Peripheral Vascular Diseases   WG 500–700
    General works   WG 500
    In infancy & childhood   WS 290
    Veterinary   SF 811
Periphlebitis see Phlebitis

Perissodactyla   QL 737.U6
Peristalsis   WI 102
    Intestinal   WI 402
Peristaltic Pumps, Implantable see Infusion Pumps,
    Implantable
Peritoneal Cavity   WI 575
Peritoneal Dialysis   WJ 378
    As treatment for diseases other than those of the
    kidney, by site or disease
Peritoneal Dialysis, Continuous Ambulatory   WJ
    378
Peritoneal Diseases   WI 575
Peritoneal Effusion see Ascitic Fluid
Peritoneal Fluid see Ascitic Fluid
Peritoneal Infusions see Infusions, Parenteral
Peritoneal Neoplasms   WI 575
Peritoneoscopy see Laparoscopy
Peritoneovenous Shunt
    In the treatment of intractable ascites   WI 575
Peritoneum   WI 575
Peritonitis   WI 575
Peritonitis, Tuberculous see Tuberculosis, Peritoneal
Perkinism see Alternative Medicine
Permeability
    Capillary see Capillary Permeability   WG 700
    Cells see Cell Membrane Permeability   QH 601,
    etc.
    Magnetic induction   QC 754.2.P4
    Other special topics, by subject
Permeability, Capillary see Capillary Permeability
Permeability, Cell Membrane see Cell Membrane
    Permeability
Permeability, Microvascular see Capillary
    Permeability
Pernicious Anemia see Anemia, Pernicious
Pernio see Frostbite
Perodicticus potto see Lorisidae
Peroperative Care see Intraoperative Care
Peroperative Complications see Intraoperative
    Complications
Peroperative Period see Intraoperative Period
Peroxidase–Antiperoxidase Complex Technique see
    Immunoenzyme Techniques
Peroxidase–Labeled Antibody Technique see
    Immunoenzyme Techniques
Peroxidases   QU 140
Peroxide, Hydrogen see Hydrogen Peroxide
Peroxides
    Inorganic chemistry   QD 181.01
    Organic chemistry   QD 305.E7
    Pharmacology   QV 60
Peroxisomes see Microbodies
Persistent Common Atrioventricular Canal see
    Endocardial Cushion Defects
Persistent Fetal Circulation Syndrome   WS 421
Persistent Ostium Primum see Endocardial Cushion
    Defects
Persistent Pulmonary Hypertension of Newborn see
    Persistent Fetal Circulation Syndrome
Persistent Vegetative State   WB 182
Personal Expenditures see Financing, Personal
Personal Health Services   W 84
Personal Hygiene see Hygiene

ALWAYS CONSULT MAIN SCHEDULES. USE NUMBER ASSIGNED ONLY WHEN
SUBJECT REPRESENTS MAJOR EMPHASIS OF WORK BEING CLASSIFIED

Personal Liability see Liability, Legal
Personal narratives
    Physicians and specialists of medically related
    fields
      Collective   WZ 112–150
      Individual   WZ 100
    Special topics, by subject
Personal Satisfaction
    Job satisfaction   HF 5549.5.J63
    Success (General)   BJ 1611–1618
    Special topics, by subject
Personal Space
    Anthropogeography   GF 51
    Psychology   BF 469
Personality   BF 698–698.9
    Dependency   BF 575.D34
    In psychoanalysis   WM 460.5.P3
    See also Antisocial Personality Disorder   WM
      190; Dual Personality   WM 173.6; Hysterical
      Personality   WM 173; Schizoid Personality
      WM 203
Personality Assessment
    Psychiatric interview   WM 141
    Psychiatric testing   WM 145
    Psychological   BF 698.4–698.8
Personality Development   BF 698
    In adolescence   WS 462
    In infancy & childhood   WS 105.5.P3
Personality Disorder, Antisocial see Antisocial
    Personality Disorder
Personality Disorder, Borderline see Borderline
    Personality Disorder
Personality Disorder, Compulsive see Compulsive
    Personality Disorder
Personality Disorder, Dependent see Dependent
    Personality Disorder
Personality Disorder, Histrionic see Histrionic
    Personality Disorder
Personality Disorder, Passive-Aggressive see
    Passive-Aggressive Personality Disorder
Personality Disorder, Schizoid see Schizoid
    Personality Disorder
Personality Disorder, Schizotypal see Schizotypal
    Personality Disorder
Personality Disorders
    General   WM 190
    In adolescence   WS 463
    In infancy & childhood   WS 350.8.P3
Personality, Hysterical see Histrionic Personality
    Disorder
Personality Inventory
    Psychology   BF 698.5–698.8
    Psychiatry   WM 145
Personality Tests
    Psychology   BF 698.5–698.8
    Psychiatry   WM 145
Personality Type A see Type A Personality
Personnel Administration, Hospital   WX 159–159.8
    In psychiatric hospitals   WM 30
    In special hospitals, with the hospital
Personnel Discipline see Employee Discipline
Personnel, Hospital   WX 159–159.8
    See also names of specific types of personnel,

e.g., Operating Room Technicians   WY 162
Personnel, Hospital, Organization and
    Administration see Personnel Administration,
    Hospital
Personnel Management   HF 5549.A2–5549.5
    Hospitals   WX 159
    Nursing   WY 30
    Special fields, by subject, e.g., Nursing,
      Supervisory   WY 105
Personnel Recruitment see Personnel Selection
Personnel Selection   HF 5549.5.S38
    Special fields, by subject
Personnel Staffing and Scheduling
    Hospitals   WX 159
    Nursing   WY 30
    Psychiatry   WM 30
Personnel Turnover
    Hospitals   WX 159
    Nursing   WY 30
    Psychiatry   WM 30
    Specific profession, by subject
Personnel Work see Personnel Management
Perspiration see Sweat
Perspiratory Glands see Sweat Glands
Persuasion see Persuasive Communication
Persuasive Communication   BF 637.P4
Perthes Disease see Legg-Perthes Disease
Pertussigen see Pertussis Toxins
Pertussis see Whooping Cough
Pertussis Toxins   WC 340
Pertussis Vaccine   WC 340
Pervasive Child Development Disorders see Child
    Development Disorders, Pervasive
Perversion, Sex see Paraphilias
Pes Cavus see Foot Deformities
Pes Planus see Flatfoot
Pessaries, Intracervical see Intrauterine Devices
Pessaries, Intrauterine see Intrauterine Devices
Pest Control   WA 240
    Agriculture   SB 950–990.5
    See also Insect Control   QX 600
Pest Control, Biological
    Agriculture   SB 975–978
    General public health   WA 240
    See also Insect Control   QX 600; names of other
      specific types of pest control
Pesticide Residues   WA 240
Pesticides
    Agriculture   SB 951–970.4
      Industrial poisoning   WA 465
    Public health   WA 240
    Toxicology   WA 240
Pet-Human Bonding see Bonding, Human-Pet
PET Scan see Tomography, Emission-Computed
Petechiae see Purpura
Pethidine see Meperidine
Petit Mal Epilepsy see Epilepsy, Absence
Petrolatum, Liquid see Mineral Oil
Petroleum
    Chemical technology   TP 690–699
    Toxicology   QV 633
Petrous Bone   WV 230
Petrous Pyramid see Petrous Bone

**ALWAYS CONSULT MAIN SCHEDULES. USE NUMBER ASSIGNED ONLY WHEN
SUBJECT REPRESENTS MAJOR EMPHASIS OF WORK BEING CLASSIFIED**

I–184

Pets see Animals, Domestic
Peyote see Mescaline
Pfaundler–Hurler Syndrome see
   Mucopolysaccharidosis I
PGE1 see Alprostadil
PGF2 see Dinoprost
PGF2alpha see Dinoprost
pH see Hydrogen–Ion Concentration
Phage lambda see Bacteriophage lambda
Phage Receptors see Receptors, Virus
Phage Typing see Bacteriophage Typing
Phages see Bacteriophages
Phages T see T–Phages
Phagocyte Bactericidal Dysfunction   QW 690
Phagocytes   QW 690
   See also Histiocytes   WH 650, etc.;
      Macrophages   WH 650, etc.; Monocytes
      WH 200, etc.; Neutrophils   WH 200, etc.
Phagocytosis   QW 690
Phantom Limb   WE 170
Pharmaceutic Aids   QV 800
Pharmaceutical Chemistry see Chemistry,
   Pharmaceutical
Pharmaceutical Ethics see Ethics, Pharmacy
Pharmaceutical Services   QV 737
   Hospital see Pharmacy Service, Hospital   WX
   179
   Insurance see Insurance, Pharmaceutical Services
      W 265, etc.
   Military
      General   UH 420–425
      Navy   VG 270–275
Pharmaceutics see Drugs
Pharmacies   QV 737
   Directories   QV 722
   Public health aspects   WA 730
   See also Pharmacy Service, Hospital   WX 179
Pharmacists
   Biography
      Collective   WZ 112.5.P4
      Individual   WZ 100
   Career books   QV 21
   Directories   QV 22
   Interprofessional and public relations   QV 21
   Registration   QV 29
Pharmacists' Aides   QV 21.5
Pharmacogenetics   QV 38
Pharmacognosy   QV 752
Pharmacokinetics   QV 38
Pharmacology   QV
   Dental   QV 50
   Drug action   QV 38
   Experimental   QV 34
   In veterinary medicine   SF 915
   Nursing texts   QV 4, etc.
   See also Psychopharmacology   QV 77, etc.
Pharmacology, Arabic see Medicine, Arabic;
   Pharmacology
Pharmacology, Clinical   QV 38
   See also Drug Therapy   WB 330, etc.
Pharmacopoeias   QV 738
Pharmacopoeias, Homeopathic   WB 930
Pharmacotherapy see Drug Therapy

Pharmacy   QV 701–835
   Instrumentation   QV 26
   Military   UH 420–425
   Naval   VG 270–275
   Nursing texts   QV 704, etc.
   Public health aspects   WA 730
   Veterinary   SF 915
Pharmacy Administration   QV 737
   Veterinary medicine   SF 915
   See also Pharmacy Service, Hospital   WX 179
Pharmacy Education see Education, Pharmacy
Pharmacy Education, Continuing see Education,
   Pharmacy, Continuing
Pharmacy Education, Graduate see Education,
   Pharmacy, Graduate
Pharmacy Schools see Schools, Pharmacy
Pharmacy Service, Clinical see Pharmacy Service,
   Hospital
Pharmacy Service, Hospital   WX 179
Pharyngeal Arches see Branchial Region
Pharyngeal Diseases   WV 400–440
   General works   WV 400
   In infancy & childhood   WV 400–440
   Nursing   WY 158.5
Pharyngeal Region see Names of organs located in
   the region: Adenoids; Nasopharynx; Palate;
   Pharynx; Tonsil; Uvula
Pharyngitis   WV 410
Pharynx   WV 410
   In respiration   WF 490
Phase–Contrast Microscopy see Microscopy,
   Phase–Contrast
Phaseolus see Legumes
Phaseolus vulgaris Lectins see Phytohemagglutinins
Phenacaine see Anesthetics, Local
Phenacetin   QV 95
Phenadone see Methadone
Phenanthrenes   QV 138.C1
   Organic chemistry   QD 395
Phenanthridines
   As antineoplastic agents   QV 269
   Organic chemistry   QD 401
Phenantoin see Phenytoin
Phencyclidine   QV 77.7
Phencyclidine Abuse   WM 270
Phenemal see Phenobarbital
Phenethylamines   QU 61
   Organic chemistry   QD 341.A8
Phenformin   WK 825
Pheniramine   QV 157
Phenobarbital   QV 88
Phenobarbitone see Phenobarbital
Phenolphthaleins   QV 75
Phenols
   As anti–infective agents   QV 223
   Organic chemistry   QD 341.P5
Phenomenon see Anaphylaxis; Arthus Reaction;
   Shwartzman Phenomenon
Phenothiazine Antipsychotic Agents see
   Antipsychotic Agents, Phenothiazine
Phenothiazine Tranquilizers see Antipsychotic
   Agents, Phenothiazine
Phenothiazines   QV 253

In veterinary pharmacology   SF 918.P5
Organic chemistry   QD 401
Phenotype
    Human genetics   QH 431
    Human variation   GN 62.8-263
        Hereditary aspects   GN 247
    See also Somatotypes   GN 66.5
Phenoxybenzamine   QV 132
Phentanyl see Fentanyl
Phenyl Ethers
    Organic chemistry   QD 341.E7
    Used for special purposes, by subject
Phenylacetates   QU 98
    Organic chemistry   QD 341.A2
Phenylalanine   QU 60
Phenylamines see Aniline Compounds
Phenylbarbital see Phenobarbital
Phenylbutazone   QV 95
Phenylenediamines   QU 61
    Carcinogenicity research   QZ 202
Phenylethylamines see Phenethylamines
Phenylglycolic Acid see Mandelic Acids
Phenylhydrazines   QV 180
    Organic chemistry   QD 341.A8
Phenylketonuria   WD 205.5.A5
Phenylmethylamine see Benzylamines
Phenylthiocarbamide see Phenylthiourea
Phenylthiourea
    In goiter experiments   WK 259
    In taste experiments   WI 210
    Organic chemistry   QD 305.T45
Phenytoin   QV 85
Pheochromocytoma   QZ 380
    Localized, by site
Pheresis see Blood Component Removal
Pheromones
    Communication   QL 776
    Secretion   QP 190
Phialophora   QW 180.5.D38
Philanthropic Funds see Fund Raising
Philately   HE 6187-6228
    Medical   WZ 340
Philocytase see Bacteriolysis; Hemolysins
Philology   P
    Chinese   PL 1001-2245
    General works   P
    English   PE
        Modern grammar   PE 1097-1400
    French   PC 2011-3761
    Latin   PA 2011-2915
    Modern (General)   PB 6-431
    Other languages in appropriate P schedule
    Special topics, by subject
    See also "phrase books" under specialty headings,
        e.g., Medicine, and names of language groups
        below
Philology, Classical   PA 1-2915
    Grammars for physicians and pharmacists   PA
        2092
    See also subheading, e.g., Latin   PA 2011-2915
        under Philology
Philology, Oriental   PJ-PL
    General works   PJ 10-187

See also names of specific oriental languages
    under Philology, e.g., Chinese   PL 1001-2245
Philology, Romance   PC
    General works   PC 6-400
    See also language subheadings, e.g., French   PC
    2011-3761 under Philology
Philosophy   B-BD
    General works   B 69-5739
    Life (Biology)   QH 501
    Of science   Q 174-175.3
    Scientology   BP 605.S2
    See also names of specific philsophies, e.g.,
        Existentialism   B 105.E8 etc.; Humanism   B
        821
Philosophy, Medical   W 61
Philosophy, Nursing   WY 86
Phimosis   WJ 790
Phlebitis   WG 610
    Pyelophlebitis   WJ 351
    Other localities, by site
Phlebography   WG 600
    Localized, by site or disease
Phlebonarcosis see Anesthesia, Intravenous
Phlebothrombosis see Thrombophlebitis
Phlebotomus Fever   WC 526
Phlebotomy see Bloodletting
Phlegmasia Alba Dolens see Thrombophlebitis
Phlegmon see Cellulitis
Phobia, School see Phobic Disorders
Phobia, Social see Phobic Disorders
Phobias see Phobic Disorders
Phobic Disorders   WM 178
Phobic Neuroses see Phobic Disorders
Phonation   WV 501
Phonation Disorders see Voice Disorders
Phonetics   P 215-240
    General   P 221
    Physiological aspects   WV 501
Phonocardiography   WG 141.5.P4
Phorbol Esters
    As carcinogens   QZ 202
Phorbol Myristate Acetate see
    Tetradecanoylphorbol Acetate
Phorias see Strabismus
Phosgene   QV 664
Phosphamidon
    Agriculture   SB 952.P5
    Public health   WA 240
Phosphatases see Phosphoric Monoester Hydrolases
Phosphates   QV 285
Phosphates, Inorganic see Phosphates
Phosphates, Organic see Organophosphorus
    Compounds
Phosphatidal Compounds see Plasmalogens
Phosphatidate Phosphatase   QU 136
Phosphatidate Phosphohydrolase see Phosphatidate
    Phosphatase
Phosphatides see Phospholipids
Phosphatidylcholines   QU 93
Phosphatidylethanolamines   QU 93
Phosphatidylinositols   QU 93
Phosphines
    As pesticides   WA 240

Inorganic chemistry   QD 181.P1
Phosphocreatine   WE 500
Phosphodiesterases see Phosphoric Diester
  Hydrolases
Phosphoglycerides see Glycerophosphates
Phosphohydrolases see Phosphoric Monoester
  Hydrolases
Phosphoinositides see Phosphatidylinositols
Phospholipase A1 see Phospholipases A
Phospholipase A2 see Phospholipases A
Phospholipases   QU 136
Phospholipases A   QU 136
Phospholipids   QU 93
Phosphomonoesterases see Phosphoric Monoester
  Hydrolases
Phosphonic Acids
    Inorganic chemistry   QD 181.P1
    Pharmacology   QV 138.P4
Phosphonomycin see Fosfomycin
Phosphopeptides   QU 68
Phosphoprotein Phosphatase   QU 136
Phosphoprotein Phosphohydrolase see
    Phosphoprotein Phosphatase
Phosphoranes
    Inorganic chemistry   QD 181.P1
    Pharmacology   QV 138.P4
Phosphorescence see Luminescence
Phosphoric Acids   QD 181.P1
    Pharmacology   QV 138.P4
Phosphoric Diester Hydrolases   QU 136
Phosphoric Monoester Hydrolases   QU 136
Phosphorus
    Inorganic chemistry   QD 181.P1
    Metabolism   QU 130
    Of bone   WE 200
    Pharmacology   QV 138.P4
    Toxicology
        As an irritant poison   QV 618
        Organic poison   QV 627
Phosphorus Isotopes
    Inorganic chemistry   QD 181.P1
    Metabolism   QU 130
    Micro-organism metabolism   QW 52
    Of bone   WE 200
    Pharmacology   QV 138.P4
Phosphorus Metabolism Disorders   WD 200.5.P4
Phosphorus Poisons, Organic see Toxicology   QV
  627 under Organophosphorus Compounds
Phosphorus Radioisotopes   WN 420
    Nuclear physics   QC 796.P1
    See also special topics under Radioisotopes
Phosphorylation   QD 281.P46
Phosphorylcholine, Acetyl Glyceryl Ether see
    Platelet Activating Factor
Phosphotransferases   QU 141
Phosphotransferases, ATP see Phosphotransferases
Phosvel
    Agriculture   SB 952.P5
    Public health   WA 240
Photoaging of Skin see Skin Aging
Photobacterium   QW 141
Photobiology see Light
Photochemistry   QD 701-731

Industrial   TP 249.5
    Other special topics, by subject
Photochemotherapy   WB 480
Photochemotherapy, Hematoporphyrin see
    Hematoporphyrin Photoradiation
Photocoagulation see Light Coagulation
Photodermatitis see Photosensitivity Disorders
Photodynamic Therapy see Photochemotherapy
Photofluorography   WN 220
    Used for diagnosis of particular disorders, with
    the disorder
Photogrammetry   TR 693-696
    For specific subjects, by subject
Photography   TR
    Dental   TR 708
    Fluorescent screen see Fluoroscopy   WN 220
    In psychotherapy   WM 450.5.P5
    Instrumentation   TR 570
    Medical   TR 708
    Roentgen-ray see Radiography   WN 200, etc.
    Used for specific subjects, by subject
Photokymography see Electrokymography
Photometry
    Analytical chemistry (General)   QD 79.P46
    Optics   QC 391
    Quantitative analysis   QD 117.P5
    Used for diagnosis of particular disorders, with
    the disorder or system
Photomicrography   QH 251
Photons see Radiation
Photoproteins see Luminescent Proteins
Photoradiation see Light
Photoradiation, Hematoporphyrin see
    Hematoporphyrin Photoradiation
Photoradiation Therapy see Phototherapy
Photoreceptors   WL 102.9
Photosensitivity Disorders   WR 160
Photosynthesis   QK 882
Phototherapy   WB 480
Phototrophic Bacteria   QW 145
Phrase Books see Medicine
Phrenic Nerve   WL 400
Phrenology   BF 866-885
    As a diagnostic technique   WB 365
Phthalein Dyes   QV 240
Phthalic Acids   QU 98
    Organic chemistry   QD 341.A2
    Toxicology   QV 612
Phthalic Anhydrides   QU 98
    Toxicology   QV 612
Phthalidyl Ampicillin see Talampicillin
Phthiraptera see Lice
Phthiriasis see Pediculosis
Phthiroptera   QX 501
Phthisis see Tuberculosis, Pulmonary
Phycomycetes   QW 180.5.P4
Phyllodes Tumor   WP 870
Phylloquinone see Phytonadione
Phylogeny   QH 367.5
Physarum   QW 180.5.M9
Physiatry see Physical Medicine
Physical Agents see Meteorological Factors; names
  of specific agents, e.g., Heat

ALWAYS CONSULT MAIN SCHEDULES. USE NUMBER ASSIGNED ONLY WHEN
SUBJECT REPRESENTS MAJOR EMPHASIS OF WORK BEING CLASSIFIED

Physical Conditioning, Human see Exercise Therapy
Physical Disability see Disabled
Physical Education and Training   QT 255
Physical Effort see Exertion
Physical Endurance   QT 255
    Special topics, by subject
Physical Examination   WB 200-288
    For legal establishment of life   W 789
    In infancy & childhood   WS 141
    In old age   WT 141
Physical Examination, Preadmission see Diagnostic
    Tests, Routine
Physical Fitness   QT 255
    For automobile driving   WA 275
    In aviation medicine   WD 705
    In space medicine   WD 752
Physical Medicine   WB 460-545
Physical Optics see Optics
Physical Therapy   WB 460-545
    General works   WB 460
    Hospital departments   WX 223
    In psychiatry   WM 405-412
    Veterinary   SF 925
Physical Therapy Department, Hospital   WX 223
Physically Challenged see Disabled
Physically Handicapped see Disabled
Physician Assignment Acceptance see Medicare
    Assignment
Physician Assistants   W 21.5
Physician Impairment
    Medicine   W 21
    For general impairment of physicians in various
    specialties, class in the number for the
    profession where applicable
Physician-Patient Relations   W 62
    In adolescence   WS 462
    In infancy & childhood   WS 105.5.I5
    In psychiatry   WM 62
    In surgery   WO 62
Physician Shortage Area see Medically Underserved
    Area
Physicians
    Arabic   WZ 80.5.A8
    Biography
        Collective   WZ 112-150
        Individual   WZ 100
    Directories   W 22
    Islamic   WZ 80.5.A8
    Liability   W 44
        See also Insurance, Liability   W 44, etc.
    Literary & artistic works   WZ 350
    Military   WZ 112.5.M4
    Social relations   W 62
    See also names of ethnic groups, e.g., Blacks
    WZ 80.5.B5, etc.; other special topics
Physicians' Assistants see Physician Assistants
Physicians' Extenders see Physician Assistants
Physicians, Family   W 89
    See also Family Practice   WB 110, etc.
Physician's Practice Patterns   W 87
Physician's Role   W 62
Physicians, Women   W 21
    Biography

        Collective   WZ 150
        Individual   WZ 100
    History of their place in medicine   WZ 80.5.W5
    See also special topics under Physicians
Physics   QC
    Biological see Biophysics   QT 34, etc.
    Radiologic see Health Physics   WN 110
Physiognomy   BF 840-861
    See also Facial Expression   WB 275, etc.
Physiologic Availability see Biological Availability
Physiological Adaptation see Adaptation,
    Physiological
Physiological Chemistry see Biochemistry
Physiological Optics see Optometry; Vision
Physiological Psychology see Psychophysiology
Physiologists see Biography   WZ 112.5.P5, etc.,
    and Directories   QT 22 under Physiology
Physiology   QT
    Bacterial   QW 52
    Biography
        Collective   WZ 112.5.P5
        Individual   WZ 100
    Cold climate   QT 160
    Desert climate   QT 150
    Directories   QT 22
    Domestic animals   SF 768-768.2
    Experimental   QT 25
    Fetus   WQ 210.5
    Hot climate   QT 150
    Human (General)   QT 104
    Labor   WQ 305
    Neurological see Neurophysiology   WL 102
    Nursing texts   QT 104
    Psychological see Psychophysiology   WL 103
    Surgical   WO 102
    Wild animals   QP, etc.
    Particular systems, organism or parts, by subject
    See also Anthropology, Physical   GN 50.2-298
Physiology, Comparative   QT 4
    Domestic animals only   SF 768-768.2
    Wild animals only   QP 33
Physiopathology see Pathology
Physiotherapy see Physical Therapy
Physostigmine   QV 124
Phytagglutinins see Lectins
Phytic Acid   QU 75
Phytin see Phytic Acid
Phytochrome   QK 898.P67
Phytohaemagglutinins see Plant Agglutinins
Phytohemagglutinins   QK 898.P8
    Hemagglutination   QW 640
Phytohormones see Plant Growth Regulators
Phytomenadione see Phytonadione
Phytomitogens see Lectins
Phytonadione   QV 195
Phytophagineae see Plant Viruses
Pia Mater   WL 200
Pial Vein see Cerebral Veins
Pica   WM 175
Picibanil
    As antineoplastic agents   QV 269
Pick's Disease of Brain see Dementia, Presenile
Pick's Disease of Heart see Pericarditis, Constrictive

**ALWAYS CONSULT MAIN SCHEDULES. USE NUMBER ASSIGNED ONLY WHEN
SUBJECT REPRESENTS MAJOR EMPHASIS OF WORK BEING CLASSIFIED**

Picloram
Public health   WA 240
Picodnaviruses see Parvoviridae
Picornaviridae   QW 168.5.P4
Picornaviridae Infections   WC 501
Picornavirus Infections see Picornaviridae Infections
Picrates   QV 223
Picric Acid see Picrates
Picrotoxin   QV 103
Pictorial Works see Form number 17 in any NLM schedule where applicable or appropriate LC number
Picture Archiving and Communication Systems see Radiology Information Systems
Picture Archiving, Radiologic see Radiology Information Systems
Picture Frustration Study see Rosenzweig Picture-Frustration Study
Piebald Skin see Albinism; Pigmentation Disorders; Vitiligo
Pig Skin Dressings see Biological Dressings
Pig-Tailed Monkey see Macaca nemestrina
Pigeon Breeder's Lung see Bird Fancier's Lung
Pigeons   QL 696.C63
Diseases   SF 994.6
Pigment Epithelium of Eye   WW 103
Of particular parts of the eye, with the part, e.g., Retinal Pigment Epithelium   WW 270
Pigmentary Retinopathy see Retinitis Pigmentosa
Pigmentation
Anthropology   GN 197
Manifestations of disease   WR 143
Physiology   WR 102
Pigmentation Disorders   WR 265-267
Manifestations of disease   WR 143
Pigments   QU 110
Animals
Domestic   SF 768-768.2
Wild   QP 670-671
Plants
Biochemistry   QD 441
Botany   QK 898.P7
See also Porphyrins   QU 110, etc.; names of other specific pigments
Pigs see Swine
Pike see Salmonidae
Pilar Cyst see Epidermal Cyst
Piles see Hemorrhoids
Pili, Bacterial see Pili, Sex
Pili, Sex   QW 51
Pills see Nostrums; Tablets
Pilocarpine   QV 122
Pilonidal Cyst   WE 750
Pilonidal Sinus see Pilonidal Cyst
Pineal Body   WK 350
Pinealoma   WK 350
Pinna see Ear, External
Pinnipedia   QL 737.P64
Pinta   WC 422
Pinworm see Oxyuroidea
Piperacillin   QV 354
Pipradol see Pipradrol

Pirenzepine
As an anti-ulcer agent   QV 69
Piroplasmosis see Babesiosis
Piroxicam   QV 95
Pit and Fissure Sealants   WU 190
Pit Viper Venoms see Crotalid Venoms
Pitch Discrimination   WV 272
Pitch Perception   WV 272
Pithecinae see Cebidae
Pituitary Adenoma, Prolactin-Secreting see Prolactinoma
Pituitary-Adrenal Function Tests   WK 510
Pituitary-Adrenal System   WK 510
Pituitary Diseases   WK 500-590
Pituitary Dwarfism see Dwarfism, Pituitary
Pituitary Function Tests   WK 502
See also Pituitary-Adrenal Function Tests   WK 510
Pituitary Gland   WK 500-590
Pituitary Gland, Anterior   WK 510
Pituitary Gland, Posterior   WK 520
Pituitary Growth Hormone see Somatotropin
Pituitary Hormone Release Inhibiting Hormones   WK 515
Pituitary Hormone-Releasing Hormones   WK 515
Pituitary Hormones   WK 502
Pituitary Hormones, Anterior   WK 515
Pituitary Hormones, Posterior   WK 520
Pituitary Neoplasms   WK 585
Pityriasis   WR 204
Linguae see Glossitis, Benign Migratory   WI 210
Pivampicillin   QV 354
PIXE see Spectrometry, X-Ray Emission
Pizotifen see Pizotyline
Pizotyline
As a serotonin antagonist   QV 126
Placebos   WB 330
Placement Agencies, Nursing see Employment
Placenta   WQ 212
Growth and Development see Placentation   QS 645
Placenta Diseases   WQ 212
Placental Extracts
Pharmacology   QV 370
Therapeutic use (General)   WB 391
Used for treatment of particular disorders, with the disorder or system
Placental Function Tests   WQ 212
Placental Hormones   WK 920
Placental Insufficiency   WQ 212
Placental Lactogen   WK 920
Placental Proteins see Pregnancy Proteins
Placental Villi see Chorionic Villi
Placentation   QS 645
Placentoma, Normal see Placenta
Placentome see Placenta
Plague   WC 350-355
Cattle see Rinderpest   SF 966
Fowl see Fowl Plague   SF 995.6.F59
Plague Vaccine   WC 350
Planigraphy, X-Ray see Tomography, X-Ray

Plankton
    Aquatic biology (General)   QH 90.8.P5
    Freshwater biology   QH 96.8.P5
    Marine biology   QH 91.8.P5
    Plant ecology   QK 933–935
    Zoology
        Freshwater   QL 143
        Ocean   QL 123
Planned Parenthood see Family Planning
Planning, Health and Welfare see Health Planning
Planning, Health Facility see Health Facility
  Planning
Planning Techniques
    Health administration   WA 525–546
    Health services   W 84–84.8
    Hospital administration   WX 150
    Hospital facility   WX 140
    In other particular areas, by subject
Planning Theories see Planning Techniques
Plant Agglutinins see Lectins
Plant Diseases   SB 599–795
    Biological control   SB 975–978
    General works   SB 731
    Trees   SB 761–767
Plant Extracts, Chinese see Drugs, Chinese Herbal
Plant Growth Regulators   QK 745
Plant Hormones see Plant Growth Regulators
Plant Lice see Aphids
Plant Microbiology see Microbiology; Plant Viruses
Plant Oils
    Biochemistry   QU 86
    Chemical technology   TP 680–684
    Public health aspects   WA 722
Plant Poisoning   WD 500–530
    Veterinary   SF 757.5
    See also Milk Sickness   WD 530
Plant Proteins   QK 898.P8
    In nutrition   QU 55
Plant Tumors   SB 741.5
    Of specific plants with the plant, e.g., tree galls
    in   SB 767
Plant Viruses   QW 163
Plantar Prints see Dermatoglyphics
Plants   QK
    Chemistry   QK 861–899
    Cytology   QK 725
    Histology   QK 671
    Lice see Aphids   QX 503, etc.
    Microbiology   QW 60
    Poisons see Plants, Toxic   WD 500–530
Plants, Edible   QK 98.5
    As a dietary supplement in health or disease
    WB 430–432
Plants, Medicinal   QV 766–770
    Atlases   QV 717
    Culture   SB 293–295
    See also specific names of medicinal plants
Plants, Toxic   WD 500–530
Plaque Therapy, Radioisotope see Brachytherapy
Plasma   WH 400
    Blood transfusion   WB 356
Plasma Cell Antigens PC-1 see Antigens,
  Differentiation, B–Lymphocyte

Plasma Cell Dyscrasias see Paraproteinemias
Plasma Cells   WH 400
Plasma Exchange   WB 356
Plasma Expanders see Plasma Substitutes
Plasma Membrane see Cell Membrane
Plasma Prokallikrein see Prekallikrein
Plasma Proteins see Blood Proteins
Plasma Substitutes   WH 450
Plasma Transglutaminase see Protein–Glutamine
  gamma–Glutamyltransferase
Plasma Volume   WG 106
Plasma Volume Expanders see Plasma Substitutes
Plasmacytes see Plasma Cells
Plasmalogens   QU 93
Plasmapheresis   WH 460
Plasmids   QW 51
Plasminogen
    Enzymology   QU 142
    Blood coagulation   WH 310
Plasminogen Activator Inhibitor 3 see Protein C
  Inhibitor
Plasminogen Activator Inhibitors see Plasminogen
  Inactivators
Plasminogen Activator, Tissue–Type see Alteplase
Plasminogen Activator, Urokinase–Type see
  Urokinase
Plasminogen Activators
    Biochemistry   QU 142
    Blood coagulation   WH 310
Plasminogen Inactivators   QU 136
Plasminokinase see Streptodornase and Streptokinase
Plasmodium   QX 135
Plasmodium Infections see Malaria
Plasmosome see Cell Nucleolus
Plaster, Adhesive see Bandages
Plaster Casts see Casts, Surgical
Plaster of Paris see Calcium Sulfate
Plasters see Dermatologic Agents; Irritants
Plastic Casts see Casts, Surgical
Plastic Surgery see Surgery, Plastic
Plasticity, Neuronal see Neuronal Plasticity
Plastics
    Chemical technology   TP 1101–1185
    Used for special purposes by subject, e.g., in
    plastic surgery   WO 640
Platelet Activating Factor   QU 93
    In blood coagulation   WH 310
Platelet Adhesiveness   WH 310
Platelet Aggregation   WH 310
Platelet Aggregation Inhibitors   QV 180
Platelet Antagonists see Platelet Aggregation
  Inhibitors
Platelet Antiaggregants see Platelet Aggregation
  Inhibitors
Platelet–Derived Growth Factor   QU 107
Platelet Function Tests   QY 410
Platelet Transforming Growth Factor see
  Transforming Growth Factor beta
Platelet Transfusion   WB 356
Plateletpheresis   WH 460
Platelets see Blood Platelets
Platelets, Blood see Blood Platelets

Platinum
    Inorganic chemistry   QD 181.P8
    Pharmacology   QV 290
Platinum Black see Platinum
Platinum Diamminodichloride see Cisplatin
Platybasia   WE 730
Platyhelminths   QX 350–422
Platyrrhina see Cebidae
Play and Playthings
    Child psychology   WS 105.5.P5
    Physical education   QT 255
    Projective techniques   WM 145.5.P8
    Preschool children   LB 1140.35.P55
    Psychology (General)   BF 717
    Recreation   QT 250
    School children   LB 1177; LB 3031
Play Therapy   WS 350.2
    Activity therapy   WM 450
    Special topics by subject, e.g., Hospitalized Child
       WS 105.5.H7
Pleasure-Pain Principle
    Psychoanalysis   WM 460.5.P5
    Psychology   BF 515
Plethysmography   WG 141.5.P7
    Special topics, by subject, e.g., in the diagnosis
      of Thrombosis   WG 610
Plethysmography, Impedance   WG 141.5.P7
    Special topics, by subject, e.g., diagnosis of
      Arteriosclerosis   WG 550
Plethysmography, Impedance, Transthoracic see
    Cardiography, Impedance
Plethysmography, Whole Body   WF 141.5.P7
    Special topics, by subject, e.g., in Tracheal
      Stenosis   WF 490
Pleura   WF 700–746
    Secretion   QY 210
    Tuberculosis see Tuberculosis, Pleural   WF 390
    See also Pleuropneumonia   WC 202
Pleural Cavity see Pleura
Pleural Effusion   WF 700
    Clinical analysis   QY 210
Pleural Fluid see Secretion   QY 210 under Pleura
Pleural Neoplasms   WF 700
Pleural Rub see Respiratory Sounds
Pleurisy   WF 744
Pleurisy, Tuberculous see Tuberculosis, Pleural
Pleuritis see Pleurisy
Pleurodynia, Epidemic   WC 500
Pleuropneumonia   WC 202
    Veterinary   SF 831
    In cattle   SF 964
Pleuropneumonia-Like Organisms see Mycoplasma
Plicamycin   QV 269
Plumbing see Sanitary Engineering
Plumbism see Lead Poisoning
Plummer-Vinson Syndrome   WI 250
Plutonium   WN 420
    Nuclear physics   QC 796.P9
    See also special topics under Radioisotopes
Pneumatosis Cystoides Intestinalis   WI 400
Pneumococcal Infections   WC 217
    See also Pneumonia, Lobar   WC 204
Pneumoconiosis   WF 654

Pneumoencephalography   WL 141
Pneumogastric Nerve see Vagus Nerve
Pneumology see Pulmonary Disease (Specialty)
Pneumomediastinum see Mediastinal Emphysema
Pneumomediastinum, Diagnostic   WF 975
Pneumonectomy   WF 668
Pneumonia   WC 202–209
    Friedlaender's pneumonia   WC 209
    Veterinary   SF 831
Pneumonia, Aspiration   WC 209
Pneumonia, Interstitial see Lung Diseases, Interstitial
Pneumonia, Lipid   WC 209
Pneumonia, Lobar   WC 204
Pneumonia, Mycoplasma   WC 209
Pneumonia, Pneumococcal see Pneumonia, Lobar
Pneumonia, Staphylococcal   WC 204
Pneumonia, Viral   WC 207
    Veterinary   SF 831
Pneumonitis, Hypersensitivity, Avian see Bird
    Fancier's Lung
Pneumonitis, Interstitial see Lung Diseases,
    Interstitial
Pneumonology see Pulmonary Disease (Specialty)
Pneumonolysis   WF 668
Pneumoperitoneum   WI 575
Pneumoperitoneum, Artificial   WI 141
    Used for diagnosis of particular disorders, with
      the disorder or system
Pneumoradiography   WN 200
Pneumoretroperitoneum see
    Retropneumoperitoneum
Pneumothorax   WF 746
Pneumothorax, Artificial   WF 768
Pocket, Periodontal see Periodontal Pocket
Podiatry   WE 890
Podophyllum
    As an antineoplastic agent   QV 269
    As a cathartic   QV 75
    As a medicinal plant   QV 767
    Poisoning   WD 500
Poetry   PN 6099–6110
    About medicine   WZ 330
    By physicians   WZ 350
    Light verse in medicine and related fields   WZ
      305–305.5
Poison Control Centers   QV 600
    Directories   QV 605
    In hospitals   WX 215
Poison Ivy see Toxicodendron
Poison Ivy Dermatitis see Dermatitis,
    Toxicodendron
Poisoning   QV 600–667
    Animal see Animals, Poisonous   WD 400–430;
      Fishes, Poisonous   WD 405; Bites and Stings
      WD 400–430
    Carbon monoxide see Carbon Monoxide
      Poisoning   QV 662
    Fluoride see Fluoride Poisoning   QV 282, etc.
    Food see Food Poisoning   WC 268
    Gas see Gas Poisoning   QV 662, etc.
    Industrial   WA 465
      Medicolegal Aspects   W 925
    Lead see Lead Poisoning   QV 292

**ALWAYS CONSULT MAIN SCHEDULES. USE NUMBER ASSIGNED ONLY WHEN
SUBJECT REPRESENTS MAJOR EMPHASIS OF WORK BEING CLASSIFIED**

Mercury see Mercury Poisoning   QV 293
Mushroom see Mushroom Poisoning   WD 520
Plant see Plant Poisoning   WD 500–530
Salmonella food see Salmonella Food Poisoning
    WC 268
Staphylococcal food see Staphylococcal Food
    Poisoning   WC 268
Veterinary   SF 757.5
See also names of particular poisonous animals,
    bacteria, chemicals, insects, plants, viruses, etc.,
    and the field Toxicology
Poisonous Animals see Animals, Poisonous
Poisonous Fishes see Fishes, Poisonous
Poisonous Gases see Gases
Poisonous Plants see Plants, Toxic
Poisons   QV 600–667
    Corrosive   QV 612
    Detection see Laboratory manuals   QV 602 and
        Methods   QV 602 under Toxicology
    Industrial protection   WA 465
    Inorganic   QV 610–618
    Organic   QV 627–633
    Public health aspects   WA 730
    Volatile   QV 633
    See also names of specific poisons
Polar Regions see Cold Climate
Polarization Microscopy see Microscopy,
    Polarization
Polarography
    Organic analysis   QD 272.E4
    Quantitative analysis   QD 116.P64
Policy Making
    General   H 97
    In special topics, by subject
Poliodystrophia Cerebri see Cerebral Sclerosis,
    Diffuse
Poliomyelitis   WC 555
    Prevention and control   WC 556
Poliomyelitis Immunization see Prevention and
    Control   WC 556 under Poliomyelitis
Poliosis see Hair Color
Poliovirus Vaccine   WC 556
Poliovirus Vaccine, Oral   WC 556
Polioviruses   QW 168.5.P4
Polioviruses, Human 1–3   QW 168.5.P4
Polishes see Industrial Oils
Polishes, Dental see Dentifrices
Political Activity see Politics
Political Systems   JC
    In psychoanalysis, psychoanalytic therapy, or
        psychoanalytic interpretation   WM 460.5.P7
    Related to special topics, by subject
    See also names of specific systems, e.g.,
        Communism   HX 72–73; 626–780.7, etc.
Politics   J (rarely used)
    Special topics, by subject
Pollen   QK 658
    As an allergen   QW 900
    As a food preparation   WB 447
Pollinosis see Hay Fever
Pollution see Names of specific kinds of pollution,
    e.g., Air Pollution
Polonium   WN 420

Nuclear physics   QC 796.P6
    See also special topics under Radioisotopes
Poly Adenosine Diphosphate Ribose   QU 57
Poly ADP Ribose see Poly Adenosine Diphosphate
    Ribose
Poly ADP Ribose Polymerase see NAD+
    ADP-Ribosyltransferase
Poly ADP Ribose Synthetase see NAD+
    ADP-Ribosyltransferase
Poly I–C
    Immunology   QW 800
    Pharmacology   QV 268.5
Polyacrylamide Gel Electrophoresis,
    Two-Dimensional see Electrophoresis, Gel,
    Two-Dimensional
Polyamides see Nylons
Polyamines   QU 61
    Organic chemistry
        Aliphatic   QD 305.A8
        Aromatic   QD 341.A8
Polyangiaceae see Myxococcales
Polyangium see Myxococcales
Polyarteritis Nodosa   WG 518
Polyarthritis see Arthritis
Polyarthritis Rheumatica see Rheumatic Fever
Polybrominated Biphenyls
    As carcinogens   QZ 202
    Toxicology   QV 633
Polybromobiphenyl Compounds see Polybrominated
    Biphenyls
Polychemotherapy see Drug Therapy, Combination
Polychlorinated Biphenyls
    As air pollutants   WA 754, etc.
    As water pollutants   WA 689
    Organic chemistry   QD 341.H9
    Toxicology (General)   QV 633
Polychlorobiphenyl Compounds see Polychlorinated
    Biphenyls
Polychloroethylene see Polyvinyl Chloride
Polycyclic Compounds
    Organic chemistry   QD 341.H9
    Toxicology   QV 633
Polycyclic Hydrocarbons
    Organic chemistry
        Aliphatic QD 305.H9
        Aromatic   QD 341.H9
    Toxicology   QV 633
Polycystic Kidney see Kidney, Polycystic
Polycystic Ovary Syndrome   WP 320
Polycythemia   WH 180
Polycythemia Vera   WH 180
Polydeoxyribonucleotide Ligases see
    Polydeoxyribonucleotide Synthetases
Polydeoxyribonucleotide Synthetases   QU 138
Polyergin see Transforming Growth Factor beta
Polyethylene Terephthalates
    Inguinal hernia repair   WI 960
    Production   TP 1180.P65
    Used for other special purposes, by subject
Polyethylenes
    Chemical technology   TP 1180.P65
    Used for special purposes, by subject, e.g., in
        drainage for middle ear surgery   WV 230

Polyglucoses see Glucans
Polyglutamate Folates see Pteroylpolyglutamic
Acids
Polygonum see Plants, Medicinal
Polyhedrosis Viruses   QW 162
Polyisocyanates see Polyurethanes
Polyisoprenyl Phosphate Sugars   QU 75
As glycolipids   QU 85
Polyisoprenyl Phosphates
Biochemistry   QU 85
Toxicology   QV 633
Polymenorrhea see Menstruation Disorders
Polymerase Chain Reaction   QH 450.3
Polymers   QD 380–388
Classify by use where possible, e.g., in dentistry
WU 190; in medicine   QT 37.5.P7
Polymorphism (Genetics)   QH 455
Polymorphonuclear Leukocytes see Neutrophils
Polymyalgia Rheumatica   WE 550
Polymyxin E see Colistin
Polyneuritis   WL 544
Polyneuritis Endemica see Beriberi
Polynuclear Aromatic Hydrocarbons see Polycyclic
Hydrocarbons
Polynucleotides   QU 57
Polyomavirus   QW 165.5.P2
Polyomavirus hominis 1   QW 165.5.P2
Polyomavirus macacae   QW 165.5.P2
Polypeptides see Peptides
Polyphosphates   QV 285
Polyploidy   QH 461
Plant breeding   SB 123
Polyposis see Polyps
Polyposis Coli, Familial see Adenomatous Polyposis
Coli
Polyposis Syndrome, Familial see Adenomatous
Polyposis Coli
Polyproteins see Proteins
Polyps   QZ 200
Localized, by site
See also Colonic Polyps   WI 529; Intestinal
Polyps   WI 430; Nasal Polyps   WV 300
Polyradiculitis   WL 400
Polyradiculoneuritis   WL 544
Polysaccharides   QU 83
Polysaccharides, Bacterial   QW 52
Polyurethanes
Chemical technology   TP 1180.P8
Used for special purposes, by subject, e.g., in
tubing for tracheal prosthesis   WF 490
Polyvidon see Povidone
Polyvinyl Chloride
Chemical technology   TP 1180.V48
Polyvinylpyrrolidone see Povidone
Polyvinylpyrrolidone Iodine see Povidone–Iodine
Polyvinyls
Chemical technology   TP 1180.V48
Used for particular purposes, by subject, e.g., in
Blood Bags   WH 460
Pompholyx see Eczema, Dyshidrotic
Pongidae   QL 737.P96
As laboratory animals   QY 60.P7
Diseases   SF 997.5.P7

Pongo pygmaeus   QL 737.P96
Diseases   SF 997.5.P7
As laboratory animals   QY 60.P7
Pons   WL 310
Pontocaine see Tetracaine
Poor, Medical Care see Medical Indigency
Popliteal Artery   WG 595.P6
See also Blood Supply   WE 870 under Knee
Popliteal Space see Knee
Popliteal Vein   WG 625.P6
See also Blood Supply   WE 870 under Knee
Poppy see Papaver
Popular works
Cardiovascular system   WG 113
Dentistry   WU 80
Digestive system   WI 113
Geriatrics   WT 120
Gynecology   WP 120
Medicine (General)   WB 120–130
Neoplasms   QZ 201
Obesity   WD 212
Obstetrics   WQ 150
Ophthalmology   WW 80
Psychiatry   WM 75
Surgery   WO 75
Special topics, by subject
Population   HB 848–3697
Genetics see Genetics, Population   QH 455, etc.
Health problems of special groups   WA 300–395
Movement   HB 1951–2577
See also Demography   HB 848–3697
Population Control   HB 848–871
Population policy   HB 883.5
See also Family Planning   HQ 763.5–767.7
Population Density   HB 1953
Population Distribution see Demography
Population Dynamics   QH 352
Special topics, by subject
Population Explosion see Population Growth
Population Growth   HB 848–871
Population Size see Population Density
Population Surveillance
Epidemiological studies   WA 105
See also names of specific types of surveys, e.g.,
Health Surveys   WA 900, etc.
Poradenitis Nostras see Lymphogranuloma
Venereum
Porcelain see Dental Porcelain
Porcine Influenza Virus Type A see Orthomyxovirus
Type A, Porcine
Porcine Xenograft Bioprosthesis see Bioprosthesis
Porcine Xenograft Dressings see Biological
Dressings
Porcupines see Rodentia
Porifera   QL 370.7–374.2
Pornography see Erotica
Porphyria   WD 205.5.P6
Special types, by system in which produced
Porphyrins   QU 110
Special types, by system in which produced, e.g.,
those related to hemorlobin   WH 190
Porpoises see Dolphins
Port Quarantine see Quarantine

**ALWAYS CONSULT MAIN SCHEDULES. USE NUMBER ASSIGNED ONLY WHEN
SUBJECT REPRESENTS MAJOR EMPHASIS OF WORK BEING CLASSIFIED**

Portacaval Shunt, Surgical   WI 720
Portal Hypertension see Hypertension, Portal
Portal System   WI 720
Portal Vein   WI 720
Portasystemic Shunt, Surgical   WI 720
Portography   WI 720
Portosystemic Encephalopathy see Hepatic
    Encephalopathy
Portosystemic Shunt, Surgical see Portasystemic
    Shunt, Surgical
Portraits   N 7575–7624.5
    Of physicians and other specialists in medically
        related fields in the appropriate biography
        number in   WZ
Position Description see Job Description
Position, Sense of see Orientation
Positioning, Radiography see Technology,
    Radiologic
Positive End-Expiratory Pressure see
    Positive–Pressure Respiration
Positive–Pressure Respiration   WF 145
    In first aid   WA 292
Positive Reinforcement see Reinforcement
    (Psychology)
Positron–Emission Tomography see Tomography,
    Emission–Computed
Positrons see Electrons
Posology see Administration & dosage   QV 748
    under Drugs; Prescriptions, Drug
Post and Core Technique   WU 515
Post–Surgical Nursing see Postanesthesia Nursing
Post–Transcriptional RNA Modification see RNA
    Processing, Post–Transcriptional
Post–Translational Protein Modification see Protein
    Processing, Post–Translational
Post–Traumatic Stress Disorders see Stress
    Disorders, Post–Traumatic
Postage Stamps see Philately
Postanesthesia Nursing   WY 154
Postcoital Contraceptives see Contraceptives,
    Postcoital
Posterior Chamber see Eye
Posterior Lobe Hormones see Pituitary Hormones,
    Posterior
Postgastrectomy Syndromes   WI 380
Postgraduate Education see Education, Graduate;
    names of specific types of graduate education, e.g.,
    Education, Pharmacy, Graduate
Postimplantation Phase   WQ 205
Postmarketing Product Surveillance see Product
    Surveillance, Postmarketing
Postmenopausal Bone Loss see Osteoporosis,
    Postmenopausal
Postmenopausal Hormone Replacement Therapy see
    Estrogen Replacement Therapy
Postmenopausal Osteoporosis see Osteoporosis,
    Postmenopausal
Postmortem Changes   QZ 35
Postmortem Examination see Autopsy
Postnatal Care   WQ 500
    See also Postnatal Nursing   WY 157.3 under
        Obstetrical Nursing
Postnidation Phase see Postimplantation Phase

Postoperative Care   WO 183
    Geriatric surgery   WO 950
    Pediatric surgery   WO 925
    See also Surgical Nursing   WY 161
Postoperative Complications   WO 184–185
    Specific complications, by site
Postoperative Period   WO 183
Postoperative Wound Infection see Surgical Wound
    Infection
Postpartum Hemorrhage   WQ 330
Postpartum Period see Puerperium
Postphlebitic Disease see Postphlebitic Syndrome
Postphlebitic Syndrome   WG 610
Postphlebitic Ulcer see Postphlebitic Syndrome
Posture   WE 103
Postviral Fatigue Syndrome see Fatigue Syndrome,
    Chronic
Potassium   QV 277
    Inorganic chemistry   QD 181.K1
    Metabolism   QU 130
    Toxicology   QV 277
Potassium Antimonyltartrate see Antimony
    Potassium Tartrate
Potassium Canrenoate see Canrenoate Potassium
Potassium Channels   QH 603.I54
Potassium Chloride
    Inorganic chemistry   QD 181.K1
    Pharmacology   QV 280
Potassium Deficiency   WD 105
    Veterinary   SF 855.P67
Potassium Isotopes
    Inorganic chemistry   QD 181.K1
    Pharmacology   QV 277
Potassium Permanganate   QV 229
Potassium Pump see Na(+)–K(+)–Exchanging
    ATPase
Pottos see Lorisidae
Pott's Disease see Tuberculosis, Spinal
Poultry
    Anatomy   SF 767.P6
    Culture   SF 481–507
    Physiology   SF 768.2.P6
Poultry Diseases   SF 995–995.6
Poultry Products
    As a dietary supplement in health or disease
        WB 426
    Public health aspects   WA 707
    See also Eggs   WA 703, etc.
Poverty
    Economic conditions   HC 79.P6
        By country   HC 94–1085
    Welfare   HV 40–4630
Poverty Areas
    Health problems (General)   WA 30
    Special topics, by subject
Povidone   WH 450
Povidone–Iodine
    As an anti–infective agent   QV 231
Powders   QV 785
    As adsorbent dermatological agents   QV 63
    As adsorbent gastrointestinal agents   QV 66
Power, Personal see Power (Psychology)
Power Plants   TJ 164

**ALWAYS CONSULT MAIN SCHEDULES. USE NUMBER ASSIGNED ONLY WHEN
SUBJECT REPRESENTS MAJOR EMPHASIS OF WORK BEING CLASSIFIED**

Prevention and control of accidents and diseases WA 440-495
Power, Professional see Power (Psychology)
Power (Psychology)
    As an expression of will   BF 608-618, etc.
      Manipulation or control by others   BF 632.5
      Self control, willpower, etc .   BF 632
    Other aspects, by subject
Power, Social see Power (Psychology)
Power Sources, Bioelectric see Bioelectric Energy Sources
Poxviridae   QW 165.5.P6
Poxviridae Infections   WC 584-590
Poxvirus Infections see Poxviridae Infections
Poxvirus myxomatis see Myxoma Virus
Poxvirus officinale see Vaccinia Virus
Poxvirus variolae see Variola Virus
PPLO see Mycoplasma
Practical Nurses see Nurses; Nursing, Practical
Practice see Family Practice; General Practice, Dental; Group Practice; Group Practice, Dental; Group Practice, Prepaid; Institutional Practice; Mortuary Practice; Partnership Practice; Private Practice; Professional Practice; See also Medicine (as practiced in particular countries)
Practice Management, Dental   WU 77-79
Practice Management, Medical   W 80
Practice Patterns, Professional see Physician's Practice Patterns
Practice (Psychology)
    Educational psychology
      Habit   LB 1061
        Memory   LB 1063
      Philosophy   B 831.3
Practolol   QV 132
Prairie Dogs see Sciuridae
Praomys see Muridae
Praying Mantis see Orthoptera
Praziquantel   QV 253
Prazosin   QV 150
Pre-Eclampsia   WQ 215
Pre-Excitation Syndromes   WG 330
Preanesthetic Medication   WO 234
Precancerous Conditions   QZ 204
Precautions, Universal see Universal Precautions
Preceptorship
    Dentistry   WU 20
    Medicine   W 20
    Nursing   WY 18.5
    Pharmacy   QV 20
    Veterinary medicine   SF 756.3-756.37
    In other fields, by subject
Precipitation   QD 547
    Antigens   QW 640
    Tests   QY 265
Precipitins   QW 640
    Diagnostic reactions   QY 265
Precocity see Child Development
Predatory Behavior   QL 758
Predental Education see Education, Predental
Prediabetic State   WK 810
Predictive Value of Tests
    Of a specific test, with the test

Prednisolone   WK 757
Prednisolone, Topical   QV 60
Prednisone   WK 757
Preferred Provider Organizations   W 130
Prefrontal Cortex   WL 307
Pregnadienes   WP 530
Pregnancy   WQ 200-260
    Breast in   WP 825
    General works   WQ 200
    Legal aspects   W 791
    Nursing   WY 157
    Popular works   WQ 150
Pregnancy, Abdominal   WQ 220
Pregnancy, Adolescent see Pregnancy in Adolescence
Pregnancy, Animal   SF 887
Pregnancy Complications   WQ 240-260
    General works   WQ 240
    Veterinary   SF 887
      See also Pregnancy, Animal   SF 887
    See also names of specific complications
Pregnancy Complications, Cardiovascular   WQ 244
Pregnancy Complications, Hematologic   WQ 252
    Veterinary   SF 887
      See also Pregnancy, Animal   SF 887
Pregnancy Complications, Infectious   WQ 256
    See also Puerperal Infection   WQ 505
Pregnancy Complications, Neoplastic   WQ 240
Pregnancy, Ectopic   WQ 220
Pregnancy in Adolescence
    Illegitimacy   WS 462
    Medical problems   WQ
    Psychological problems   WS 462
    Welfare   WA 310-352
Pregnancy in Diabetes   WQ 248
Pregnancy, Multiple   WQ 235
Pregnancy Outcome   WQ 240
Pregnancy, Prolonged   WQ 240
Pregnancy Proteins   WK 920
Pregnancy, Teenage see Pregnancy in Adolescence
Pregnancy Tests   QY 335
Pregnancy Toxemias   WQ 215
Pregnancy, Tubal   WQ 220
Pregnancy, Unwanted   WQ 200
Pregnanediol   WP 530
Pregnanediones   QV 81
Pregnanes   WP 530
Pregnanetriol   WP 530
Prehospital Emergency Care see Emergency Medical Services
Preimplantation Phase   WQ 205
Prejudice   BF 575.P9
    In adolescence   WS 462
    In infancy & childhood   WS 105.5.S6
    Specific prejudice, by subject
Prekallikrein   QU 136
Premarin see Estrogens, Conjugated
Premarital Examinations
    General   WB 200
    Female   WP 141
    Male   WJ 700
Premature Beat see Extrasystole
Premature infants see Infant, Premature

Premedical Education see Education, Premedical
Premedication
    In anesthesia see Preanesthetic Medication WO 234
    In surgery WO 179
    Used for special purposes, by subject
Premenstrual Syndrome WP 560
Premenstrual Tension see Premenstrual Syndrome
Prenatal Care WQ 175
Prenatal Diagnosis WQ 209
    For hereditary diseases specifically QZ 50
Prenatal Diagnosis, Ultrasonic see Ultrasonography, Prenatal
Prenatal Exposure Delayed Effects WQ 210
Prenidation Phase see Preimplantation Phase
Preoperative Care WO 179
    Geriatric surgery WO 950
    Pediatric surgery WO 925
    Preparation of patient for anesthesia WO 234
Prepaid Dental Care see Insurance, Dental
Prepaid Group Health Organizations see Health Maintenance Organizations
Prepaid Group Practice see Group Practice, Prepaid
Preparatory Manipulation, Obstetric see Methods WQ 415–430 under Delivery
Prepayment Medical Plans see Insurance, Health
Preprosthetic Oral Surgery see Surgery, Oral, Preprosthetic
Prepuce see Penis
Presbyopia WW 300
Presbytis see Cercopithecidae
Prescription Fees QV 736
Prescription Insurance see Insurance, Pharmaceutical Services
Prescriptions, Drug
    Dental WU 166
    Formularies QV 740
    Pharmacopoeias QV 738
    Veterinary SF 916.5
    Writing QV 748
Prescriptions, Non–Drug
    For specific subjects, with the subject, e.g.,
      Hearing aids WV 274
Presentation, Breech see Breech Presentation
Presentation, Fetal see Labor Presentation
Presentation (Obstetrics) see Labor Presentation
Preservation, Biological QH 324
    Blood see Blood Preservation WH 460, etc.
    Dead bodies see Embalming WA 844
    Drugs see Drug Storage QV 754, etc.
    Food see Food Preservation WA 710
    Organs see Tissue Preservation WO 665, etc.
Preservation, Food see Food Preservation
Preservatives, Pharmaceutical QV 820
Pressoreceptors WL 102.9
Pressure
    Therapeutic use WB 890
    See also Atmospheric pressure WD 710, etc.;
      Blood Pressure WG 106, etc.; Intracranial
      Pressure WL 102, etc.; Intraocular
      Pressure WW 103, etc.
Pressure Sore see Decubitus Ulcer
Pressure Ulcer see Decubitus Ulcer

Prevalence Studies see Cross–Sectional Studies
Prevention of accidents see Accident Prevention
Prevention of Infectious Diseases see Communicable Disease Control; names of specific diseases
Prevention, Primary see Primary Prevention
Preventive Dentistry WU 113–113.7
Preventive Health Services WA 108
    See also Immunization QW 800–815, etc.
Preventive Inoculation see Immunization
Preventive Medicine WA 108–245
Preventive Psychiatry WM 31.5
Priapism WJ 790
Primaquine QV 258
Primary Care Physicians see Physicians, Family
Primary Health Care W 84.6
Primary Nursing Care WY 101
Primary Prevention WA 108–245
    Of particular conditions, by subject
Primates QL 737.P9–737.P968
    As laboratory animals QY 60.P7
    Diseases SF 997.5.P7
    Human emphasis, in NLM schedules, by subject
Printers' Marks Z 235–236
Printing Z 116–264.5
Prinzmetal's Angina see Angina Pectoris, Variant
Prion Diseases WL 300
Prion Proteins see Prions
Prions QU 55
Priorities, Health see Health Priorities
Prisoners
    Human experimentation QV 20.5
      In special areas, by subject
    Psychology of prisoners of war BF 727.P7
    Reform of HV 9261–9430.7
    Special topics, by subject, e.g., Psychotherapy of Prisoners WM 420
Prisoner's Dilemma see Game Theory
Prisons HV 8301–9025
    Hygiene and medical service HV 8833–8844
    Psychiatric services HV 8841
    Sex in prisons HV 8836
Privacy Act see Civil Rights
Privacy of Space see Personal Space
Private Nursing see Nursing, Private Duty
Private Practice W 89
    By country WB 50
    Nursing see Nursing, Private Duty WY 127
    Textbooks for WB 100
Privatization
    In special fields, by subject, e.g. Mental Health Services WM 30, etc.
Privileged Communication see Confidentiality
PRL–Secreting Pituitary Adenoma see Prolactinoma
PRO Professional Review Organizations see Professional Review Organizations
Probabilistic Models see Models, Statistical
Probability QA 273–274.8
Probability Learning QA 273.2
    Educational psychology LB 1051
Probability Theory QA 273–274.8
    Special topics, by subject
Problem–Oriented Medical Records see Medical Records, Problem–Oriented

ALWAYS CONSULT MAIN SCHEDULES. USE NUMBER ASSIGNED ONLY WHEN SUBJECT REPRESENTS MAJOR EMPHASIS OF WORK BEING CLASSIFIED

Problem Solving   BF 449
    In infancy & childhood   WS 105.5.D2
Problems
    (Form number 18.2 in any NLM schedule where
    applicable)
Probucol   QU 95
    Organic chemistry   QD 341.P5
Procaine   QV 115
    In veterinary pharmacology   SF 918.P75
    In veterinary anesthesiology   SF 914
Procarbazine
    Antineoplastic agent   QV 269
        Therapeutic use   QZ 267
    Other special topics, by subject
Procolobus see Colobus
Proconvertin see Factor VII
Proctitis   WI 600
Proctocolitis, Hemorrhagic see Colitis, Ulcerative
Proctocolitis, Ulcerative see Colitis, Ulcerative
Proctological Surgery see Surgery   WI 650 under
    Rectum
Proctology see Colon and Rectal Surgery (Specialty)
Proctoscopy   WI 620
Proctosigmoidoscopy see Sigmoidoscopy
Prodrugs   QV 785
Product Labeling   WA 250
    Of specific products, by subject
    See also Drug Labeling   QV 835
Product Labeling, Drug see Drug Labeling
Product Surveillance, Postmarketing
    Of specific product, with the product
Productivity see Efficiency
Proenzymes see Enzyme Precursors
Proerythroblasts see Erythroblasts
Professional Competence   W 21
    Dentists   WU 21
    Nurses   WY 16
    Pharmacists   QV 21
    As an educational measurement
        Works about (Form number 18 in any NLM
        schedule where applicable)
        Actual tests (Form number 18.2 in any NLM
        schedule where applicable)
Professional Corporations   W 87
Professional Impairment
    Medicine   W 21
    For general impairment in other specialties, class
    in the number for the profession where
    applicable
Professional Liability see Liability, Legal
Professional-Patient Relations
    Allied health personnel   W 21.5
    Hospital personnel   WX 159
    Particular specialty, with the specialty
    See also specific professional relationships with
    the patient, e.g. Physician-Patient Relations
    W 62, etc.
Professional Practice
    Medicine as a career   W 21
    Types of professional practice   W 87
    See also names of specialties in medicine and
    allied fields, e.g., Nursing   WY 16; form
    number 21 in any other NLM schedule where

applicable
Professional Review Organizations   W 84
    By specialty, in the number for the profession,
    e.g.,   QV 21
Professional Staff Committees
    In schools
        (Form number 19-20 in any NLM schedule
        where applicable)
    In hospitals   WX 159
Professional Standards Review Organizations see
    Professional Review Organizations
Professions see Names of Professions, e.g., Nursing
Profibrinolysin see Plasminogen
Proflavine
    As a local anti-infective agent   QV 220
Progenitor Cells see Stem Cells
Progenitor Cells, Hematopoietic see Hematopoietic
    Stem Cells
Progestational Hormones   WP 530
Progesterone   WP 530
Progesterone Receptors see Receptors, Progesterone
Progestin Receptors see Receptors, Progesterone
Progestins see Progestational Hormones
Progestogens see Progestational Hormones
Proglumide Receptors see Receptors,
    Cholecystokinin
Prognathism   WU 440
Prognosis   WB 142
    See also names of particular diseases
Prognostic Nutritional Index (PNI) see Nutrition
    Assessment
Program Evaluation
    Health Services   W 84
    Other special topics, by subject being evaluated
Program Evaluation, Nursing see Nursing
    Evaluation Research
Programmable Implantable Insulin Pump see Insulin
    Infusion Systems
Programmable Implantable Medication Systems see
    Infusion Pumps, Implantable
Programmed Instruction   LB 1028.5-1028.7
    (Form number 18.2 in any NLM schedule where
    applicable)
Programmed Instruction, Computerized see
    Computer-Assisted Instruction
Programmed Learning see Programmed Instruction
Programming, Linear   T 57.74-57.79
    Special topics, by subject
Progressive Lenticular Degeneration see
    Hepatolenticular Degeneration
Progressive Lipodystrophy see Lipodystrophy
Progressive Muscular Atrophy see Muscular
    Atrophy, Spinal
Progressive Muscular Dystrophy see Muscular
    Dystrophy
Progressive Patient Care   W 84.7-84.8
    Of hospital patients   WX 162-162.5
Proinsulin   WK 820
Projection   WM 193.5.P7
    In adolescence   WS 463
    In infancy & childhood   WS 350.8.D3
Projections and Predictions see Forecasting
Projective Techniques   WM 145.5.P8

In adolescence   WS 462
In infancy & childhood   WS 105.5.E8
See also Psychological Tests   BF 176
Prokaryotic Cells   QW 51
Prolactin   WK 515
Veterinary medicine   SF 768.3
Prolactin-Producing Pituitary Adenoma see
Prolactinoma
Prolactinoma   WK 585
Prolapsed Disk see Intervertebral Disk Displacement
Proliferative Phase see Menstrual Cycle
Proline   QU 60
Prolongation of life see Longevity; Rejuvenation
Prolonged-Action Preparations see Delayed-Action
Preparations
Promethium   WN 420
Nuclear physics   QC 796.P5
See also special topics under Radioisotopes
Promoter (Genetics) see Promoter Regions
(Genetics)
Promoter Regions (Genetics)   QH 450.2
Promotion of Health see Health Promotion
Promyelocytes see Granulocytes
Pronormoblasts see Erythroblasts
PROPAC see Prospective Payment Assessment
Commission
Propafenone   QV 150
Propaganda   HM 263
Propamidine see Antiprotozoal Agents
Propanidid   QV 81
Propanol see Alcohol, Propyl
Propanolamines
Organic chemistry   QD 305.A4
Pharmacology   QV 82
Used for specific purposes, by subject, e.g., as
a betablocker   QV 132
Properdin   WH 400
Clinical analysis   QY 455
Complement action   QW 680
In other biological processes, by subject
Prophage Integration see Lysogeny
Propheniramine see Pheniramine
Prophenpyridamine see Pheniramine
Prophylactic Immunization see Vaccination
Prophylaxis see Dental Prophylaxis; diseases for
which prevention and control measures are
prescribed
Propionates   QU 98
Propionibacteriaceae   QW 120
Propionibacterium   QW 120
Propionic Acids   QU 98
Propiophenones
Organic chemistry   QD 341.K2
Pharmacology   QV 150
Propolis
Used for special purposes, by subject
Propranolol   QV 132
Proprioception   WE 103
Proptosis see Exophthalmos
Propyl Gallate
As a carcinogen   QZ 202
Prosencephalon see Embryology   WL 300 under
Brain

Prosimii see Strepsirhini
Prospective Payment Assessment Commission
Prospective Payment System
Hospitals   WX 157
Prospective Pricing see Prospective Payment System
Prospective Reimbursement see Prospective
Payment System
Prospective Studies
In epidemiology   WA 105
Special topics, by subject
Prostacyclins see Epoprostenol
Prostaglandin Antagonists   QU 90
Prostaglandin-Endoperoxide Synthase   QU 140
Prostaglandin Endoperoxides   QU 90
Prostaglandin E1 see Alprostadil
Prostaglandin F2 see Dinoprost
Prostaglandin F2alpha see Dinoprost
Prostaglandin Inhibitors see Prostaglandin
Antagonists
Prostaglandin Receptors see Receptors,
Prostaglandin
Prostaglandin Synthesis Antagonists see
Anti-Inflammatory Agents, Non-Steroidal
Prostaglandins   QU 90
Prostaglandins A   QU 90
Prostaglandins E   QU 90
Prostaglandins F   QU 90
Prostaglandins I see Epoprostenol
Prostaglandins I2 see Epoprostenol
Prostaglandins X see Epoprostenol
Prostanoic Acids   QU 90
Prostate   WJ 750
Prostatectomy   WJ 768
Prostatectomy, Transurethral see Prostatectomy
Prostatic Diseases   WJ 752
Prostatic Hyperplasia see Prostatic Hypertrophy
Prostatic Hypertrophy   WJ 752
Prostatic Hypertrophy, Benign see Prostatic
Hypertrophy
Prostatic Neoplasms   WJ 752
Prostatitis   WJ 752
Prosthesis   WE 172
Blood vessels see Blood Vessel Prosthesis   WG
170
Cleft palate see Palatal Obturators   WV 440
Dental see Dental Prosthesis   WU 500-530
Heart valve see Heart Valve Prosthesis   WG
169
Joint see Joint Prosthesis   WE 312
Mandibular see Mandibular Prosthesis   WU 600
Maxillofacial see Maxillofacial Prosthesis   WU
600
Ocular see Eye, Artificial   WW 358; Lenses,
Intraocular   WW 358
Periodontal see Periodontal Prosthesis   WU 240
Plastic surgery   WO 640
Veterinary   SF 901
Prosthesis, Dental see Dental Prosthesis
Prosthesis Design   WE 172
Localized, by site
Prosthesis Failure
Equipment failure (General)   W 26
Of particular prosthesis, with the prosthesis

Prosthesis Loosening see Prosthesis Failure
Prosthodontics   WU 500
    See also Dental Prosthesis   WU 500–530
Prostitution   HQ 101–440.7
Protactinium   WN 420
    Nuclear physics   QC 796.P2
    See also special topics under Radioisotopes
Protease Antagonists see Protease Inhibitors
Protease Inhibitors   QU 136
Proteases see Peptide Hydrolases
Protective Clothing   WA 260
    In industry   WA 485
Protective Devices   WA 260
    In hospitals   WX 185
    In industry   WA 485
      Aviation   WD 740
      Ophthalmology   WW 505
      Professions   WA 487
    In ophthalmology (General)   WW 113
    Respiratory   WF 26
    For particular parts of the body (when not covered by above) use form number 26 in any schedule where applicable
Protectives see Dermatologic Agents; Radiation–Protective Agents
Protein A see Staphylococcal Protein A
Protein Binding   QU 55
Protein–Bound Iodine Test   WK 202
Protein C
    As an anticoagulant   QV 193
Protein C Inhibitor   QU 136
Protein–Calorie Malnutrition see Protein–Energy Malnutrition
Protein Conformation   QU 55
Protein Deficiency   WD 105
    Veterinary   SF 855.P76
Protein Denaturation   QU 55
Protein–Energy Malnutrition   WD 105
Protein Engineering   TP 248.65.P76
Protein–Glutamine gamma–Glutamyltransferase   WH 310
    Clinical examination   QY 410
    Pharmacology   QV 195
Protein Hydrolysates   QU 55
Protein–Losing Enteropathies   WI 400
Protein Methylases see Protein Methyltransferases
Protein Methyltransferases   QU 141
Protein Phosphatase see Phosphoprotein Phosphatase
Protein Processing, Post–Translational   QH 450.6
Protein Sensitization see Hypersensitivity
Protein Structure, Primary see Amino Acid Sequence
Protein Structure, Quaternary see Protein Conformation
Proteinase Inhibitors see Protease Inhibitors
Proteins   QU 55
    Antigens and antibodies   QW 570–680
    Bacterial see Bacterial Proteins   QW 52
    Blood see Blood Proteins   QY 455, etc.
    Carrier see Carrier Proteins   QU 55
    Cerebrospinal fluid see Cerebrospinal Fluid Proteins   WL 203, etc.
    Dietary see Dietary Proteins   QU 55, etc.
    Eye see Eye Proteins   WW 101
    Milk see Milk Proteins   WA 716, etc.
    Muscle see Muscle Proteins   WE 500
    Myeloma see Myeloma Proteins   WH 540
    Neoplasm see Neoplasm Proteins   QZ 200
    Nerve tissue see Nerve Tissue Proteins   WL 104
    Plant see Plant Proteins   QK 898.P8
    Viral see Viral Proteins   QW 160
    With drug action on a particular system in   QV
    Localized elsewhere, by site
    See also names of other specific proteins
Proteins, Acute Phase see Acute Phase Proteins
Proteinuria   WJ 343
Proteinuria–Edema–Hypertension Gestosis see Gestosis, EPH
Proteoglycans   QU 55
Proteolytic Enzymes see Peptide Hydrolases
Protestantism see Christianity
Proteus   QW 138.5.P7
Prothrombin   WH 310
    Clinical analysis   QY 410
Prothrombin Time   QY 410
Protirelin   WK 515
Proto–Oncogenes   QZ 202
Protocol–Directed Therapy, Computer–Assisted see Therapy, Computer–Assisted
Protocols, Clinical see Clinical Protocols
Protoheme see Heme
Proton–Induced X–Ray Emission Spectrometry see Spectrometry, X–Ray Emission
Proton–Translocating ATPase Complex see H(+)–Transporting ATP Synthase
Protons   WN 415–420
    In health physics   WN 110
    In nuclear physics (General)   QC 793.5.P72–793.5.P729
Protoplasts
    Bacteria   QW 51
    Plants   QK 725
Protoporphyrins
    General   QU 110
    Special types, by system in which produced
Protozoa   QX 50–151
Protozoan Infections   WC 700–770
    Veterinary   SF 780.6
Protracted Pregnancy see Pregnancy, Prolonged
Proverbs see Aphorisms and Proverbs
Proverbs, Medical see Aphorisms and Proverbs
Provocation Tests, Bronchial see Bronchial Provocation Tests
Provocation Tests, Nasal see Nasal Provocation Tests
Prurigo   WR 282
Pruritus   WR 282
Pruritus Ani   WI 600
Pruritus Vulvae   WP 200
Psammomys see Gerbillinae
Pseudarthrosis   WE 180
Pseudobulbar Paralysis see Paralysis
Pseudoephedrine see Ephedrine
Pseudoglobulins see Serum Globulins

Pseudohypoparathyroidism   WD 200.5.C2
  Inborn error   WD 205.5.M3
Pseudomonadaceae   QW 131
Pseudomonas   QW 131
Pseudomonas aeruginosa   QW 131
Pseudomonas fluorescens   QW 131
Pseudomonas Infections   WC 330
Pseudoneurotic Schizophrenia see Schizotypal
  Personality Disorder
Pseudonyms see Anonyms and Pseudonyms
Pseudopelade see Alopecia
Pseudopolyarthritis, Rhizomelic see Polymyalgia
  Rheumatica
Pseudopsychopathic Schizophrenia see Schizotypal
  Personality Disorder
Pseudorabies   SF 809.A94
Pseudorabies Virus see Herpesvirus 1, Suid
Pseudosclerosis see Hepatolenticular Degeneration
Pseudotuberculosis Infections, Yersinia see Yersinia
  pseudotuberculosis Infections
Pseudotuberculosis, Pasteurella see Yersinia
  pseudotuberculosis Infections
Pseudotumor Cerebri   WL 348
Psilocybine   QV 77.7
  Indian ritual use   E 98.R3
Psilosis see Celiac Disease
Psittacosis see Ornithosis
Psittacosis-Lymphogranuloma Group see Chlamydia
Psoralen Ultraviolet A Therapy see PUVA Therapy
Psoralens   QV 60
  As sunscreens   QV 63
Psoriasis   WR 205
PSRO see Professional Review Organizations
Psychasthenia see Neurasthenia
Psychedelic Agents see Hallucinogens
Psychiatric Aides   WY 160
Psychiatric Aspects of Aerospace Medicine see
  Aerospace Medicine
Psychiatric Department, Hospital   WM 27–28
  In a children's hospital   WS 27–28
Psychiatric Nursing   WY 160
  Education   WY 18–18.5
Psychiatric Social Work see Social Work,
  Psychiatric
Psychiatric Status Rating Scales   WM 141
Psychiatrist–Patient Relations see Physician–Patient
  Relations
Psychiatrists see Biography   WZ 112.5.P6, etc., and
  Directories   WM 22 under Psychiatry
Psychiatry   WM
  Adolescents see Adolescent Psychiatry   WS 463
  Biography
    Collective   WZ 112.5.P6
    Individual   WZ 100
  Case studies   WM 40–49
    In mental retardation   WM 302
  Children see Child Psychiatry   WS 350–350.8
  Counseling   WM 55, etc.
  Directories   WM 22
  Experimental   WM 20
    Techniques   WM 25
  Geriatric see Geriatric Psychiatry   WT 150
  Insurance see Insurance, Psychiatric   W 270,

  etc.
  Legislation & jurisprudence   WM 32–33
  Medicolegal see Forensic Psychiatry   W 740
  Nursing see Psychiatric Nursing   WY 160
  Office management   WM 30
  Old age   WT 150
  Preventive see Community Psychiatry   WM
    31.5, etc.
  Social see Psychiatry, Community   WM
    30.6–31.5; Socioenvironmental Therapy   WM
    428
  See also Forensic Psychiatry   W 740
Psychiatry, Biological see Biological Psychiatry
Psychiatry, Community see Community Psychiatry
Psychiatry, Geriatric see Geriatric Psychiatry
Psychiatry, Military see Military Psychiatry
Psychic Energizers see Antidepressive Agents
Psychic Maladjustment see Personality Disorders
Psychical Research see Parapsychology
Psychoacoustics   WV 270
Psychoactive Agents see Psychotropic Drugs
Psychoanalysis   WM 460–460.5
  In adolescence   WS 463
  In infancy & childhood   WS 350.5
  In old age   WT 150
Psychoanalytic Interpretation   WM 460.7
  In adolescence   WS 463
  In infancy & childhood   WS 350.5
  In old age   WT 150
  Of art and literature   WM 49
  Of famous people from their works   WZ 313
Psychoanalytic Theory   WM 460
Psychoanalytic Therapy   WM 460.6
  In adolescence   WS 463
  In infancy & childhood   WS 350.2
Psychodrama   WM 430.5.P8
  In infancy & childhood   WS 350.2
Psychogenetics see Genetics, Behavioral
Psychogeriatrics see Geriatric Psychiatry
Psychoimmunology see Psychoneuroimmunology
Psycholinguistics   BF 455–463
  In infancy & childhood   WS 105.5.C8
  Language development   LB 1139.L3
Psychological aspects of Aerospace Medicine see
  Aerospace Medicine
Psychological Tests   BF 176
  In infancy & childhood   WS 105.5.E8
  In psychiatry   WM 145
  Projective Techniques   WM 145.5.P8
  Intelligence Tests   BF 431–433
Psychological Theory   BF 38–64
Psychological Warfare   UB 275–277
Psychology   BF
  Abnormal   WM
  Adolescent see Adolescent Psychology   WS 462
  As a career   BF 75–76
  Biography   WZ 100
  Biography, Collective   BF 109
  Child see Child Psychology   WS 105
  Counseling   WM 55
  Criminal see Criminal Psychology   HV
    6080–6113
  Crowd   HM 281–283

Directories   BF 30
Geriatric   WT 145
In aviation medicine   WD 730
In space medicine   WD 754
Mass   HM 281-283
Nursing   WY 87
Pathological see Psychopathology   WM, etc.
Phenomenological   BF 204.5
Physiological see Psychophysiology   WL 103
Sex   BF 692
War see Psychology, Military   U 22.3;
    Psychological Warfare   UB 275-277
Psychology, Applied   BF 636-637
Psychology, Clinical   WM 105
    In infancy & childhood   WS 105
Psychology, Comparative
    Animals (primarily)   QL 751
    Human   BF 660-685
Psychology, Criminal see Criminal Psychology
Psychology, Educational   LB 1051-1091
Psychology, Experimental   BF 181-198.7
    In infancy & childhood   WS 105
    Laboratory manuals   BF 79
    Works about research   BF 76.5
Psychology, Industrial   HF 5548.8
    Mental health of working people   WA 495
Psychology, Medical   WB 104
    Special topics, by subject
Psychology, Military   U 22.3
Psychology, Pastoral see Pastoral Care
Psychology, Physiological see Psychophysiology
Psychology, Schizophrenic see Schizophrenic
    Psychology
Psychology, Social   HM 251-291
    In adolescence   WS 462
    In infancy & childhood   WS 105
Psychometrics   BF 39
Psychomotor Disorders   WM 197
    Of the retarded child   WS 107.5.P7
    See also names of specific disorders
Psychomotor Performance   WE 104
Psychoneuroimmunology   WL 103.7
Psychoneuroses see Neuroses
Psychopathic Personality see Antisocial Personality
    Disorder
Psychopathology   WM
    In infancy & childhood   WS 350
Psychopharmaceuticals see Psychotropic Drugs
Psychopharmacology   QV 77
    Drug therapy of mental disorders   WM 402
Psychophysics   WL 702
Psychophysiologic Disorders   WM 90
    In infancy & childhood   WM 90
    Sex disorders   WM 611
Psychophysiology   WL 103
Psychoses see Psychotic Disorders
Psychoses, Alcoholic   WM 274
Psychoses, Drug see Psychoses, Substance-Induced
Psychoses, Manic Depressive see Bipolar Disorder
Psychoses, Organic see Organic Mental Disorders,
    Psychotic
Psychoses, Paranoid see Paranoid Disorders
Psychoses, Presenile see Dementia, Presenile

Psychoses, Senile see Dementia, Senile
Psychoses, Substance-Induced   WM 220
Psychoses, Toxic see Psychoses, Substance-Induced
Psychoses, Traumatic see Psychoses, Organic
Psychosexual Development   BF 692
    In adolescence   WS 462
    In infancy & childhood   WS 105.5.P3
Psychosexual Disorders   WM 611
Psychosexual Dysfunctions   WM 611
Psychosis, Brief Reactive see Psychotic Disorders
Psychosis, Involutional see Depression, Involutional
Psychosis, Manic-Depressive see Bipolar Disorder
Psychosocial Deprivation   HM 291
    Adolescents   WS 462
    Children   WS 105.5.D3
        Psychological aspects   WS 105.5.D3
        Welfare   WA 320
Psychosocial Support Systems see Social Support
Psychosomatic Disorders see Psychophysiologic
    Disorders
Psychosomatic Medicine   WM 90
    Diseases see Psychophysiologic Disorders   WM
    90, etc.
Psychosurgery   WL 370
Psychotherapy   WM 420
    In adolescence   WS 463
    In infancy & childhood   WS 350.2
    In old age   WT 150
Psychotherapy, Brief   WM 420.5.P5
Psychotherapy, Cognitive see Cognitive Therapy
Psychotherapy, Group   WM 430-430.5
    In infancy & childhood   WS 350.2
    See also names of specific types of group therapy,
        e.g., Sensitivity Training Groups   WM
        430.5.S3, etc.
Psychotherapy, Multiple   WM 420.5.P7
Psychotherapy, Rational see Psychotherapy,
    Rational-Emotive
Psychotherapy, Rational-Emotive   WM 420.5.P8
Psychotic Disorders   WM 200-220
    Functional   WM 202
    In adolescence   WS 463
    In infancy & childhood   WS 350-350.8
    Presenile see Dementia, Presenile   WM 220
Psychotomimetic Agents see Hallucinogens
Psychotomimetic Drugs see Hallucinogens
Psychotropic Drugs   QV 77.2-77.9
PTCA see Angioplasty, Transluminal, Percutaneous
    Coronary
PtdIns see Phosphatidylinositols
Pteridines
    In folic acid   QU 188
    Organic chemistry   QD 401
Pterins   QU 110
Pteroylglutamic Acid see Folic Acid
Pteroylpolyglutamic Acids   QU 188
Pterygium   WW 212
Ptomaine Poisoning see Food Poisoining
Ptosis, Eyelid see Blepharoptosis
PTSD see Stress Disorders, Post-Traumatic
Puberty   WS 450
Puberty, Delayed   WS 450
Puberty, Precocious   WS 450

**ALWAYS CONSULT MAIN SCHEDULES. USE NUMBER ASSIGNED ONLY WHEN
SUBJECT REPRESENTS MAJOR EMPHASIS OF WORK BEING CLASSIFIED**

Pubic Bone   WE 750
    Surgery to facilitate delivery   WQ 430
Pubic Symphysis   WE 750
    Surgery   WE 750
        To facilitate delivery   WQ 430
    See also Symphysiotomy   WQ 430
Pubiotomy see Surgery   WQ 430 under Pubic Bone
Public Advocacy see Consumer Advocacy
Public Assistance   HV 687-4630
        For maternal and child welfare (Public health
        aspects)   WA 310-320
        For medicosocial problems of the aged   WT
        30
        See also more specific headings, e.g., Medicaid
        W 250
Public Baths see Baths
Public Carriers see Transportation
Public Health   WA
    As a profession   WA 21
    Statistics   WA 900
        See also Morbidity   WA 900; Vital statistics
        HB, etc.
    Workers see Allied Health Personnel   W 21.5,
    etc.; Health Manpower   W 76
Public Health Administration   WA 525-590
Public Health Dentistry   WU 113
Public Health Nursing   WY 108
    Education   WY 18
    Government (General)   WY 130
    Indian services   WY 130
    See also Military Nursing   WY 130
Public Health Schools see Schools, Public Health
Public Health Surveillance see Population
Surveillance
Public Housing
    Hotels   WA 799, etc.
    Low cost housing   HD 7288.77-7288.78
    Rural   HD 7289
    Sanitary control   WA 795-799
Public Opinion   HM 261
    Specific topics, by subject
Public Policy
    Abortion   HQ 767
    Laetrile   QZ 267
    Other areas, by subject
Public Relations   HM 263
    Specific relations by subject, professions, or
    named group of persons involved
Publishers' Catalogs see Catalogs, Publishers'
Publishing   Z 278-544
    Medical   WZ 345
Puericulture see Child Care
Puerperal Disorders   WQ 500-505
Puerperal Infection   WQ 505
Puerperium   WQ 500-505
Puerto Ricans see Hispanic Americans
Pulex see Fleas
Pulmonary Alveolar Proteinosis   WF 600
Pulmonary Alveoli   WF 600
Pulmonary Artery   WG 595.P8
    See also Blood Supply   WF 600 under Lungs;
    Pulmonary Circulation   WF 600
Pulmonary Circulation   WF 600

Pulmonary Coin Lesion see Coin Lesion, Pulmonary
Pulmonary Diffusing Capacity   WF 141
Pulmonary Disease, Chronic Obstructive see Lung
Diseases, Obstructive
Pulmonary Disease (Specialty)   WF 100
Pulmonary Diseases see Lung Diseases
Pulmonary Edema   WF 600
Pulmonary Embolism   WG 420
Pulmonary Emphysema   WF 648
Pulmonary Fibrosis   WF 600
Pulmonary Function Tests see Respiratory Function
Tests
Pulmonary Gas Exchange   WF 102
    Used for diagnostic aspects   WF 141
Pulmonary Heart Disease   WG 420
Pulmonary Incompetence see Pulmonary Valve
Insufficiency
Pulmonary Medicine see Pulmonary Disease
(Specialty)
Pulmonary Neoplasms see Lung Neoplasms
Pulmonary Nodule, Solitary see Coin Lesion,
Pulmonary
Pulmonary Regurgitation see Pulmonary Valve
Insufficiency
Pulmonary Stenosis see Pulmonary Valve Stenosis
Pulmonary Surfactants   WF 600
Pulmonary Tuberculosis see Tuberculosis,
Pulmonary
Pulmonary Valve   WG 269
Pulmonary Valve Incompetence see Pulmonary
Valve Insufficiency
Pulmonary Valve Insufficiency   WG 269
Pulmonary Valve Stenosis   WG 269
Pulmonary Veins   WG 625.P8
    See also Blood Supply   WF 600 under Lungs;
    Pulmonary Circulation   WF 600
Pulmonology see Pulmonary Disease (Specialty)
Pulp see Dental Pulp
Pulp Canal see Dental Pulp Cavity
Pulp Capping see Dental Pulp Capping
Pulp Chamber see Dental Pulp Cavity
Pulpitis   WU 230
Pulpotomy   WU 230
Pulsatile Flow   WG 106
Pulse
    Cardiovascular diagnosis   WG 141
    General diagnosis   WB 282
    Hemodynamics   WG 106
Pulse Oximetry see Oximetry
Pulse Radiolysis   QD 643.P84
Pulsus Alternans see Arrhythmia
Pulverization see Drug Compounding; Powders
Pumping, Intra-Aortic Balloon see Intra-Aortic
Balloon Pumping
Pumps, Heart-Assist see Heart-Assist Devices
Pumps, Infusion see Infusion Pumps
Punched-Card Systems   Z 695.92
    Special topics, by subject
Puncture Biopsy see Biopsy, Needle
Puncture Fluids see Body Fluids; Diagnosis,
Laboratory; Exudates and Transudates
Punctures   WB 373-377
    Cisternal   WB 377

ALWAYS CONSULT MAIN SCHEDULES. USE NUMBER ASSIGNED ONLY WHEN
SUBJECT REPRESENTS MAJOR EMPHASIS OF WORK BEING CLASSIFIED

Sternal   WH 380
Ventricular   WB 377
See also Amniocentesis   WQ 209; Biopsy,
  Needle   WB 379, etc.; Spinal Puncture   WB
  377, etc.
Punishment
In adolescence   WS 462-463
In infancy & childhood   WS 105.5.C3
Conditioned response   BF 319.5.P8
Theory of (Penology)   K 5103
Pupil   WW 240
Dilatation   WW 240
See also Dilatation, Pathologic   WW 240, etc.
Dilators   QV 134
Pupillary Reflex see Reflex, Pupillary
Puppets see Play and Playthings
Purchasing, Hospital   WX 157
Pure Food Laws see Food and drug laws   WA
  697 under Legislation, Drug
Pure Red-Cell Aplasia see Red-Cell Aplasia, Pure
Purgatives see Cathartics
Purification see Environment, Controlled;
  Sterilization
Purine-Nucleoside Phosphorylase   QU 141
Purine Nucleosides   QU 57
Pharmacology   QV 185
Purine-Pyrimidine Metabolism, Inborn Errors
  WD 205.5.P8
See also Gout   WE 350
Purine Receptors see Receptors, Purinergic
Purinergic Receptors see Receptors, Purinergic
Purines
Constituents of nucleic acids   QU 58
Organic chemistry   QD 401
Stimulants   QV 107
Purkinje Cells   WL 320
Purple Membrane see Bacteriorhodopsin
Purpura   WH 314-320
Purpura, Thrombocytopenic   WH 315
Purpura, Thrombopenic see Purpura,
  Thrombocytopenic
Pursuit, Saccadic see Saccades
Pus see Suppuration
Pustulants see Irritants
Pustular Dermatosis, Subcorneal see Skin Diseases,
  Vesiculobullous
Pustular Psoriasis of Palms and Soles see Psoriasis
Pustulosis of Palms and Soles see Psoriasis
Pustulosis Palmaris et Plantaris see Psoriasis
PUVA Therapy   WB 480
PVP-Iodine see Povidone-Iodine
Pyelitis   WJ 351
Pyelography see Urography
Pyelonephritis   WJ 351
Pyelonephritis, Acute Necrotizing see Kidney
  Papillary Necrosis
Pyelophlebitis see Phlebitis
Pyemia see Septicemia
Pygathrix see Cercopithecidae
Pyknolepsy see Epilepsy, Absence
Pyloric Antrum   WI 387
Pyloric Stenosis   WI 387
Pylorospasm see Spasm

Pylorus   WI 387
Pyoctanium aureum see Benzophenoneidum
Pyoderma   WR 220
Pyonephrosis see Pyelonephritis
Pyopneumothorax see Pneumothorax
Pyorrhea Alveolaris see Periodontal Diseases
Pyothorax see Empyema
Pyramidal Tracts   WL 400
Pyrans   QV 138.C1
Organic chemistry   QD 405
Pyrazinopyrimidines see Pteridines
Pyrazoles
Organic chemistry   QD 401
Pharmacology   QV 95
Pyrethrum
As an insecticidal plant   SB 292.P8
Public health aspects   WA 240
Pyretotherapy see Hyperthermia, Induced
Pyrexia see Fever
Pyridazines   QV 150
As antirheumatoid agents   QV 95
Organic chemistry   QD 401
Pyridines
Enzyme inhibitors   QU 143
Organic chemistry   QD 401
Pyridinium Compounds
Enzymology   QU 135
Organic chemistry   QD 401
Pyridinones see Pyridones
Pyridones
As anti-arteriosclerosis agents   QV 150
Organic chemistry   QD 401
Pyridoxal   QU 195
Pyridoxine   QU 195
Pyridoxine Deficiency   WD 120
Pyrimethamine   QV 256
Pyrimidines
Constituents of nucleic acids   QU 58
Organic chemistry   QD 401
Pyrocatechols see Catechols
Pyrogallol   QV 223
Pyrogens
As substances causing fever   WB 152
Special topics, by subject
Pyromania see Firesetting Behavior
Pyrophosphatases   QU 136
Pyrophosphates see Diphosphates
Pyrosis see Heartburn
Pyrroles
As antirheumatoid agents   QV 95
In heme and porphyrin chemistry   WH 190
Organic chemistry   QD 401
Pyrrolidines
As antineoplastic agents   QV 269
Organic chemistry   QD 401
Pyruvaldehyde   QU 98
Pyruvate Oxidase   QU 140
Pyruvates   QU 98
Organic chemistry
Aliphatic compounds   QD 305.A2
Pyuria   WJ 151
In urine analysis   QY 185

ALWAYS CONSULT MAIN SCHEDULES. USE NUMBER ASSIGNED ONLY WHEN
SUBJECT REPRESENTS MAJOR EMPHASIS OF WORK BEING CLASSIFIED

Q

Q Fever   WC 625
Quackery   WZ 310
   Supposed antineoplastic agents   QV 269
Quadrigeminal Plate see Corpora Quadrigemina
Quadriplegia   WL 346
   Veterinary   SF 895
Quality Assessment, Health Care see Quality
   Assurance, Health Care
Quality Assurance, Health Care   W 84
   Special topics, by subject
Quality Circles see Management Quality Circles
Quality Control
   Drugs   QV 771
     Public health aspects   WA 730
   Food (Flavor, texture, appearance)   TP 372.5
     Public health aspects   WA 695–722
   Health services   W 84
   Hospitals   WX 153
     See also Facility Regulation and Control   WX 153
   Nursing   WY 16
   Psychiatry   WM 30
   Sanitation   WA 672
   Other particular products or procedures, by subject
   Of other specialty fields, in the number for the profession, e.g. Dentistry   WU 21
Quality of Health Care
   General   W 84
   Hospitals   WX 153
   Private practice   WB 50
   Public health   WA 525–546
Quality of Life   WA 30
   Specific topics, by subject
Quantum Theory   QC 173.96–174.52
Quarantine   WA 230
   Law   WA 32–33
   Port and maritime   WA 234
   Veterinary medicine   SF 740
     By locality   SF 621–723
Quarantine Hospitals see Hospitals, Special
Quartz
   Toxicology   QV 610
Questionnaires
   Research (Form number 20 or 20.5 in any NLM schedule where applicable)
   Statistical methods in psychology   BF 39
   Surveys
     Health   WA 900
     Nutrition   QU 146
   Special topics, by subject
Queuing Theory see Systems Theory
Quick Test see Prothrombin Time
Quinacrine   QV 258
Quinalbarbitone see Secobarbital
Quinazolines
   As antihypertensive agents   QV 150
   Organic chemistry   QD 401
Quincke's Edema see Angioneurotic Edema
Quinidine   QV 155
Quinine   QV 257

Quinolines
   As anti–infective agents   QV 250
   Organic chemistry   QD 401
Quinolinic Acids
   Biochemistry   QU 65
   Organic chemistry   QD 401
Quinolinium Compounds
   As anti–infective agents   QV 250
   Organic chemitry   QD 401
Quinolinols see Hydroxyquinolines
Quinolinones see Quinolones
Quinolone Anti–Infective Agents see Anti–Infective Agents, Quinolone
Quinolones   QV 250
Quinones
   Organic chemistry   QD 341.Q4
Quinoxalines
   As anti–infective agents   QV 250
   Organic chemistry   QD 401
Quintan Fever see Trench Fever
Quinuclidines
   As autonomic drugs (general)   QV 120
   Organic chemistry   QD 401
Quokkas see Kangaroos

R

R Factors   QW 51
R Plasmids see R Factors
Rabbit Aorta Contracting Substance see Thromboxane A2
Rabbit Fever see Tularemia
Rabbits
   As laboratory animals   QY 60.L3
   Culture   SF 451–455
   Diseases (Domestic and Wild)   SF 997.5.R2
   Wild   QL 737.L32
Rabies   WC 550
   Veterinary   SF 797
Rabies Vaccine   WC 550
Rabies Virus   QW 168.5.R2
Raccoon Dogs see Carnivora
Race see Racial Stocks
Race Psychology see Ethnopsychology
Race Relations   HT 1503–1595
   Adolescent   WS 462
   Children   WS 105.5.S6
   Discrimination (non–MeSH usage)
     In education   LC 212–212.73
     In employment   HD 4903–4903.5
     In housing   HD 7288.75–7288.76
     In particular countries (General) by country D, E, or F schedules
Races, Diseases of see Diseases   WB 720 under Ethnic Groups
Rachitis see Rickets
Racial Stocks   GN 537–673
   Miscegenation   GN 254
   See also special topics under Ethnic Groups
Radar   TK 6573–6595
   Special topics, by subject
Rademacherism see Alternative Medicine
Radial Keratotomy see Keratotomy, Radial

ALWAYS CONSULT MAIN SCHEDULES. USE NUMBER ASSIGNED ONLY WHEN SUBJECT REPRESENTS MAJOR EMPHASIS OF WORK BEING CLASSIFIED

Radiant Warmers, Infant see Incubators, Infant
Radiation   WN
    As a cause of disease (Pathology)   QZ 57
    Physics (General)   QC 474–496.9
Radiation Biology see Radiobiology
Radiation Counters see Instrumentation   WN 150
    under Technology, Radiologic; Scintillation
    Counting; Whole–Body Counting
Radiation Dosage
    Measurement, tolerance, safety measures   WN
    665
    See also Radiotherapy Dosage   WN 250, etc.
Radiation Effects   WN 610–630
    See also names of organs, organisms, chemicals,
    drugs, or processes affected
Radiation Genetics   WN
    Animal   WN 620
    General works   WN 610
    Human   WN 620
    Plant   WN 630
Radiation–Induced Dermatitis see Radiodermatitis
Radiation Injuries   WN 610–650
    In industry   WA 470
    Prevention & control   WN 650
    Veterinary   SF 757.8
    See also Adverse effects   WN 200 under
    Radiography; Adverse effects   WN 250 under
    Radiotherapy; Adverse Effects   WN 300
    under Radium
Radiation Injuries, Experimental   WN 620
Radiation, Ionizing
    General works   WN 105
Radiation Monitoring   WN 650
Radiation, Non–Ionizing
    Diseases caused by   WD 605
    Diagnostic use   WB 288
    General medical use   WB 117
    General physiological effects   QT 162.U4
    Therapeutic use   WB 480
    Used for special purposes, by subject
    See also names of specific forms of non–ionizing
    radiation, e.g., Light   WB 117, etc.
Radiation Protection   WN 650
    In industry   WA 470
    See also Radioactive Waste   WA 788
Radiation–Protective Agents   WN 650
Radiation Sensitivity see Radiation Tolerance
Radiation–Sensitizing Agents   WN 610
Radiation Sickness see Radiation Injuries
Radiation Syndrome see Radiation Injuries
Radiation Therapy, Computer–Assisted see
    Radiotherapy, Computer–Assisted
Radiation Tolerance   WN 650
    In treating particular conditions, with the
    condition, e.g., in the radiotherapy of neoplasms
    QZ 269
Radiation, Visible see Light
Radiation, Whole–Body see Whole–Body Irradiation
Radicular Cyst   WU 240
Radiculitis   WL 400
Radiesthesia   WB 960
Radio
    In general education   LB 1044.5–1044.6

In special fields of education
    (Form number 18.2 in any NLM schedule
    where applicable)
    Influence on adolescent   WS 462
    Influence on child   WS 105.5.E9
    Special topics, by subject
Radio–Hippuran see Iodohippuric Acid
Radio Waves   QC 676–678.6
    Adverse effects (General)   WD 605
    General physiological effects   QT 162.U4
Radioactive Air Pollutants see Air Pollutants,
    Radioactive
Radioactive Fallout   WN 610–650
Radioactive Pollutants   WN 615
    Environmental
        Industrial   WA 788
        Atomic bomb   WN 610–650
    In industry   WA 470
        See also Radioactive Waste   WA 788; names
    of other types of pollutants
Radioactive Pollution see Air Pollution, Radioactive;
    Food Contamination, Radioactive; Water
    Pollution, Radioactive; also various types of
    pollutants, e.g., Radioactive Fallout
Radioactive Substances see Radium; Radioisotopes;
    Radioactive Pollutants; Air Pollutants,
    Radioactive; Radiation, Ionizing   WN 100, etc.
    and names of specific substances, e.g., Gold
    Colloid, Radioactive
Radioactive Tracers   WN 415–450
Radioactive Waste   WA 788
Radioactivity   WN 415–450
    Safety measures   WN 650
        In industry
            Waste material   WA 788
            Workers   WA 470
Radioallergosorbent Test   QW 525.5.R15
Radioautography see Autoradiography
Radiobiology   WN 600
Radiochemistry   QD 601–655
Radiocinematography see Cineradiography
Radiodermatitis   WR 160
Radiographic Film see X–Ray Film
Radiographic Image Enhancement   WN 160
    Localized, by site
Radiographic Intensifying Screens see X–Ray
    Intensifying Screens
Radiographic Magnification   WN 160
    Localized, by site
Radiography   WN 180–240
    Adverse effects   WN 200
    In infancy & childhood   WN 240
    Instrumentation   WN 150
    Veterinary   SF 757.8
    See also Diagnostic use   WN 445 under
    Radioisotopes; names of specific radiographic
    techniques; names of organs, regions, and
    diseases being diagnosed
Radiography, Body–Section see Tomography,
    X–Ray
Radiography, Dental   WN 230
Radiography, Insufflation see Pneumoradiography
Radiography, Interventional   WN 200

**ALWAYS CONSULT MAIN SCHEDULES. USE NUMBER ASSIGNED ONLY WHEN
SUBJECT REPRESENTS MAJOR EMPHASIS OF WORK BEING CLASSIFIED**

I–205

Radiography, Panoramic   WN 230
Radioimmunoassay   QW 525.5.R2
  Assay of hormones   QY 330
  Used for diagnostic, monitoring or evaluation
    tests in special fields, with the field
Radioimmunodetection   WN 203
Radioimmunoimaging see Radioimmunodetection
Radioimmunoscintigraphy see
  Radioimmunodetection
Radioimmunosorbent Assay of Allergens see
  Radioallergosorbent Test
Radioisotope Brachytherapy see Brachytherapy
Radioisotope Dilution Technique   WG 141
  Blood volume   WG 106
Radioisotope Generators see Radionuclide
  Generators
Radioisotope Renography   WJ 302
Radioisotope Scanning see Radionuclide Imaging
Radioisotope Teletherapy   WN 450
Radioisotopes   WN 415-450
  Adverse effects   WN 610-650
  Diagnostic use   WN 445
  General works slanted toward the biological
    sciences   WN 420
  Nuclear engineering   TK 9400-9401
  Nuclear medicine (General)   WN 440
  Nuclear physics
    General   QC 795.6-795.8
    Specific, A-Z (like QD 181)   QC 796
  Therapeutic use   WN 450
  Used for special purposes, by subject
  See also Radioactive Waste   WA 788;
    Radionuclide Imaging   WN 203
Radiologic Physics see Health Physics
Radiologic Services in Hospitals see Hospital
  Departments; Mass Chest X-Ray
Radiology   WN
  Veterinary medicine   SF 757.8
Radiology Department, Hospital   WN 27-28
Radiology, Diagnostic X-Ray see Radiography
Radiology Information Systems   WN 26.5
Radiology, Interventional
  As a profession   WN 21
Radiometry   WN 660
  Equipment   WN 150
Radionuclide Generators   WN 150
Radionuclide Imaging   WN 203
  Cardiovascular diseases (General)   WG
    141.5.R3
  Localized, by site
Radionuclide Tomography, Computed see
  Tomography, Emission-Computed
Radionuclide Tomography, Single-Photon
  Emission-Computed see Tomography,
  Emission-Computed, Single-Photon
Radionuclides see Radioisotopes
Radiopaque Media see Contrast Media
Radiopharmaceuticals see Nuclear Medicine;
  Radioisotopes; Radionuclide Imaging; names of
  drugs or chemicals to which the radioactive
  substance is attached
Radioscopy see Fluoroscopy
Radiosensitivity see Radiation Tolerance

Radiotherapy
  Adverse effects   WN 250
  Anti-neoplastic see Radiotherapy   QZ 269
    under Neoplasms
  Dermatology   WR 660
  General works   WN 250
  Radioisotopes see Therapeutic use   WN 450
    under Radioisotopes
  Radium see Therapeutic use   WN 340 under
    Radium
  Veterinary   SF 757.8
  X-ray therapy   WN 250.5.X7
  See also names of diseases for which therapy is
    used
Radiotherapy, Computer-Assisted   WN 250.5.R2
Radiotherapy Dosage
  Radioisotopes   WN 450
  Radium   WN 340
  X-rays   WN 250.5.X7
  See also Radiation Dosage   WN 665
Radiotherapy, High-Energy   WN 250.5.R3
  See also special topics under Radiotherapy
Radiotherapy, Interstitial see Brachytherapy
Radiotherapy, Intracavity see Brachytherapy
Radiotherapy Planning, Computer-Assisted   WN
  250.5.R2
Radiotherapy, Surface see Brachytherapy
Radium   WN 300-340
  Adverse effects   WN 300
  Inorganic chemistry   QD 181.R1
  Therapeutic use   WN 340
Radius   WE 820
Radius Fractures   WE 820
Radon   WN 300-340
  General works   WN 300
  Therapeutic use   WN 340
Rage   BF 575.A5
  In adolescence   WS 462
  In infancy & childhood   WS 105.5.E5
Raillietina see Cestoda
Raillietiniasis see Cestode Infections
Railroads
  Accidents   WA 275
  Occupational medicine   WA 400-495
  Nursing service   WY 143
  Sanitary control of public carriers   WA 810
Rain
  Meteorology   QC 924.5-926.2
  Special topics, by subject, e.g., Air Pollution
    WA 754
Rales see Respiratory Sounds
Raman Spectroscopy see Spectrum Analysis, Raman
Ramps see Architectural Accessibility
Ramsay Hunt Paralysis Syndrome see Parkinson
  Disease
Random Allocation
  (Form number 20 or 20.5 in any NLM schedule
    where applicable)
Randomization see Random Allocation
Randomized Controlled Trials
  Special topics, by subject
  See also Clinical Trials

Ranitidine
    As an anti-ulcer agent   QV 69
Rape
    Criminology   HV 6558-6569
    Medicolegal aspects   W 795
    Therapy for victims   WM 401
Rapeseed see Brassica
Raphe Nuclei   WL 310
Rapid Eye Movements see Sleep, REM
Rare Books
    Works about   Z 688.R3
    Medical books by period (if old)   WZ 220-270
    By subject, if post 1801 or post-Americana
ras Genes see Genes, ras
Rat-Bite Fever   WC 390
Rat Virus see Parvovirus
Rate Setting and Review
    General   W 74
    Hospitals   WX 157
Rational-Emotive Psychotherapy see
Psychotherapy, Rational-Emotive
Rationalization   WM 193.5.R1
Rationing, Health Care see Health Care Rationing
Rats
    Diseases   SF 997.5.R3
    As laboratory animals   QY 60.R6
    Public health aspects see Rodent Control   WA
    240
Rats, Bandicoot see Muridae
Rats, Brattleboro
    As laboratory animals   QY 60.R6
Rats, Inbred CDF see Rats, Inbred F344
Rats, Inbred Fischer 344 see Rats, Inbred F344
Rats, Inbred F344
    As laboratory animals   QY 60.R6
Rats, Inbred SHR
    As laboratory animals   QY 60.R6
Rats, Inbred Strains
    As laboratory animals   QY 60.R6
Rats, Laboratory see Rats
Rats, Mutant Strains
    As laboratory animals   QY 60.R6
Rats, Norway see Rats
Rats, Sand see Gerbillinae
Rats, Spontaneously Hypertensive see Rats, Inbred
    SHR
Rattlesnake Venoms see Crotalid Venoms
Rattus see Muridae
Rattus norvegicus see Rats
Rauwolfia   QV 150
Rauwolfia Alkaloids   QV 150
Rauwolscine see Yohimbine
Raw Food Diet see Diet
Raynaud's Disease   WG 570
Reactants, Acute Phase see Acute Phase Proteins
Reaction, Acute-Phase see Acute-Phase Reaction
Reaction Time   BF 317
Reactive Disorders see Adjustment Disorders
Reactive Site see Binding Sites
Readiness Potential see Contingent Negative
    Variation
Reading
    Education (General)   LB 1050-1050.75

Children with learning disabilities   LC
    4704-4803
Mentally disabled children   LC 4620
Medical aspects of problems associated with poor
    vision   WW 480
Psychology   BF 456.R2
See also Dyslexia   WL 340.6; Dyslexia,
    Acquired   WL 340.6
Reading Disability, Acquired see Dyslexia, Acquired
Reading Disability, Developmental see Dyslexia
Reading, Therapeutic see Bibliotherapy
Reagent Kits, Diagnostic   QY 26
    Used for particular tests, by subject, e.g., for
    hemoglobin examination   QY 455
Reagents see Indicators and Reagents
Reagins   QW 575
    Associated with hypersensitivity   QW 900
Real-Time Systems see Computer Systems
Reality Testing
    Child psychology   WS 105.5.S3
    Psychoanalysis   WM 460.5.E3
Recall   BF 370-385
    In infancy & childhood   WS 105.5.M2
Receptor-Mediated Signal Transduction see Signal
    Transduction
Receptors, Acetylcholine see Receptors, Cholinergic
Receptors, Adenosine see Receptors, Purinergic P1
Receptors, ADP see Receptors, Purinergic P2
Receptors, Adrenergic   WL 102.8
Receptors, Adrenergic, alpha   WL 102.8
Receptors, Adrenergic, beta   WL 102.8
Receptors, alpha-Adrenergic see Receptors,
    Adrenergic, alpha
Receptors, Angiotensin   QU 68
Receptors, Antigen   QW 573
Receptors, Antigen, T-Cell   QW 573
Receptors, ATP see Receptors, Purinergic P2
Receptors, Benzodiazepine see Receptors, GABA-A
Receptors, Benzodiazepine-GABA see Receptors,
    GABA-A
Receptors, beta-Adrenergic see Receptors,
    Adrenergic, beta
Receptors, Caerulein see Receptors, Cholecystokinin
Receptors, Caffeine see Receptors, Purinergic
Receptors, Cell Surface
    Biochemistry   QU 55
    Immunochemistry   QW 504.5
    Pharmacology   QV 38
Receptors, Cholecystokinin   WK 170
Receptors, Cholinergic   WL 102.8
Receptors, Complement   QW 680
Receptors, Corticosteroid see Receptors,
    Glucocorticoid
Receptors, Diazepam see Receptors, GABA-A
Receptors, Diiodotyrosine see Receptors, Thyroid
    Hormone
Receptors, Dopamine   WL 102.8
Receptors, Drug   QV 38
Receptors, Endogenous Substances see Receptors,
    Cell Surface
Receptors, Epidermal Growth Factor-Urogastrone
    WK 170
Receptors, Estrogen   WP 522

Receptors, Fc   QW 601
Receptors, GABA-A   QU 60
Receptors, GABA-Benzodiazepine see Receptors, GABA-A
Receptors, gamma-Aminobutyric Acid see Receptors, GABA
Receptors, Gastrin see Receptors, Cholecystokinin
Receptors, Gastrointestinal Hormone   WK 170
Receptors, Glucocorticoid   WK 150
Receptors, Growth Hormone see Receptors, Somatotropin
Receptors, Histamine   QV 157
   See also Histamine H1 Receptor Blockaders QV 157
Receptors, Histamine H2   QV 157
Receptors, Hormone   WK 102
   Localized, by site
   See also names of specific hormone receptors
Receptors, IL-2 see Receptors, Interleukin-2
Receptors, Immunologic   QW 570
   Immunochemistry   QW 504.5
Receptors, Interleukin-2   QW 568
Receptors, LDL   QU 95
Receptors, Low Density Lipoprotein see Receptors, LDL
Receptors, Muscarinic   WL 102.8
Receptors, Muscimol see Receptors, GABA-A
Receptors, N-Methyl-D-Aspartate   QU 60
   As neurotransmitter   QV 126
   In synaptic transmission   WL 102.8
Receptors, Neural see Receptors, Sensory
Receptors, Neurohumor see Receptors, Neurotransmitter
Receptors, Neurotransmitter   WL 102.8
Receptors, Nicotinic   WL 102.8
Receptors, Pancreozymin see Receptors, Cholecystokinin
Receptors, Pheromone see Chemoreceptors
Receptors, Progesterone   WP 530
Receptors, Progestin see Receptors, Progesterone
Receptors, Proglumide see Receptors, Cholecystokinin
Receptors, Prostaglandin   QU 90
Receptors, Purinergic   QU 58
Receptors, Purinergic P1   QU 58
Receptors, Purinergic P2   QU 58
Receptors, Sensory   WL 102.9
Receptors, Sincalide see Receptors, Cholecystokinin
Receptors, Somatotropin   WK 515
Receptors, Steroid   WK 150
Receptors, Stretch see Mechanoreceptors
Receptors, Synaptic see Receptors, Neurotransmitter
Receptors, T-Cell Growth Factor see Receptors, Interleukin-2
Receptors, Tetragastrin see Receptors, Cholecystokinin
Receptors, Theophylline see Receptors, Purinergic
Receptors, Thyroid Hormone   WK 202
Receptors, Thyroxine see Receptors, Thyroid Hormone
Receptors, Transforming Growth Factor Alpha see Receptors, Epidermal Growth Factor-Urogastrone

Receptors, Triiodothyronine see Receptors, Thyroid Hormone
Receptors, Urogastrone see Receptors, Epidermal Growth Factor-Urogastrone
Receptors, Virus   QW 160
Receptosomes see Endosomes
Recklinghausen's Disease of Bone see Osteitis Fibrosa Cystica
Recklinghausen's Disease of Nerve see Neurofibromatosis
Recombinant DNA see DNA, Recombinant
Recombinant Interferon Alfa-2c see Interferon Alfa, Recombinant
Recombinant Proteins   QU 55
   Biotechnology   TP 248.65.P76
Recombination, Genetic   QH 443-450.6
Record Linkage, Medical see Medical Record Linkage
Records
   Bibliographical on magnetic tape   Z 699-699.5
   Government administration   JF 1521
   Hospital see Hospital Records   WX 173
   Public records and privacy   JC 596-596.2
   Statistical   HA 38-39
   See also Dental Records   WU 95; Medical Records   WX 173, etc.; Nursing Records WY 100.5
Records Control see Forms and Records Control
Recovery Period, Anesthesia see Anesthesia Recovery Period
Recovery Room   WX 218
Recovery Room Nursing see Postanesthesia Nursing
Recreation   QT 250
   Centers (General works)   GV 182
     For physical education and outdoor games QT 250
Recrudescence see Recurrence
Rectal Diseases   WI 600
Rectal Drug Administration see Administration, Rectal
Rectal Fistula   WI 605
   See also Rectovaginal Fistula   WP 180
Rectal Neoplasms   WI 610
Rectal Prolapse   WI 600
Rectal Surgery (Specialty) see Colon and Rectal Surgery (Specialty)
Rectocolitis, Hemorrhagic see Colitis, Ulcerative
Rectocolitis, Ulcerative see Colitis, Ulcerative
Rectovaginal Fistula   WP 180
Rectum   WI 600-650
   Anesthesia by see Anesthesia, Rectal   WO 290
   Feeding by see Tube feeding   WB 410
   Medication by see Enema   WB 344; Suppositories   QV 785
   Surgery   WI 650
Recurrence   QZ 140
   Of specific diseases, with the disease
Red Blood Cell Count see Erythrocyte Count
Red Blood Cell Membrane Sialoglycoprotein see Glycophorin
Red Blood Cell Transfusion see Erythrocyte Transfusion
Red Blood Cells see Erythrocytes

ALWAYS CONSULT MAIN SCHEDULES. USE NUMBER ASSIGNED ONLY WHEN SUBJECT REPRESENTS MAJOR EMPHASIS OF WORK BEING CLASSIFIED

Red Bugs see Trombiculid Mites
Red-Cell Aplasia, Pure   WH 155
Red Cell Ghost see Erythrocyte Membrane
Red Cell Mass see Erythrocyte Volume
Red Cell Substitutes see Blood Substitutes
Red Cross
    Army services   UH 535–537
    Disasters   HV 560–583
    Navy services   VG 457
    Nursing   WY 137
Red Marrow see Bone Marrow
Red Mites see Trombiculid Mites
Red Monkey see Erythrocebus patas
Red Nucleus   WL 310
Red Tide see Dinoflagellida
Redox see Oxidation–Reduction
Reductases see Oxidoreductases
Reductive Enzymes see Oxidoreductases
Reeler Mice see Mice, Neurologic Mutants
Reference Books
    General   Z 711
    On special topics, by subject
Reference Books, Medical
    Bibliography   ZWB 100
    On special topics, by subject, e.g., Dictionary of
    Nutrition   QU 13
Reference Ranges see Reference Values
Reference Standards
    Drugs   QV 771
    Of other products, by subject
Reference Values
    (Form number 16 in any NLM schedule where
    applicable)
Referral and Consultation
    Initiated by the nurse practitioner   WY 90
    Initiated by the physician   W 64
    Initiated by the psychiatrist   WM 64
    Initiated by the surgeon   WO 64
    In other specific specialties, in the number for
    interpersonal relationships or lacking that, in
    the general works number
    Specific conditions discussed, by subject
Reflex   WL 106
    Psychogalvanic see Galvanic Skin Response
    WM 145, etc.
    See also Conditioning, Classical   BF 319 and
    other types of conditioning
Reflex, Abnormal   WL 340
Reflex, Acoustic
    In hearing assessment   WV 274
Reflex, Conditioned see Conditioning, Classical
Reflex Epilepsy see Epilepsy
Reflex, Pharyngeal see Gagging
Reflex, Psychogalvanic see Galvanic Skin Response
Reflex, Pupillary   WW 240
Reflex, Stretch   WL 106
Reflex Sympathetic Dystrophy   WL 600
Reflex, Tendon see Reflex, Stretch
Reflex, Vestibulo–Ocular   WV 255
Reflexology see Massage
Reflexotherapy   WB 962
Refraction, Ocular   WW 300–320
Refractive Disorders see Refractive Errors

Refractive Errors   WW 300–320
    Diagnosis   WW 300
Refractive Index see Refractometry
Refractometry   QC 387
Refrigeration
    Biological products   WA 730
    Blood   WH 460
    Chemical technology   TP 490–497
    Drugs   WA 730;   QV 754
    Food   WA 710
    Organs   WO 665
    Specimen handling   QY 25, etc.
Refrigeration Anesthesia see Anesthesia,
    Refrigeration
Refugees
    Health problems   WA 300
    Mental health problems   WA 305
    Relief   HV 640–640.5
Refuse Disposal
    Industrial bacteriology   QW 75
    Public health aspects
        General   WA 780
        Industrial   WA 788
        Solid and fluid waste combined (General)
        WA 778
    See also names of specific types of waste and
    waste disposal, e.g., Industrial Waste,
    Radioactive Waste, Medical Waste, Medical
    Waste Disposal, etc.
Regeneration
    Biology   QH 499
    Bone see Bone Regeneration   WE 200
    Liver see Liver Regeneration   WI 702
    Local reaction to injury (Pathology)   QZ 150
    Nerve see Nerve Regeneration   WL 102
    Other specific areas, with the area affected
    See also Wound Healing   WO 185, etc.
Regional Anatomy see Anatomy, Regional
Regional Anesthesia see Anesthesia, Conduction
Regional Blood Flow   WG 106
Regional Health Planning   WA 541
Regional Hospital Planning see Hospital Planning
Regional Medical Programs   WA 541
Regional Perfusion see Perfusion, Regional
Regional Surgery see Surgery; names of organs or
    regions treated
Registration see Birth Certificates; Death
    Certificates; Licensure; Notifiable disease
    registration   WA 55 under Communicable
    Disease Control
Registries
    Of mental diseases
        Administration of registries   WM 30
        Statistics themselves   WM 16
    Of neoplastic diseases   QZ 200
    Of notifiable diseases   WA 55, etc.
    Of other diseases or types of data
    (Form number 16 in any NLM schedule where
    applicable)
Regression Analysis   QA 278.2
    Special topics, by subject
Regression Diagnostics see Regression Analysis
Regression (Psychology)   WM 193.5.R2

**ALWAYS CONSULT MAIN SCHEDULES. USE NUMBER ASSIGNED ONLY WHEN
SUBJECT REPRESENTS MAJOR EMPHASIS OF WORK BEING CLASSIFIED**

In adolescence   WS 463
In infancy & childhood   WS 350.8.D3
Regulation of Gene Expression see Gene Expression
   Regulation
Regulation of Gene Expression, Bacterial see Gene
   Expression Regulation, Bacterial
Regulation of Gene Expression, Enzymologic see
   Gene Expression Regulation, Enzymologic
Regulation of Gene Expression, Neoplastic see Gene
   Expression Regulation, Neoplastic
Regulation of Gene Expression, Viral see Gene
   Expression Regulation, Viral
Regurgitation, Gastric see Gastroesophageal Reflux
Rehabilitation   WB 320
   Disabled veterans   UB 360–366
   Educational   LC 4001–4824
   General works on physically disabled   WB 320
   Of the blind   HV 1573–2349
     Medical   WW 276
   Of the deaf, etc.   HV 2353–2990.5 etc.
     Medical rehabilitation   WV 270–280
   Orthopedic devices for see Orthopedic
     Equipment   WE 172
   Physical therapy   WB 460
   Physically disabled child   WS 368
     Psychological problems   WS 105.5.H2
   Retarded child see Mental Retardation   WS
   107.5.R3
   Sociological aspects   HD 7255–7256
   Videotherapy in psychiatry   WM 450.5.V5
   See also names of particular disabilities or diseases
     being treated
Rehabilitation Centers
   For the mentally disabled; alcoholics and drug
     addicts   WM 29
   For the physically disabled   WB 29
   See also Halfway houses   WM 29, etc.; Sheltered
     workshops   WB 29, etc.
Rehabilitation, Vocational   HD 7255–7256
   See also Occupational Therapy   WB 555, etc.
Rehydration see Fluid Therapy
Rehydration, Oral see Fluid Therapy
Rehydration Solutions   QV 786
   Used for special purposes, by subject
Reimbursement, Health Insurance see Insurance,
   Health, Reimbursement
Reimbursement, Incentive
   Hospitals   WX 157
Reimbursement Mechanisms
   Dentistry   WU 77
   Hospitals   WX 157
   Medicine   W 80
   Nursing   WY 77
   Pharmacy   QV 736
   In other specific fields, by subject
Reimbursement, Prospective see Prospective
   Payment System
Reimplantation see Replantation
Reimplantation, Tooth see Tooth Replantation
Reindeer   QL 737.U55
   Diseases   SF 997.5.D4
Reinforcement (Psychology)   BF 319.5.R4
   Associated with psychoanalysis   WM 460.5.R2

Reinforcement Schedule   BF 319.5.R4
Reinforcement, Social   HM 291
Reinforcement, Verbal   LB 1065
Rejuvenation   WJ 875
rel Genes see Oncogenes
Relapse see Recurrence
Relapsing Fever   WC 410
Relationship, Blood see Consanguinity; Family;
   Paternity; Twins
Relative Risk see Risk
Relative Value Scales
   Dental   WU 77
   Hospital   WX 157
   Medical   W 74
   Nursing   WY 77
   Pharmaceutical   QV 736
   For other services, by subject
Relative-Value Schedules see Relative Value Scales
Relaxation
   Hygiene   QT 265
   Mental health   WM 75, etc.
   Physical therapy   WB 545
Relaxation Techniques
   Behavior therapy   WM 425.5.R3
   Hygiene   QT 265
   Mental health   WM 75
   Physical therapy   WB 545
Relaxation Therapy see Relaxation Techniques
Reliability and Validity see Reproducibility of
   Results
Relief Work   HV 553–555
   Hospital emergency service   WX 215
   See also special topics under Disasters
Religion   BL–BX
   In psychoanalysis   WM 460.5.R3
     See also Religion and Psychology   BL 53,
     etc.
Religion and Medicine
   Ethical considerations
     Church's   BL 65.M4
     Doctor's   W 50
   In literature   WZ 330
   Mental healing aspects   WB 885
   Mental health aspects   WM 61
   Other aspects, by subject
   See also specific religions, e.g., Christian Science
     BX 6903–6997, etc.
Religion and Psychology
   Psychology of religion   BL 53
   Therapeutic aspects   WM 61
   See also Mental Healing   WB 880–885; Pastoral
     Care   WM 61
Religion and Science   BL 239–265
Religion and Sex   HQ 63
   In psychoanalysis   WM 460.5.R3
Religious Beliefs see Religion
REM   WL 108
Remedial Teaching   LB 1029.R4
   Special students, by type, e.g., the deaf   HV
   2417–2990.5
Remedies see Therapeutics
Remission Induction   WB 300
   Special topics, by subject

Remission, Spontaneous   QZ 140
  In specific diseases, with the disease
Remission, Spontaneous Neoplasm see Neoplasm
  Regression, Spontaneous
Renal Aminoaciduria see Aminoaciduria, Renal
Renal Artery   WG 595.R3
  See also Blood Supply   WJ 301 under kidney
Renal Artery Obstruction   WJ 300
Renal Artery Stenosis see Renal Artery Obstruction
Renal Calculi see Kidney Calculi
Renal Circulation   WJ 301
Renal Dialysis, Home see Hemodialysis, Home
Renal Disease, End-Stage see Kidney Failure,
  Chronic
Renal Failure, Acute see Kidney Failure, Acute
Renal Failure, Chronic see Kidney Failure, Chronic
Renal Failure, End-Stage see Kidney Failure,
  Chronic
Renal Function Tests see Kidney Function Tests
Renal Hormones see Hormones
Renal Hypertension see Hypertension, Renal
Renal Insufficiency see Kidney Failure, Acute;
  Kidney Failure, Chronic
Renal Insufficiency, Acute see Kidney Failure,
  Acute
Renal Insufficiency, Chronic see Kidney Failure,
  Chronic
Renal Osteodystrophy   WD 200.5.C2
Renal Papillitis, Necrotizing see Kidney Papillary
  Necrosis
Renal Transplantation see Kidney Transplantation
Renal Tubular Transport   WJ 301
Renal Tubular Transport, Inborn Errors   WJ 301
Renal Veins   WG 625.R3
  See also Blood Supply   WJ 301 under kidney
Renin   WK 180
  Enzymology   QU 136
Renin-Angiotensin-Aldosterone System see
  Renin-Angiotensin System
Renin-Angiotensin System
  Enzymology   QU 136
  In hemodynamics   WG 106
Renin-Substrate see Angiotensinogen
Rennin see Chymosin
Renography see Radioisotope Renography
Reoperation   WO 500
  For specific condition, with the condition
Reoviridae   QW 168.5.R15
Reoviruses see Reoviridae
Reperfusion Injury   QZ 170
  Localized, by site
    As a postoperative complication   WO 184
Reperfusion Injury, Myocardial see Myocardial
  Reperfusion Injury
Reperfusion, Myocardial see Myocardial
  Reperfusion
Repetition Strain Injury   WE 175
Replacement Therapy, Estrogen see Estrogen
  Replacement Therapy
Replantation   WO 700
  Localized, by specific organ or tissue
Replantation, Tooth see Tooth Replantation
Repression   WM 193.5.R4

In adolescence   WS 463
In infancy & childhood   WS 350.8.D3
Reproducibility of Results
  Used for special purposes, by subject
Reproduction
  Animals, Domestic
    General   SF 887
    Specific   SF 768.2.A-Z
  Animals, Wild
    General   QP 251-285
    Specific   QL 364-739.2
  Bacteria   QW 52
  Drugs affecting   QV 170-177
  Fishes   SH 165
  General biology   QH 471-489
  Human   WQ 205-208
  Plant ecology   QK 925-929
  Plant physiology   QK 825-830
  See also Genitalia   WJ 100, etc.; Urogenital
    System   WJ, etc.
Reproductive System see Genitalia; Reproduction;
  Urogenital System
Reptile Poisons see Snake Venoms
Reptiles   QL 665-666
  As poisonous animals   WD 410
  Diseases   SF 997.5.R4
Research
  (Form number 20 or 20.5 in any NLM schedule
  where applicable)
  Anesthesia   WO 220
  Genetics   QH 440
    For the biochemist   QU 20
  Internal medicine   WB 25
  Neoplasms   QZ 206
  Radiology   WN 20
  Scientific   Q 179.9-180.6
  Other fields outside the NLM area, in appropriate
  LC number
Research, Clinical Nursing see Clinical Nursing
  Research
Research Design
  (Form number 20-20.5 in any NLM schedule
  where applicable)
  Science   Q 180.A1, etc.
Research, Health Services see Health Services
  Research
Research Institutes see Academies and Institutes
Research, Nursing see Nursing Research
Research, Nursing Administration see Nursing
  Administration Research
Research, Nursing Education see Nursing Education
  Research
Research, Nursing Evaluation see Nursing
  Evaluation Research
Research, Nursing Methodology see Nursing
  Methodology Research
Research Personnel
  Medical   W 20.5
  Scientific (General)   Q 180.A5-Z [by country]
    Directories   Q 145
  See also names of fields in which research is done
Research Protocols, Clinical see Clinical Protocols

ALWAYS CONSULT MAIN SCHEDULES. USE NUMBER ASSIGNED ONLY WHEN
SUBJECT REPRESENTS MAJOR EMPHASIS OF WORK BEING CLASSIFIED

Research Support
    (Form number 20-20.5 in any NLM schedule
      where applicable)
    Science   Q 180-180.5
Reserpine   QV 150
Residence Characteristics
    Demography   HB 1951-2577
    Housing   HD 7285-7391
        Public health aspects   WA 795
        Public housing   HD 7288.77-7288.78
Residencies see Internship and Residency
Residency, Dental see Internship and Residency
Residency, Medical see Internship and Residency
Residency, Nonmedical see Internship, Nonmedical
Residential Facilities
    For children   WS 27-28
    For the mentally ill   WM 29
    For the physically ill   WB 29
    See also Foster home care   HV 875, etc.
Residential Mobility   HB 1954
    Of health manpower   W 76
    Of other special groups, by subject
Residential Treatment
    Institutions
        General   WM 29
        In adolescence   WS 27-28
        In infancy & childhood   WS 27-28
    Programs
        General   WM 445
        In adolescence   WS 463
        In infancy & childhood   WS 350.2
Resins
    Chemical technology   TP 978-979.5
    In dentistry   WU 190
    Pharmaceutical preparation   QV 785
    Used for special purposes, by subject, e.g., in the
      treatment of mandibular fractures   WU 610
Resins, Synthetic
    Chemical technology   TP 978-979.5
    Dentistry   WU 190
    Pharmaceutic preparation   QV 785
    Used for special purposes, by subject
    See also Acrylic Resins   WU 190, etc;
        Composite Resins   WU 190; Epoxy Resins
        WU 190, etc.
Resistance Factors see R Factors
Resistance, Natural see Immunity, Natural
Resistance to Infection see Infection
Resistance Transfer Factor see F Factor
Resorcinols   QV 223
Resorts see Health Resorts
Resorts, Health see Health Resorts
Resource Allocation see Health Care Rationing
Resource-Based Relative Value Scale see Relative
    Value Scales
Respiration   WF 102
    Anesthesia see Anesthesia, Inhalation   WO 277
    Biochemistry   WF 110
    In physical examination   WB 284
    Skin   WR 102
Respiration, Artificial
    Anesthesia complications   WO 250
    First Aid   WA 292

Respirators see Ventilators, Mechanical
Respirators, Air-Purifying see Respiratory
    Protective Devices
Respirators, Industrial see Respiratory Protective
    Devices
Respiratory Acidosis see Acidosis, Respiratory
Respiratory Airflow   WF 102
Respiratory Alkalosis see Alkalosis, Respiratory
Respiratory Care Units   WF 27-28
Respiratory Center   WL 310
Respiratory Chain see Electron Transport
Respiratory Diseases see Respiratory Tract Diseases
Respiratory Distress Syndrome   WS 410
Respiratory Distress Syndrome, Adult   WF 140
Respiratory Drug Administration see
    Administration, Inhalation
Respiratory Exchange see Respiration
Respiratory Failure see Respiratory Insufficiency
Respiratory Function Tests
    General physical examination   WB 284
    Respiratory diagnosis   WF 141
Respiratory Hypersensitivity   WF 150
    See also Asthma   WF 553; Farmer's Lung
      WF 652; Hay Fever   WV 335
Respiratory Insufficiency   WF 140
Respiratory Mechanics   WF 102
Respiratory Muscles   WF 101-102
Respiratory Paralysis   WF 140
Respiratory Protective Devices   WF 26
Respiratory Sounds   WF 102
Respiratory Syncytial Viruses   QW 168.5.P2
Respiratory System   WF
    Children   WS 280
    Drugs affecting see names of particular agents
      or groups of agents, e.g., Antibiotics   QV 350
Respiratory Therapy   WB 342
    For disease of the respiratory system   WF 145
    For disease of the respiratory system in animals
      SF 831
Respiratory Therapy Department, Hospital   WF
    27-28
Respiratory Tract Diseases   WF 140-900
    In infancy & childhood   WS 280
    Nursing   WY 163
    Veterinary   SF 831
    See also names of specific diseases
Respiratory Tract Infections
    General   WF 140
    In infancy & childhood   WS 280
    Veterinary   SF 831
    Viral   WC 505-510
      General works   WC 505
    See also name of specific infections
Respiratory Tract Neoplasms   WF 450
Response, Acute-Phase see Acute-Phase Reaction
Response Latency see Reaction Time
Response Time see Reaction Time
Responsibility for Injuries see Forensic Medicine
Responsibility, Social see Social Responsibility
Rest
    Hygienic   QT 265
    Therapeutic   WB 545
Restaurants   WA 799

Resting Phase see Interphase
Resting Potentials see Membrane Potentials
Restraint, Physical
    Of mental patients WM 35
    Veterinary (Surgery) SF 911
    See also Immobilization WE 168; Protective
      Devices WX 185, etc.
Restriction Endonucleases see DNA Restriction
  Enzymes
Resume, Job see Job Application
Resurrectionists see Cadaver
Resuscitation
    Accidents in anesthesia WO 250
    First aid WA 292
    In infancy & childhood WS 100
    Of the newborn WQ 450
Resuscitation Decisions see Resuscitation Orders
Resuscitation Orders
    General works W 84.7
    In hospitals WX 162
    Ethical aspects W 50
    See also Right to Die
Retarded Child see Mental Retardation
Retention (Psychology) BF 370-385
    Physiology WL 102
    In infancy & childhood WS 105.5.M2
Reticular Formation WL 310
Reticulocytes WH 150
Reticuloendothelial Cytomycosis see Histoplasmosis
Reticuloendothelial System WH 650
Reticuloendotheliosis WH 650
Reticuloendotheliosis, Leukemic see Leukemia,
  Hairy Cell
Reticulolymphosarcoma see Lymphoma
Reticulosis see Reticuloendotheliosis
Reticulum-Cell Sarcoma see Lymphoma,
  Large-Cell
Retina WW 270
Retinal Artery WG 595.R38
Retinal Degeneration WW·270
Retinal Detachment WW 270
Retinal Diseases WW 270
Retinal Ganglion Cells WW 270
Retinal Hemorrhage WW 270
Retinal Pigment Epithelium see Pigment Epithelium
  of Eye
Retinal Pigments WW 270
Retinal Vein WG 625.R38
Retinal Vessels WW 270
    See also Retinal artery WG 595.R38; Retinal
    Vein WG 625.R38
Retinitis WW 270
Retinitis Pigmentosa WW 270
Retinoblastoma WW 270
Retinoic Acid see Tretinoin
Retinoids QU 167
Retinol see Vitamin A
Retinopathy of Prematurity WW 270
Retinoscopy see Diagnosis WW 300 under
  Refractive Errors
Retirement HQ 1062-1063.2
    As a problem of aging WT 30
    Housing for HD 7287.9-7287.92

    Pensions, etc. HD 7105-7105.45
Retirement Benefits see Pensions
Retrognathism WU 440
Retrolental Fibroplasia see Retinopathy of
  Prematurity
Retroperitoneal Fibrosis WI 575
Retroperitoneal Neoplasms WI 575
Retroperitoneal Space WI 575
Retropneumoperitoneum WI 575
Retrospective Studies
    Epidemiology WA 105
    Other special topics, by subject
Retroviridae QW 168.5.R18
Retroviridae Infections WC 502
Retrovirus Infections see Retroviridae Infections
Retroviruses see Retroviridae
Reuptake Inhibitors, Neurotransmitter see
  Neurotransmitter Uptake Inhibitors
Reverse Immunoblotting see Immunoblotting
Reverse Transcription see Transcription, Genetic
Review Literature
    On special topics, by subject
Revision, Joint see Reoperation
Revision, Surgical see Reoperation
Reward
    Conditioned response BF 319
    School management LB 3025
Reye's Syndrome WS 340
Rh Factors see Rh-Hr Blood-Group System
Rh-Hr Blood-Group System WH 425
Rh Isoimmunization WH 425
Rhabdomyolysis WE 550
Rhabdomyosarcoma QZ 345
    Localized, by site
Rhabdoviridae QW 168.5.R2
Rhamnus
    As a medicinal plant QV 766
    Poisoning WD 500
Rhenium
    Inorganic chemistry QD 181.R4
    Pharmacology QV 290
Rheography see Plethysmography, Impedance
Rheology QC 189.5
    Blood WG 106
Rhesus Blood-Group System see Rh-Hr
  Blood-Group System
Rhesus Monkey see Macaca mulatta
Rhetinic Acid see Glycyrrhetinic Acid
Rheum see Rhubarb
Rheumatic Diseases WE 544
    Acute articular see Rheumatic Fever WC 220
Rheumatic Fever WC 220
Rheumatic Heart Disease WG 240
Rheumatism see Rheumatic Diseases
Rheumatism, Articular, Acute see Rheumatic Fever
Rheumatism, Muscular see Fibromyalgia
Rheumatism, Peri-Extra-Articular see Polymyalgia
  Rheumatica
Rheumatoid Arthritis see Arthritis, Rheumatoid
Rheumatoid Factor WE 346
Rheumatoid Spondylitis see Spondylitis, Ankylosing
Rheumatology WE 140
    See also names of specific musculoskeletal
    disease

Rhinencephalon see Limbic System
Rhinitis   WV 335
   Veterinary   SF 891
Rhinitis, Allergic, Nonseasonal see Rhinitis, Allergic,
   Perennial
Rhinitis, Allergic, Perennial   WV 335
Rhinitis, Allergic, Seasonal see Hay Fever
Rhinitis, Atrophic   WV 335
   Veterinary   SF 891
Rhinitis, Vasomotor   WV 335
Rhinology see Otolaryngology
Rhinopharynx see Nasopharynx
Rhinoplasty   WV 312
Rhinoscleroma   WV 300
Rhinosporidiosis   WC 450
Rhinovirus   QW 168.5.P4
Rhizanesthesia see Anesthesia, Conduction
Rhizobium   QW 131
Rhodanates see Thiocyanates
Rhodopsin   WW 270
Rhombencephalic Sleep see Sleep, REM
Rhonchi see Respiratory Sounds
Rhubarb
   As a medicinal plant   QV 766
   As a cathartic   QV 75
Rhus see Toxicodendron
Rhus Dermatitis see Dermatitis, Toxicodendron
Rhythm Method   WP 630
Rhythmicity see Periodicity
Ribavirin
   As an antiviral agent   QV 268.5
Riboflavin   QU 191
Riboflavin Deficiency   WD 124
Ribonucleases   QU 136
Ribonucleic Acid see RNA
Ribonucleoproteins   QU 56
Ribonucleoside Diphosphate Reductase   QU 140
Ribosomal RNA see RNA, Ribosomal
Ribosomes   QH 603.R5
Ribovirin see Ribavirin
Ribozymes see RNA, Catalytic
Ribs   WE 715
Rice
   As a dietary supplement in health or disease
   WB 431
   Cultivation   SB 191.R5
Ricin
   As a toxin   QW 630.5.R5
Ricinus   QV 75
Rickets   WD 145
Rickets, Renal see Renal Osteodystrophy
Rickettsia   QW 150
   As a cause of disease   QZ 65
Rickettsia Infections   WC 600-660
   General works   WC 600
   Mite-borne   WC 630-635
   Tick-borne   WC 620-625
   Veterinary   SF 809.R52
Rickettsiaceae   QW 150
Rickettsiaceae Infections   WC 600-635
Rickettsial Vaccines   WC 600
Rickettsiales   QW 150

Rickettsialpox   WC 635
Rickettsias see QW 149 for works including
   Rickettsias and Chlamydias treated together
Rifampicin see Rifampin
Rifampin   QV 268
Rifamycins   QV 350
Rifomycins see Rifamycins
Rift Valley Fever   WC 524
Rift Valley Fever Virus   QW 168.5.B9
Right to Die   W 85.5
Right to Treatment see Patient Advocacy
Rigidity, Decerebrate see Decerebrate State
Riley-Day Syndrome see Dysautonomia, Familial
Rinderpest   SF 966
Ringworm see Tinea
Risk
   In specific topics, by subject
Risk Behavior see Risk-Taking
Risk Factors
   In a particular subject, with the subject
Risk Management
   Hospitals   WX 157
   For other topics, class by subject if specific; if
     general, in economics number where available
Risk-Taking
   Psychology   BF 637.R57
Ritodrine
   Used in controlling premature labor   WQ 330
RNA   QU 58.7
RNA, Antisense   QU 58.7
RNA, Bacterial   QW 52
RNA Caps   QU 58.7
RNA, Catalytic   QU 58.7
RNA-Dependent RNA Polymerase see RNA
   Replicase
RNA, Double-Stranded   QU 58.7
RNA, Messenger   QU 58.7
RNA, Messenger, Splicing see RNA Splicing
RNA, Neoplasm
   In cancer research   QZ 206
RNA Nucleotidyltransferases   QU 141
RNA Polymerases   QU 141
RNA Processing, Post-Transcriptional   QH 450.2
RNA Replicase   QU 141
RNA, Ribosomal   QU 58.7
RNA, Ribosomal, Self-Splicing see RNA, Catalytic
RNA Rodent Viruses see RNA Viruses
RNA Sequence see Base Sequence
RNA Sequence Analysis see Sequence Analysis,
   RNA
RNA, Small Nuclear   QU 58.7
RNA Splicing   QH 450.2
RNA, Transfer   QU 58.7
RNA, Transfer, Amino Acyl   QU 58.7
RNA, Viral   QW 168
RNA Viruses
   General works   QW 168
   Specific viruses   QW 168.5.A-Z
RNase see Ribonucleases
Ro 10-9359 see Etretinate
Ro 15-1788 see Flumazenil
Robotics   TJ 210.2-211.47
   Biomedical engineering   QT 36

Used for special purposes, by subject, e.g., in
clinical laboratory procedures   QY 23
Rock Fever see Brucellosis
Rocky Mountain Spotted Fever   WC 620
Rod–Cone Dystrophy see Retinitis Pigmentosa
Rodent Control   WA 240
Rodent Diseases   SF 997.5.R64
Rodentia   QL 737.R6–737.R688
   As laboratory animals   QY 60.R6
Rodenticides
   Agriculture   SB 951.8
   Public health aspects   WA 240
Rods and Cones   WW 270
Roentgen Radiation see Radiation, Ionizing
Roentgen Rays see X–Rays
Roentgenkymography see Electrokymography
Roentgenograms see Radiography
Roentgenography see Radiography
Roentgenography, Dental see Radiography, Dental
Roentgenology see Radiation, Ionizing
Roentgenotherapy see X–Ray Therapy
Roeteln see Rubella
Rogerian Therapy see Nondirective Therapy
Role
   Parents   WS 105.5.F2
   Physician   W 62
   Sexual psychology   BF 692–692.5
   Social   HM 131
   See also Self Concept   BF 697, etc.
Role Concept see Role
Role Playing   WM 430.5.P8
   In infancy & childhood   WS 350.2
   In adolescence   WS 463
Romano–Ward Syndrome see Long QT Syndrome
Root Canal see Dental Pulp Cavity
Root Canal Filling Materials   WU 190
Root Canal Therapy   WU 230
Root Resection see Apicoectomy
Root Resorption   WU 230
Root Scaling see Dental Scaling
Rorschach Test   WM 145.5.R7
Rosa see Plants, Medicinal
Rosacea see Acne Rosacea
Rosaniline Dyes   QV 240
Rose Bengal   QV 240
Rosenzweig Picture–Frustration Study   WM
145.5.R8
   In adolescence   WS 462
   In infancy & childhood   WS 105.5.E8
   In psychology   BF 698.8.R6
Roseola, Epidemic see Measles
Roseola Infantum see Exanthema Subitum
Rotation
   Aviation medicine   WD 720
   Motion sickness   WD 630
   Of the eye   WW 103
   Special topics, by subject
Rotavirus Infections   WC 501
Roughage see Dietary Fiber
Round Window   WV 250
Roundworms see Nematoda
Rous–Associated Virus see Leukosis Virus, Avian
Rous Sarcoma see Sarcoma, Avian

Rous Sarcoma Virus see Sarcoma Viruses, Avian
Roussy–Levy Syndrome see Charcot–Marie Disease
Routine Diagnostic Tests see Diagnostic Tests,
   Routine
Roxithromycin   QV 350.5.E7
Royal Free Disease see Fatigue Syndrome, Chronic
RU–486 see Mifepristone
Rubber
   Agriculture   SB 289–291
   Industry   TS 1870–1935
   Used in artificial parts, with specific part
Rubber Silicone see Silicone Elastomers
Rubefacients see Irritants
Rubella   WC 582
Rubella Vaccine   WC 582
Rubella Virus   QW 168.5.R8
Rubeola see Measles
Rubidium
   Inorganic chemistry   QD 181.R3
   Metabolism   QU 130
   Pharmacology   QV 275
Rubinstein–Taybi Syndrome   QS 675
Rubivirus   QW 168.5.R8
Ruffini's Corpuscles see Thermoreceptors
Rumen   QL 862
   Domestic animals   SF 851
Ruminantia see Ruminants
Ruminants   QL 737.U5
   Diseases   SF 997.5.U5
   Physiology   SF 768.2.R8
Rumination, Obsessive see Compulsive Behavior
Runaway Reaction
   Adolescents   WS 463
   Children   WS 350.8.R9
Running   QT 260.5.R9
Runt Disease see Graft vs Host Disease
Rupture   QZ 55
   Localized, by site
Rural Health   WA 390
Rural Population
   Demography   HB 2371–2577
   Health problems see Rural Health   WA 390
   Other aspects, by subject
   See also Housing   HD 7289, etc.; Public Housing
      HD 7288.77–7288.78
Russell's Viper Venom Time see Prothrombin Time
Russian Baths see Baths
Ruthenium
   Inorganic chemistry   QD 181.R9
   Pharmacology   QV 290
Rutin   QU 220

S

S–Adenosylhomocysteine   QU 60
S–Adenosylmethionine   QU 57
Sabin Vaccine see Poliovirus Vaccine, Oral
Saccades   WW 400
Saccadic Eye Movements see Saccades
Saccharide–Mediated Cell Adhesion Molecules see
   Cell Adhesion Molecules
Saccharides see Carbohydrates; Disaccharides;
   Monosaccharides; Oligosaccharides;
   Polysaccharides

Saccharin   WA 712
Saccharomyces   QW 180.5.A8
Sacral Plexus see Lumbosacral Plexus
Sacral Region see Sacrococcygeal Region
Sacrococcygeal Region   WE 750
Sacroiliac Joint   WE 750
Sadism   WM 610
Sadomasochism see Sadism; Masochism
Safety   WA 250-288
Safety, Consumer Product see Consumer Product
   Safety
Safety Devices see Protective Devices
Safety Equipment see Protective Devices
Safety, Equipment see Equipment Safety
Safety Glasses see Eye Protective Devices
Safety Lenses see Eye Protective Devices
Saimiri   QL 737.P925
   Diseases   SF 997.5.P7
   As laboratory animals   QY 60.P7
Saimirine Herpesvirus 2 see Herpesvirus 2, Saimirine
Salaam Seizures see Spasms, Infantile
Salamanders see Urodela
Salaries and Fringe Benefits
   Economic theory   HD 4909-4912
      Fringe benefits (General)   HD 4928.N6
   In hospitals   WX 157
   Of dentists   WU 77
   Of nurses   WY 77
   Of physicians   W 79
   Of other specialties, by type, e.g., of psychiatric
      nurses   WY 160
Salicylates   QV 95
Salicylic Acids   QV 60
Salientia see Anura
Saline see Sodium Chloride
Saline Infusion see Infusions, Parenteral; Sodium
   Chloride
Saline Solution, Hypertonic   WB 354
Saliva   QY 125
Salivary Duct Calculi   WI 230
Salivary Duct Stones see Salivary Duct Calculi
Salivary Gland Diseases   WI 230
Salivary Gland Fistula   WI 230
Salivary Gland Neoplasms   WI 230
Salivary Gland Virus Disease see Cytomegalovirus
   Infections
Salivary Gland Viruses see Cytomegalovirus
Salivary Glands   WI 230
Salk Vaccine see Poliovirus Vaccine
Salmonella   QW 138.5.S2
Salmonella arizonae   QW 138.5.S2
Salmonella Food Poisoning   WC 268
Salmonella Infections   WC 269
Salmonella Infections, Animal   SF 809.S24
Salmonella paratyphi B see Salmonella
   schottmuelleri
Salmonella schottmuelleri   QW 138.5.S2
Salmonella typhi   QW 138.5.S2
Salmonella typhosa see Salmonella typhi
Salmonellosis see Salmonella Infections
Salmonidae
   Anatomy and physiology   QL 638.S2

Diseases   SH 179.S3
Salpingography see Hysterosalpingography
Salt-Free Diet see Diet, Sodium-Restricted
Salts
   Inorganic chemistry   QD 189-193
   Microorganism metabolism   QW 52
   See also names of specific salts, e.g. Sodium
      Chloride   QV 273, etc.
Sampling Studies
   Epidemiology   WA 105-106, etc.
   Psychology   BF 39
   Research
      (Form number 20 or 20.5 in any NLM schedule
         where applicable)
   Surveys
      Health   WA 900
      Nutrition   QU 146
   Special topics, by subject
Sanatorium Regimen in Tuberculosis see
   Rehabilitation   WF 330, etc. under Tuberculosis,
   Pulmonary
Sand Baths see Ammotherapy
Sand-Dollar see Sea Urchins
Sandfly Fever see Pappataci Fever
Sanitary Codes see Legislation   WA 32 under
   Sanitation
Sanitary Conditions, Epidemic Factor see
   Communicable Disease Control; Public health
   WA 30 under Socioeconomic Factors
Sanitary Control see Environment, Controlled
Sanitary Engineering   WA 671
   See also specific topics, e.g. Refuse Disposal
      WA 780, etc.
Sanitation   WA 670-847
   Housing   WA 795
   Occupational   WA 440
   Inspection   WA 672
      See also Food Inspection   WA 695; Quality
         Control   WA 672, etc.
   Legislation   WA 32-33
   Rural   WA 390
   School   WA 350-351
   Surveys   WA 672
Santonin   QV 253
Sao Paulo Typhus see Rocky Mountain Spotted
   Fever
Saphenous Vein   WG 625.S2
Sapogenins
   Biochemistry   QU 85
Saponins   QU 75
Saralasin   QU 68
Sarcodina   QX 55
Sarcoidosis   QZ 140
   Localized, by site
Sarcolemma   WE 500
Sarcoma   QZ 345
   Localized, by site
Sarcoma, Avian
   Experimental in the interest of humans   QZ 345
Sarcoma, Ewing's   WE 258
   Localized, by site
Sarcoma, Germinoblastic see Lymphoma
Sarcoma, Kaposi's   QZ 345
   Localized, by site

**ALWAYS CONSULT MAIN SCHEDULES. USE NUMBER ASSIGNED ONLY WHEN
SUBJECT REPRESENTS MAJOR EMPHASIS OF WORK BEING CLASSIFIED**

Sarcoma, Lymphatic see Lymphoma, Diffuse
Sarcoma, Osteogenic see Osteosarcoma
Sarcoma, Reticulum-Cell see Lymphoma, Large-Cell
Sarcoma, Rous see Sarcoma, Avian
Sarcoma, Synovial   WE 300
    Localized, by site
Sarcoma Virus, Feline   QW 166
Sarcoma Viruses, Avian   QW 166
Sarcoptes scabiei   QX 475
Sarcoptidae see Mites; Sarcoptes scabiei
Sarcosomes see Mitochondria, Muscle
Satellite DNA see DNA, Satellite
Satire see Wit and Humor
Sauna see Baths, Finnish
Savanna Baboons see Papio
Scabies   WR 365
    Veterinary   SF 810.S26
Scalded Skin Syndrome, Nonstaphylococcal see Epidermal Necrolysis, Toxic
Scalds see Burns
Scalenus Anticus Syndrome see Thoracic Outlet Syndrome
Scaling, Dental see Dental Scaling
Scaling, Root see Dental Scaling
Scaling, Subgingival see Dental Scaling
Scaling, Supragingival see Dental Scaling
Scalp   WR 450
Scalp Dermatoses   WR 450
Scanning Electron Microscopy see Microscopy, Electron, Scanning
Scanning, Radioisotope see Radionuclide Imaging
Scapula   WE 810
Scarlatina see Scarlet Fever
Scarlet Fever   WC 214
Scarpa's Ganglion see Vestibular Nerve
Scars see Cicatrix
Scattering, Radiation
    Biomedical uses   WB 117
    Physical optics   QC 427.4
Schamberg's Disease see Pigmentation Disorders
Schaumann's Disease see Sarcoidosis
Schedules, Patient see Appointments and Schedules
Scheie's Syndrome see Mucopolysaccharidosis I
Scheuermann's Disease   WE 725
Schistosoma   QX 355
Schistosomiasis   WC 810
Schistosomiasis, Intestinal see Schistosomiasis mansoni
Schistosomiasis japonica   WC 810
Schistosomiasis mansoni   WC 810
Schizoaffective Disorder see Psychotic Disorders
Schizoid Personality Disorder   WM 203
Schizomycetes see Bacteria
Schizophrenia   WM 203
Schizophrenia, Borderline see Schizotypal Personality Disorder
Schizophrenia, Catatonic   WM 203
Schizophrenia, Childhood   WM 203
Schizophrenia, Disorganized   WM 203
Schizophrenia, Hebephrenic see Schizophrenia, Disorganized

Schizophrenia, Latent see Schizotypal Personality Disorder
Schizophrenia, Paranoid   WM 203
Schizophrenia, Pseudoneurotic see Schizotypal Personality Disorder
Schizophrenic Disorders see Schizophrenia
Schizophrenic Language   WM 203
Schizophrenic Psychology   WM 203
Schizophreniform Disorders see Psychotic Disorders
Schizosaccharomyces   QW 180.5.A8
Schizotypal Personality Disorder   WM 203
Scholarships see Fellowships and Scholarships
School Admission Criteria   LB 2351-2351.6
    (Form number 18 in any NLM schedule where applicable)
School Dentistry
    Services offered   WA 350-351
    Specific dental problems   WU
School Dropouts see Student Dropouts
School Health Services   WA 350
    Mental health   WA 352
    See also Student Health Services   WA 350-353
School Nursing   WY 113
    Education   WY 18-18.5
Schools   L
    (Form number 19 in any NLM schedule where applicable)
    For exceptional children   LC 3951-4801
    For the blind   HV 1618-2349
    For the deaf   HV 2417-2990.5
    For the deaf-mute   HV 2417-2990.5
Schools, Dental   WU 19
Schools, Health Occupations   W 19
Schools, Library see Library Schools
Schools, Medical   W 19
Schools, Nursery   LB 1140-1140.5
    Public health aspects   WA 350-352
Schools, Nursing   WY 19
Schools, Pharmacy   QV 19
Schools, Public Health   WA 19
Schools, Veterinary   SF 756.3-756.37
Schueller-Christian Disease see Hand-Schueller-Christian Syndrome
Schwalbe's Nucleus see Vestibular Nuclei
Schwannoma see Neurilemmoma
Schwannoma, Acoustic see Neuroma, Acoustic
Schwartz-Jampel Syndrome see Osteochondrodysplasias
Sciatic Nerve   WL 400
Sciatica   WE 755
Science   Q
    Biography
        Collective   Q 141
        Individual   WZ 100
    Directories   Q 145
    General works   Q 158-158.5
    History (General)   Q 125
Scientific Misconduct   Q175.37
    Special topics, by subject
Scientific Societies see Societies, Scientific
Scientology see Alternative Medicine; Philosophy
Scintigraphy see Radionuclide Imaging
Scintigraphy, Computed Tomographic see
Tomography, Emission-Computed

Scintillation Counting   WN 660
Scintiphotography see Radionuclide Imaging
Sciuridae   QL 737.R68
    As laboratory animals   QY 60.R6
Sclera   WW 230
    Abnormalities   WW 230
    Scleritis   WW 230
Scleral Buckling   WW 230
Scleroderma, Circumscribed   WR 260
Scleroderma, Diffuse see Scleroderma, Systemic
Scleroderma, Localized see Scleroderma,
    Circumscribed
Scleroderma, Systemic   WR 260
Scleroma, Nasal see Rhinoscleroma
Scleroproteins (Non MeSH)   QU 55
Sclerosing Solutions   QV 786
Sclerosis   QZ 190
    Disseminated see Multiple Sclerosis   WL 360
    Hereditary spinal see Friedreich's Ataxia   WL
    390
    Presenile see Dementia, Presenile   WM 220
    Progressive systemic see Scleroderma, Systemic
    WR 260
Sclerosis, Disseminated see Multiple Sclerosis
Sclerosis, Hereditary Spinal see Friedreich's Ataxia
Sclerosis, Presenile see Dementia, Presenile
Sclerosis, Progressive Systemic see Scleroderma,
    Systemic
Sclerostomy
    For glaucoma   WW 290
Sclerotherapy   WB 354
    Special topics, by subject
Sclerotinia see Ascomycetes
Scoliosis   WE 735
Scopolamine   QV 134
Scopolamine Derivatives   QV 134
Scopolamine-Morphine Anesthesia see Anesthesia,
    Obstetrical; Preanesthetic Medication
Scorbutus see Scurvy
Scorpion Venoms   WD 420
Scorpions   QX 469
    Sting see Arachnidism   WD 420
Scrapie Agent see Prions
Scrapie-Associated Fibrils see Prions
Scrapie Virus see Prions
Screen-Film Systems, X-Ray see X-Ray
    Intensifying Screens
Screens, Radiographic see Instrumentation   WN
    150 under Radiography
Scrofula see Tuberculosis, Lymph Node
Scrofuloderma see Tuberculosis, Cutaneous
Scrotum   WJ 800
Scrub Typhus   WC 630
Sculpture
    Related to medicine   WZ 330
    Related to psychiatry   WM 49
Scurvy   WD 140
Sea Anemone Venoms see Coelenterate Venoms
Sea Bathing see Balneology; Swimming;
    Thalassotherapy
Sea Pollution see Seawater; Water Pollution
Sea Urchins   QL 384.E2

Sealants, Tooth see Pit and Fissure Sealants
Sealed Cabin Ecology see Ecological Systems,
    Closed
Seasickness see Motion Sickness
Seasons
    Astronomical geography   QB 637.2-637.8
    Atmospheric temperature   QC 903-906
    Folklore   GR 930
    Medical climatology   WB 700
Seawater
    Balneology   WB 525
    Ecology   QH 541.5.S3
    Marine biology   QH 91-95.9
    Microbiology see Plankton   QH 90.8.P5, etc.;
      Water Microbiology   QW 80
    Oceanography   GC 100-181
    Pollution
      Bathing beaches   WA 820
      Industrial waste   WA 788
        See also Water Pollution   WA 689
Seaweed   QK 564-580
Sebaceous Cyst see Epidermal Cyst
Sebaceous Gland Neoplasms   WR 410
Sebaceous Glands   WR 410
Seborrhea see Dermatitis, Seborrheic
Secobarbital   QV 88
Second-Look Surgery see Reoperation
Second Messenger Systems   QU 120
Second Opinion see Referral and Consultation
Secretaries, Medical see Medical Secretaries
Secretin   WK 170
Secretory Granules see Cytoplasmic Granules
Secretory Phase see Menstrual Cycle
Secretory Rate   QU 120
Security Measures
    Hospitals   WX 185
    Libraries   Z 679.6
Sedation, Conscious see Conscious Sedation
Sedatives see Hypnotics and Sedatives
Sedimentation of Blood see Blood Sedimentation
Seeds
    As a dietary supplement in health and disease
    WB 431
    Botany   QK 661
    Plant culture   SB 113.2-118.46
    Toxic   WD 500
Seizures   WL 340
Seizures, Febrile see Convulsions, Febrile
Selection (Genetics)   QH 455
    See also Natural Selection   QH 375
Selegiline
    As an antiparkinson agent   QV 80
Selenium
    Inorganic chemistry   QD 181.S5
    Metabolism   QU 130.5
    Pharmacology   QV 138.S5
Self see Ego
Self Assessment (Psychology)   BF 697
    In infancy & childhood   WS 105.5.S3
Self Care   WB 327
    For particular conditions, with the condition
Self Care (Rehabilitation) see Activities of Daily
    Living

Self–Care Units   WX 200
Self Concept   BF 697
      In infancy & childhood   WS 105.5.S3
Self Determination see Freedom
Self Disclosure   BF 697.5.S427
      In infancy & childhood   WS 105.5.S3
Self Esteem see Self Concept
Self–Evaluation Programs
      In a particular field (Form number 18–18.2 in
        any NLM schedule where applicable)
      Other special topics, by subject
Self–Examination   WB 120
      For specific conditions, with the condition
Self–Help Devices   WB 320
      Catalogs   W 26
      For particular disability, by the disability
      See also specific types of devices
Self–Help Groups
      In mental disorders   WM 426
      In other areas, by subject
Self–Instruction Programs see Programmed
   Instruction
Self–Instruction Programs, Computerized see
   Computer–Assisted Instruction
Self Medication   WB 120
      Popular works   WB 120
Self–Monitoring, Blood Glucose see Blood Glucose
   Self–Monitoring
Self Mutilation   WM 100
      Special topics, by subject
Self Perception see Self Concept
Self Realization see Achievement
Sella Turcica   WE 705
Selye Syndrome see General systemic reaction   QZ
   160 under Wounds and Injuries; Stress
Semantic Differential
      Used in psycholinguistics   BF 463
      As a personality test   BF 698.5
Semantics   P 325
Semen
      Analysis   QY 190
         Medicolegal   W 750
      Secretion
         Genital physiology   WJ 702
         Spermatozoa   WJ 834
Semen Preservation   WJ 834
      Artificial insemination   WQ 208
Semicircular Canals   WV 255
Semiconductors
      Electronics   TK 7871.85–7871.99
      Medical engineering   QT 36
      Photoelectronics   TK 8320–8334
      Physics   QC 610.9–611.8
Semilunar Bone   WE 830
Semilunar Cartilages see Menisci, Tibial
Seminal Vesicles   WJ 750
Seminiferous Tubules   WJ 830
Seminoma see Dysgerminoma
Semiochemicals see Pheromones
Semiology see Symptomatology   WB 143 under
   Diagnosis
Semisynthetic Vaccines see Vaccines, Synthetic
Semliki Forest Virus   QW 168.5.A7

Sendai Virus see Parainfluenza Virus Type 1
Senescence see Aging
Senile Osteoporosis see Osteoporosis
Senility see Aged; Psychoses, Senile
Sensation   WL 702
      Disorders
         Dermatological   WR 280
         General   WL 710
      See also Touch   WR 102; Smell   WV 301 and
        other sensations
Sense see Hearing; Orientation; Pain; Proprioception;
   Smell; Taste; Temperature Sense; Touch; Vision
Sense Organs   WL 700–710
Sensibilisinogens see Anaphylaxis
Sensitinogens see Allergens; Anaphylaxis
Sensitivity, Contact see Dermatitis, Contact
Sensitivity Training Groups
      Psychiatry   WM 430.5.S3
      Social psychology   HM 134
Sensitization see Anaphylaxis; Hypersensitivity
Sensitization, Immunologic see Immunization
Sensitizer see Antibodies
Sensory Aids
      Catalogs   W 26
      General   WL 26
      See also Eyeglasses   WW 350–354; Hearing Aids
        WV 274; other specific types in the
        equipment number, usually 26, for the field
Sensory Deprivation   WL 710
Sensory Motor Performance see Psychomotor
   Performance
Sensory Thresholds   WL 705
      See also names of specific thresholds, e.g.,
        Auditory Threshold   WV 272, etc.
Seoul Virus see Hantavirus
Separation, Drugs see Drug Compounding
Septal Nuclei   WL 314
Septic Sore Throat see Streptococcal Infections
Septicemia   WC 240
      Puerperal see Puerperal Infection   WQ 505
      Veterinary   SF 802
Septum, Nasal see Nasal Septum
Septum Pellucidum   WL 314
Sequence Analysis
      As a genetic technique (General)   QH 441
      Special topics, by subject
Sequence Analysis, DNA
      As a genetic technique (General)   QH 441
      Special topics, by subject
Sequence Analysis, RNA
      As a genetic technique (General)   QH 441
      Special topics, by subject
Sequence Data, Molecular see Molecular Sequence
   Data
Sequence Homology, Nucleic Acid   QU 58
Serial Learning   LB 1059
Serial Publications (Non Mesh) see Periodicals
Serine   QU 60
Serine Proteases see Serine Proteinases
Serine Proteinases   QU 136
Serodiagnosis   QY 265–275
Seroepidemiologic Methods
      Used for the detection of a specific disease, with
        the disease

Serology   QW 570
Seromucoid see Orosomucoid
Serotherapy see Immunization, Passive
Serotonin   QV 126
Serotonin Antagonists   QV 126
Serotonin Blockaders see Serotonin Antagonists
Serpin Superfamily see Serpins
Serpins   QU 136
Serratia   QW 138.5.S3
Sertoli Cell Tumor   WJ 858
Serum see Blood; Immune Sera; Serum Albumin;
   Serum Globulins
Serum Albumin   WH 400
   Clinical analysis   QY 455
Serum Globulins   WH 400
   Immunoglobulins   QW 601
Serum Markers see Biological Markers
Serum Proteins see Blood Proteins
Serum Sialomucin see Orosomucoid
Serum Sickness   WD 330
Serum Thymic Factor see Thymic Factor,
   Circulating
Servicemen see Military Personnel
Set (Psychology)   BF 321
Sewage
   Bacteriology   QW 80
   Disposal   WA 785
      General waste disposal   WA 778
   Water pollution   WA 689
Sex
   Counseling   WM 55
   General   HQ 12-25
   Hygiene
      Female   WP 120
      Male   WJ 700
   In mental retardation   WM 307.S3
   Medicolegal aspects   W 795
   Organs see Genitalia   WJ 700, etc.
   Psychoanalysis   WM 460.5.S3
   Psychology   BF 692
   Research   HQ 60
Sex Behavior
   Human   HQ 12-472
   In adolescence   WS 462
   In infancy & childhood   WS 105.5.S4
   Psychology   BF 692
Sex Behavior, Animal   QL 761
   Domestic animals   SF 195-518
   Wild animals   QL 364-739.3
Sex Characteristics
   Physical   QS, QT
      Female   WP 101
      Male   WJ 101-102
   Psychological   BF 692
Sex Chromatin   QH 599
Sex Chromosome Abnormalities   QS 677
Sex Chromosomes   QH 600.5
Sex Counseling   WM 55
Sex Determination
   Diagnostic   WQ 206
   Embryogenic   QS 638
Sex Deviations see Paraphilias

Sex Differences see Sex Characteristics
Sex Differentiation
   Embryogenic   QS 640
Sex Differentiation Disorders   WJ 712
   Veterinary   SF 871
Sex Dimorphism see Sex Characteristics
Sex Disorders
   Female   WP 610
   Male   WJ 709
   Problems of mentally retarded   WM 307.S3
   Psychophysiologic (General)   WM 611
Sex Education   HQ 34-59
   Of the mentally retarded   LC 4601-4640.4 or
      HQ 54.3
      Sex problems   WM 307.S3
   School texts   QT 225
Sex Factor, Bacterial see F Factor
Sex Factor F see F Factor
Sex Factors
   As a cause of disease   QZ 53
      See also Sex Ratio   QH 455, etc.
   Demography   HB 1741-1947
   Other special topics, by subject
Sex Hormones   WK 900
   Female   WP 520-530
   Male   WJ 875
   See also names of specific hormones
Sex Manuals   HQ 31
Sex Offenses
   Criminology   HV 6556-6593
   Medicolegal aspects   W 795
Sex Pili see Pili, Sex
Sex Predetermination see Sex Preselection
Sex Preselection   WQ 205
   Using genetic engineering techniques   QH 44:
Sex Ratio
   Animals
      Domestic (Breeding)   SF 105
      Wild   QH 352
   Population genetics   QH 455
   Population statistics
      At birth by country   HB 911-1107
      General   HB 1741-1947
   Other special topics, by subject, e.g., Sex Ratic
      of children born with Huntington Chorea   WI
      390
Sex Reversal, Gonadal   WK 900
Sex Role see Gender Identity
Sex Selection see Sex Preselection
Sexology see Sex
Sexual Abuse, Child see Child Abuse, Sexual
Sexual Adjustment see Sex Disorders; Sex Manual
Sexual Dysfunctions, Psychological see
   Psychosexual Dysfunctions
Sexual Harassment   HD 6060.3
Sexual Intercourse see Coitus
Sexual Partners
   Special topics, by subject
Sexually Transmitted Diseases   WC 140-185
   General works   WC 140
   Gonorrhea   WC 150
      In the female   WP 157
SGOT see Aspartate Aminotransferase

ALWAYS CONSULT MAIN SCHEDULES.   USE NUMBER ASSIGNED ONLY WHEN
SUBJECT REPRESENTS MAJOR EMPHASIS OF WORK BEING CLASSIFIED

SGPT see Alanine Aminotransferase
Shadow Test see Refraction, Ocular
Shame   BF 575.S45
    In adolescence   WS 462
    In infancy & childhood   WS 105.5.E5
Shared Paranoid Disorder   WM 205
Sharks   QL 638.9–638.95
Sharp Syndrome see Mixed Connective Tissue Disease
Sheathed Bacteria (Non Mesh) see Bacteria
Sheehan's Syndrome see Hypopituitarism
Sheep
    Domestic   SF 371–379
      Anatomy   SF 767.S5
      Physiology   SF 768.2.S5
    Wild   QL 737.U53
Sheep Diseases   SF 968–969
Shellfish
    As a dietary supplement in health or disease   WB 426
    Culture   SH 365–380.92
    Diseases   SH 179.S5
    Poisoning   WD 405
    See also Crustacea   QX 463; Mollusca   QX 675
Sheltered Workshops
    For the mentally disabled   WM 29
    For the physically disabled   WB 29
Sherman Antitrust Act see Antitrust Laws
Shigella   QW 138.5.S4
Shigella Infections see Dysentery, Bacillary
Shingles see Herpes Zoster
Ships
    Naval science   V
    Nursing service   WY 143
    Public health aspects   WA 810
    Quarantine   WA 234
Shivering   WB 152
Shock   QZ 140
    Anaphylactic see Anaphylaxis   QW 900
    Electric see Electric Injuries   WD 602, etc.
Shock, Anaphylactic see Anaphylaxis
Shock, Cardiogenic   WG 300
Shock, Endotoxic see Shock, Septic
Shock, Hemorrhagic
    Surgical complications   WO 149
    Injury   WO 700
Shock Lung see Respiratory Distress Syndrome, Adult
Shock, Septic   QZ 140
    In pregnancy   WQ 240
    In septicemia   WC 240
    Other special topics, by subject
Shock, Surgical   WO 149
Shock Therapy see Convulsive Therapy
Shock Therapy, Electric see Electroconvulsive Therapy
Shock Therapy, Insulin see Convulsive Therapy
Shock, Toxic see Shock, Septic
Shock, Traumatic   WO 700–820
Shockwaves, Ultrasonic see Ultrasonics
Shoes   QT 245
    Orthopedic   WE 880–890

Protective
    In sports   QT 260
    In industry   WA 485
Short-Term Psychotherapy see Psychotherapy, Brief
Short Waves see Radio Waves
Shorthand   Z 53–102
    Medical   W 80
      Dictionaries   W 13
Shoulder   WE 810
Shoulder Dislocation   WE 810
Shoulder Fractures   WE 810
Shoulder–Girdle Neuropathy see Cervico–Brachia Neuralgia
Shoulder–Hand Syndrome   WE 810
Shoulder Joint   WE 810
Shrimp   QX 463
Shwartzman Phenomenon   QW 900
Shyness   BF 575.B3
SI Units see International System of Units
Sialadenitis   WI 230
Sialidase see Neuraminidase
Sialography   WI 230
Sialolithiasis, Ductal see Salivary Duct Calculi
Sialyltransferases   QU 141
Siamang see Hylobates
Siamese Twins see Twins, Conjoined
Sibling Relations   WS 105.5.F2
Sicca Syndrome see Sjogren's Syndrome
Sick Building Syndrome see Air Pollution, Indoor
Sick Role   WM 178
    Special topics, by subject
Sick Sinus Syndrome   WG 330
Sickle Cell Anemia see Anemia, Sickle Cell
Sickle Cell Trait   WH 170
Sickness Insurance see Insurance, Health
SID see Sudden Infant Death
Siderophilin see Transferrin
Siderosis   WF 654
    Localized, by site, e.g., of the cornea,   WW 220
Sight see Vision
Sigma Element see Sigma Factor
Sigma Factor   QU 141
Sigma Initiation Factor see Sigma Factor
Sigma Subunit see Sigma Factor
Sigmoid   WI 560
Sigmoid Neoplasms   WI 560
Sigmoidoscopy   WI 620
Sign Language   HV 2474–2476
Signal Interpretation, Computer–Assisted see Signal Processing, Computer–Assisted
Signal Pathways see Signal Transduction
Signal Peptides   QU 68
Signal Processing, Computer–Assisted
    As equipment in special fields (Form number 26.5 in any NLM schedule where applicable; e.g. Nursing   WY 26.5)
Signal Processing, Digital see Signal Processing, Computer–Assisted
Signal Sequences, Peptides see Signal Peptides
Signal Transduction
    Cytology   QH 601
Signs and Location Directories see Location Directories and signs

Silastics see Silicone Elastomers
Silica see Silicon Dioxide
Silicate Cement   WU 190
    Used for special purposes, by subject, e.g., in
      dental cavity treatment   WU 350
Silicate Fillings see Silicate Cement
Silicic Acid
    Toxicology   QV 610
Silicon
    Inorganic chemistry   QD 181.S6
    Metabolism   QU 130.5
    Toxicology   QV 618
Silicon Dioxide
    Inorganic chemistry   QD 181.S6
    Toxicology   QV 610
Silicone Elastomers
    Artificial organ construction (General)   WO 176
    Chemical technology   TP 248.S5
    Dental materials   WU 190
    Plastic surgery   WO 600-640
    Used in other particular procedures, with the
      procedure
Silicone Oils
    Chemical technology   TP 685
    Public health aspects   WA 722
    In the treatment of retinal detachment   WW 270
Silicones
    Analytical chemistry   QD 139.S5
    Chemical technology   TP 248.S5
    Plastic surgery   WO 600-640
    Used in other particular procedures, with the
      procedure
Silicopolyacrylate Cement see Glass Ionomer
  Cements
Silicosis   WF 654
Silicotuberculosis   WF 654
Silver   QV 297
    Metabolism   QU 130
Silver Nitrate
    Inorganic chemistry   QD 181.A3
    Pharmacology   QV 297
Simian Immunodeficiency Viruses see SIV
Simian T-Lymphotropic Virus Type III see SIV
Simian Virus 40 see Polyomavirus macacae
Simmonds' Disease see Hypopituitarism
Simplexvirus   QW 165.5.H3
Simuliidae   QX 505
Simulium see Simuliidae
SIN-10 see Molsidomine
Sinapis see Mustard
Sincalide Receptors see Receptors, Cholecystokinin
Single Parent   HQ 759.915
    Special topics, by subject
Single-Parent Family see Single Parent
Single Person   HQ 800-800.4
    Widows and widowers   HQ 1058-1058.5
    Relations to adolescents   WS 462
    Relations to children   WS 105.5.F2
Single-Photon Emission-Computed Tomography
  see Tomography, Emission-Computed,
  Single-Photon
Single-Stranded DNA see DNA, Single-Stranded

Single-Stranded DNA Binding Proteins see
  DNA-Binding Proteins
Sinoatrial Node   WG 201-202
Sinus Arrhythmia see Arrhythmia, Sinus
Sinus Arrythmia see Arrythmia, Sinus
Sinus Thrombosis   WL 355
Sinuses, Cranial see Cranial Sinuses
Sinuses, Paranasal see Paranasal Sinuses
Sinusitis   WV 340
Sinusitis, Maxillary see Maxillary Sinusitis
Siphonaptera see Fleas
Sipunculida see Nematoda
sis Genes see Oncogenes
Sisomicin   QV 350.5.G3
Sisomycin see Sisomicin
Sissomicin see Sisomicin
Sister Chromatid Exchange   QH 445
Site-Directed Mutagenesis see Mutagenesis,
  Site-Directed
Site-Specific Mutagenesis see Mutagenesis,
  Site-Directed
Situational Ethics see Ethics
Situational Therapy see Milieu Therapy
Situs Inversus   QS 675
Situs Transversus see Situs Inversus
SIV   QW 166
SIV-1 see SIV
SIV-2 see SIV
Sixth Disease see Exanthema Subitum
Size Perception   WW 105
Sjogren's Syndrome   WE 346
Skeletal Age Measurement see Age Determination
  by Skeleton
Skeletal Fixation see Fracture Fixation
Skeletal Muscle Relaxants see Neuromuscular
  Agents
Skeletal System see Musculoskeletal System
Skeleton   WE 100-102
Skiascopy see Diagnosis   WW 300 under Refractive
  Errors; Fluroscopy
Skid Row Alcoholics
    Medical aspects   WM 274
    Sociological problems   HV 5050
Skiing   QT 260.5.S6
Skilled Nursing Facilities   WX 27-28
Skin   WR
    Drugs affecting see Dermatologic Agents   QV
      60-65
    Epidermis   WR 101
Skin Absorption   WR 102
Skin Aging   WR 102
Skin Appendage Diseases   WR 390-475
Skin Diseases   WR
    General   WR 140
      Diagnosis   WR 141
    Genetic (General)   WR 218
    In infancy & childhood   WS 260
    Nursing   WY 154.5
    Papulosquamous   WR 204
    Radiotherapy   WR 660
    Veterinary   SF 901
Skin Diseases, Bullous see Skin Diseases,
  Vesiculobullous

**ALWAYS CONSULT MAIN SCHEDULES. USE NUMBER ASSIGNED ONLY WHEN
SUBJECT REPRESENTS MAJOR EMPHASIS OF WORK BEING CLASSIFIED**

Skin Diseases, Fungal see Dermatomycoses
Skin Diseases, Infectious   WR 220–245
   Bacterial   WR 220–245
   Fungal see Dermatomycosis   WR 300–340
   General works   WR 220
   Veterinary   SF 901
   Viral   WC 570–590, etc.
     General works   WC 570
Skin Diseases, Parasitic   WR 345
   Veterinary   SF 901
Skin Diseases, Vesicular see Skin Diseases,
   Vesiculobullous
Skin Diseases, Vesiculobullous   WR 200
Skin Drug Administration see Administration,
   Cutaneous
Skin Electric Conductance see Galvanic Skin
   Response
Skin Glands see Exocrine Glands
Skin Grafts see Skin Transplantation
Skin Manifestations   WR 143
Skin Neoplasms   WR 500
   Veterinary   SF 901
   See also Sebaceous Gland Neoplasms   WR 410;
     Sweat Gland Neoplasms   WR 400
Skin Pigmentation   WR 102
   Disorders   WR 265
Skin Syphilis see Syphilis, Cutaneous
Skin Temperature   WR 102
Skin Tests   QY 260
Skin Transplantation   WO 610
Skin Tuberculosis see Tuberculosis, Cutaneous
Skin Ulcer   WR 598
Skin Wrinkling see Skin Aging
Skinfold Thickness
   Malnutrition   WD 105
   Obesity diagnosis   WD 210
Skull   WE 705
   Animal   QL
     Domestic   SF 901
     Wild   QL 822
   Anthropology   GN 71–131
Skull Fractures   WL 354
Skull Neoplasms   WE 707
Slang see Language; Philology; Vocabulary
Slaughter Houses see Abattoirs
Slaughterhouses see Abattoirs
Sleep   WL 108
   Drugs promoting   QV 85
   In personal hygiene   QT 265
   Physiology   WL 108
Sleep Apnea Syndromes   WF 143
Sleep Deprivation
   Experimental   WL 108
   In personal hygiene   QT 265
Sleep Disorders   WM 188
   See also names of specific disorders
Sleep, REM   WL 108
Sleep Stages   WL 108
Sleep Talking see Sleep Disorders
Sleep Terror Disorder see Sleep Disorders
Sleep Therapy see Rest; specific conditions for which
   therapy is used
Sleep Walking see Somnambulism

Sleeping Sickness see Encephalitis, Epidemic;
   Trypanosomiasis, African
Slime Bacteria see Myxococcales
Slime Molds see Myxomycota
Slipped Disk see Intervertebral Disk Displacement
Slit–Lamp Microscopy see Microscopy
Slotted Attachment, Dental see Denture, Precision
   Attachment
Slow Virus Diseases   WC 500
   See also names of specific diseases, e.g., Kuru
     WC 540
Slums see Poverty Areas
Small Nuclear RNA see RNA, Small Nuclear
Smallpox   WC 585–590
   Prevention & control   WC 588
Smallpox Vaccine   WC 588
   Used in the treatment of other diseases, with the
     disease
Smallpox Virus see Variola Virus
Smell   WV 301
Smith, Theobald, Phenomenon see Anaphylaxis
Smittia see Chironomidae
Smoke
   Air pollution   WA 754
   Tobacco   QV 137
     Public health aspects   WA 754
   Toxicology   QV 665
Smoke Inhalation Injury   WO 704
Smokeless Tobacco see Tobacco, Smokeless
Smokers' Patches see Leukoplakia, Oral
Smoking
   Dependence   WM 290
   Effects   QV 137
   General   HV 5725–5770
Smoking, Passive see Tobacco Smoke Pollution
Snails   QX 675
Snake Bites   WD 410
Snake Poisons see Snake Venoms
Snake Venoms   WD 410
Snakeroot Poisoning see Milk Sickness
Snakes   QL 666.O6–666.O694
   Diseases   SF 997.5.R4
Sneddon–Wilkinson Disease see Skin Diseases,
   Vesiculobullous
Sneezing Gas see Toxicology   QV 665 under
   Smoke
Snoring   WF 143
Snuff see Tobacco, Smokeless
Soaps   QV 233
Soccer   QT 260.5.S7
Social Accountability see Social Responsibility
Social Adjustment   HM 291
   In adolescence   WS 462
   In infancy & childhood   WS 105.5.A8
Social Alienation
   In adolescence   WS 463
   In infancy & childhood   WS 350.8.S6
   Psychiatry   WM 600
   Sociology   HM 291
Social Behavior   HM 251
   Animals   QL 775
   In adolescence   WS 462
   In infancy & childhood   WS 105.5.S6

Social Behavior Disorders
    In adolescence   WS 463
    In infancy & childhood   WS 350.8.S6
      See also Child Behavior Disorders   WS 350.6
    Psychiatry (General)   WM 600
    Sociology   HM 291
    Television influence   HE 8700.6
Social Breakdown Syndrome   WM 600
    In adolescence   WS 463
    In infancy & childhood   WS 350.8.S6
    Sociology   HM 291
Social Change
    Progress   HM 101
    Reform   HN
Social Class   HT 603–1445
    Adolescents   WS 462
    Children   WS 105.5.S6
Social Clubs, Therapeutic see Self-Help Groups
Social Conditions   HN
Social Conformity   HM 291
Social Control, Formal
    Penology   HV 7240–9960
    Social elements, forces, laws   HM 201–221
    Special topics, by subject
Social Control, Informal   HM 291
    Primitive customs, e.g., Taboo   GN 493–495.2
    Special topics, by subject
Social Desirability   HM 132
Social Discrimination see Prejudice
Social Disorganization see Anomie
Social Distance   HM 132
    In adolescence   WM 462
    In infancy & childhood   WS 105.5.S6
Social Dominance
    Anthropology
      Matriarchy   GN 479.5
      Patriarchy   GN 479.6
    In animals   QL 775
    Sociology   HM 132
    Leadership   BF 637.L4
Social Environment   HM 206
    Mental Health   WM 31
Social Facilitation   BF 774
Social Identification
    In adolescence   WS 462
    In infancy & childhood   WS 105.5.S6
Social Insurance see Social Security
Social Interaction see Interpersonal Relations
Social Isolation
    In infancy & childhood   WS 105.5.D3
    Psychology   BF 575.L7
    Social psychology   HM 291
Social Justice
    Special topics, by subject
Social Medicine   WA 31
Social Perception   HM 132
Social Planning   HN
Social Policy see Public Policy
Social Problems   HN
    In old age   WT 30
    Of the mentally retarded   WM 307.S6
    Of children   WS 107.5.P8
    Of the normal child   WS 105.5.S6

Social Psychiatry see Community Psychiatry
Social Psychology see Psychology, Social
Social Reinforcement see Reinforcement, Social
Social Responsibility
    Medical ethics   W 50
    Medical research   W 20.5
    Specific topics, by subject
Social Sciences   H
Social Security   HD 7090–7250.7
    Medical benefits   W 225–275
      See also Medicare   WT 31
Social Service see Social Work
Social Service, Psychiatric see Social Work,
  Psychiatric
Social Support
    Special topics, by subject
Social Values   HM 73
Social Welfare   HV 1–4959
    General works   HV 30–31
      By country   HV 85–525
Social Work
    As a preventive health measure   WA 108
    Children   WA 310–320
    General works   HV 6–696
    Hospitals   W 322
    Maternity   WA 310
    Medical   W 322
    Periodicals   W1
Social Work Department, Hospital   W 322
Social Work, Psychiatric   WM 30.5
Social Workers see Social Work
Socialization   HM 131
    Adolescents   WS 462
    Children   WS 105.5.S6
Socialized Dentistry see State Dentistry
Socialized Medicine see State Medicine
Societies
    (Form number 1 in any NLM schedule where
      applicable. Include history)
    Fraternities in medicine and allied fields   W 20.9
    Other societies in appropriate LC number
Societies, Dental   WU 1
Societies, Hospital   WX 1
Societies, Medical   WB 1
    Fraternities   W 20.9
    Specialties (Form number 1 in any NLM schedule
      where applicable)
Societies, Nursing   WY 1
Societies, Pharmaceutical   QV 701
Societies, Scientific   Q 10–99
    See also types of societies above or subheading
      societies under specialty headings, e.g., Zoology
      QL 1
Sociocultural Change see Acculturation
Socioeconomic Factors
    Mental health   WM 31
    Public health   WA 30
    Other topics, by subject
Socioeconomic Status see Social Class
Socioenvironmental Therapy   WM 428–445
Sociology   HM-HX
    See also Social Medicine   WA 31; Social Work
      W 322, etc.; Social Work, Psychiatric
      WM 30.5

ALWAYS CONSULT MAIN SCHEDULES. USE NUMBER ASSIGNED ONLY WHEN
SUBJECT REPRESENTS MAJOR EMPHASIS OF WORK BEING CLASSIFIED

Sociology, Medical   WA 31
Sociometric Techniques   HM 48
Sociopathic Personality see Antisocial Personality Disorder
Sodium
    Inorganic chemistry   QD 181.N2
    Pharmacology   QV 275
Sodium Bicarbonate see Bicarbonates
Sodium Cephalothin see Cephalothin
Sodium Channels   QH 603.I54
Sodium Chloride
    Metabolism   QU 130
        Water–electrolyte balance   QU 105
        Water–electrolyte imbalance   WD 220
    Pharmacology   QV 273
    Solution   QV 786
    Infusion   WB 354
Sodium Chloride Solution, Hypertonic see Saline Solution, Hypertonic
Sodium Cromoglycate see Cromolyn Sodium
Sodium, Dietary
    Metabolism   QU 130
    Pharmacology   QV 273
    Relation to a particular disorder, with the disorder
Sodium Glutamate
    Biochemistry   QU 60
    As a food additive   WA 712
Sodium Iodohippurate see Iodohippuric Acid
Sodium Isotopes
    Inorganic chemistry   QD 181.N2
    Pharmacology   QV 275
Sodium Nitroprusside see Nitroprusside
Sodium, Potassium Adenosinetriphosphatase see Na(+)-K(+)-Exchanging ATPase
Sodium, Potassium ATPase see Na(+)-K(+)-Exchanging ATPase
Sodium-Potassium Pump see Na(+)-K(+)-Exchanging ATPase
Sodium Pump see Na(+)-K(+)-Exchanging ATPase
Sodium Valproate see Valproic Acid
Sodoku see Rat-Bite Fever
Soft Contact Lenses see Contact Lenses, Hydrophilic
Soft Tissue Neoplasms   WD 375
    Localized, by site
Soft Tissue Radiography see Technology, Radiologic
Softball see Baseball
Softening, Brain see Encephalomalacia; Paresis
Software   QA 76.75-76.765
    In medicine (General)   W 26.55.S6
    In other special fields (Form number 26.5 in any NLM schedule where applicable)
Software Engineering see Software
Software Tools see Software
Soil   S 590-599.9
Soil Microbiology   QW 60
Soil Pollutants
    General public health aspects   WA 785
    Radioactive   WN 615
Soil Pollutants, Radioactive   WN 615
Solar Aging of Skin see Skin Aging

Solar Fever see Dengue
Solcoseryl see Actihaemyl
Soldiers see Military Personnel
Soldier's Heart see Neurocirculatory Asthenia
Sole, Foot see Foot
Solo Practice see Private Practice
Solubility   QD 543
    Pharmaceutical chemistry   QV 744
Solutions   QV 786
    Used for special purposes, by subject
Solvents
    Pharmaceutical chemistry   QV 744
    Solution chemistry   QD 544-544.5
    Toxicology   QV 633
Soman
    Biochemistry   QU 131
    Toxicology   QV 627
Somatic Cell Hybrids see Hybrid Cells
Somatic Gene Therapy see Gene Therapy
Somatization Disorder see Somatoform Disorders
Somatization Syndromes see Psychophysiologic Disorders
Somatoform Disorders   WM 170
Somatomammotropin, Chorionic see Placental Lactogen
Somatomammotropin Receptors see Receptors, Somatotropin
Somatomedin C see Insulin–Like Growth Factor I
Somatomedin MSA see Insulin–Like Growth Factor II
Somatosensory Cortex   WL 307
Somatosensory Evoked Potentials see Evoked Potentials, Somatosensory
Somatostatin   WK 515
Somatostatin-14 see Somatostatin
Somatotropin   WK 515
    Deficiency   WK 550
        As a cause of a particular disorder, with the disorder
Somatotropin Receptors see Receptors, Somatotropin
Somatotropin Release Inhibiting Hormone see Somatostatin
Somatotypes   GN 66.5
Somnambulism   WM 188
Somniloquism see Sleep Disorders
Sonography, Speech see Sound Spectrography
Soporifics see Hypnotics and Sedatives; names of specific drugs
Sorbitol   QV 160
Sorbitol Dehydrogenase see Iditol Dehydrogenase
Sore Throat see Pharyngitis
Sore Throat, Septic see Streptococcal Infections
Sotalol   QV 132
Sound   QC 221-246
    Animal   QL 765
    Insect   QL 496.5
    See also Acoustics   WA 776, etc.; Hearing   WV 270; Noise   WA 776, etc.; Ultrasonics   WN 208, etc.; other particular topics associated with sound
Sound Localization   WV 272
Sound Spectrography   QC 246
    In a specific field, by subject

ALWAYS CONSULT MAIN SCHEDULES. USE NUMBER ASSIGNED ONLY WHEN SUBJECT REPRESENTS MAJOR EMPHASIS OF WORK BEING CLASSIFIED

Southern Blotting see Blotting, Southern
Soy Beans see Soybeans
Soybeans
    As a dietary supplement in health or disease
      WB 430
    Cultivation   SB 205.S7
    Sanitary control   WA 703
Space Biology see Extraterrestrial Environment
Space Flight   WD 750–758
    Standards
        Physical   WD 752
        Psychological   WD 754
Space Medicine see Space Flight
Space Perception   WW 105
    Concept formation in children   WS 105.5.D2
    Psychological aspects   BF 469
Spanish Americans see Hispanic Americans
Spasm   WL 340
    Bronchial see Bronchial Spasm   WF 500
    Drugs affecting   QV 85
    Pyloric   WI 150
    Affecting other parts of the body, with the part
Spasmolytics see Parasympatholytics
Spasmophilia see Tetany
Spasms, Infantile   WS 340
Spasmus Nutans see Spasms, Infantile
Spastic Paralysis see Muscle Spasticity
Spastic Paraplegia see Paraplegia
Spasticity, Muscle see Muscle Spasticity
Spatial Behavior
    Anthropogeography   GF 51
    Psychology   BF 469
Spatial Orientation see Orientation
Spatial Vectorcardiography see Vectorcardiography
Specialism   W 90
Specialization see Specialism; Specialties, Dental;
    Specialties, Medical; Specialties, Nursing
Specialties, Dental   WU 21
Specialties, Medical   W 90
    See also names of particular specialties
Specialties, Nursing   WY 101–164
    Government   WY 130
    Indian service   WY 130
    Institutional   WY 125
    See also specific types of nursing, e.g.,
      Occupational Health Nursing   WY 141
Specialty Boards
    (Form number 21 in any NLM schedule where
     applicable)
Species Specificity
    Bacteriology   QW 700
    Special topics, with the affecting organism or the
     organism affected
Specimen Handling   QY 25
    In field other than clinical pathology, with the
     field
SPECT see Tomography, Emission-Computed,
    Single-Photon
Spectacles see Eyeglasses
Spectrin   WH 400
Spectrometry, Mass see Spectrum Analysis, Mass
Spectrometry, Particle-Induced X-Ray Emission see

Spectrometry, X-Ray Emission
Spectrometry, Proton-Induced X-Ray Emission see
    Spectrometry, X-Ray Emission
Spectrometry, X-Ray Emission
    Analysis of drinking water   WA 686
    Analytical chemistry   QD 96.X2
    Radiation physics   QC 482.S6
    Used for other purposes, by subject
Spectrometry, X-Ray Emission, Electron
    Microscopic see Electron Probe Microanalysis
Spectrometry, X-Ray Emission, Electron Probe see
    Electron Probe Microanalysis
Spectrometry, X-Ray Fluorescence see
    Spectrometry, X-Ray Emission
Spectrophotometry
    Analytical chemistry (General)   QD 95
    Quantitative analysis   QD 117.S64
    Used for special purposes, by subject, e.g.,
     Analysis of hormones   QY 330
Spectrophotometry, Atomic Absorption   QC
    454.A2
    Used for special purposes, by subject, e.g., for
     blood chemical analysis   QY 450–490, etc.
Spectrophotometry, Infrared
    Organic chemistry   QD 272.S57
    Physics   QC 457
    Used for special purposes, by subject, e.g., for
     measuring impurities in the air   WA 754
Spectroscopy see Spectrum Analysis
Spectroscopy, Magnetic Resonance see Nuclear
    Magnetic Resonance
Spectroscopy, Mass see Spectrum Analysis, Mass
Spectroscopy, Nuclear Magnetic Resonance see
    Nuclear Magnetic Resonance
Spectrum Analysis
    Analytical chemistry   QD 95
    Organic analysis   QD 272.S6
Spectrum Analysis, Mass   QC 454.M3
Spectrum Analysis, Raman   QC 454.R36
Speech   WV 501
    Development see Language Development   WS
     105.5.C8, etc.
Speech Acoustics   WV 501
Speech, Alaryngeal   WV 540
Speech Articulation Tests   WV 501
    In disorders of psychogenic origins   WM 475
    In disorders of neurologic origins   WL 340.2
Speech Discrimination see Speech Perception
Speech Discrimination Tests   WV 272
Speech Disorders
    Associated with the larynx and other organs
     involved with speech   WV 500
    Neurologic   WL 340.2
    Psychogenic   WM 475
    Therapy   WL 340.2; WM 475; WV 500
     See also Speech Therapy   WM 475, etc.
    See also Deaf-Mutism   WV 280
Speech, Esophageal   WV 540
Speech Intelligibility
    In adolescence   WS 462
    In infancy & childhood   WS 105.5.C8
    Physiological aspects   WV 501
    Speech disorders   WM 475, etc.

**ALWAYS CONSULT MAIN SCHEDULES. USE NUMBER ASSIGNED ONLY WHEN
SUBJECT REPRESENTS MAJOR EMPHASIS OF WORK BEING CLASSIFIED**

Speech–Language Pathology
  Neurologic   WL 340.2
  Psychogenic   WM 475
Speech Pathology see Speech–Language Pathology
Speech Perception   WV 272
Speech Production Measurement   WV 501
  In disorders of psychogenic origins   WM 475
  In disorders of neurologic origins   WL 340.2
Speech Reception Threshold Test   WV 272
Speech Sounds see Phonetics
Speech Synthesizers see Communication Aids for
  Disabled
Speech Therapy
  General   WL 340.2
  For disorders of neurologic origins   WL 340.2
  For disorders of psychogenic origins   WM 475
  See also Therapy   WL 340.2, etc., under Speech
    Disorders
Speechreading see Lipreading
Speed see Accidents, Traffic; Aircraft
Sperm see Spermatozoa
Sperm Immobilizing Agents   QV 177
Sperm–Ovum Interactions   WQ 205
Sperm Penetration see Sperm–Ovum Interactions
Spermatic Cord   WJ 780
Spermatic Cord Torsion   WJ 780
Spermatocidal Agents   QV 177
Spermatocytes   WJ 834
Spermatogenesis   WJ 834
Spermatogonia   WJ 834
Spermatophores see Spermatogonia
Spermatozoa   WJ 834
  Drugs destroying see Spermatocidal Agents
    QV 177
  Drugs immobilizing see Sperm–Immobilizing
    Agents   QV 177
Spermicidal Agents see Spermatocidal Agents
Spermiocytes see Spermatocytes
Spermophilus see Sciuridae
Sphaerophorus see Fusobacterium
Sphaerophorus Infections see Fusobacterium
  Infections
Sphagnum see Plants
Sphenoid Bone   WE 705
Sphenoid Sinus   WV 358
Spherocytosis, Hereditary   WH 170
Spheroplasts   QW 51
Sphingolipidoses   WD 205.5.L5
  See also names of specific forms, e.g.,
    Niemann–Pick Disease   WD 205.5.L5
Sphingolipids   QU 85
Sphingomyelins   QU 93
Sphygmography see Blood Pressure Determination
Sphygmomanometers, Continuous see Blood
  Pressure Monitors
Spider Bite see Arachnidism
Spider Monkey see Cebidae
Spider Venoms   WD 420
Spiders   QX 471
  Bites see Arachnidism   WD 420
Spin Labels
  Biological research   QH 324.9.S62
Spina Bifida see Spinal Dysraphism

Spina Bifida Aperta see Spina Bifida Cystica
Spina Bifida Cystica   WE 730
Spina Bifida Manifesta see Spina Bifida Cystica
Spina Bifida Occulta   WE 730
Spina Bifida, Open see Spina Bifida Cystica
Spinal Accessory Nerve see Accessory Nerve
Spinal Anesthesia see Anesthesia, Spinal
Spinal Bifida, Closed see Spina Bifida Occulta
Spinal Canal   WE 725
Spinal Cord   WL 400
Spinal Cord Compression   WL 400
Spinal Cord Diseases   WL 400
Spinal Cord Injuries   WL 400
Spinal Cord Neoplasms   WL 400
Spinal Cord Syphilis see Tabes Dorsalis
Spinal Diseases   WE 725
  Veterinary   SF 901
Spinal Dysraphism   WE 730
Spinal Fluid Pressure see Cerebrospinal Fluid
  Pressure
Spinal Fractures   WE 725
Spinal Fusion   WE 725
Spinal Injuries   WE 725
Spinal Muscular Atrophy see Muscular Atrophy,
  Spinal
Spinal Neoplasms   WE 725
Spinal Nerve Roots   WL 400
Spinal Nerves   WL 400
Spinal Osteophytosis   WE 725
  Veterinary   SF 901
Spinal Puncture
  Anesthesia see Anesthesia, Spinal   WO 305
  Clinical pathology
    Cerebrospinal fluid   QY 220, etc.
  General diagnosis   WB 377
  In neurology
    Cerebrospinal   WL 203, etc.
Spinal Stenosis   WE 725
Spine   WE 725–740
Spiral and Curved Bacteria (Non Mesh) see Bacteria
Spiral Ganglion   WV 250
Spiral Organ see Organ of Corti
Spirillum   QW 154
Spiritual Healing see Mental Healing
Spiritualism   BF 1228–1389
Spiro Compounds
  As tranquilizing agents   QV 77.9
  Organic chemistry   QD 341.H9
Spirochaeta   QW 155
Spirochaetales   QW 155
Spirochaetales Infections   WC 400–425
  General works   WC 400
  Veterinary   SF 809.S6
Spirochete Infections see Spirochaetales Infections
Spirochetosis see Spirochaetales Infections
Spirolactone see Spironolactone
Spirometry
  General physical examination   WB 284
  Respiratory diagnosis   WF 141
Spironolactone   QV 160
Splanchnic Circulation   WI 900
Splanchnic Nerves   WL 610
Splanchnoptosis see Visceroptosis

Spleen   WH 600
    Blood supply   WH 600
Splenectomy   WH 600
Splenic Anemia see Hypersplenism
Splenic Artery   WG 595.S7
    See also Blood supply   WH 600 under Spleen
Splenic Diseases   WH 600
Splenic Neoplasms   WH 600
Splenic Rupture   WH 600
Splenic Vein   WI 720
Splenomegaly   WH 600
    Febrile tropical see Leishmaniasis, Visceral   WC 715
Splenoportography see Portography
Spliced Leader Peptides see Signal Peptides
Splicing, RNA see RNA Splicing
Splints   WE 26
Splints, Periodontal see Periodontal Splints
Split Genes see Genes
Spondylarthritis Ankylopoietica see Spondylitis, Ankylosing
Spondylitis   WE 725
Spondylitis, Ankylosing   WE 725
Spondyloepiphyseal Dysplasia see Osteochondrodysplasias
Spondylolisthesis   WE 730
Spondylosis see Spinal Osteophytosis
Spondylosis Deformans see Spinal Osteophytosis
Spontaneous Generation see Biogenesis
Spores   QW 190
    Of bacteria only in   QW 51
    Of cryptogams (other than fungi) in   QK 506
    Of fungi in   QW 180
Spores, Bacterial   QW 51
Spores, Fungal   QW 180
Sporotrichosis   WC 475
Sporozoa see Sporozoea
Sporozoea   QX 123–140
Sports   QT 260
Sports Medicine   QT 261
    First aid   WA 292
Spotted Fever, Rocky Mountain see Rocky Mountain Spotted Fever
Spouse Abuse
    Counseling   WM 55
    Crime against the person   HV 6626
    Effect on family   HQ 809–809.3
Spouse Caregivers see Caregivers
Sprains and Strains   WE 175
Spreading Cortical Depression   WL 307
Sprue see Celiac Disease
Sprue, Tropical   WD 175
Sputum   QY 120
SQ 14225 see Captopril
Squalene   QU 85
    Organic chemistry   QD 416
Squint see Strabismus
Squirrel Monkey see Saimiri
Squirrels see Sciuridae
St. Anthony's Fire see Ergotism
St. Vitus' Dance see Chorea
STA–MCA Bypass see Cerebral Revascularization
Stabilizing Agents see Excipients

Stable Factor see Factor VII
Staff Development
    Job enrichment   HF 5549.5.J616
    Training of employees   HF 5549.5.T7
    In special fields, by subject
    See also Personnel Management
Staffing and Scheduling see Personnel Staffing and Scheduling
Staggerer Mice see Mice, Neurologic Mutants
Staging, Neoplasm see Neoplasm Staging
Stains and Staining
    Bacteriology   QW 25
    Microscopy (General)   QH 237
    In medicolegal examination   W 750
Stammering see Stuttering
Standard Preparations see Reference Standards
Standardization, Drugs see Standards   QV 771 under Drugs
Standards see Name of specialties with subheading standards or, lacking that, the number for the specialty as a profession, e.g., in psychiatry; Hospitals; Professional standards review organizations; Quality control
Standards, Reference see Reference Standards
Stannum see Tin
Stapedectomy see Stapes Surgery
Stapedius   WV 230
Stapes   WV 230
Stapes Surgery   WV 230
    Treatment of otosclerosis   WV 265
Staphylocoagulase see Coagulase
Staphylococcal Clumping Factor see Coagulase
Staphylococcal Food Poisoning   WC 268
Staphylococcal Infections   WC 250
    Veterinary   SF 809.S72
Staphylococcal Phages see Staphylococcus Phages
Staphylococcal Pneumonia see Pneumonia, Staphylococcal
Staphylococcal Protein A   QW 52
Staphylococcal Toxoid   WC 250
Staphylococcal Vaccines   WC 250
Staphylococcus   QW 142.5.C6
Staphylococcus Phages   QW 161.5.S8
Starch   QU 83
Starvation   WD 100
Stasis Ulcer see Varicose Ulcer
State Dentistry   W 260
    By political jurisdiction   W 275
State Government
    Special topics, by subject
State Health Planning and Development Agencies   WA 540
State Health Planning, United States see Health Planning
State Health Plans   WA 540
State Medicine   W 225
    By political jurisdiction   W 275
State-of-the-Art Review see Review Literature
Statewide Health Coordinating Councils see Health Planning Councils
Statistical Computing see Mathematical Computing
Statistical Models see Models, Statistical
Statistical Regression see Regression Analysis

ALWAYS CONSULT MAIN SCHEDULES.   USE NUMBER ASSIGNED ONLY WHEN SUBJECT REPRESENTS MAJOR EMPHASIS OF WORK BEING CLASSIFIED

Statistics   HA
    Biometry (General)   QH 323.5
    Mathematical methods (General)   QA 276–280
    Medical   WA 900
      By specialty or particular disease (Form number 16 in any NLM schedule where applicable)
      Theory and methods   WA 950
        By specialty (Form number 25 in any NLM schedule where applicable)
    Nursing   WY 31
    Periodical government documents   W2
    Vital see Vital statistics,   HB, etc.
    Special topics, by subject
Status Asthmaticus   WF 553
Status Dysraphicus see Spinal Dysraphism
Status Lymphaticus see Lymphatic Diseases
Stealing see Theft
Steam   TJ 268–280.7
    See also Baths, Finnish   WB 525; Sterilization   WX 165, etc.
Steatorrhea see Celiac Disease
Steatorrhea, Idiopathic see Celiac Disease
Steele–Richardson–Olszewski Syndrome see Supranuclear Palsy, Progressive
Stegomyia see Aedes
Stein–Leventhal Syndrome see Polycystic Ovary Syndrome
Stellate Ganglion   WL 600
Stem Cell Assay see Colony-Forming Units Assay
Stem Cell Assay, Tumor see Tumor Stem Cell Assay
Stem Cells   QH 581.2
Stem Cells, Hematopoietic see Hematopoietic Stem Cells
Stem Cells, Neoplastic see Tumor Stem Cells
Stenocardia see Angina Pectoris
Stenosis see Constriction, Pathologic; names of various types of stenosis, e.g., Pulmonary Valve Stenosis
Step Test see Exercise Test
Stereognosis   WR 102
Stereophotogrammetry see Photogrammetry
Stereopsis see Depth Perception
Stereoscopic Vision see Depth Perception
Stereoscopy see Optics
Stereotyped Behavior   WM 165
    In a particular situation, with the situation
Stereotyping   BF 323.S63
Sterility see Infertility
Sterility, Female see Infertility, Female
Sterility, Male see Infertility, Male
Sterilization
    In dentistry   WU 300
    In hospitals   WX 165
    In mortuary practice   WA 840
    In organ transplantation   WO 665
    In preventive medicine   WA 240
    In surgery   WO 113
Sterilization, Involuntary
    Social aspects   HV 4989
Sterilization, Sexual
    Family planning   HQ 767.7
    Female   WP 660

    See also Castration   WP 660; Sterilization, Tubal   WP 660
    Insect   QX 600
    Male   WJ 868
    See also Castration   WJ 868; Vasectomy   WJ 780
Sterilization, Tubal   WP 660
Sternum   WE 715
Steroid Receptors see Receptors, Steroid
Steroidal Anti–Inflammatory Agents see Anti–Inflammatory Agents, Steroidal
Steroids
    Biochemistry   QU 85
    Organic chemistry   QD 426–426.7
    Hormones   WK 150
    See also names of specific steroids, e.g., Anabolic Steroids   WK 150, etc.
Steroids, Anabolic see Anabolic Steroids
Sterols   QU 95
Stethoscopy see Auscultation
Stevens–Johnson Syndrome   WR 150
Sticklebacks see Fishes
Stigmatization   BV 5091.S7
Stilbenes
    As contraceptives   QV 177
    Organic chemistry   QD 341.H9
Stilbestrol see Diethylstilbestrol
Stillbirth see Fetal Death
Still's Disease, Juvenile–Onset see Arthritis, Juvenile Rheumatoid
Stimulants see Analeptics; Convulsants; Parasympathomimetics; Sympathomimetics; Xanthines; names of specific stimulants
Stimulation, Chemical   QV 38
Stimulation, Electric see Electric Stimulation
Stings see Bites and Stings
Stippled Epiphyses see Chondrodysplasia Punctata
STLV–III see SIV
Stochastic Processes   QA 274–274.76
    Special topics, by subject
Stockings, Compression see Bandages
Stockings, Elastic see Bandages
Stoicism see Philosophy
Stokes–Adams Attacks see Adams–Stokes Syndrome
Stomach   WI 300–387
    Acidity see Gastric Acidity Determination   QY 130; Gastric Juice   WI 302, etc.; Antacids   QV 69
    Analysis   QY 130
    Desiccated see Tissue Extracts   QV 370, etc.
Stomach Dilatation   WI 300
    Veterinary   SF 851
Stomach Diseases   WI 300–387
    General works   WI 300
    Veterinary   SF 851
Stomach Neoplasms   WI 320
Stomach, Ruminant   QL 862
    Domestic animals   SF 851
Stomach Rupture   WI 300
Stomach Ulcer   WI 360
Stomach Volvulus   WI 300
Stomatitis
    General works for the dentist   WU 140

General works for the gastroenterologist   WI 200

Veterinary   SF 852

Stomatitis, Aphthous

General works for the dentist   WU 140

General works for the gastroenterologist   WI 200

Stomatitis, Herpetic   WC 578

Stomatitis, Ulcerative see Gingivitis, Necrotizing Ulcerative

Stomatology see Mouth; Mouth Diseases

Storerooms see Materials Management, Hospital

Strabismus   WW 415

Strabismus, Convergent see Esotropia

Strains see Sprains and Strains

Stramonium   QV 134

Strapping, Wounds see Bandages

Stratigraphy, X-Ray see Tomography, X-Ray

Stream Pollution see Water Pollution

Street Drug Testing see Substance Abuse Detection

Street Drugs

Abuse   WM 270

General works   QV 55

Pharmacology   QV 38

Street People see Homeless Persons

Streetcars, Public Health Aspects see Public Health Aspects   WA 810 under Transportation

Strepsirhini   QL 737.P95

Diseases   SF 997.5.P7

Streptococcal Infections   WC 210

Food poisoning   WC 268

Streptococcal OK-432 see Picibanil

Streptococcal Preparation OK-432 see Picibanil

Streptococcus   QW 142.5.C6

Streptococcus mutans   QW 142.5.C6

Streptococcus pneumoniae Infections see Pneumococcal Infections

Streptodornase see Deoxyribonucleases

Streptodornase and Streptokinase   QU 136

Streptomyces   QW 125.5.S8

Streptomycetaceae   QW 125.5.S8

Streptomycin   QV 356

Streptozocin Diabetes see Diabetes Mellitus, Experimental

Streptozotocin Diabetes see Diabetes Mellitus, Experimental

Stress   QZ 160

Physiology   QT 162.S8

Special topics, by subject

Stress Disorders, Post-Traumatic   WM 170

Stress Fractures see Fractures, Stress

Stress, Mechanical

Biophysics   QT 34

Bone   WE 140

Other special topics, by subject

Stress Proteins see Heat-Shock Proteins

Stress, Psychological   WM 172

In aviation medicine   WD 730

In infancy & childhood   WS 350

In space medicine   WD 754

Stress Test see Exercise Test

Stressful Events see Life Change Events

Striate Cortex see Visual Cortex

Striated Border see Microvilli

Stridor see Respiratory Sounds

Strikes, Employee   HD 5306-5450.7

Hospital personnel   WX 159.8

Occupational health services   WA 412

Mental health services   WA 495

Nurses   WY 30

Dealings with hospitals   WX 159.8

Special fields, by profession, industry, or specialty

See also Labor Unions

Stroke see Cerebrovascular Disorders; Heat Exhaustion; Lightning; Sunstroke

Stroke Volume   WG 106

Strongyloidea   QX 243

Strongyloidiasis   WC 865

Strontium

Inorganic chemistry   QD 181.S8

Metabolism   QU 130

Pharmacology   QV 275

Strontium Isotopes

Inorganic chemistry   QD 181.S8

Pharmacology   QV 275

Strontium Radioisotopes   WN 420

Nuclear physics   QC 796.S8

See also special topics under Radioisotopes

Strophanthins   QV 153

Structure-Activity Relationship

Biochemistry   QU 34

Pharmaceutical chemistry   QV 744

Structure, Molecular see Molecular Structure

Struma see Goiter

Struma Ovarii   WP 322

Strychnine   QV 103

Toxicology   QV 628

Student Dropouts   LC 142-145

Adolescent psychology and psychiatry   WS 462-463

Student Health Services   WA 350-353

Universities and colleges   WA 351

Mental health   WA 353

See also Mental Health Services   WM 30, etc.; School Health Services   WA 350, etc.

Student Loans see Training Support

Student Selection see School Admission Criteria

Students

Substance abuse   WM 270, etc.

School mental health services   WA 352-353

School public health services   WA 350-351

Sexual behavior   HQ 27-29

See also Adolescence   WS 460, etc.; Child WS, etc.

Students, Dental   WU 18

Students, Health Occupations   W 18

Students, Medical   W 18

Supervision of student assistants in a mental hospital   WM 30

Other special topics, by subject

Students, Nursing   WY 18

Supervision in hospitals   WY 105

In mental hospitals   WM 30

Students, Premedical   W 18

Stuttering   WM 475

Stye see Hordeolum

Styrenes
  Organic chemistry   QD 341.H9
  Toxicology   QV 633
Subarachnoid Hemorrhage   WL 200
Subarachnoid Pressure see Intracranial Pressure
Subarachnoid Space   WL 200
Subcellular Fractions   QH 581-581.2
Subchondral Cysts see Bone Cysts
Subclavian Artery   WG 595.S8
Subclavian Steal Syndrome   WL 355
Subclavian Vein   WG 625.S8
Subconscious see Unconscious (Psychology)
Subcorneal Pustular Dermatosis see Skin Diseases, Vesiculobullous
Subcutaneous Tissue, Medication by see Injections, Subcutaneous
Subdiaphragmatic Abscess see Subphrenic Abscess
Subject Headings   Z 695-695.1
  Medicine   Z 695.1.M48
Sublimation   WM 193.5.S8
  In adolescence   WS 463
  In infancy & childhood   WS 350.8.D3
Sublimation, Drugs see Drug Compounding
Subliminal Perception see Subliminal Stimulation
Subliminal Projection see Subliminal Stimulation
Subliminal Stimulation   BF 323.S8
  In psychoanalysis   WM 460
  Perception   WL 705
  Suggestion   BF 1156.S8
Sublingual Gland   WI 230
Sublingual Region see Mouth Floor
Submandibular Gland   WI 230
Submarine Medicine   WD 650
Submaxillary Gland see Submandibular Gland
Submersion see Immersion
Subphrenic Abscess   WI 575
Subsidies, Educational see Training Support
Subsidies, Government see Financing, Government
Subsidies, Health Planning see Health Planning Support
Subsidies, Research see Research Support
Substance Abuse   WM 270-290
  Autopsy to determine   WM 270-290
  Social aspects   HV 5800-5840
  See also Doping in Sports   QT 261
Substance Abuse Detection   HV 5823-5823.5
  Of specific substance, with the substance
  Through urine screening   QY 185
Substance Abuse, Intravenous   WM 270
  Special topics, by subject
Substance Abuse Testing see Substance Abuse Detection
Substance Dependence   WM 270-290
  Cannabis   WM 276
  Cocaine   WM 280
  Narcotics   WM 284
  Nicotine   WM 290
  Opium alkaloids   WM 286
  See also Heroin Dependence   WM 288;
    Morphine Dependence   WM 286
Substance Use Disorders   WM 270-290
Substance Withdrawal, Neonatal see Neonatal Abstinence Syndrome

Substance Withdrawal Syndrome   WM 270-290
Substantia Nigra   WL 310
Substrate Specificity   QU 135
Subtrochanteric Fractures see Hip Fractures
Success see Achievement
Succinate Dehydrogenase   QU 140
Succinates   QU 98
  Organic chemistry
    Aliphatic compounds   QD 305.A2
Succinbromimide see Bromosuccinimide
Succinic Oxidase see Succinate Dehydrogenase
Succinimides   QV 85
Succinylcholine   QV 140
Succinyldicholine see Succinylcholine
Sucralfate   QV 66
Sucrase   QU 136
Sucrose   QU 83
Suction
  Drainage in surgery   WO 188
  Puncture technique in diagnosis   WB 373
Suction Curettage see Vacuum Curettage
Suction Lipectomy see Lipectomy
Sudden Deafness see Deafness, Sudden
Sudden Infant Death   WS 430
Sudeck's Atrophy   WE 250
Sudorifics see Sweating
Suffocating Gases see Phosgene; names of other specific gases
Suffocation see Asphyxia
Sugar Acids   QU 84
Sugar Alcohol Dehydrogenases   QU 140
Sugar Alcohol Oxidoreductases see Sugar Alcohol Dehydrogenases
Sugar Alcohols
  Biochemistry   QU 75
  Organic chemistry   QD 305.A4
  Pharmacology   QV 82
Sugar Phosphates   QU 75
  See also Glycerophosphates   QU 93
Sugar Substitutes see Sweetening Agents
Sugars see Carbohydrates
Suggestion   WM 415
  See also Counseling   WM 55, etc.; Mental Healing   WB 880-885; related special topics
Suicide   HV 6543-6548
  Medicolegal aspects   W 864
  Specific mental disorders associated with suicide, with the disorder
  See also Crisis Intervention   WM 401
Suicide, Assisted   W 50
Suipoxvirus   QW 165.5.P6
Sulbactam   QV 350
Sulfadiazine   QV 265
Sulfadoxine   QV 265
Sulfamethoxazole   QV 265
Sulfamethoxypyridazine   QV 265
Sulfamethylisoxazole see Sulfamethoxazole
Sulfamyl Diuretics see Diuretics, Sulfamyl
Sulfanilamides   QV 265
Sulfaninylbutylurea see Carbutamide
Sulfates   QV 280
Sulfates, Inorganic see Sulfates
Sulfates, Organic see Sulfuric Acids

Sulfathiazoles   QV 265
Sulfhydryl Compounds
    Biochemistry   QU 130
    Organic chemistry
        Aliphatic compounds   QD 305.S3
        Aromatic compounds   QD 341.S3
Sulfhydryl Compounds Antagonists see Sulfhydryl
    Reagents
Sulfhydryl Compounds Inhibitors see Sulfhydryl
    Reagents
Sulfhydryl Reagents   QU 143
Sulfides   QV 280
    Inorganic chemistry   QD 181.S1
Sulfobromophthalein   QV 240
Sulfonamides   QV 265
Sulfones
    Biochemistry   QU 130
    Organic chemistry
        Aliphatic compounds   QD 305.S6
        Aromatic compounds   QD 341.S6
    Pharmacology   QV 265
Sulfonethylmethane see Hypnotics and Sedatives
Sulfonic Acids   QU 98
    Inorganic chemistry   QD 181.S1
    Organic chemistry
        Aliphatic   QD 305.S3
        Aromatic   QD 341.S3
Sulfonmethane see Hypnotics and Sedatives
Sulfonyldianiline see Dapsone
Sulfonylurea Compounds
    As hypoglycemic agents   WK 825
    Organic chemistry
        Aliphatic compounds   QD 305.S6
Sulformethoxine see Sulfadoxine
Sulforthomidine see Sulfadoxine
Sulfoxides
    Organic chemistry
        Aliphatic compounds   QD 305.S3
        Aromatic compounds   QD 341.S6
    Pharmacology   QV 265
Sulfur
    Inorganic chemistry   QD 181.S1
    Pharmacology   QV 265
    Mineral waters   WB 442
Sulfur Amino Acids see Amino Acids, Sulfur
Sulfur Dioxide
    Inorganic chemistry   QD 181.S1
    Toxicology   QV 618
Sulfur Isotopes
    Inorganic chemistry   QD 181.S1
    Pharmacology   QV 265
Sulfur Mustard see Mustard Gas
Sulfur Oxides
    As air pollutants   WA 754
    Inorganic chemistry   QD 181.S1
Sulfuric Acids   QD 181.S1
    Toxicology   QV 612
Sulindac
    As an anti–inflammatory analgesic   QV 95
Sulph–
    For words beginning thus, see those beginning
    with Sulf–
Sulpiride   QV 77.5

Sumac see Toxicodendron
Sun Baths see Sunlight; Heliotherapy
Sun Fever see Dengue
Sunbathing see Heliotherapy
Sunburn   WR 160
Sunlight
    As an aid to health   QT 230
    Therapeutic use see Heliotherapy   WB 480, etc.
Sunscreening Agents   QV 63
Sunstroke   WD 610
    See also Heat Exhaustion   WD 610
Superego   WM 460.5.R3
    In adolescence   WS 463
    In infancy & childhood   WS 350.5
Superfecundation see Pregnancy, Multiple
Superfetation   WQ 235
Superior Vena Cava Obstruction see Superior Vena
    Cava Syndrome
Superior Vena Cava Syndrome   WG 625.V3
Superior Vena Cava Thrombosis see Superior Vena
    Cava Syndrome
Superiority Complex see Personality Disorders
Supernumerary Organs see Abnormalities
Superoxide Dismutase   QU 140
Superoxides   QV 312
Superpalite see Phosgene
Supersonic Waves see Ultrasonic Therapy;
    Ultrasonics
Superstitions
    Curiosities   WZ 308
    Medical   WZ 309
    Occult sciences   BF 1405–1999
    Popular delusions   AZ 999
    Religion   BL 490
Supplies, Pharmaceutical see Equipment and
    Supplies; Pharmacy; Catalogs, Drug; specific
    types of pharmaceutical supplies, e.g., Drug
    packaging
Supply Catalogs see Catalogs, Commercial; names
    of other specific types of catalogs
Suppositories
    Administration of medicines   WB 344
    Drug forms   QV 785
Suppressor Cells see T–Lymphocytes,
    Suppressor–Effector
Suppressor–Effector T–Lymphocytes see
    T–Lymphocytes, Suppressor–Effector
Suppressor Factor, T–Cell, Glioblastoma–Derived
    see Transforming Growth Factor beta
Suppressor Transfer RNA see RNA, Transfer
Suppuration   QZ 150
    Clinical examination   QY 210
    See also Infection   WC 195, etc.
Supranuclear Palsy, Progressive   WL 359
Suprarenal Glands see Adrenal Glands
Suprarenalin see Epinephrine
Suprasellar Cyst see Craniopharyngioma
Supratentorial Neoplasms   WL 358
Suprofen   QV 95
Surface–Active Agents   QV 233
    See also Pulmonary Surfactant   WF 600; Surface
    Tension   QC 183
Surface Anesthesia see Anesthesia, Local

**ALWAYS CONSULT MAIN SCHEDULES. USE NUMBER ASSIGNED ONLY WHEN
SUBJECT REPRESENTS MAJOR EMPHASIS OF WORK BEING CLASSIFIED**

Surface Antigens see Antigens, Surface
Surface Glycoproteins see Membrane Glycoproteins
Surface Markers, Immunological see Antigens,
    Surface
Surface Properties   QD 506.A1A–508
    Dental chemistry   WU 170
    In other areas, by subject
Surface Proteins see Membrane Proteins
Surface Tension   QC 183
    See also Pulmonary Surfactant   WF 600; Surface
        Active Agents   QV 233
Surfactants see Surface–Active Agents
Surfactants, Pulmonary see Pulmonary Surfactants
Surgeon–Patient Relations see Physician–Patient
    Relations
Surgeons see Biography   WZ 112.5.S8, etc., and
    Directories   WO 22 under Surgery
Surgeons, Oral, Directories see Directories   WU
    22 under Surgery, Oral
Surgery   WO
    Abdominal see Surgery   WI 900–970 under
        Abdomen
    Animal see Surgery   SF 911 under Veterinary
        Medicine
    Atlases see Surgery, Operative   WO 517, etc.
    Barber surgeons   WO 11
    Biography
        Collective   WZ 112.5.S8
            Military   WZ 112.5.M4
        Individual   WZ 100
    Cardiac problems   WG 460
    Cardiovascular see Surgery   WG 168, etc.,
        under Cardiovascular System
    Care plans see Insurance, Health   W 100–275
    Case Studies   WO 16
    Cryogenic see Cryogenic Surgery   WO 510, etc.
    Dental see Dentistry, Operative   WU 300–360,
        etc.; Surgery, Oral   WU 600–640, etc.
    Directories   WO 22
    Diseases   WO 140
    Emergency   WO 700–820
    Experimental   WO 50
    Exploratory   WO 141
    Humor about   WZ 305.5
    In adolescence   WO 925
    In infancy & childhood   WO 925
    In old age   WO 950
    Industrial   WO 700–820
    Infection   WO 184–185
    Insurance see Insurance, Health   W 100–275
    Military   WO 800
    Naval   WO 800
    Obstetrical   WQ 400–450
    Ophthalmological see Surgery   WW 168 under
        Eye
    Orthopedic see Orthopedics   WE 168–190, etc.
    Otorhinolaryngologic see Surgery   WV 168
        under Otorhinolaryngologic Diseases; or
        Surgery   WV 200 under Ear; Surgery   WV
        300 under Nose; Surgery   WV 540 under
        Larynx
    Proctological see Surgery   WI 650 under
        Rectum

    Thoracic see Thoracic Surgery   WF 980
    Traumatic   WO 700–820
    Urologic see Urinary Tract   WJ 168, etc.; or
        Urogenital System   WJ 168, etc.
    Veterinary see Surgery   SF 911 under
        Veterinary Medicine
    See also Electrosurgery   WO 198, etc.;
        Neurosurgery   WL 368; names of other
        diseases, organs or systems; names of other
        types of surgery
Surgery, Cosmetic see Surgery, Plastic
Surgery Department, Hospital   WO 27–28
Surgery, Esthetic see Surgery, Plastic
Surgery, Laparoscopic
    General works   WO 500
    For specific diseases, with the disease
Surgery, Laser see Laser Surgery
Surgery, Minor   WO 192
Surgery, Office see Ambulatory Surgery
Surgery, Operative   WO 500–517
    Atlases   WO 517
    Obstetrical   WQ 400
    Veterinary   SF 911
    Localized, by site
Surgery, Oral   WU 600–640
    Directories of oral surgeons   WU 22
    In infancy & childhood   WU 480
Surgery, Oral, Preprosthetic   WU 500
Surgery, Orthopedic see Orthopedics
Surgery, Outpatient see Ambulatory Surgery
Surgery, Plastic   WO 600–640
    Nose   WV 312
    Other locations, by site
Surgery, Repeat see Reoperation
Surgery, Veterinary   SF 911–914.4
Surgical Anastomosis see Anastomosis, Surgical
Surgical Atlases see Surgery, Operative
Surgical Blood Loss see Blood Loss, Surgical
Surgical Care Plans see Insurance, Health
Surgical Diathermy see Electrocoagulation
Surgical Diseases see Surgery
Surgical Equipment   WO 162–170
    Catalogs   W 26
Surgical Flaps   WO 610
    Used in surgery for a particular condition, with
        the condition
Surgical Infection see Surgical Wound Infection
Surgical Instruments   WO 162
    Catalogs   W 26
Surgical Mesh   WO 162
Surgical Nursing   WY 161–162
    Education   WY 18–18.5
    See also Operating Room Nursing   WY 162;
        Nursing   WY 154, etc. under Critical Care
Surgical Pathology see Pathology, Surgical
Surgical Replantation see Replantation
Surgical Revision see Reoperation
Surgical Scrub see Handwashing
Surgical Staplers   WO 162
Surgical Wound Dehiscence   WO 185
Surgical Wound Infection   WO 185
Surrogate Markers see Biological Markers
Surrogate Mothers   HQ 759.5
    Special topics, by subject

**ALWAYS CONSULT MAIN SCHEDULES. USE NUMBER ASSIGNED ONLY WHEN
SUBJECT REPRESENTS MAJOR EMPHASIS OF WORK BEING CLASSIFIED**

Surveillance, Immunologic see Immunologic
Surveillance
Survey Methods see Data Collection
Surveys see Dental Health Surveys; Health Surveys;
Library Surveys; Nutrition Surveys; subject of
other specific surveys, e.g., Nursing
Survival
Arctic and antarctic   QT 160
Atomic warfare   WN 650
Aviation accidents   WD 740
Civil defense   UA 926–929
First aid   WA 292
Shipwrecks
Navies and merchant marines   VK 1250–1299
Private ships   G 525–530
Space flight   WD 740
Wilderness   WA 250
From other accidents and disasters, by subject
Survival Analysis   WA 950
Special topics, by subject
Survival Rate   WA 900
Special topics, by subject
Survivorship see Survival Rate
Suspending Agents see Excipients
Suspensions   QV 785
Sustained-Release Preparations see Delayed-Action
Preparations
Suture Techniques   WO 166
Sutures   WO 166
Suxamethonium see Succinylcholine
SV40 Virus see Polyomavirus macacae
Swallowing see Deglutition
Swamp Fever see Equine Infectious Anemia
Sweat   WR 400
Sweat Gland Diseases   WR 400
Sweat Gland Neoplasms   WR 400
Sweat Glands   WR 400
Sweating   WR 102
Drugs inducing   QV 122
Swedish Gymnastics see Gymnastics; Exercise
Therapy
Sweetening Agents   WA 712
Swimbladder see Air Sacs
Swimming   QT 260.5.S9
Accidents   QT 260.5.S9
Swimming Pools   WA 820
Swine
Anatomy   SF 767.S95
Culture   SF 391–397.83
As laboratory animals   QY 60.S8
Physiology   SF 768.2.S95
Swine Diseases   SF 971–977
Swine Herpesvirus 1 see Herpesvirus 1, Suid
Swine Influenza Virus see Orthomyxovirus Type A,
Porcine
Swinepox Virus see Suipoxvirus
Swing Beds see Bed Conversion
Swiss Mice see Mice
Sydnones
Organic chemistry   QD 401
Used for particular diseases, with the disease
Sylvian Vein see Cerebral Veins

Symbiosis
Ecology and general   QH 548
Microbial   QW 52
Plant   QK 918
Symbiotes see Rickettsiaceae
Symbiotic Relations (Psychology) see Object
Attachment
Symbolism (Psychology)   BF 458
Psychoanalysis   WM 460.5.D8
See also Emblems and Insignia   WZ 334, etc.
Sympathectomy   WL 610
Sympathetic-Blocking Agents see Sympatholytics
Sympathetic Ganglia see Ganglia, Sympathetic
Sympathetic Nerve Block see Autonomic Nerve
Block
Sympathetic Nervous System   WL 610
Children   WS 340
Sympathetic Transmitter Releasers see
Sympathomimetics
Sympathins see Catecholamines
Sympatholytics   QV 132
Sympathomimetics   QV 129
Symphalangus see Hylobates
Symphysiotomy   WQ 430
Symptomatology see Diagnosis
Synapses   WL 102.8
Synaptic Membranes   WL 102.8
Synaptic Potentials see Synaptic Transmission
Synaptic Receptors see Receptors, Neurotransmitter
Synaptic Transmission   WL 102.7–102.8
Synaptosomes   WL 102.8
Syncope   WB 182
Syndactyly   WE 835
Syndrome   QZ 140
Of specific disorders, with the disorder
Synergism see Drug Synergism
Synostosis   WE 250
Synovia see Synovial Fluid
Synovial Fluid   WE 300
Synovial Membrane   WE 300
Synovioma see Sarcoma, Synovial
Synovitis   WE 300
Synovitis, Pigmented Villonodular   WE 300
Synstigmin see Neostigmine
Synthetases see Ligases
Synthetic Vaccines see Vaccines, Synthetic
Syphacia see Oxyuroidea
Syphilids see Syphilis, Cutaneous
Syphilis   WC 160–170
Antisyphilitics   QV 261–262
Cerebrospinal see Neurosyphilis   WC 165
Drug therapy   WC 170
In pregnancy   WQ 256
Syphilis, Cardiovascular   WC 168
Syphilis, Congenital   WC 161
Syphilis, Cutaneous   WC 160
Syphilis, Latent   WC 160–164
Syphilis Serodiagnosis   QY 275
Syphilis, Spinal Cord see Tabes Dorsalis
Syringadenoma see Adenoma, Sweat Gland
Syringe Sharing see Needle Sharing
Syringes   W 26
Syringomyelia   WL 400

ALWAYS CONSULT MAIN SCHEDULES. USE NUMBER ASSIGNED ONLY WHEN
SUBJECT REPRESENTS MAJOR EMPHASIS OF WORK BEING CLASSIFIED

Systematics see Classification
Systeme International d'Unites see International System of Units
Systemic Poisons see Poisons
Systems Analysis
    Analytical methods connected with physical problems   QA 402–402.37
    Industrial engineering   T 57.6–57.97
Systems Theory   QA 402–402.37
    Of other special topics, by subject
Systole   WG 280
Systolic Click–Murmur Syndrome see Mitral Valve Prolapse
Systolic Time Interval see Systole
Szondi Test   WM 145.5.S9
    In adolescence   WS 462
    In infancy & childhood   WS 105.5.E8
    In psychology   BF 698.8.S85

T

T Antigens see Antigens, Viral, Tumor
T–Cell Growth Factor see Interleukin–2
T–Cell Growth Factor Receptors see Receptors, Interleukin–2
T–Cell Leukemia Virus I, Human see HTLV–I
T–Cell Leukemia Viruses, Human see HTLV–BLV Viruses
T–Cell Receptors see Receptors, Antigen, T–Cell
T–Cells see T–Lymphocytes
T–Cells, Suppressor–Effector see T–Lymphocytes, Suppressor–Effector
T–Groups see Sensitivity Training Groups
T–Lymphocytes   WH 200
    Cellular immunity   QW 568
T–Lymphocytes, Cytotoxic   WH 200
    In cellular immunity   QW 568
T–Lymphocytes, Suppressor–Effector   WH 200
    In cellular immunity   QW 568
T–Lymphotropic Virus Type III Antibodies, Human see HIV Antibodies
T–Lymphotropic Virus Type III Infections, Human see HIV Infections
T–Lymphotropic Virus, Type III, Simian see SIV
T–Phages   QW 161.5.C6
Tabacosis see Pneumoconiosis
Tabes Dorsalis   WC 165
Tables
    (Form number 16 in any NLM schedule where applicable or appropriate LC number, e.g., tables illustrating general science   Q 199)
    See also name of specific subject of the table
Tablets   QV 787
    As medication for particular diseases, with the disease
Tablets, Enteric–Coated   QV 787
Taboo   GN 471.4
Tac Peptide see Receptors, Interleukin–2
Tac P55 Peptide see Receptors, Interleukin–2
Tachyarrhythmia see Tachycardia
Tachycardia   WG 330
Tachycardia, Paroxysmal   WG 330
Tachypleus see Horseshoe Crabs

Taenia   QX 400
Taenia Infections see Taeniasis
Taeniacides see Anticestodal Agents
Taeniarhynchus see Taenia
Taeniasis   WC 838
    Veterinary   SF 810.C5
Tahyna Virus see California Group Viruses
Talampicillin   QV 354
Talc
    Adverse effects   WF 654
    Dosage form   QV 785
Talipes Cavus see Foot Deformities
Talipes Equinovarus see Clubfoot
Tamarin, Golden see Callitrichinae
Tamias see Sciuridae
Tamoxifen
    As an estrogen antagonist   WP 522
    Used in the treatment and prevention of breast neoplasms   WP 870
Tampons
    In surgery   WO 162
Tanning
    Occupational medicine   WA 400–495
Tannins   QV 65
Tantalum
    Inorganic chemistry   QD 181.T2
    Pharmacology   QV 290
Tape Recording
    Catalogs and works about (Form number 18.2 in any NLM schedule where applicable)
    Recordings, by subject
Tape Recording, Video see Videotape Recording
Tapetoretinal Degeneration see Retinitis Pigmentosa
Tapeworm Infection see Cestode Infections
Tapeworms see Cestoda
Tapioca see Cassava
Tapping see Punctures
Tarantulas see Spiders
Targeted Toxins see Immunotoxins
Tars   QV 241
    As dermatologic agents   QV 60
    See also Coal Tar   QV 60, etc.
Tarsal Joint   WE 880
Tartar see Dental Calculus
Tartar Emetic see Antimony
Taste   WI 210
Taste Buds   WI 210
TAT see Thematic Apperception Test
Tattooing   GN 419.3
Taurine   QU 60
    Organic chemistry   QD 305.A8
Taxes
    General   HJ 2240–7390
    Dentistry   WU 77
    Hospitals   WX 157
    Medicine   W 74
    Nursing   WY 77
    Pharmacy   QV 736
    Tax aspects of legislation, in number for discussion of legislation, e.g., of black lung legislation   WF 33
Taxonomy see Classification
Tc–99m MDP see Technetium Tc 99m Medronate

TCGF see Interleukin–2
TDE see DDD
Tea
    As a beverage used as a dietary supplement in
        health or disease   WB 438
    As a medicinal plant   QV 766
    Chemical technology   TP 650
    Cultivation of plant   SB 271–272
    See also Theophylline   QV 107
Teachers' Manuals see Teaching Materials
Teaching
    (Form number 18 in any NLM schedule where
        applicable)
    As a medical profession   W 88
    Nursing   WY 105
    Of the blind   HU 1618–2349
    Of the deaf   HV 2417–2990.5
    Of the deaf-mute   HV 2417–2990.5
    Of other groups in education, number for the
        group
Teaching Materials   LB 1027
    (Form number 18.2 in any NLM schedule where
        applicable)
    Physiology   QT 200
    Special topics, by subject
Team Nursing see Nursing, Team
Tear Gases   QV 665
Tears   WW 208
    Secretion   WW 208
        See also Crying   WS 105.5.E5, etc.
Tears, Artificial see Ophthalmic Solutions
Teas, Herbal see Beverages
Teas, Medicinal see Beverages
Technetium   WN 420
    Nuclear physics   QC 796.T35
    See also special topics under radioisotopes
Technetium Methylene Diphosphonate see
    Technetium Tc 99m Medronate
Technetium Tc 99m Medronate   WN 420
    Diagnostic use   WN 445
Technical Services, Library see Library Technical
    Services
Technology   T–TX
    Chemical (General)   TP 144–145
    General works   T 44–51
    Special topics, by subject
Technology Assessment, Biomedical
    General   W 74
    Special topics, by subject
Technology, Dental   WU 150
Technology, Food see Food Technology
Technology, High–Cost
    Medicine   W 74
    Other topics, class by subject if specific; if general,
        in economics number where available
Technology, Medical
    As a profession   QY 21
    Clinical pathology   QY
    Diagnostic and therapeutic techniques   WB 365
Technology, Pharmaceutical   QV 778
Technology, Radiologic   WN 160
    Instrumentation   WN 150
    Veterinary   SF 757.8

Tectum Mesencephali see Corpora Quadrigemina
Tedelparin   QV 193
Teenage Pregnancy see Pregnancy in Adolescence
Teeth see Tooth
Teeth-Straightening see Orthodontics
Teething see Tooth Eruption
Tegafur   QV 269
Telangiectasia, Hereditary Hemorrhagic   WG 700
Telangiectasis   WG 700
Telecommunication Networks see Computer
    Communication Networks
Telecommunications   TK 5101–5105.9
Teleconference see Telecommunications
Telemetry
    Biomedical (General)   QT 34
    General   TK 399
    Space flight   WD 750
    Monitoring special systems, in the diagnosis
        number for the system
Telencephalon   WL 307
Teleological Ethics see Ethics
Telepathy   BF 1161–1171
Telephone Hotlines see Hotlines
Teleradioisotope Therapy see Radioisotope
    Teletherapy
Teletherapy, Radioisotope see Radioisotope
    Teletherapy
Television
    Educational (General)   LB 1044.7–1044.8
    Effect on adolescents   WS 462
    Effect on children   WS 105.5.E9
    In special fields of education
        (Form number 18.2 in any NLM schedule
            where applicable)
    Special topics, by subject
Tellurium
    Inorganic chemistry   QD 181.T4
    Metabolism   QU 130
Temperament   BF 795–811
Temperance   HV 5701–5722
Temperature
    Medical climatology   WB 700
    Meteorology   QC 901–913.2
    Physiological effects on animals   QP 82.2.T4
    Physiological effects on humans   QT 145–160
    See also Body Temperature   WB 270, etc.; Cold
        Climate   QT 160, etc.; Desert Climate   QT
        150, etc.; Heat   QZ 57, etc.
Temperature Sense   WL 103
Templates
    Biochemistry   QU 58
    Dental see Dental Materials   WU 190
    Genetics   QH 450.2
Temporal Arteries   WG 595.T3
Temporal Arteritis   WG 595.T3
Temporal Bone   WE 705
    For the otolaryngologist   WV 201
Temporal Lobe   WL 307
Temporary Threshold Shift, Auditory see Auditory
    Fatigue
Temporomandibular Joint   WU 101–102
Temporomandibular Joint Diseases   WU 140.5
Temporomandibular Joint Syndrome   WU 140.5

Tendinitis   WE 600
Tendon Injuries   WE 600
    Veterinary   SF 901
Tendon Reflex see Reflex, Tendon
Tendon Sheaths see Tendons
Tendon Transfer   WE 600
Tendons   WE 600
    Achilles see Achilles Tendon   WE 880
Teniasis see Taeniasis
Tenicides see Anticestodal Agents
Tennis   QT 260.5.T3
Tenosynovitis   WE 600
    Veterinary   SF 901
TENS see Transcutaneous Electric Nerve
    Stimulation
Tensile Strength
    Biophysics   QT 34
    Bone   WE 103
Tension–Discharge Disorders see Personality
    Disorders
Tension, Intraocular see Intraocular Pressure
Tensor Tympani   WV 230
Teratogenesis see Etiology   QS 675 under
    Abnormalities; Abnormalities, Drug–Induced;
    Chromosome Abnormalities
Teratogens   QS 675–679
Teratoid Tumor see Teratoma
Teratology see Abnormalities
Teratoma   QZ 310
    Localized, by site
Teratoma, Cystic see Dermoid Cyst
Teratoma, Mature see Dermoid Cyst
Terminal Addition Enzyme see DNA
    Nucleotidylexotransferase
Terminal Care
    In infancy & childhood   WS 200
    Medical aspects   WB 310
    Nursing   WY 152
    Of patients with particular disease, with the
        disease
    See also Attitude to Death   BF 789.D4;
        Hospices   WX 28.6–28.62
Terminal Deoxyribonucleotidyltransferase see DNA
    Nucleotidylexotransferase
Terminals, Computer see Computer Terminals
Terminology
    (Form number 15 in any NLM schedule where
        applicable)
Terpene Phosphates see Polyisoprenyl Phosphates
Terpenes
    Biochemistry   QU 85
    Toxicology   QV 633
Territoriality
    Animal   QL 756.2
    Human   HM 132
Terrorism see Violence
Test–Tube Fertilization see Fertilization in Vitro
Testicular Diseases   WJ 800–875
    General Works   WJ 830
    Monorchidism   WJ 840
Testicular Feminization   WJ 712
Testicular Hormones   WJ 875
Testicular Neoplasms   WJ 858

Testicular Torsion see Spermatic Cord Torsion
Testing, Biocompatible Materials see Materials
    Testing
Testis   WJ 830
    Abnormalities   WJ 840
    Diseases see Testicular Diseases   WJ 830, etc.
    Feminization see Testicular Feminization   WJ
        712
    Hormones see Testicular Hormones   WJ 875
    Neoplasms see Testicular Neoplasms   WJ 858
    Surgery   WJ 868
    Tunica Vaginalis   WJ 800
    See also Castration   WJ 868, etc.; Epididymis
        WJ 800
Testis, Undescended see Cryptorchidism
Testosterone   WJ 875
Testosterone Propionate see Testosterone
Tests see Diagnosis Laboratory; Psychological Tests
    WM 145, etc; Serodiagnosis; names of other
    specific tests
Tetanus   WC 370
    Veterinary   SF 804
Tetanus Antitoxin   WC 370
Tetanus Toxoid   WC 370
Tetanus Vaccine see Tetanus Toxoid
Tetany   WD 200.5.C2
    Veterinary   SF 910.T47
Tethered Cord Syndrome see Spina Bifida Occulta
Tetracaine   QV 115
Tetracemate see Edetic Acid
Tetrachlorodibenzodioxin
    As an herbicide   WA 240
Tetrachloroethylene   QV 253
Tetracycline   QV 360
Tetradecanoylphorbol Acetate
    As a carcinogen   QZ 202
Tetraethylammonium Compounds   QV 132
Tetraethylthiuram Disulfide see Disulfiram
Tetragastrin Receptors see Receptors,
    Cholecystokinin
Tetrahydrocannabinol   QV 77.7
Tetrahydrofolate Dehydrogenase   QU 140
Tetrahydronaphthalenes
    Organic chemistry   QD 391
    Pharmacology   QV 241
Tetrahymena   QX 151
Tetrakain see Tetracaine
Tetralins see Tetrahydronaphthalenes
Tetralogy of Fallot   WG 220
Tetramon see Tetraethylammonium Compounds
Tetraplegia see Quadriplegia
Tetrylammonium see Tetraethylammonium
    Compounds
Textbooks, Programmed see Programmed
    Instruction
Textile Industry
    Occupational accidents   WA 485
    Occupational medicine   WA 400–495
    Industrial waste   WA 788
Textiles
    Fire prevention   WA 250
TGF–beta see Transforming Growth Factor beta
Thalamencephalon see Diencephalon

Thalamic Nuclei   WL 312
Thalamostriate Vein see Cerebral Veins
Thalamus   WL 312
Thalassemia   WH 170
Thalassotherapy   WB 750
Thalidomide   QV 85
   Adverse effects   QS 679
Thalidomide Children see Abnormalities,
   Drug-Induced
Thallium
   Toxicology   QV 618
Thallium Radioisotopes   WN 415-450
Thanatology   HQ 1073-1073.5
THC see Tetrahydrocannabinol
Thea see Tea
Thebaine   QV 92
Theca Cell Tumor see Thecoma
Thecoma   WP 322
Theft
   Special topics, by subject
Theileriasis   SF 809.T5
Thematic Apperception Test   WM 145.5.T3
Theobroma see Cacao
Theobromine   QV 107
Theology see Religion
Theophylline   QV 107
Theophylline Receptors see Receptors, Purinergic
Therapeutic Abortion see Abortion, Therapeutic
Therapeutic Community   WM 440
Therapeutic Cults see Alternative Medicine
Therapeutic Equivalency   QV 38
Therapeutics   WB 300-962
   Animals (General works)   SF 743-745
     See also Drug Therapy   SF 915-919.5
   Anesthetics   WO 375
   Cardiovascular diseases   WG 166
   Eye diseases   WW 166
   Gynecologic diseases   WP 650
   Home remedies   WB 120
   Hormones   WK 190
   In infancy & childhood   WS 366
   In old age   WT 166
   Mental disorders   WM 400-460.7
     In infancy & childhood   WS 350.2
   Mouth diseases   WU 166
   Neoplasms   QZ 266-269
   Physical see Physical Therapy   WB 460-545,
     etc.
   Radioisotopes   WN 450
   Radium   WN 340
   Roentgen ray see X-Ray Therapy   WN
   250.5.X7
   Skin diseases   WR 650-660
   Special systems see Alternative Medicine   WB
   890-962, etc.; other specific types of therapy,
   by name
   Tooth diseases   WU 166
   Urologic diseases   WJ 166
   For therapy of other diseases see general works
     number for disease, organ, or system
Therapy, Combined Modality see Combined
   Modality Therapy
Therapy, Computer-Assisted   WB 365

Special topics, by subject
Thermocoagulation see Electrocoagulation
Thermodynamics
   Biochemistry   QU 34
   Physical and theoretical chemistry   QD 504
   Physics   QC 310.15-319
Thermoelectric Power Plants see Power Plants
Thermography   WN 205
   Used for diagnosis of specific diseases, with the
   disease
Thermogravimetry   QD 79.T4
   In clinical pathology   QY 90
Thermoluminescent Dosimetry   WN 660
Thermometers
   As equipment   WB 26
   In physical examination   WB 270
Thermopenetration see Diathermy
Thermoreceptors   WL 102.9
Thermoregulation see Body Temperature Regulation
   QT 165, etc
Thermotherapy see Hyperthermia, Induced;
   Therapeutic use   WB 469 under Heat
Theropithecus gelada   QL 737.P93
   Diseases   SF 997.5.P7
   As laboratory animals   QY 60.P7
Theses see Dissertations, Academic
Thiabendazole   QV 253
Thiamine   QU 189
Thiamine Deficiency   WD 122
   Veterinary   SF 855.V58
Thiamine Diphosphate see Thiamine Pyrophosphate
Thiamine Pyrophosphate   QU 135
Thiamphenicol   QV 350.5.C5
Thiazines
   Dyes   QV 240
     Chemical technology   TP 918
     Chemistry   QD 441
   Organic chemistry   QD 403
Thienamycins   QV 350
Thigh   WE 865
Thin Sectioning see Microtomy
Thinking   BF 441-449.5
   In adolescence   WS 462
   In infancy & childhood   WS 105.5.D2
Thinness
   Anthropology   GN 66-67.5
   Nutrition disorders   WD 100
   Symptomatology   WB 146
Thio-Tepa see Thiotepa
Thiobacillus   QW 135
Thiobacteriaceae see Gram-Negative
   Chemolithotrophic Bacteria
Thioctic Acid   QU 135
Thiocyanates   WK 202
Thioethers see Sulfides
Thiols see Sulfhydryl Compounds
Thiomebumal see Thiopental
Thiopental   QV 88
Thiopentobarbital see Thiopental
Thiophenes
   Acting on the nervous system   QV 76.5
   As anthelmintics   QV 253
   Organic chemistry   QD 403

**ALWAYS CONSULT MAIN SCHEDULES. USE NUMBER ASSIGNED ONLY WHEN
SUBJECT REPRESENTS MAJOR EMPHASIS OF WORK BEING CLASSIFIED**

Thiophenicol see Thiamphenicol
Thiophosphamide see Thiotepa
Thioredoxin   QU 55
Thiosemicarbazones   QV 268
Thiosulfates
    Inorganic chemistry   QD 181.S1
    Pharmacology   QV 280
Thiotepa   QV 269
Thiothixene   QV 77.9
Thiourea   WK 202
Third–Party Payments see Insurance, Health,
    Reimbursement
Thirst
    Neurophysiology   WI 102
Thomsonian Medicine see Alternative Medicine
Thoracentesis see Punctures
Thoracic Arteries   WG 595.T4
Thoracic Cyst see Mediastinal Cyst
Thoracic Diseases   WF 970–985
    In infancy & childhood   WS 280
    See also Empyema   WF 745
Thoracic Duct   WH 700
Thoracic Injuries   WF 985
Thoracic Neoplasms   WF 970
Thoracic Nerves   WL 400
Thoracic Outlet Syndrome   WL 500
Thoracic Radiography   WF 975
    In infancy & childhood   WS 280
    See also Mass Chest X-Ray   WF 225
Thoracic Surgery   WF 980
Thoracic Vertebrae   WE 725
Thoracoplasty   WF 980
Thoracotomy   WF 980
Thorax
    Anatomy and physiology   WE 715
    Bone structure and abnormalities   WE 715
    Diseases of the organs within (General)   WF
    970–975
    Funnel see Funnel Chest   WE 715
    Mass X-ray see Mass Chest X-Ray   WF 225
    Surgery see Thoracic Surgery   WF 980
    Wounds see Thoracic Injuries   WF 985
Thorium   WN 420
    Nuclear physics   QC 796.T5
    See also special topics under Radioisotopes
Thornapple see Stramonium
Thorny–Headed Worms see Acanthocephala
Threadworms see Nematoda
Three–Day Fever see Phlebotomus Fever
Three–Day Sickness see Ephemeral Fever
Threshold Limit Values see Maximum Permissible
    Exposure Level
Throat see Pharynx
Thrombase see Thrombin
Thrombelastography   QY 410
Thrombin   QV 195
    In the mechanism of blood coagulation   WH
    310
Thromboangiitis Obliterans   WG 520
Thrombocytapheresis see Plateletpheresis
Thrombocytes see Blood Platelets
Thrombocytopathy see Blood Platelet Disorders
Thrombocytopenia   WH 300

Thromboelastography see Thrombelastography
Thromboembolism   QZ 170
    Venous   WG 610
Thromboendarterectomy see Endarterectomy
Thrombolysis, Therapeutic see Thrombolytic
    Therapy
Thrombolytic Agents see Fibrinolytic Agents
Thrombolytic Therapy   QZ 170
    See also Fibrinolytic Agents   QV 190
Thrombopenia see Thrombocytopenia
Thrombopenic Purpura see Purpura, Thrombopenic
Thrombophlebitis   WG 610
Thromboplastin   WH 310
    Clinical analysis   QY 410
Thrombosis   QZ 170
    Arterial   WG 540
    Cerebral see Cerebral Embolism and Thrombosis
        WL 355
    Carotid artery see Carotid Artery Thrombosis
        WL 355
    Coronary see Coronary Disease   WG 300
    Meningeal vessels   WL 200
    Pulmonary see Pulmonary Embolism   WG 420
    Sinus see Sinus Thrombosis   WL 355
    Venous see Thrombophlebitis   WG 610
Thrombosis, Coronary see Coronary Thrombosis
Thrombosis, Venous see Thrombophlebitis
Thrombotest see Prothrombin Time
Thromboxane A Synthase see Thromboxane
    Synthetase
Thromboxane A2   QU 90
Thromboxane Synthetase   QU 137
Thromboxanes   QU 90
    Perinatology   WQ 210–211
Thrombus see Thrombosis
Thrush see Moniliasis, Oral
Thulium
    Inorganic Chemistry   QD 181.T8
    Pharmacology   QV 290
Thumb   WE 835
Thumbsucking see Fingersucking
Thyme see Herbs
Thymectomy   WK 400
Thymic Cyst see Mediastinal Cyst
Thymic Factor, Circulating   WK 400
Thymic Group Viruses see Herpesviridae
Thymidine   QU 57
    Pharmacology   QV 185
Thymidine Kinase   QU 141
Thymine   QU 58
Thymins see Thymopoietins
Thymoanaleptics see Antidepressive Agents
Thymol   QV 250
Thymoleptics see Antidepressive Agents
Thymoma   WK 400
    Veterinary   SF 910.T8
Thymopoietins   WK 400
Thymosin   WK 400
Thymotaxin see beta 2–Microglobulin
Thymus–Dependent Lymphocytes see
    T–Lymphocytes
Thymus Extracts
    Pharmacology   QV 370

Therapeutic use (General)   WB 391
Used for treatment of particular disorders, with
   the disorder or system
Thymus Gland   WK 400
Thymus Hyperplasia   WK 400
Thymus Neoplasms   WK 400
Thyrocalcitonin see Calcitonin
Thyroglobulin   WK 202
Thyroglossal Cyst   WK 270
Thyroid Antagonists   WK 202
Thyroid Diseases   WK 200–280
Thyroid Function Tests   WK 202
Thyroid Gland   WK 200–280
Thyroid Hormone Receptors see Receptors, Thyroid
   Hormone
Thyroid Hormones   WK 202
   Deficiency   WK 250
   As a cause of particular disorders, with the
      disorder
   See also Hypothyroidism   WK 250
Thyroid Neoplasms   WK 270
Thyroid Peroxidase see Iodide Peroxidase
Thyroid–Stimulating Hormone see Thyrotropin
Thyroidectomy   WK 280
Thyroiditis   WK 200
Thyroliberin see Protirelin
Thyrotoxicosis see Hyperthyroidism   WK 265
Thyrotropin   WK 515
Thyrotropin–Releasing Hormone see Protirelin
Thyroxine   WK 202
Thyroxine–Binding Globulin see Thyroxine–Binding
   Proteins
Thyroxine–Binding Prealbumin see
   Thyroxine–Binding Proteins
Thyroxine–Binding Proteins   WK 202
Thyroxine Receptors see Receptors, Thyroid
   Hormone
Thyroxine 5'–Deiodinase see Iodide Peroxidase
Thyroxine 5'–Monodeiodinase see Iodide Peroxidase
Tiabendazol see Thiabendazole
Tibia   WE 870
Tibial Fractures   WE 870
Tibial Menisci see Menisci, Tibial
Tic   WM 197
   Neurologic manifestation   WL 340
Tic Douloureux see Trigeminal Neuralgia
Ticarcillin   QV 354
Tick–Borne Diseases   WC 600
Tick–Borne Rickettsial Fevers see Rickettsia
   Infections
Tick Control   QX 600
   Animal culture   SF 810.T5
Tick Infestations   WC 900
   Disinfestation   WC 900
   Veterinary   SF 810.T5
Ticks   QX 479
Time   QB 209–224
   Factor in ability to infect   QW 700
   In relation to particular topics, by subject
Time and Motion Studies
   Special topics, by subject
Time Factors
   Factor in ability to infect   QW 700

In relation to particular topics, by subject
Time Perception   BF 468
   In infancy & childhood   WS 105.5.D2
Time–Resolved Immunofluorometric Assay see
   Fluoroimmunoassay
Timed–Release Preparations see Delayed–Action
   Preparations
Timidity see Shyness
Timolol   QV 132
Tin
   As a trace element   QU 130.5
   Dental use   WU 180
   Toxicology   QV 618
   Used in particular procedures, with the procedure
Tinctures, Pharmacy see Solutions
Tinea   WR 310
   Veterinary   SF 809.R55
Tinea Capitis   WR 330
Tinea Favosa   WR 330
Tinea Pedis   WR 310
Tinidazole   QV 254
Tinnitus   WV 272
Tiotixene see Thiothixene
Tissue
   Aging   WT 104
   Composition   QU 100
   Specific types   QS 532–532.5
   Susceptibility to infection   QW 700
   Transplantation   WO 660–690
   See also Histology   QS 504–539, etc.
Tissue Adhesives   WO 166
Tissue Banks   QS 523–524
   Organ banks   WO 23–24
   Tooth banks   WU 24.5
   See also Eye Banks   WW 23–24
Tissue Compatibility see Histocompatibility
Tissue Culture
   General works   QS 530
   Plant   QK 725
   Technique   QS 525
Tissue Distribution   QV 38
Tissue Donors   QS 523–524
Tissue Extracts
   Pharmacology   QV 370
   Therapeutic use (General)   WB 391
   Used for the treatment of particular disorders,
      with the disorder or system
Tissue Factor see Thromboplastin
Tissue Preservation
   Histology   QS 525
   Transplantation   WO 665
Tissue Therapy   WB 391
Tissue Thromboplastin see Thromboplastin
Tissue Transplantation   WO 660–690
Tissue–Type Plasminogen Activator see Alteplase
Tissue Typing see Histocompatibility Testing
Titanium
   Inorganic chemistry   QD 181.T6
   Dentistry   WU 180
Titration, Conductometric see Conductometry
TLV see Maximum Permissible Exposure Level
TMJ Syndrome see Temporomandibular Joint
   Syndrome

Tn Elements see DNA Insertion Elements
TNF-alpha see Tumor Necrosis Factor
Toad, Fire-Bellied see Anura
Toad Venoms see Amphibian Venoms
Toads and Frogs see Anura
Toads, True see Bufonidae
Tobacco
    Cultivation   SB 273-278
    Dependence   WM 290
      See also Smoking   WM 290
    Pharmacology   QV 137
      See also Nicotine   QV 137; Smoking   WM 290, etc.
Tobacco Dependence see Tobacco Use Disorder
Tobacco Mosaic Virus   QW 163
Tobacco Smoke see Smoke; Tobacco
Tobacco Smoke Pollution   WA 754
Tobacco, Smokeless
    Dependence   WM 290
    Pharmacology   QV 137
Tobacco Use Disorder   WM 290
Tobramycin   QV 350
Tocodynamometry see Uterine Monitoring
Tocography see Uterine Monitoring
Tocolysis   WQ 330
Tocolytic Agents
    Pharmacology   WK 102
Tocolytic Therapy see Tocolysis
Tocopherol see Vitamin E
Tocopherols see Vitamin E
Toenails see Nails
Toes   WE 835
    Abnormalities   WE 835
Togaviridae   QW 168.5.A7
Togaviridae Infections   WC 501
Togavirus Infections see Togaviridae Infections
Toilet Facilities   WA 830
Toilet Training   WS 113
Token Economy   BF 319.5.R48
    In behavior therapy   WM 425
Token Reinforcement see Token Economy
Tolbutamide   WK 825
Tolerance of Drugs see Drug Tolerance
Tolmetin   QV 95
Tolonium Chloride   QV 195
Tolosa-Hunt Syndrome see Ophthalmoplegia
Toluene
    As indicators and reagents   QV 240
    Organic chemistry   QD 341.H9
    Toxicology   QV 633
Toluene 2,4-Diisocyanate   QV 280
Toluidine Blue O see Tolonium Chloride
Tolylene Diisocyanate see Toluene 2,4-Diisocyanate
Tombs, Public Health Aspects see Burial
Tomodensitometry see Tomography, X-Ray Computed
Tomography   WN 206
    Cardiovascular diseases (General)   WG 141.5.T6
    Used in the examination of particular organs, with the organ or region
Tomography, Computed, Scanners see Tomography Scanners, X-Ray Computed
Tomography, Emission-Computed   WN 206

Tomography, Emission-Computed, Single-Photon   WN 206
    Localized by site
Tomography, NMR see Magnetic Resonance Imaging
Tomography, Positron-Emission see Tomography, Emission-Computed
Tomography, Proton Spin see Magnetic Resonance Imaging
Tomography, Radionuclide-Computed see Tomography, Emission-Computed
Tomography Scanners, X-Ray Computed   WN 150
    Used in the examination of particular organs, with the organ or region
Tomography, Single-Photon, Emission-Computed see Tomography, Emission-Computed, Single-Photon
Tomography, Transmission see Tomography, X-Ray
Tomography, Transmission Computed see Tomography, X-Ray Computed
Tomography, X-Ray   WN 206
    Used in the examination of particular organs, by organ or region
Tomography, X-Ray Computed   WN 206
    Used in the examination of particular organs, with the organ or region
Tomography, X-Ray Computed, Scanners see Tomography Scanners, X-Ray Computed
Tongue   WI 210
Tongue Diseases   WI 210
Tongue, Geographic see Glossitis, Benign Migratory
Tongue Habits
    In adolescence   WS 463
    In adulthood   WM 172
    In infancy & childhood   WS 350.6
    Malocclusion etiology   WU 440
Tongue, Hairy   WI 210
Tongue Neoplasms   WI 210
Tonofilaments see Intermediate Filaments
Tonometry   WW 143
Tonsil   WV 430
Tonsil, Palatine see Tonsil
Tonsillar Neoplasms   WV 430
Tonsillectomy   WV 430
Tonsillitis   WV 430
Tonsils see Tonsil
Tooth   WU
    Banks   WU 24.5
    Canine see Cuspid   WU 101
    Devitalized see Dental Pulp Devitalization   WU 230
    Injuries   WU 158
    Medicolegal aspects   W 705
    Microbiology   QW 65
    Pathology   WU 140
    Transplantation   WU 640
Tooth Abnormalities   WU 101.5
Tooth Abrasion   WU 140
Tooth Apex see Tooth Root
Tooth, Artificial   WU 515
Tooth Avulsion see Tooth Luxation
Tooth Cleaning see Toothbrushing
Tooth Crowding see Malocclusion

Tooth, Deciduous   WU 480
Tooth Diseases   WU 140
Tooth Erosion   WU 140
Tooth Eruption   WU 102
   Teething   WU 480
Tooth Extraction   WU 605
Tooth Fractures   WU 158
Tooth Germ   WU 101
Tooth, Impacted   WU 101.5
Tooth Luxation   WU 158
Tooth Mobility   WU 102
   Orthodontics   WU 400
   Periodontics   WU 240
Tooth Movement, Minor   WU 400
Tooth Reimplantation see Tooth Replantation
Tooth Remineralization   WU 166
Tooth Replantation   WU 640
Tooth Root   WU 230
Tooth Supporting Structures see Periodontium
Tooth, Wisdom see Molar, Third
Toothache   WU 140
Toothbrushing   WU 113
Topectomy see Psychosurgery
Topical Infiltration see Topical Anesthesia   WO
  340 under Anesthesia, Local
Topographic Brain Mapping see Brain Mapping
Topography, Moire see Moire Topography
Tornadoes see Natural Disasters
Torsion   QZ 150
   Ovarian   WP 320
   Testicular see Spermatic Cord Torsion   WJ 780
Torsion Dystonia see Dystonia Musculorum
  Deformans
Torticollis   WE 708
Torture
   As a form of punishment   HV 8593-8599
Torula see Cryptococcus
Torulopsis see Candida
Torulosis see Cryptococcosis
Total Body Clearance Rate see Metabolic Clearance
  Rate
Total Body Irradiation see Whole-Body Irradiation
Total Communication Methods see Communication
  Methods, Total
Total Parenteral Nutrition see Parenteral Nutrition,
  Total
Total Quality Management   HD 62.15
   In special fields by subject, in number for
   professions where available
Touch   WR 102
Tourette Syndrome   WM 197
Tourette's Disorder see Tourette Syndrome
Tourniquet Pain Test see Pain Measurement
Town Planning see City Planning
Toxaphene
   Agriculture   SB 952.C44
   Public health   WA 240
Toxemia   WC 240
   In pregnancy see Pregnancy Toxemias   WQ 215
   Intestinal   WI 405
Toxic Shock Syndrome see Shock, Septic
Toxic Substances, Environmental see Hazardous
  Substances

Toxicodendron   WD 500
  See also Dermatitis, Toxicodendron
Toxicodendron Dermatitis see Dermatitis,
  Toxicodendron
Toxicology   QV 600-667
   Industrial   WA 465
   Laboratory manual   QV 602
   Medicolegal aspects   W 750
   Methods   QV 602
   Nursing texts   QV 600
   Public health aspects   WA 730
   Veterinary   SF 757.5
   See also Poisoning   QV 600-667, etc.; names
    of types of poisoning, e.g. Plant poisoning
    WD 500-530; names of particular poisons
Toxin-Antibody Conjugates see Immunotoxins
Toxin-Antibody Hybrids see Immunotoxins
Toxin-Antitoxin Reaction see Antitoxins; Toxins
Toxin Carriers see Immunotoxins
Toxin Conjugates see Immunotoxins
Toxins   QW 630
   See also names of specific toxins
Toxins, Chimeric see Immunotoxins
Toxins, Deactivated see Toxoids
Toxins, Targeted see Immunotoxins
Toxoids   QW 805
   Used for particular diseases, with the disease
   See also names of specific toxoids
Toxoplasma   QX 140
Toxoplasma gondii see Toxoplasma
Toxoplasma gondii Infection see Toxoplasmosis
Toxoplasmosis   WC 725
Toxoplasmosis, Animal   SF 809.T6
Toxoplasmosis, Congenital   WC 725
Toxoplasmosis, Ocular   WW 140
Toys see Play and Playthings
Trabeculectomy
   For glaucoma   WW 290
Trabeculoplasty see Trabeculectomy
Trace Elements
   Biochemistry   QU 130.5
   Analytical chemistry   QD 139.T7
Tracers, Radioactive see Radioisotopes
Trachea   WF 490
Tracheal Cyst see Mediastinal Cyst
Tracheal Diseases   WF 490
Tracheal Neoplasms   WF 490
Tracheal Stenosis   WF 490
Tracheitis   WF 546
Tracheoesophageal Fistula   WI 250
Tracheotomy   WF 490
Trachoma   WW 215
Track and Field   QT 260.5.T7
Traction   WE 190
Trade Unions see Labor Unions
Trades, Diseases see Occupational Diseases
Traditional Birth Attendant see Midwifery
Traditional Medicine, Chinese see Medicine, Chinese
  Traditional
Traditional Medicine, Oriental see Medicine,
  Oriental Traditional
Traffic Accidents see Accidents, Traffic
Training, Athletic see Sports

Training of Children see Child Care; Child Rearing
Training Programs see Education
Training Support
  (Form number 18 in any NLM schedule where
    applicable)
  Directories (Form number 22 in any NLM
    schedule where applicable)
  Science Q 181–183.4
Tranquilizing Agents QV 77.9
  In anesthesia WO 297
Tranquilizing Agents, Major see Antipsychotic
  Agents
Tranquilizing Agents, Minor see Anti–Anxiety
  Agents
Transactional Analysis WM 460.6
  Special topics, by subject
Transaminases see Aminotransferases
Transcendental Meditation see Relaxation
  Techniques
Transcriptases see RNA Polymerases
Transcription, Genetic QH 450.2
Transcriptional Regulatory Elements see Genes,
  Regulator
Transcultural Nursing WY 107
Transcultural Studies see Cross–Cultural
  Comparison
Transcutaneous Administration see Administration,
  Cutaneous
Transcutaneous Blood Gas Monitoring see Blood
  Gas Monitoring, Transcutaneous
Transcutaneous Capnometry see Blood Gas
  Monitoring, Transcutaneous
Transcutaneous Electric Nerve Stimulation WB
  495
Transcutaneous Oximetry see Blood Gas Monitoring,
  Transcutaneous
Transdermal Administration see Administration,
  Cutaneous
Transdermal Electrostimulation see Transcutaneous
  Electric Nerve Stimulation
Transducers, Pressure QT 26
Transduction, Genetic QW 51
Transfection QW 51
Transfer Factor
  In cellular immunity QW 568
  Other special topics, by subject
Transfer (Psychology) LB 1059
Transfer RNA see RNA, Transfer
Transfer RNA, Amino Acyl see RNA, Transfer,
  Amino Acyl
Transferases QU 141
Transference (Psychology) WM 62
Transferrin WH 400
  Clinical analysis QY 455
Transformation, Bacterial QH 448.4
Transformation, Genetic QW 51
Transforming Genes see Oncogenes
Transforming Growth Factor Alpha Receptors see
  Receptors, Epidermal Growth
  Factor–Urogastrone
Transforming Growth Factor beta QU 107
Transforming Growth Factors QU 107
Transforming Region see Base Sequence

Transfusion see Blood Transfusion
Transgenic Animals see Animals, Transgenic
Transgenic Mice see Mice, Transgenic
Transglutaminase see Protein–Glutamine
  gamma–Glutamyltransferase
Transient Ischemic Attack see Cerebral Ischemia,
  Transient
Transient Situational Disturbance see Adjustment
  Disorders
Transients and Migrants
  Demography HB 1951–2577
  Labor HD 5855–5856
  Health problems WA 300, etc.
  See also Emigration and immigration JV
    6008–6348
Transillumination WW 143
  Used for other special purposes, by subject
Transketolase QU 141
Translating PN 241–245
  Directories of translators PN 241
  Machine translating P 307–310
  Science Q 124
  Technology T 11.5
  See also Automatic Data Processing W
    26.55.A9, etc.
Translation, Genetic QH 450.5
Translations
  Bibliography Z 6514.T7
    Classical Z 7018.T7
    Medical NLM subject number preceded by
      Z
    National
      Great Britain and Ireland Z 2014.T7
      Latin and South America Z 1609.T7
      United States Z 1231.T7
  Individual works, with the original work, by
    subject
Translocation, Chromosomal see Translocation
  (Genetics)
Translocation (Genetics) QH 462.T7
Transluminal Coronary Balloon Dilatation see
  Angioplasty, Transluminal, Percutaneous
  Coronary
Transmembrane Potentials see Membrane Potentials
Transmissible Gastroenteritis of Swine see
  Gastroenteritis, Transmissible, of Swine
Transmission Electron Microscopy see Microscopy,
  Electron
Transmission of Infectious Diseases see Carrier State;
  Disease Outbreaks; Epidemiology; Infection;
  specific types of vectors, e.g., Insect Vectors;
  names of particular diseases
Transmitter Uptake Inhibitors, Neuronal see
  Neurotransmitter Uptake Inhibitors
Transphosphorylases see Phosphotransferases
Transplacental Exposure see Maternal–Fetal
  Exchange
Transplantation WO 660–690
  Legal, ethical, or religious aspects WO 690
    (Laws WO 32)
  Skin WO 610
  Tube grafts WO 610
  Specific organs, with the organ

  See also Tissue preservation WO 665

**ALWAYS CONSULT MAIN SCHEDULES. USE NUMBER ASSIGNED ONLY WHEN
SUBJECT REPRESENTS MAJOR EMPHASIS OF WORK BEING CLASSIFIED**

Transplantation, Allogeneic see Transplantation, Homologous
Transplantation, Autologous   WO 660
Transplantation, Bone see Bone Transplantation
Transplantation, Bone Marrow see Bone Marrow Transplantation
Transplantation, Brain Tissue see Brain Tissue Transplantation
Transplantation, Cardiac see Heart Transplantation
Transplantation, Heart see Heart Transplantation
Transplantation, Heart–Lung see Heart–Lung Transplantation
Transplantation, Hepatic see Liver Transplantation
Transplantation, Heterologous   WO 660
Transplantation, Homologous   WO 660
    Veterinary   SF 911
Transplantation Immunology   WO 680
Transplantation, Islets of Langerhans see Islets of Langerhans Transplantation
Transplantation, Kidney see Kidney Transplantation
Transplantation, Liver see Liver Transplantation
Transplantation, Lung see Lung Transplantation
Transplantation, Organ see Organ Transplantation
Transplantation, Pancreas see Pancreas Transplantation
Transplantation, Pancreatic Islets see Islets of Langerhans Transplantation
Transplantation, Renal see Kidney Transplantation
Transplantation, Skin see Skin Transplantation
Transplantation, Tissue see Tissue Transplantation
Transport, Biological see Biological Transport
Transport of Wounded and Sick see Transportation of Patients
Transport Proteins see Carrier Proteins
Transportation
    Hazardous materials   WA 810
    Mentally disabled   HV 3005.5
    Nursing services   WY 143
    Of elderly   WT 30
    Physically disabled   HV 3022
    Public Health aspects   WA 810
    See also Automobiles   TL 1–390, etc.; Wheelchairs   WB 320, etc.; names of other modes of transportation
Transportation of Patients
    Ambulance service (general or hospital)   WX 215
    War   UH 500–505
    See also Ambulances   WX 215 etc.
Transposable Elements see DNA Insertion Elements
Transposition of Great Vessels   WG 220
Transposons see DNA Insertion Elements
Transsexualism   WM 611
Transudates see Exudates and Transudates
Transvestism   WM 610
Tranylcypromine   QV 77.5
Trauma see Wounds and Injuries
Trauma, Multiple see Multiple Trauma
Trauma Severity Indices
Traumatology   WO 700
Travel   QT 250
    First aid   WA 292

    Medical   W 10
    See also Expeditions   W 10, etc.
Trazodone
    As an antidepressant   QV 77.5
Treacher–Collins Syndrome see Mandibulofacial Dysostosis
Treadmill Test see Exercise Test
Treatment Costs see Health Care Costs
Treatment Protocols see Clinical Protocols
Trees
    Botany   QK 475–493.5
    Conservation   SD 411–428
    Damage from natural elements   SB 781–795
    Diseases   SB 761–767
    Forestry   SD
    Toxic   WD 500
Trematoda   QX 353
Trematode Infections   WC 805–810
    Veterinary   SF 810.F3
Tremor   WL 340
    Veterinary   SF 895
Trench Fever   WC 602
Trench Foot see Immersion Foot
Trench Mouth see Gingivitis, Necrotizing Ulcerative
Trephining   WE 705
Treponema   QW 155
Treponemal Infections   WC 422
Tretamine see Triethylenemelamine
Tretinoin   QU 167
    Used in treating a particular skin disease, with the disease
Triacylglycerol Lipase see Lipase
Triacylglycerols see Triglycerides
Trials, Medicolegal see Forensic Medicine
Triamcinolone   WK 757
Triamcinolone Acetonide   WK 757
Triamterene   QV 160
Triazines
    As analgesics   QV 95
    As herbicides   WA 240, etc.
    Organic chemistry   QD 401
Triazoles
    Organic chemistry   QD 401
Tribavirin see Ribavirin
Tributyrinase see Lipase
Tricarboxylic Acid Cycle see Citric Acid Cycle
Trichina see Trichinella
Trichinella   QX 207
Trichinelliasis see Trichinosis
Trichinelloidea see Trichuroidea
Trichinosis   WC 855
    Veterinary   SF 810.T7
Trichlorbutanol see Chlorobutanol
Trichlormethane see Chloroform
Trichloroacetic Acid   QU 98
    Organic chemistry   QD 305.A2
Trichloroethanes
    Toxicology   QV 633
Trichloroethylene   QV 81
Trichloromethylchloroformate see Phosgene
Trichobezoars see Bezoars
Trichocephaliasis see Trichuriasis
Trichocephalus see Trichuris

Trichomonas   QX 70
Trichomonas Infections   WC 700
 Veterinary   SF 810.T73
 Localized, by site
Trichomonas vaginalis   QX 70
Trichomonas Vaginitis   WP 258
Trichomoniasis see Trichomonas Infections
Trichophytosis see Tinea
Trichosanthin
 As an abortifacient agent   QV 175
Trichostrongyloidea   QX 248
Trichothecene Epoxides see Trichothecenes
Trichothecenes
 As mycotoxins   QW 630.5.M9
Trichuriasis   WC 860
Trichuris   QX 207
Trichuris trichiura see Trichuris
Trichuroidea   QX 207
Tricuspid Incompetence see Tricuspid Valve
 Insufficiency
Tricuspid Regurgitation see Tricuspid Valve
 Insufficiency
Tricuspid Valve   WG 268
Tricuspid Valve Incompetence see Tricuspid Valve
 Insufficiency
Tricuspid Valve Insufficiency   WG 268
Tricuspid Valve Stenosis   WG 268
Triethylenemelamine   QV 269
Triethylenethiophosphoramide see Thiotepa
Trifluoperazine   QV 77.9
Trifluoroperazine see Trifluoperazine
Trifluperidol   QV 77.9
Trifluralin
 Public health aspects   WA 240
 Toxicology   QV 633
Triftazin see Trifluoperazine
Trigeminal Nerve   WL 330
Trigeminal Neuralgia   WL 544
Trigeminal Nuclei   WL 310
Trigger Points, Myofascial see Myofascial Pain
 Syndromes
Triglyceride Lipase see Lipase
Triglycerides   QU 85
Triiodobenzoic Acids
 Biochemistry   QU 98
 As plant growth regulators   QK 745
Triiodothyronine   WK 202
Triiodothyronine Receptors see Receptors, Thyroid
 Hormone
Trimepranol   QV 132
Trimeprimine see Trimipramine
Trimethoprim   QV 256
Trimethoxyphenethylamine see Mescaline
Trimipramine   QV 77.5
Triolein   QU 85
Trional see Ethyl Methanesulfonate
Triparanol   QU 95
Triphosphopyridine Nucleotide see NADP
Triple-Symptom Complex see Behcet's Syndrome
Triplets   WQ 235
 Embryology   QS 642
 Psychology   WS 105.5.F2
Tris Buffer see Tromethamine

Trisaccharides   QU 83
Trisamine see Tromethamine
Trismus   WC 370
Trisomy   QH 461
 Associated with abnormalities, with the
 abnormality, e.g., Chromosome Abnormalities
 QS 677
Trisomy 21 see Down Syndrome
Triterpenes
 Organic chemistry   QD 416
 Pharmacognosy   QV 752
 Pharmacology   QV 66
Triticum see Wheat
Tritium   WN 420
 Inorganic chemistry   QD 181.H1
 See also special topics under Radioisotopes
Trituration see Drug Compounding
tRNA see RNA, Transfer
tRNA-Amino Acyl see RNA, Transfer, Amino Acyl
Trochanter see Femur
Trochanteric Fractures see Hip Fractures
Trombicula see Trombiculid Mites
Trombiculiasis   WC 900
Trombiculid Mites   QX 483
Trombididae see Mites
Trometamol see Tromethamine
Tromethamine
 In acid-base equilibrium   QU 105
Trophoblast   QS 645
Trophoblastic Neoplasms   WP 465
 Pathology   QZ 310
Trophoblastic Tumor see Trophoblastic Neoplasms
Tropical Climate
 Hygiene   QT 150
 Meteorology   QC 993.5
 Physiological effects   QT 150
Tropical Hygiene see Tropical Climate
Tropical Medicine   WC 680
 In infancy & childhood   WC 680
 Of the skin   WR 350
 See also names of particular diseases
Trunk see Musculoskeletal System
Trusses   WO 162
Trustees
 Hospitals   WX 150
 Of other organizations and institutions, in the
 administration number for the agency or lacking
 that, in the general number, e.g., Trustees of
 the American Medical Association   WB 1.
Truth Disclosure
 In drug research   QV 20.5
 In medical research   W 20.5
 In other fields, in research number if applicable
 and available; elsewhere, by subject
Trypanosoma   QX 70
Trypanosomiasis   WC 705
 Veterinary   SF 807
Trypanosomiasis, African   WC 705
 Veterinary   SF 807
Trypanosomiasis, Bovine   SF 967.T78
Trypanosomiasis, Cardiovascular see Chagas
 Cardiomyopathy
Trypanosomiasis, South American see Chagas
 Disease

**ALWAYS CONSULT MAIN SCHEDULES. USE NUMBER ASSIGNED ONLY WHEN
SUBJECT REPRESENTS MAJOR EMPHASIS OF WORK BEING CLASSIFIED**

Tryparsamide   QV 254
Trypsin   WI 802
Trypsin Inhibitor, alpha 1-Antitrypsin see alpha
   1-Antitrypsin
Trypsin Inhibitor, Kunitz, Pancreatic see Aprotinin
Trypsin Inhibitors   WI 802
Tryptamines
   Biochemistry   QU 61
   Organic chemistry   QD 401
   Serotonin antagonists   QV 126
Tryptophan   QU 60
Tryptophan Oxygenase   QU 140
Tryptophan Pyrrolase see Tryptophan Oxygenase
Tsetse Flies   QX 505
Tsetse Fly Disease see Trypanosomiasis, African
TSH see Thyrotropin
Tsutsugamushi Disease see Scrub Typhus
Tsutsugamushi Fever see Scrub Typhus
Tuba Uterina see Fallopian Tubes
Tubal Embryo Transfer see Embryo Transfer
Tubal Ligation see Sterilization, Tubal
Tubal Pregnancy see Pregnancy, Tubal
Tube Feeding see Tube Feeding see Enteral Feeding
Tube Grafts see Transplantation
Tube Ileostomy see Ileostomy
Tubercle Bacillus see Mycobacterium tuberculosis
Tuberculin   WF 250
Tuberculin Test   WF 220
   Veterinary   SF 808
Tuberculin-Type Hypersensitivity see
   Hypersensitivity, Delayed
Tuberculoid Infections see Mycobacterium
   Infections, Atypical
Tuberculoma   WF 200
   Localized (other than the lungs), by site or
      associated disease
Tuberculosis   WF 200-415
   Drugs for see Antitubercular Agents   QV 268,
      etc.
   Genital see Tuberculosis, Female Genital   WP
      160, etc.; Tuberculosis, Male Genital   WJ 700,
      etc.
   In pregnancy   WQ 256
   Industrial   WF 405
   Laws   WF 200
   Nursing   WY 163
   Oral see Tuberculosis, Oral   WI 200, etc.
   Skin see Tuberculosis, Cutaneous   WR 245
   Veterinary   SF 808
      See also Paratuberculosis   SF 809.J6
   Other localities, by site
   See also Silicotuberculosis   WF 654
Tuberculosis, Avian   SF 995.6.T8
Tuberculosis, Bovine   SF 967.T8
Tuberculosis, Cardiovascular   WG 100
   Localized, by site
Tuberculosis, Cutaneous   WR 245
Tuberculosis, Endocrine   WK 140
   Localized, by site
Tuberculosis, Female Genital   WP 160
   Localized, by site
Tuberculosis, Gastrointestinal   WI 140

Localized, by site
Tuberculosis, Hepatic   WI 700
Tuberculosis in Childhood   WF 415
Tuberculosis, Laryngeal   WV 500
Tuberculosis, Lymph Node   WF 290
Tuberculosis, Male Genital   WJ 700
   Localized, by site
Tuberculosis, Meningeal   WL 200
Tuberculosis, Miliary   WF 380
Tuberculosis, Ocular   WW 160
   Localized, by site
Tuberculosis, Oral   WI 200
   For the dentist   WU 140
Tuberculosis, Osteoarticular   WE 253
   Localized, by site
Tuberculosis, Peritoneal   WI 575
Tuberculosis, Pleural   WF 390
Tuberculosis, Pulmonary   WF 300-360
   Rehabilitation
      At home   WF 315
      At hospital   WF 330
Tuberculosis, Renal   WJ 351
Tuberculosis Societies   WF 1
Tuberculosis, Spinal   WE 253
Tuberculosis, Splenic   WH 600
Tuberculosis, Urogenital   WJ 140
   Localized, by site
Tuberculostatic Agents see Antitubercular Agents
Tuberous Sclerosis   QS 675
Tubocurarine   QV 140
Tubulin   QU 55
Tuftsin   QW 806
   As Immunologic Factors   WH 400
Tularemia   WC 380
Tullidora see Rhamnus
Tumescence, Penile see Penile Erection
Tumor Antibodies see Antibodies, Neoplasm
Tumor Antigens see Antigens, Neoplasm
Tumor Antigens, Viral see Antigens, Viral, Tumor
Tumor-Associated Carbohydrate Antigens see
   Antigens, Tumor-Associated, Carbohydrate
Tumor Cells, Cultured
   Special topics, by subject
Tumor Cells, Embolic see Neoplasm Circulating
   Cells
Tumor Initiators see Carcinogens
Tumor Markers, Biochemical see Tumor Markers,
   Biological
Tumor Markers, Biological
   In the diagnosis of neoplasms   QZ 241
Tumor Metabolite Markers see Tumor Markers,
   Biological
Tumor Necrosis Factor   QW 630
   See also Antibiotics, Antineoplastic QV 269;
      names of toxins specific to particular cells, e.g.
      Enterotoxins QW 630 (jcn added)
Tumor Necrosis Factor-alpha see Tumor Necrosis
   Factor
Tumor Promoters see Carcinogens
Tumor Staging see Neoplasm Staging
Tumor Stem Cell Assay
   Used in testing antineoplastic agents   QV 269
Tumor Stem Cells   QZ 202

**ALWAYS CONSULT MAIN SCHEDULES. USE NUMBER ASSIGNED ONLY WHEN
SUBJECT REPRESENTS MAJOR EMPHASIS OF WORK BEING CLASSIFIED**

Tumor Suppressor Genes see Genes, Suppressor,
Tumor
Tumor Virus Infections   QZ 200
Tumor Viruses see Oncogenic Viruses
Tumor Viruses, Murine   QW 166
Tumoricidal Activity, Immunologic see
Cytotoxicity, Immunologic
Tumorigenicity Tests see Carcinogenicity Tests
Tumors see Neoplasms
Tungsten
    Inorganic chemistry   QD 181.W1
    Metabolism   QU 130
    Pharmacology   QV 290
Tunica Vaginalis see Testis
Tunnel Anemia see Ancyclostomiasis
Turbellaria   QX 352
Turbidimetry see Nephelometry and Turbidimetry
Turbinates   WV 301
Turkeys
    Culture   SF 507
    Diseases   SF 995.4
Turkish Baths see Baths
Turner's Syndrome   QS 677
Turpentine   QV 65
Turtles   QL 666.C5-666.C587
    Diseases   SF 997.5.T87
Twenty-Four Hour Rhythm see Circadian Rhythm
Twilight Sleep see Anesthesia, Obstetrical
Twinning see Embryology
Twins   WQ 235
    Embryology   QS 642
    Psychology   WS 105.5.F2
Twins, Conjoined   QS 675
Twins, Dizygotic   WQ 235
    Special topics, by subject
    See also Twins
Twins, Fraternal see Twins, Dizygotic
Twins, Identical see Twins, Monozygotic
Twins, Monozygotic   WQ 235
    Special topics, by subject
    See also Twins
Two-Parameter Models see Models, Statistical
Tympanic Cavity see Ear, Middle
Tympanic Membrane   WV 225
Tympanometry see Acoustic Impedance Tests
Tympanoplasty   WV 225
Tympanostomy Tube Insertion see Middle Ear
Ventilation
Tympanum see Ear, Middle
Type A Personality   BF 698.3
    Medical aspects, with the disease
Type I Hypersensitivity see Hypersensitivity,
Immediate
Type III Hypersensitivity see Immune Complex
Diseases
Type IV Hypersensitivity see Hypersensitivity,
Delayed
Typhoid   WC 270
Typhoid Bacillus see Salmonella typhi
Typhoid-Paratyphoid Vaccines
    For paratyphoid   WC 266
    General and for typhoid   WC 270
Typhus see Typhus, Epidemic Louse-Borne

Typhus, Abdominal see Typhoid
Typhus, Endemic Flea-Borne   WC 615
Typhus, Epidemic Louse-Borne   WC 605-610
Typhus, Murine see Typhus, Endemic Flea-Borne
Typhus, Sao Paulo see Rocky Mountain Spotted
Fever
Typhus, Scrub see Scrub Typhus
Typing, Bacteriophage see Bacteriophage Typing
Typology see Somatotypes
Tyramine   QV 174
Tyrocidine   QV 220
Tyrosine   QU 60
Tyrosine Aminotransferase see Tyrosine
Transaminase
Tyrosine Transaminase   QU 141
Tyrothricin   QV 350
Ty1 Transposon see DNA Insertion Elements
T3 Receptors see Receptors, Thyroid Hormone
T4 Antigens, T-Cell see Antigens, CD4
T4 Receptors see Receptors, Thyroid Hormone

U

Ubiquinone   QU 135
Ubiquitin   QU 56
Udder see Mammae
UDP Glucose see Uridine Diphosphate Glucose
UDP Sugars see Uridine Diphosphate Sugars
UDPG see Uridine Diphosphate Glucose
Ulcer
    Corneal see Corneal Ulcer   WW 220
    Decubitus see Decubitus Ulcer   WR 598
    Duodenal see Duodenal Ulcer   WI 370
    Gastric see Stomach Ulcer   WI 360
    Leg see Leg Ulcer   WE 850
    Pathology   QZ 150
    Peptic see Peptic Ulcer   WI 350-370
    Skin see Skin Ulcer   WR 598
    Varicose see Varicose Ulcer   WG 620
Ulcer, Aphthous see Stomatitis, Aphthous
Ulna   WE 820
Ulnar Nerve   WL 400
    See also names of organs innervated, e.g.,
    Forearm   WE 820
Ultracentrifugation
    Biological research   QH 324.9.C4
    Chemical engineering   TP 159.C4
    Chemical techniques   QD 54.C4
    Clinical chemistry   QY 90
    See also Centrifugation   QD 54.C4, etc.
Ultradian Cycles see Activity Cycles
Ultramicrotomy see Microtomy
Ultrasonic Diagnosis see Ultrasonography
Ultrasonic Imaging see Ultrasonography
Ultrasonic Lithotripsy see Lithotripsy
Ultrasonic Therapy   WB 515
Ultrasonics
    Biophysics   QT 34
    Diagnostic use (General) see Ultrasonography
    WN 208
    Physics   QC 244
    Used for other special purposes, by subject
Ultrasonography   WN 208

Used for special purposes, by subject
Ultrasonography, Fetal see Ultrasonography, Prenatal
Ultrasonography, Prenatal   WQ 209
Ultraviolet Microscopy see Microscopy, Ultraviolet
Ultraviolet Rays
   Adverse effects (General)   WD 605
   Diagnostic use   WB 288
   General physiological effects   QT 162.U4
   Medical use (General)   WB 117
   Meteorology   QC 976.U4
   Therapeutic use see Ultraviolet Therapy   WB 480
Ultraviolet Therapy   WB 480
Umbilical Arteries   WG 595.U6
Umbilical Cord   WQ 210
Umbilical Hernia see Hernia, Umbilical
Umbilical Veins   WI 720
   Embryology   QS 604
   Obstetrics   WQ 210
Umbilicus   WI 940
   See also Umbilical Cord   WQ 210
Umbra see Salmonidae
Uncinaria see Hookworms
Uncinaria stenocephala see Ancylostomatoidea
Uncinariasis, Human see Necatoriasis
Unconscious (Psychology)   BF 315
   In adolescence   WS 462
   In infancy & childhood   WS 105
   Psychoanalysis   WM 460.5.U6
Unconsciousness
   General diagnosis   WB 182
   Neurological manifestation   WL 341
Underachievement   BF 637.U53
   Academic   LC 4661
      Relation to personality   BF 698.9.A3
Underpopulation see Population Density
Undertaking see Mortuary Practice
Undulant Fever see Brucellosis
Unemployment   HD 5707.5–5710.2
Unipolar Depression see Depressive Disorder
United States National Health Insurance see National Health Insurance, United States
Universal Precautions
   Precaution against a specific communicable disease, by disease
Universities   LB 2301–2430
University Health Services see Student Health Services
Unknown Primary Tumors see Neoplasms, Unknown Primary
Unsaturated Dietary Fats see Dietary Fats, Unsaturated
Unsaturated Fats see Fats, Unsaturated
Unsaturated Oils see Fats, Unsaturated
Unwed Fathers see Illegitimacy
Unwed Mothers see Illegitimacy
Uphill Transport see Biological Transport, Active
Upper Extremities see Extremities; names of particular parts
Upper Extremity see Arm
Upper Respiratory Infections see Respiratory Tract Infections

Urachus   WQ 210.5
Uracil
   In nucleic acids   QU 58
Uragoga see Ipecac (Syrup)
Uralenic Acid see Glycyrrhetinic Acid
Uranium   WN 420
   Nuclear physics   QC 796.U7
   See also special topics under Radioisotopes
Urban Development see Urban Renewal
Urban Health   WA 380
Urban Planning see City Planning
Urban Population
   Demography   HB 2161–2367
   Health Problems   WA 380
   Other aspects, by subject
   See also Housing   HD 257, etc.; Public Housing HD 7288.77–7288.78
Urban Renewal   HT 170–178
   Architecture and engineering   NA 9000–9428
   Public health aspects in   WA
Urea
   In animal nutrition   SF 98.U7
   In blood   QY 455
   In protein metabolism   QU 55
   In urine   QY 185
   Organic chemistry   QD 315
Urease   QU 136
Uremia   WJ 348
Ureter   WJ 400
Ureteral Calculi   WJ 400
Ureteral Diseases   WJ 400
Ureteral Neoplasms   WJ 400
Ureteral Obstruction   WJ 400
Ureteritis see Ureteral Diseases
Ureterolithiasis see Ureteral Calculi
Urethane   QV 269
Urethra   WJ 600
   Surgery   WJ 600
Urethral Diseases   WJ 600
Urethral Stenosis see Urethral Stricture
Urethral Stricture   WJ 600
   In infancy & childhood   WS 320
Urethritis   WJ 600
Urethrotomy see Surgery   WJ 600 under Urethra
Uric Acid   WJ 303
   In urine   QY 185
   Organic chemistry   QD 401
Uricosuric Agents   QV 98
Uridine   QU 57
Uridine Diphosphate Glucose
   Biochemistry   QU 57
   Pharmacology   QV 185
Uridine Diphosphate Sugars
   Biochemistry   QU 57
   Pharmacology   QV 185
Uridine Diphosphoglucose see Uridine Diphosphate Glucose
Urinalysis   QY 185
Urinary Calculi   WJ 140
   See also Bladder Calculi   WJ 500; Kidney Calculi   WJ 356; Ureteral Calculi   WJ 400
Urinary Catheterization   WJ 141

Urinary Diversion
    Surgery of the kidney   WJ 368
    Surgery of the penis   WJ 790
    Surgery of the ureter   WJ 400
    Surgery of the urethra   WJ 600
    By organ used as conduit if more appropriate
      for the work
Urinary Fistula   WJ 140
    See also Bladder Fistula   WJ 500; Vesicovaginal
      Fistula   WP 180
Urinary Incontinence   WJ 146
Urinary Incontinence, Stress   WJ 146
Urinary Tract   WJ
    Animals, Domestic   SF 871
    Antiseptics see Anti-Infective Agents, Urinary
      QV 243
    Children   WS 320–322
    Drugs affecting see Diuretics   QV 160;
      Vasopressin   QV 160, etc.
    Surgery   WJ 168
Urinary Tract Diseases see Urologic Diseases
Urinary Tract Infections   WJ 151
    In infancy & childhood   WS 320
    Veterinary   SF 871
Urination   WJ 146
Urination Disorders   WJ 146
    Veterinary   SF 871
Urine
    Analysis   See Urinalysis   QY 185
    Secretion   WJ 303
    Sugars see Diabetes Mellitus   WK 810–850;
      Glycosuria   WK 870
    Urine therapy see Alternative Medicine   WB
      890, etc.
Urine Concentrating Ability see Kidney
    Concentrating Ability
Urodela   QL 668.C2–668.C285
    As laboratory animals   QY 60.A6
Urodynamics   WJ 102
Urogastrone see Epidermal Growth
    Factor–Urogastrone
Urogastrone Receptors see Receptors, Epidermal
    Growth Factor–Urogastrone
Urogenital Diseases
    General   WJ 140
Urogenital Neoplasms   WJ 160
    Localized, by site
    See also names of specific urogenital neoplasms
Urogenital System   WJ
    Animals, Domestic   SF 871
    Children   WS 320–322
    Surgery   WJ 168
Urography   WJ 141
    In infancy & childhood   WS 320
    Pyelography   WJ 302
Urokinase   QU 142
Urokinase–Type Plasminogen Activator see
    Urokinase
Urolithiasis see Urinary Calculi
Urologic Diseases   WJ
    Diagnosis   WJ 141
    General   WJ 140
    Gynecology   WJ 190

    In infancy & childhood   WS 320–322
    In pregnancy   WQ 260
    Nursing   WY 164
    Therapy   WJ 166
    Veterinary   SF 871
Urologic Neoplasms   WJ 160
    Localized, by site
Urology   WJ
    Pediatric   WS 320–322
Urology Department, Hospital   WJ 27–28
Uropepsin   QU 136
Urotropin see Methenamine
Ursodeoxycholic Acid
    Bile acid   WI 703
    As a Cholagogue and choleretic   QV 66
Urticaria   WR 170
Urticaria, Giant see Angioneurotic Edema
Urticaria Pigmentosa   WR 267
User–Computer Interface   QA 76.9.U83
Uterine Contraction   WQ 305
Uterine Diseases   WP 440–480
    General works   WP 440
Uterine Endoscopy see Hysteroscopy
Uterine Hemorrhage   WP 440
Uterine Inertia   WQ 330
Uterine Inversion see Uterine Diseases
Uterine Monitoring   WQ 209
Uterine Muscle see Myometrium
Uterine Neoplasms   WP 458–465
    Leiomyoma   WP 459
Uterine Prolapse   WP 454
Uterus   WP 400–480
    Anatomy & histology   WP 400
    During puerperium   WQ 500
    Drugs affecting   QV 170–174
    See also Oxytocics   QV 173–174
Utilitarianism see Ethics
Utilization and Quality Control Peer Review
    Organizations see Professional Review
    Organizations
Utilization Review   WX 153
    Of special hospitals, by type
Utopias   HX 806–811
Uvea   WW 240–245
Uveal Diseases   WW 240
Uveal Neoplasms   WW 240
Uveitis   WW 240
Uveitis, Sympathetic see Ophthalmia, Sympathetic
Uvula   WV 410
U1 Small Nuclear RNA see RNA, Small Nuclear
U2 Small Nuclear RNA see RNA, Small Nuclear
U3 Small Nuclear RNA see RNA, Small Nuclear
U4 Small Nuclear RNA see RNA, Small Nuclear
U5 Small Nuclear RNA see RNA, Small Nuclear
U6 Small Nuclear RNA see RNA, Small Nuclear
U7 Small Nuclear RNA see RNA, Small Nuclear

V

v–Ha–ras Genes see Genes, ras
v–Ki–ras Genes see Genes, ras
Vaccination   QW 806
    BCG see BCG Vaccine   WF 250

In infancy & childhood   WS 135
Poliomyelitis see Prevention & control   WC 556
   under Poliomyelitis
Smallpox see Prevention & control   WC 588
   under Smallpox
Veterinary medicine   SF 757.2
Other diseases, with the disease
See also Vaccines and particular types of vaccines
Vaccination Encephalitis see Encephalomyelitis,
   Acute Disseminated
Vaccine Therapy see Immunotherapy, Active
Vaccines   QW 805
   Bacterial see Bacterial Vaccines   WC 200
   BCG see BCG Vaccine   WF 250
   Brucella see Brucella Vaccine   WC 310
   Cholera see Cholera Vaccine   WC 262
   Fungal see Fungal Vaccines   WC 450
   Influenza see Influenza Vaccine   WC 515
   Measles see Measles Vaccine   WC 580
   Mumps see Mumps Vaccine   WC 520
   Pertussis see Pertussis Vaccine   WC 340
   Plague see Plague Vaccine   WC 350
   Poliovirus see Poliovirus Vaccine   WC 556
   Rabies see Rabies Vaccine   WC 550
   Rickettsial see Rickettsial Vaccines   WC 600
   Rubella see Rubella Vaccine   WC 582
   Smallpox see Smallpox Vaccine   WC 588
   Staphylococcal see Staphylococcal Vaccines
    WC 250
   Tuberculosis see BCG Vaccine   WF 250
   Typhoid-Paratyphoid see Typhoid-Paratyphoid
    Vaccines   WC 270, etc.
   Viral see Viral Vaccines   WC 500
Vaccines, Recombinant see Vaccines, Synthetic
Vaccines, Synthetic
   As a vaccine   QW 805
   As an antigen   QW 573
Vaccinia   WC 584
Vaccinia Virus   QW 165.5.P6
Vacuolating Agent see Polyomavirus macacae
Vacuoles   QH 591
   In plant cells   QK 725
Vacuum Curettage   WP 470
   Used for special purposes, by subject
Vagina   WP 250-258
Vaginal Birth after Cesarean   WQ 415
Vaginal Diseases   WP 250-258
   General works   WP 250
Vaginal Fistula   WP 250
   See also Rectovaginal Fistula   WP 180;
   Vesicovaginal Fistula   WP 180
Vaginal Neoplasms   WP 250
Vaginal Prolapse see Uterine Prolapse
Vaginal Smears   WP 141
Vaginismus see Dyspareunia; Hyperesthesia; Vaginal
   Diseases
Vaginitis   WP 255
   See also Trichomonas Vaginitis   WP 258;
   Vulvovaginitis   WP 200
Vagotomy   WL 330
Vagotomy, Parietal Cell see Vagotomy, Proximal
   Gastric
Vagotomy, Proximal Gastric   WL 330

Vagotomy, Selective Proximal see Vagotomy,
   Proximal Gastric
Vagus Nerve   WL 330
   Vagotonia   WL 330
Valerates   QU 90
Valerian   QV 767
   As sedative   QV 85
Validity of Results see Reproducibility of Results
Valine   QU 60
Valproic Acid   QV 85
Vanadium
   Inorganic chemistry   QD 181.V2
   Metabolism   QU 130.5
   Pharmacology   QV 290
Vanillin   QV 810
Vanylglycol see Methoxyhydroxyphenylglycol
Vapor Baths see Baths
Vaporization, Laser see Laser Surgery
Vaporizers see Nebulizers and Vaporizers
Vaquez's Disease see Polycythemia Vera
Variation (Genetics)   QH 401-411
   Animal   QH 408
   Microbial genetics
    Bacteria   QW 51
    Fungi   QW 180
    Viruses   QW 160
   Plants   QK 983
Varicella see Chickenpox
Varicella-Zoster Virus see Herpesvirus 3, Human
Varices see Varicose Veins
Varicocele   WJ 780
Varicose Ulcer   WG 620
Varicose Veins   WG 620
   In pregnancy   WQ 244
Variola see Smallpox
Variola Virus   QW 165.5.P6
Varnish see Paint
Vas Deferens   WJ 780
Vascular Access Ports see Catheters, Indwelling
Vascular-Assist Devices see Heart-Assist Devices
Vascular Dementia see Dementia, Vascular
Vascular Diseases   WG 500-700
   General works   WG 500
   In infancy & childhood   WS 290
   Varices   WG 620
   Veterinary   SF 811
   See also Cardiovascular Diseases   WG, etc.;
    names of specific organs or systems (for their
    blood supply) or specific vascular diseases
Vascular Diseases, Peripheral see Peripheral
   Vascular Diseases
Vascular Endothelium see Endothelium, Vascular
Vascular Headache   WL 344
   See also specifics, e.g., Migraine   WL 344y
Vascular Permeability see Capillary Permeability
Vascular Prosthesis see Blood Vessel Prosthesis
Vascular Resistance   WG 106
Vascular Surgery   WG 170
   Children   WS 290
Vasculitis   WG 515
   Of the veins only   WG 610
Vasculitis, Allergic Cutaneous   WG 515
   Emphasis on skin hypersensitivity   WR 160

Vasculitis, Churg–Strauss see Churg–Strauss
Syndrome
Vasectomy   WJ 780
Vasoactive Agonists see Vasoconstrictor Agents
Vasoactive Antagonists see Vasodilator Agents
Vasoactive Intestinal Peptide   WK 170
As a Peptide   QU 68
As a Vasopressin   WK 520
Vasoconstriction   WG 106
See also Constriction, Pathologic   WG 560, etc.
Vasoconstrictor Agents   QV 150
Vasoconstrictor Agents, Nasal   QV 150
Vasodilation   WG 106
See also Dilatation, Pathologic   WG 578, etc.
Vasodilator Agents   QV 150–156
Vasodilator Disorders see Dilatation, Pathologic
Vasomotor Disorders see Vasomotor System; names
of specific disorders
Vasomotor Regulation see Vasomotor System
Vasomotor Rhinitis see Rhinitis, Vasomotor
Vasomotor System   WL 610
Disorders   WG 560
Spastic see Raynaud's Disease   WG 570
Vasodilator   WG 578
See also Constriction, Pathologic   WG 560,
etc.
Regulation   WG 560
Vasopressin, Arginine see Argipressin
Vasopressin, Deamino Arginine see Desmopressin
Vasopressin, Isoleucyl–Leucyl see Oxytocin
Vasopressin, Lysine see Lypressin
Vasopressins   WK 520
Diuretic   QV 160
Vasopressor Agents see Vasoconstrictor Agents
Vasospastic Disorders see Raynaud's Disease
Vasotocin, Leucyl see Oxytocin
Vater's Ampulla   WI 750
Vectorcardiography   WG 140
Vectors see Disease Vectors
Vectors, Genetic see Genetic Vectors
Vecuronium see Vecuronium Bromide
Vecuronium Bromide   QV 140
Vegetable Oils see Plant Oils
Vegetables
As a dietary supplement in health and disease
WB 430
Cultivation   SB 320–353.5
Drugs see Plants, Medicinal   QV 766, etc.
Poisonous see Plants, Toxic   WD 500–530
Processing   TX 801–807
Purgatives see Cathartics   QV 75
Sanitation and other public health aspects   WA
703
See also names of specific vegetables
Vegetarianism   WB 430
Vegetative Nervous System see Autonomic Nervous
System
Vegetative State, Persistent see Persistent Vegetative
State
Vehicles   QV 800
Veiled Cells see Dendritic Cells
Vein Anesthesia see Anesthesia, Local
Vein of Galen see Cerebral Veins

Veins   WG 600–625
Coronary see Coronary Vessels   WG 300
Medication by see Injections, Intravenous   WB
354
Portal see Portal Vein   WI 720
Velocimetry see Rheology
Velopharyngeal Insufficiency   WV 410
Vena Cava, Inferior   WG 625.V3
Vena Cava, Superior   WG 625.V3
Venae Cavae   WG 625.V3
Venereal Diseases see Sexually Transmitted Diseases
Venereology   WC 140–185
Venesection see Bloodletting
Venipuncture see Bloodletting
Venoclysis, Medication see Injections, Intravenous
Venography see Phlebography
Venoms
Poisoning   WD 400–430
Therapeutic use see name of disease being treated;
Alternative Medicine   WB 890, etc.
See also specific venoms, e.g., Bee Venoms   WD
430
Venous Catheterization, Peripheral see
Catheterization, Peripheral
Venous Insufficiency   WG 600
Venous Pressure   WG 106
Venous Pressure, Central see Central Venous
Pressure
Venous Thrombosis see Thrombophlebitis
Venous Ulcer see Varicose Ulcer
Venovenous Hemofiltration see Hemofiltration
Ventilation   WA 770
Hospitals   WX 165
Industrial   WA 450
Ventilation, High Frequency Jet see
High–Frequency Jet Ventilation
Ventilation, Intermittent Positive-Pressure see
Intermittent Positive-Pressure Ventilation
Ventilation, Maximal Voluntary see Respiratory
Airflow
Ventilation, Mechanical see Respiration, Artificial
Ventilation, Middle Ear see Middle Ear Ventilation
Ventilation–Perfusion Ratio   WF 141
Ventilation Tests see Respiratory Function Tests
Ventilators, Mechanical   WF 26
Ventilators, Pulmonary see Ventilators, Mechanical
Ventilatory Muscles see Respiratory Muscles
Ventral Hernia see Hernia, Ventral
Ventricle-Assist Device see Heart-Assist Devices
Ventricular Ejection Fraction see Stroke Volume
Ventricular End–Diastolic Volume see Stroke
Volume
Ventricular End–Systolic Volume see Stroke
Volume
Ventricular Fibrillation   WG 330
Ventricular Puncture see Punctures
Ventricular System see Cerebral Ventricles
Ventriculography, Cerebral see Cerebral
Ventriculography
Verapamil   QV 150
Veratrum   QV 150
Veratrum Alkaloids   QV 150

Verbal Behavior
   In adolescence   WS 462
   In infancy & childhood   WS 105.5.C8
   General psychology   BF 455
   Physiological aspects   WV 501
   Social psychology   HM 258
   Verbal ability   BF 463.V45
   Verbal self-defense   BF 637.V47
   Speech disorders   WM 475, etc.
Verbal Learning   LB 1139.L3
Vermifuges see Anthelmintics
Vermin, Public Health Aspects see Parasites
Veronal see Barbiturates
Verruga Peruana see Bartonella Infections
Verse's Disease see Calcinosis; Intervertebral Disk
Version, Fetal   WQ 415
Vertebrae see Spine
Vertebral Artery   WG 595.V3
Vertebral Artery Insufficiency see Vertebrobasilar Insufficiency
Vertebrate Viruses
   General works   QW 164
   DNA see DNA Viruses   QW 165
   RNA see RNA Viruses   QW 168
   See also names of other specific vertebrate viruses
Vertebrate Viruses, Unclassified   QW 169
Vertebrates
   Anatomy
      Domestic animals   SF 761–767
      Fishes   QL 639
      Wild animals   QL 801–950.9
         Specific animals or groups of animals, with animal or group
   Diseases   SF 600–997.5, etc.
   Human see specific topics
   Physiology   QP
      Domestic animals   SF 768–768.2
      Fishes   QL 639.1
      Wild animals   QP
   See also other specific topics relating to vertebrates, e.g., Embryology   QL 959, etc.
Vertebrobasilar Insufficiency   WL 355
Verticillium see Hyphomycetes
Vertigo   WV 255
   Aural see Ménire's Disease   WV 258
   Manifestation of disease   QZ 140
Vertigo, Aural see Meniere's Disease
Vervet Monkey see Cercopithecus aethiops
Vesical Calculi see Bladder Calculi
Vesical Fistula see Bladder Fistula
Vesicants see Irritants
Vesication see Blister
Vesico-Ureteral Reflux   WJ 500
   In infancy & childhood   WJ 500
Vesicovaginal Fistula   WP 180
Vesicular Exanthema of Swine   SF 977.V3
Vesicular Palmoplantar Eczema see Eczema, Dyshidrotic
Vesicular Skin Diseases see Skin Diseases, Vesiculobullous
Vesiculitis, Seminal see Seminal Vesicles
Vesiculobullous Skin Diseases see Skin Diseases, Vesiculobullous

Vespid Venoms see Wasp Venoms
Vestibular Apparatus see Vestibule
Vestibular Aqueduct   WV 255
Vestibular Diseases   WV 255
Vestibular Function Tests   WV 255
Vestibular Nerve   WL 330
   Physiology of hearing   WV 272
Vestibular Nuclei   WV 255
Vestibule   WV 255
Vestibulo-Ocular Reflex see Reflex, Vestibulo-Ocular
Veterans   UB 356–405
   Hospitalization   UH 460–485
   Lists of veterans   UA 37–39
   Provision for vetrans   UB 356–405, etc.
Veterans Disability Claims   UB 368–369.5
Veterans Hospitals see Hospitals, Veterans
Veterans Nursing see Hospitals, Veterans; Military Nursing
Veterinary Anatomy see Anatomy, Veterinary
Veterinary Bacteriology see Veterinary Science QW 70 under Bacteriology
Veterinary Clinics see Hospitals, Animal
Veterinary Education see Education, Veterinary
Veterinary Histology see Histology
Veterinary Hospitals see Hospitals, Animal
Veterinary Medicine   SF 600–1100
   Education   SF 756.3–756.37
   Immunology   SF 757.2
   Military see Veterinary Service, Military   UH 650–655
   Surgery   SF 911–914.4
   See also Veterinary under particular topics and specific animals being treated
Veterinary Microbiology see Microbiology
Veterinary Pathology see Pathology, Veterinary
Veterinary Schools see Schools, Veterinary
Veterinary Service, Military   UH 650–655
Veterinary Toxicology see Toxicology
Vibration
   Adverse effects (General)   WD 640
   As a cause of disease   QZ 57
   In aviation   WD 735
   In industry
      Diseases   WA 400
      Prevention & control   WA 470
   Therapeutic use   WB 535
Vibrio   QW 141
Vibrio fetus see Campylobacter fetus
Vibrio Infections   WC 200
   Veterinary   SF 809.V52
   See also Cholera   WC 262–264
Vibrio parahaemolyticus   QW 141
Vibrionaceae   QW 141
Vibrocardiography see Kinetocardiography
Vicarious Menstruation see Menstruation Disorders
Vichy Water see Mineral Waters
Vidarabine   QU 57
   As an antiviral agent   QV 268.5
Video Display Terminals see Computer Terminals
Video Games see Play and Playthings
Video Recording   TK 6655.V5
   Recording by subject

ALWAYS CONSULT MAIN SCHEDULES. USE NUMBER ASSIGNED ONLY WHEN SUBJECT REPRESENTS MAJOR EMPHASIS OF WORK BEING CLASSIFIED

Videodisc Recording   TK 6685
    Catalogs and works about (Form number 18.2
    in any NLM schedules where applicable)
    Actual recordings, by subject
Videotape Recording
    Catalogs and works about (Form number 18.2
    in any NLM schedule where applicable)
    Actual recordings, by subject
Videotherapy
    In psychiatry   WM 450.5.V5
Vidine see Choline
Vigilance see Attention
Vigilance, Cortical see Arousal
Village Health Worker see Community Health Aides
Vinblastine   QV 269
Vinca Alkaloids   QV 269
Vincaleukoblastine see Vinblastine
Vincent's Angina see Gingivitis, Necrotizing
    Ulcerative
Vincent's Infection see Gingivitis, Necrotizing
    Ulcerative
Vincristine   QV 269
Vinyl Chloride
    As carcinogen   QZ 202
Vinyl Chloride Polymer see Polyvinyl Chloride
Vinyl Compounds
    Organic chemistry   QD 305.H7
    Toxicology   QV 633
Vinyl Ether   QV 81
Vinylidene Chlorides see Dichloroethylenes
Violence
    In adolescence   WS 463
    In infancy & childhood   WS 350.8.A4
        Influence of television   WS 105.5.E9
    Criminal (Medicolegal aspects)   W 860
    Political theory   JC 328.6
    Psychology (General)   BF 575.A3
    Sociology   HM 281-283
Viper Venoms   WD 410
Viral Antibodies see Antibodies, Viral
Viral Antigens see Antigens, Viral
Viral DNA see DNA, Viral
Viral Gene Expression Regulation see Gene
    Expression Regulation, Viral
Viral Gene Products see Viral Proteins
Viral Gene Proteins see Viral Proteins
Viral Genes see Genes, Viral
Viral Hepatitis Vaccines   WC 536
Viral Interference   QW 160
Viral Markers see Biological Markers
Viral Proteins   QW 160
Viral RNA see RNA, Viral
Viral Tumor Antigens see Antigens, Viral, Tumor
Viral Vaccines   WC 500
    Used for particular disease, with the disease
    See also names of specific vaccines
Virales see Viruses
Viremia   WC 500
Virilism   WK 770
Virilizing Adenoma see Adenoma, Virilizing
Viroids   QW 160
Virology   QW 160
    See also numbers   QW 1-85 (except 5, 7, 9, 20.5,

50, 51 and 52)
    Veterinary medicine   QW 70
        Specific viruses, in number for the group
        QW
        Virus diseases of animals (General)   SF 780.4
Virulence   QW 730
Virus Cultivation   QW 25.5.V7
Virus Diseases   WC 500-593
    Affecting the nerve tissues   WC 540-556
    Affecting the skin see Skin Diseases, Infectious
    WC 570-590
    In infancy & childhood   WC 500-593, etc.
    In plants   SB 736
    Veterinary (individual virus diseases)   SF
    781-809
Virus Inhibitors   QW 160
Virus Pneumonia see Pneumonia, Viral
Virus Receptors see Receptors, Virus
Virus Replication   QW 160
Virus Transforming Antigens see Antigens, Viral,
    Tumor
Viruses   QW 160-170
    As a cause of disease   QZ 65
    Bacteria see Bacteriophages   QW 161
    Insect see Insect Viruses   QW 162
    Of animals   QW 70
    Plant see Plant Viruses   QW 163
    Vertebrate see Vertebrate Viruses   QW 164, etc.
    See also names of other specific viruses
Visammin see Khellin
Viscera
    In the abdomen   WI 900
    In the thorax   WF 970
    In the pelvis   WE 750
        Gynecological   WP 155
Visceral Arches see Branchial Region
Visceroptosis   WI 900
    Of the intestines   WI 450
    Other localities, by site
Viscosity
    Of blood   WH 400
        Clinical analysis   QY 408
    Of gases   QC 167
    Of liquids   QC 145.4.V5
Vision   WW 103
    Acuity see Visual Acuity   WW 145
    Binocular see Eye Movements   WW 400-460;
        Accommodation, Ocular   WW 109
    Conservation   WW 113
    Fields see Visual Fields   WW 145
    Measurement see Vision Tests   WW 145;
        Optometry   WW 704, etc.
    Night see Dark Adaptation   WW 109
    Perception see Visual Perception   WW 105
    Physiology   WW 103
    See also Perimetry   WW 145
Vision, Binocular   WW 400
Vision Disorders   WW 140
    Corrective devices   WW 350-358
    In infancy & childhood   WW 600
    Neuromuscular   WW 410-460
    Orthoptics   WW 405
    Refractive errors   WW 300-320

See also Blindness   WW 276; Color Blindness
    WW 150
Vision, Low see Vision, Subnormal
Vision, Subnormal   WW 140
Vision Tests   WW 145
Visiting Nurse Associations see Home Care Services
Visiting Nurses see Community Health Nursing
Visna–Maedi Virus   QW 166
    As pathogen, with the specific disease
Visna Virus see Visna–Maedi Virus
Visual Acuity   WW 145
Visual Aids see Audio–Visual Aids
Visual Analogue Pain Scale see Pain Measurement
Visual Contrast Sensitivity see Contrast Sensitivity
Visual Cortex   WL 307
Visual Evoked Response see Evoked Potentials,
    Visual
Visual Fields   WW 145
Visual Motor Coordination see Psychomotor
    Performance
Visual Pathways   WW 103
Visual Perception   WW 105
Visual Purple see Rhodopsin
Vital Statistics   HB 848–3697
    Deaths, by disease   WA 900
    See also Birth Rate   HB 901–1108; Divorce
        HQ 811–960.7; Marriage   HB 1111–1317;
        Morbidity   WA 900; Mortality   HB
        1321–1528, etc.
Vitamin A   QU 167
Vitamin A Acid see Tretinoin
Vitamin A Deficiency   WD 110
    Veterinary   SF 855.V58
Vitamin B Complex   QU 187–195
    See also names of specific vitamins
Vitamin B Deficiency   WD 120–126
Vitamin B T see Carnitine
Vitamin B 1 see Thiamine
Vitamin B 12   QU 194
Vitamin B 12 Deficiency   WD 120
Vitamin B 2 see Riboflavin
Vitamin B 6 see Pyridoxine
Vitamin C see Ascorbic Acid
Vitamin Content of Food see Analysis   QU 160
    under Vitamins; Nutrition
Vitamin D   QU 173
Vitamin D Deficiency   WD 145
Vitamin D 2 see Ergocalciferols
Vitamin D 3 see Cholecalciferol
Vitamin Deficiency see Avitaminosis
Vitamin E   QU 179
Vitamin E Deficiency   WD 150
Vitamin G see Riboflavin
Vitamin H see Biotin
Vitamin K   QU 181
Vitamin K Deficiency   WD 155
Vitamin K 1 see Phytonadione
Vitamin M see Folic Acid
Vitamin P Complex see Bioflavonoids
Vitamin PP see Niacinamide
Vitamins   QU 160–220
    Analysis   QU 160
        Clinical assay   QY 350

Animal nutrition   SF 98.V5
Animal physiology
    Domestic   SF 768–768.2
    Wild   QP 771–772
Fat soluble   QU 165–181
Plant constituents   QK 898.V5
Water soluble   QU 185–210
See also names of specific vitamins
Vitiligo   WR 265
Vitrectomy   WW 250
Vitreous Body   WW 250
    Opacity   WW 250
Vitreous Fluorophotometry see Fluorophotometry
Vivisection
    Experimental surgery   WO 50
    Sociological aspects   HV 4915
Vocabulary   P 305
    Special topics, by subject
Vocabulary Tests see Language Tests
Vocal Cord Paralysis   WV 535
Vocal Cords   WV 530–535
Vocal Fold see Vocal Cords
Vocalization, Animal   QL 765
Vocational Education   LC 1041–1048
    Exceptional children   LC 3976
Vocational Guidance   HF 5381–5382.5
    Dentistry   WU 21
    Dietetics   WB 400
    For the blind   HV 1652–1658
    For the deaf   HV 2452–2458
    For the mentally disabled   HV 3005
    For the physically disabled   HD 7255–7256; HV
        3018–3019
    Hospital administration   WX 155
    Hospital work (General)   WX 159
    Nurses' aides   WY 193
    Nursing   WY 16
        See also special types of nursing
    Ophthalmology   WW 21
    Opticianry   WW 721
    Optometry   WW 721
    Physicians   W 21
    Psychiatry   WM 21
    Surgery   WO 21
    In other areas, with the number for the profession
        or lacking that, in a general works number
Vocational Rehabilitation see Rehabilitation,
    Vocational
Vocations see Occupations
Voice
    Care   WV 500
    Physiology   WV 501
Voice Disorders   WV 500
    Psychogenic   WM 475
Voice Production, Alaryngeal see Speech,
    Alaryngeal
Voice Prosthesis see Larynx, Artificial
Voice Quality   WV 501
Voice Training   WV 500
Volatile Oils see Oils, Volatile
Volatile Poisons see Poisons
Volcanic Ash see Volcanic Eruption

Volcanic Eruption
First aid   WA 292
Hospital emergency service   WX 215
Medical emergencies   WB 105
Volcanic Gases see Volcanic Eruption
Voles see Microtinae
Volhynia Fever see Trench Fever
Volition   BF 608–635
Volkmann Contracture see Compartment Syndromes
Volkmann's Contracture see Compartment Syndromes
Volume Index see Blood Volume
Voluntary Health Agencies   WA 1
(Form number 1 in any NLM schedule where applicable)
See also Red Cross   HV 560–583, etc.; names of specialties
Voluntary Health Insurance see Insurance, Health
Voluntary Sterilization see Sterilization, Sexual
Voluntary Workers
In hospitals see Hospital Volunteers   WX 159.5, etc.
In psychiatry   WM 30.5
In social service   HV 41
In other areas, by subject
Volunteers see Voluntary Workers
Volvulus see Intestinal Obstruction
Volvulus, Stomach see Stomach Volvulus
Vomer see Nasal Septum
Vomiting   WI 146
Drugs promoting see Emetics   QV 73
In pregnancy   WQ 215
See also Adverse effects   WO 245 under Anesthesia
Von Gierke's Disease see Glycogen Storage Disease Type I
von Willebrand Factor   WH 310
von Willebrand's Disease   WH 312
Voyages see Expeditions; Travel
VP 16–213 see Etoposide
Vulva   WP 200
Vulvar Neoplasms   WP 200
Vulvitis   WP 200
Vulvovaginal Glands see Bartholin's Glands
Vulvovaginitis   WP 200
VZ Virus see Heepesvirus 3, Human

W

Wages see Salaries and Fringe Benefits
Waiting Lists
In hospitals   WX 159
Practice management
Dental   WU 77
Medical   W 80
Wakefulness   WL 108
In personal hygiene   QT 265
Waldenstrom's Macroglobulinemia   WH 400
Clinical pathology   QY 455
Walking
As locomotion   WE 103
As a sport   QT 260.5.W2
Wallabies see Kangaroos

War   U; V
Adolescent psychology   WS 462
Atomic warfare   U 263
Bacterial warfare   UG 447.8
For the bacteriologists   QW 300
Biological warfare   UG 447.8
For the bacteriologists   QW 300
Chemical warfare   UG 447–447.65
Child psychology   WS 105.5.E9
Civil defense   UA 926–929
Combat psychiatry   UH 629–629.5
Military dentistry   UH 430–435
Naval   VG 280–285
Military medical services   UH 201–630
Morale   U 22
Naval medical services   VG 100–475
Psychiatry see Military Psychiatry   UH 629–629.5
Psychological warfare   UB 275–277
Psychology see Psychology, Military   U 22.3
Rehabilitation   UB 360–366
Surgery   WO 800
Veterinary services   UH 650–655
War crimes   JX 5419.5
Wounded, Transportation   UH 500–505
See also Military Hygiene   UH 600–627; Military Medicine   UH 201–515, etc.
War Gases see Chemical Warfare Agents
War Neuroses see Combat Disorders
Ward Administration see Hospital Administration
Ward Attendants see Nurses Aides; Personnel, Hospital; Psychiatric Aides
Ward Secretaries see Personnel, Hospital
Wards, Hospital see Hospital Units; also special topics under Manuals and Nursing, Supervisory
Warfare, Biological see Biological Warfare
Warfarin   QV 193
Wart-Hog Disease Virus see African Swine Fever Virus
Warthin Tumor see Adenolymphoma
Wasp Venoms   WD 430
Wasps   QX 565
Waste Disposal, Fluid   WA 785
Waste Disposal, Industrial see Industrial Waste
Waste Disposal, Solid see Refuse Disposal
Waste Products   WA 670
Utilization   TP 995–996
Special topics, by subject
See also names of particular products, e.g., Radioactive Pollutants   WN 615, etc.
Water
Analysis   WA 686–689
Bacteriological see Water Microbiology   QW 80
Pharmacology   QV 270–273
As a beverage   WB 442
See also Drinking   WI 102; Water Supply   WA 675–690
Bacteriology see Water Microbiology   QW 80
Balance see Water-Electrolyte Balance   QU 105
Imbalance see Water-Electrolyte Imbalance   WD 220
Metabolism   QU 120

Mineral see Mineral Waters   WB 442
Officinal   QV 785
Pharmacology   QV 270–273
Therapeutic use see Hydrotherapy   WB 520;
  Balneology   WB 525
See also Seawater   WB 525, etc.
Water Buffaloes see Buffaloes
Water Consumption see Drinking
Water Deprivation
  Experimental biochemistry   QU 34
  Experimental pharmacology   QV 34
  Experimental physiology   QT 25
  See also Dehydration   WD 220, etc.; Thirst
  WI 102
Water–Electrolyte Balance   QU 105
Water–Electrolyte Imbalance   WD 220
Water Intake see Drinking
Water Microbiology   QW 80
Water Pollutants   WA 689
  See also names of specific pollutants
Water Pollutants, Chemical   WA 689
Water Pollutants, Radioactive   WN 615
Water Pollution   WA 689
  See also Sewage   WA 785, etc.
Water Pollution, Chemical   WA 689
Water Pollution, Radioactive   WN 615
Water Softening   TP 263
  Public health aspects   WA 675–689
Water Supply   WA 675–690
  Analysis
    Bacteriological see Water Microbiology   QW
    80
    General works   WA 686
  Purification   WA 690
  Sanitation   WA 675
Waterborne Diseases see Communicable Diseases;
  Water Pollution
Waterhouse-Friderichsen Syndrome   WC 245
Waxes   QU 85
Weaning   WS 125
Weather
  Meteorology (Physics)   QC 980–999
  Relation to disease   WB 700–710
    Of animals   SF 760.C55
  See also Acclimatization   QT 145–160
Weaver Mice see Mice, Neurologic Mutants
Webbed Fingers and Toes see Abnormalities   WE
  835. under Fingers and under Toes
Weber-Christian Disease see Panniculitis, Nodular
  Nonsuppurative
Wechsler Scales
  For adults   BF 432.5.W4
  For children   BF 432.5.W42
Wegener's Granulomatosis   WF 600
Weight Gain
  In infancy & childhood   WS 103
Weight Lifting   QT 260.5.W4
Weight Loss
  In infancy & childhood   WS 103
Weight Perception   WE 104
Weight Reduction see Weight Loss
Weight Tables for Children see Tables   WS 16
  under Body Weight

Weightlessness   WD 752
Weights and Measures   QC 81–114
  Pharmaceutical   QV 16
  See also Metric System   QC 90.8–94
Weil's Disease   WC 420
  Veterinary   SF 809.L4
Welding
  Occupational accidents   WA 485
  Occupational medicine   WA 400–495
Welfare Work see Social Work; Social Welfare
Wellness Programs see Health Promotion
Wens, Sebaceous see Epidermal Cyst
Wernicke Area see Temporal Lobe
Wernicke's Encephalopathy   WD 122
West Syndrome see Spasms, Infantile
Western Blotting see Blotting, Western
Western Immunoblotting see Blotting, Western
Wet Lung see Pulmonary Edema
Whales   QL 737.C4
  Diseases   SF 997.5.M35
Wheat
  As a dietary supplement in health or disease
  WB 431
  Cultivation   SB 191.W5
  See also Bread   WB 431, etc.
Wheelchairs   WB 320
  Catalogs   W 26
  For particular disability, by the disability
Wheezing see Respiratory Sounds
Whiplash Injuries   WE 725
Whirlpool Baths see Hydrotherapy
White Blood Cell Count see Leukocyte Count
White Blood Cell Transfusion see Leukocyte
  Transfusion
White Blood Cells see Leukocytes
White Spots see Dental Caries
Whitefish see Salmonidae
Whites
  Anthropology   GN 537
  Other special topics, by subject, e.g., Alcohol
  problem   WM 274
Whitmore's Disease see Melioidosis
Whole-Body Counting   WN 660
Whole-Body Irradiation
  Adverse effects   WN 620
  Therapeutic use   WN 450
  Other aspects, by subject
Whooping Cough   WC 340
Widowers see Widowhood
Widowhood   HQ 1058–1058.5
  Special topics, by subject
Widows see Widowhood
Widows and Widowers see Widowhood
Wife Abuse see Spouse Abuse
Wild Animals see Animals, Wild
Will see Volition
Wilms' Tumor see Nephroblastoma
Wilson's Disease see Hepatolenticular Degeneration
Wind   QC 930.5–959
Wine
  As a dietary supplement in health or disease
  WB 444
  Chemical technology   TP 544–561
  See also Grapes   WB 430, etc.

**ALWAYS CONSULT MAIN SCHEDULES. USE NUMBER ASSIGNED ONLY WHEN
SUBJECT REPRESENTS MAJOR EMPHASIS OF WORK BEING CLASSIFIED**

Wing   QL 950.7
   Birds   QL 697–698.9
   Insects   QX 500
Wirsung's Duct see Pancreatic Ducts
Wit and Humor   PN 6147–6231
   Medicine and related subjects   WZ 305–305.5
   Satire on medicine   WZ 305–305.5
Withdrawal Symptoms see Substance Withdrawal
   Syndrome
Wittenborn Scales see Psychiatric Status Rating
   Scales
Wolff–Parkinson–White Syndrome   WG 330
Wolfram see Tungsten
Women
   As physicians see Physicians, Women   W 21;
     WZ 80.5.W5
   As dentists see Dentists, Women   WU 21
   In industry   HD 6050–6220.7
   In history of medicine   WZ 80.5.W5
     Protection   WA 491
   In marriage   HQ
   In medicine see Physicians, Women   W 21, etc.
   Psychoanalysis   WM 460.5.W6
   See also Gynecology   WP, etc.; Obstetrics
     WQ, etc.; other specific subjects
Women Physicians see Physicians, Women
Women, Working
   Special topics, by subject
Women's Health   WA 309
Women's Liberation see Women's Rights
Women's Rights   HQ 1236–1236.5
   As executives   HD 6054.3–6054.4
   As educators   LB 2837
   In industry   HD 6050–6220.7
   U.S.   HQ 1236.5.U6
   See also Physicians, Women   W 21, etc.
Wood
   Industrial accidents among wood workers   WA
     485
   Occupational disease of wood workers   WA
     400–495
Wool   SF 377
   Animal anatomy   QL 942
     Domestic animals   SF 761–767
   Textile fibers   TS 1547
Woolly Monkey see Cebidae
Woolsorters' Disease see Anthrax
Word Association Tests
   Psychiatry   WM 145.5.W9
   Psychology   BF 698.8.A8
Word Processing
   In particular fields (Form number 26.5 in any
     NLM schedule where applicable)
   Used for special purposes, by subject
Work
   Health see Occupational Health   WA 400–495,
     etc.
   Physical effects   WE 103
   Psychology   BF 481
Work Capacity Evaluation
   Medicolegal aspects   W 925
   Special topics, by subject

Work of Breathing   WF 102
Work Satisfaction see Job Satisfaction
Work Schedule Tolerance
   Occupational health aspects   WA 400–495
   Physiological effects   WE 103
   Psychological aspects   BF 481
Workers' Compensation   HD 7103.6–7103.65
   Medicolegal aspects   W 925
Working Women see Women, Working
Workmen's Compensation see Workers'
   Compensation
World Health   WA 530
Worms see Helminths
Wound Healing   WO 185
   Pathology   QZ 150
   Surgical wounds   WO 185
Wound Infection   WC 255
   See also Surgical Wound Infection   WO 185
Wounded, Transportation see Transportation of
   Patients
Wounds and Injuries   WO 700–820
   As a cause of disease   QZ 55
   Closure   WO 188
   General systemic reaction   QZ 160
   Local reaction   QZ 150
   Medicolegal aspects in death   W 843
   Minor injuries   WA 292
   Minor surgery   WO 192
   Veterinary   SF 914.3–914.4
   See also Surgical Wound Dehiscence   WO 185;
     Surgical Wound Infections   WO 185; Wound
     Infection   WC 255; names of various types of
     injury, by cause or site, e.g., Blast Injuries
     WO 820; Facial Injuries   WE 706
Wounds, Gunshot   WO 807
Wounds, Multiple see Multiple Trauma
Wounds, Penetrating   WO 700–820
WPW Syndrome see Wolff–Parkinson–White
   Syndrome
WR–2721 see Amifostine
Wrestling   QT 260.5.W9
Wrist   WE 830
Wrist Injuries   WE 830
Wrist Joint   WE 830
Writing
   English (General)   PE 1402–1497
   In psychotherapy   WM 450.5.W9
   Medical   WZ 345
   Rules (English)   PE 1411
   See also Handwriting   Z 105–115.5, etc.
Wryneck see Torticollis
Wuchereria   QX 301

X

X Chromosome   QH 600.5
X–Linked Lymphoproliferative Syndrome see
   Lymphoproliferative Disorders
X–Ray Departments see Radiology Department,
   Hospital
X–Ray Diagnosis see Radiography
X–Ray, Diagnostic see Radiography
X–Ray Emission Spectrometry see Spectrometry,
   X–Ray Emission

ALWAYS CONSULT MAIN SCHEDULES. USE NUMBER ASSIGNED ONLY WHEN
SUBJECT REPRESENTS MAJOR EMPHASIS OF WORK BEING CLASSIFIED

X-Ray Emission Spectrometry, Electron
Microscopic see Electron Probe Microanalysis
X-Ray Emission Spectrometry, Electron Probe see
Electron Probe Microanalysis
X-Ray Film   WN 150
Used for specific purpose, by subject
X-Ray Film–Screen Systems see X-Ray Intensifying
Screens
X-Ray Fluorescence Spectrometry see
Spectrometry, X-Ray Emission
X-ray Information Systems see Radiology
Information Systems
X-Ray Intensifying Screens   WN 150
Used for specific purpose, by subject
X-Ray Measurement in Obstetrics see Pelvimetry
X-Ray Microanalysis, Electron Microscopic see
Electron Probe Microanalysis
X-Ray Microanalysis, Electron Probe see Electron
Probe Microanalysis
X-Ray Service, Hospital see Radiology Department,
Hospital
X-Ray Therapy   WN 250.5.X7
X-Ray Tomography see Tomography, X-Ray
X-Ray Tomography, Computed see Tomography,
X-Ray Computed
X-Rays
General works   WN 105
Diagnostic use (General)   WN 200
Therapeutic use   WN 250.5.X7
Physics   QC 480.8–482.3
Xanthines   QV 107
Xanthinol Niacinate   QV 150
Xanthinol Nicotinate see Xanthinol Niacinate
Xanthomatosis   WD 205.5.X2
Xanthotoxin see Methoxsalen
Xantinol Nicotinate see Xanthinol Niacinate
Xenoantibodies see Antibodies, Heterophile
Xenobiotics
As carcinogens   QZ 202
Metabolism   QU 120
Xenograft see Transplantation, Heterologous
Xenograft Bioprosthesis see Bioprosthesis
Xenograft Dressings see Biological Dressings
Xenon
Inorganic chemistry   QD 181.X4
Pharmacology   QV 310
Xenopus   QL 668.E265
As laboratory animals   QY 60.A6
Xeroderma see Ichthyosis
Xeroderma Pigmentosum   WR 265
Xeromammography   WP 815
Xerophthalmia   WW 208
Xeroradiography, Breast see Xeromammography
Xerostomia   WI 230
Xiphosura see Horseshoe Crabs
Xylenes
As antiseptics   QV 223
Organic chemistry   QD 341.H9
Xylitol
Organic chemistry   QD 305.A4
Pharmacology   QV 82
Xylose   QU 75

XYY Karyotype   QS 677

Y

Y Chromosome   QH 600.5
Yaws   WC 425
Yeast, Dried   WB 447
Yeast, Fission see Schizosaccharomyces
Yeasts
As a dietary supplement in health or disease
WB 447
Microbiology   QW 180.5.Y3
Processing   TP 433
Yellow Fever   WC 530–532
Yellow Jackets see Wasps
Yellow Marrow see Bone Marrow
Yersinia   QW 138.5.Y3
Yersinia enterocolitica   QW 138.5.Y3
Yersinia Infections   WC 350–355
Yersinia pseudotuberculosis   QW 138.5.Y3
Yersinia pseudotuberculosis Infections   WC
350–355
Yoga   QT 255
Philosophy   B 132.Y6
Therapeutics see Alternative Medicine   WB 890,
etc.
Yogurt   SF 275.Y6
As a dietary supplement in health or disease
WB 428
Bacteriology   QW 85
Sanitation   WA 715
Yohimbans
As cardiovascular agents   QV 150
Organic chemistry   QD 421
Yohimbine   QV 132
Yolk Proteins see Egg Proteins
Yolk Sac Tumor see Endodermal Sinus Tumor
Youth see Adolescence
Yttrium Isotopes
Inorganic chemistry   QD 181.Y1
Pharmacology   QV 290

Z

Z-DNA see DNA
Zea see Corn
Zearalenone
As a mycotoxin   QW 630.5.M9
As an estrogen   WP 522
Special topics, by subject
Zidovudine   QV 185
Special topics, by subject
Zimeldine
As an antidepressant   QV 77.5
Zimelidine see Zimeldine
Zimmermann's Corpuscles see Blood Platelets
Zinc
Inorganic chemistry   QD 181.Z6
Pharmacology   QV 298
Zinc Isotopes
Inorganic chemistry   QD 181.Z6
Pharmacology   QV 298
Ziram
As an industrial fungicide   WA 240
Toxicology   QV 298

**ALWAYS CONSULT MAIN SCHEDULES. USE NUMBER ASSIGNED ONLY WHEN
SUBJECT REPRESENTS MAJOR EMPHASIS OF WORK BEING CLASSIFIED**

ALWAYS CONSULT MAIN SCHEDULES. USE NUMBER ASSIGNED ONLY WHEN
SUBJECT REPRESENTS MAJOR EMPHASIS OF WORK BEING CLASSIFIED

Appendix 1

Numbers Added or Deleted

The following is a list of new classification numbers added to the *NLM Classification* since the publication of the fourth edition, revised in 1981. It includes numbers added for this revision and those previously announced in "Additions and Changes to the NLM Classification" issued as part of the "Notes for Medical Catalogers" prior to 1986, or since 1986 in the *NLM Technical Bulletin*. It does not include those numbers added for general coverage following a Table G number.

The column on the right reflects where materials on the subject were most often classified. "Various places" indicates that no "most often used" number was found. "None" identifies new numbers for concepts new to the *Classification*.

Although a notation may indicate that a subject was formerly classed in a particular number, that number may still be acceptable for material that represents another aspect of the subject.

Added Numbers

New	Subjects	Old
	QS Human Anatomy	
18.2	Educational materials	QS 18
39	Handbooks	None
518.2	Educational materials [Histology]	QS 518
529	Handbooks [Histology]	QS 539
618.2	Educational materials [Embryology]	QS 618
629	Handbooks [Embryology]	QS 639
	QT Physiology	
18.2	Educational materials	QT 18
29	Handbooks	QT 39
36	Biomedical engineering	QT 34
37	Biomedical and biocompatible materials	QT 34
37.5	Specific materials, A-Z	QT 34
260.5	Specific activities, A-Z [Athletics. Sports]	QT 260
261	Sports medicine	QT 260
	QU Biochemistry	
18.2	Educational materials	QU 18
39	Handbooks	None
54	Nitrogen and related compounds	QU 55
56	Nucleoproteins	QU 58
57	Nucleosides. Nucleotides	QU 58
58.5	DNA	QU 58
58.7	RNA	QU 58
61	Amines. Amidines	QU 60
62	Amides	QU 60
86	Fats. Oils	QU 85

Added Numbers

New	Subject	Old
	QU Biochemistry Continued	
107	Growth substances. Growth inhibitors	QU 100
130.5	Trace elements	QU 130
145.5	Nutritive values of food	QU 145
	QV Pharmacology	
18.2	Educational materials	QV 18
39	Handbooks	None
77.2	Psychotropic drugs	QV 77
350.5	Specific drugs, A-Z	QV 350
	QV 600 Toxicology	
607	Handbooks	None
	QV 700 Pharmacy and Pharmaceutics	
715	Classification. Nomenclature. Terminology	Various places
717	Atlases. Pictorial works	QV 17
722	Directories	QV 22
732	Laws	QV 32
733	Discussion of law. Jurisprudence	QV 33
735	Handbooks	None
760	Materia medica	None
	QW Microbiology and Immunology	
18.2	Educational materials	QW 18
25.5	Specific techniques, A-Z [Laboratory manuals. Technique]	Various places
39	Handbooks	None
50	Bacteria. Bacteriology	QW 4
55	Environmental microbiology	None
518.2	Educational materials [Immunology]	QV 518
525.5	Specific techniques, A-Z [Laboratory manuals. Technique]	Various places
539	Handbooks [Immunology]	None
540	Immunity (General)	QV 504
545	Autoimmunity	QV 504
573.5	Specific antigens, A-Z	QV 573
575.5	Specific antibodies, A-Z	QV 575
630.5	Specific toxins and antitoxins, A-Z	QV 630
	QX Parasitology	
18.2	Educational materials	QX 18
39	Handbooks	None
45	Host-parasite relations	Various places

Added Numbers

New	Subject	Old
	QY Clinical Pathology	
18.2	Educational materials	QY 18
39	Handbooks	None
	QZ Pathology	
18.2	Educational materials	QZ 18
39	Handbooks	None
275	Pediatric oncology. Adolescent oncology	QZ 200-269
	W Health Professions	
18.2	Educational materials	W 18
20.55	Special topics, A-Z [Medical research]	Various places
26.55	Special topics, A-Z [Medical informatics...]	Various places
49	Handbooks	W 39
85.5	Right to die. Advance directives. Living wills	Various places
130	Managed care plans	Various places
132	Health maintenance organizations	W 125
160	Hospitalization insurance...	W 100-275
255	Nursing insurance	None
	W 600 Forensic Medicine and Dentistry	
618.2	Educational materials	W 618
639	Handbooks	None
	WA Public Health	
18.2	Educational materials	WA 18
39	Handbooks	None
309	Women's health	Various places
530	International health administration	WA 540
790	Medical waste. Dental waste	Various places
	WB Practice of Medicine	
18.2	Educational materials	WB 18
39	Handbooks	None
101	Ambulatory care (General)	Various places
102	Clinical medicine	None
103	Behavioral medicine	None
104	Medical psychology	None
327	Self care	None
422	Macrobiotic diet	None

Added Numbers

New	Subject	Old
	WC Communicable Diseases	
18.2	Educational materials	WC 18
39	Handbooks	None
501	RNA virus infections	WC 500
502	Retroviridae infections	WC 500
503	Acquired immunodeficiency syndrome. HIV infections	WD 308
	WD 100 Nutrition Disorders	
101	Handbooks	None
	WD 200 Metabolic Diseases	
200.1	Handbooks	None
	WD 300 Immunologic and Collagen Diseases. Hypersensitivity	
301	Handbooks	None
	WD 400 Animal Poisons	
401	Handbooks	None
	WD 500 Plant Poisons	
501	Handbooks	None
	WD 600 Diseases and Injuries Caused by Physical Agents	
601	Handbooks	None
	WD 700 Aviation and Space Medicine	
701	Handbooks	WD 704
704	Research	None
	WD 750 Space Medicine	
751	Research	None
751.6	Medical informatics. Automatic data processing. Computers	None
	WE Musculoskeletal System	
18.2	Educational materials	WE 18
39	Handbooks	None
304	Joint diseases	WE 300
	WF Respiratory System	
18.2	Educational materials	WF 18
39	Handbooks	None
141.5	Specific techniques, A-Z [Examination. Diagnosis...]	Various places

Added Numbers

New	Subject	Old
	WG Cardiovascular System	
18.2	Educational materials	WG 18
39	Handbooks	None
120	Cardiovascular diseases	WG 100
166.5	Specific therapeutic methods, A-Z	Various places
210	Heart diseases	WG 200
	WH Hemic and Lymphatic Systems	
18.2	Educational materials	WH 18
39	Handbooks	None
120	Hematologic diseases	WH 100
	WI Digestive System	
18.2	Educational materials	WI 18
39	Handbooks	None
140	Diseases	WI 100
529	Neoplasms. Polyps [Colon]	WI 520
830	Surgery (General) [Pancreas]	WI 800
	WJ Urogenital System	
18.2	Educational materials	WJ 18
39	Handbooks	None
140	Urologic diseases	WJ 100
706	Neoplasms (General) [Male genitalia]	WJ 700
	WK Endocrine System	
18.2	Educational materials	WK 18
39	Handbooks	None
140	Endocrine diseases	WK 100
	WL Nervous System	
18.2	Educational materials	WL 18
39	Handbooks	None
103.5	Neuropsychology	WL 103
103.7	Psychoneuroimmunology	None
105	Neuroendocrinology	None
140	Nervous system diseases	WL 100
160	Nervous system neoplasms	Various places
340.2	Communicative disorders. Speech-language pathology	WL 340

Added Numbers

New	Subject	Old
	WM Psychiatry	
18.2	Educational materials	WM 18
34	Handbooks	None
102	Biological psychiatry	WM 100
140	Mental disorders	WM 100
145.5	Specific tests, A-Z [Psychologic]	WM 145
165	Behavioral symptoms	Various places
284	Narcotics	WM 270
290	Nicotine	Various places
420.5	Special types, A-Z [Psychotherapy]	WM 420
425.5	Special types, A-Z [Behavior therapy]	WM 425
475.5	Aphasia [Psychogenic]	WM 475
475.6	Dyslexia [Psychogenic]	WM 475
	WN Radiology. Medical Imaging	
18.2	Educational materials	WN 18
39	Handbooks	None
105	Ionizing radiation	WN 100
180	Diagnostic imaging	Various places
185	Magnetic resonance imaging	Various places
203	Radionuclide imaging	WN 445
205	Thermography	WB 270
206	Tomography	WN 160
208	Ultrasonography	WB 289
250.5	Special types, A-Z [Radiotherapy]	WN 250
600	Radiobiology	WN 610
660	Radiometry	WN 650
665	Radiation dosage	WN 650
	WO Surgery	
18.2	Educational materials	WO 18
39	Handbooks	None
	WO 200 Anesthesia	
218.2	Educational materials	WO 218
231	Handbooks	None
	WO 500 Operative Surgery and Surgical Techniques	
511	Laser surgery	WO 500

Added Numbers

New	Subject	Old
	WP Gynecology	
18.2	Educational materials	WP 18
34	Malpractice	WP 32-33
39	Handbooks	None
440	Uterine diseases	WP 400
	WQ Obstetrics	
18.2	Educational materials	WQ 18
34	Malpractice	WQ 32-33
39	Handbooks	None
152	Natural childbirth	WQ 150
155	Home childbirth	WQ 415
	WR Dermatology	
18.2	Educational materials	WR 18
39	Handbooks	None
141	Diagnosis. Monitoring	WR 140
	WS Pediatrics	
18.2	Educational materials	WS 18
39	Handbooks	None
104	Growth disorders. Failure to thrive	Various places
205	Pediatric emergencies	WS 200
421	Diseases of newborn infants	WS 420
	WT Geriatrics. Chronic Disease	
18.2	Educational materials	WT 18
31	Medical care plans. Long term care	WT 30
39	Handbooks	None
115	Nutritional requirements. Nutrition disorders	QU 145
116	Longevity. Life expectancy. Death	WT 104
141	Physical examination and diagnosis	Various places
145	Geriatric psychology. Mental health	WT 150
155	Senile dementia. Alzheimer's disease	WT 150, WM 220
166	Therapeutics	WT 100
	WU Dentistry. Oral Surgery	
18.2	Educational materials	WU 18
49	Handbooks	WU 39
105	Dental emergencies	WU 100
140.5	Jaw diseases	WU 140

Added Numbers

New	Subject	Old
	WU Dentistry. Oral Surgery Continued	
141.5	Specific diagnostic methods, A-Z [Examination. Diagnosis...]	WU 141
317	Atlases [Operative Dentistry]	WU 17
417	Atlases [Orthodontics]	WU 17
426	Orthodontic appliances	WU 400-440
470	Dental care for the disabled	Various places
507	Atlases [Prosthodontics]	WU 17
600.7	Atlases [Oral Surgery]	WU 17
	WV Otolaryngology	
18.2	Educational materials	WV 18
39	Handbooks	None
140	Otorhinolaryngologic diseases	WV 100
190	Otorhinolaryngologic neoplasms	WV 100
	WW Ophthalmology	
18.2	Educational materials	WW 18
21.5	Ophthalmic assistants	Various places
39	Handbooks	None
	WX Hospitals and Other Health Facilities	
18.2	Educational materials	WX 18
39	Handbooks	None
157.8	Diagnosis-related groups	Various places
	WY Nursing	
15	Classification. Nomenclature. Terminology	None
18.2	Educational materials	WY 18
26.5	Medical informatics. Automatic data processing. Computers	None
49	Handbooks	WY 39
100.4	Nursing assessment. Nursing diagnosis	WY 100
107	Transcultural nursing	None
153.5	AIDS/HIV nursing	Various places
158.5	Otolaryngological nursing	WY 158
160.5	Neurological nursing	WY 160
	WZ History of Medicine	
18.2	Educational materials	WZ 18
39	Handbooks	WZ 29

Deleted Numbers

Deleted	Subject	Moved to
QS 539	Handbooks [Histology]	QS 529
QS 639	Handbooks [Embryology]	QS 629
QT 39	Handbooks [Physiology]	QT 29
QW 167	Oncolytic viruses	QW 160
QW 168.5.R6	RNA rodent viruses	QW 168
W 39	Handbooks [Health Professions]	W 49
WB 289	Diagnostic use of ultrasonics	WN 208
WG 595.I6	Innominate artery	WG 595.B72
WG 625.I6	Innominate vein	WG 625.B7
WM 612	Masturbation	HQ 447; WM 611
WM 615	Homosexuality	HQ 75-76.8; WM 611
WU 39	Handbooks [Dentistry]	WU 49
WY 39	Handbooks [Nursing]	WY 49
WZ 29	Handbooks [History of Medicine]	WZ 39

Appendix 2

Bibliography of Principal Sources
for Classification Decisions

Bergey's manual of determinative bacteriology. 9th ed. Baltimore: Williams & Wilkins; c1994. 787 p.

Bergey's manual of systematic bacteriology. 1st ed. Baltimore: Williams & Wilkins; c1984- v.

Diagnostic and statistical manual of mental disorders: DSM-IV. 4th ed. Washington, D.C.: American Psychiatric Association; 1994. 886 p.

Diagnostic and statistical manual of mental disorders: DSM-III-R. 3rd ed., rev. Washington, D.C.: American Psychiatric Association; 1987. 567 p.

Dorland's illustrated medical dictionary. 27th ed. Philadelphia: Saunders; 1988. 1888 p.

The International classification of diseases: 9th revision, clinical modification: ICD-9-CM. 4th ed. Washington, D.C.: U.S. Dept. of Health and Human Services, Public Health Service, Health Care Financing Administration: For sale by the Supt. of Docs., U.S. G.P.O.; 1991- v.

Medical subject headings: annotated alphabetical list, 1994. Bethesda, Md.: National Library of Medicine; 1993. I-230, 1066 p.

Medical subject headings: tree structures, 1994. Bethesda, Md.: National Library of Medicine; 1993. I-124, 865 p.

The Merck index; an encyclopedia of chemicals and drugs. 11th ed. Rahway, N.J.: Merck and Co.; 1989. 1 v. (various pagings)

National Library of Medicine classification. 4th ed., rev. 1981. Bethesda, Md.: U.S. Dept. of Health and Human Services, Public Health Service, National Institutes of Health, National Library of Medicine; Washington, D.C.: For sale by the Supt. of Docs., U.S. G.P.O.; 1981. 397 p.

Shortliffe, Edward H.; Perreault, Leslie E., editors. Medical informatics: computer applications in health care. Reading, Mass.: Addison-Wesley Pub. Co.; c1990. 715 p.

The Systematized nomenclature of human and veterinary medicine: SNOMED international. Northfield, Ill.: College of American Pathologists; Schaumburg, Ill.: American Veterinary Medical Association; c1993. 4 v.

Walker, John M.; Cox, Michael. The language of biotechnology, a dictionary of terms. Washington, D.C.: American Chemical Society; 1988. 255 p.

Appendix 3

NLM Staff Contributors
to the
NLM Classification, 5th edition

Arenales, Duane W., Chief, Technical Services Division
Armstead, Karen, Librarian, Technical Services Division
Bain, Evelyn S., Librarian, Technical Services Division
Charen, Thelma G., Technical Information Specialist, Medical Subject Headings Section
Charuhas, Joe C., Public Affairs Specialist, Office of Public Information
Chung, Chong C., Librarian, Technical Services Division
Clausen, Carol, Librarian, History of Medicine Division
Colaianni, Lois Ann, Associate Director, Library Operations
Coleman, Ann D., Technical Information Specialist, Technical Services Division
Coligan, Nelda C., Librarian, Technical Services Division
Conkle, Yhorda, Secretary, Technical Services Division
Cox, John W., Computer Specialist, Office of Computer and Communications Systems
Demsey, Andrea M., Librarian, Technical Services Division
Detweiler, Victoria L., Library Technician, Technical Services Division
Eannarino, Judith C., Librarian, Technical Services Division
Emanuele, Lora A., Library Technician, Technical Services Division
Feng, Margaret S.C., Librarian, Technical Services Division
Fitzgerald, Joe P., Visual Information Officer, Lister Hill Center
Freidin, Mark, Librarian, Technical Services Division
Gilkeson, Roger L., Assistant Chief, Office of Public Information
Goodson, Luanne M., Librarian, Technical Services Division
Gordner, Ronald L., Librarian, Public Services Division
Hoffmann, Christa F.B., Head, Cataloging Section, Technical Services Division
Horan, Meredith L., Librarian, Technical Services Division
Humphreys, Betsy L., Deputy Associate Director, Library Operations
Jacobs, Alice E., Assistant Head, Cataloging Section, Technical Services Division
Kao, Wen-Min C., Principal Cataloger, Technical Services Division
Kingsland, Lawrence C., Chief, Computer Sciences Branch, Lister Hill Center
Kraly, Karen A., Computer Specialist, Office of Computer and Communications Systems
Kurth, Sabra M., Librarian, Technical Services Division
Licht, Pamela C., Librarian, Technical Services Division
Lindsay, Schendell A., Clerk, Technical Services Division
Murtagh, Eileen, Librarian, Technical Services Division
Nguyen, Hien P., Librarian, Technical Services Division
Nguyen, Janet C., Librarian, Technical Services Division
Pothier, Patricia, Research Analyst, Bibliographic Services Division
Powell, Tammy, Technical Information Specialist, Medical Subject Headings Section
Rawsthorne, Grace C., Librarian, Technical Services Division
Savage, Allan G., Technical Information Specialist, Medical Subject Headings Section
Schuyler, Peri L., Head, Medical Subject Headings Section, Technical Services Division
Sinn, Sally K., Deputy Chief, Technical Services Division
Van Lenten, Elizabeth J., Technical Information Specialist, Bibliographic Services Division

White, Dorothy C., Librarian, Technical Services Division
Willis, Sharon R., Librarian, Technical Services Division
Wright, Nancy D., Head, Index Section, Bibliographic Services Division
Zellner, Varonica, Library Technician, Technical Services Division

ISBN 0-16-045397-6

9 780160 453977   90000